The Times
DIARY & INDEX OF THE WAR.

CONTENTS.

ABBREVIATIONS.

A.C.   ..... Army Corps.
Adm.   ..... Admiral.
A.M.C. .... Armed Merchant Cruiser.

B.I. .... British India (Co.).

C.-in-C. .... Commander-in-Chief.
C.M.B. .... Coastal Motor Boat.
Comm...... Commodore.
C.V. ...... Cap Verde.

D.F.C. .... Distinguished Flying Cross.
D.S.C. ..... Distinguished Service Cross.
D.S.M. .... Distinguished Service Medal.
D.S.O. .... Distinguished Service Order.

E. .... East.

F. .... Flag (—ship).
F.F. ...... Fleet Flagship.
F.M. ...... Field Marshal.

G.E. ...... German East (Africa).
Gen. ...... General.
G.H.Q. .... General Headquarters.

H.I.M.S. .. German Warship.
H.I.J.M.S... Japanese Warship.
H.M.S. .... British Warship.
H.M.T. .... British Transport.
H.Q. ...... Headquarters.
H.S. ...... Hospital Ship.

L. .... German Naval Airship.
LZ. ...... German Army Airship.

M.C. ...... Military Cross.
M.L. ...... Motor Launch.

N. .... North.
N.F.L. .... Newfoundland.

P. & O. .... Peninsular & Oriental (Co.).
P.E. ...... Portuguese East (Africa).

Q. .... Decoy Ship.
QF. ...... Quick-firing.

R. .... River.
R.A. ...... Royal Artillery.
R.A.F. .... Royal Air Force.
R.F.C. .... Royal Flying Corps.
R.H.A. ... Royal Horse Artillery.
R.M. ..... Royal Marines.
R.N. ...... Royal Navy.
R.N.A.S. .. Royal Naval Air Service.
R.N.D. .... Royal Naval Division.
R.N.R. .... Royal Naval Reserve.
R.N.V.R. .. Royal Naval Volunteer Reserve

S. .... South.
S.L. .... Schütte-Lanz Airship.
S.M. ...... Submarine.
S.N.O. .... Senior Naval Officer.
S.S. ...... Steamship.
S.V. ...... Sailing Vessel.

T.B. ...... Torpedo Boat.
T.B.D. .... Destroyer.

U-Boat .... German Submarine.
UB-Boat. .. German (Mine) Submarine.
UC-Boat .. German (Mine) Submarine.
UK-Boat .. German Submarine Cruiser.
U.S. ...... United States.
U.S.N. .... United States Navy.

V.C. ...... Victoria Cross.

W. .... West.

Z. .... Zeppelin (Army) Airship.

The Times
Diary and Index of the War.

*June 28, 1914.

Archduke Francis Ferdinand and his wife, Duchess of Hohenberg, assassinated at Serajevo (Bosnia).

H.I.M.S. *Goeben* off Syrian Coast.

June 29.

Anti-Serb riots throughout Bosnia.

June 30.

German Ambassador at Vienna, Herr von Tschirschky, reported to Berlin Foreign Office. Austrian desire for "thorough reckoning" with Serbs. This dispatch the Kaiser endorsed, "*Now or never*"!

July 1.

Austrian Dreadnought *Viribus Unitis* arrived at Trieste with bodies of murdered Archduke Francis Ferdinand and Consort.

July 2.

Kaiser abandoned intention of attending murdered Archduke's funeral, in view of Austrian rumours of a plot to attempt his own life in Vienna.

July 4.

Archduke's funeral at Artstetten (near Vienna).

Count Hoyos, Chef de Cabinet to Count Berchtold, left Vienna for Berlin with autograph letter from Emperor Francis Joseph to Kaiser and a Ballplatz Memorandum on Balkan policy.

*July 5.

The Potsdam Conferences.

Austrian Ambassador in Berlin, Count Szögyény, presented Emperor Francis Joseph's letter and the Balkan Memorandum to Kaiser at New Palace, Potsdam. Kaiser promised unconditional German support for Austrian action against Serbia; and later conferred with his Chancellor, Herr von Bethmann Hollweg, and Foreign Under-Secretary, Herr Zimmermann; also with War Minister, Gen. von Falkenhayn (of whom the Kaiser inquired whether the Army was ready for every eventuality); Chief of Military Cabinet, Gen. von Lyncker, and representative of Naval Staff, Capt. Zenker.

July 6.

In early morning, in Park of New Palace Kaiser, before leaving for Kiel on Northern cruise, conferred with Adm. von Tirpitz's deputy at Berlin Navy Office, Adm. Capelle, and with other official personages.

As result of Potsdam conferences on July 5-6 it was resolved to take preparatory war measures.

H.I.M.S. *Goeben* ordered to Pola for boiler repairs; German dockyard hands sent to expedite work.

H.I.M.SS. *Scharnhorst* and *Gneisenau* (Adm. Spee), *en route* to Samoa, ordered to await instructions at Truck or Ponape.

July 6 (*continued*).

During afternoon Counts Szögyény and Hoyos conferred with Chancellor and Herr Zimmermann in Berlin.

July 7.

Joint Ministerial Council in Vienna to consider, in light of assurances of German support, chances of war with Serbia and eventually also with Russia. Principle of Ultimatum to Belgrade adopted.

July 8.

Count Szögyény informed at Berlin Foreign Office that Herr von Tschirschky had been reprimanded for his "lukewarmness" towards Count Berchtold.

Count Tisza, Hungarian Premier, in Budapest Chamber pledged Government to safeguard Monarchy's prestige.

July 9.

Count Berchtold reported to Emperor Francis Joseph at Ischl.

Austro-Hungarian Press campaign against Serbia.

July 10.

Death of M. Hartwig, Russian Minister at Belgrade.

Herr von Tschirschky, German Ambassador at Vienna, reported to Berlin that Count Berchtold contemplated addressing to Belgrade an inacceptable formula with 48 hours' time-limit, in order that Serbia might not have time effectively to consult Russia.

July 11.

Kaiser advised by Berlin Foreign Office to address his usual congratulations to King Peter of Serbia, on the occasion of the latter's birthday on July 12, in order not to excite "premature apprehension."

*July 12.

Demonstrations in Ulster.

Herr von Jagow informed Count Berchtold that both Russia and Serbia had received confidential information of Austrian military movements on their frontiers.

Herr von Jagow instructed Prince Lichnowsky, German Ambassador in London, to influence British Press in German sense.

July 13.

President Poincaré sailed from Dunkirk in the Dreadnought *France* on visit to Tsar.

Revelations in French Senate regarding deficiencies in French military equipment.

Count Berchtold's agent at Serajevo reported that inquiry into murder of Archduke had disclosed nothing even to suggest Serbian Government's complicity in the crime.

July 14.

Lords passed Government of Ireland Amending Bill.

Sundays marked with Asterisk (*).

B

July 14, 1914 *(continued)*

German Second High Sea Squadron left Kiel to *rendezvous* off Skagen with new Third High Sea Squadron from Wilhelmshaven.

Count Berchtold and Count Tisza, the Hungarian Minister President, reached complete agreement regarding form and tenor of Austro-Hungarian demands to Serbia.

July 15

Count Tisza in Hungarian Chamber declared that Serbian question must be settled, even if by the "*ultima ratio.*"

July 16.

British Home Fleets, 460 pennants, under Adm. Sir G. A. Callaghan, assembled at Portland for test mobilisation.

July 17.

Much to Kaiser's regret, Count Berchtold decided to postpone presentation of Austrian Note until after close of President Poincaré's visit to Russia, *i.e.*, until July 23.

Adm. Spee at Ponape.

July 18.

King George reviewed Fleet at Spithead.

Berlin Foreign Office, in view of mobilisation and similar prospective decisions, asked to be kept advised of exact whereabouts of Kaiser's yacht *Hohenzollern*, now in Norwegian waters with German High Sea Fleet.

⚓July 19.

King George summoned Home Rule Conference.

Kaiser ordered High Sea Fleet not to disperse before July 25.

Kaiser instructed Herr von Jagow to warn directors of Hamburg-Amerika Line and of North-German Lloyd that coming events might endanger their ships in distant seas.

Second Joint Ministerial Council in Vienna approved final draft of Austrian Note to Serbia.

July 20.

President Poincaré at Kronstadt.

July 21.

Count Berchtold in audience at Ischl.

Austrian Note to Serbia confidentially communicated in advance to German Ambassador at Vienna.

H.I.M.S. *Nürnberg* left San Francisco to join Adm. Spee in the Pacific.

July 22.

Austrian Note received and read at Berlin Foreign Office between 7 and 8 p.m.

July 23.

Herr Ballin visited London and conversed with Lord Haldane and Sir E. Grey.

Austrian Note presented at Belgrade. Time limit to expire at 6 p.m. on July 25.

Herr von Jagow instructed German Minister at Stockholm to inform Swedish Government that war was imminent between Germany and Russia in connexion with Austro-Serbian conflict, and to express the hope that Sweden might discern how grave was the moment also in her own destiny.

July 24.

Home Rule Conference failed.

Sir E. Grey proposed Four-Power mediation in Austro-Serbian conflict.

Serbia appealed to the Tsar.

Strikes in St. Petersburg.

July 25.

H.I.M.SS. *Dresden* and *Karlsruhe* at Port-au-Prince.

Adm. von Pohl, German Chief of Naval Staff, returned to Berlin from leave. Naval Staff advised Berlin Navy Office to expedite dockyard work, completion of Kiel Canal, &c.

Austria refused to accept Russian proposal for extension of time-limit to Serbia.

At 6 p.m. Serbian reply, conciliatory but not unconditional acceptance, handed to Austrian Minister, who left Belgrade at 6.30 p.m.

Austrian mobilisation ordered.

Serbia mobilised ; Government removed to Nish.

Russia prepared to mobilise on Austrian frontier, to meet eventual pressure on Serbia.

⚓July 26.

Riots in Dublin.

British Fleet ordered not to disperse.

Kaiser and Fleet returned from Norway.

German warships abroad "warned."

Germany, while professing to believe that the conflict would be "localised," and that Russia would not fight, threatened mobilisation (*i.e.*, war) if Russia did not suspend her military preparations.

Austria mobilised on Russian frontier.

Montenegro ordered mobilisation.

July 27.

Sir E. Grey in Commons explained his conference proposal.

Kaiser at Potsdam.

Adm. von Tirpitz returned to Berlin.

Count Berchtold urged Emperor Francis Joseph immediately to declare war on Serbia, in order to forestall Triple Entente's efforts.

Tsar informed Serbia that Russia could not remain indifferent to her fate.

July 28.

British First Fleet ordered to Scapa.

Austria refused mediation and declared war on Serbia.

Austrian general mobilisation.

Kaiser, feeling himself at disadvantage in view of "skilful" Serbian reply, wired to Tsar not to intervene on Serbia's behalf.

July 29.

British First Fleet put to sea from Portland, and proceeded east-about up the North Sea to Scapa.

Sir E. Grey warned Germany that Britain could not in all circumstances stand aside.

Kaiser held War Council at Potsdam, and instructed Chancellor to make the "infamous offer" that Germany would not annex French territory if Britain remained neutral.

German ships at Kiel mobilising.

M. Poincaré in Paris.

Kaiser and Tsar exchanged telegrams without effect, but Emperor Nicholas at 11 p.m. sought to stop Russian general mobilisation, which had been ordered earlier in day on German threat of war in event of Russian partial mobilisation against Austria.

Austrians began to bombard Belgrade.

July 30.

Adm. Jellicoe turned over the duties of Second Sea Lord, and prepared to take up his new appointment as Second in Command to Adm. Callaghan, C.-in-C. Home Fleets.

Adm. Milne (F. *Inflexible*), C.-in-C. Mediterranean Fleet, at Malta, ordered to assist in covering transport of French African Army.

For List of Abbreviations see page iv.

July 30, 1914 (*continued*).

Sir J. French designated C.-in-C. of eventual B.E.F. to France.

Mr. Asquith moved adjournment of second reading of Government of Ireland Amendment Bill in House of Commons.

Sir E. Grey repudiated Germany's " infamous proposal " of the day before.

Kaiser instructed Chancellor in event of war to inflame the Mahomedan world against Britain, for " if we are to bleed to death, England shall at the very least lose India."

German mobilisation " prematurely " announced.

Austrians again bombarded Belgrade.

Russia proposed to Germany to stop mobilising if Austria waived demands touching Serbian Sovereignty. Proposal not communicated to Vienna.

July 31.

Sir E. Grey, in reply to direct inquiry, received assurance from France that she would respect Belgian neutrality ; Germany returned no answer.

Belgian mobilisation decreed for August 1.

Germany declared a state of " danger of war," and challenged France to intimate within 18 hours whether she would remain neutral, in which event Toul and Verdun to be pledged to Germany. M. Viviani replied that France would act as her interests dictated.

H.I.M.S. *Friedrich der Grosse* (F.F. Adm. von Ingenohl, C.-in-C. High Sea Fleet) passed through Kiel Canal into North Sea.

M. Jaurès assassinated in Paris.

Germany at midnight (C.E.T.) summoned Russia to stop mobilising within 12 hours.

Russian general mobilisation announced.

Austrian general mobilisation announced.

Vienna Cabinet meeting passed over Sir E. Grey's final proposals.

Turkey began to mobilise.

H.I.M.S. *Emden* left Tsingtau.

H.I.M.S. *Königsberg* left Dar-es-Salaam.

August 1.

Canada formally offered help.

First Phase of U-Boat War :

Two German U-Boat Flotillas, U5, U6, U7, U8, U9, U10, U11, U12, U13, U14, U15, U16, U17, U18, U19, U20, U21, U22, U23, U24, and U25 assembled off Heligoland.

German High Sea Fleet concentrated in Jade anchorage.

Mobilisation proceeding in Belgium, who announced determination to uphold neutrality

General mobilisation ordered in France.

Germany declared war on Russia.

Austria claimed Italian support

British Mediterranean Fleet (Adm. Milne) concentrated at Malta.

H.I.M.S. *Goeben* arrived from Pola at Brindisi, where she was joined by H.I.M.S. *Breslau* from Durazzo.

*August 2.

Adm. Jellicoe arrived at Scapa Flow.

British Naval Reserves mobilised.

Lord Lansdowne and Mr. Bonar Law offered Mr. Asquith support of Opposition in national emergency.

Seven German Armies forming in the West : First Army, Gen. von Kluck ; Second Army, Gen. von Bülow ; Third Army, Gen. von Hausen ; Fourth Army, Duke Albrecht of Wurtemberg ; Fifth Army, German Crown Prince ; Sixth Army, Bavarian Crown Prince ; Seventh Army, Gen. von Heeringen.

*August 2 (*continued*).

Germany demanded right of way from Belgium. Reply required within 12 hours.

Germans violated French territory.

Libau bombarded by H.I.M.S. *Augsburg*.

German Eighth Army, Gen. von Prittwitz und Gaffron, concentrated on Russian Front.

Russian forces crossed German frontier at Schwidden, S.E. of Biala (E. Prussia).

Germans invaded Russian Poland.

Turkey signed offensive and defensive treaty with Germany at Constantinople.

Adm. Milne to remain at Malta ; Adm. Troubridge (F. *Defence*), with 1st Cruiser Squadron, reinforced by H.M.S.S *Indomitable Indefatigable*, and *Gloucester*, to shadow H.I.M.S. *Goeben* and watch Adriatic.

August 3.

British First Battle Cruiser Squadron and Third Cruiser Squadron put to sea to cruise S. of Fair Island Channel on reports that German transports had passed Great Belt.

French 2nd Cruiser Squadron, Adm. Rouyer (F. *Marseillaise*) on guard in Dover Straits.

British s.s. *San Wilfrido* mined off Cuxhaven ; crew made prisoners.

Moratorium in England.

Sir E. Grey in Commons defined British attitude ; announced mobilisation of Fleet and Army ; German naval operations against French N. coast to be disputed.

Australia offered 20,000 men.

Belgium rejected German ultimatum.

King Albert appealed to King George.

Luxemburg invaded by VIIIth German Army Corps.

Germany declared war on France.

German Ambassador left Paris.

French Ambassador left Berlin.

Lunéville bombed by German aeroplanes.

Grand Duke Nicholas, Russian Vice-Generalissimo for the Tsar in the field.

Germans occupied Tchenstochowa, Bendzin and Kalish (Russian Poland).

Adm. Boué de Lapeyrère took French Fleet to sea from Toulon to watch H.I.M.S. *Goeben* and protect transport of French African Army.

H.I.M.SS. *Goeben* and *Breslau* (Adm. Souchon), cruising in Mediterranean, ordered by Berlin W. T. to make for Constantinople.

August 4.

Adm. Jellicoe, under Admiralty orders took over Adm. Callaghan's command with the new designation of C.-in-C. of the Grand Fleet, and hoisted his flag in H.M.S. *Iron Duke*. Adm. Madden Chief of Staff.

The Grand Fleet put to sea at 8.30 a.m.

Dover and Cross-Channel Patrols at war stations.

H.I.M. minelayer *Königin Luise* at 7.30 p.m. left Ems R. to mine Thames mouth ; A.M.C. *Kronprinz Wilhelm* also left port.

Dutch s.s. *Tubantia*, with German gold and reservists, brought into Plymouth by H.M.S. *Highflyer*.

German troops entered Belgium.

Visé set on fire ; attack on Liége begun by Gen. von Emmich, Xth Corps, Second Army.

Kaiser opened Reichstag with speech from the Throne in Berlin Palace.

Chancellor in Reichstag announced invasion of Belgium : " necessity knows no law. . . . We must hack our way through."

Sundays marked with Asterisk (*).

August 4, 1914 (*continued*).

German Socialists in Reichstag voted first 5,000,000,000 marks war credit.

Amnesty proclaimed in Prussia.

Britain demanded from Germany assurance by midnight (11 p.m., G.M.T.) that neutrality of Belgium would be respected.

Sir E. Goschen's "scrap of paper" interview with Chancellor von Bethmann Hollweg in Berlin.

Britain declared war on Germany.

Bône and Philippeville (Algeria) bombarded by H.I.M.SS. *Goeben* and *Breslau* at dawn. A few hours later the German cruisers were sighted west of Galita Is. by H.M.SS. *Indomitable*, *Indefatigable*, and *Dublin*. British ships outdistanced.

Enver Pasha intimated that Dardanelles would be open to German warships, but Grand Vizier, fearing complications, demurred.

Austro-German terms for Treaty of Alliance with Bulgaria signed at Sofia.

August 5.

Grand Fleet holding North Sea.

H.I.M. minelayer *Königin Luise* sunk off Outer Gabbard by H.M. T.B.D. *Lance* and *Landrail*, with H.M.S. *Amphion* in company.

British submarine Heligoland Patrol instituted.

British authorities cut German down-Channel cables from Emden to Vigo and Azores.

New Zealand force accepted by Home Government ; New Zealand naval forces placed under Admiralty.

War Council at 10, Downing Street.

Lord Kitchener appointed War Secretary in the room of Mr. Asquith.

Raid by Z VI. on Liége.

Kaiser in Berlin re-instituted the Iron Cross decoration for war services, "1914."

Skirmish with Russian cavalry at Soldau.

Montenegro declared war on Austria.

Austria-Hungary declared war on Russia.

H.I.M.SS. *Goeben* and *Breslau* at Messina first ordered to make for Pola or Atlantic ; later ordered to exercise own discretion.

British s.s. *Craigforth* mined in Bosporus.

August 6.

H.I.M.S. *Karlsruhe* sighted north-westward of Bahamas by H.M.S. *Suffolk* (F. Adm. Cradock), pursued and engaged by H.M.S. *Bristol*, but escaped.

Three British ships stopped and released by H.I.M.S. *Dresden* in N. Atlantic.

North-German Lloyd s.s. *Schlesien* captured at sea off Cape Ortegal by H.M.S. *Vindictive* (Adm. de Robeck) ; sent to Plymouth with prize crew.

Adm. de Chair, with 10th Cruiser Squadron, established Northern (Blockade) Patrol in Latitude of the Shetlands.

H.M.S. *Amphion* mined in North Sea.

Kaiser's first order to Admiralty Staff : "High Sea Fleet to remain on defensive ; work only with U-Boats and torpedo boats."

U5, U6, U7, U8, U9, U10, U11, U12, U13, U14, U15, U16, U17, and U18 proceeded on first scouting cruise in North Sea.

Canada called for 20,000 volunteers.

Additional 500,000 men for British Army sanctioned by Parliament.

Commons voted £100,000,000 credit.

Gen. Ludendorff, Quarter-Master Second Army, penetrated Liége with 14th German infantry brigade, which had lost its commander on the march into the city.

Gen. Sordet's French Cavalry Corps co-operating in Belgium against Gen. von der

August 6 (*continued*).

Marwitz's cavalry screen in advance of invading German armies.

French entered German Lorraine.

Austrians attacked Serbians at Obrenovatz.

Adm. Boué de Lapeyrère in command Anglo-French naval forces in Mediterranean, with Malta as advanced base, by virtue of Anglo-French naval convention assigning direction to British Admiralty in other waters.

H.I.M.SS. *Goeben* and *Breslau* left Messina for Constantinople in the evening ; sighted off Taormina by H.M.S. *Gloucester* ; chased and held throughout the night.

H.I.M.S. *Königsberg* sank s.s. *City of Winchester* (6,601 tons) 280 miles E. from Aden.

Adm. Spee left Ponape for Ladrones.

August 7.

British fishing vessel *Tubal Cain* sunk by gunfire by German A.M.C. *Kaiser Wilhelm der Grosse*, 50 miles W.N.W. from Stalberg (Iceland).

British Channel Fleet, Adm. Burney (F.F *Lord Nelson*), constituted in readiness to cover passage of B.E.F. to France.

H.M.SS. *Russell*, *Albemarle* and *Exmouth*, from Channel, joined Grand Fleet at Scapa.

Prince of Wales appealed for National Relief Fund.

Lord Kitchener called for first 100,000 men.

British Expeditionary Force began to embark.

Gen. von Emmich entered Liége after Gen. Ludendorff had occupied the citadel single-handed. Both generals received Pour le Mérite Order.

French entered Altkirch (Alsace).

Russian First Army under Gen. Rennenkampf invaded East Prussia.

Austrians occupied Kielce (Poland).

Serbians invaded Bosnia.

H.I.M.SS. *Goeben* and *Breslau* holding eastward past Cape Matapan, with H.M.S. *Gloucester* (Capt. W. A. H. Kelly) in pursuit. After challenging *Goeben* by engaging *Breslau*, breaking off the action, and later continuing to shadow, Capt. Kelly, by order of Adm. Milne, abandoned chase off Cape Matapan.

August 8.

Canada's 20,000 men accepted.

Belgian retirement on Dyle R.

French entered Mülhausen (Alsace).

Mobilisation in Switzerland.

Montenegrins crossed into Bosnia.

H.I.M.SS. *Goeben* and *Breslau* coaling at Denusa, E, of Naxos.

Franco-British force in Togoland.

British column left Nigeria for Cameroons.

H.M.SS. *Astrœa* and *Pegasus* shelled Dar-es-Salaam wireless station.

*August 9.

H.I.M.S. *Karlsruhe* put into Puerto Rico to coal.

H.M.S. *Highflyer* at Lisbon ; German ships dismantled in Tagus.

Adm. Jellicoe requested that movements of Commodore (T) and Commodore (S) might be directed from Admiralty.

Adm. Christian's Southern Force formed.

U15 rammed and sunk by H.M.S. *Birmingham* in North Sea.

U13 posted missing on same cruise.

*August 9, 1914 (*continued*).

First British troops landed at Boulogne.

Belgium rejected German peace offer.

German cavalry fighting in streets of St. Trond.

First battle of Mülhausen. German Seventh Army engaged. French retirement.

August 10.

Adm. Miller appointed S.N.O., Scapa.

H.M.SS. *Hannibal* and *Magnificent* arrived at Scapa to act as guardships against eventual T.B.D. attacks.

H.M.S. *Southampton* (F. Commodore Goodenough) visited Stavanger to inquire into reports of U-Boat base in the Fjord.

French military mission, under Col. Huguet, arrived in London.

French advance in Lorraine.

France declared war on Austria-Hungary.

Z IV. raided Mlava.

Austrian Gen. Dankl entered Poland at Krasnik.

H.M.SS. *Inflexible* (F. Adm. Milne), *Indefatigable*, and *Indomitable* entered Ægean.

H.I.M.SS. *Goeben* and *Breslau* in Dardanelles at 8.30 p.m.

Germans from S.W. Africa raided Cape Colony. Germans abandoned Swakopmund and Lüderitz Bay.

Australian naval forces in Imperial service. Adm. Patey's flag in H.M.S. *Australia*.

Russian volunteer s.s. *Ryasan* captured and brought into Tsingtau a few days earlier by H.I.M.S. *Emden*, armed as German raider and renamed *Cormoran*, left Tsingtau, preceded by raider *Prinz Eitel Friedrich*.

August 11.

Adm. Purefoy in charge of new alternative coaling base for Grand Fleet at Loch Ewe.

H.M.S. *Arethusa* commissioned at Chatham as Flagship to Commodore Tyrrwhitt, commanding Harwich Force.

During first week of war at sea British Fleet engaged in sweeping and blockading operations, while German activities confined to U-Boat and other patrols in North Sea.

U-Boats returned to Heligoland from scouting cruise.

British Press Bureau formed.

Montenegro at war with Germany.

Z V. raided Lodz.

August 12.

H.I.M.S. *Karlsruhe* at Curaçao.

Great Britain declared war on Austria-Hungary.

Kaiser attempted to buy off Japan.

Germans took Huy (Belgium), but failed at Haelen and Dinant.

French preliminary concentration completed.

. Serbo-Montenegrin attack on Vishegrad.

Adm. Milne to hand over Mediterranean command to Adm. Carden.

French Fleet at Malta after covering transfer of Algerian Army Corps to France.

Gold Coast Force landed at Lome, Togoland.

H.M.S. *Minotaur* (F.Adm. Jerram) destroyed Yap wireless station.

H.I.M.S. *Emden* with *Markomannia* and *Prinz Eitel Friedrich*, joined Adm. Spee at Pagan Island.

August 13.

Adm. Cradock at Halifax transferred his flag to H.M.S. *Good Hope*.

August 13 (*continued*).

British R.F.C., concentrated at Dover, proceeded to France ; 56 machines landed at Amiens and flew to Maubeuge, where they began to operate with B.E.F.

German cavalry attack at Tirlemont.

Fall of four more Liége forts, including Fléron, where Germans first employed their trench-mortars.

Austrians crossed Drina into Serbia.

Austrian Lloyd s.s. *Baron Gautsch* mined in Adriatic.

British shelled Dar-es-Salaam (G.E. Africa) and sank H.I.M.S. *Moewe*.

German steamer *Von Wissmann* captured by British launch *Gwendolen* on Lake Nyassa.

August 14.

Admiralty reported passage across Atlantic to be safe ; British trade running as usual.

National Relief Fund £1,000,000.

First English liquor restrictions.

Three U-Boats detached to watch Firth of Forth and Humber.

Sir John French landed at Boulogne.

French forces, part of Gen. Lanrezac's Fifth Army, entered Belgium near Chimay.

Gen. von Kluck's leading Corps reached Meuse N. of Liége ; Reserve Corps crossing Belgian frontier W. of Aix.

German concentration on W. Front completed : First Army, 5 Corps (Gen. von Kluck), S.W. of Crefeld ; Second Army, 7 Corps (Gen. von Bülow), S. of Aix-la-Chapelle ; Third Army, 4 Corps (Gen. von Hausen), in the Eifel ; Fourth Army, 5 Corps (Duke of Wurtemberg), in Luxemburg and Rhineland ; Fifth Army, 5 Corps (German Crown Prince), E. of Metz-Diedenhofen ; Sixth Army, 5 Corps (Bavarian Crown Prince), about Metz-Saarburg ; Seventh Army, 3 Corps (Gen. von Heeringen), about Strassburg. Total : 22 Active Corps, 12 Reserve Corps ; numbering, with 10 cavalry divisions, &c., in all 1,600,000 men.

Gen. Dubail's French First Army reached Donon Crest.

Gen. Pau re-occupied Thann.

Gen. Russky entered Sokol (Galicia).

Grand Duke Nicholas's Proclamation to Poland.

August 15.

Panama Canal inaugurated.

British s.s. *Galician* captured and released by German A.M.C. *Kaiser Wilhelm der Grosse* in N. Atlantic.

Kaiser called up Landsturm.

Last Liége fort, Loncin, destroyed ; Belgian Gen. Leman taken prisoner.

Prussian Guard Cavalry Division checked at Dinant by Gen. d'Esperey's 1st Corps French Fifth Army.

French advance towards Sambre R.

French holding Vosges passes.

Sir J. French visited President Poincaré in Paris.

Japanese Ultimatum to Germany.

Adm. Boué de Lapeyrère's Main Fleet joined Adm. Troubridge's squadron at entrance to Adriatic for combined operation against Austrians.

Hamburg-Amerika s.s. *Istria* and *Südmark* captured by H.M.S. *Black Prince* in Red Sea.

Gen. von Lettow took Taveta (B.E. Africa).

*August 16.

R.M.S.P.SS. *Arlanza* (15,044 tons), from Buenos Ayres, captured and released by

Sundays marked with Asterisk (*).

*August 16, 1914 (*continued*).

Kaiser Wilhelm der Grosse in N. Atlantic. S.S. *Kaipara* (7,392 tons) and *Nyanza* (3,066 tons) sunk S.E. from Teneriffe.

Grand Fleet swept North Sea down to southward of Horn Reef. One U-Boat sighted. This operation was carried out so that on this critical day, when the bulk of the British Expeditionary transport was passng to France, the Heligoland Bight was completely blockaded. During Aug. 15, 16, and 17 the transports made 137 passages, the tonnage being over half a million.

First B.E.F. landed in France.

Sir J. French's first conference with Gen. Joffre at Vitry-le-François; latter declined to place under British orders the French cavalry and Reserve forces posted behind British left.

Kaiser, with Army and Navy Staffs, left Berlin for German G.H.Q. at Coblenz.

German IXth Corps transferred from Second to First Army.

French Second Army (Gen. de Castelnau) invaded Lorraine.

French First Army at Schirmeck.

Russian Niemen Army crossed E. Prussian frontier in force.

Austrians took Shabatz (Serbia).

Austrian cruiser *Zenta* sunk near Cattaro by French squadron, having been brought to a standstill by first salvos of *Courbet* (F.F. Adm. Boué de Lapeyrère.)

Adm. Souchon (H.I.M.S. *Goeben*) asked Berlin Admiralty Staff to send out to Constantinople 2 Admirals, 10 other naval officers, 10 engineers, and 500 men for Turkish Fleet and defence of Dardanelles.

August 17.

German A.M.C. *Kaiser Wilhelm der Grosse* at Rio de Oro.

R.N.D. to be formed.

H.I.M.SS. *Stralsund* and *Strassburg* within 40 sea miles of Yarmouth; chased later by British light forces.

H.I.M.SS. *Augsburg* and *Magdeburg* minelaying in Gulf of Finland.

Belgian Government at Antwerp.

Sir J. French at Le Cateau.

Gen. Grierson, 2nd Army Corps, died on his way to Amiens; succeeded by Gen. Smith-Dorrien.

Austrian set-back at Shabatz.

Kaiser, on receiving Japanese Ultimatum at Coblenz, sought to induce U.S. to " neutralise " E. Asia, the Eastern Seas, and the Pacific.

Tsar at Moscow.

August 18.

British s.s *Bowes Castle* (4,650 tons) sunk by H.I.M.S. *Karlsruhe* N.W. from Cape Orange, Brazil.

Dreadnought Battle Fleet at Loch Ewe. H.M.SS. *Invincible* and *New Zealand* stationed in the Humber.

L3 scouting over Hanstolm-Ryvingen.

Gen. von Kluck's First Army placed under command of Gen. von Bülow, Second Army, together with Gen. von der Marwitz's 2nd Cavalry Corps.

Battle at Tirlemont.

Gen. Maudhuy's 16th Division, 8th Corps, of Gen. Dubail's First Army, took Saarburg, supporting Gen. de Castelnau's Second Army in its attack on Mörchingen positions held by Bavarians of German Sixth Army.

Russian invasion of Galicia continued.

August 18 (*continued*).

Serbians under Crown Prince Alexander defeated Austrians on Yadar R. and drove them back across Drina R.

H.M.S. *Inflexible* left Malta for home.

Adm. Carden S.N.O. Malta; Adm. Troubridge to command ships at sea in Mediterranean ; both under French C.-in-C.

August 19.

Germans destroyed Aerschot.

Germans occupied Louvain, where Gen. von Kluck remained for two days.

King Albert at Malines.

French cavalry checked at Perwez.

French driven from Saarburg.

Second battle of Mülhausen.

Battle at Gumbinnen (E. Prussia).

Austrian defeat on Yadar R. completed.

Morocco broke with Germany.

H.M.S. *Indomitable* ordered to leave Dardanelles for Gibraltar. Blockade maintained by H.M.SS. *Indefatigable* (F. Adm. Troubridge) and *Defence*.

Adm. Spee in Marshall Islands.

August 20.

Order in Council on conditional contraband.

Germans occupied Brussels.

Gen. von Lüttwitz appointed Military Commandant of the city of Brussels.

French evacuated Saarburg, and, after heavy fighting before Mörchingen, Gen. Foch's 20th Corps fell back with remainder of Second Army.

End of Gumbinnen battle. Gen. von François (1st Prussian Corps) retiring on Königsberg ; while Gen. von Prittwitz informed German G.H.Q. that he could no longer maintain himself E. of the Vistula.

Germans seized Taveta (B.E. Africa).

August 21.

Belgians evacuated Ostend.

Battle of Charleroi begun.

Gen. von Kluck advancing from Brussels.

Gen. Allenby's Cavalry Division holding Condé Canal line with four Brigades ; Gen. Chetwode's 5th Cavalry Brigade at Binche. Gen. Haig's 1st Corps at Maubeuge—Givry ; Gen. Smith-Dorrien's 2nd Corps at Maubeuge —Sars la Bruyères.

Gen. de Castelnau falling back to Grand Couronné positions on Meurthe R.

Germans still retiring on Königsberg. Gen. Samsonoff's Second Army invaded Allenstein district (E. Prussia).

August 22.

H.I.M.SS. *Rostock* and *Strassburg*, with T.B.D. Flotilla, sank eight British fishingboats in North Sea ; crews taken prisoners.

Adm. Christian at Ostend.

Kaiser at Coblenz ordered Admiralty Staff to begin preparations for campaign against England from Franco-Belgian coast.

Levy of £8,000,000 on Brussels.

Gen. von Kluck at Hal, S. Brussels.

Gen. von Gallwitz's Army Group, with Second Army's siege train and 42-centimetre howitzers, besieging Namur.

First British cavalry contact with Germans at Casteau N.E. of Mons.

First British aeroplane shot down near Enghien.

British on Mons line on Allied left. At Condé was French 84th Territorial Division ; British 19th Brigade on right along canal,

August 22, 1914 (*continued*).

with British 5th Division next on right and British 3rd Division holding salient round Mons to Villers-Ghislain. British 1st Corps extended S.E. to Peissant.

French Fifth Army retired from Charleroi.

French Fourth and Third Armies unsuccessfully engaged astride Belgian frontier between Givet—Longwy, about Neufchâteau.

Germans entered Lunéville.

French in Alsace brought down Zeppelin.

Z IV. raided Gumbinnen.

Z V. raided Novo-Georgievsk.

Gen. von Hindenburg to command Eighth Army in E. Prussia, vice Gen. von Prittwitz, with Gen. Ludendorff as Chief of Staff, vice Gen. Count Waldersee.

German naval contingent, with Adm. Usedom, left for Constantinople.

*August 23.

H.M.S. *Carnarvon* (F.Adm. Stoddart) captured German s.s. *Professor Woermann* off Cape Verde.

Marshal von der Goltz Governor General of occupied Belgium.   Herr von Sandt, of Aix-la-Chapelle, appointed Civil Administrator.

Germans entered Namur.

Gen. von der Marwitz's cavalry on Scheldt, W. of Renaix.

Gen. von Kluck at Soignies.

Mons Battle begun. British 3rd and 5th Divisions attacked by six German Divisions of Gen. von Kluck's First Army. British 1st Corps attacked only by artillery. British retired at nightfall.

French attacked at Charleroi-Dinant.

Germans evacuated Insterburg and were defeated at Frankenau.

Gen. von Hindenburg and Gen. Ludendorff arrived at Marienburg.

Japan declared war on Germany.

Japanese 2nd Squadron, Adm. S. Kato, proceeded to blockade Tsingtau; while 1st Squadron, Adm. T. Kato, held route for transport of Gen. Kamio's Expeditionary Force.

H.M. T.B.D. *Kennet* damaged in action with German T.B.D. off Tsingtau.

August 24.

Z IX. raided Antwerp.

Belgians drove Germans out of Malines.

Allies abandoned Sambre line.

Sir J. French at Bavai.

Retreat from Mons: British fell back to Maubeuge-Jenlain. Tournai taken by German 4th Cavalry Division; Gen. d'Amade's 61st and 62nd Territorial Divisions falling back.

Gen. von der Marwitz's Cavalry Corps placed under direct orders of German First Army and diverted from Courtrai to Tournai and Denain.

German Third Army intervened on Second Army front.

Noske and Liebknecht visiting Belgium.

Russian advance in E. Prussia.

August 25.

H.M.S. *Agincourt* (ex-Turkish *Osman I.*) joined Grand Fleet.

H.M.S. *King Edward VII.* left Scapa for Devonport to replace two cracked 12-inch guns. H.M.S. *Dominion* reported similar defect.

Austrian s.s. *Attila* captured by British 3rd Battle Squadron in North Sea.

Lord Kitchener announced first 100,000 practically secured.

August 25 (*continued*).

Prusso-German XXIInd, XXIIIrd, XXIVth, XXVth, XXVIth, and XXVIIth Reserve Corps formed.

Portsmouth. Plymouth, and Chatham Marine Battalions ordered to Ostend to create diversion on flank of German advance. Covering movement to be carried out in Heligoland Bight (see 28-viii.-14).

Battle at Malines.

Prusso-German IXth Reserve Corps fighting in Louvain streets.

Gen. Joffre ordered Allied retreat. French G.H.Q. at Vitry-le-François.

Retreat from Mons: British falling back to Le Cateau, where 4th Division arrived; German attack at Landrecies beaten off by 4th Guards Brigade.

Germans entered Sedan. Maubeuge invested.

Gen. Dubail's First Army holding fast on Vosges front.

French again evacuated Mülhausen.

First German air-raid on Belfort.

Cattaro bombarded by French squadron.

Z IV. raided Nordenburg.

Z V. raided Rypin.

Russians beaten at Krasnik.

British force in Cameroons.

August 26.

British s.s. *Holmwood* (4,223 tons) sunk by H.I.M.S. *Dresden* off Cape Santa Marta Grande.

H.I.M. A.M.C. *Kaiser Wilhelm der Grosse* sunk by H.M.S. *Highflyer* off Rio de Oro.

H.I.M. minelayers *Albatross* and *Nautilus*, with T.B.Ds. during this week mined approaches to Tyne and Humber; 16 British fishing vessels captured by these raiders; all British fishing vessel losses off E. Coast during next three months due to mines.

Prussian Guard Reserve (Gen. von Gallwitz) and XIth Army Corps (Gen. von Plüskow) transferred from W. to E. Front.

Germans began to destroy Louvain.

German cavalry in Lille.

Fall of last two Namur forts.

Fall of Longwy to German Fifth Army.

Gen. Ruffey's Third Army falling back across the Meuse.

Battle of Le Cateau. Allied forces engaged: British 2nd Corps, with 19th Brigade, its right at Le Cateau; 4th Division, its left at Esnes; Gen. Sordet's Cavalry Corps and British 4th Cavalry Brigade prolonged to Cambrai, through which French 84th Territorial Division retiring. British retiring.

Gen. von Kluck at Solesmes resumed independent command of First Army.

Gen. Galliéni, Governor of Paris.

French fell back in Alsace-Lorraine.

H.I.M.S. *Magdeburg* ashore and blown up off Odensholm in Finland Gulf. Part of crew rescued by T.B.D. V 26, while H.I.M.S. *Augsburg* and U3 engaged Russian cruisers *Pallada* and *Bogatyr*.

Russians occupied Tilsit.

Battle of Tannenberg (E. Prussia) begun. Gen. Samsonoff engaged Hindenburg at Allenstein-Mlava.

Austrians evacuated Novi Bazar.

H.I.J.M.SS. *Ibuki* and *Shikuma* sent to Singapore to join Adm. Jerram's China squadron.

Togoland conquered.

August 27.

Chatham and Portsmouth Marine Battalions landed at Ostend under Gen. Aston.

Sundays marked with Asterisk (*).

August 27, 1914 (continued).

Malines bombarded by Germans.

Lille abandoned by the French.

Gen. Maunoury, new French Sixth Army, took over from Gen d'Amade on Allied left in Somme Valley.

British reached St. Quentin line.

French Meuse line giving way.

Gen. Foch's new Ninth Army interposed between Gen. Lanrezac's Fifth Army and Gen. de Langle's Fourth Army.

M. Millerand, French War Minister; M. Delcassé, Foreign Minister.

At Tannenberg Gen. Samsonoff's right being turned by Hindenburg's Army. Gen. Rennenkampf still feeling his way westward.

Z V. raided Mlava.

Gen. Brusiloff took Tarnopol (Galicia). Austrians fell back on Lemberg.

Japanese occupied islands off Tsingtau.

Blockade of Kiaochow Bay declared by Adm. S. Kato, and maintained by Japanese 2nd Squadron, together with H.M.S. *Triumph* and T.B.D. *Usk*.

August 28.

Battle of Heligoland Bight. Commodore Tyrwhitt, commanding Harwich Force, swept into Bight during early morning with H.M.SS. *Arethusa* and *Fearless* and T.B.D.s of 3rd and 1st Flotillas, and with Commodore Goodenough's Light Cruiser Squadron and Adm. Beatty's five battle cruisers in support, surprised German outposts, engaged and sank T.B.D. Leader V 187 and H.I.M.S. *Mainz*. Adm. Beatty with Battle Cruisers intervened shortly after noon, relieved disabled *Arethusa* and sank H.I.M.SS. *Köln* (F. Adm. Maass, commanding T.B.D. flotillas) and *Ariadne;* two other German light cruisers, *Stettin* and another, and three T.B.D.s damaged; Adm. von Tirpitz's son, among 348 survivors of *Mainz*, taken prisoner, and brought to England. H.M. submarine E4 (which was in position with E5 and E9, and E6, E7, and E8) later rescued other survivors of the action.

Plymouth Marine Battalion joined Chatham and Portsmouth Battalions at Ostend.

Kaiser ordered advance on Paris.

Sir J. French at Compiègne.

Germans made first organised aerial bombing raid on Compiègne during the retreat.

British retiring on La Fère—Noyon.

Battle on the Meuse.

Austria declared war on Belgium.

Battle of Tannenberg continued.

Gen. Plehwe's Army Group moved forward from Lublin-Lutsk.

Gens. Russky, Ivanoff, and Brusiloff advancing in Galicia.

Main Indian convoy preparing to sail from Bombay and Karachi for Marseilles.

August 29.

British base to be transferred to St. Nazaire, with Le Mans as advanced base. Communications with Havre threatened.

Sir J. French conferred with Gen. Joffre.

Gen. von Kluck at Péronne.

British fell back from La Fère—Noyon.

Battle of Guise. Three German Corps heavily defeated by French Fifth Army.

French retired behind Aisne R.

Tannenberg battle turning in Hindenburg's favour, German ring closing about Neidenburg—Willenberg—Passenheim.

Gen. Brusiloff occupied Halicz.

British at Archibong (Cameroons).

Adm. Spee proceeded E. of Marshall Is.

*August 30.

British s.s. *Holtby*, mined off Seaham reached Tyne.

Belgian troops from Namur transferred to Antwerp, via Ostend.

British 3rd Army Corps (Gen. Pulteney) formed in France: 4th Division and 19th Infantry Brigade.

German First Army, having reached with its right wing Amiens, started wheeling towards the Oise in support of Second Army.

Germans reached Noyon, La Fère, and Laon.

Germans across the Meuse.

First German aeroplane raid on Paris.

German G.H.Q. at Luxemburg.

At Tannenberg, Gen. Samsonoff killed; his army routed.

British at Carus (Cameroons) driven back; Nsanakong captured from Germans.

New Zealand troops convoyed by Adm. Patey, landed at Apia, Samoa; British flag hoisted.

August 31.

British s.s. *Strathroy* (4,336 tons) sunk by H.I.M.S. *Karlsruhe* N.N.E. from Cape St. Roque, Brazil.

At the end of August all ships of Grand Fleet disembarked 50 per cent. of their rifle ammunition to help cover Army deficiency.

During August the British Admiralty commissioned three armed merchant ships, *Mantua, Alsatian* and *Oceanic*, to reinforce 10th (Blockade) Cruiser Squadron.

During August U21 covered 1,600 sea miles on a scouting cruise *via* S. Norway to Moray Firth and Firth of Forth.

R.M. Brigade withdrawn from Ostend.

German Naval Corps formed under Adm. von Schröder, in first place for garrison of Liége.

Givet fell under bombardment of Austro-German heavy guns.

Gen. von Kluck at Noyon.

Sir J. French at Dammartin.

German aeroplane raid on Paris.

French Armies on Aisne—Reims—Verdun line.

Battle of Grand Couronné (Nancy).

Battle of Tannenberg ended; Narev Army destroyed; two Russian corps commanders and over 80,000 men prisoners. Gen. Rennenkampf retiring on Insterburg.

Gen. von Hindenburg ordered by German G.H.Q. to clear E. Prussia, and to relieve threat to Silesia by striking towards Warsaw.

H.I.M.S. *Nürnberg* at Honolulu.

H.M.SS *Australia* (F.Adm. Patey) and *Melbourne*, with French cruiser *Montcalm*, felt Samoa to escort Australian force to Rabaul and Herbertshöhe.

September 1.

Z IX. raided Belgian coast.

Aeroplane raid on Paris.

Sir J. French conferred with Lord Kitchener in Paris.

Gen. Joffre's G.H.Q. at Bar-sur-Aube.

British rearguard action in Compiègne—Villers-Cotterets Woods; "L" battery's heroic stand at Néry, N.W. Crépy-en-Valois.

British 4th Guards Brigade and 6th Infantry Brigade attacked by Gen. von Kluck's IInd Corps and Gen. von. der Marwitz's Cavalry Corps. German 4th Cavalry Division heavily hit, losing two-thirds of its guns at Néry and abandoning rest in Ermenonville Wood. These two actions were the

September 1, 1914 (continued).

only serious German attempt to interfere with B.E.F. in retreat after Le Cateau.

St. Petersburg renamed " Petrograd."

Russian retirement towards Bug R.

Battle of Lemberg (Galicia) going against Austrians.

September 2.

H.M.S. *King Edward VII.* rejoined Grand Fleet after exchanging defective guns at Devonport, whereupon *Dominion* sent south for similar work.

Malines church tower shelled and destroyed.

Gen. von Kluck at Compiègne. During the night he was instructed by G.H.Q. that : " The intention is to drive the French S.E. from Paris. First Army to follow in echelon behind Second Army and secure flank of the Armies."

German First Army engaged about Creil—Senlis ; Second Army moving through Soissons towards Château-Thierry, which, however, was first reached by Gen. von Kluck's IXth Corps. Marne crossed.

Allies hardening on Seine, Marne (British at Lagny-Meaux), and Meuse above Verdun.

Kaiser on Crown Prince's front, where first battle of Varennes begun.

First captured French and Russian guns paraded in Berlin.

Austrian check near Lublin (Poland).

Austrian defeat at Lemberg (Galicia).

Japanese landed at Tsingtau.

September 3.

British s.s. *Maple Branch* (4,338 tons) sunk by H.I.M.S. *Karlsruhe* S.W. from St. Paul Rocks.

H.M.S. *Speedy* mined off Humber R.

British 7th and 8th Battle Squadrons joined Channel Fleet.

U19, U20, U21, and U22, with U24 and U28, transferred to the Ems.

Prince Henry of Prussia hoisted his flag in H.I.M.S. *Blücher* for a " Demonstration " cruise in the Baltic.

French Government at Bordeaux.

Gen. von Kluck at Laferté-Milon.

German First Army swinging S.E. within 30 miles of Paris ; Second Army a day's march behind.

German Third Army at Reims.

British retired across Marne.

Crown Prince took St. Ménéhould.

Pope Benedict XV. elected.

Austrians evacuated Lemberg.

French again attacked Cattaro.

Prince William (Wied) left Albania.

Gen. Stewart arrived at Nairobi (B.E. Africa). Von Lettow at Moshi preparing for Kilimandjaro campaign.

September 4.

British s.s. *Indian Prince* sunk by German A.M.C. *Kronprinz Wilhelm* 210 miles E. by N. from Pernambuco.

British cruiser squadrons swept down to entrance of the Skagerrak.

Belgians delaying German advance on Antwerp.

Germans took Termonde.

Sir J. French at Mortcerf and Melun.

Allied left and left centre behind Marne.

German right crossed Ourcq. Kluck's First Army towards Paris drawing S.E. across the Marne and across the front of Bülow's Second Army towards Montmirail.

German XIXth Corps, Third Army, at Châlons, converging on Troyes.

September 4 (continued).

Gen. Joffre instructed his commanders to prepare to take advantage of German First Army's exposed situation :—

Gen. Maunoury's Sixth Army to attack on 5th, towards Château-Thierry ; British Army on 6th towards Montmirail ; Fifth Army, Gen. Franchet d'Espérey (vice Lanrezac), to prepare to attack northward ; Gen. Foch's Ninth Army towards Sézanne-Fère ; Gen. de Langle de Cary's Fourth Army to hold German Fourth Army, while Gen. Sarrail (vice Gen. Ruffey) with Third Army to strike westward from S.W. of Verdun. Gen. de Castelnau's Second Army covering Nancy, and Gen. Dubail's First Army holding Vosges sector.

British s.s. *Southport* (3,588 tons) captured by H.I.M.S. *Geier* off Caroline Is. ; engines disabled and ship left at Kusaie ; engines repaired by Sept. 18, when ship left for Brisbane.

September 5.

Grand Fleet after cruising for three days off N.E. Scotland and Norway proceeded to Loch Ewe to coal.

Pact of London : Triple Entente Powers agreed not to make separate peace.

H.M.S. *Pathfinder* torpedoed by U21 off east coast of Scotland. First warship sunk by submarine.

British s.s. *Runo* mined off the Tyne ; 29 lost.

Gen. von Kluck at Rebais, about 35 miles due E. Paris, with 2nd Cavalry Corps scouting to southward N.E. Provins, with IVth, IIIrd, and IXth Corps, pressing S.E., and with IInd Corps covering his flank E. of Paris, while IVth Reserve Corps covered Army to N.E.

Sir J. French and Gen. Joffre at Melun.

Allied retirement ended.

At noon Maunoury's Sixth Army began Battle of Ourcq by attack on Kluck's IVth Reserve Corps, which had halted N. of Meaux ; at end of day Kluck had been compelled to order successive withdrawal of his marching corps from S. of Marne.

German aeroplane raid on Paris.

Kaiser watched German attack on Gen. de Castelnau's Second Army at the Grand Couronné, before Nancy.

Masurian Lakes battle. Two Prussian Corps from W. Front (26-viii.-14) also in line on Hindenburg's Eighth Army Front against Gen. Rennenkampf.

British driven from Nsanakong in Cameroons, Germans following across Nigerian frontier.

German attacks on Abercorn and Karonga, Northern Rhodesia, failed.

*September 6.

Portsmouth floating dock arrived at Invergordon (Cromarty Firth), the new repairing base for Grand Fleet.

Gen. von Kluck at Charly-sur-Marne with his IInd, IVth, and IVth Reserve Corps facing Maunoury in some confusion, and his IIIrd and IXth Corps transferred to Second Army.

Gen. Joffre's Army Order ; offensive to be resumed ; " no flinching to be tolerated."

First Marne Battle begun ; general Allied offensive ; left, including British, in progress ; centre standing, right giving slightly.

Russian offensive from Vistula to Upper Dniester.

Serbians invaded Syrmia.

Sundays marked with Asterisk (*).

September 7, 1914.

Adm. Colville placed in general command of Orkneys and Shetlands.

Grand Fleet put to sea from Loch Ewe.

Fall of Maubeuge after bombardment by Austro-German heavy guns.

Gen. von Kluck at Vendrest (Ourcq) with his IInd, IVth, and IVth Reserve Corps hard pressed between the Thérouane and Gergogne streams ; at 11.15 a.m. he urgently begged Gen. von Bülow, Second Army, to return the IIIrd and IXth Corps to the First Army and to transfer them from the Morin sector to Crouy—Laferté Milon. With the Second Army pivoted on its right flank at Montmirail, the withdrawal of the IIIrd and IXth Corps opened a gap in the German front which, when once the British had pierced the cavalry screen, widened to 30 miles.

On Marne Allied left progressed ; Germans along Ourcq driven back by French Sixth Army. British took Coulommiers. Von Kluck retired from Grand Morin. French Fifth Army passed through La Ferté Gaucher. On Allied right heavy fighting round Nancy.

H.I.M.SS. *Augsburg, Strassburg, Gazelle,* and T.B.D. V 25 holding up shipping in Gulf of Bothnia.

Hindenburg advancing towards the Niemen, his right penetrating Masurian Lake line.

Austrians (Marshal Potiorek) again across Save and Drina into Serbia.

Germans repulsed on River Tsavo (E. Africa).

Adm. Spee at Christmas Island.

H.I.M.S. *Nürnberg,* off Fanning Island ; destroyed cable station ; cut cable.

September 8.

Mr. Lloyd George's " Silver Bullet " speech.

First R.N.V.R. drafts for R.N.D. moved into Crystal Palace for training.

H.M.A.M.C. *Oceanic* (17,274 tons) wrecked off Shetland Is.

Gen. von Kluck at Laferté-Milon holding the front Cuvergnon—Changis with IXth Corps on his right wing and Gen. von der Marwitz's 2nd Cavalry Corps guarding southern flank of First Army on the Marne.

On Marne German right falling back. British left reached Marne-Petit-Morin line. French Fifth Army crossed Petit-Morin. Foch's Ninth Army thrust back on the right.

Germans bombarded Fort Troyon.

Fighting round Nancy.

Masurian Lake battle continued.

Gen. Botha in Union Parliament announced offensive against G.S.W. Africa.

September 9.

Chilian battleship *Almirante Latorre,* building at Elswick, purchased by Admiralty : renamed *Canada.*

H.M.S. *Orion* rejoined Grand Fleet after 21 days' absence to repair condenser trouble.

Sir J. French's first dispatch.

Sir J. French at Coulommiers.

Gen. von Kluck at Mareuil instructed by G.H.Q. to conform to a general retirement from Marne to Aisne.

Marne Battle : French Sixth Army, reinforced by fresh troops sent from Paris by Gen. Galliéni, drove Germans across Ourcq. British crossed Marne. French Fifth Army made good advance to Marne at Château-Thierry—Mézy. Foch carried Sézanne Plateau and attacked Fère—Champenoise, driving a wedge between Bülow and Saxons which

September 9 (*continued*).

caused precipitate retirement of both towards Epernay—Châlons.

Germans bombarded Nancy.

Fort Troyon refused to surrender.

H.I.M.S. *Blücher* and 4th (*Wittelsbach*) Squadron returned from Baltic to North Sea.

Z IV. raided Insterburg.

Masurian Lake battle ; Germans pressing Gen. Rennenkampf's left wing about Lyck.

September 10.

Adm. Wemyss (F. *Charybdis*), Western Patrol, to proceed to St. Lawrence to escort Canadian contingent.

British 42nd Division, first T.F. Division for overseas, embarked at Southampton for Egypt.

The Harwich Force, with the Battle Cruisers, including H.M.SS. *Invincible, Inflexible* and *New Zealand,* and Grand Fleet in support, swept out the Bight from a position ten or twelve miles off Heligoland. No German ships sighted. H.M.S. *Zealandia* reported having rammed and apparently sunk a U-Boat.

Parliament sanctioned additional 500,000 men.

German G.H.Q. admitted retirement of German right wing on Marne.

Gen. von Kluck at Cœuvres (S.W. Soissons) again under von Bülow.

Marne Battle ended. Germans retreated all along line except Crown Prince's Army. British beyond Marne at Laferté Milon—Neuilly St. Front—Rocourt. Gen. Foch at Fère-Champenoise. Vitry occupied by French Fourth Army.

German attack on Fort Troyon failed.

Gen. Rennenkampf withdrawing his centre about Gerdauen.

Austrians under Archduke Joseph defeated and retired towards the San.

Russians holding Kolomea oil-fields.

Serbians occupied Semlin.

Germans took Kisi (Nyassaland).

H.I.M.S. *Emden* in Bay of Bengal.

September 11.

H.M.S. *Hibernia* reported 12-inch gun cracked ; fifth such defect since outbreak of war.

British 6th Division landed at St. Nazaire.

Gen. von Moltke's last war-council at Reims.

Gen. von Kluck at Fontenoy (Aisne).

Allied left advancing on Compiègne. British reached Aisne near Soissons. Foch entered Châlons. Sarrail retook Revigny.

Germans retook Insterburg.

Russians closing on Grodek.

Australians captured German Headquarters at Herbertshöhe (New Guinea).

H.I.M.S. *Leipzig* sank British s.s. *Elsinore* (6,542 tons) off Cape Corrientes.

September 12.

H.I.M.A.M.C. *Spreewald* captured by H.M.S. *Berwick* in North Atlantic.

H.I.M.S. *Hela* torpedoed and sunk by H.M. submarine E9 six miles S.S.W. from Heligoland.

H.I.M.SS. *König* and *Grosser Kurfürst* (25,390 ton battleships), having joined High Sea Fleet, Adm. von Ingenohl, German C.-in-C. at Wilhelmshaven, asked German Admiralty Staff to authorise transfer of 3rd High Sea Squadron to Baltic, in order to exercise new ships in waters free from submarines.

Sir J. French at Fère-en-Tardenois,

September 12, 1914 (*continued*).

Gen. von Kluck at Juvigny. Position warfare began on front of German First Army which in some thirty days had marched and fought over 375 miles from Aix to E. of Paris and thence back to Aisne.

Gen. von Einem to command German Third Army vice Gen. von Hausen.

Gen. von Heeringen's Seventh Army (which, like German Sixth Army on Moselle, had failed before Epinal) transferred from St. Dié to Aisne to close gap between First and Second Armies.

Gen. von Deimling's XVth (Prussian) Corps transferred from Lorraine to Aisne on new Seventh Army front.

Germans in position along Aisne evacuated Reims. Siege of Troyon raised by Crown Prince's retirement. French reoccupied Lunéville.

Russians evacuated Tilsit. Prussian 3rd Reserve Division reached Suvalki.

Vistula-Dniester Battle ended. Austrian rout.

Serbians took Jarak (Syrmia).

Germans driven from Kisi (Nyassaland).

＊September 13.

Dreadnought Battle Fleet at Loch Ewe.

Four days' battle N. of Brussels begun.

Battle of the Aisne opened.

Reims and Soissons recaptured by Allies.

French Sixth Army crossed Aisne; British at Venizel and between Venizel and Missy, at Vailly, Chavonne, Pont-Arcy and Bourg.

Nancy-Vosges sector cleared.

Germans checked on Niemen R., but reached Prusso-Russian frontier at Eydtkuhnen.

British s.s. *Diplomat* (7,615 tons) sunk by H.I.M.S. *Emden* 480 miles N.E. from Madras.

Japanese captured Kiaochow railway station.

Australians occupied Bougainville, Solomon Islands.

September 14.

H.M.A.M.C. *Carmania* sank off Brazil H.I.M.A.M.C. *Cap Trafalgar*, which had been fitted out by H.I.M.S. *Eber*, now at Bahia.

H.I.M.S. *Karlsruhe* sank British s.s. *Highland Hope* (5,150 tons) S.W. from St. Paul Rocks.

Adm. Cradock ordered to concentrate a squadron strong enough to meet *Scharnhorst* and *Gneisenau*, with Falkland Is. as his base.

Gen. von Falkenhayn German Acting Chief of Staff, vice Gen. von Moltke, invalided.

Gen. von Stein to command Prussian XIVth Reserve Corps; succeeded later as Quarter-Master General by Gen. Wild von Hohenborn.

French Sixth Army carried Aisne line at Compiègne—Soissons, and advanced against plateau beyond. British dug in on slopes, except First Corps on right under Sir D. Haig, which advanced to Troyon—Cour-de-Soupir, facing Chemin-des-Dames. French Fifth Army attacked Craonne Plateau. Germans clinging to Berry-au-bac. French Ninth and Fourth Armies advanced; latter took Souain. Crown Prince's Army in retreat; headquarters removed from St. Ménéhould to Montfaucon. Châlons-Verdun line clear.

British 6th Division now concentrated S. of Marne; proceeding to Aisne front.

Gen. Rennenkampf extricated bulk of his Niemen Army from Hindenburg's grip with loss of 45,000 prisoners and 150 guns.

September 14 (*continued*).

Russians holding Drohobycz oil-fields (Galicia); San R. forced behind retreating Austrians.

Serbo-Montenegrins at Vishegrad,

H.I.M.S. *Emden* sank British s.s. *Trabboch* and *Ulan Matheson* off Mouth of Hooghli.

Adm. Spee appeared off Samoa.

September 15.

Gen. von Kluck at Vauxaillon.

On Aisne Germans drove back French Sixth Army; French flank attack towards Noyon continued and held by newly-arrived German IXth Reserve Corps. Soissons shelled and on fire.

Masurian Lake battle ended on E. Prussian frontier.

Gen. Ludendorff designated Chief of Staff of new Ninth Army to be formed in Upper Silesia.

Russians took Czernowitz (Bukovina).

Serbians before continuous Austrian attacks fell back from Drina, but first invasion at this date partially exhausted.

British defeated Germans at Ramans Drift (S.W. Africa).

Complete capitulation of German New Guinea to Adm. Patey.

September 16.

Adm. von Tirpitz in memorandum to Adm. von Pohl expressed opinion that High Sea Fleet's best chance of an effective blow against England had passed during the first two or three weeks of the war.

By this date British Naval Transport Service had cleared Boulogne, Havre, and Rouen. During preceding six days there had left Havre 20,000 officers and men, 4,000 horses, and 60,000 tons of stores.

British armed motor-cars under Commander Samson cut up Uhlans near Doullens.

Brig.-Gen. Haking, British 5th Infantry Brigade, wounded.

Lull in British Aisne sector. French Fifth Army before Craonne Plateau. French Sixth Army clinging to German flank about Noyon.

Tsar prohibited sale of alcohol.

Russian advance on Przemysl (Galicia).

September 17.

Mr. Churchill, First Lord of Admiralty, accompanied by Adm. Sturdee, Chief of War Staff, Commodore (S) Keyes, and Commodore (T) Tyrwhitt, conferred at Loch Ewe with Adm. Jellicoe, and discussed bombardment and capture of Heligoland. All Flag Officers except one opposed. Large-scale operations in Baltic also discussed.

H.M.S. *Erin* (ex-Turkish *Resha iiey*) joined Grand Fleet, which once more put to sea.

H.M.S. *Fisgard II.* lost off Portland.

Malines—Aerschot Battle ended. Belgians retired on Antwerp.

Gen. von Beseler's Antwerp Army Group formed.

Gen. Bridoux, who had taken over Gen. Sordet's 1st Cavalry Corps, killed in a raid on German communications E. from Roye.

French Sixth Army regained ground between Soissons—Compiègne.

British before Chemin-des-Dames repelled Germans. French lost Craonne. French Ninth Army fell back on Reims.

Serbians evacuated Semlin.

French Adriatic Squadron bombarded Lissa and Pelagosa.

Small British force at Nakob (G.S.W. Africa) overcome by German raiders.

September 18, 1914.

Parliament prorogued. King's Speech : " We are fighting for a worthy purpose."

Cape Garrison at Southampton.

Gen. Maunoury to stand at Soissons—Bailly, pending formation of fresh Army under Gen. de Castelnau N.W. of Noyon.

Allies held up on Aisne. British pressed at Troyon and French Ninth Army at Reims. Bombardment of Reims begun.

Brig.-Gen. the Earl of Cavan arrived in France to command 4th (Guards) Brigade, vice Brig.-Gen. Scott-Kerr, wounded.

Hindenburg (with Ludendorff as Chief of Staff) to take over new German Ninth Army for combined Austro-German movement against Russian centre in Poland.

Gen. von Schubert to command depleted German Eighth Army, vice Hindenburg.

Russians took Sandomir.

Russo-Rumanian Agreement signed.

Lüderitz Bay (G.S.W. Africa) occupied by British.

September 19.

Grand Fleet in North Sea proceeding southward.

German attacks on Aisne and on Meuse Heights.

Reims Cathedral bombarded.

Adm. Troubridge recalled for inquiry into escape of H.I.M.SS. *Goeben* and *Breslau.*

British Tsingtau Force under Gen. Barnardiston left Tientsin.

H.M. Submarine AE 1 lost on patrol in Bismarck Archipelago ; cause unknown.

S.S. *Ortega* (8,075 tons) chased by H.I.M.S. *Dresden* in S. Atlantic, escaped, doubling the Horn through uncharted Nelson Straits.

*September 20.

Grand Fleet in support of Battle Cruisers engaged in examining trawlers off Little Fisher Bank.

R.M. Brigade and Oxfordshire Hussars, under Gen. Aston, landed at Dunkirk.

U9 left Heligoland to operate against British Channel transports.

French Second Army (Gen. de Castelnau) re-formed N.W. of Noyon.

Reims Cathedral bombarded.

German attack on Fort Troyon (Meuse) repulsed.

Gen. Ivanoff attacked Jaroslav (Galicia).

Adm. Carden C.-in-C. Mediterranean.

H.I.M.S. *Königsberg* sank H.M.S. *Pegasus* off Zanzibar.

Second Indian convoy, 29 transports, sailed from Bombay, escorted by H.M.SS. *Swiftsure, Fox* and *Dufferin.*

September 21.

Grand Fleet swept back to northward on a front of 40 miles, with cruisers prolonging to E. and W.

Gen. Rawlinson in temporary command 4th Division, vice Gen. Snow, invalided.

German Eighth Army pushed forward to Niemen at Druskeniki—Kovno.

H.I.M.S. *Breslau* entered Black Sea.

September 22.

Gen. Alderson in command First Canadian Division.

H.M.SS. *Aboukir, Cressy* and *Hogue* (12,000 tons each) sunk in succession by U 9 (Kapitän-Leutnant Otto Weddigen) with five torpedoes about 30 miles W. by S. from Ymuiden. Some 60 officers and 1,400 men

September 22 (*continued*).

lost. German U-Boat commander received Pour le Mérite Order.

British air raid on Düsseldorf Zeppelin sheds.

Russian investment of Przemysl (Galicia).

Serbs moved on Serajevo (Bosnia).

H.I.M.S. *Goeben* in Black Sea.

H.I.M.S. *Emden* bombarded Madras.

H.I.M.SS. *Scharnhorst* and *Gneisenau* bombarded Papeete (Tahiti) and sank French gunboat *Zélée.*

September 23.

H.I.M. minelayer *Kaiser* left Wilhelmshaven for Rattray Head.

H.I.M. minelayer *Berlin*, which also left Wilhelmshaven, ran into a fog N.W. Heligoland and returned to port.

Bavarian Crown Prince's Sixth Army completed transfer from Lorraine to Artois ; reinforced on 1-x.-14 by Prussian Guard.

Aisne battle extending northwards along Oise R.

Germans attacked St. Mihiel (Meuse), S. of Verdun.

Jaroslav (Galicia) fell to Russians.

British under Gen. Barnardiston landed at Laoshan Bay to co-operate with Japanese in attack on Tsingtau.

Gen. Dobell off Duala, Cameroons.

September 24.

Germans mined Langeland Belt on report that British warships had passed Great Belt.

Z IX. raided Ostend.

Germans occupied Péronne.

Z IV. raided Bialystok.

German raid on Belgian post in Lake Kiwu (Ruanda).

Adm. Patey (F.H.M.S. *Australia*) occupied Friedrich Wilhelm, Kaiser Wilhelm's Land (New Guinea).

September 25

U-Boat fired two torpedoes at H.M.S. *Stag* and another at a T.B. off May Island.

Albert Battle begun. De Castelnau driven out of Lassigny—Noyon. Heavy fighting at Ribécourt—Albert.

Bavarians, after taking Fort Camp-des-Romains, occupied St. Mihiel and formed salient, which they maintained for four years.

Russians driven across Niemen R.

Z IV. raided Warsaw.

H.I.M.S. *Emden* captured and sank two British steamers off Point de Galle and Colombo.

H.I.M.S. *Leipzig* sank British s.s. *Bankfields* in Gulf of Guayaquil.

September 26.

British 1st Battle Cruiser Squadron swept down Norwegian coast to the Naze in search of German commerce destroyers.

Z IX. raided Boulogne.

Germans besieging Antwerp.

Gen. von Lüttwitz, Military Commandant of Brussels, ordered arrest of M. Max, Burgomaster of the city.

Malines bombarded and set on fire.

Germans driven out of Audeghem.

Fierce Oise-Somme fighting.

Gen. de Castelnau halted at Ribécourt—Roye—Chaulnes—Bray-sur-Somme ; to await formation of new Army on his left flank.

Mr. Churchill visited Sir J. French on the Aisne.

Germans failed to cross Meuse at St. Mihiel.

For List of Abbreviations see page iv.

September 26, 1914 (*continued*).

Indian E.F. landed at Marseilles.

French battleships *Suffren* (Adm. Gué-pratte), and *Vérité* joined Adm. Milne's squadron outside Dardanelles.

British Mesopotamia Expedition originated in a minute of this date by Gen. Barrow, Military Secretary India Office, suggesting that a force be sent from India to occupy Basra, in the event of Turkey's entering the war.

Japanese drove in Tsingtau outposts.

British reverse at Sandfontein (G.S.W. Africa).

* September 27.

H.M.S. *Attentive* in Dover Straits attacked with torpedo and missed by U18, first German submarine in the Channel.

M. Max conveyed to Namur.

Antwerp forts bombarded ; siege begun.

Germans reoccupied Malines ; driven back at Labbeke.

Aisne Battle dying down.

Battle of Albert continued.

German air raid on Paris.

Hindenburg's Ninth Army concentrated for advance on Warsaw : XIth Corps N.E. Cracow ; Gallwitz's Guard Reserve Corps, the XXth Corps, and Mackensen's XVIIth Corps between Kattowitz—Kreuzburg ; and Frommel's mixed group between Kempen—Kalish.

Franco-British force at Duala (Cameroons), which surrendered after bombardment.

H.M.S. *Princess Royal* left 1st Battle Cruiser Squadron to meet and protect in Atlantic first convoy of Canadian troops proceeding to England.

German liner *Brandenburg* interned at Trondhjem.

Attack on Antwerp continued.

Aisne Battle ended ; Albert Battle continued.

Gen. Sixt von Armin's IVth (Prussian) Corps transferred from First Army front to Sixth Army before Arras.

French counter-attack about Reims.

German G.H.Q. at Charleville.

Austrian First Army and German Ninth Army in advance on general line Radom—Lodz.

Krosno and Dukla Pass (Galicia) taken by Russians.

All Galician oil-fields in Russian hands.

Russian cavalry raid into Hungary.

Japanese carried Prince Heinrich Hill, Tsingtau.

September 29.

Antwerp Fort Wavre Ste. Catherine silenced.

Albert Battle ended.

Sir J. French proposed to Gen. Joffre immediate transfer of British forces from Aisne to left flank of Allied line in the West.

Ossowietz relieved. Russians pursuing Hindenburg from Niemen.

Russians 100 miles from Cracow.

Tsingtau bombarded.

H.I.M.S. *Emden* off Pondicherry.

Adm. Yamaya occupied Jaluit.

September 30.

Antwerp waterworks destroyed.

During September there arrived in France the London Scottish and the H.A.C. infantry battalion.

September 30 (*continued*).

First recorded air-combat took place on W. Front during September, and during this period the R.F.C. first fitted an aeroplane with a gun.

French Tenth Army (Gen. Maud'huy) brought up round Arras—Lens, extending Allied flanking movement. Group formed by French Second and Tenth Armies placed under Gen. Foch.

German attack at Tsingtau failed.

H.I.M.S. *Emden* off Malabar coast.

October 1.

H.M.S. *Theseus* returning from White Sea, where she had been to fetch some Russian officers.

Admiralty closed E. Coast ports to neutral fishing craft.

Kaiser's message on " General French's Contemptible Little Army " published.

At Antwerp : fall of Forts Waelhem, Koningshoyckt, and Lierre. Belgians retiring N. of the Nethe.

Gen. Maud'huy advancing on Douai.

Battle before Arras.

Preliminary orders issued for transfer of B.E.F. from Aisne to left of Allied line.

Russians pursuing Hindenburg harassed Germans in Augustovo Woods.

Turkey closed Dardanelles.

October 2.

Mr. Asquith at Cardiff on German overtures in 1912.

Admiralty ordered defensive minefield to be laid in Southern area of North Sea.

H.M. submarine B3 (Dover Patrol) attacked by U-Boat off Goodwins.

Kaiser at G.H.Q. Charleville, instructed Adm. von Pohl that he reserved to himself control of High Sea Fleet which must for the present be preserved intact ; torpedo boats, U-Boats and mines must continue to be used until further notice.

R.M. Brigade (Gen. Paris, vice Gen. Aston, invalided) to proceed from Dunkirk to Antwerp.

Fighting near Roye.

Fighting near Augustovo.

British attacked at Gazi (E. Africa).

H.M.S. *Cumberland* captured nine German liners in Cameroon R.

October 3.

Adm. Wemyss escorted first Canadian convoy (31 ships) out of St. Lawrence ; two more ships, with Newfoundland contingent and 2nd Lincolns from Bermuda, joined off Cape Race.

Grand Fleet in position in North Sea to secure protection of first convoy of Canadian troops crossing Atlantic from Halifax.

British North Sea minefield notified.

Adm. von Pohl conveyed Kaiser's order (2-x.-14) to Adm. von Ingenohl and to the latter's Chief of Staff, Adm. Eckermann, at Wilhelmshaven, and informed them that the battle cruisers might be used for offensive raids.

Mr. Churchill arrived at Antwerp to concert measures for delaying withdrawal of Belgian Field Army.

Antwerp outer defences fell ; German attempt to cross Nethe at Waelhem failed.

Germans reached Ypres.

Transfer of British Army to West Flanders begun.

Sundays marked with Asterisk (*).

October 3, 1914 (*continued*).

Gen. Willcocks, G.O.C. Indian Contingent, reported himself at British G.H.Q. on arrival in France.

At Orleans, the Indian advance base, there had now arrived the 15th Lancers, one artillery brigade, and two infantry brigades.

Crown Prince's attack towards St. Ménéhould repulsed ; French at Varennes.

Austro-German invasion of Poland begun.

*October 4.

R.N.D. arrived at Dunkirk for Antwerp under command of Gen. Paris, vice Gen. Aston, invalided.

Germans reached Poperinghe.

Gen. de Maud'huy retired on Arras ; Germans occupied Lens.

Austro-German advance against Russian centre in Poland supported by Austrian advance in Galicia.

Serbs falling back in Bosnia.

German Professors' Manifesto issued.

October 5.

British s.s. *Farn* captured by H.I.M.S. *Karlsruhe* 140 miles S.W. from St. Paul's Rock ; interned at San Juan P.R.

National Relief Fund £3,000,000.

Germans crossed Nethe.

President Poincaré visited Sir J. French at Fère-en-Tardenois.

Action near Radom.

Essad Pasha to administer Albania.

October 6.

H.I.M.T.B.D. S116 sunk by H.M. submarine E9 off the Ems.

R.N.D. at Antwerp.

Gen. Rawlinson, who had come up from the Aisne to assume command of British reinforcements in Belgium, attended with Mr. Churchill a war council at Antwerp.

Belgian Government left Antwerp. Germans across Nethe. Belgian Army withdrawn across Scheldt. Large German cavalry forces about Lille—Armentières in race to sea.

Arras bombarded.

German line in France hardening about Lille, E. of Arras, W. of Baupaume and Roye, S. of Noyon, N. of Aisne to Craonne, Brimont, Somme-Py, N.E. Verdun.

Russians retiring in Poland and Galicia.

Marshall Islands occupied by Adm. Yamaya's 1st Japanese South Seas Squadron.

October 7.

U-Boat sighted in Loch Ewe.

British 7th Division, Gen. Capper, landed at Zeebrugge.

Belgian Government at Ostend. Evacuation of Antwerp. Germans across Scheldt at Termonde, but held up at Zele. Bombardment of city begun. Gen. Rawlinson at Bruges covering retreat.

Adm. Ronarc'h's Marine Brigade left Paris for Belgian front.

Russians withdrawing from Carpathian passes.

October 8.

British 3rd Cavalry Division (Gen. Byng) landed at Zeebrugge, and moved to Ostend, before which 7th Division in position. Gen. Rawlinson's H.Q. at Bruges.

Antwerp inner forts fell.

French Marine Brigade reinforcing Allied ne at Ghent.

October 8 (*continued*).

Gen. Foch at Doullens.

Sir J. French transferred his G.H.Q. from Fère-en-Tardenois to Abbeville, N.E. of which British 2nd Corps concentrating.

Germans at Douai—Lens. Lille bombarded.

German air raid on Paris.

Zeppelin destroyed in its shed at Düsseldorf by Flight-Lieut. Marix, R.N.A.S.

Gen. von François to command German Eighth Army, vice Gen. von Schubert.

Z IV. over Shavli (Lithuania).

Russians took Lyck (E. Prussia).

October 9.

H.M.S. *Antrim* off Stavanger just failed to ram U-Boat that fired two torpedoes at her.

Germans entered Antwerp. Gen. von Beseler received Pour le Mérite Order.

Part of R.N.D. and 18,000 Belgians crossed into Holland ; interned.

British Cavalry Corps in France formed under Gen. Allenby. Gen. de Lisle 1st Division ; Gen. Gough 2nd Division.

Gen. von Hollen's 4th Cavalry Corps attacked Hazebrouck.

German defeat at Augustovo (E. Prussia).

Austro - Germans nearing Ivangorod. Mackensen's XVIIth Corps engaged at Grojetz, S. of Warsaw, newly arrived Russo-Siberian Corps.

Russians fell back from Przemysl.

French T.B. 347 and T.B. 348 lost by collision at Toulon.

October 10.

H.M.S. *Princess Royal* met Canadian convoy in Mid-Atlantic. *Majestic* in support.

Capitulation of Antwerp.

R.N.D. re-embarked at Ostend and sent into camp at Deal.

German Second Army (von Bülow) transferred from Reims sector to St. Quentin.

Duke Albrecht of Wurtemberg transferred his Fourth Army H.Q. from Champagne to Belgium, reinforced by young troops of new Prussian XXIInd, XXIIIrd, XXVIth, and XXVIIth Corps.

Gen. Rawlinson's force (7th Division and 3rd Cavalry Division) to form British Fourth Army Corps, under the orders of Sir J. French.

Lille again bombarded.

Z IV. over Tauroggen.

Battle before Ivangorod.

Gen. Russky in Galicia falling back.

Austrians at Tarnov.

King Carol of Rumania died ; nephew Ferdinand succeeded.

*October 11.

Grand Fleet W. of Orkneys.

French Marine Brigade fell back from Ghent to Thielt.

Gen. Byng's 3rd Cavalry Division at Thourout.

British from Aisne aligning on Gen. Maud'huy's left. Gen. Smith-Dorrien on La Bassée Canal.

Three French and British Cavalry Corps (Gens. Conneau, de Mitry, and Allenby) sweeping N. and N.E. between Vermelles and W. of Hazebrouck.

Prussian Guard Cavalry engaged at La Bassée.

British 1st Corps left the Aisne for St. Omer.

Air raid on Paris ; Notre Dame hit.

For List of Abbreviations see page iv.

*October 11, 1914 (*continued*).

Russian cruiser *Pallada* sunk by U26 in Baltic ; cruiser *Bayan* escaped.

Austrians relieved Przemysl and recovered Jaroslav.

October 12.

Grand Fleet returned to Scapa. Cruisers swept down to Dogger Bank.

Admiral of Patrols reconstituted himself on Humber to organise anti-U-Boat measures.

Adm. Hood to be Rear-Admiral commanding Dover Patrol, including 6th T.B.D. Flotilla and Downs Boarding Flotilla, and S. N. O. Dover.

New British (ex-Brazilian) monitors *Mersey*, *Severn* and *Humber* ordered to proceed from Dover to Ostend.

Belgian Government withdrew by sea from Ostend to Havre.

Gen. von Beseler's troops from Antwerp entered Ghent. Gen. Rawlinson's cavalry at Roulers covering Belgian retreat. Allies evacuated Ostend—Zeebrugge. British 7th Division and French Marine Brigade at Thielt.

Sir J. French transferred G.H.Q. from Abbeville to St. Omer.

British 3rd Corps at Hazebrouck.

German XIXth Corps at Lille.

Prussian Guard Cavalry at Festubert—Givenchy.

German aeroplane dropped six bombs on Paris.

M. Max interned in Prusso-Silesian fortress of Glatz.

Mackenzen S.E. of Blonie (Warsaw) position.

Martial law in S. Africa.

October 13.

British 1st Battle Cruiser Squadron, with light forces, swept on broad front down to Dogger Bank and Norwegian coast.

H.M. T.B.116 sighted and just missed ramming U-Boat off the Isle of Wight.

Belgian Government at Havre.

Germans levied £20,000,000 on Antwerp.

French Marine Brigade at Thourout.

Gen. Byng's 3rd Cavalry Division at Ypres.

Gen. Smith-Dorrien wheeling S. round La Bassée ; hard fighting, especially at Festubert. Gen. Pulteney carried Meteren.

German air raids on Reims and Nancy.

Germans retook Lyck (E. Prussia).

Lt.-Col. Maritz, commanding Union detachment on Orange R., rebelled.

Adm. Spee at Easter Island.

October 14.

First Canadian Convoy at Plymouth.

H.I.M. auxiliary minelayer *Berlin* left Wilhelmshaven (27-x-14).

Germans passed Bruges. Gen. Byng's 3rd Cavalry Division joined Gen. Gough's 2nd Cavalry Division in front of Kemmel, which these two Divisions captured and secured. Gen. Pulteney at Bailleul. Gen. Hubert Hamilton killed near La Bassée.

Hindenburg's left in advance on Warsaw, at Mlava, and Plock ; centre beyond Lovicz, right S.E. of Radom.

October 15.

H.M.S. *Theseus* attacked and H.M.S. *Hawke* (7,350 tons) torpedoed and sunk by U 9 in North Sea.

H.M.S. *Swift* sent to pick up survivors of *Hawke* (one officer 20 men) also attacked.

October 15 (*continued*).

Two British E submarines working in the Baltic.

U16 returned to Heligoland after fortnight's cruise.

Gen. von Beseler's IIIrd Reserve Corps entered Ostend—Zeebrugge.

First Battle of Ypres. First phase.

French Marine Brigade at Dixmude.

Belgian Army behind Yser.

King Albert at La Panne.

Three German Cavalry Corps, including Prussian Guard Cavalry Division, now on right wing of German Sixth Army, southward of Messines.

Gen. Pulteney reached Lys R. towards Armentières.

Gen. Smith-Dorrien's left wheeling on La Bassée ; pushed Germans off Estaires—La Bassée Road ; his right at Givenchy.

Germans in Argonne captured La Barricade and St. Hubert.

First Warsaw battle begun along Vistula.

Austrian cruiser *Kaiserin Elizabeth* sunk at Kiaochow.

Japanese permitted non-combatants to leave Tsingtau.

Rebel Maritz's forces defeated at Ratedrai (S. Africa).

October 16.

U-Boats reported inside Scapa Flow ; Grand Fleet moved out to W. of Orkneys.

Battle of Yser begun : German attack on Dixmude held by French Marine Brigade under Adm. Ronarc'h and (later also) French 89th Territorial Division.

Houthulst Forest abandoned.

Gen. Rawlinson in front of Ypres.

Allied fleets bombarded Cattaro.

Germans 7 miles from Warsaw.

General Allied attack at Tsingtau.

H.I.M.S. *Emden's* collier *Markomannia* destroyed by H.M.S. *Yarmouth*.

October 17.

Grand Fleet bases transferred to Lough Swilly and Loch-na-Keal.

H.M.SS. *Undaunted* and *Lance*, *Legion*, *Lennox* and *Loyal* sank German Ems T.B.D.s S115, 117, 118, and 119 off Dutch coast while bound on minelaying enterprise in Channel.

H.I.M.S. *Ophelia* sent to rescue survivors of above action was captured by British next day.

H.I.M. auxiliary minelayer *Berlin* left port on mine-laying expedition to N. Scotland.

H.M. monitors *Humber*, *Severn*, and *Mersey* with Adm. Hood (F. *Attentive*) supporting Belgians in Yser Battle.

Fierce fighting on Yser. Gen. von Beseler's IIIrd Reserve Corps engaged on extreme German right. This corps formed right wing of Fourth German Army, now in position from coast to Lys with four young Reserve Corps (10-x-14), Gen. von Deimling's XVth Active Corps, Naval Corps, &c., and Prussian Guard Cavalry Division.

Gen. Pulteney halted on Bois Grenier—Nieppe—Le Gheir. Gen. Smith-Dorrien took Aubers and Herlies.

German air raid on Paris.

Warsaw saved by arrival of Russian reinforcements on completion of Russian Main Army mobilisation.

Japanese cruiser *Takachiho* sunk by German T.B.D. S90 in Kiaochau Bay.

*October 18.

H.M. submarine E3 torpedoed off Ems R. by U27, which had been lying in wait all day.

Sundays marked with Asterisk (*).

*October 18, 1914 (continued).

H.M. submarine E1, having passed into Baltic the day before, attacked German patrol cruiser *Fürst Bismarck.*

H.M. monitors *Severn, Mersey,* and *Humber,* with H.M.S. *Attentive* later H.M.S. *Amazon* as F. Adm. Hood, shelled Belgian coast towards Westende.

Yser line held.

King Albert at Dixmude.

Gen. Bidon, with Dunkirk Territorial Divisions, before Ypres.

Germans, after three days' struggle, occupied Roulers.

Gen. Pulteney at Armentières.

German counter-attacks against Gen. Smith-Dorrien before La Bassée.

Mackensen during night of Oct. 18-19 began to fall back from Warsaw on to the line Rawa—Lovicz.

Austrian attempts to cross San R. (Galicia).

October 19.

British Naval D.S.M. instituted.

British ships off Belgian coast in support of Allied flank.

British transfer from Aisne to Flanders completed. Allied line to coast formed. Road to Calais barred.

Indian troops near Béthune supporting Gen. Smith-Dorrien.

Gen. Allenby's cavalry N. of Gen. Pulteney from Le Gheir to Hollebeke. Gen. Rawlinson advancing from Ypres against Menin—Roulers, finding Germans too strong, fell back in front of Ypres. Sir D. Haig reinforced N. of Ypres. Belgians and French (Gen. d'Urbal) on Yser between Dixmude—Nieuport. Strong German attacks at Dixmude on French marines (Adm. Ronarc'h).

Sir J. French's dispatches of Sept. 17 and Oct. 8 published.

Germans retiring in Poland.

October 20.

British s.s. *Glitra* sunk off Norwegian coast by U 17. First U-Boat victim.

H.M. submarine E9 passed into Baltic.

H.M. submarine E1 in Danzig Bay.

H.M.S. *Amazon* hit off Westende ; Adm. Hood transferred flag to H.M.S. *Cossack.*

German fire destroyed British naval machine-gun detachment landed to hold Bamburg Farm. Lombaertzyde evacuated.

German Naval Corps began and continued until Armistice its occupation of Flanders coast.

Belgians preparing to flood Yser region. Germans took Poelcapelle.

Heavy fighting at Arras and La Bassée German Sixth Army in position on Arras—Lille front.

Lahore Division (Gen. Watkins) concentrated W. of Hazebrouck.

French Dreadnoughts *Flandre* and *Normandie* (25,000 tons each) launched at Brest and St. Nazaire.

Russian offensive before Warsaw.

October 21.

German s.s. *Crefeld* reached Teneriffe with crews of thirteen vessels captured or sunk by H.I.M.S. *Karlsruhe.*

Cromarty now U-Boat proof.

Adm. Hood (F.H.M.S. *Foresight)* bombarded Lombaertzyde and Groote Bamburg.

Germans failed at Dixmude.

Sir D. Haig's 1st Corps at Zonnebeke—St. Julien—Langemarck—Bixschoote after

October 21 (continued).

hard fight. French Territorials, Gen. de Mitry's 1st Cavalry Corps, Belgian forces, and French Marines on his left, in coast sector ; on his right, from Ypres to La Bassée, Gen. Rawlinson's 4th Corps, Gen. Allenby's Cavalry Corps, Gen. Pulteney's 3rd Corps with 19th Brigade, Gen. Conneau's 2nd Cavalry Corps, and Gen. Smith-Dorrien's 2nd Corps.

French recovery in Argonne.

H.M. submarine E1 at Libau.

German retreat from Warsaw.

October 22

H.M.S. *Iron Duke* at Lough Swilly.

Two military convoys from India and Egypt diverted to Liverpool.

H.M. submarine E9 at Libau.

H.M. submarine E11, having failed to pass into Baltic, returned to her base.

Belgians reoccupied Lombaertzyde.

Germans captured British trenches N. of Pilkem (Ypres).

Gen. Smith-Dorrien retired on Givenchy—Neuve Chapelle—Fauquissart.

Gen. Morland to command British 5th Division, vice Gen. Fergusson, invalided.

Lahore Division (Gen. Watkins) at Bailleul.

Gen. Russky crossed Vistula R. in pursuit of Germans.

Rebel Maritz repulsed at Keimoes (S. Africa).

October 23.

Lough Swilly temporarily obstructep against U-Boat attack. Grand Fleet for first time since declaration of war securely based.

Sugar imports into U.K. prohibited.

The Times Red Cross Fund = £500,000.

H.M.S. *Crusader,* flying the flag of Adm. Hood, reconnoitred and bombarded Ostend.

Germans (who from Yser to Lys were now attacking in dense columns, singing " *Die Wacht am Rhein*") repulsed at Dixmude.

French reinforced at Nieuport.

Heavy fighting round Langemarck (Ypres) ; British recovered Pilkem trenches.

Russians relieved Ivangorod and recovered Jaroslav.

Austrian gunboat *Temes* mined in Danube.

October 24.

First Newfoundland contingent arrived.

H.M.S. *Badger* rammed U19 in North Sea.

Germans occupied Polygon Wood (Ypres).

At La Bassée violent German attack. Indians in line. Climax of German attack at Arras.

De Wet, having joined rebellion, seized Heilbron (New Free State).

*October 25.

British 2nd Battle Cruiser Squadron in support of projected air raid on Cuxhaven Zeppelin sheds by Harwich Force ; operation prevented by heavy rain.

Vain German efforts to break through at Dixmude, Ypres, La Bassée, and Arras.

Germans reoccupied Vermelles.

Germans in retreat reached Radom (Poland) ; outflanked by Gen. Russky between Radom and Pilitza R.

Further defeat of Maritz near Galvinia (S. Africa).

October 26.

S.S. *Vandyk* (10,328 tons) captured and sunk by H.I.M.S. *Karlsruhe* 690 miles W. by S.

*For List of **Abbreviations** see page iv.*

October 26, 1914 (*continued*).

from St. Paul Rocks ; largest British ship sunk by Germans in 1914.

S.S. *Manchester Commerce* mined 20 miles N.E. from Tory Island.

French s.s. *Amiral Ganteaume* with 2,500 refugees torpedoed without warning in Channel and sunk.

Adm. Hood transferred flag to H.M.S. *Venerable*, which arrived to reinforce British Squadron off Belgian coast.

Fierce fighting on Yser. German attack at Pervyse.

At Arras Germans pushed back by Gen. Maud'huy.

Maritz driven into German territory.

Allies occupied Edea (Cameroons).

October 27.

British s.s. *Royal Sceptre* captured and released by H.I.M.S. *Karlsruhe* 500 miles W. from St. Paul Rocks.

H.M.S. *Audacious* (23,000 tons) sunk by mines off N. Ireland. Germans attributed loss to mines laid by German auxiliary *Berlin*.

White Star s.s. *Olympic* (46,359 tons), Capt. Haddock, U.S. to Liverpool, stood by *Audacious* all day and with a number of H.M. ships attempted to take her in tow ; attempts abandoned ; *Audacious* blew up and sank at 9 p.m.

Prince Maurice of Battenberg died of wounds.

Battle of Ypres : Second phase :

Nieuport sluices opened.

Nieuport—Dixmude front maintained.

French 9th Corps relieved British 1st Corps in N. sector of Ypres salient.

Gen. Rawlinson's 4th Corps broken up ; 7th Division attached 1st Corps.

Gen. Willcocks assumed command of Indian Corps in the field.

Germans took Neuve Chapelle.

Germans repulsed E. of Nancy.

Germans retiring on Czenstochau.

Maritz defeated, and Gen. Beyers with another rebel force routed by Gen. Botha.

October 28.

First Sea Lord Prince Louis of Batten·berg resigned.

British squadron off Belgian coast with H.M.S. *Venerable* (F. Adm. Hood) heavily engaged. H.M.SS. *Falcon, Mersey, Brilliant* and *Wildfire* hit and damaged.

Germans retook Lombaertzyde.

Indian Corps relieved British Second Corps on Neuve Chapelle front.

Russians regained Lodz and Radom (Poland).

H.I.M.S. *Emden* destroyed Russian cruiser *Zhemchug* at Penang and French T.B.D. *Mousquet*.

October 29.

Lord Fisher First Sea Lord.

Order in Council on conditional contraband.

Belgian coast bombardment continued.

Germans took Ramscapelle.

German mass attacks on British 1st and 7th Division front about Gheluvelt beaten off ; ground gained to E. of Gheluvelt.

Heavy fighting at Festubert, Germans captured trenches.

Brig.-Gen. F. S. Maude to command 14th Infantry Brigade, vice Gen. Rolt, invalided.

Turco - German warships bombarded Odessa and Sebastopol, where Russian mine-layer *Prut* sunk.

October 29 (*continued*).

Bedouin raid in Sinai.

Turkey entered war on Central side.

October 30.

H.S. *Rohilla* (7,891 tons) wrecked off Whitby.

Adm. Hood hoisted his flag in French T.B.D. *Intrépide*, and with *Aventurier* engaged German positions at Lombaertzyde.

Yser floods compelled German retreat.

Ypres close pressed by Germans. Bavarians at Hollebeke.

Gen. von Deimling's XVth Army Corps now fighting at Gheluvelt—Zandvoorde. By this date between Nieuport and La Bassée some 12 German Corps were opposed to 7 Allied Corps.

H.M. submarines E1 and E9 at Lapvig, under Russian Baltic Adm. Essen's orders.

Russian successes in Poland.

Entente Ambassadors to Turkey asked for passports.

H.I.M.S. *Königsberg* discovered hiding in Rufiji R. (E. Africa) shelled by H.M.S. *Chatham*.

S. African rebel Maritz again defeated.

October 31.

At the end of October the Dreadnought Fleet was reduced for a period to 17 effective battleships and 5 battle cruisers, against 15 German battleships, 4 battle cruisers and the *Blücher*.

During October the Rosyth base was provided with an effective obstruction against U-Boat attack.

H.M.S. *Hermes* (aircraft carrier, 5,600 tons) sunk by U27 eight miles off Calais.

During October U20 accomplished first German submarine voyage round British Isles ; cruise occupied eighteen days.

Yser floods extending. Allies drove Germans from Ramscapelle into flooded territory, and advanced along coast. Germans in disastrous situation ; many drowned.

Crisis at Ypres : British lost Gheluvelt ; recaptured with the bayonet towards 3 p.m. by 2nd Worcesters (Major Hankey), who were sent forward by Brig.-Gen. FitzClarence, V.C., 1st Guards Brigade. At outset of attack which broke British 1st Division line N. of Ypres—Menin road, Gen. Lomax, G.O.C. 1st Division, fatally wounded ; Gen. Monro, G.O.C. 2nd Division, temporarily disabled. Gen. Bulfin took over 1st Division. Less than half an hour before recapture of Gheluvelt, Gen. Haig issued orders that, failing Klein Zillebeke—Westhoek, the line Verbranden Molen—Potijze was to be held to the last.

Gen. Allenby's Cavalry Corps on Wytschaete Messines Ridge.

London Scottish—first Territorial infantry in action—engaged at Messines, where they sustained " unshaken " losses amounting to 278 out of 26 officers and 786 men.

Russians reoccupied Czernowitz (Bukovina).

Land bombardment of Tsingtau.

German Muanza (Victoria Nyanza) Expedition dispersed by British lake flotilla.

*November 1.

Adm. Jellicoe left Lough Swilly to confer with Mr. Churchill and Lord Fisher in London.

Queen's Westminsters embarked for France ; later joined 7th Division, relieving Artists' Corps, which became O.T.C.

Sundays marked with Asterisk (*).

#November 1, 1914 (*continued*).

German guns now mounted among dunes from Westende to Ostend and beyond.

Battle of Ypres. Third Phase :

Violent German attacks in Ypres region ; Germans took Messines and Wytschaete, W. part of latter regained by French 16th Army Corps, whose arrival saved Kemmel position.

Gen. Bulfin wounded.

British aeroplane bombed German Headquarters at Thielt.

Air raids on Paris and Reims.

Gen. von Hindenburg C.-in-C. in the East.

Mackensen in command Ninth Army.

British Ambassador left Constantinople.

Tsingtau Bismarck Forts silenced by H.M.S. *Triumph*.

Australian Convoy sailed for Colombo, escorted by H.M.SS. *Minotaur*, *Melbourne* and *Sydney*, and H.I.J.M.S. *Ibuki*.

Battle of Coronel : H.M.SS. *Monmouth* and *Good Hope* (Adm. Cradock) sunk off Chile by Adm. Spee's squadron : *Scharnhorst*, *Gneisenau*, *Leipzig*, *Dresden*. and *Nürnberg*. H.M.S. *Glasgow* and A.M.C. *Otranto* escaped.

British s.s. *Colusa* chased in Pacific by German A.M.C. *Prinz Eitel Friedrich* escaped.

November 2.

Admiralty proclaimed North Sea a military area.

French mined N.E. Channel.

Kaiser witnessed continued German offensive on Franco-Belgian frontier.

German aeroplane bombed Furnes.

German air raid on Reims.

Russians re-entered E. Prussia.

French and Russian Ambassadors left Constantinople.

H.M. T.B.D.s *Wolverine* and *Scorpion* destroyed Turkish minelayer in Smyrna Gulf.

Imperial Service Cavalry Brigade and five Infantry Brigades left India for France and Egypt.

At Tsingtau Austrian cruiser *Kaiserin Elizabeth* sunk.

British landed near Tanga (G.E. Africa).

Adm. von Spee at Valparaiso.

November 3.

Adm. Jellicoe on return to Lough Swilly from London put to sea, and subsequently proceeded with the Fleet to Scapa.

German battle cruisers bombarded Yarmouth, attacked H.M.S. *Halcyon*, and scattered mines, one of which destroyed H.M. submarine D5.

Gen. von Falkenhayn confirmed as German Chief of Staff.

Anglo-French squadron, including H.M.SS. *Indefatigable* and *Indomitable*, bombarded Dardanelles forts.

Montenegrins bombarded Cattaro.

Serbia broke with Turkey. Bulgaria announced neutrality.

Austro-German defeat at Kielce (Poland).

Russians from Persia crossed Turkish frontier and occupied Bayazid.

Action at Ras Kasone (Tanga).

November 4.

H.I.M.S. *Karlsruhe* destroyed by internal explosion off Barbados.

Grand Fleet returned to Scapa.

H.I.M.S. *Yorck* mined near Wilhelmshaven on return from Yarmouth.

Germans lost and retook Lombaertzyde.

November 4 (*continued*).

French 20th Corps (Gen. Balfourier) began detraining in Ypres area.

Russians drove back Germans on E. Prussian front.

Austrian defeat at Jaroslav (Galicia).

British reverse at Tanga (G.E. Africa).

November 5.

H.M.SS. *Invincible* and *Inflexible* left Cromarty and Devonport to sail under Admiral Sturdee, who had been specially commissioned as C.-in-C. in S. Atlantic and Pacific, to search out Adm. Spee's squadron.

Kaiser and Prince Henry of Prussia removed from British Royal Navy List.

British 1st Grenadier Battalion withdrawn from 7th Division line before Ypres with a strength of one officer and fewer than 90 men. On withdrawal the battalion proceeded to reform the King's Company, and did an hour's steady drill.

Germans repulsed near Roye.

German air raid on Reims.

Baron Sonnino, Italian Foreign Minister in new Salandra Cabinet.

Great Britain declared war on Turkey, " owing to hostile acts committed by Turkish forces under German officers."

Cyprus annexed by Great Britain.

France declared war on Turkey.

November 6.

H.M.S. *Tiger* (28,500 tons, 29 knots, eight 13.5 inch guns) arrived at Scapa to join 1st Battle Cruiser Squadron.

Lieut. Lody, German spy, shot in the Tower of London.

Germans ordered internment of British subjects of military age.

German attack at Klein Zillebeke (Ypres) repulsed.

San line again in Russian hands. Austrians retreating on Cracow.

Tsingtau inner forts stormed.

November 7.

British counter-attacks at Klein Zillebeke.

British violently attacked at Givenchy. Heavy fighting at Arras.

Gen. Otto von Below to command German Eighth Army, vice Gen. von François.

Russians bombarded Turkish Black Sea ports.

Belgium declared war on Turkey.

Tsingtau fell ; 2,300 prisoners.

Rebel De Wet defeated Union troops at Doornberg.

#November 8.

British ships off Belgian coast recalled to England.

Dixmude—Ypres—Arras battle continued.

French occupied Vregny on Aisne front.

Russians reached Eydtkuhnen—Stallupönen (E. Prussia).

Austrians invaded Serbia a third time. Serbians evacuated Matchva Plain and fell back fighting towards Kolubara line.

British troops from India and Marines from H.M.S. *Ocean* occupied Fao (Persian Gulf) after bombardment by H.M.S. *Odin* and armed launch *Sirdar*.

S. African rebels defeated at Sandfontein and Kroonstadt.

H.M.SS. *Canopus* and *Glasgow* reached Falklands which former was directed to defend.

November 9, 1914.

Mr. Asquith, speaking at Guildhall on Allied aims, says, " We shall never sheathe the sword . . .''

King George's Message to B.E.F.

Sir J. French inspected H.A.C. upon latter's joining Indian Corps in the line.

British again in danger at Ypres.

Germans abandoned Kalish and Czenstochowa (Poland); Russian cavalry entered Posen and cut railway at Pleschen.

Artillery fight between Russians and Turks around Kuprukeui (Caucasus).

H.M.S. *Duke of Edinburgh*, with s.s. *City of Manchester* and two other transports detached from Indian Convoy (2-xi.-14).

H.I.M.S. *Emden* at Cocos Island (Pacific); destroyed wireless station, but was herself caught and destroyed by H.M.A.S. *Sydney*, together with British collier *Buresk*, which was captured by *Emden* 27-ix.-14. H.M.A.S. *Sydney* formed, with H.M.A.S. *Melbourne* and H.I.J.M.S. *Ibuki*, part of escort to New Zealand troop transports then under convoy.

H.I.M.S. *Geier* interned by U.S.A. at Honolulu after having been under observation by H.I.J.M.SS. *Hizen* and *Asama*.

November 10.

Germans took Dixmude after three weeks battle.

Germans took St. Eloi (Ypres).

Russians took Goldap (E. Prussia). They penetrated 20 miles into German territory between Kalish and Thorn.

Mackensen (Ninth Army) supported by Austrian Second, First, and Fourth Armies to the southward, in position on Vistula and Warta for new thrust from Prussian frontier into Poland at about Lowicz-Lodz, against Russian First, Second, Fifth, Fourth, and Ninth Armies now forward of Warsaw.

Russian success in Armenia.

Gen. Delamain's 16th Brigade (6th Poona Division) established on Shatt-al-Arab.

H.I.M.S. *Königsberg* blocked in Rufiji R. (G.E. Africa) and shelled by H.M.S. *Chatham*.

November 11.

King opened Parliament.

Adm. Sturdee left Portland for Falkland Is. ; (see 8-xii.-14).

H.M.S. *Princess Royal* left Scapa for Halifax to reinforce North American Squadron if Adm. von Spee's ships should break north.

H.M.S. *Niger* sunk by U12 off Deal.

Battle of Ypres. Fourth Phase : Desperate Prussian Guard attack against Gheluvelt salient. Gallant British resistance ; Germans by night retained only small portion of Polygon Wood. Gen. FitzClarence killed ; 1st Guards Brigade mustered at night only four officers and 300 men.

Mackensen began battle of Wloclawek.

Russians investing Przemysl (Galicia).

Serbian Headquarters removed from Valievo to Kraguyevatz.

Home Counties Territorial Division bound for India detained at Port Said.

British attacked at Saniyeh (Mesopotamia); Turks driven off.

De Wet routed by Gen. Botha in Mushroom Valley.

Japanese T.B. 33 mined in Kiaochau Bay.

November 12.

Scapa seaplane sheds wrecked by heavy gales.

Remaining old *Edgar* cruisers of 10th Squadron found to be strained and unsuited to Northern winter ; withdrawn from service.

November 12 (*continued*).

Sailing vessel *Kwango* arrived in Downs, manned mostly by German reservists ; sent to Gravesend.

Before Ypres Allies continued to hold the enemy firmly.

Brig.-Gen. Shaw, 9th Infantry Brigade, wounded.

Russian cavalry at Miechov (N. of Cracow).

November 13.

H.I.M.SS. *Leipzig* and *Dresden* at Valparaiso.

German onslaught at Ypres slackening.

French took Tracy-le-Val (N. of Aisne R.).

Russians threatening Thorn.

Russians on Dunayetz line advancing on Cracow.

Russians retiring in Caucasus.

November 14.

Adm. Troubridge honourably acquitted by court-martial of neglect in allowing H.I.M.SS. *Goeben* and *Breslau* to escape.

F.M. Lord Roberts died of pneumonia at British G.H.Q., St. Omer, while inspecting Indian troops in France.

Yser and Ypres battles declining.

Russians checked in E. Prussia.

Mackensen began battle of Kutno.

Turkey declared war on Russia.

Gen. Barrett, G.O.C. 6th (Poona) Division, joined Gen. Delamain at Bahrein Is.

S. African rebels again defeated at Bultfontein.

*November 15.

Last serious attack by Prussian Guard at Ypres beaten off.

Indian Corps heavily engaged between Armentières—La Bassée.

Russians levied in E. Prussia war taxes similar to German imposts in Belgium.

Russians retired on Gombin—Lodz.

Action at Sahain on way to Basra.

November 16.

Loss of H.M.S. *Audacious* (27-x.-14) described in New York Press.

German auxiliary *Berlin* interned at Trondhjem.

Mr. Asquith moved £225,000,000 war credit. British war expenditure estimated at £900,000-£1,000,000 a day. Parliament sanctioned additional 1,000,000 men.

First award of V.C. ; five officers and four men decorated.

Prince of Wales joined B.E.F.

Yser fighting ended by rain and flood. French Marine Brigade relieved.

Germans failed to cross Aisne at Vailly.

H.I.M.S. *Friedrich Karl* sunk off Memel.

Battle of Lodz begun.

Gen. A. Wilson in command Suez Canal zone.

H.M. collier *North Wales* (3,691 tons) sunk by H.I.M.S. *Dresden* 360 miles S.W. from Valparaiso.

November 17.

Mr. Lloyd George announced £350,00 000 War Loan.

Sharp fighting round Plotsk.

Germans reached Strykow (N.E. Lodz).

Sundays marked with Asterisk (*).

November 17, 1914 (continued).

Turks defeated at Sahil (Mesopotamia).
Adm. Sturdee at St. Vincent, Cape Verde.

November 18.

British mine-sweeping gunboats in Fair Island Channel sighted U-Boat on surface, chased at 18 knots, but failed to overhaul before German submarine dived.
Local skirmishes in the West.
German squadron shelled Libau.
Russian defeat at Soldau (E. Prussia).
Germans approaching Lodz ; towards Warsaw they occupied Leczca and Orlov on Bzura R.
Russian Black Sea Fleet engaged H.I.M.SS. *Goeben* and *Breslau*.

November 19.

Lord Roberts's funeral at St. Paul's.
Renewed activity in Flanders.
French repulse counter-attack against Tracy-le-Val (N. of Aisne R.).
Germans, under Mackensen, crossed Bzura R. and drove Russians from Piontek (Poland).
Austrians took Valievo (Serbia).

November 20.

Admiralty proclaimed extension of North Sea minefield.
Gun accident in H.M.S. *Achilles* ; 11 men injured.
British 3rd Battle Squadron and 3rd Cruiser Squadron based on Rosyth to cope with eventual German attempts to land on E. Coast.
Sir J. French's Ypres dispatch issued.
German attack in Flanders slackening ; five weeks' struggle for Calais failed.
Germans fighting E. and S.E. Lodz.
Austrians took Milovatz and Strazhara Height (Serbia).
Russians occupied Kuprukeui (Caucasus).

November 21.

First Battle of Ypres ended. All British troops now withdrawn from salient to refit. British 1st Corps between 15-x.-14 and 21-xi.-14 lost 197 officers and 2,424 men killed ; and suffered total casualties of 839 officers and 20,874 men. German casualties in the battle were estimated by German G.H.Q. on 14-ix.-14 at 100,000.
First " Trench Feet " cases in B.E.F. developed during third week of November ; during following winter over 20,000 men invalided from this cause.
Allies harassed Germans entrenching on Aisne R. and in Champagne.
British air raid at Friedrichshaven ; Squad.-Comm. Briggs, R.N., brought down.
German XXVth Reserve Corps, with 3rd Prussian Guard Division heavily engaged at Rzgov, S.E. Lodz.
Skirmish at Katiyeh (Suez Canal) between Bikanir Camel force and Bedouins.
Turks evacuated Basra (Mesopotamia).

*November 22.

Trench warfare on whole West front.
Battle for Lodz continued.
Austrians defeated between Cracow-Czestochowa.
Serbians retired on Babuna—Glava-Rajac.
British occupied Basra (Mesopotamia).

November 23.

U21 sank British s.s. *Malachite* in Channel ; first submarine merchant victim in Channel.
British naval squadron bombarded Zeebrugge.
Ypres violently bombarded by Germans ; Cathedral and Cloth Hall damaged.
Gen. von Bissing Governor of Belgium, vice Marshal von der Goltz.
Gen. von Kraewel Commandant of Brussels, vice Gen. von Lüttwitz.
Russians drove wedge through German line E. of Lodz (Poland), about Brzeziny.

November 24.

U18 rammed by British trawler off Scapa Flow ; officers and crew saved. U16 earlier visited Lerwick and U22 the Minch.
British cruisers off Heligoland. H.M.S. *Liverpool* bombed by aeroplane.
Belgian coast fighting desultory.
Indian troops recaptured lost trenches.
During night of Nov. 24-25 German XXVth Reserve Corps and 3rd Guard Division cut off S.E. of Lodz broke through Russian line to northward at Brzeziny.

November 25.

British Government accepted amendments limiting Press Censor's powers.
U16 sighted off Dundee.
H.M. submarine D2 lost in North Sea.
At Ypres farms harbouring German snipers blown up by British.
Germans bombard Arras.
Germans in Poland on defensive about Strykow-Glowno and westward of Lowicz.

November 26.

H.M.S. *Bulwark* (15,000 tons) blown up by internal explosion in Medway R. ; 800 lost.
U21 sank s.s. *Primo* in Channel.
Kaiser and Admiralty Staff at G.H.Q. Charleville learned loss of H.M.S. *Audacious* on 27-x.-14.
German attack on Yser Canal failed.
French repulsed an attack at Missy (Aisne R.).
German retreat near Rzgov (Poland) completed after desperate fighting. German advance on Lovicz-Lodz—Petrikov.
Austrians again evacuated Czernowitz (Bukovina).

November 27.

Defence of the Realm Act (D.O.R.A.).
£350,000,000 War Loan over-subscribed.
Reims Cathedral again shelled.
Russians evacuating Lodz (Poland).
Hindenburg promoted Field Marshal.

November 28.

Germans concentrating on Arras.
Russian successes towards Cracow.
Carpathian passes again held by Gen. Brusiloff.
Austro-Serbian battle at Lazarevatz.
Turks advancing on Suez Canal.
British ships shelled Dar-es-Salaam.

*November 29.

King George left for France.
First Q Ship commissioned.
U-Boats appeared off Havre.

For List of Abbreviations see page iv.

*November 29, 1914 (*continued*).

French advance between Somme and Chaulnes.

French retook Bagatelle (Argonne), completing recovery of lost ground which began Oct. 21, excepting the Barricade, French repulsed counter-attacks in Ban-de-Sapt (Vosges).

Germans bombarded Lodz (Poland).

Serbians began to evacuate Belgrade.

North Waziristan Militia engaged in Tochi Valley.

November 30.

King George visited British W. front.

German date for end of Yser Battle.

Artillery duels at Dixmude—Ypres—Arras.

During November R.F.C. took first successful aerial photograph over Neuve Chapelle.

Mackensen, reinforced by XXIVth Reserve Corps from Ypres on his right about Lask—Pabiance, S.W. Lodz, began battle of Lowicz.

December 1.

H.M.SS. *Emperor of India* and *Benbow* arrived at Berehaven to work up after commissioning.

French " Yellow Book " issued.

King in France visited Indian troops and wounded.

Gens. Joffre and Foch created G.C.B.

French recovered Vermelles Château.

German attack at Berry-au-Bac failed.

Battle for Belgrade Ridges.

Germans in suburbs of Lodz (Poland).

Russians nearing Cracow.

Russians took Bashkal and Sarai (Caucasus).

De Wet surrendered 100 miles from Mafeking.

December 2.

National Relief Fund = £4,001,000.

King George and Prince of Wales on 70 miles tour of British front in France.

Germans failed to cross Yser on rafts near Dixmude.

French advanced in direction of Metz and took Xon signal station and Lesmésnils.

French occupied Aspach-le-Haut and Aspach-le-Bas (Alsace).

Chancellor, in Reichstag, accused England of originating the war.

Reichstag voted second war credit of 5,000,000,000 marks ; Socialists also voted credits ; Liebknecht voted against.

Russian cavalry raid on Bartfeld (Hungary).

Austrians took Belgrade.

December 3.

Adm. de Chair hoisted his flag in H.M. A.M.C. *Alsatian*, as commander of 10th (Merchant) Cruiser Squadron in Northern waters for Blockade duties.

H.M. T.B.D. *Garry* engaged U-Boat at Holm Sound entrance to Scapa Flow in heavy gale ; *Garry* and U-Boat fired torpedoes at each other, but missed.

King George in France invested Sir J. French with O.M., and witnessed British artillery in action.

French advance near Altkirch (Alsace).

Russians nearer to Cracow.

Austrians gained footing on Rudnik Ridge (Belgrade) ; Serbian counter-attack.

December 4.

Grand Fleet's mine-sweeping gunboats detached from Scapa to Sheerness for service on Belgian coast.

Antwerp dispatches published.

King George in France inspected British G.H.Q., visited Belgian H.Q., and invested King Albert with Garter.

French took Langemarck.

Germans repulsed in Argonne.

Russians took Wielitza, near Cracow.

Serbian counter-attack in Battle of Ridges.

British force, with naval flotilla, failed to take Kurna (Tigris), 50 miles N. of Basra. Mezera destroyed by H.M. ships.

Gen. Botha's operations round Reitz culminated in capture of 900 rebels.

December 5.

King George inspected R.F.C. and returned from France.

Reims again bombarded.

French airmen bombed airsheds at Freiburg (Breisgau).

Austrians began battle of Limanowa in support of Mackensen's attack at Lowicz.

Austrians routed in Serbian Battle of Ridges.

Gen. Botha demanded unconditional surrender of Wessels, Serfontein, and Vancoller, three S. African rebel leaders.

First Australian troops in Egypt.

Last Indian units for defence of Suez Canal arrived.

British s.s. *Charcas* (5,067 tons) sunk by German A.M.C. *Prinz Eitel Friedrich* 70 miles S.W. from Valparaiso.

*December 6.

U16 at Esjberg (Denmark), damaged.

Long-distance bombardment of Dunkirk at over 20 miles range by German 38 centimetre naval guns in Flanders.

German air raid on Reims.

Germans entered Lodz (Poland).

Austrian retreat from Serbian Ridges.

Pope sought to promote Christmas truce

December 7.

New 1st Cruiser Squadron formed at Scapa : *Leviathan* (F. Adm. Moore), *Duke of Edinburgh*, *Warrior*, and *Black Prince*.

S.S. *Michigan* and *City of Oxford*, disguised as men of war, arrived at Scapa, where they later formed nucleus of Special Service Squadron, under Commodore Haddock, R.N.R., formerly of s.s. *Olympic*.

Mr. Churchill's second visit to Sir J. French in France.

Germans again failed to cross Yser near Pervyse.

French recovered Vermelles, Le Rutoire, and trenches S. of Carency.

Further German counter-attacks against Tracy-le-Val (Aisne R.) failed.

Second German attack on Warsaw.

Russians bombarded N. Cracow forts.

Russians drove back Turks S. of Batum.

British routed Turks opposite Kurna (Tigris).

Gen. Beyers shot while trying to swim Vaal R. after defeat at Bothaville.

Japanese Diet opened. Emperor's speech : " The alliance with Great Britain and the *ententes* with France and Russia have been cemented."

December 8.

H.M.S. *Thunderer* left Scapa for Devonport to refit and retube condensers.

Sundays marked with Asterisk (*).

December 8, 1914 (*continued*).

German long-distance bombardment of Furnes (Belgium).

S. of La Bassée fighting close to " The Labyrinth."

French penetrated into Bois-le-Prêtre, near Pont-à-Mousson.

Austrian defeat S. of Belgrade.

Austrian counter-attack to save Cracow ; battle in outskirts. Russians fell back between Niditza R. and Dunayetz R.

Collapse of S. African rebellion ; Wessels, Serfontein, and Vancoller, with 1,200 men, surrendered.

Off Falkland Islands British squadron, H.M.SS. *Invincible* (F. Adm. Sturdee), *Inflexible, and Carnarvon*, sank H.I.M.SS. *Scharnhorst* (F. Adm. Spee) and *Gneisenau* ; *Leipzig* sunk by H.M.SS. *Glasgow* and *Cornwall* ; *Nürnberg* sunk by H.M.S. *Kent* ; *Dresden* escaped ; two transports sunk by H.M.S. *Bristol* and A.M.C. *Macedonia*.

December 9.

Nicholaus Ahlers, ex-German consul at Sunderland, sentenced to death at Durham for high treason.

British Government proposed to French Government at Bordeaux that B.E.F. be moved to extreme left of Allied line. so as to be able to co-operate with British Fleet in any offensive operations along Belgian coast. This proposal was not accepted by French military authorities.

Warsaw battle continued.

Serbians pursued Austrians and retook Valievo.

Turks surrendered Kurna (Tigris).

December 10.

H.M.SS. *Benbow* and *Emperor of India* joined 4th Battle Squadron at Scapa.

U-Boat raid on Dover. U11 lost.

German attack on Ypres failed.

French advance near Perthes (Champagne).

French Government returned from Bordeaux to Paris.

Gen. Botha on suppression of S. African rebellion : " Now more than ever it is for the people of S. Africa to practise the wise policy of forgive and forget."

December 11.

Serbians still pursuing Austrians.

Russian stand at Lovicz (Poland).

H.I.M.S. *Goeben* bombarded Batum.

December 12.

H.M.S. *King George V.* returned to Grand Fleet, after being absent since the end of November to repair condenser defects ; work not completed, owing to Grand Fleet's small margin over High Sea Fleet at this time.

H.M.S. *Liverpool* first ship in Grand Fleet to develop serious boiler trouble, which was later to incapacitate many other ships in turn for a period of two or three months.

Montenegrins took Vishegrad (Bosnia).

Austrians retreating in Serbia recrossed Drina R.

Austrians seized Dukla Pass (Carpathians). Russians from Cracow fell back almost to R. San.

Brig.-Gen. Barnardiston, British commander at Tsingtau, welcomed in Tokyo.

✱December 13.

Adm. Hood visited Sir J. French at St. Omer.

✱December 13 (*continued*).

Germans withdrew from Yser Canal.

Battle for Warsaw continued.

Battle for Cracow ending.

Austrian rout in Serbia.

H.M. submarine B11 (Lieut. N. Holbrook, R.N.) entered Dardanelles, dived under nets, and torpedoed Turkish battleship *Messudiyeh.*

December 14.

French 32nd and 16th Corps attacked from Klein Zillebeke southwards.

British attacked S. of Wytschaete (Ypres) and gained footing in Petit Bois.

German 4th Cavalry Corps Command broken up.

H.M. submarine B9 entered Dardanelles, but forced to retire.

December 15.

H.M.SS. *Blanche* and *Boadicea* seriously damaged by heavy seas in Pentland Firth while accompanying 2nd Battle Squadron on a sweep from Scapa. Battle Squadron continued to southward to meet battle cruisers from Cromarty at rendezvous in North Sea.

German battle cruisers under Adm. Hipper left Jade for raid on English E. Coast, supported later in the day by High Sea Fleet.

Allies crossed Yser, advanced towards Lombaertzyde.

Austrian sortie from Przemysl (Galicia) failed.

King Peter returned to Belgrade ; third Austrian invasion ended. Marshal Putnik, having cleared Serbian territory, claimed over 60,000 prisoners and nearly 200 guns.

H.M.S. *Doris* raided Ascalon (Syria).

December 16.

German battle cruisers *Seydlitz, Moltke,* and *Blücher* in early morning bombarded W. Hartlepool, while *Derfflinger* and *Von der Tann* shelled Scarborough and Whitby, killing 127 civilians (including 39 women and 39 children), and wounding 567. Raiders escaped in the mist. *Moltke* and *Blücher* hit by shore batteries.

Before daylight H.M.T.B.D.s *Lynx, Ambuscade, Unity, Hardy, Shark, Acasta,* and *Spitfire,* 10 miles ahead of Adm. Warrender's 2nd Battle Squadron, sighted German light forces in advance of High Sea Fleet. While German Fleet at 4.45 a.m. immediately turned on S.E. course, H.I.M.S. *Hamburg* and consorts engaged British T.B.Ds, disabling *Hardy,* and damaging *Ambuscade* and *Lynx.* During forenoon German battle cruisers, returning eastward from raid on English coast, passed some miles astern of 2nd Battle Squadron, which at 12.16 p.m., in Lat. 54° 23′N., Long. 2° 14′E., sighted German ships, turned to close, but failed to overtake them. Adm. Beatty's 1st Battle Cruiser Squadron did not sight any German ships. Adm. Jellicoe, on learning of early morning encounter, put to sea with Grand Fleet from Scapa at about this time. The 3rd Battle Squadron from Rosyth had put to sea at 10 a.m. to intercept any German ships passing to northward.

British warships bombarded Westende (Belgium).

Russian T.B.D.s *Letuchi* and *Ispoluitelni* foundered in Gulf of Finland.

Russian stand 30 miles S.W. of Warsaw.

December 17, 1914.

H.M.SS. *Bellona* and *Broke* seriously damaged by collision in North Sea.

Gen. de Maud'huy attacked Germans N. of Arras.

Germans bombarded Armentières.

Germans took Lowicz (Poland).

Mackensen (Ninth Army), after fighting battles of Wloclawek, Kutno, Lodz, and Lowicz, forced Russians behind Bzura, Rawka, Pilitza, Nida line with an estimated loss of over 250,000 in prisoners and casualties.

Turks drove Russians out of Kuprukeui (Armenia).

British Protectorate over Egypt proclaimed; Sir A. H. McMahon High Commissioner.

December 18.

Court of Criminal Appeal quashed conviction of Nicholaus Ahlers, ex-German Consul at Sunderland.

Five days battle at Givenchy begun.

Germans crossed Bzura R.

Austrians regained Lupkov Pass (Galicia).

Prince Hussein Kamel Pasha appointed Khedive with title of Sultan of Egypt, in room of Abbas Hilmi Pasha, deposed for adhering to King's enemies.

December 19.

British s.s. *Tritonia* (4,272 tons) sunk by mine off Tory Island.

Grand Fleet returned to Scapa and cruisers to Cromarty.

Allied airmen bombed Brussels airsheds.

Indian attack near Cuinchy and Givenchy. German counter-attack. German attack broken near Lihons, N. of Somme R.

Germans attacked Russians along Lower Bzura—Ravka line (Poland). Austrian sortie at Przemysl (Galicia) failsed.

Two Fourie brothers, S. African ring-leaders, found guilty of treason.

＊December 20.

Mr. Churchill, First Lord of Admiralty, in letter to Mayor of Scarborough, stigmatised German raiders as " baby-killers."

Mr. Churchill telegraphed to Sir J. French: " We are receiving almost daily requests from the French for naval support on the Belgian coast. We regret we are unable to comply. The small vessels by themselves cannot face the new shore batteries, and it is not justifiable to expose battleships to submarine perils unless to support a land attack of primary importance.

Germans attacked Indians near La Bassée, and took part of Givenchy, later retaken by British.

German air raid on Reims.

First battle of Perthes.

Russian stand on Lower Bzura (Poland) ; counter-attack towards Cracow and Carpathian passes.

Turks defeated near Lake Van (Caucasus).

S. African rebel Capt. Fourie shot ; brother's sentence commuted.

December 21.

Adm. Burney arrived at Scapa in H.M.S. *Marlborough* to assume command of 1st Battle Squadron, vice Adm. Bayly, transferred to Channel Fleet.

Following upon Scarborough raid, Admiralty ordered 1st Battle Cruiser Squadron and 1st Light Cruiser Squadron to be based on Rosyth.

Round Givenchy British re-established line. British troops supported Indians.

December 21 (*continued*).

Germans failed to cross Lower Bzura (Poland).

French Dreadnought *Jean Bart* damaged by Austrian U-Boat torpedo in Adriatic.

Lieut. N. Holbrook, R.N., received V.C. for his action in the Dardanelles. (13-xii.-14.)

Landing-party from H.M.S. *Doris* blew up bridge near Deurt Yol (Syria).

December 22.

Adm. Callaghan to command at the Nore Givenchy battle dying down.

British First Corps relieved Indian Corps in Givenchy sector. Givenchy secured.

French advance towards Noyon, and near Beauséjour (Champagne).

Fresh Austrian sortie from Przemysl (Galicia) failed.

December 23.

British 2nd and 4th Battle Squadrons, with H.M.S. *Iron Duke*, proceed from Scapa to westward of Orkneys for target practice N. of the Hebrides.

Home Government to relieve victims of E. Coast raid.

Kaiser at G.H.Q., Charleville, heard Adm. von Pohl's report on Scarborough raid. Adm. von Pohl's appointment in place of Adm. von Ingenohl was at this date already under discussion.

At Wilhelmshaven captain of H.I.M.S. *Yorck* sentenced to two years' detention for loss of ship (4-xi.-14.), commander one year's imprisonment.

Belgians crossed Yser S. of Dixmude.

British 27th Division arrived and concentrated near St. Omer.

Near Givenchy British completed recapture of lost positions.

Germans before Warsaw crossed Bzura R., but failed to advance.

December 24.

British 2nd and 4th Battle Squadrons again in North Sea on sweep to southward.

First German air raid on England : German aeroplane dropped one bomb at Dover, making hole in a garden. No casualties.

British airman bombed Brussels airshed.

French success at Perthes-les-Hurlus (Champagne).

German air raid on Nancy.

Prussian XXXIXth (Gen. von Lauenstein), XLth (Gen. Litzmann), and XLIst (Gen. von François) Reserve Corps formed.

H.M.S. *Doris* destroyed German s.s. *Odessa* (German Levant Line) near Mortalik, Ayas Bay (Asia Minor).

Britain recognised French Protectorate in Morocco.

Germans invaded Angola (Portuguese S.W. Africa).

December .25.

British 1st (Adm. Colville in temporary command, vice Adm. Burney, ill), and 3rd Battle Squadrons joined 2nd and 4th Squadrons in North Sea, with 1st Battle Cruiser Squadron.

Second air raid on England : German aeroplane over Sheerness ; driven off.

Seven British naval airmen, assisted by H.M.SS. *Arethusa* and *Undaunted*, and submarines, attacked German warships off Cuxhaven, and encountered two Zeppelins, three or four seaplanes, and U20, U22, and U30.

Sundays marked with Asterisk (＊).

December 25, 1914 (*continued*).

Flight-Commander Hewlett missing; no other casualties. Five British airmen taken on board H.M. submarine E11 under fire from German airships.

Sir J. French ordered formation of first two British armies on W. Front: Gen. Haig to command First Army (1st, 4th, and Indian Corps); Gen. Smith-Dorrien to command Second Army (2nd, 3rd, and 5th Corps).

Christmas "fraternisation" episode on W. Front.

Zeppelins over Nancy.

Italians occupied Avlona (Albania).

German offensive against Warsaw arrested.

Russians recovered Lupkov and Dukla Passes (Carpathians). Austrians defeated at Tarnov (Galicia).

Turks reached Khorasan — Sarikamish (Armenia).

December 26.

Whole gale blowing from S.E. in North Sea. Grand Fleet abandoned sweep. One man washed overboard from H.M.S. *Caroline*.

H.M.S. *Indomitable* joined Battle Cruiser Fleet at Rosyth from Mediterranean.

Adm. Scheer transferred from 2nd to 3rd German High Sea Squadron at Wilhelmshaven, now comprising: F. *Prinz Regent Luitpold*, *König*, *Grosser Kurfürst*, *Markgraf*, *König Albert*, *Kaiser*, *Kaiserin*, and, a week later, *Kronprinz*.

German air raid on Reims.

French airmen bombed airship sheds at Frescati (Metz).

French advance near Cernay (Alsace).

Germans abandoned direct attack on Warsaw.

Austro-German offensive in Galicia broken.

* December 27.

H.M.SS. *Conqueror* and *Monarch* disabled by collision in heavy gale off Scapa Flow. Three T.B.D.s damaged and docked.

H.M.S. *Success* wrecked off Fifeness.

Sir J. French conferred with Gen. Joffre at Chantilly.

Belgians near Lombaertzyde took German trenches.

French success at Carency.

St. Dié (Vosges) bombarded by Germans.

Germans defeated at Skiernevice on Ravka R. (Poland).

December 28.

British s.s. *Hemisphere* (3,486 tons) sunk by German A.M.C. *Kronprinz Wilhelm* 400 miles N.E. from Pernambuco.

Adm. Burney resumed command of 1st Battle Squadron.

New British 2nd Light Cruiser Squadron formed : *Falmouth* (F. Adm. Napier), *Gloucester*, *Yarmouth*, and *Dartmouth*.

Two U-Boats sighted off the Tay.

British "Military Cross" instituted.

Londoners warned to take refuge in basements in case of air attacks.

German mines in North Sea destroyed eight vessels.

Sir J. French proposed amalgamation of British and Belgian Armies; this proposal fell through.

Allies on Yser recovered St. Georges.

French submarine *Curie* captured by Austrians near Pola (Adriatic).

December 28 (*continued*).

German 2nd Cavalry Corps broken up; Gen. von der Marwitz to command XXXVIIIth Reserve Corps.

Germans before Warsaw retired from Dzura—Ravka line.

Turks withdrew from Sarikamish (Caucasus).

December 29.

U.S. Note to Britain on treatment of American sea-borne trade.

First line of anti-U-Boat obstructions in Hoxa entrance to Scapa Flow completed.

H.M.S. *Monarch* left Scapa for Devonport for repair. As H.M.SS. *Conqueror* and *King George V.* also undergoing repairs, 2nd Battle Squadron at this period reduced to four ships.

British ships active off Belgian coast.

German counter-attack at St. Georges (Yser) fails.

French success at Apremont (Argonne).

Austrians retreating fast in Galicia.

December 30.

German Ostend bombing aeroplanes raided Dunkirk.

Allies consolidating at Ypres.

Germans fighting rearguard action at Bolimov and Inovlodz (Poland).

December 31.

Flight-Commander Hewlett landed at Ymuiden, having been picked up by Dutch trawler after Cuxhaven raid (25-xii.-14).

During December U5 was posted lost; probably mined off Zeebrugge.

During December no British merchantman were sunk by U-Boat.

During December Gen. Seely assumed command of Canadian Cavalry Brigade.

By the end of 1914 about 24 T.F. Battalions had joined B.E.F. in France.

Artillery active from Yser to Verdun.

French recovered part of Steinbach (Alsace).

Austro-German retreat in Poland and Galicia.

Russians again raided Hungary.

Union Government appealed for men for S.W. African campaign.

January 1, 1915.

H.M.S. *Princess Royal* returned to Grand Fleet from N. American waters.

H.M.S. *Formidable* (15,000 tons) torpedoed by U24 in English Channel; over 200 survivors.

First 12 British sloops of Flower (" Herbaceous Border ") Class ordered ; 118 ultimately built.

At New Year 20 U-Boats in North Sea and 7 U-Boats (Courland Flotilla) in Baltic.

Army Order on new organisation of British Western Armies (three corps each).

Artillery duel at Nieuport and Zonnebeke.

French took wood near Mesnil-les-Hurlus (Champagne).

Russian advance on Uzok Pass (Carpathians) and in Bukovina.

Fiji volunteers left for England.

January 2.

Mr. Churchill in telegram to Sir J. French, explained difficulties created for British Admiralty by development of Zeebrugge as U-Boat base.

For List of Abbreviations see page iv.

January 2, 1915 (*continued*).

Rain impeded Flanders operations.

French progress near Vermelles.

Further Russian successes on Bzura front (Poland); in Carpathians; and in Bukovina.

Turkish transport mined in Bosporus.

Second bombardment of Dar-es-Salaam (G.E. Africa) by H.M.SS. *Fox* and *Goliath*.

*January 3.

Sir J. French, in Memorandum to War Council, suggested an offensive for recapture of Ostend and Zeebrugge.

British 1st Battle Cruiser Squadron on three days' cruise in centre of North Sea.

Cardinal Mercier, Archbishop of Malines, forbidden by Germans to circulate his Pastoral Letter.

French gained ground near Arras and near Cernay (Alsace), and retook more of Steinbach.

German attack on Boureuilles (Argonne).

Austrians occupied Ada Tsiganlia Island, near Belgrade.

Russians took Suczava (Bukovina).

Russians destroyed two Turkish Army Corps at Ardahan (Caucasus), and captured Commander-in-Chief, and many other prisoners.

January 4.

London Stock Exchange, closed since July 30, reopened.

H.M.S. *King George V.* rejoined 2nd Battle Squadron.

First unit of Drifter Patrol arrived at Dover; by June Patrol numbered 132 drifters and 3 yachts.

H.M. submarine C31 lost off Belgian Coast.

French advanced opposite Nieuport and consolidated at St. Georges.

French completed recapture of Steinbach (Alsace).

German airmen over British camp in G.S.W. Africa.

January 5.

Adm. von Pohl at German G.H.Q., Charleville, discussed with Chancellor von Bethmann-Hollweg preliminaries of air-campaign against London.

French attack near Courtechasse (Argonne).

French progress N. Altkirch (Alsace).

Turkish transport sunk in Black Sea.

January 6.

Arrangements made, through U.S., for exchange of disabled British and German prisoners.

In the House of Lords Lord Kitchener reviewed the military situation.

Three Zeppelins off Calais—Gravelines.

Dunkirk raided.

Allies at this date " have the advantage almost constantly " from sea to Lys R.

French still advancing N. of Altkirch.

Germans 30 miles from Warsaw; steel shields used to approach Russian positions.

Russians took Kimpolung (Bukovina).

January 7.

British preliminary reply to U.S. Note of 29-xii.-14.

French Decree confirming prohibition of absinthe.

January 7 (*continued*).

Germans repulsed in Argonne and about Verdun.

French took Burnhaupt-le-Haut (Alsace).

German attacks on Ravka R. (Poland) repulsed by Russians.

January 8.

Summary of preliminary report on German atrocities in France published in *The Times.*

N. of Soissons Gen. Maunoury's troops took Hills 132 and 151.

Second battle of Perthes (Champagne).

Germans regained Burnhaupt-le-Haut.

British raid on Shirati, Victoria Nyanza.

January 9.

War Council in Memorandum to Sir J. French adumbrated possibility of stalemate in France and Flanders, and eventual necessity for seeking fresh and more decisive theatre.

King George and Queen Mary visited wounded Indians in hospital at Brighton.

Kaiser at G.H.Q., Charleville, authorised Adm. von Pohl, Chief of Naval Staff, to use airships for raids on London docks and works.

Germans bombarded Soissons Cathedral.

German counter-attacks in Soissons area and at Perthes (Champagne) repulsed.

*January 10.

British s.s. *Potaro* (4,419 tons) captured and scuttled by German A.M.C. *Kronprinz Wilhelm* 560 miles E. by N. from Pernambuco.

Dreadnought Battle Fleet on three days' cruise westward of Orkneys and Shetlands for gunnery and battle exercises.

Sixteen German aeroplanes seen in English Channel, but owing to bad weather they return towards Dunkirk, upon which 30 bombs are dropped during the day.

German aeroplanes prevented by French airmen from flying over Paris.

Further French progress in Soissons area at Hill 132 and N. of Perthes (Champagne).

British force occupied Mafia Is., off mouth of Rufiji (G.E. Africa).

January 11.

Death sentence on Private Lonsdale, a prisoner of war, for striking a guard in a German camp, commuted to 20 years' imprisonment.

President Poincaré presented colours to Adm. Ronarc'h's (Dixmude) Marine Brigade.

German reinforcements launched in counter-attack N. of Soissons. Aisne overflowed; bridges behind French carrried away.

Heavy fighting round Beauséjour Farm (Champagne).

New Russian advance on E. Prussia.

German Southern Army formed on E. front under Gen. von Linsingen.

Arab attack on British outpost line in Oman repelled.

January 12.

First line of anti-U-Boat obstructions in Switha Sound, Scapa Flow, completed.

Near Soissons French being pushed back from Hills 132 and 151 to Aisne R.; only Venizel bridge retained.

Germans and Austrians leaving Rome.

In E. Prussia Russians advancing.

Union Forces occupied Raman's Drift on G.S.W. African frontier.

Sundays marked with Asterisk (*).

January 13, 1915.

H.M. merchant cruiser *Viknor* (5,386 tons) lost off Irish coast.

Gens. Haig and Smith-Dorrien appointed Grand Officers of Legion of Honour.

Near Soissons Germans recaptured Hills 132 and 151 and gained Vregny heights ; French in retreat across Aisne.

Kaiser conferred Pour le Mérite Order on Gen. von Lochow, IIIrd (Brandenburg) Army Corps, whose Chief of Staff, Gen. von Seeckt, had planned Soissons operation.

Baron Burian succeeded Count Berchtold as Austro-Hungarian Minister for Foreign Affairs.

Russians advancing along Middle Vistula took Serpets, N. of Plock.

Turks seized Tabriz (Persia).

Turks near Erzrum temporarily checked Russian advance round Kara Urgan.

January 14.

British s.s. *Highland Brae* (7,634 tons) captured and scuttled by German A.M.C. *Kronprinz Wilhelm* 630 miles N.E. by E. from Pernambuco. British s.v. *Wilfrid M.* captured and rammed by same raider in same latitude.

East of Soissons, round Venizel and Missy, French withdrew to S. of Aisne R.

Russians progressing on Lower Vistula, 45 miles E. of Thorn.

Swakopmund, principal port of G.S.W. Africa, occupied by Union Forces.

January 15.

Hamburg-Amerika liner *Dacia*, sheltering in American waters, transferred to American registry. British warning.

Adm. Leveson to be Rear-Admiral in 2nd Battle Squadron, vice Adm. Arbuthnot, transferred to 1st Cruiser Squadron (F. *Defence*), vice Adm. Moore, transferred to reconstituted 2nd Battle Cruiser Squadron (F. *New Zealand*).

German progress at Soissons checked. South of La Bassée ; Germans recovered some trenches on Notre Dame de Lorette Ridge and at Carency lost in December.

In Champagne since Nov. 15 French had advanced 1,000 yards in region of Prunay and 2,000 yards in region of Perthes.

Russians took 5,000 prisoners and nearly 10,000 head of cattle from defeated Turks near Kara Urgan (Caucasus).

January 16.

Higher wheat prices in U.K.

French artillery drove Germans from Nieuport dunes.

At Blangy (Arras) village taken by Germans and recovered by French. French gained ground in Perthes region (Champagne).

Russians continued to advance on right bank of the Lower Vistula ; they occupied Kirlibaba Pass (Bukovina).

Turks invaded Sinai Peninsula ; Suez Canal Defence troops reinforced.

Turkish rout near Kara Urgan (Caucasus) complete.

* January 17.

Adm. Beatty's cruisers from Rosyth in position to support Commodore Tyrwhitt in carrying out reconnaissance in Heligoland Bight. Nothing sighted beyond a German airship and seaplane.

Slight French gain at La Boisselle (N. of Somme R.).

In Soissons district German attacks near Autrêches beaten off.

* January 17 (*continued*).

Whole of Bois-le-Prêtre (Pont-à-Mousson) in French hands.

French submarine *Saphir* sunk in attempt to pass up Dardanelles.

January 18.

H.M.S. *Superb* left Scapa for Portsmouth to remedy turbine defects (11-iii.-15).

Since 26-xii.-14 the 10th (Northern Blockade) Cruiser Squadron, now 21 ships strong, had intercepted 80 vessels, 52 being eastward bound.

H.M. submarine E10 lost in North Sea.

French progressed near Bois-le-Prêtre, but failed to hold new positions.

French airmen bombed Arnaville Station (Thiaucourt-Metz Railway).

Russians drove Turks back west of Chorok river (Caucasus).

Von Lettow's force attacked British post at Jasin (B.E. Africa) ; action lasted all day.

January 19.

First German airship, L3, from Cuxhaven, over England : Yarmouth, King's Lynn, Snettisham, and other Norfolk towns and villages attacked, 4 civilians killed, including 2 women, 15 injured, including 4 women and 2 children, and one soldier injured.

Adm. Beatty's 1st and 2nd Battle Cruiser Squadrons and 1st Light Cruiser Squadron supported Commodore Tyrwhitt in reconnaissance off Heligoland.

Gen. Joffre in Memorandum to Sir J. French expressed the opinion that, in view of a fresh German offensive in the near future, operations towards Ostend—Zeebrugge were for the moment secondary ; primary need was collection of reserves.

Snowstorms impeded operations in Flanders. French attacked on Hartmannsweilerkopf (Alsace).

Pursuit of Turks Army in Caucasus continued.

British forced to surrender at Jasin (E. Africa) owing to want of ammunition. German losses included six regular officers killed.

January 20.

H.M.S. *Monarch* returned to Scapa after repairs at Devonport.

France to issue Treasury and National Defence Bonds up to £120,000,000.

French still improving position in Bois-le-Prêtre. Heavy fighting near Hartmannsweilerkopf (Alsace).

Russian protest against German atrocities including use of explosive bullets.

Russians advancing took Skempe (Poland).

Austrian counter-offensive in Bukovina ; Russians repelled attacks in Kirlibaba Pass.

January 21.

U.S. Press stigmatised German air raid on England as senseless barbarism.

British decision regarding s.s. *Dacia*.

H.M.S. *Conqueror*, after temporary repairs, left Scapa for a southern dockyard, but is compelled to put in at Invergordon.

Capt. Tomlin appointed S.N.O. Ramsgate in charge of Downs Boarding Flotilla, under Admiral Dover Patrol.

British s.s. *Durward* stopped by U19 near Maas Lightship, crew ordered to leave, and vessel sunk with bombs.

Infantry actions at Beauséjour (Champagne), where French took woods, but ground lost in Bois-le-Prêtre.

January 21, 1915 (continued).

Germans carried Hartmannsweilerkopf.
Russians holding Kirlibaba Pass.

January 22.

M. Millerand, French Minister of War. inspected new armies in England.

German IIIrd High Sea Squadron passed through Kiel Canal into Baltic for exercises.

German Ostend bombing aeroplanes over Dunkirk; one brought down by Allied airmen.

British airmen bombed Zeebrugge.

Heavy fighting at Fontaine Madame and St. Hubert (Argonne).

Struggle round Hartmannsweilerkopf.

Austrians recaptured Kirlibaba Pass.

British landing-party from H.M.S. *Doris* distributed food to destitute inhabitants of Ruad Island (Asia Minor).

January 23.

M. Millerand, in England, received by King George, and confers with Ministers.

British Battle Cruisers left Rosyth for a sweep in southern North Sea, in conjunction with Harwich Force, and with Grand Fleet in support.

U21 left Ems R. for cruise in Irish Sea.

More fighting in Alsace and Argonne; slight French progress in Nieuport area.

On Aisne Germans bombarded Berry-au-Bac.

Retreating Turks further defeated by Russians at Khorasan (Armenia).

*January 24.

Mr. Bryan denied that American Government had shown partiality to Allies.

U.K. food supply and prices under consideration by Cabinet Committee, presided over by Prime Minister.

Battle of Dogger Bank. British Battle Cruisers *Lion*, *Princess Royal*, *Tiger*, *New Zealand*, and *Indomitable* patrolling in North Sea sighted three German battle-cruisers, *Seydlitz* (F. Adm. Hipper), *Moltke*, and *Derfflinger*, an armoured cruiser, the *Blücher*, six light cruisers, and a number of destroyers steering westward. The German warships turned and made for home, but were pursued at 28.5 knots and brought to action at 9 a.m. E. of Dogger Bank. H.M.S. *Lion* (Vice-Adm. Beatty) led British line, but later fell out owing to injury. Adm. Beatty transferred flag to *Princess Royal*. *Blücher* sunk, *Derfflinger* and *Seydlitz* seriously damaged. *Lion* towed home by *Indomitable*. H.M.S. *Meteor* also towed back damaged. British casualties: 6 killed and 11 wounded in *Tiger*, 11 wounded in *Lion*. German casualties heavy in *Blücher*, *Derfflinger* and *Seydlitz*.

S. African rebels Maritz and Kemp beaten off at Upington.

January 25.

Battle Fleet, after cruising in North Sea returned to Scapa, except H.M.S. *Iron Duke*. which proceeded to Cromarty for refit, accompanied by *Centurion* as stand-by Flagship.

Keels of H.M.SS. *Repulse* and *Renown* officially laid down.

British repulsed an attack on Givenchy, near La Bassée and French near Ypres.

French lost ground on Craonne Plateau (Aisne R.)

Fog interfered with fighting in Alsace.

January 25 (continued).

Chancellor issued new apologia for his " scrap of paper " suggestion.

German Government decreed seizure of all stocks of grain and flour.

Russian submarine damages H.I.M.S. *Gazelle* in Baltic near Rügen.

Z XIX. shot down by Libau forts; crew captured.

Russians advancing in neighbourhood of Pillkallen (E. Prussia). Hard fighting in Carpathians.

Alexandretta raided by H.M.S. *Doris*. Party landed and telegraph wires cut.

January 26.

H.M.S. *Lion* reached Rosyth.

H.M.S. *Britannia* aground for 36 hours in fog in Firth of Forth; damage necessitated dockyard repairs.

Admiralty stated that all the British ships in action on 24-i.-15 had returned safely to port.

King George decorated first Indian soldier to receive V.C.

French recovered ground at Craonne.

Austrians beaten near Dukla Pass (Carpathians).

Turkish advance on Egypt begun. Skirmish near El Kantara (Suez Canal).

Turks recovering from Kara Urgan defeat and counter-attacking in Armenia.

New German Tenth Army formed for Masurian Campaign, consisting of XXIst Corps and young XXXVIIIth, XXXIXth and XLth Reserve Corps, under Gen. von Eichhorn.

January 27.

Vice-Adm. Beatty's preliminary telegraphic report to Admiralty on Dogger Bank action issued.

Second Q. ship commissioned.

German Ostend bombing aeroplanes raided Dunkirk.

Germans in Argonne repulsed.

French artillery destroyed German bridge at St. Mihiel (Meuse).

French advance near Senones (Vosges).

Gen. von Bülow (Second German Army) created Field Marshal.

Gen. von Cramon appointed German Army representative at Austro-Hungarian G.H.Q., Teschen, vice Gen. von Freytag-Loringhoven, appointed Quarter - Master General, vice Gen. Wild von Hohenborn, to be War Minister in Berlin, in the room of Gen. von Falkenhayn, Chief of Staff.

British £5,000,000 loan to Rumania.

January 28.

U.S. sailing ship *William P. Frye* sunk in S. Atlantic by German A.M.C. *Prinz Eitel Friedrich*.

H.M.SS. *Princess Royal* and *Queen Mary* left Rosyth to support operations by Commodores Tyrwhitt and Keyes in Heligoland Bight; operations abandoned owing to fog.

Allies carried Great Dune near Nieuport.

German attack at Bellacourt (Arras).

Russians beaten back by Austrians near Beskid Pass (Carpathians).

Russian T.B.D. shelled Trebizond and Riza (Black Sea).

January 29.

Germans again checked by British near La Bassée at Cuinchy.

Near Soissons Germans failed to cross Aisne.

Sundays marked with Asterisk (*).

January 29, 1915 (*continued*).

H.M. submarine E9 (Comdr. Horton) sank German T.B.D. in Baltic.

Russian advance towards Tilsit.

Battle in Beskid Pass (Carpathians).

Turkish advance posts reported at Katieh, and on roads leading to Suez Canal.

French took Bertua (Cameroons).

January 30.

U21 shelled Vickers works, Walney Is., and off Fleetwood (Lancashire) sank three British steamers, *Ben Cruachan* (3,092 tons), *Linda Blanche*, and *Kilcoan*. Crews rescued.

U20 off Havre sank, without warning, s.s. *Tokomaru* (6,084 tons), *Ikaria* (4,335 tons), and *Oriole* (1,489 tons). First officially recorded U-Boat attack without warning.

Japanese sword of honour presented to King Albert in Belgium.

French reverse near Fontaine Madame (Argonne).

German offensive near Lipno (Poland).

Russians defeated Turks at Sufian (Persia) and drove them from Tabriz.

* January 31.

At the end of January F.F. *Iron Duke* was refitting; *Superb* was away from 1st Battle Squadron; *Conqueror* from 2nd Battle Squadron; *Commonwealth* and *Britannia* of 3rd Battle Squadron were refitting; 4th Battle Squadron was complete; of the Battle Cruisers *Lion* was repairing, and *Tiger* and *Indomitable* were refitting.

During January U7 and U31 were posted lost: the former was torpedoed by another U-Boat which mistook her signals; the latter was found adrift in the North Sea, with her crew dead inside the closed hull.

Germans, during January, perfected and completed their first 6-inch gas-shell.

Germans gained slight success near Bolimov (Poland).

First French Syrian Squadron, of three battleships amd two cruisers, formed under Adm. Dartige du Fournet.

First French Dardanelles Squadron, *Suffren* (F. Adm. Guépratte), *Bouvet*, *Gaulois*, and *Charlemagne*, placed under orders of Adm. Carden.

February 1.

Irish Sea sailings restricted owing to U-Boat menace.

H.M.S. *Tiger* arrived in Tyne for refit.

H.S. *Asturias* attacked by U20 off Havre.

Strenuous fighting near Cuinchy; trenches rushed by British.

Third battle of Perthes (Champagne).

Z IV raided Lyck, E. Prussia.

German offensive along Ravka line near Bolimov (Poland).

Russian advance between Dukla Pass and Upper San R. (Carpathians).

Russian Government proclaimed bombardment of unfortified towns to be piracy.

February 2.

Highest wheat prices at Chicago since 1898.

Arrest in Maine (U.S.) of German officer, Werner Horne, for partially blowing up C.P.R. bridge across St. Croix R.

Sailings from Irish ports resumed.

British Parliament reassembled.

German pressure at Bolimov (Poland).

German £3,000,000 loan to Bulgaria.

Turks appeared opposite Ismailia (Suez Canal); desultory action.

February 3.

H.M. A.M.C. *Clan MacNaughton* (4,985 tons) believed foundered N. Atlantic.

Adm. von Pohl assumed command of High Sea Fleet, vice Adm. von Ingenohl, and hoisted his flag in H.I.M.S. *Friedrich der Grosse* at Wilhelmshaven.

Vain German attack near Perthes (Champagne); and attempt to use fireships on Ancre R., N. of Albert.

Russians regained Gumin near Bolimov (Poland). German offensive weakening.

Russians retired from Tucholka and Beskid Passes, but advanced near the Uzok Pass (Galicia).

Turks attempted to bridge Suez Canal at El Kantara, Tussum and Serapeum; repelled by British. Djemal Pasha's force numbered some 12,000-15,000 men. The Canal Defence force at this time had risen to 30,000 men.

S. African rebel Kemp with 500 men surrendered at Upington.

February 4.

Kaiser addressed U-Boat Commanders at Wilhelmshaven.

Second Phase of U-Boat War:

German official "Blockade" of Great Britain announced for Feb. 18.

Germans now had 23 U-Boats in North Sea, 7 U-Boats in Baltic, and on order: 42 large U-Boats and 127 small U-Boats, including the so-called "canal-fleas" for Flanders.

Slight French advance at Ecuries, between Arras—La Bassée.

In Carpathians Russians retired.

British crossed Suez Canal in pursuit of Turks.

Union Forces repulsed German attack on Kakamas, in N.W. of Cape Colony.

February 5.

British Army estimates for 3,000,000 men, exclusive of India.

Hostile shelling of British left and centre in the West decreased. Aircraft on both sides active.

French bombed German aeroplane sheds at Habsheim.

Hindenburg at Insterburg, whither German Eastern H.Q. removed from Posen, issued orders for Masurian Winter Battle. Gen. Ludendorff now back again from Southern Army to which he had been attached during January.

February 6.

H.M.S. *Erne* lost off Rattray Head.

S.S. *Lusitania* arrived at Liverpool, flying American flag.

Adm. Bachmann, Chief of German Naval Staff, vice Adm. von Pohl.

Triple Entente finance agreement.

Successful British attack on two German sap-heads S. of La Bassée Canal, near Cuinchy.

Germans exploded 3 mines in La Boiselle, N.E. of Albert.

Austrians recaptured Kimpolung (Bukovina).

* February 7.

Germans attacked Bagatelle (Argonne).

Masurian Winter Battle begun in Kaiser's presence. Hindenburg with German Tenth and Eighth Armies attacked Russian Tenth Army (Gen. Sievers) on Pilkallen—Gumbinnen—Johannisburg front.

Austrians held near Tucholka Pass (Carpathians); but reached Suczava Valley (Bukovina).

February 8, 1915.

H.M.S. *Tiger* left the Tyne for Rosyth.

King George received M. Delcassé, French Foreign Minister, at Buckingham Palace.

King of Belgians visited British front in Flanders.

Germans still attacking Bagatelle.

Germans in Johannisburg (E. Prussia).

No Turks within 20 miles of Suez Canal.

H.M.S. *Philomel* raided Bab Yunus (near Alexandretta).

Russian Black Sea destroyers sank over 50 Turkish sailing vessels ; German cruisers again bombarded Trebizond.

H.I.M.S. *Breslau* bombarded Yalta (Crimea).

February 9.

H.M.S. *Lion* arrived for repairs in the Tyne, and remained until end of February.

U.S. s.s. *Wilhelmina* arrived at Falmouth from America with food consigned to Germany.

King George received M. Bark, Russian Finance Minister, at Buckingham Palace.

French took St. Rémy (Woevre).

Gen. von Gallwitz's new Army Group formed on Mlawa front. Old Prussian Guard Reserve Corps merged in this formation.

Germans took Biala and outflanked Russian right near Pillkallen (E. Prussia).

Russians retired before Austrians across Suczava R. (Bukovina).

Russian Orange Book on Armenia.

February 10.

Further British reply to U.S. Note on treatment of neutral shipping.

British s.s. *Laertes* escaped from U-Boat.

Germans attacked Marie-Thérèse in La Grurie Wood (Argonne) and at Ban-de-Sapt.

Germans took Eydtkuhnen and Wirballen (Prusso-Russian frontier).

Austrians repulsed at Koziova (Carpathians).

February 11.

U.S. Note to Germany described German threat to sink neutral vessels in British waters as " unprecedented in naval warfare " and " indefensible violation of neutral rights."

U.S. Note to Britain on use of American Flag by British ships.

S.S. *Wilhelmina's* cargo seized at Falmouth.

Germans repulsed at Marie-Thérèse.

Germans took Serpets (Poland).

Austrians reached Sereth (R. Bukovina).

February 12.

British air attack on Bruges, Zeebrugge, Blankenberghe, and Ostend ; 34 naval aeroplanes and seaplanes engaged ; great damage to Ostend Railway Station.

French Chamber by 481 votes to 52 adopted absinthe prohibition Bill.

Germans advanced towards Lyck (E. Prussia) and took Mariampol and Kalvaria.

Austrian advance through Yablonitza Pass (Galicia).

Turkish force at Tor (Sinai) annihilated

February 13.

Allied line E. of Givenchy pushed forward ; British guns and infantry co-operating in French advance on right.

French attack near Souain (Champagne).

February 13 (*continued*).

Germans took Xon—Norroy (Moselle).

German offensive in Lauch Valley.

Germans near Lyck (E. Prussia).

*February 14.

German Government urgently requested Kaiser's Naval Staff to instruct U-Boat commanders until further notice not to attack ships flying neutral flags.

German artillery active in Northern France. Germans captured trenches at St. Eloi (Ypres). French recovery at Norroy (Moselle).

Germans took Sengern and Remsbach in Lauch Valley (Alsace).

Germans wrested Lyck from 3rd Siberian Corps. Russians completely out of E. Prussia.

Austrians took Nadvorna (Galicia).

February 15.

Kaiser at German G.H.Q. ordered postponement of U-Boat action against neutrals in the proclaimed area.

Exchange of British and German disabled prisoners.

Canadians began to arrive in France.

British regained St. Eloi trenches.

German advance in E. Prussia and N. of Vistula R. continued ; enemy took Plock.

Mutiny of Indian Light Infantry at Singapore.

February 16.

German reply to U.S. Note on U-Boat blockade holding out prospect of eventual revision, provided Great Britain be induced to observe Declaration of London.

Captain of H.I.M.S. *Blücher* died at Edinburgh.

Sir J. French's dispatch covering operations from November, 1914, to February, 1915, issued.

French s.s. *Ville de Lille* sunk off Barfleur

Fresh British air attack by 40 aeroplanes and seaplanes, on Ostend, Middelkerke, Ghistelles, and Zeebrugge.

Fourth battle of Perthes (Champagne).

Russians from E. Prussia retired on Niemen R.

Fresh Austrian reverse at Koziova (Carpathians). Austrians retook Kolomea (E. Galicia).

February 17.

H.M.S. *Australia* joined Battle Cruisers at Rosyth.

L3 and L4 wrecked off Danish coast.

German attack on Indians near La Bassée repulsed.

Slight French progress in Arras region ; success at Perthes (Champagne) and N.W. of Verdun.

French began attack on important Les Eparges spur (Woevre), on W. side of St. Mihiel salient.

Russians defeated at Plock-Ratsioni.

Austrians retook Czernowitz (Bukovina). Heavy fighting near Nadvorna and Kolomea (Galicia)

February 18.

H.M.SS. *Bellona, Blanche, Boadicea*. and *Blonde*, with four T.B.D.s, left Scapa for four days patrol off Norwegian coast.

U-Boat " blockade " of Great Britain.

U30 and U16 in Irish Sea.

German Naval Staff exempted a marked route between Lindesnäs and the Tyne in the proclaimed U-Boat area for Danish and Swedish ships.

Sundays marked with Asterisk (*).

February 18, 1915 (*continued*).
German counter-attack at Perthes.
French regained Xon—Norroy (Moselle).
Germans took Tauroggen (E. Prussia).
Austrians advanced on Dunayetz R. near Tarnov (Galicia).

February 19.—200*TH DAY OF WAR.*
British reply to U.S. on use of American flag by British ships.
Second British Note to U.S. on seizure of s.s. *Wilhelmina.*
First line of anti-U-Boat obstructions in Hoy Sound, Scapa Flow, completed.
H.M.S. *Goldfinch* wrecked off Orkney Is.
H.M.S. *Fearless* and two T.B.D. divisions from Harwich reinforced Grand Fleet, bringing up to 48 total destroyer strength of Grand Fleet.
Norwegian s.s. *Belridge* torpedoed by U-Boat in Channel.
French success at Les Eparges (Woevre).
Germans took Reichsackerkopf (Vosges), and entered Metzeral—Sondernach, but driven from summit between Lusse—Wissenbach.
Austrian sortie at Przemysl (Galicia).
Forts at entrance to Dardanelles at Kum Kale and Cape Helles bombarded by Franco-British Naval Squadron (Vice-Admiral Carden). R.N.A.S. seaplanes and aeroplanes assist.

February 20.
The Times Fund over £1,000,000.
German Naval Staff ordained U.S. and Italian flags to be immune even in North Sea and Channel. A free route for Scandinavian ships to be fixed.
Slight German gain near Ypres.
French captured wood near Perthes.
German advance near Sulzern (Alsace).
Gen. von Gallwitz's Army Group engaged by Russians at Przasnysz.
Austrians again repulsed at Koziova.
Dardanelles bombardment continued.

*February 21.
German aeroplanes dropped bombs on Colchester, Coggeshall, and Braintree at night.
ZX. and LZ35 raided Calais.
French progress near Perthes.
Germans took Hochrod and Stossweiler.
Russians counter-attacked near Plock and Lomja (Poland) ; in Carpathians they drove Austrians from Lupkov and Wyzkov Passes and attacked successfully near Stanislau.

February 22.
German Naval Staff issued U-Boat instruction for western British waters ; caution enjoined in dealing with U.S. and Italian ships.
Reims Cathedral violently bombarded.
Masurian Winter Battle ended ; Germans claimed 100,000 prisoners ; no strategic development.
Russians giving before German attacks at Przasnysz, N. of Warsaw.
Battle at Stanislau—Dolina (Galicia).
French cruiser *Desaix* landed marines at Akabah (Red Sea) ; Turks driven out.
Union Forces occupied Garub (G.S.W. Africa).

February 23.
Admiralty proclaimed prohibited area in Irish Channel.
U-Boat attack on Folkestone—Boulogne night-packets failed.

February 23 (*continued*).
Two wrecked German airmen picked up in North Sea by British trawler.
German Tenth Army re-engaged on the Bobr.

February 24.
Landship (Tank) Committee formed under Director of Naval Construction.
S.S. *Harpalion* and *Rio Parana* torpedoed in Channel.
French artillery successes on the Meuse.
Fighting at Les Eparges (Woevre).
Germans crossed Niemen R. near Sventsiansk, and stormed Przasnysz (N. of Warsaw).
Russians took Mozely near Bolimov (Poland).
German air raid on Alexandrovo.
French T.B.D. *Dague* mined off Montenegrin coast.

February 25.
Admiralty War Staff issued instructions regarding submarines applicable to vessels carrying a defensive armament.
H.S. *St. Andrew* chased by U-Boat off Boulogne.
Slight British advance near La Bassée.
French gain near Le Mesnil.
Germans bombarded Ossovietz (Poland) ; Russians struggling to regain Przasnysz.
Dardanelles bombardment resumed. Sedd-ul-Bahr and Cape Helles forts at entrance shattered by Allied squadron, including H.M.S. *Queen Elizabeth* (completed in January, oil-fired, and first British ship to mount 15-inch guns). Straits swept by trawlers for four miles up.

February 26.
Welsh Guards to be formed.
French took trenches near Le Mesnil.
German attack with " flame-throwers " in Bois de Malancourt, N. E. of Verdun.
Germans giving way at Przasnysz.
German air raid on Warsaw.
At Dardanelles on Asiatic side H.M.SS. *Albion, Majestic,* and *Vengeance* proceeded to limit of swept area and bombarded Fort Dardanos. Marines landed at Kum Kale and Sedd-ul-Bahr to complete destruction of forts.

February 27.
King George visited Rosyth.
S.S. *Dacia* brought by French warship to Brest.
French took Beauséjour (Champagne).
Russians recaptured Przasnysz (Poland).
British blockade of G.E. Africa.

*February 28.
During February the Battle Cruiser Fleet was constituted under Adm. Beatty.
During February Adm. Sturdee, after Falkland Is. victory, joined Grand Fleet and succeeded Adm. Gamble in command 4th Battle Squadron.
During February the construction of the first S.S. airship was approved ; 27 of this type were completed during the year.
During February no British fishing vessels were lost by enemy action.
S.S. *Thordis* rammed U-Boat off Beachy Head, awarded prize for first British steamer to sink German submarine.
Germans bombarded Soissons and Reims.
Further French progress near Perthes.
French success at Hill 263 (Argonne).

For List of Abbreviations see page iv.

March 1, 1915.

In reply to German campaign of "piracy and pillage," Allied Fleets to prevent all commodities from reaching or leaving Germany.

Soissons heavily bombarded.

French established new line 2,000 yards forward from previous positions between Perthes—Beauséjour (Champagne), as a result of their gain on Feb. 16.

French entered Vauquois.

German offensive on Niemen R. stopped. Retreat beginning; heavy fighting round Grodno and Ossovietz.

German air raid on Warsaw.

Russians in Carpathians holding firm.

Progress in Dardanelles. H.M.SS. *Triumph, Ocean,* and *Albion,* further up Straits, bombarded forts on Cape Kephez and opposite on European shore.

French warships shelled Bulair from Xeros Gulf.

March 2.

Germany notified of new Anglo-French blockade.

Adm. von Pohl exercised the 2nd and 3rd High Sea Squadrons off Heligoland.

German counter-attacks near Perthes.

Russian counter-offensive from Niemen R. continued; Germans retired from Przasnysz (Poland), yielding 10,000 prisoners.

H.M.SS. *Canopus, Swiftsure,* and *Cornwallis* engaged Dardanelles Forts No. 8 and No. 9. French battleship *Suffren* bombarded Fort Sultan on Bulair Lines; *Gaulois* bombarded Fort Napoleon; *Bouvet* damaged bridge over Carack R.

March 3.

Admiral Sturdee's Falkland Islands Battle Dispatch and Admiral Beatty's Dogger Bank Dispatch published.

Reims again bombarded.

Russians recaptured Stanislau (Galicia), and began repelling Austrians in Carpathians.

In Dardanelles, H.M.SS. *Irresistible, Albion, Prince George,* and *Triumph* resumed attack. H.M.S. *Dublin* destroyed observation station on Gallipoli. H.M.S. *Sapphire* bombarded Turkish troops in Adramyti Gulf (Asia Minor).

Heavy fighting N.W. of Basra (Mesopotamia) between Indian troops and Turks.

March 4.

U8 sunk off Dover at 5 p.m. by H.M.SS. *Ghurka* and *Maori,* after hunt by 12 T.B.D.s; crew taken prisoners. Admiralty decided that these 29 officers and men could not be allowed "honourable treatment," as they had probably attacked unarmed ships.

At Dardanelles demolition parties again landed. H.M.S. *Sapphire* silenced field battery at Dikeli, between Mitylene and mainland; Besika shelled by H.M.S. *Prince George.*

March 5.

Issue of £50,000,000 3 per cent. Exchequer Bonds announced.

L8 wrecked near Tirlemont.

Three heavy German counter-attacks failed against positions won by French on Feb. 28 at Hill 263 near Boureuilles (Argonne).

French attacked Germans on Hartmannsweilerkopf (Alsace); success at Sülzern.

Germans massing forces between Thorn and Mlava (Poland).

March 5 (*continued*).

German Ninth Army engaged in ten days battle about Stolniki.

Russians crossed Bistritza R. (Galicia).

New Dardanelles attack opened with indirect fire by H.M.S. *Queen Elizabeth* from Gulf of Xeros over Gallipoli Peninsula on Kilid Bahr and Chanak Forts. This attack supported by H.M.SS. *Inflexible* and *Prince George* and controlled by seaplanes. *Queen Elizabeth* fired 29 rounds; magazine in Fort L blown up; other two forts damaged. Some ships of the East Indies Squadron (Vice-Admiral Peirse in H.M.S. *Euryalus*) in Smyrna Gulf bombarded Yeni Kale.

March 6.

H.M.S. *Conqueror* rejoined Grand Fleet, after repairs at Liverpool.

Austrian retreat in Bukovina.

Progress in Dardanelles. H.M.S. *Queen Elizabeth* again attacked forts, by indirect fire, across Gallipoli Peninsula (about 12 miles). Fort Dardanus in Narrows again bombarded. Smyrna Gulf bombardment continued. H.M.S. *Euryalus* hit. Smyrna Forts silenced.

Greek crisis; M. Venizelos resigned.

* March 7.

British s.s. *Bengrove* (3,840 tons) sunk by U-Boat off Ilfracombe; no warning.

Dreadnought Battle Fleet on three days cruise in northern part of North Sea, and Battle Cruiser Fleet in central North Sea.

German Naval Staff abolished free route for Scandinavian ships; but designated area to be free from mines.

British air raid on Ostend; Kursaal bombed.

French gained footing in Sabot Wood (Champagne).

Germans in W. Poland using liquid fire.

French battleships, *Gaulois, Charlemagne, Bouvet,* and *Suffren* (Admiral Guépratte), entered Dardanelles to cover bombardment of Narrows by H.M.SS. *Agamemnon* and *Lord Nelson,* with direct fire at 12,000-14,000 yards; two forts out of action.

March 8.

German attack about Dixmude failed.

Germans forced back at Ossovietz.

H.M.S. *Queen Elizabeth,* supported by four battleships, entered Dardanelles and bombarded Fort Rumeli Medjidieh Tabia, S. of Kilid Bahr.

Russian Black Sea Fleet bombarded Heraclea (Asia Minor).

March 9.

British s.s. *Tangistan* (3,738 tons) sunk by U-Boat off Flamborough Head; no warning; 38 lost.

French progress near Le Mesnil.

Struggle between Four de Paris—Bolante (Argonne).

German Eleventh Army formed; Gen. von Fabeck, ex-XIIIth (Prussian) Corps, in temporary command.

Germans began new offensive with fresh troops from Thorn—Przaznyz (Poland). Russians advancing from Ossovietz.

Russian success in Transchorok (Caucasus).

M. Gounaris formed new Greek Ministry.

German reverse on Mara R. (E. Africa).

Sundays marked with Asterisk (*).

March 10, 1915.

U12 rammed and sunk by H.M.S. *Ariel* off Aberdeen coast. *Ariel* docked for repair.

Battle of Neuve Chapelle begun.

British attacked at 8 a.m. and Sir J. French reported : "Before noon we had captured the whole of the village of Neuve Chapelle, and our infantry at once proceeded to confirm and extend the local advantage gained. By dusk the whole labyrinth of trenches on a front of about 400 yards was in our hands beyond the enemy's advanced trenches. The number of German prisoners captured and brought in during the day was 750."

German attack towards Niemen R.

LZ34 raided Warsaw.

H.M.S. *Doris* bombarded barracks at Deurt Yol (Syria) ; 450 Turkish casualties.

March 11.

German auxiliary *Prinz Eitel Friedrich* arrived at Newport News, U.S.A., disarmed.

H.M.S. *Superb* returned to Scapa from Portsmouth.

H.M. A.M.C. *Bayano* (5,948 tons) sunk by U-Boat off Clyde.

Blockade of Germany took effect.

Commander Otto Weddigen in U29 captured British s.s. *Adenwen* off Casquets. Ship towed in damaged.

Battle of Neuve Chapelle ; German attempts to recover lost ground repulsed.

French warships bombarded Bulair Lines (Gallipoli).

March 12.

H.M.S. *Faulknor* and six T.B.D.s detached from Grand Fleet to hunt U-Boats in Irish Sea.

British s.s. *Andalusian* (2,349 tons) sunk by U-Boat off Bishop Rock.

British s.s. *Headlands* (2,988 tons) and *Indian City* (4,645 tons) torpedoed and sunk by U-Boat off Scilly Is.

British Government acquired indigo crop.

Ypres bombarded.

Battle of Neuve Chapelle ended ; counter-attacks easily repulsed by 4th and Indian Corps ; L'Epinette captured by 3rd Corps. British consolidated.

Gen. Maunoury directing Soissons operations wounded in eye ; invalided.

German attacks repulsed at Augustovo—Przasnysz (Poland).

March 13.

Gen. Sir Ian Hamilton left London for Dardanelles.

In Neuve Chapelle region progress by 7th Division towards Aubers ; Germans reinforced ; British took 612 prisoners. British aircraft bombed Don—Douai junctions.

German offensive at Augustovo—Przasnysz (Poland) checked.

Russians penetrated outer defences of Przemysl (Galicia).

H.M.S. *Amethyst* damaged by Turkish gunfire in Sari Siglar Bay (Dardanelles).

∗March 14.

H.I.M.S. *Dresden* sunk off Juan Fernandez (Chile) by H.M.SS. *Glasgow* and *Kent* with A.M.C. *Orama.*

Belgian Relief Ship s.s. *Sutton Hall* attacked with torpedo by U-Boat in Channel.

Belgian progress about Dixmude.

Germans attacked near Ypres and took part of St. Eloi.

∗March 14 (*continued*).

Most of Sabot Wood (Champagne) in French hands.

Germans failed to take Przasnysz, and, though severe fighting continued between that town and Niemen R., they made no appreciable progress.

French submarine *Coulomb* on reconnaissance in Dardanelles.

March 15.

First aircraft attack on British merchantman ; s.s. *Blonde* bombed by Taube aeroplane three miles off N. Foreland ; missed.

British recovery at St. Eloi.

Russian counter-attack along Orzec R. (N. Poland).

Russians broke Austrian line near Smolnik (Galicia).

March 16.

In House of Lords Lord Crewe announced that considerable reinforcements were proceeding to Ahwaz—Kurna (Mesopotamia).

Vice-Admiral Carden relinquished Dardanelles command ; succeeded by Rear-Admiral de Robeck with rank of Vice-Admiral.

March 17.

U.S. notified that British cruiser cordon would effectively control all passage to and from Germany.

H.M.SS. *Nemesis* and *Nymphe* in collision in North Sea ; both docked.

Z XII., fitted with observation " basket," raided Calais.

Further German attack at St. Eloi repulsed.

Austrians failed to cross Pruth R. (Bukovina).

Sir Ian Hamilton at Tenedos met French commander Gen. D'Amade.

Approaches to Dardanelles swept by Allied minesweepers.

March 18.

U29 (Comdr. Weddingen), after attempting to attack ships of 1st Battle Squadron, rammed and sunk by H.M.S. *Dreadnought* in North Sea shortly after noon, while Battle Fleet was carrying out a strategical exercise.

Russians occupied Memel (E. Prussia).

Last Austrian sortie from Przemysl (Galicia) fails.

Allied naval attack on Dardanelles forts by three squadrons of battleships. H.M.SS. *Irresistible* (15,000 tons) and *Ocean,* and French *Bouvet* mined ; H.M.S. *Inflexible* and French *Gaulois* damaged. Losses made good by H.M.SS. *Queen* and *Implacable.*

March 19.

Grand Fleet returned to bases.

Home Government and trade unions agreed that during war there should be no cessation of work upon munitions and equipments.

March 20.

Between Arras—La Bassée Germans took trenches near Notre Dame de Lorette.

Z X. and LZ.35 raided Paris.

Reichstag voted 10,000,000,000 marks (third war credit) ; Socialist Minority of 30 abstained ; Liebknecht and another voted against.

Przemysl (Galicia) defence ending.

Further Russian success near Smolnik.

British ships shelled Lindi (G.E. Africa).

For List of Abbreviations see page iv.

March 20, 1915 (*continued*).

Gen. Botha took over 200 prisoners and some field guns at Riet, near Swakopmund (G.S.W. Africa).

＊March 21.

Dutch s.s. *Batavier V.* and *Zaanstroom* seized at sea and taken to Zeebrugge by Germans.

Belgian Relief Ship s.s. *Strathfillan* bombed by aircraft off North Hinder ; missed.

Two other steamers also bombed by German aircraft in North Sea ; missed.

French recovered ground near Notre Dame de Lorette.

Germans retook Memel (E. Prussia). They abandoned Ossovietz (Poland).

H.M. T.B. 064 wrecked in Ægean.

March 22.

British steamer bombed by German aircraft in North Sea ; missed.

Soissons Cathedral bombarded.

Fall of Przemysl (Galicia), besieged since Nov. 11 ; Russians took 126,000 prisoners and 700 big guns.

Austro-Germans in Wyszkow Pass.

March 23.

British steamer attacked by aircraft with bombs and darts in North Sea ; missed.

French courts declared *Dacia* seizure valid.

Belgians on E. bank of Yser R.

Reims and Soissons bombarded by Germans.

Another Turkish raid in Suez Canal zone stopped near El Kubri by Indian troops supported by a Lancashire T.F. Battery.

March 24.

Chile protested against destruction of H.I.M.S. *Dresden* off Juan Fernandez.

H.M.S. *Indefatigable,* from Mediterranean, joined H.M.S. *Invincible* at Rosyth, where latter, on return from Falkland Is., became Flag of 3rd Battle Cruiser Squadron, which was completed in June by arrival of H.M.S. *Indomitable* from Gibraltar.

British air raid on German U-Boat workshops at Hoboken (Antwerp).

French reached German second line at Hartmannsweilerkopf (Alsace).

Sir Ian Hamilton at Alexandria to superintend transports for Gallipoli.

March 25.

Dutch s.s. *Medea* sunk by U-Boat off Beachy Head.

Between La Bassée—Arras French re-established on Notre Dame de Lorette Ridge ; German counter-attack repulsed.

Russian cruiser *Askold* arrived at Dardanelles from Far East.

March 26.

French air raid on Metz—Frescati.

French carried fortified summit of Hartmannsweilerkopf (Alsace).

Germans in Alsace used liquid fire.

Russians, after capturing Lupkov Pass (Carpathians), advanced and took 1,700 prisoners.

Bannu Movable Column and North Waziristan Militia, under Gen. Fane, defeated a large Khostwal *lashkar* threatening Miranshah.

March 27.

Sir J. French in a statement published in *The Times* :

"The protraction of the war depends entirely upon the supply of men and munitions."

March 27 (*continued*).

British s.s. *Aguila* sunk by U28 off the Smalls.

British s.s. *Vosges* shelled and sunk by U-Boat in Channel.

British steamer bombed by aircraft in North Sea ; missed.

German air raid on Calais—Dunkirk.

German air raid on Verdun—Nancy.

French progress at Les Eparges (Woevre).

French battleship *Henri IV.* arrived at Dardanelles.

＊March 28.

H.M.S. *Courageous* laid down.

S.S. *Falaba*, outward from Liverpool torpedoed by U28 (Commander von Forstner), off Milford, 104 lives lost. Germans jeered at drowning people.

G.E.R. s.s. *Brussels* (Capt. Fryatt) chased by U133 off Maas Lightship ; escaped.

Gen. von Fabeck in command of German First Army, vice Gen. von Kluck, wounded.

German counter-attack at Les Eparges (Woevre) repulsed.

German air raid on Nancy.

German Beskid Corps formed.

Russian Black Sea Fleet bombarded outer Bosporus forts.

French battleship *Jauréguiberry* (F. Adm. Guépratte) arrived at Dardanelles.

March 29.

Adm. von Pohl put to sea with 1st and 3rd High Sea Squadrons and Battle Cruisers.

Germans in Tauroggen near Tilsit.

Action E. of Taveta (B.E. Africa).

March 30.

German Naval Staff suspended all favoured treatment of Scandinavian ships.

Reims Cathedral bombarded.

March 31.

During March Adm. Pakenham succeeded Adm. Moore in command 2nd Battle Cruiser Squadron (F. *Australia*).

King George informed Chancellor of Exchequer that H.M. would set example by giving up alcoholic liquors himself and in Royal Household.

French Absinthe Prohibition law.

German air raid on Belfort.

Germans bombarded Libau (Courland).

Heavy fighting in Carpathians.

At the end of March Gen. von Conrad issued from Austrian G.H.Q., Teschen, an Army Order reprehending surrender of 28th (Prague) Infantry Regiment to Russians.

During March Australian R.F.C. was inaugurated by dispatch of flying unit to Mesopotamia.

April 1.

Three Tyne trawlers *Jason, Gloxinia,* and *Nelly,* sunk by U10.

British s.s. *Seven Seas* torpedoed off Beachy Head.

British air raid on Zeebrugge and Hoboken.

Germans took Cloister—Hoek (Dixmude).

German aeroplane bombing Reims brought down.

German State nitrogen plant at Piesteritz (Elbe), with annual capacity of 175,000 metric tons, laid down.

Bulgarian irregulars attacked Serbians at Valandovo.

Sundays marked with Asterisk (*).

D

April 1, 1915 (*continued*).

British ships shelled Pangani coast (G.E. Africa).

Union forces occupied Hasuur (G.S.W. Africa).

April 2.

Germany threatened reprisals if U-Boat crews were segregated by British authorities.

German Naval Staff, irritated by successive loss of U8, U12, and especially U29 during March, ordered all U-Boat commanders primarily to look out for themselves; ships no longer need be challenged.

German attack at Bagatelle (Argonne).

French air raid on Neuenburg and Mülheim.

Austria offered Italy rectification of Trentino frontier.

Easter battle in Laborcza Valley begun.

April 3.

Near Cuinchy 100 yards of German trench blown in by mine.

French took Regniéville (Woevre).

German air raid on Novo-Georgievsk.

Turkish cruiser *Medjidieh* mined off Odessa.

Off Crimea, Russian Fleet exchanged shots at long range with H.I.M.SS. *Goeben* and *Breslau*.

Union Forces occupied Warmbad (G.S.W. Africa).

*April 4.

Germans took Driegrachten from Belgians and crossed Yperlee Canal.

Gen. F. von Below in command of German Second Army (W. Front), vice Marshal von Bülow, retired.

Gen. von Hutier to command XXIst (Prussian) Army Corps, vice Gen. F. von Below.

Gen. von Falkenhayn instructed Gen. von Cramon at Teschen to report on possibilities of an Austrian offensive in Galicia, eventually reinforced by four German Army Corps.

Russians occupied Cisna and Sztropko (Carpathians). Heavy fighting at Okna, near Czernowitz (Bukovina).

Turks defeated by Russians at Olti (Armenia).

April 5.

U.S. Note to Germany demanding £45,610 indemnity for sinking of American ship *William P. Frye*.

Battle Cruiser Fleet on four days' cruise in northern part of North Sea.

Belgians failed to retake Driegrachten.

French attacked Les Eparges crest and took part of Ailly Wood, S. of St. Mihiel.

Union forces occupied Kalkfontein and Kamus (G.S.W. Africa).

April 6.

King George commanded that henceforth no wines, spirits, or beer be consumed in any of his houses.

Near Furnes Belgians drove Germans back across Yperlee Canal on Merckem.

French completed capture of Ailly Wood S. of St. Mihiel.

Russians occupied Artvin (Caucasus).

Smyrna bombarded by warships and aeroplanes.

German defeat at Karunga (E. Africa).

April 7.

H.M.S. *Lion* returned to Rosyth, on completion of all repairs.

April 7 (*continued*).

French advance at Les Eparges (Woevre).

Russians reached southern side of Rostoki Pass (Galicia).

British skirmish with Turks N.E. of El Kantara (Suez Canal).

Sir Ian Hamilton returned from Egypt to Mudros.

April 8.

German A.M.C. *Prinz Eitel Friedrich* interned at Newport News, U.S.

Allied airmen bombed Zeebrugge.

Germans failed to retake Beauséjour (Champagne).

French took part of Les Eparges heights (St. Mihiel).

French "Croix de Guerre" instituted.

Allied naval attack on Enos (Ægean).

Attempted assassination of Sultan of Egypt, Hussein Kamel.

April 9.

Germans on rafts attacked St. Jacques Cappelle, S. of Dixmude; repulsed by French marines.

French carried Les Eparges crest (Woevre).

Russians advancing towards Suvalki (N. Poland).

Russians holding Carpathian crest from Dukla to Uzok Pass.

April 10.

Belgian relief ship *Harpalyce* (5,940 tons) torpedoed and sunk by U-Boat off N. Hinder; 15 lost.

French progress in Bois de Montmare.

Belgrade shelled by Austrian gunboat.

Durazzo bombarded by Albanians.

*April 11.

101,000 Canadians under arms.

German A.M.C. *Kronprinz Wilhelm* arrived at Newport News, U.S.

Harrison s.s. *Wayfarer* torpedoed by U-Boat off Scilly; towed into Queenstown.

Whole Grand Fleet on three days cruise in centre of North Sea.

British steamer bombed by aircraft in North Sea; missed.

French air raid on Bruges.

Heavy fighting near Albert.

German counter-attacks at Les Eparges (Woevre) repulsed.

Russians took Wysocko Nizhne in fight for Uzok Pass (Carpathians).

British attacked by Turks at Kurna and Ahwaz (Mesopotamia).

April 12.

British steamer bombed by aircraft in North Sea; missed.

Germans placed under arrest 39 captured British officers as reprisal for special treatment of U-Boat prisoners.

German attack near Dixmude failed.

French failed at Hartmannsweilerkopf.

Russians held in Uzok Pass (Carpathians).

Strong Turkish attacks on British at Shaiba, S.W. of Basra (Mesopotamia).

Gaza (Syria) bombarded by French cruiser *St. Louis*.

April 13.

H.M.S. *Warspite* (27,500 tons, eight 15-inch guns), sister-ship of H.M.S. *Queen Elizabeth*, joined Grand Fleet at Scapa.

April 13, 1915 (*continued*).
Adm. Bacon succeeded Adm. Hood in command Dover Patrol.
French gain near Berry-au-Bac (Aisne R.). Near Maizeray (Woevre) their attacks fail.

April 14.
Dutch s.s. *Katwyk* sunk without warning by U-Boat off Dutch Coast.
L9 raided Tyne district.
LZ35 raided Poperinghe—Cassel—Hazebrouck.
French nearing Ablain St. Nazaire.
French airmen bombed German G.H.Q. at Mézières—Charleville.
Germans accused French of using mines emitting asphyxiating gases N.W. of Verdun.
Germans repulsed at Ossovietz (N. Poland).
French T.B.D. Flotilla at Dardanelles.
Turks routed at Shaiba (Mesopotamia).

April 15.
Allied aeroplanes bombed Ostend.
French progress 1,600 yards N. of Lauch.
French airmen bombed Metz and Freiburg.
LZ34 raided Warsaw.
German air raid on Novo-Georgievsk.
H.M. submarine E15 wrecked in Dardanelles and sunk by Turkish gunfire in making first attempt to enter Sea of Marmora.
H.M.SS. *Majestic* and *Swiftsure* bombarded Turkish post at Gaba Tepe (Gallipoli).
Russian Black Sea Fleet again bombarded Heraclea (Anatolia).

April 16.
British apology to Chile for sinking H.I.M.S. *Dresden* off Juan Fernandez.
Sir J. French's dispatch of April 5 issued.
German aeroplane raid on Faversham—Sittingbourne; airship dropped bombs in Essex and Suffolk.
French air raid on Strassburg.
Gen. von Mackensen in command of new Eleventh German Army (reinforced by Prussian Guard Corps and XLIst Reserve Corps from W. Front) in Galicia, with Gen. von Seeckt as Chief of Staff.
Prince Leopold of Bavaria took over Ninth Army from Gen. von Mackensen.
Turkish torpedo boat attacked in Ægean British transport *Manitou*; attack failed; Turkish T.B. chased ashore by Allied ships.
British air raid on Turkish camps in Sinai.
Turks reached Urmia (Persia).

April 17.
S.S. *La Rosarina* (8,332 tons) chased by U-Boat off S. Ireland; first officially recorded escape of British ship by use of her gun.
British took Hill 60 on Ypres—Comines railway near St. Eloi, after exploding mines.
German air raid on Belfort.
British advancing from Shaiba occupied Nakaila (Mesopotamia).

*April 18.
Grand Fleet in North Sea, sweeping down to Little Fisher Bank.
German Naval Staff issued fresh instruction to U-Boat commanders to treat neutrals with discrimination.
German counter-attacks against Hill 60 (Ypres) repulsed. British consolidated.
German air raid on Belfort.
Frontier raid in Peshawar repulsed by Khaibar Moveable Column.
Union Forces occupied Seeheim (G.S.W. Africa).

April 19.
German attempt on Hill 60 (Ypres).
French advance along Fecht R. (Alsace).
French airships bombed Strassburg and Mannheim.
Germans evacuated Keetmanshoop (G.S.W. Africa).

April 20.
Mr. Asquith at Newcastle on munitions.
Ypres bombarded by German heavy guns. Germans still attacking Hill 60.
Reims bombarded with incendiary shells.
Germans retook Embermènil (Lorraine).
Turks besieging Van (Armenia).
Anglo-French force took Mandera (Cameroons).
Union Forces occupied Keetmanshoop and defeated Germans at Kebus (G.S.W. Africa).

April 21.
Grand Fleet returned to bases, fuelled, and again put to sea for sweep towards Danish coast.
Adm. von Pohl took High Sea Fleet for a run of 120 sea miles to N.W. of Heligoland.
H.I.M.S. *Hamburg* rammed and cut down German T.B. 21 in North Sea.
Violent German attacks on Hill 60.
Slight French advance near St. Mihiel.
French airmen bombed Mannheim and Mülheim.
Russians took Hill 1002 near Lubonia (Carpathians).

April 22.
War Office directed Sir J. French that 20 per cent. of his ammunition reserves were to be shipped to Dardanelles.
First German gas-attack on W. Front:
Second battle of Ypres begun: Germans used asphyxiating gas against French Colonials, supported on right by Canadians, near St. Julien in northern sector of Ypres Salient.
Germans advanced behind gas clouds wearing respirators in Bixschoote-Langemarck sector.
French between Steenstraate and E. of Langemarck retired to canal. Germans captured wood W. of St. Julien. Canadians gallantly retook wood, but failed to hold.
Gen. von Lauenstein (XXXIXth Reserve Corps) to command independent force of three cavalry divisions and three infantry divisions for German thrust into Lithuania and Courland.
Russians repulsed at Uzok Pass (Carpathians).
Austrian monitor *Körös* torpedoed by British picket-boat on the Danube.
Anglo-French force at Enos (Ægean).
Smyrna forts again bombarded.

April 23.
Second Battle of Ypres. Germans took Langemarck, bridge at Steenstraate, and works S. of Lizerne. Canadians maintaining resistance. More gas used by Germans.
At Ypres Lance-Cpl. F. Fisher (13th Battln) was first Canadian to win V.C. in Great War.
German aeroplane raid on Warsaw.
Allied Fleet bombarded Turkish coast in Saros Gulf (Ægean).
Gen. Townshend arrived from India at Basra to take command of 6th (Poona) Division, vice Gen. Barrett, invalided.
Cameroons blockaded by British.

Sundays marked with Asterisk (*).

April 24, 1915.

German Naval Staff once more enjoined upon U-Boat commanders caution in dealing with neutrals.

Second Battle of Ypres continued. Germans took St. Julien. French and Belgians recovered Lizerne. Canadian counter-attacks checked German advance at St. Julien.

French repulsed German attacks at Les Eparges (Woevre).

Austrians took Ostraij (Carpathians).

French cruiser *Jeanne d'Arc* arrived at Dardanelles.

British Expeditionary Force left Mudros for Dardanelles.

Fighting round Kilimanjaro (E. Africa).

＊April 25.

Second Battle of Ypres: Germans re-captured Lizerne

Allied landing in Gallipoli Peninsula, supported by Fleet; British at Cape Helles and N. of Gaba Tepe; French at Kum Kale, on Asiatic side of Dardanelles, to create diversion. Helles landings (Rear-Admiral Wemyss) at Beaches S, V, W, X, Y by Imperial troops and R.N.D. Feint at S. Beach; De Tott's Battery carried; feint at Y Beach N. of Cape Tekke; men reached heights and dug in. Landing at X Beach covered by H.M.SS. *Swiftsure* and *Implacable*. Hill 114 captured and junction effected with forces from Beach W. Gallant landing at W Beach (Lancashire Landing); men charged through wire entanglements on beach, stormed heights, and joined with forces from X, then took Hill 138. At V Beach (Sedd-ul-Bahr) collier s.s. *River Clyde* run ashore to help landing. Heavy casualties here and little progress. Australians and New Zealanders landed N. of Gaba Tepe at Anzac Cove, under direction of Rear-Admiral Thursby with H.M.SS. *Triumph*, *Majestic*, and *Bacchante*; troops carried ridges and held line against Turkish counter-attacks.

French landing at Kum Kale supported by French warships and Russian cruiser *Askold*.

French cruiser *Latouche-Tréville* arrived at Dardanelles.

H.M.A. submarine AE2 entered Dardanelles, torpedoing Turkish gunboat.

Some 600 prominent Armenians deported from Constantinople.

April 26.

Triple Entente's secret convention with Italy signed in London.

Second Battle of Ypres: British counter-attack; Canadians relieved by Lahore Division of Indian Corps, who attacked despite gas. Northumberland Brigade entered for a time southern part of St. Julien; Gen. Riddell killed.

Germans attacked Franco-Belgians with gas S. of Dixmude, but failed to break through.

British airmen destroyed Courtrai junction and attacked Tourcoing, Courtrai, and Roubaix railways.

Germans recaptured Hartmannsweilerkopf (Alsace), but French regained crest.

Germans invaded Russian Baltic Provinces; advance on Shavli (Lithuania).

In Gallipoli British at V Beach advanced, took Sedd-ul-Bahr village and old fort, and carried Castle and Hill 141. Men from W and X Beaches joined up with V Beach forces. French at Kum Kale re-embarked after capturing 500 prisoners and diverting fire from British landings. Main French force

April 26 *(continued).*

disembarked at V Beach to relieve British party at S.

H.M.A. submarine AE2 in Sea of Marmora.

April 27.

Second Battle of Ypres: Allies regaining ground; Lahore Division pushing north; French back in Lizerne.

Gen. von Lauenstein's mixed force in three columns invaded Lithunia and Courland, with Shavli as general objective.

In Gallipoli Allied advance from Cape Helles to line across Peninsula from Hill 236 to mouth of nullah. H.M.S. *Queen Elizabeth* sank Turkish transport off Maidos in Narrows.

H.M. submarine E14 (Lieut.-Com. Boyle) entered Sea of Marmora through Dardanelles; sank Turkish gunboat.

French cruiser *Léon Gambetta* torpedoed in Otranto Straits by Austrian U5, with loss of Rear-Adm. Serrès and over 600 officers and men.

Union Forces occupied Aus (G.S.W. Africa).

April 28.

U.S. s.s. *Flushing* bombed by German aeroplane.

Germans at Ypres "definitely stopped."

Dunkirk bombarded from near Dixmude.

French airmen bombed Friedrichshaven and Leopoldshöhe.

In Gallipoli further Allied advance from Cape Helles on Krithia, reaching line 3 miles N. of Tekke Burnu to one mile N. of Eski Kissarlik Point. Reinforcements reached Anzac; Australians in front trenches relieved.

Union forces defeated Germans at Gibeon (G.S.W. Africa).

April 29.

Mr. Lloyd George in Commons outlined liquor control proposals.

Second Battle of Ypres: Allies still holding.

New British line fixed. Gen. Foch asked Sir J. French to await result of French attack on morrow.

Belgian artillery near coast destroyed 3 German boat-bridges on Yser R.

German air raid on Belfort.

Germans reached Libau—Dvinsk railway. Russians near Shavli retired on Mitau.

In Gallipoli Allies straightening line. Turkish counter-attacks repulsed.

H.M. submarine E14 sank Turkish transport in Sea of Marmora.

Brig.-Gen. Tighe (Temp. Major-Gen.) appointed C.-in-C. in E. Africa.

April 30.

German warning against sailing in s.s. *Lusitania* published in U.S. Press.

During April H.M.S. *Invincible* was sent to the Tyne to change some of her 12-inch guns which had become worn in Falkland Is. Battle.

During April Germans mined southern part of North Sea, so as to impede Grand Fleet's movements if endeavouring to bring High Sea Fleet to action.

LZ38 raided Ipswich and Bury St. Edmunds.

French attack at Ypres; no substantial result.

During the five months ended 30-iv.-15 there had arrived in France the 46th (North Midland), 47th (London), 48th (South Midland), 49th (West Riding), 50th (Northumbrian) and 51st (Highland) T.F. Divisions.

April 30, 1915 (*continued*).

Allied airmen bombed Valenciennes Station.

Germans reached Shavli and Muravievo and Radzivilishki, on Libau—Dvinsk railway.

In Gallipoli Allied artillery landed.

H.M.A. submarine AE2 sunk by Turks in Sea of Marmora.

During April Ali Dinar, Sultan of Darfur, renounced allegiance to Sudan Government.

May 1.

H.M.S. *Glorious* laid down.

U.S. oil-tanker *Gulflight* sunk by U-Boat.

H.M. destroyer *Recruit I.* and trawler *Columbia* torpedoed and sunk in North Sea. Two German torpedo-boats sunk by British destroyer off Dutch coast.

Second Battle of Ypres: German gas attack on Hill 60 repulsed; British ordered to withdraw to new line.

French Dreadnought *Languedoc* (25,500 tons) launched at Bordeaux.

Germans entered Shavli and advanced on Libau. German torpedo-boats in Riga Gulf.

Austro-German mass-offensive in Galicia from Dunayetz R. to San R., Gorlice—Tarnow.

French submarine *Joule* mined in Dardanelles.

Violent Turkish attacks on Anglo-French positions in Gallipoli.

Union Forces occupied Kubas (G.S.W. Africa).

* May 2.

Second Battle of Ypres: German gas attacks near St. Julien—Fortuin repulsed.

German Ninth Army delivers unsuccessful gas-attack before Skiernievice.

Dunayetz Battle; Austro-Germans, after massed bombardment by over 1,000 guns, took Gorlice and Ciezkovice (Galicia) and crossed Biala R.; Russians retired on Visloka R.

Allied counter-attack in Gallipoli; heavy Turkish losses.

Russian Black Sea Fleet bombarded Bosporus forts.

Union Forces took Otimbingwe (G.S.W. Africa).

May 3.

Second Battle of Ypres: Further German attacks against northern part of salient repulsed.

German advance on Mitau (Courland) contained S.W. of the town.

Dunayetz crossing begun.

French repulsed Turkish attack in Gallipoli.

H.M. submarine E14 torpedoed Turkish gunboat in Sea of Marmora.

May 4.

Sir J. French officially reported that Germans had definitely decided to use gases as a normal procedure, and that protests would be useless.

Second Battle of Ypres French advance between Lizerne—Het Sas. British withdrawal completed. Germans thereupon occupied Zonnebeke, Westhoek, and Zevenkote. New British line: Shell-trap Farm—Frezenberg Ridge—Hooge—Zillebeke Ridge—Hill 60.

German G.H.Q. moved to Pless (Silesia).

Russians on Visloka R. (Galicia); Austro-German pursuit begun.

May 5.

Second Battle of Ypres: Germans recaptured Hill 60 after heavy gas attack.

German advance on Mitau checked.

LZ34 raided Grodno.

Union Forces occupied Karibib (G.S.W. Africa).

May 6.

H.M. minelayer *Orvieto*, with eight T.B.D.s, started from Scapa for Heligoland Bight and ran into dense fog in which H.M.SS. *Comet* and *Nemesis* collided; latter seriously damaged; force returned.

British s.s. *Candidate* (5,858 tons) sunk by U-Boat off Coningbeg Light.

British s.s. *Centurion* (5,945 tons) sunk by U-Boat off Barrel Light.

Second Battle of Ypres: British regained some trenches on Hill 60.

French dented German line E. of Forêt de l'Aigle (Aisne).

Dunayetz Battle: Austrians entered Tarnov (Galicia).

Second attack on Krithia (Gallipoli); Allies bombarded Turkish lines, warships assisted. French advanced towards Kereves Dere, and made gains.

Gen. Bailloud's Algerian Division reinforcing at Dardanelles.

Mr. Harcourt's statement on well-poisoning by Germans in S.W. Africa.

May 7.

S.S. *Lusitania* (30,396 tons) torpedoed and sunk by U20 (Kapitän-Leutnant Schwieger), off Old Head of Kinsale, near Queenstown; 1,198 drowned, including many women and children and 124 U.S. citizens.

H.M.S. *Maori* mined off Belgian coast; H.M.S. *Crusader* damaged in rescuing crew.

Germans occupied Libau; Gen. von Pappritz, Governor of Königsberg, appointed Governor of Libau.

Germans retired further from Mitau.

Dunayetz Battle: Austro-Germans crossed Visloka R. at Jaslo. Russians retired on San R.

In Gallipoli, after land and sea bombardment of Achi Baba, British attacked towards Krithia and French again towards Kereves Dere. Turkish opposition strong.

May 8.

H.M. minelayer *Orvieto* again set out from Scapa for the Bight.

Second Battle of Ypres: Germans took Frezenberg Ridge after violent bombardment of British 5th Corps front. Princess Patricia's Canadian Light Infantry stuck to their trenches.

German destroyer mined outside Libau harbour. At Zejny on Libau—Vilna railway Germans forced back.

Allies failed to take Krithia (Gallipoli). Total gain in 3 days' battle averaged 500 yards along whole front.

* May 9.

Second Battle of Ypres: British retook Wieltje. Heavy German bombardment.

Germans bombarded Nieuport.

British airmen attacked St. André junction N. of Lille and Don canal bridge.

Battle of Festubert begun. British Fourth Corps attacked Aubers Bridge at Rougebanc, N.W. of Fromelles, and British

Sundays marked with Asterisk (*).

✳May 9, 1915 (continued).

First and Indian Corps between Neuve Chapelle—Givenchy. Neither attack very successful.

British ammunition supply permitted only 40 minutes' artillery preparation before these attacks.

Battle of Artois begun between Notre Dame de Lorette—Ecurie. French fired 17 mines near Carency, and captured three trench lines on Notre Dame de Lorette Ridge, White Works, La Targette, and half of Neuville St. Vaast.

Gen. Pétain's 33rd Army Corps mentioned in Army Orders for its fine work before Carency.

Russian counter-attack on Dniester R.

In Gallipoli Australians at Anzac carried three trench lines in front of Quinn's Post.

May 10.

President Wilson at Philadelphia in speech to 4,000 naturalised aliens, said : " There is such a thing as a man being too proud to fight."

Anti-German riots in London and Liverpool provoked by *Lusitania* outrage.

LZ38 and LZ39 raided Southend, Leigh-on-Sea, and Westcliff in early morning. About 100 bombs dropped : one person killed, 2 injured ; £20,000 damage.

Second Battle of Ypres : Slight German gain after severe shelling.

Battle of Festubert. British withdrew from Rougebanc trenches. Festubert attack suspended.

Battle of Artois : French took Neuville St. Vaast cemetery and part of Carency.

Dunayetz Battle : Russians checked Austro-Germans at Sanok (Galicia).

Turks retook trenches near Quinn's Post (Gallipoli) from Anzacs ; further advance checked.

H.M. submarine E14 sank Turkish transport *Gujdjemal* with 6,000 soldiers.

French battleship *Saint Louis* arrived at Dardanelles.

Franco-Italian Naval Convention giving Italy initiative in Adriatic.

May 11.

More anti-German riots in London.

German airmen bombed St. Denis (Paris).

Belgians on E. bank of Yser R.

Battle of Artois : French took wood E. of Carency.

Germans retired from Shavli (Lithuania). Russians retiring to San line.

First advance on Yaunde (Cameroons).

May 12.

H.M. minelayer *Orvieto* returned to Scapa after mine-laying operation in Heligoland Bight during night of May 10-11.

Climax of anti-German riots in London.

Bryce Report on German outrages published.

Battle of Artois : French completed capture of Carency, and carried Notre Dame de Lorette fort and chapel, and part of Ablain St. Nazaire.

Austro-Germans took Kielce (Poland).

Russian G.H.Q ordered Przemysl to hold, " for political reasons."

In Gallipoli British, chiefly Gurkhas, took bluff at Cape Tekke on extreme left, afterwards called Gurkha Bluff.

Gen. Botha occupied Windhuk (G.S.W. Africa).

May 13.

Both Kaisers and other enemy Sovereigns, etc., struck off Garter roll.

Mr. Asquith announced adult male enemy aliens to be interned or repatriated ; women and children also to be repatriated.

Second Battle of Ypres ; Gallant resistance by Gen. de Lisle's dismounted Cavalry Force between Verlorenhoek—Bellewarde. Line bent slightly in that region after heaviest bombardment.

Battle of Artois : French failed to take White Way Spur.

Whole Bois-le-Prêtre (Meuse) in French hands.

H.M. submarine E14 drove Turkish steamer ashore in Sea of Marmora.

H.M.S. *Goliath* sunk by Turkish T.B. off Cape Helles (Dardanelles).

May 14.

First U.S. *Lusitania* Note to Germany.

Lord Fisher's resignation as First Sea Lord refused.

The Times Military Correspondent : " The want of an unlimited supply of high explosive was a fatal bar to our success at Festubert."

This statement was sent from British G.H.Q. in France by desire of Sir J. French, who further endorsed it by commissioning his Military Secretary to proceed to London in order to lay the facts regarding the ammunition supply of the B.E.F. before Mr. Lloyd George, Mr. Balfour, and Mr. Bonar Law.

Second Battle of Ypres : French progress near Steenstraate—Het Sas.

Prussian Guard took Jaroslav (Galicia). Russians behind San R. ; they recovered Kolomea (E. Galicia).

May 15.

N. of Ypres French recovered Het Sas and drove Germans from W. bank of Yperlee Canal.

Canadian Division moved from Gen. Plumer's Second Army (Ypres) front to Gen. Haig's Festubert front.

Battle of Festubert resumed. Indian Corps held up before Richebourg l'Avoué.

Germans failed at Ville-sur-Tourbe (Champagne).

Russians forced back Germans on Dniester front and recovered Nadvorna (Galicia).

Adm. Nicol to command reinforced French Dardanelles Squadron.

✳May 16.

ZXII. and LZ39 raided Calais.

Battle of Ypres ; French progress.

Battle of Festubert : British advance.

Russians defeated Austro-Germans near Kielce (Poland).

Austro-German San crossing begun.

May 17.

Whole Grand Fleet on two days sweep in central North Sea.

High Sea Fleet started on a brief excursion in North Sea, and returned next day.

LZ38 raided Ramsgate.

Zeppelin over Ostend attacked and damaged by R.N.A.S., Dunkirk.

Battle of Ypres : French advance.

Battle of Festubert : British consolidated.

Austro-Germans crossed San R. at Jaroslav and Lezachov (Galicia).

In Gallipoli slight British advance.

French battleship *Suffren* returned to Dardanelles from Toulon.

May 17, 1915 (*continued*).
Russians occupied Ardjiche on Lake Van (Armenia).
Skirmish near Fife (Nyasaland).

May 18.
H.I.M.S. *Danzig* mined off Hellgoland; returned to port.
Two German T.B.D.s collided during night in North Sea; one sunk.
Lord Kitchener in Lords announced British would use gas; discussed munitions shortage, and asked for 300,000 more recruits.
Battle of Festubert: British reached La Quinque Rue—Béthune road, taking du Bois and Cour l'Avoué farms.
Russians on San R. driven from Sieniava (Galicia).
Anzac (Gallipoli) heavily bombarded by Turks.
H.M. submarine E14 returned from Sea of Marmora after 21 days. Lieut.-Com. Boyle given V.C.; crew decorated.

May 19.
Mr. Asquith announced coming reconstruction of Government on broader basis.
Liquor Control Bill passed.
On Gen. Haig's front Canadian Division relieved 7th Division and 51st (Highland) Division relieved 2nd Division.
M. Albert Thomas Under-Secretary in French War Ministry.
Turkish attack at Anzac (Gallipoli) repulsed.
Russians took Van (Armenia).

May 20.
LZ39 raided Béthune.
Battle of Ypres: French progress.
Near Festubert Canadians captured outstanding orchard position near La Quinque Rue.
Italian Chamber voted Government a free hand against Austria and Germany.
Adm. Essen, C.-in-C. Russian Baltic Fleet, died.
LZ34 raided Kovno.
Austro-Germans bombarded Przemysl (Galicia).
Negotiations at Anzac (Gallipoli) for truce to bury dead.

May 21.
H.I.M.S. *Ophelia* condemned by Prize Court (18-x.-14).
British Fleet minesweepers sent from Aberdeen to locate German minefield in southern North Sea; two sweepers collide in a fog; a third ashore.
Battle of Artois: French captured White Way Spur near Souchez and most of Ablain St. Nazaire.
Prusso-Bavarian Alpine Corps formed, under Gen. Krafft von Delmensingen, for service in Tirol.
Austrians cut communications between Italy and Austria.
Turkish attack on Quinn's Post (Gallipoli).
Turks retired on Bitlis (Kurdistan).

May 22.
Lord Fisher's resignation accepted.
Adm. Jackson First Sea Lord.
H.M. T.B.D. *Rifleman*, of Grand Fleet, aground in a fog; docked for repairs.
Battle of Festubert: British gain S. of Quinque Rue.
German aeroplane raid on Paris: 8 bombs near Eiffel Tower.

May 22 (*continued*).
Mobilisation ordered in Itay.
Russian battleship *Panteleimon* torpedoed in Black Sea.

May 23.
Adm. Lowry, C.-in-C. Coast of Scotland, inaugurated new anti-U-Boat operation; two " C " class submarines acting with decoy trawler.
Battle of Festubert: German counter-attacks near Festubert failed.
German aeroplane bombed Paris suburbs.
Italy declared war on Austria-Hungary.
Austro-German San crossing ended.
H.M. submarine E11 sank Turkish gunboat off Constantinople. H.M.S. *Albion* ashore near Dardanelles and under fire; towed off by H.M.S. *Canopus*.

May 24.
Last German attack but one in Second Battle of Ypres—gas used; Germans gained trenches near Shelltrap Farm; some of these recovered. Violent shelling all day.
Captured ground secured by British near Festubert. In Artois French took Les Corneilles, near Angres.
German aeroplane raid on Paris.
Raid on Italian Adriatic coast by Austrian ships from Pola. Railway from Brindisi damaged.
Cruiser *Novara* shelled Porto Corsini.
Cruiser *St. George* shelled Rimini.
Battleship *Zrinyi* shelled Sinigaglia.
Battleship *Radetsky* destroyed bridge S. of Ancona.
Cruisers *Admiral Spaun* and *Helgoland* bombarded railway and coast round Viesti—Manfredonia.
Italians raided island of Porto Buso.
Italian T.B.D. *Turbine* sunk in Adriatic.
Austrians blew up two bridges on Adige R. (Trentino). Italians occupied Monte Pasubio. On Isonzo front Italian advance on Gorizia. Left wing at Caporetto. In Carnic Alps Italians seized Val d'Inferno.
First German troops in line on Serbian front.
Nine hours' truce at Anzac (Gallipoli) to bury dead.
H.M. submarine E11 sank Turkish transport in Sea of Marmora and a Turkish storeship in Rodosto Harbour.

May 25.
Gen. Steele in command Second Canadian Division.
British Coalition Ministry.
U.S. s.s. *Nebraskan* torpedoed; reached port.
H.M.T. *Marquette* (7,057 tons) chased by U-Boat in Channel; escaped.
Lieut. Warneford, R.N.A.S., Dunkirk, bombed Gontrode Zeppelin sheds.
British line before Ypres consolidated at Wieltje-Hooge.
Battle of Festubert ended.
Italians occupied Monte Altissimo (Trentino) and Val Raccolana (Carnia).
Austro-Germans took Zagrody in advance on Przemysl (Galicia).
H.M.S. *Triumph* torpedoed off Gallipoli by U21, which had been sent out from the North Sea to the Mediterranean during April. *Swiftsure* and *Vengeance* attacked.
H.M. submarine E11 torpedoed Turkish steamer alongside Constantinople Arsenal.
Russians occupied Miandob (Persia).

Sundays marked with Asterisk (*).

May 26, 1915.

Adm. Jellicoe conferred with Adm. Jackson at Rosyth.

Adm. Hood hoisted his flag in H.M.S. *Invincible.*

H.M.S. *Queen Elizabeth* arrived at Scapa from Dardanelles.

Liquor Control Board appointed.

LZ38 raided Southend.

German aeroplane raid on Dunkirk.

Two years' position warfare on Yser begun.

French air raid on Ludwigshafen.

German Niemen Army formed from Lauenstein force, &c., under Gen. O. von Below, who is succeeded in command of Eighth Army by Gen. von Scholtz.

May 27.

H.M. auxiliary *Princess Irene* accidentally destroyed by explosion at Sheerness.

U-Boat fired two torpedoes at s.s. *Argyllshire* (12,097 tons) off Havre ; missed.

Gen. Joffre inspected British 7th Division (Gen. Gough) on W. Front.

Between La Bassée—Arras French took Les Quatre Bouquetaux, near Souchez.

Italians captured Ala and Grado (Trentino). Flooded Isonzo R. impeded their advance against Carso.

Russians took Kindovary near Shavli (Lithuania) and recaptured Sieniava on San R. (Galicia).

Austrian G.H.Q. accused 36th (Jungbunzlau) Regiment of treason.

H.M.S. *Majestic* torpedoed off Cape Helles, Gallipoli, by U21.

Turkish " Provisional " Law for deportation of political suspects.

May 28.

French progress in " The Labyrinth " and towards Souchez, N. of Arras.

Capture of Ablain St. Nazaire.

First Reichstag debate on " annexation " principle ; Chancellor spoke of " guarantees "; Ebert against annexations.

French took Haricot Redoubt (Gallipoli).

H.M. submarine E11 sank Turkish supply-ship in Sea of Marmora.

Russians took Vastan on Lake Van.

May 29.

Grand Fleet again swept for two days down to Dogger Bank.

High Sea Fleet put out from Wilhelmshaven and returned next day.

Russian success S. of Dniester R.

Italians occupied Avlona (Albania).

Mine sprung at Quinn's Post (Gallipoli) followed by Turkish attack which was eventually repulsed.

French drove Germans from Njok (Cameroons).

*May 30.

German reply to U.S. *Lusitania* Note asserting she carried guns, etc.

S.S. *Megantic* (14,878 tons), chased by U-Boat off S. Ireland.

H.I.M. auxiliary cruiser *Meteor* left Kiel for raid into White Sea.

Mr. Asquith visited British G.H.Q. in France.

Italian air raid on Pola.

Italians took Cortina (Dolomites).

Austro-Germans attacked Przemysl.

British naval attack on Sphinxhaven, Lake Nyassa ; town taken and German armed steamer *Von Wissmann* destroyed.

May 31.

British s.s. *Demerara* (11,484 tons) warded off pursuing U-Boat by gunfire off S. Ireland.

LZ38, first Zeppelin over London, bombed East End : 7 killed, 35 injured.

British captured Hooge Château stables.

At Souchez French took Mill Malon and sugar refinery ; advance in " The Labyrinth " sector.

Two years position warfare in Lorraine begun.

Kaiser at German G.H.Q., Pless, conferred with military, naval and political advisers on first U.S. *Lusitania* Note, decided that U-Boats should continue to operate against British passenger ships.

Fresh German gas-attack on E. Front (Nieboroff) failed disastrously.

Austro-Germans took Stryj on Dniester front and northern Przemysl forts on San front.

H.M. submarine E11 torpedoed Turkish steamer in Panderma Roads.

British victory at Kurna (Tigris).

German surrender at Monso (Cameroons).

June 1.

83,000 Australian troops trained since outbreak of war.

French progress at Souchez and in " The Labyrinth " (Artois).

Italians across Isonzo on Monte Nero ; advance in Adige Valley (Trentino).

Brindisi and Bari bombed by Austrian aeroplanes.

Before Warsaw German gas attack on Bzura-Ravka line repulsed.

British reached Bahran (Tigris).

June 2.

Berlin Government informed by Count Bernstorff (Washington) that President Wilson would regard abandonment of U-Boat Blockade as an appeal to the public conscience.

Italians reached highest point of Monte Nero (Isonzo).

Austrian defeat at Mikalojov on Dniester.

Austro-Germans attacking Przemysl (Galicia).

H.M. submarine E11 sank Turkish storeship in Sea of Marmora.

Turkish Tigris gunboat *Marmariss* set on fire and run ashore.

June 3.

Ypres shelled. Remnant of St. Martin's spire destroyed.

British recaptured outbuildings at Hooge.

At Givenchy British took trenches.

Przemysl (Galicia) retaken by German and Austrian forces.

Turks repulsed in Gallipoli.

Turkish surrender at Amarah (Tigris).

June 4.

Zeppelin raid on Kent, Essex, and Yorkshire.

H.M. submarine E9 sank German transport in Baltic.

Russian minelayer *Yenisei* sunk by U-Boat in Baltic.

British abandoned trenches won day before near Givenchy.

German aeroplane raid on Nancy.

Isonzo floods subsiding.

Third Allied attack on Krithia and Achi Baba (Gallipoli) ; advance averaged 300 yards on 3-mile front. French captured and lost Haricot Redoubt for fourth time.

British column from Quetta reached Kalat to carry out a demonstration in Baluchistan.

For List of Abbreviations see page iv.

June 5, 1915.

First Q ship in action.

U14 rammed and sunk by H.M. armed trawler *Hawk* of Peterhead Patrol off E. Scotland.

Kaiser, in deference to Chancellor, agreed that no large passenger ships should be sunk.

French repulsed German attacks E. of Notre Dame de Lorette Ridge.

German aeroplane raid on Nancy.

Italians crossed Isonzo R. near Pieris and advanced on Monfalcone.

Italian fleet bombarded Dalmatian Islands and Monfalcone.

On Dniester front Austro-Germans took Zuravno and Hill 247.

*June 6.

Zeppelin raid on Hull, Grimsby, and E. Riding, 24 killed, and 40 injured.

LZ39 over Harwich.

LZ37 raided Calais.

Adm. von Pohl instructed that U-Boats should not attack any large passenger ships whatever.

Austro-German Army across Dniester R. at Zuravno.

H.M. store-carrier *Immingham* sunk in collision off Mudros.

June 7.

H.M. armed steamer *Duke of Albany* aground in thick fog on Lother Rock, Pentland Firth.

First aeroplane victory over airship. Flight Sub.-Lieut. Warneford, R.N., destroyed Zeppelin between Ghent—Brussels.

Zeppelin destroyed by British airmen at Evere, near Brussels.

French advance N. of Arras and near Hébuterne, S. of Arras.

German attacks on Aisne repulsed.

H.M. submarine E11 torpedoed Turkish troopship on way back from Sea of Marmora.

June 8.

Mr. Robert Lansing succeeded Mr. Bryan as U.S. Secretary of State.

H.M.S. *Furious* laid down.

H.M. collier *Strathcarron* sunk by U-Boat 60 miles W. of Lundy Is.

H.S. *Llandovery Castle* (11,423 tons) chased by U-Boat off Finisterre.

In Artois French gained in " The Labyrinth " and completed capture of Neuville St. Vaast ; further progress at Hébuterne.

June 9.

Second U.S. *Lusitania* Note to Germany.

High Sea Fleet exercised off Heligoland.

Italian submarine *Medusa* sunk by Austrian U-Boat in Adriatic.

Italians captured Monfalcone (Isonzo). Fighting near Plava. In Carnic Alps they took Pal Piccolo, Freikofel and Pal Grande.

Germans checked near Shavli (Lithuania), defeated near Zuravno (Galicia), and driven across Dniester R.

June 10.

H.M. T.B.s 10 and 12 sunk by U-Boat in North Sea.

Italians attacked Gradisca and Sagrada.

Russian victory on Dniester R. near Zuravno developing.

Garua (Cameroons) surrendered to Anglo-French force.

June 11.

British s.s. *Arndale* (3,583 tons) mined in entrance to White Sea.

Grand Fleet put to sea for battle exercises in northern waters, accompanied by sea-plane carrier s.s. *Campania*.

G.E.R. s.s. *Brussels* chased by U-Boat in North Sea ; escaped ; second encounter.

S. of Arras round Hébuterne French advanced on 2,000 yards front and maintained captured positions.

Italians holding Gradisca (Isonzo).

Russians retook Zuravno (Dniester).

June 12.

LZ39 over Harwich.

Germany was informed that U-Boat crews were again treated as ordinary prisoners.

British s.s. *Desabla* (6,047 tons) sunk by U-Boat off Tod Head.

N. of Arras French captured Souchez Station.

Austro-Germans across Pruth R. at Kolomea (E. Galicia).

H.M. oiler *Desabla* sunk by U-Boat 12 miles E. from Tod Head.

*June 13.

French repulse at Souchez (Artois) ; further success near Hébuterne.

Austro-German advance between San R. and Moscisca (Galicia).

Greek Elections : Venizelist victory.

June 14.

Belgians S. of Dixmude crossed Yser R. and captured German blockhouse.

Italians carried Vrata Ridge and Kozliak (Upper Isonzo).

Russians back on Grodek line before Lemberg. Austro-Germans at Moscisca.

Armenians deported from Erzrum.

June 15.

H.M. special service ship *Zylpha* (Q) sunk by U-Boat off S.W. Ireland.

G.E.R. s.s. *Brussels* chased by U-Boat off Sunk Light ; escaped ; third encounter.

Zeppelin raid on Northumberland and Durham : 18 killed, 72 injured.

Near Festubert British attacked N.E. of Givenchy, but failed to hold.

German air raid on Nancy.

French airmen bombed Karlsruhe.

Italians attacked Podgora spur (Isonzo), they again failed to cross river at Sagrado.

Austro-Germans advancing on right bank of San R. (Galicia).

Turks, having again occupied Shaikh Sa'id, attempted to land on Perim ; attack driven off by Sikh garrison.

June 16.

Mr. Lloyd George Minister of Munitions.

At Ypres British success N. of Hooge on Bellewaarde Ridge, reaching edge of lake ; 1,000 yards gained ; success E. of Festubert.

N. of Arras French gained ground.

French advance in Fecht Valley (Alsace).

Italians progressed on Monte Nero (Isonzo) ; took summit of Hill 383 above Plava.

June 17.

French T.B. 331 sunk.

N. of Arras French took Fond-de-Buval.

Germans evacuated Metzeral (Alsace).

Villach—Gorizia railway (Isonzo) cut by Italians near Plava.

Battle before Lemberg begun.

Sundays marked with Asterisk (*).

June 18, 1915.

Plava positions (Isonzo) held by Italians.
Austrian warships raided Italian Adriatic coast at Fano.

June 19.

H.M.S. *Inflexible* joined Battle Cruiser Fleet from Gibraltar.
French progress near Souchez (Artois).
French entered Metzeral (Alsace) and bombarded Münster.
Haase, Bernstein and Kautsky published manifesto declaring war no longer defensive and could not therefore be supported by true Socialists.
Russian retreat from Grodek line (Galicia).

*June 20.

H.M.S. *Roxburgh* hit by U-Boat torpedo in North Sea while engaged in light cruiser sweep across to Skagerrak and back to Rosyth. This was second attack on *Roxburgh*. Two torpedoes also fired at *Nottingham*, missed ; and one at *Argyll*, also missed ; *Birmingham* was attacked on day before.
H.I.M. auxiliary cruiser *Meteor* returned to Kiel from three weeks' raid in White Sea.
Further French gains at Souchez (Artois).
German Crown Prince began attack towards Vienne-le-Chateau (Argonne).
Italians consolidated round Monte Nero.
Austro-Germans took Rava Russka and Zolkiev (Galicia).
H.M. submarine E14 sinking dhows in Sea of Marmora.

June 21.

French stand near Souchez (Artois).
French regained Haricot Redoubt and took heights above Kereves Dere (Gallipoli).
Successful British raid on Bukoba, Victoria Nyanza.

June 22.

U37 sunk in Ems R. ; commander and one man saved.
Germans took Hill 627 near Ban de Sapt (Vosges).
French captured Sondernach. S. of Metzeral (Alsace).
Austro-Germans recaptured Lemberg.
Mackensen promoted Field-Marshal.

June 23.

U40 torpedoed and sunk by H.M. submarine C24, working in company with a trawler, 50 miles S.E. by S. of Girdle Ness.
During night of June 23-24 a U-Boat attacked fishing fleet some 50 miles E. of Shetlands and sank 16 drifters by bombs and gunfire.
British s.s. *Tunisiana* (4,220 tons) sunk by U-Boat off Lowestoft ; no warning.
Austro-Germans again checked round Zuravno (Dniester).

June 24.

British s.s. *Drumloist* (3,118 tons) mined in entrance to White Sea.
British Memorandum on Neutral Trade.
German attack on Meuse Heights.

June 25.

French airmen bombed Douai Station.
Italians gained crossing of Isonzo R. at Sagrado and captured the town.
Russians in retreat from Lemberg, Armenians deported from Sivas.
British captured Bukoba, on Victoria Nyanza (E. Africa).

June 26.

Archbishop of York visited Grand Fleet at Scapa.
Adm. von Pohl urged German naval authorities not to make any concessions in conduct of U-Boat Blockade.
German Crown Prince still attacking in Argonne.
Italian T.B. 5 P.N. sunk by U-Boat in Adriatic.
Gen. Polivanoff succeeded Gen. Sukhomlinoff as Russian War Minister.
Armenians deported from Trebizond.

*June 27.

H.M. submarine S1 returned to Yarmouth from Heligoland Bight, towing, although partly disabled, German trawler *Ost*, captured by her on June 24.
French repulsed German attacks at Metzeral (Alsace).
Russians retreating from Lemberg and Dniester R. ; Austro-Germans occupied Halicz (Galicia).
H.M.S. *Hussa* bombarded Turkish coast opposite Chios.
Armenians deported from Samsun.

June 28.

S.S. *Armenian* (8,825 tons) sunk by U-Boat 20 miles W. from Trevose Head ; 29 lost.
French advanced near Souchez (Artois).
Italians captured Castello Nuovo bridgehead (Isonzo).
Germans bombarded Windau (Courland) and lost a torpedo-boat.
In Gallipoli Battle of Gully Ravine (Saghir Dere) British attacked near coast and gained ground on Turkish flank. Boomerang and Turkey Trot Redoubts captured.
German attack on Abercorn, N. Rhodesia.

June 29.

British s.s. *Scottish Monarch* (5,043 tons) sunk by U-Boat off Ballycottin Light ; 15 lost.
G.E.R. s.s. *Brussels* chased by U-Boat off Sunk Light ; escaped ; fourth encounter.
National Registration Bill introduced.
Austro-German offensive between Vieprz and Bug (Poland).
Ngaundere (Central Cameroons) occupied by Anglo-French forces.

June 30.

New British 4th Light Cruiser Squadron formed : *Calliope* (F. Commodore Le Mesurier), *Constance*, *Comus*, *Caroline*, and *Royalist*.
H.M.S. *Lightning* mined in North Sea.
German attacks at Bagatelle (Argonne).
In Galicia, S. of Lemberg, Germans stormed Gnila—Lipa line and crossed near Rohatyn. N. of Lemberg, Austro-German advance from Tomaszow and Russian retreat.
French captured Turkish trench lines in Gallipoli. Gen. Gouraud wounded ; relieved by Gen. Bailloud. Turkish attack on Anzac repulsed.
H.M. submarine E7 in Sea of Marmora.

July 1.

H.M.S. *Hampshire* attacked by U-Boat with torpedo in Moray Firth.
British s.s. *Welbury* (3,591 tons) sunk by U-Boat W. from Fastnet.
British s.s. *Inglemoor* (4,331 tons) and *Caucasian* (4,656 tons) sunk by U-Boat S.W. from Lizard.

For List of Abbreviations see page iv.

July 1, 1915 (*continued*).

British s.s. *Craigard* (3,286 tons), *Gadsby* (3,497 tons), and *Richmond* (3,214 tons) sunk by U-Boat off Wolf Rock.

Austrian U11 bombed by French airman in Adriatic.

Kaiser at Posen ordered Hindenburg and Ludendorff to resume offensive in Poland.

Austro-Germans captured Zamosc and Krasnik (Poland).

Union Forces occupied Otavi (G.S.W. Africa).

July 2.

Allied aircraft bombed German airship sheds at Ghistelles (Belgium).

Germans progressed near Four de Paris (Argonne), but were repulsed near Blanleuil.

Italian Battle for Carso Plateau begun.

H.M. submarine E9 torpedoed and damaged H.I.M.S. *Prinz Adalbert* off Danzig.

German minelayer *Albatross* chased ashore by Russian men-of-war off Gothland.

Italian T.B. 17 O.S. damaged by explosion in Adriatic and destroyed.

Turkish attacks repulsed by Allies in Gallipoli.

H.M. submarine E7 sank Turkish steamer and two dhows in Rodosto Bay.

Armenian massacre at Bitlis.

July 3.

Norwegian s.s. *Oscar II.* sunk off Stornoway after collision with s.s. *Patuca.*

British s.s. *Renfrew* (3,488 tons) and *Larchmore* (4,355 tons) sunk by U-Boat S.W. from Wolf Rock.

German aeroplane over E. Suffolk.

Germans rushed advanced trenches on Verlorenhoek road (Ypres salient) ; ejected.

German attacks on Calonne Trench, Meuse Heights, repulsed.

Italian attack on Podgora Ridge (Carso).

Russians retiring from Gnila—Lipa to Zlota—Lipa line (Galicia).

Turks in Gallipoli heavily reinforced.

British column from Aden moved out to Shaikh Othman.

S. Africa offered Overseas Contingent.

*July 4.

S.S. *Anglo-Californian* (7,333 tons) attacked and shelled by U-Boat about 90 miles S. from Queenstown ; 21 lives lost, including master ; remainder rescued.

German attacks in Arras region repulsed.

German Crown Prince's Argonne attack slackening, having failed to break line.

Italian advance in Carso.

Serbians entered Durazzo (Albania).

Austro-German offensive towards Lublin (Poland) stayed near Krasnik.

Austro-Germans reached Zlota—Lipa line.

Turkish attack in Gallipoli.

French transport *Carthage* torpedoed off Cape Helles (Dardanelles).

British force at Lahez (Arabia) attacked.

H.I.M.S. *Königsberg* attacked up Rufiji R. (E. Africa) by H.M. monitors *Severn* and *Mersey.*

Germans defeated at Gaub (G.S.W. Africa).

July 5.

Lord Fisher Chairman Inventions Board.

Austro-Germans defeated N.E. of Krasnik.

Turkish attack from Krithia (Gallipoli).

British retired from Lahej towards Aden.

Union Forces took Tsumeb (G.S.W. Africa).

July 6.

H.M. collier *African Monarch* (4,003 tons) mined at entrance to White Sea.

High Sea Fleet cruised to Heligoland and back.

Lord Kitchener visited Western Front.

British captured trenches between Boesinghe—Ypres.

Slight German success at Vaux Féry, near St. Mihiel.

German attack on Ravka R. (Poland).

German Bug Army formed under Gen. von Linsingen.

Count Bothmer assumed command of German Southern Army.

First attack by British warships and aeroplanes on H.I.M.S. *Königsberg* discovered in Rufiji R. (G.E. Africa).

July 7.

King visited Grand Fleet at Scapa.

French success at Souchez (Artois).

German Crown Prince advanced between Fontaine Madame and Haute Chevauchée, capturing La Fille Morte Mill (Argonne).

Italians attacked Gorizia (Isonzo).

Italy blockaded E. Adriatic coasts.

Austro-Germans held at Krasnostav.

H.M. submarine E7 in action with Turkish gunboat in Sea of Marmora.

July 8.

German reply to second U.S. *Lusitania* Note.

Lord Kitchener returned to England from W. Front.

Germans recaptured trenches at Souchez.

French recaptured trenches between Feyen-Haye and Bois-le-Prêtre, also Hill 627 near Ban de Sapt (Vosges).

Italians took Monticello (Trentino).

Italian Cruisers *Amalfi* and *G. Garibaldi* sunk by Austrian U-Boat in Mediterranean.

July 9.

Italians captured Malga Sarta and Costa Bella (Trentino).

Austro-German defeat N. of Krasnik.

Bomb thrown at Sultan of Egypt.

G.S.W. Africa conquered. Governor Seitz surrendered to Gen. Botha.

July 10.

Skirmish near Ferryman's House (Yser).

Austro-German attack at Krasnik.

Russians attacked by Turks near Karadezbent (Caucasus).

H.M. submarine E7 sank Turkish steamer at Mudania in Sea of Marmora.

Armenian massacre at Mush.

*July 11.

Dreadnought Battle Fleet started on three days cruise near Shetlands, while Battle Cruiser Fleet swept down to Dogger Bank.

French lost ground S. of Souchez (Artois).

German attacks on Fresnes (St. Mihiel).

Russian counter-attacks at Lublin.

Germans held on Zlota Lipa—Dniester.

H.M. submarine E7 sank two dhows in Sea of Marmora.

Allies occupied Tingr (Cameroons).

H.I.M.S. *Königsberg* destroyed in Rufiji R (E. Africa). Germans, later, mounted her guns at Tanga and Dar-es-Salaam.

July 12.

German attack in " The Labyrinth " repulsed ; French regained trenches at Souchez.

Italian air raid on Pola.

Sundays marked with Asterisk (*).

July 12, 1915 (*continued*).

Germans again bombarded Ossovietz.

Anglo-French advance in Gallipoli against Krithia and Achi Baba; some 400 yards gained. French on right reached mouth of Kereves Dere.

Fighting in Northern Rhodesia.

July 13.

Second British War Loan—£570,000,000.

German temporary gain at Vienne-le-Château and La Fille Morte (Argonne).

Great Austro-German offensive between Baltic and Bukovina opened.

Further progress in Gallipoli; Krithia not reached.

Over 100,000 Australians at the front or in training at this date.

July 14.

National Registration Act passed.

German attack on Belgians along Yser Canal repulsed.

French captured trenches S. of Souchez.

Germans captured Przasnysz (Poland); Russians retired on Narev R. German thrust towards Riga.

Austrian attack at Grahovo (Montenegro). repulsed.

Fighting at Nasiriyeh (Euphrates); Turks driven off by British from Kurna.

Action E. of Taveta (B.E. Africa).

July 15.

Welsh miners strike. The strike considerably handicapped the movements of the Grand Fleet during July and August.

Germans repulsed in Argonne.

Italian offensive in Upper Cadore.

H.M. submarine E7 fired torpedo at Constantinople Arsenal and shelled Zeitunlik powder mills.

July 16.

H.M.S. *Speedwell* reported having rammed U-Boat at 15 knots N. of Shetlands.

German attack at Fontenoy, near Soissons; and in Parroy Forest (Lorraine).

Prussian Guard Cavalry Division now transferred from Belgium and fighting on Eleventh Army Front in Poland.

Heavy Austro-German losses on Vieprz and Dniester.

July 17.

Adm. von Pohl's Fleet Flagship H.I.M.S. *Friedrich der Grosse* and three other ships developed engine defects which detained whole High Sea Fleet in port.

Italian successes on Cadore front.

Russians in Poland forced back towards Narev Fortress line by Gen. von Gallwitz.

Serbians evacuated Durazzo (Albania).

H.M. submarine E7 in Sea of Marmora shelled Turkish trains near Kaya Burnu.

#July 18.

British Army losses to date: 330,995.

German attacks at Souchez (Artois).

Big Italian attack on Carso.

H.M. submarine E7 shelled Mudania in Sea of Marmora.

Russian retreat to Blonie line before Warsaw. Austro-Germans crossed Bug R. near Sokal, and took Krasnostav on Vieprj.

July 19.

High Sea Fleet put out as far as Eider Light, where Fleet turned back owing to engine trouble in a number of ships.

July 19 (*continued*).

Adm. Eckermann, Chief of Staff both to Adm. von Ingenohl and Adm. von Pohl, invalided. Adm. Schmidt succeeded.

British mined German redoubt at Hooge.

German attack S.E. of Les Eparges.

Italian success on Carso.

Heavy fighting on Lublin front (Poland).

Germans reoccupied Radom.

H.M. submarine E7 sank four dhows in Sea of Marmora.

July 20.

R.N. casualties to date: 9,106.

U23 torpedoed and sunk by H.M. submarine C27 off Fair Island.

G.E.R. s.s. *Brussels* missed by U-Boat's torpedo off Inner Gabbard; fifth encounter.

French advance towards Münster along Fecht Valley (Alsace).

Italian success about Gorizia and in Carso. Part of Podgora ridge captured.

Heavy fighting on Narev line before Rozhan, Pultusk, and Novo Georgievsk.

Z XII. raided Bialystok.

July 21.

British success at Hooge.

Italians advancing at Plava (Isonzo).

Germans took Shavli.

New Beseler Army Group formed for siege of Novo-Georgievsk.

Warsaw threatened. Ivangorod invested.

Austro-Germans driven back across Bug R. near Sokal by Russian counter-attacks.

H.M. submarine E7 sank a dhow in Sea of Marmora.

H.M. motor-boat *Dorothea* destroyed by fire in E. Mediterranean.

Turkish forces in Aden district driven back to Lahej from Shaikh Othman.

July 22.

French progress near Bagatelle (Argonne).

French near Metzeral (Alsace) attacked.

Italians advanced from Tolmino to Monfalcone (Isonzo); in Carso they took and held ground just below San Michele Ridge.

Z XII. raided Malkin.

LZ39 raided Warsaw.

Russians driven across Vistula, N. of Ivangorod.

H.M. submarine E7 again shelled Turkish trains at Kaya Burnu.

Turkey, at instance of Central Powers, modified Treaty of Pera (Sept. 1913) in favour of Bulgaria.

July 23.

Third U.S. *Lusitania* Note.

Italian advance on Luznica Ridge.

Austrian destroyers in Adriatic bombarded Ortona, Tremiti, and coast railway.

Germans crossed Narev R. between Pultusk and Rozhan.

Turkish attack in Gallipoli repulsed.

Senussi tribesmen under Turco-German leadership massacred Italians in Tripoli.

July 24.

British repulsed Germans near Hooge.

French stormed German La Fontenelle—Launois defences (Vosges).

Germans stormed Rozhan and Pultusk.

Germans checked at Lublin—Kholm.

H.M. submarine E7 returned from her cruise in Sea of Marmora.

Turks and Arabs heavily defeated near Nasiriyeh (Euphrates) by Gen. Gorringe.

*July 25, 1915.

U.S. s.s. *Leelanaw* torpedoed by U-Boat.
U36 sunk by H.M.S. *Prince Charles* near
N. Rona Is.

Italians occupied Pelagosa Island.

Russians preparing to evacuate Warsaw.

Germans took Poniewiecz.

Nasiriyeh captured by British.

French occupied Lomie (Cameroons).

July 26.

British armed trawler *Taranaki* engaged
and claimed to have sunk U-Boat about 120
miles E. of Dundee.

German T.B.D., believed of G196 class,
sunk by British submarine in North Sea.

Germans in Argonne repulsed.

French advance on Lingenkopf (Alsace);
second battle of Münster (see 19-ii.-15).

Italians established on Monte San
Michele and Monte de Sei Busi (Carso).

French submarine *Mariotte* sunk in Dardanelles.

German troops across Narev R. checked.

Germans besieging Abercorn (Northern
Rhodesia).

July 27.

British armed trawler No. 83 engaged
and claimed to have hit U-Boat by gunfire S.
of St. Kilda.

French success towards Münster at
Lingenkopf (Alsace).

Armenians deported from Cilicia.

July 28.

British 2nd Battle Cruiser Squadron with
light forces from Rosyth, Scapa and Harwich,
carried out operation in Skagerrak.

British s.s. *Mangara* (1,821 tons) torpedoed and sunk by U-Boat off Aldeburgh ;
no warning ; 11 lost.

Austrians repulsed by Italians in Carnia.

Italians retired near Gorizia (Isonzo).

Germans forced Vistula between Warsaw
and Ivangorod.

July 29.

Four British ships sent from Scapa to
Bear Island and Spitzbergen to search for
reported U-Boat base and W.-T. station ; no
trace found.

H.M. submarine E1 (Comdr. Laurence)
sank German transport in Baltic.

Germans broke Russian line on Lublin—
Kholm Railway at Biscupice (S.E. Poland).

German East African liner s.s. *Präsident*
blown up in Lukuledi R.

July 30.

Leyland s.s. *Iberian* (5,223 tons) sunk by
U-Boat off Fastnet ; 7 lost.

German success at Hooge by use of
flame-throwers ; trenches taken on Menin
road.

French air raids on Freiburg and Pfalz-
burg.

Italian attack E. of Gradisca (Isonzo).

Russians retiring on whole Polish front.

Austro-Germans in Lublin (Poland).

Baron von Wangenheim, German
Ambassador to the Porte, invalided.

July 31.

H.M. Fleet Messengers *Nugget* and *Turquoise* sunk by U-Boat S.W. of Scilly Isles.

During 12 months ended July 31 there
were completed 19 U-Boats aggregating
16,075 tons.

German aeroplane raid on Nancy.

German aeroplane raid on Warsaw.

Austro-Germans at Kholm (Poland).

*August 1.

British s.s. *Benvorlich* (3,381 tons), *Clin-
tonia* (3,830 tons), and *Ranza* (2,320 tons)
sunk by U-Boat S.W. from Ushant.

British counter-attack at Hooge failed.

German aeroplane raid on Nancy.

Austrian attacks on Monte Medetta
(Carnic Alps) repulsed.

Battle-cruiser *Hindenburg* launched at
Wilhelmshaven.

Mitau (Courland) occupied by Germans.

Germans held on Blonie line, W. of
Warsaw. German progress on Narev R.

Tsar convened Duma.

British submarine blew up Galata
Bridge, Constantinople.

British reinforcements relieved Abercorn
(Northern Rhodesia).

August 2.

H.M. Fleet Messenger *Portia* sunk by
U-Boat 70 miles S. from Scilly Isles.

German success at Hill 213 (Argonne).

Germans attacked French at Lingenkopf
and Barrenkopf (Alsace).

Italians progressed near Monte de Sei
Busi (Carso) ; repulsed on Polazzo Plateau.

British submarine in Baltic sank German
transport with a regiment of von Below's
army.

German gunboat near Windau attacked
by Russian seaplanes.

Russians retired E. of Poniewiecz, near
Dvinsk.

Z XII. raided Malkin.

August 3.

German attacks in Argonne failed.

Germans forced Narev line near Ostrolenka. Prince Leopold of Bavaria attacking
Warsaw. Austro-German success near Kholm.

Smyrna coast at Sighadjik bombarded
by French warships.

Italian Note to Turkey demanding free
departure of Italians from Asia Minor towns

August 4.

H.M. submarine C33 lost in North Sea.

Italians captured Carso entrenchments ;
gained footing on Col de Lana (Dolomites).
Austrians destroyed Lizzana Castle.

Battle of Goworowo begun.

Civilians evacuating Warsaw. Russians
retired from Blonie line and Ivangorod.

Rumanian Cabinet voted £4,000,000
credit for military purposes.

Turkish coast opposite Samos bombarded
by French warships.

August 5.

Cmdr. Lambe, R.N., appointed to command Dover—Dunkirk air forces. later amalgamated as No. 1 Wing R.N.A.S.

Miss Edith Cavell arrested in Brussels.

Fierce fighting round Hill 213 (Argonne).

Herr Helfferich, in memorandum to
Chancellor, suggested that U-Boat Blockade
might be suspended for a period up to three
months in order to induce U.S. to enter into
working maritime agreement with Germany.

Hindenburg (with Ludendorff as Chief of
Staff) and Prince Leopold Army Groups
formed on E. Front.

Germans entered Warsaw.

Austrians entered Ivangorod.

Z XII. raided Bialystok.

Russians evacuating Riga.

August 6.

British 4th Light Cruiser Squadron left
Scapa to cruise off Norwegian coast.

Sundays marked with Asterisk (*).

August 6, 1915 (*continued*).

Struggle for Hill 213 (Argonne).

German success on Bobr R. near Ossovietz (Poland). Advancing round Novo Georgievsk, Germans reached junction of Bug and Narev. Austrians bombarded Hill 183, near Lubartov, on Vieprz R., N. of Lublin.

Z XII. raided Siedlec.

LZ39 raided Novo-Minsk.

Gen. Sarrail to command French Dardanelles force, vice Gen. Gouraud, invalided.

Big Allied movement in Gallipoli. New surprise landing at Suvla Bay, N. of Anzac, under Gen. Stopford. Lala Baba Hill and Hill 10 stormed and carried (dawn Aug. 7).

Advance from Anzac against Sari Bair Ridge. Lone Pine, Wauchop's Hill, Tblea Top and entrance to Chailak valley taken.

August 7.

Mr. Asquith and Mr. McKenna visited Adm. Jellicoe on board *Iron Duke* at Cromarty.

H.M. T.B.D. *Christopher* in action with U-Boat in Moray Firth.

British minesweepers reported new minefield in Moray Firth, northward of Banff. These were, later, found to have been laid by *Meteor*, a German minelayer. During next six weeks 222 out of 480 mines laid were accounted for.

Germans repulsed at Hill 213 (Argonne), and on Lingenkopf Ridge (Alsace).

Italians on Ercavallo Peak (Trentino).

Germans driven back before Riga.

New German Twelfth Army formed in Poland from Gallwitz Army Group, with Gen. von Gallwitz in command.

Austrians took Hill 183 near Lubartov.

In Gallipoli at new Suvla landing British took Chocolate Hill (Yilghin Burnu), but did not advance to support Anzacs, attacking Sari Bair Ridge.

Another Allied attack from Helles; vineyard captured E. of Krithia road.

H.M. submarines E11 and E14 shelled Turkish reinforcements marching to Gallipoli.

✱August 8.

H.M. armed steamer *Ramsey* sunk by German minelayer *Meteor* in North Sea.

H.M. A.M.C. *India* (7,940 tons) sunk by U-Boat off Norway; 120 lost.

German naval retreat from Riga Gulf.

Germans attacking Kovno repulsed. Russians forced back across Vieprz R.

Turkish reinforcements arrived on Suvla front (Gallipoli). Gen. Hamilton at Suvla investigating delay. At Anzac heroic N.Z. attack gained footing on Chanuk Bair crest.

August 9.

H.M.S. *Lynx* mined off Moray Firth.

Zeppelin raid on Yorkshire, Suffolk, and Dover; 17 killed, 21 wounded. L12 damaged by land guns, finally destroyed near Ostend by aircraft.

In North Sea German auxiliary *Meteor*, chased by British ships, abandoned, and blown up. Crew rescued by Swedish sailing ship, which U28 tows into List.

High Sea Fleet moved from Brunsbüttel to Cuxhaven.

Important British success N. and W. of Hooge, " extending the front of the trenches captured to 1,200 yards," including recapture of trenches lost on July 30.

German attack in Bois le Prêtre (Meuse).

French air raid on Saarbrücken.

August 9 (*continued*).

German attack again fails on Kovno. Russians evacuated Ossovietz. Germans broke through and stormed Fort 4 at Lomzha (Narev).

Russians driven out of Praga, E. Warsaw. S. of Warsaw Russians cross Vieprz.

Desperate British attack at Sari Bair (Gallipoli). Progress, but Turks too strong. At night Anzacs still clung to part of Chanuk Bair crest. At Suvla slight advance towards Anafarta.

Turkish battleship *Kheir-ed-Din-Barbarossa* sunk by British submarine.

August 10.

British positions at Hooge secured.

Kaiser at German G.H.Q., Pless, conferred Pour le Mérite Order on Adm. von Tirpitz on occasion of 25th anniversary of German installation in Heligoland.

German fleet in Riga Gulf again driven off after shelling city.

Russians evacuating Kovno and Dvinsk. Germans took Lomzha and Ostrov.

LZ39 raided Novo-Georgievsk.

LZ79 raided Brest-Litovsk.

Italian submarine *Jalea* mined in Gulf of Trieste.

In Gallipoli another attack from Suvla on Anafarta failed. At Anzac Turks recovered Chanuk Bair ridge. Other gains held.

Admiralty announced Turkish gunboat *Berk-i-Salvet* sunk by British submarine in Dardanelles.

Russians captured hill in Passin Valley, on Upper Euphrates.

August 11.

UB4 sunk by British armed trawler *G and E* near Smith's Knoll Spar Buoy.

Germans repulsed at Marie-Thérèse and La Fontaine-aux-Charmes (Argonne).

Austrian U12 sunk by Italian submarine.

Russians evacuated Dvinsk.

Germans E. of Warsaw took junction of Ostrolenka—Petrograd—Warsaw railways.

Z XII. raided Bialystok.

August 12.

Zeppelin raid on Suffolk and Essex: 6 killed, 24 injured. One naval airship reached E. Coast; three others turned back owing to engine trouble.

Germans driven beyond Courland Aa. Germans in Poland entered Siedlce, seized Lukov railway junction, and progressed towards Bug R., 60 miles E. of Warsaw. Advance on Bialystok; Zombrovo taken.

Belgrade again bombarded.

British progress at Suvla (Gallipoli).

Turkish transport sunk by British seaplane (Flight-Lieut. Edmonds) in Dardanelles.

Russians again at Alashgerd (Armenia).

Armenians deported from W. Anatolia.

August 13.

Italian advance in Sexten Valley (Carnic Alps).

Austrian U3 sunk in Adriatic by French torpedo-boat *Bisson*, after being rammed by Italian auxiliary cruiser.

Siege of Novo-Georgievsk begun.

Russian centre retired from Siedlce towards Bug.

Germans repulsed from Vlodava on Upper Bug.

For List of Abbreviations see page iv.

August 14, 1915.

British s.s. *Highland Corrie* (7,583 tons) mined off N. Foreland ; reached Tilbury.

Adm. von Tirpitz visited Libau.

Russians retiring from Siedlce (Poland) reached Losice. Germans bombarded Novo Georgievsk.

Fighting on Zlota Lipa (Galicia) and near Czernovitz (Bukovina).

H.M.T. *Royal Edward* sunk by U-Boat in Ægean ; 800 out of 1,400 lost.

*August 15.

British National Register taken.

R.N.D. at this date reached *maximum* strength of 24,300 officers and men.

Russian minelayer *Ladoga* sunk by U-Boat in Gulf of Finland.

Germans reached Briansk heights between Narev and Bug ; Leopold of Bavaria and Mackensen closing in on Brest Litovsk ; Losice entered ; Austro-Germans at Vlodava, where they crossed Upper Bug.

Venice bombed by Austrian seaplane.

Italian submarine *Nereide* sunk by Austrian U-Boat in Adriatic.

Further 500 yards advance at Suvla Bay (Gallipoli) ; Kiretch Tepe Sirt ridge captured. Gen. Stopford succeeded at Suvla by Gen. de Lisle.

H.M.S. *Hyacinth* bombarded Tanga.

August 16.

U-Boat shelled Parton, Harrington, and Whitehaven on the Cumberland coast.

British light forces from Scapa and Rosyth started on two days sweep towards Skagerrak.

British s.s. *Serbino* (2,205 tons) torpedoed and sunk by U-Boat off Worms Light House, Baltic.

Germans in Riga Gulf repulsed.

Second German assault on Kovno ; small outlying fort taken. Some outer forts at Novo Georgievk carried. Russians partially evacuated Bialystok. Germans over Bug at Drohiczyn, N.W. of Brest Litovsk, which garrison ordered to evacuate.

Russians entered Van (Armenia).

Armenians deported from Konia.

August 17.

Gen. Turner in command Second Canadian Division, vice Gen. Steele.

British s.s. *Kirkby* (3,034 tons) and *Paros* (3,596 tons) sunk by U-Boat off Bardsey Island.

Second Zeppelin raid on London by new naval airships, L10, L11, and L14, also over Kent and Essex. Bombs dropped on Leyton and Leytonstone : 10 killed and 48 injured.

French gained footing on Sondernach crest (Vosges).

Italian advance on Bacher Valley (Dolomites) ; progress at Vrsik Crest, Santa Maria and Santa Lucia (Julian Alps).

Austrian attack on Pelagosa Island.

German ships entered Riga Gulf under cover of fog.

Kovno fell after desperate resistance ; heavy German losses. Mackensen's army cut Kholm—Brest-Litovsk railway.

Attack by border tribes near Peshawar.

August 18.

H.M. Fleet minesweeper *Lilac* mined in Moray Firth ; fore part destroyed ; vessel towed to Peterhead.

H.M. submarine E13 wrecked off Saltholm and interned, after being shelled by German T.B.D.s ; crew fired on while in water.

August 18 (*continued*).

French took trenches on Ablain—Angres road (Artois).

French captured trenches on Schratzmännele crest (Vosges).

Italian advance towards Tolmino.

Russian naval victory in Riga Gulf ; H.M.S. *Moltke* torpedoed by H.M. submarine E1 ; Russian gunboat *Sivoutch* sunk.

Gen. von Garnier's 6th German Cavalry Corps formed on Niemen front.

Brest-Litovsk outer defences pierced by Austro-Germans. Brest-Litovsk—Bialystok railway cut by Germans at Bielsk.

Kaiser visited Teschen.

H.M. submarine E11 shelled Turkish reinforcements marching to Gallipoli.

August 19.

White Star s.s. *Arabic* (15,800 tons) Liverpool to New York, torpedoed and sunk by U27 S.W. from Old Head of Kinsale ; some American passengers among 44 drowned. British s.s. *Dunsley* (4,930 tons) also sunk hereabouts ; 2 lost.

H.M.S. *Baralong* sank U27, which had sunk *Arabic* and attacked s.s *Nicosian* (6,369 tons), 73 miles S. by W. from Old Head of Kinsale.

British s.s. *New York City* (2,970 tons) sunk by U-Boat S.S.E. from Fastnet.

British s.s. *Ben Vrackie* (3,908 tons) sunk by U-Boat N.W. from Scilly Isles.

British s.s. *Baron Erskine* (5,585 tons), *Gladiator* (3,359 tons), and *Samara* (3,172 tons) sunk by U-Boat N.W. from Bishop Rock.

Norwegian s.s. *Haakon VII.* stopped by U-Boat in North Sea ; mails seized.

Germans regained some trenches on Ablain—Angres and Béthune—Arras roads (Artois).

Fall of Novo Georgievsk (Vistula), with 700 guns and 85,000 prisoners. Russians driven back between Augustovo and Ossovietz. Germans between Bug—Jasiolda.

Italians prevented from leaving Smyrna.

Armenian massacre at Urfa.

August 20.

Two British steamers and one British sailing vessel sunk by U-Boat off Ushant.

Reichstag Socialists divided on vote for new 10,000,000,000 marks credit ; some 30 deputies abstained. Liebknecht alone voted against.

Attempted German landing at Pernau. N. of Riga, surprised by Russian torpedo craft and all troops captured or killed.

Gen. von Beseler's Novo-Georgievsk Army Group dissolved.

Italy declared war on Turkey.

August 21.

British and French Governments declared cotton absolute contraband.

S.S. *San Melito* (10,160 tons) shelled by U-Boat 70 miles S.W. from Lizard ; rescued.

British s.s. *Windsor* (6,055 tons) sunk by U-Boat S.W. from Wolf.

British s.s. *Ruel* (4,029 tons) sunk by U-Boat S.W. from Bishop Rock.

British s.s. *Cober* (3,060 tons) sunk by U-Boat S.S.W. from Scilly Isles.

German fleet left Riga Gulf.

Count Schmettow's 5th Cavalry Corps formed on Dvina front.

In Gallipoli another British attack on Anafarta from Suvla failed. Fine advance in open across plain by dismounted Yeomanry. Troops from Anzac advanced, took Kabak

Sundays marked with Asterisk (*).

August 21, 1915 (continued).

Kuyu well and gained footing on Kaiajik Aghala.

Lieut. Hughes, R.N., of H.M. submarine E11 landed and blew up portion of Anatolian railway in Gulf of Ismid.

M. Venizelos Greek Premier.

Gen. Townsend returned to Basra after two months' sick-leave in India.

Gen. Woodyatt's Brigade (Peshawar Division), at Rustam, began ten days' operations against hostile tribesmen.

*August 22.

British s.s. *Palmgrove* (3,100 tons) sunk by U-Boat W. by N. from Bishop Rock.

British s.s. *Diomed* (4,672 tons) sunk by U-Boat W.N.W. from Scilly Isles ; 10 lost.

German destroyer sunk off Ostend by two French torpedo-boats. Admiral Bacon left for Belgian Coast with 80 vessels.

French carried Schratzmännele Crest (Vosges) ; trenches captured on the Linge and Barrenkopf.

Ossovietz (Poland) occupied by 11th Prussian Landwehr Division ; Russian retirement from Niemen—Bobr line. German advance S. of Bielsk.

August 23.

British s.s. *Silvia* (5,268 tons) and *Trafalgar* (4,572 tons) sunk by U-Boat W. from Fastnet.

Zeebrugge bombarded by H. M. monitors *Prince Rupert*, *John Moore* and *Lord Clive* (12-inch guns).

Austro-Germans advancing E. from Lublin (Poland), entered Kovel (Volhynia).

British submarine torpedoed Turkish supply ship *Isfahan* near Constantinople.

Gen. Townsend instructed by Gen. Nixon to occupy Kut-el-Amara.

August 24.

Adm. Gaunt to command 1st Battle Squadron, vice Adm. Evan-Thomas designated for command of new 5th (*Queen Elizabeth*) Battle Squadron.

German apology to U.S. in *Arabic* case, (see 19-viii.-15), and to Denmark in case of H.M. Submarine E13 (see 18-viii.-15).

Restrictions imposed upon German U-Boat commanders in regard to passenger ships.

Austrian offensive on Italian front.

Skupshtina at Nish recognised " the sacrifices indispensable for the protection of the vital interests of our people."

Gen. von Beseler appointed Governor-General at Warsaw.

Germans penetrated Russian line near Brest-Litovsk at Dobrynka.

Assemblage of *Firefly* gunboat class begun at Abbadan (Tigris).

August 25.

British ships bombarded Belgian coast between Ostend—Zeebrugge.

British, French, and Belgian aeroplanes set on fire Houthoulst Forest, where German reinforcements reported.

Austrian aeroplanes bombed Brescia.

Brest-Litovsk fell to Bug Army. Kaiser decorated co-operating Austrian Gen. von Arz with Pour le Mérite Order.

Allied blockade of Syria and Asia Minor.

Armenian massacres reported.

Gen. Townsend left Basra for Amarah.

August 26.

Count Bernstorff at Washington said U-Boats ordered not to attack passenger ships without warning.

Lord Selborne announced that Navy had submarine menace " well in hand."

British aeroplane (Squad. Com. Bigsworth, R.N.) destroyed U-Boat off Ostend.

French consolidated at Sondernach.

Allied airmen bombarded German poison-gas factory at Dornach and Mülheim station.

Olita (Niemen) evacuated by Russians.

Bialystok taken by 1st (Prussian) Army Corps, Gen. von Eben.

August 27.

Adm. von Pohl ordered, until further notice, not to send out any more U-Boats on Blockade duty.

Kaiser refused to accept resignations of Adms. von Tirpitz and Bachmann.

French took trenches between Sondernach and Landersbach (Alsace).

Italians stormed Monte Rombon, near Plezzo (Julian Alps).

Montenegrins repulsed Austrians at Grahovo.

German advance N.E. of Brest-Litovsk drove Russians nearly to Kobryn. Austro-German offensive against Zlota—Lipa line (Galicia) ; Russian line broken N. and S. of Brzezany.

Anzac advance against Hill 60 north of Kaiajik Aghala (Gallipoli).

August 28.

H.M. motor-boat *Dolores* destroyed by fire, Douglas Harbour (Isle of Man).

German aeroplane raid on Paris.

Italians took Monte Cista in Val Sugana.

Further advance at Suvla Bay (Gallipoli) ; an " important tactical feature commanding the Biyuk Anafarta valley to the East and North " captured.

Gen. Townsend at Amarah.

*August 29.

H.M. submarine C29 mined in North Sea.

Violent artillery struggle in Argonne.

Bombardment of German Western line.

Germans stormed Lipsk, 20 miles from Grodno ; attacked Friedrichstadt bridgehead on Dvina, commanding Riga railway ; and progressed towards Vilna.

In Gallipoli, Hill 60 north of Kaiajik Aghala secured by Anzacs.

Malakand Moveable Column, Gen. Beynon, engaged on Swat R.

August 30.

British s.s. *Honiton* (4,914 tons) mined and sunk off Longsand Light.

Adm. von Pohl instructed that, until further notice, also small passenger ships are not to be sunk by U-Boats without warning.

Austrians driven by Italians from Monte Maronia (Julian Alps).

Russian success on Strypa R. (Galicia) ; 3,000 prisoners, 30 guns, and 24 machine-guns captured.

French aeroplanes bombed Akbachi Sliman and Chanak (Dardanelles).

August 31.

British Guards Division constituted.

By the arrival in France during July and August of the 3rd, and of a new 4th, Grenadier Battalion, the Brigade of Guards, for the first time in British military history, became the Division of Guards—three Brigades of four Battalions each.

For List of Abbreviations see page iv.

August 31, 1915 (*continued*).

French airman Pégoud killed in air duel near Belfort.

In advance on Vilna Germans reached Orany ; they occupied Lutsk and crossed Styr.

During August U26 was lost in the Baltic and UB1 in the Mediterranean.

During August and onwards the new German submarines U33, U34, U35, U36, U38, and U39 were sent to the Mediterranean and based on Pola.

Talaat Pasha informed Prince Hohenlohe, acting German Ambassador at the Porte, that Armenian question " no longer exists."

September 1.

Eight T.B.D.s fitted for mine-sweeping swept waters westward of Pentland Firth. First occasion on which T.B.D.s used for this purpose.

Gen. Alexeieff appointed Russian Chief of Staff.

Grodno outer forts captured by 1st Prussian Landwehr Division. Austrians enter Brody, N.E. of Lemberg (Galicia).

French occupied Ruad Island, off Syria.

September 2.

Prussian Guard Corps returned from Eleventh Army to Sixth Army on W. Front.

Grodno fell to German Eighth Army after house-to-house fight. Fierce fighting at Orany, between Grodno—Vilna. Austrian advance from Brody ; Russians on Sereth.

Rumanian grain exports stopped.

H.M.T. *Southland* (11,899 tons) torpedoed in Ægean ; beached at Mudros.

German intrigues in Persia ; British Consul-General at Ispahan attacked.

September 3.

Kaiser refused resignation of Adm. von Pohl, tendered in view of U-Boat blockade restrictions.

Adm. von Holtzendorff Chief of German Naval Staff, vice Adm. Bachmann, transferred to Baltic command.

Gen. Joffre visited the Italian front.

Germans stormed Friedrichstadt bridge-head (Dvina).

Russian local recovery at Grodno.

Austrians in E. Galicia reached Sereth.

September 4.

Allan s.s. *Hesperian* (10,920 tons) torpedoed by U-Boat off Fastnet ; sunk ; 32 lost.

British s.s. *Cymbeline* (4,505 tons) and *Mimosa* (3,466 tons) sunk by U-Boat westward from Fastnet.

H.M. minesweeping sloop *Dahlia* mined in Moray Firth ; ship badly damaged.

Italian successes in Trentino and in Plezzo Basin (Julian Alps).

Bulgaria signed military convention with Central Powers.

H.M. submarine E7 sunk in Dardanelles.

British s.s. *Natal Transport* (4,107 tons) sunk by U-Boat off Gavdo Island, Crete.

*September 5.

British s.s. *Dictator* (4,116 tons) sunk by U-Boat westward from Fastnet.

French air raid on Dieuze and Mörchingen.

Zimmerwald Internationalist Socialist Conference met ; ended by resolving, under impulse of Radek, in favour of peace without annexations or indemnities.

Tsar assumed supreme command of Russian Armies ; Grand Duke Nicholas transferred to Caucasus as Viceroy and C.-in-C.

*September 5 (*continued*).

German Eleventh Army concentrating on Serbian front.

At Anzac (Gallipoli) Australians repulsed Turkish night attack.

Two Russian destroyers repelled Turkish cruiser *Hamidieh* in Black Sea.

Frontier raid in Mohmand country repulsed by composite British Force, including Gen. Dunsterville's Brigade.

September 6.

Indignation in U.S. following discovery of documents carried by American journalist, James Archibald, compromising Dr. Dumba, Austrian Ambassador at Washington.

H.M. monitor M25 joined Dover Patrol.

British s.s. *John Hardie* (4,372 tons) sunk by U-Boat W. by S. from Cape Finisterre.

British s.s. *Fulmer* bombed by German aircraft off North Hinder ; missed.

French bombed Saarbrücken in Lorraine with 40 aeroplanes ; military railway blown up, 75 persons reported killed. French air raid on Freiburg-in-Breisgau.

Russians forced across Galician border between Brody—Dubno.

Turkish destroyer *Yar Hissar* reported sunk in Sea of Marmora by submarine.

Fighting near Saisa on Rhodesian frontier between Germans and Belgians.

September 7.

Third Zeppelin (including L10, L11, L13, L14, L15, L16, and LZ74) raid on London, also over Suffolk : 18 killed, 38 injured.

Belgian coast round Ostend and West-ende bombarded by British squadron under Adm. Bacon (*Lord Clive*). Monitors under fire of Tirpitz Battery (four 11-inch guns at 18,000-22,000 yards. H.M.S. *Attentive* hit by German aircraft bomb while under weigh.

French and British airships bombarded Ostend.

S.S. *Leicestershire* (8,095 tons) chased by U-Boat in Bay of Biscay ; escaped.

Kaiser addressed Cabinet Order to Navy, enjoining officers not to presume to criticise his U-Boat policy, which was governed by considerations that they could not understand, and assuring them that he, above all others, would be only too happy to throw the Fleet without reserve into the scale.

Russian victory near Tarnopol—Trembovla on Sereth R.—8,000 prisoners. Austrians from Galicia invaded Russia, took Dubno. Germans striking N.W. of Vilna at Novo Troki and took Volkovisk, S.E. of Grodno.

Turks repulsed by Russians on Arkhave R., and a Turkish force again routed at Olti.

September 8.

Fourth Zeppelin (including LZ77) raid on London, also over Norfolk and North Riding ; 26 killed, 94 injured. Over £2,000,000 damage.

Two Grand Fleet T.B.D.s damaged and docked as result of collision with steamers in a fog.

Two German T.B.D.s collided in North Sea ; one sunk.

British s.s. *Mora* (3,047 tons) sunk by U-Boat W. by S. from Belle Ile.

Heavy German attack in Argonne repulsed.

German aeroplane raid on Nancy.

Italians repulsed at Doberdo (Carso) ; advance in Cadore.

Further Russian successes at Tarnopol—Trembovla ; total captures, 383 officers,

September 8, 1915 (*continued*).
17,000 men, 33 guns, and 66 machine-guns ; Austrians driven back towards Strypa R.
French auxiliary s.s. *Indien* torpedoed off Rhodes.

September 9.
U.S. demand for recall of Dr. Dumba, Austro-Hungarian Ambassador at Washington.
German attacks from Lingenkopf to Barrenkopf (Vosges) repulsed.
French air raids on Lütterbach and Grand Pré.
Austrians shelled Monfalcone dockyard.
British s.s. *Cornubia* sunk by U-Boat S.E. from Cartagena.
Battle on Vilna—Dvinsk front begun.
Further Russian successes on Sereth R. between Trembovla and Chortkoff ; 5,000 more prisoners.
British Vice-Consul at Shiraz killed.

September 10.
H.M.S. *Lion* with 1st and 2nd Battle Cruiser Squadrons and light forces covered mine-laying operations in the Bight.
H.M.S. *Fearless* at sea damaged by collision with a destroyer.
Germans shelled Ramskapelle and Steenstraate (Belgium).
Z XII. raided Vileika (Vilna).
S.S. *Antilochus* (9,039 tons) warded off U-Boat by gunfire in Mediterranean.
Fighting near Songwe R. (E. Africa).

September 11.
H.M. A.M.CS. *Patia* and *Oropesa*, of 10th (Blockade) Cruiser Squadron, collided ; former attacked by U-Boat while being convoyed into port.
LZ77 raided Essex ; no casualties.
High Sea Fleet put out and returned next day.
Russians attacked on Dvina ; retired N.W. of Vilna ; German concentration on Dvinsk—Vilna line.
Austro-Germans retired from Sereth R. to Strypa R. (Galicia).
Europeans left Ispahan (Persia).

*September 12.
H.M. submarine E16, attached Grand Fleet, left Aberdeen for coast of Norway to deal with U-Boat reported there.
LZ74 raided Essex and Suffolk ; no casualties.
Belgian Relief Ship *Pomona* sunk by U-Boat.
Germans towards Vilna reached Utsiany. Russians forced back E. of Grodno.
Independent Austrian offensive collapsed behind Styr and Strypa (Galicia).

September 13.
Admiral Sir Percy Scott in command of London air defences.
LZ77 raided Suffolk ; no casualties. German aeroplane bombed Margate : 2 killed, 6 injured.
Gen. Alderson first commander of Canadian Corps ; succeeded by Gen. Currie in command First Canadian Division.
French air raids on Bernsdorf and Langemarck.
Z XII. raided Lida.
Germans cut Vilna—Dvinsk—Petrograd railway at Svientsiany ; Russians at Vilna threatened with envelopment.
Russian advance at Tarnopol (Galicia).

September 14.
German aeroplane raid on Belfort.
Further Russian offensive along Sereth R. (Galicia) ; 40,000 prisoners to date.
Entente Note to Bulgaria.
British success at Maktan (E. Africa).

September 15.
U6 torpedoed and destroyed by H.M. submarine E16 off Norwegian Coast.
Lord Kitchener stated that 11 New Army Divisions had been sent to France, and that British now held additional 17 miles of French front.
Germans across Vilia, N.E. of Vilna Austro-Germans occupied Pinsk. In Galicia Germans being driven back across Strypa R German offensive towards Rovno developing
British s.s. *Patagonia* (6,011 tons) sunk by U-Boat off Odessa.

September 16.
Vilna almost encircled ; in attempt to cut off Russian retreat German cavalry reached Vilna—Minsk railway between Molodechna and Polotsk.

September 17.
Dr. Dumba recalled to Austria from U.S.
German First Army in suspense until 19-vii.-16
Gen. von Fabeck with First Army H.Q goes East to take over Twelfth Army from Gen. von Gallwitz.
Russians retiring between Vilia R.— Pripet R.
Austro-German offensive towards Rovno checked.

September 18.
British s.s. *Nigretia* (3,187 tons) mined off S. Foreland ; beached.
British s.s. *San Zeferino* (6,430 tons mined off S. Goodwins ; beached ; 2 lost.
Fall of Vilna. Renewed attacks on Dvinsk. Prince Leopold of Bavaria, attacking Russian centre, repulsed at Slonim.
Austro-Germans retiring near Rovno.
Mackensen took over new Army Group against Serbia.
Swedish Gendarmerie in Persia disbanded

*September 19.
French guns and British ships bombarded German positions on Belgian coast.
Germans reached Smorgon (Vilna—Minsk railway).
Russian counterstroke at Smorgon— Molodechna to secure retreat.
Bulgaria mobilised, and announced armed neutrality.
H.M.T. *Ramazan* sunk by U-Boat in Ægean ; 300 Indian troops lost.

September 20.
French on Aisne—Marne Canal ; progress at Hartmannsweilerkopf (Alsace).
Heavy fighting at Vilna—Dvinsk—Riga
Sir I. Hamilton's Gallipoli dispatch of 26-viii.-15 published.
H.M. collier *Linkmoor* (4,306 tons) sunk by U-Boat 50 miles W. from Cape Matapan.

September 21.
Kaiser issued Army Order prescribing "field-grey" for German uniforms in peace as well as in war.
Successful Russian retreat from Vilna Germans repulsed, driven out of Smorgon Russian success at Lennewaden (Dvina).

September 22, 1915.

Dutch s.s. *Koningin Emma* mined ; towed into Thames.

White Paper on " Archibald " documents. Von Papen on " idiotic Yankees."

French raid on Stuttgart ; King of Wurtemberg's palace bombed.

Russians holding in Northern sector.

Gen. von Fabeck assumed command of German Twelfth Army, vice Gen. von Gallwitz.

September 23.

King George inspected Dover Patrol.

Three British steamers (total tonnage, 13,000) sunk by U-Boat off Fastnet.

Russians retook Vileika, E. of Vilna.

Russians re-occupied Lutsk (Volhynia) ; over 6,000 prisoners.

Austro-Germans driven behind Oginski Canal (Pinsk).

Greece mobilised like Bulgaria.

September 24.

Liquor Control in Greater London.

British s.s. *Urbino* (6,651 tons) sunk by U-Boat off Bishop Rock.

U41 sunk by H.M.S. *Baralong* in Western Channel.

British monitors bombarded Knocke, Heyst, Zeebrugge, Blankenberghe, and Ostend.

German Champagne front reinforced by 5th Brandenburg Division from the Aisne.

German assault between Lake Drisviaty (Dvinsk) and Dvina R. repulsed.

September 25.

Middelkerke and Westende shelled by British monitors, including H.M.S. *Marshal Ney* (15-inch guns), which fired 17 rounds, while 12-inch monitors fired 102 rounds.

H.M. yacht *Sanda* sunk by gunfire off Zeebrugge ; all officers killed, including Lieut.-Commander Gartside Tipping, over 70 years, oldest naval officer serving at sea.

Battle of Loos. After 25 days' bombardment, British attacked S. of Le Bassée Canal to E. of Grenay—Vermelles ; penetrated German line 4,000 yards, and captured part Hohenzollern Redoubt, W. outskirts of Hulluch, Loos village and Hill 70. French gained cemetery at Souchez and remainder of Labyrinth. British ships continued shelling Belgian coast ; feint attacks made on Yser R. ; near Ypres—Comines Canal ; Bois Grenier ; Moulin du Piétre (Neuve Chapelle), and near Givenchy.

British used gas for first time. Germans, later, admitted that they were completely surprised by this attack at Loos.

French took offensive in Champagne ; penetrated German lines 2 miles along 15 mile front ; W. of Souain they reached Harem trench, passed Gretchen trench and followed on towards Navarin Farm ; in Perthes district they reached Souain—Tahure road ; in front of Beauséjour they reached slopes of Maisons de Champagne. On extreme right they topped Massiges Plateau.

Gen. von Emmich's Xth (Prussian) Corps arrived on Champagne front from White Russia.

Russian fleet bombarded German positions on Riga Gulf.

German reverse near Dvinsk. Russians retook Drisviaty.

Turco-Arab force driven from Waht by British Aden column.

*September 26.

British pilot cutter *Vigilant* mined off Harwich ; 14 lost.

*September 26 *(continued)*.

Monitors again shelled Belgian Coast.

Loos Battle : Anglo-French gains consolidated ; counter-attacks repulsed. French captured Souchez ; reached La Folie.

In Champagne French reached Vedegrange and Maisons de Champagne farm.

German Crown Prince's Army Group on W. Front formed.

Russian success round Vileika (Vilna).

Germans again repulsed near Pinsk.

Russians straightened line N.W. of Dubno.

September 27.

British naval receiving-ship *Caribbean* sunk in heavy weather off Cape Wrath ; 15 lives lost.

Monitors again shelled Belgian coast.

Loos battle : British attack progresses E. of Loos, but pushed back between Fosse 8 and Hohenzollern Redoubt.

French before German second line in Champagne ; they take Sabot Wood (Souain) ; on left of line they take wood on St. Hilaire—St. Souplet road and Vedegrange position.

German offensive in Argonne repulsed.

German attacks at Eckau (Riga) and W. of Vileika (Vilna) repulsed.

Italian battleship *Benedetto Brin*, with Adm. Rubin, sunk by internal explosion at Brindisi.

Battle of Kut-al-Amara (Tigris) began.

September 28.

£100,000,000 Anglo - French Five Per Cents. to be issued at 98 in U.S.

Loos Battle : Further British progress facing German third line. Chalk pit near Hill 70 carried by Guards. French took over line at Double Crassier—Loos, owing to heavy British losses.

German Third Army Front in Champagne reinforced by Gen. von Watter's XIIIth (Prussian) Army Corps (1st Guard Reserve and 4th Guard Divisions), from Twelfth Army Front in Lithuania.

In Pripet area Russians forced back ; Germans lost heavily in marshes.

Russians again evacuated Lutsk (Volhynia).

H.M. oiler *H. C. Henry* (4,219 tons) sunk by U-Boat 59 miles S.E. from Cape Matapan.

Turks defeated at Kut-el-Amara (Tigris) in retreat towards Baghdad.

September 29.

British trenches lost at Hooge (Ypres).

Loos Battle : German pressure near Hohenzollern Redoubt ; French carried Hill 140 on Vimy crest.

French engaged German second line at Butte de Tahure—Navarin Farm.

Two years position warfare on Lower Dvina begun.

Dvinsk fighting continued.

British s.s. *Haydn* (3,923 tons) sunk by U-Boat S.E. from Gavdo Island, Crete.

September 30.

Second Phase of U-Boat War ended inconclusively during September.

King George's Message to Sir J. French.

Sir J. French's " Order of the Day."

British regained most of Hooge trenches.

Loos Battle continued.

Further French progress in Champagne.

Mackensen massed 250,000 men and 2,000 guns on Serbian frontier.

Sundays marked with Asterisk (*).

September 30, 1915 (*continued*).
Gen. von Gallwitz in command of new German Eleventh Army against Serbia.
German advance in Russia stayed.

October 1.
H.M.S. *Iron Duke* at Invergordon for 10 days refit.
British 3rd Light Cruiser Squadron from Rosyth swept down to Little Fisher Bank.
British monitors bombarded Lombaertzyde and Middelkerke.
Gen. von Sauberzweig, Commandant of Brussels vice Gen. von Kraewel.
French progress on La Folie heights on Vimy Ridge.
Further French advance N. of Massiges (Champagne); German counter-attacks on Maisons de Champagne repulsed.
Germans again attacked Dvinsk and Smorgon.
German officers arriving in Bulgaria.
White Star s.s. *Olympic* (46,359 tons), chased by U-Boat 40 miles W. from Cape Matapan; escaped by speed; first encounter.

October 2.
H.M.S. *Barham* arrived at Scapa as Flagship of new 5th (*Queen Elizabeth*) Battle Squadron under Adm. Evan-Thomas.
British ships bombarded Westende.
Fresh German threat to Dvinsk.
German battalion attempting to cross Danube at Semendria repulsed by Serbians.
Bulgarians massing on Serbian frontier.
British s.s. *Arabian* (2,744 tons) sunk by U-Boat off Cerigo Island.
British s.s. *Sailor Prince* (3,144 tons) sunk by U-Boat S.E. from Cape Sidero, Crete; 2 lost.

*October 3.
British ships bombarded Zeebrugge.
Germans recaptured part of Hohenzollern Redoubt (Loos).
LZ77 raided Châlons-sur-Marne.
Desperate fighting S. of Dvinsk.
Russian ultimatum to Bulgaria; Russian Minister to leave Sofia if Bulgaria " does not within 24 hours openly break with the enemies of the Slav cause and of Russia," and expel all German and Austrian officers.
Turks retreating from Kut reached Ctesiphon position, where they were reinforced. Gen. Townshend's advanced forces reached Aziziyeh, 30 miles E. of Ctesiphon.

October 4.
Russian advance between Smorgon—Lake Drisviati (Dvinsk).
Artillery action on Belgrade—Save front.
Allied Ultimatum to Bulgaria.
British s.s. *Craigston* (2,617 tons) sunk by U-Boat off Ovo Island.

October 5.
Lord Derby Director of Recruiting.
French T.B.D. *Branlebas* mined off Nieuport.
Indecisive actions in Artois and Champagne.
Fighting near Smorgon.
Allied Forces, including British 10th Division under Gen. Mahon, landed at Salonika at invitation of Greek Government; M. Venizelos, informed by King Constantine that he could not support his policy, resigned.
H.M. collier *Bursfield* (4,037 tons) sunk by U-Boat 70 miles W. from Cape Matapan.

October 6.
Commodore Tyrwhitt, with 5th Ligh Cruiser Squadron from Harwich, swep towards Skagerrak and captured 14 Germa trawlers suspected of acting as outposts; on other trawler sunk.
H.M. minesweeper *Brighton Queen* mine and sunk off Nieuport.
New French advance in Champagne Tahure Butte taken.
German assaults on Dvinsk; desperat fighting at Grünwald, near Illukst; attemp to cut Riga—Dvinsk railway.
Austro-German invasion of Serbia b German Eleventh Army (Gen. von Gallwit: and Austro-Hungarian Third Army (Gen. vc Koevess), both under Marshal Mackensen.
British s.s. *Scawby* (3,658 tons) an *Silverash* (3,753 tons) sunk by U-Boat eas ward from Malta.
800,000 Armenians reported massacre since May.

October 7.
H.M. monitor M24 joined Dover patrol
Miss Edith Cavell tried before Germa Brussels Court Martial.
LZ77 raided Suippes—St. Hilaire.
French gain S.E. of Tahure (Champagne
Fighting at Garbunovka, 9 miles fro Dvinsk.
Austro-Germans began to cross Dvin. Save, and Danube.
20,000 Allied troops at Salonika.
M. Zaimis, Greek Premier.
British s.s. *Halizones* (5,093 tons) sun by U-Boat S.S.E. from Cape Martello, Cret Two Russian Black Sea destroyers san 19 Turkish supply ships off Anatolia.

October 8.
Anglo-French Munitions Agreement.
Strong German counter-attack on Loc front repulsed; British gain German trenc 500 yards W. of Cité St. Éloi.
French lost ground near Double Crassi (Loos).
Germans failed at Navarin Farm—But de Tahure (Champagne).
Close fighting before Dvinsk.
British submarine destroyed Germa transport in Baltic
Austro-Germans entered Belgrade.
British s.s. *Thorpwood* (3,184 tons) sun by U-Boat S. from Cape Martello, Crete.
British forces at Shabkadar repulse another Mohmand raid. In this operatic armoured cars were used for first time : action in India. In the course of this year fighting mechanical transport also was use for first time on Indian Frontier.

October 9.
Severe fighting near Loos.
Desperate struggle for Garbunovk N.W. of Dvinsk.
Russians under Gen. Ivanoff aga: advancing in Galicia.
Austrians occupied Belgrade.
Gen. von Gallwitz crossed Danube belo Semendria.
Montenegrin frontier attacked.
British s.s. *Apollo* (3,774 tons) sunk b U-Boat S. from Gavdo Island, Crete.
British took Wum Biagas (Cameroons).

*October 10.
British 3rd Light Cruiser Squadron fro Scapa swept down to Little Fisher Bank.
British s.s. *Newcastle* (3,403 tons) mine off Folkestone Pier.

For List of Abbreviations see page iv.

*October 10, 1915 (*continued*).

French progress in Souchez Valley (Artois), Givenchy-en-Gohelle Wood, and the ridges towards La Folie ; French gains in Champagne extended.

Russians drove Germans from Garbunovka (Dvinsk).

British submarine sank German s.s. *Lulea* off Lübeck.

Belgrade heights captured by Austro-Germans, who crossed Danube in force at Semendria.

S.S. *Ajax* (7,040 tons) shelled by U-Boat in Mediterranean ; rescued.

October 11.

Lord Derby's Recruiting Scheme.

French progressed N.E. of Souchez (Artois) and on La Folie heights ; they dominated La Boutte ravine (Champagne).

Adm. D'Artiges du Fournet succeeded Adm. Boué de Lapeyrère as French C.-in-C. in E. Mediterranean.

Bulgarians crossed Serbian frontier E. and S.E. of Nish.

Gen. Ivanoff pierced Austro-German line near Hajvoronka, on Strypa R. (Galicia), taking 2,000 Austrians, and crossed river.

Turks advanced at Ichkau (Caucasus).

October 12.

Miss Edith Cavell shot by order of Gen. von Sauberzweig, German Military Commandant of Brussels, for harbouring Allied soldiers and helping them to escape. M. Philippe Baucq also shot.

French progress in Champagne.

German aeroplane raid on Verdun.

Italian success in Carnia.

Austro-German progress S. of Belgrade.

New Greek Government declined to assist Serbia.

H.M. ammunition ship *Combe* lost on voyage from U.K. to Archangel.

Russian attack at Dvinsk—Smorgon.

LZ85 raided Dvinsk.

LZ39 raided Rovno.

On Strypa R. (Galicia) Russians took Visniovtchyk.

Turks repulsed in Van Pass and at Arkhava (Caucasus).

October 13.

Dreadnought Battle Fleet exercised in northern part of North Sea. H.M. T.B.D.s *Mandate* damaged by heavy sea, *Ardent* by collision with *Fortune*.

Fifth Zeppelin (including all naval airships) raid on London district, also over Norfolk, Suffolk, and Home Counties. 71 killed, 128 injured—highest casualties in 1915.

M. Delcassé, French Foreign Minister, resigned.

British took trenches behind the Vermelles—Hulluch road, and main trench of Hohenzollern Redoubt (Loos). North Midland T.F. (46th Division) engaged.

LZ77 raided Château-Thierry.

Prusso-Bavarian Alpine Corps transferred from Tirol to Serbian front.

Gen. Sarrail at Salonika.

Russians driven back across Strypa R.

October 14.

German counter-attack repulsed at Hohenzollern Redoubt (Loos).

H.M. submarine E19 sank German T.B.D. near Eaxö (Denmark).

Germans advanced, crossing Ekau R. near Grünwald, S.E. of Mitau (Courland). Russian success at Vessolovo (Dvinsk).

October 14 (*continued*).

LZ85 raided Minsk.

Fighting on Strypa R. at Hajvoronka (Galicia) ; Austro-Germans checked.

Pozarevatz stormed and taken by Austro-German forces S. of Danube.

Bulgaria declared war on Serbia.

October 15.

H.M.S. *Canada* (28,000 tons, ten 14-inch guns), new battleship of Emergency War Programme, joined Grand Fleet at Scapa.

French success on Hartmannsweilerkopf.

Great Britain at war with Bulgaria.

Heavy fighting between French and Bulgarians at Valandovo (Salonika—Nish line). Bulgarians occupied Vrania.

October 16.

German aeroplane raid on Belfort.

Five German transports sunk in the Baltic by British submarine and sixth driven ashore.

Russians repulsed at Gross Ekau.

Austro-German forces 10 miles S. of Belgrade. Franco-Serbian forces repulsed Bulgarians at Valandovo.

France at war with Bulgaria.

British blockade of Bulgarian Ægean.

Sir I. Hamilton recalled from Gallipoli.

British terminated occupation of Bushire.

*October 17.

Zeebrugge bombarded from the sea.

German aeroplane raid on Belfort.

Germans active on Dvina line.

Italy declared war on Bulgaria.

Austro-Germans 15 miles S. of Belgrade.

Bulgarians forced Timok Valley, captured Egri Palanka, and cut Nish—Uskub railway at Vrania.

British Government's offer of Cyprus to Greece in return for participation in the war.

October 18.

Sir E. Carson resigned from Cabinet.

Harwich Force sailed to operate off Danish coast N. of Horn Reef ; H.M.S. *Lion* and 1st Battle Cruiser Squadron in support ; no German ships sighted.

Two German steamers torpedoed by British submarine in Baltic.

German advance on Dvina R.

Heavy fighting on Styr R. ; Russians captured Chartorysk (Galicia).

Austro-Germans 20 miles S. of Belgrade ; Obrenovats (Save) taken. Fierce fighting between Bulgars and Serbs at Vrania ; 20 miles of railway in Bulgarian hands.

Gen. Monro in command Mediterranean E.F., *vice* Sir Ian Hamilton.

October 19.

H.M. monitor M26 joined Dover Patrol.

German attacks failed against British positions from Quarries to Hulluch and at Hohenzollern Redoubt (Loos).

German gas attack near Reims—La Pompelle—Prosnes.

Two more German steamers torpedoed in Baltic by British submarine.

Fighting at Olai, 12 miles S.W. of Riga.

Japan adhered to Pact of London.

October 20.

Admiralty War Staff issued revised instructions for defensively-armed merchant ships.

Lord Derby on his 46 " Groups."

Further German gas attack near Reims

Sundays marked with Asterisk (*).

October 20, 1915 (*continued*).

Germans captured Dvina bank 10 miles E. of Riga.

Russians carried German positions E. of Baranovitchi ; 3,500 prisoners.

Germans 25 miles S. of Belgrade. Bulgarians occupied Veles ; Allied forces at Strumnitza—Krivolak.

Gen. Botha's victory in South African elections.

October 21.

British s.s. *Cape Antibes* (2,549 tons) mined in entrance to White Sea ; 6 lost.

King George proceeded to France.

Italian attack on Isonzo front at Doberdo—San Martino ; trenches captured on Podgora ridge.

Serbian H.Q. removed to Krushevatz.

Bulgarian attack on Salonika—Uskub— Nish railway progressing ; 100 miles of line captured ; Kumanovo occupied. Bulgarians repulsed by French near Rabrovo, S. of Strumnitza.

British Fleet bombarded Dedeagatch.

Russian Fleet bombarded Varna and Burgas (Black Sea).

Greece refused offer of Cyprus.

October 22.

King George's Message to the Nation.

Italian advance ; 1,000 prisoners on Isonzo.

Russian troops landed at Domesnes (Riga Gulf) repulsed Germans.

LZ85 raided Riga.

German success near Dvinsk.

Bulgarians occupied Uskub and Austrians Shabatz ; Allied forces in touch with Bulgarians at Krivolak ; Bulgarians again repulsed by French at Rabrovo.

Gen. Monro left for Gallipoli.

Allies took Bamenda (Cameroons).

October 23.

H.I.M.S. *Prinz Adalbert* torpedoed and sunk by H.M. submarine E8 off Libau.

Germans took Illukst (Dvinsk).

Germans crossed Danube at Orsova ; Bulgarian advance on Prahovo—Negotin.

H.M.T. *Marquette* (7,057 tons) sunk by U-Boat off Salonika Bay ; 29 lost.

Gen. Townshend's main force advancing on Ctesiphon reached Aziziyeh (Mesopotamia).

*October 24.

German High Sea Fleet put out as far as Horn Reef. This was Adm. von Pohl's fifth and last outing in 1915.

French captured " La Courtine " (Champagne) S. of Tahure, on Butte de Mesnil Salient.

Austrian aeroplanes bombed Venice.

Furious fighting before Riga ; Germans captured Dahlen Island (Dvina), but were repulsed on Aa R. (Courland).

Bulgarians took Prahovo and Negotin (N.E. Serbia.)

October 25.

H.M.S. *Velox* mined off Nab Light.

German counter-attack failed at " La Courtine " (Champagne).

Franco-Serbians recaptured Veles, and threatened Uskub ; Bulgarians retired on Ishtip ; Austrians occupied Kladovo (N.E. Serbia),

Death of Baron von Wangenheim, German ambassador to the Porte.

French took Sende (Cameroons).

October 26.

Slight German progress near Dvinsk.

Austro-German and Bulgarian forces i touch at Liubichevatz (Danube) ; Austro Germans within 20 miles of Kraguievatz Serbians retiring through Zaitchar—Kraguie vatz.

Persian Cossacks sent to aid British an Russian consuls at Kengaver.

Mr. Hughes Australian Prime Minister in the room of Mr. Fisher, appointed High Commissioner in London.

October 27.

King George visited French Armies a front and issued Order of Day.

Germans repulsed in Champagne.

British submarine sank four more Germa steamers in Baltic.

Austrians across Drina E. of Vishegrad Montenegrins fighting in this sector. Bul garians took Zaitchar.

Russian Fleet shelled Varna (Black Sea)

Gen. Townsend's night attack on Turkish advanced camp at El Kutunich (Tigris).

Malakand Moveable Column at Chakdar repulsed fresh raid and captured a standard

October 28.

H.M.S. *Argyll* wrecked on Bell Rock near Dundee, in thick weather.

King George in France thrown from hi horse and injured.

Viviani Ministry resigns. M. Briand Premier and Foreign Minister ; Gen. Galliéni War Minister.

German success at Garbunovka (Dvinsk)

Gen. Mahon G.O.C. Salonika Army.

Gen. Monro assumed command of British Mediterranean E.F.

H.M. minesweeper *Hythe* sunk in collision off Cape Helles (Gallipoli).

October 29.

H.M. merchant cruiser *Arlanza* mined i White Sea ; reached Yukanski anchorage.

Gen. Joffre in London.

British casualties to Oct. 9—493,294.

Bulgarians recaptured Veles ; French occupied Strumnitza.

October 30.

British s.s. *Avocet* (1,408 tons) attacked by aircraft with bombs and machine-gun of North Hinder ; bombs missed.

Germans recaptured Butte de Tahure (Champagne), but failed at " La Courtine."

Further Russian success near Tarnopol (Galicia) ; several thousand prisoners.

Prusso-Bavarian Alpine Corps arrived on Serbian front.

British in action on the Gevgeli—Doiran front ; Bulgarian attack on Krivolak (Vardar) repulsed.

French submarine *Turquoise* sunk in Dardanelles.

Allies re-occupied Eseka (Cameroons).

*October 31.

H.M. patrol yacht *Aries* mined off Leathercoat.

Commodore Tyrwhitt's Harwich Force passed before daylight some 70 miles N.W. of Heligoland, steered for Little Fisher Bank, and thence home. One neutral ore-steamer intercepted.

During October UC9 was blown up by her own mines.

Steel helmets issued to British on W. front.

For List of Abbreviations see page iv.

*October 31, 1915 (*continued*).

Russians forced back between Kemmern —Lake Babit (Riga Gulf).

Russian counter-offensive between Lakes Sventen—Ilse (Dvinsk).

Fighting on Strypa R. (Galicia); Russians took Siemikovice.

Russian Fleet again shelled Varna (Black Sea).

H.M.S. *Louis* wrecked in Suvla Bay.

November 1,

S.S. *Hocking* under U.S. flag, but German control, seized by British and taken into Halifax (N.S.).

King George returned from France.

Armlet scheme under Derby system.

Sir J. French's Loos Dispatch issued.

H.M. T.B. 96 sunk in collision off Gibraltar.

Italian successes near Gorizia and Zagora (Isonzo).

Russians crossed Strypa R. (Galicia) near Siemikovice in boats and took Bakovice.

Polish Legion fighting as Austrian unit on Linsingen's front in Galicia.

Kraguievatz, chief Serbian arsenal, fell to Austro-Germans. Bulgarians advanced from Veles on Monastir; Serbians holding between Veles—Prilep.

November 2.

Dreadnought Battle Fleet left Scapa for cruise W. of Orkneys.

Mr. Asquith on new War Committee.

Gen. Maunoury Governor of Paris.

Bulgarians occupied Izvor.

More disturbances engineered by Germans in Persia; large Russian force at Kazvin.

November 3.

M. A. Thomas French Munitions Minister.

Germans took trenches on Hill 199 (Champagne).

Important Russian success near Platonovka between Lakes Sventen—Ilsen (Dvinsk) and at Siemikovice (Strypa); 5,000 prisoners.

Bulgarians took Kalavat, N.E. of Nish (Serbia).

Greek (Zaimis) Ministry resigned.

British s.s. *Woolwich* (2,936 tons) sunk by U-Boat off Cape Sidero, Crete.

British s.s. *Woodfield* (3,584 tons) sunk by U-Boat E.S.E. from Ceuta, Morocco; 8 lost.

November 4.

S.S. *Dotterel* (1,596 tons) attacked by aircraft with bombs and machine-gun off North Hinder; bombs missed (see 29-xi.-15).

Fighting in Champagne.

Russians approached Illukst (Dvinsk).

Austro-Germans at Parachin, between Kraguievatz—Nish. Bulgarians defeated at Izvor by Serbians, French and British. Danube navigation re-opened; Austrian munitions for Bulgaria.

M. Skouloudis Greek Premier.

Turkish attacks at Anzac (Gallipoli).

November 5.

U.S. Note on British blockade.

Mr. Asquith at War Office while Lord Kitchener visited Near East.

Fierce fighting round Massiges (Champagne).

German reverse at Platonovka (Dvinsk).

Nish fell to Bulgarians, who joined Germans at Krivivir.

Two British steamers warded off U-Boat by gunfire in Mediterranean.

November 5 (*continued*).

British s.s. *Lady Plymouth* chased by U-Boat for two days off Algerian coast.

British s.s. *Moorina* (4,994 tons) sunk by U-Boat S. from Cape Martello, Crete.

H.M. armed steamer *Tara* sunk by U-Boat in E. Mediterranean.

November 6.

British 1st and 2nd Light Cruiser Squadrons, with H.M.S. *Lion* and Battle Cruisers in support, swept out Skagerrak.

H.M.S. *Birkenhead* joined 3rd Light Cruiser Squadron at Rosyth.

During the night of November 6-7, H.M.SS. *Hibernia* (Adm. Fremantle), *Zealandia*, and *Albemarle*, while outward bound to Mediterranean, encountered heavy sea in Pentland Firth; *Albemarle's* fore-bridge carried away, and roof of conning-tower displaced; all three ships returned to Scapa.

H.M. monitor M27 joined Dover Patrol.

U8's crew interned by Dutch.

Russian counter-attack near Lake Babit (Riga), warships supporting. Germans extended to Ragassen (Riga Gulf) to avoid being outflanked. Russians took Olai (Riga —Mitau railway).

Four British steamers sunk by U-Boat in Mediterranean—s.s. *Caria* (3,032 tons), *Clan Macalister* (4,835 tons) and *Lumina* (5,950 tons) 120 miles S.E. from Cape Martello, Crete, and s.s. *Glenmoor* (3,075 tons) 5 miles N.E. from Cap de Fer, Tunis.

H.M. submarine E20 sunk by U-Boat in Dardanelles.

British took German positions at Banyo Mt. (Cameroons).

*November 7.

H.I.M.S. *Undine* sunk by British submarine off S. Sweden.

Gen. von der Marwitz to command VIth (Prussian) Army Corps.

Russian advance on Kemmern between Shlock and Lake Babit (Riga Gulf).

Italians captured crest of Col di Lana (Dolomites).

Italian s.s. *Ancona*, for New York, sunk off Sardinia by U-Boat; great loss of life, including many Americans.

Austro-Germans reached Krushevatz; across W. Morava R. at Kralievo (Serbia).

November 8.

H.M. auxiliary *Princess Margaret* laid mines in Heligoland Bight.

Germans in Russia on defensive; lost positions near Kolki (Styr).

Serbians held Bulgarians in Katchanik Pass.

British s.s. *Den of Crombie* (4,949 tons) sunk by U-Boat off Cape Martello, Crete.

November 9.

Mr. Asquith's second war speech at Guildhall.

H.M.S. *Matchless* damaged by mine in North Sea.

British Trinity House Yacht *Irene* mined off Tongue Light; 21 lost.

French T.B.D. *Branlebas* mined off Flanders coast.

Russian victory at Kolki (Styr); 3,500 prisoners.

Bulgarians took Leskovatz (Salonika—Nish Railway).

S.S. *Kashgar* (8,840 tons) warded off U-Boat attack by gunfire in Mediterranean.

Sundays marked with Asterisk (*).

November 9, 1915 (*continued*).

S.S. *Californian* (6,223 tons) sunk by U-Boat off Cape Matapan.

Japanese steamer sunk by U-Boat off Morocco.

November 10.

Germans forced from Kemmern; Russian warships shelled Germans on Riga Gulf coast.

German line dented at Chartorysk (Styr); 2,000 prisoners.

French troops occupied Gradsko (Macedonia).

Russian forces advancing on Teheran; Persian gendarmerie revolted and imprisoned British subjects.

November 11.

War Committee to consist of Messrs. Asquith, Lloyd George, Balfour, Bonar Law and McKenna.

British s.s. *Rhineland* mined off Southwold; 20 lost.

Russian success W. of Riga; Kemmern occupied, fleet co-operating. German attack near Dahlen Island (Dvina).

Bulgarian attack on French positions S. of Veles repulsed.

H.M.T. *Mercian* (6,305 tons) attacked by U-Boat in Mediterranean; 103 casualties.

Greek Chamber dissolved.

Gen. Townshend advanced from Aziziyeh and occupied Kutunieh (Mesopotamia).

November 12.

H.M. auxiliary yacht *Resource II.* (1,000 tons) destroyed by fire at Southampton.

H.M. submarine E17 proceeded on a week's reconnoitring cruise in the Kattegat.

French mining successes in Argonne.

Russian advance W. of Kemmern (Riga).

Serbians retook Kalkandelen (Tetovo).

British within 7 miles of Ctesiphon.

Shah of Persia received Allied Ministers.

November 13.

Lord Kitchener visited Gallipoli.

Serbians retired to new capital, Mitrovitza.

＊November 14.

French repulsed viole   attacks on " The Labyrinth " (Artois).

Weimar Socialists censured Scheidemann for having visited Belgi m under auspices of German G.H.Q.

Verona bombed by Austrian aircraft; 30 killed, 49 injured.

German retreat from Kemmern (Riga Gulf).

Gallwitz fighting in Toplitza Valley, S.W. of Nish. Bulgarians took Krushevo; advanced on Prilep; recovered Tetovo.

Turco-German schemes in Persia frustrated. Turkish Ambassador and German and Austrian Ministers left Teheran.

November 15.

H.M. A.M.C. *Teutonic,* on night of November 15-16, intercepted Norwegian-American liner s.s. *Kristianiafjord* steaming fast, without lights, in high latitudes, and trying to break blockade; liner sent to Kirkwall.

LZ86 raided Dvinsk.

Russians driven out of Chartorysk across Styr R. (Galicia).

Serbians resisting at Babuna Pass.

British gained nearly 300 yards of trenches between Vineyard and Gully Ravine (Gallipoli).

Count Wolff-Metternich new German ambassador to the Porte.

November 16.

Germans again attacking near Dahlen Island (Dvina).

Prilep fell to Bulgarians. Allies evacuated Monastir.

November 17.

H.M.S. *Donegal* left Scapa to cruise along White Sea route and protect Archangel trade; large consignments of arms and ammunition passing from France to Russia. Other cruisers swept along Norwegian coast.

H.S. *Anglia* mined in Channel; 85 lost.

War Committee in Paris for conference.

Austro-Germans at Kurshumlia, threatening Mitrovitza (Serbia).

November 18.

Canadian raid near Messines (Ypres).

M. Denys Cachin, French Envoy to Greece, received by King Constantine.

Gen. Townshend's forces concentrated at Kutunieh (Mesopotamia).

November 19.

Three Harwich submarines proceeded to Kattegat to reconnoitre.

Anglo-Danish Agreement signed.

Russians re-occupied Chartoryisk (Styr).

Allied " Peaceful Blockade " of Greece.

Gen. Townshend left Kutunieh and occupied Zeur (Mesopotamia).

November 20.

Italian assaults on Gorizia (Isonzo); Oslavia stormed; ground won in Carso.

Novi Bazar fell. Bulgarians checked towards Monastir.

Lord Kitchener visited King Constantine at Athens.

Gen. Townshend reached Lajj (Tigris), 9 miles from Ctesiphon.

＊November 21.

Gen. Townshend advanced from Lajj (Tigris) on Ctesiphon.

Persian Government took steps against German intrigues.

Allies occupied Tibati (Cameroons).

November 22.

From this date until December 7, H.M.SS. *Donegal* and *Hampshire* protected White Sea route, coaling at Alexandrovsk.

Germans took Bersemunde Farm, near Dahlen Island (Dvina).

French attack at Krivolak; Brusnik occupied.

M. Venizelos to abstain from elections.

Ctesiphon battle, 18 miles from Baghdad; British captured Turkish front positions.

November 23.

H.M.S. *Warspite* rejoined Grand Fleet after some weeks repairing in the Tyne, owing to injuries caused by grounding in Firth of Forth.

Russians retook Bersemunde Farm.

Mitrovitza and Prishtina fell; Serbian Army retreated towards Albania.

S.S. *City of Marseilles* (8,250 tons) warded off U-Boat by gunfire in Mediterranean.

At Ctesiphon British repulsed Turkish counter-attack; Turks reinforced.

British operating towards Yaunde (Cameroons).

November 24, 1915.

Germans recovered Bersemunde (Dvina). Russians took Yanopol Farm, N. of Illukst (Dvinsk). Germans retired.

Serbian Government moved to Scutari (Albania).

S.S. *City of Lahore* (6,048 tons) warded off U-Boat by gunfire 10 miles E. from Cape de Gata.

Marshal von der Goltz assumed Turco-German command in Mesopotamia. At Ctesiphon British consolidated; Turks fell back on second position. More Turkish re-inforcements.

November 25.

250,000 Russian troops on Rumanian frontier.

Dedeagatch - Constantinople railway bombed by British aeroplanes.

Greece guaranteed security of Allied troops.

British, retiring from Ctesiphon to Kut-el-Amara owing to large Turkish reinforcements, reached Lajj (Tigris).

November 26.

German camp near Albert raided by 23 Allied aeroplanes.

Lord Kitchener visited Italian front.

Bulgarians crossed Tcherna R. and threaten Monastir.

November 27.

British s.s. *Balgownie* (1,061 tons) attacked near North Hinder by aircraft with bombs and machine-guns; bombs missed.

German attack N. of the " Labyrinth " (Artois), repulsed by French.

M. Max transferred from Glatz to Celle.

Storm in Gallipoli followed by frost; 10,000 sick during week—frost-bite, etc.

*November 28.

U-Boat destroyed off Middelkerke by British seaplane.

German memorandum on *Baralong* case.

German aeroplane raid on Verdun.

Italian successes in Carso.

Russian success near Pinsk, German 82nd Divisional Staff, including 2 generals, captured.

German H.Q. reported: " With the flight of the scanty remnants of the Serbian Army into the Albanian mountains our main operations are closed." Bulgarians and Austro-Germans advancing on Monastir.

Gen. Townshend in retreat from Ctesiphon reached Aziziyeh (Tigris). H.M.S. *Shaitan* aground; abandoned.

November 29.

British s.s. *Dotterel* (1,596 tons) mined off Boulogne Pier; 5 lost.

Lord Kitchener in Paris.

Russian success near Illukst (Dvinsk). German counter-attack failed. Russians in outskirts of town.

British cavalry (14th Hussars and 7th Hariana Lancers) in rearguard action E. of Kutunieh (Mesopotamia).

November 30.

Lord Kitchener returned to London.

First Motor Launches, under Cmdr. Hamilton Benn, arrived at Dover during November.

November 30 (*continued*).

German aeroplane raid on Dunkirk.

Italian progress towards Gorizia (Isonzo).

Prizrend taken by Bulgarians.

Three British steamers (over 10,000 tons in all) sunk by U-Boat in Mediterranean.

British in retreat to Kut reached Umm-Al-Tubal (Mesopotamia).

December 1.

Grand Fleet proceeded to sea for battle exercises, during which H.M.SS. *Barham* and *Warspite* were damaged in collision and had to leave for Invergordon and Devonport for repairs.

Italian adhesion to Pact of London announced.

Marshal Mackensen detached 105th Prussian Division from his Army and transferred it from Nish to Black Sea coast.

S.S. *Clan Macleod* (4,796 tons) and *Umeta* (5,312 tons) sunk by U-Boat off Malta; 14 lost.

Gen. Townshend fought rearguard action at Umm-Al-Tubal (Mesopotamia); H.M.SS. *Comet* and *Firefly* disabled and abandoned. British Force marched 36 miles to Shadieh.

December 2.

H.M. motor-boat *Nita Pita* destroyed by fire at Poole.

Austro-Germans driven back across Styr R. (Galicia).

Serbian retreat along Ochrida road towards Albania.

S.S. *Commodore* (5,858 tons) sunk by U-Boat off Malta.

Gen. Townshend's Force, after 40-mile march, reached Shumran bend of Tigris, six miles W. of Kut.

Allies took Fumban (Cameroons).

December 3.

Captains Boy-Ed and von Papen, German Naval and Military Attachés at Washington, requested to leave U.S.

Gen. Joffre appointed French C.-in-C.

Serbians defeated by Bulgarians on White Drin R.

Turkish T.B.D. *Yar Hissar* sunk by British submarine in Sea of Marmora.

British s.s. *Helmsmuir* (4,111 tons) sunk by U-Boat off Gavdo Island.

In Mediterranean s.s. *Benalla* (11,118 tons) warded off U-Boat by gunfire; s.s. *Torilla* (5,205 tons) and s.s. *Andania* (13,405) attacked and chased by U-Boat; rescued.

Gen. Townshend reached Kut-el-Amara (Tigris) after a retreat of 90 miles.

December 4.

Mr. Henry Ford's " Peace Mission " left U.S.A. in Danish liner.

Lord Kitchener at Calais conference.

Italian T.B.D. *Intrepido* mined off Avlona.

Fresh British forces at Salonika.

British submarine in Sea of Marmora sank Turkish supply ship and several sailing vessels.

Russian troops at this date three marches from Hamadan and 23 marches from Baghdad.

\#December 5.

Austro-Germans and Bulgarians, pursuing Serbian Army, entered Montenegro and Albania; Bulgarian attack on French bridgehead at Demir Kapu repulsed.

French submarine *Fresnel* destroyed by Austrian warship off San Giovanni di Medua.

Sundays marked with Asterisk (*).

*December 5, 1915 (continued).

American s.s. *Petrolite* shelled by Austrian U-Boat in Mediterranean.

Siege of Gen. Townshend's force at Kut-el-Amara by Turks under Nur-ed-Din begun. Gen. Nixon hoping to relieve Kut within two months.

December 6.

Allied War Council at Chantilly.

Austro-Germans captured Ipek (Montenegro). French retired to Demir Kapu Pass. Bulgarians attacked British at Strumnitza. British lost front trenches.

Austrian naval squadron bombarded Durazzo.

Capt. Stanley Wilson, M.P., captured by Austrian U-Boat while carrying dispatches in a Greek ship.

Gen. Townshend's cavalry sent down Tigris. British force thus reduced to 8,990 combatants, of whom 7,000 infantry.

December 7.

President Wilson's Message denouncing pro-Germans.

Yser floods forced Germans to abandon trenches.

French lost and recaptured advanced work near St. Souplet (Champagne).

British retired from Strumnitza. Bulgarians occupied Demir Kapu.

U.S. s.s. *Communipaw* attacked by an Austrian U-Boat off Tripoli.

British s.s. *Veria* (3,229 tons) sunk by U-Boat about 24 miles N.W. from Alexandria.

Austrian request for safeguard for Austrian passengers in s.s. *Golconda* against danger from their own U-Boats.

Investment of Kut-el-Amara by Turks complete. Nur-ed-Din summoned Gen. Townshend to surrender; he refused. Turks attacked and temporarily gained North Fort.

Russians advancing from Teheran drove German-led rebels from Aveh (Persia).

December 8.

British 2nd Light Cruiser Squadron left Rosyth for two days sweep to eastward of Little Fisher Bank.

Further fighting in Champagne.

Fierce Bulgarian attacks on Allied Macedonian front; Allies withdrew towards Greek frontier.

Kut heavily bombarded; Turkish attacks repulsed by British garrison.

December 9.

Allied War Council in Paris.

Gen. de Castelnau French Chief-of-Staff.

Peace Debate in Reichstag; Chancellor Bethmann - Hollweg described occupied territories as "pawns." Socialist leader Scheidemann opposed annexations.

German gas attack on Riga front.

Allied retreat from Vardar R. (Macedonia); British lost eight guns—1,500 casualties; Bulgarian irregulars over Greek frontier.

British s.s. *Orteric* (6,535 tons) sunk by U-Boat off Gavdo Island.

British s.s. *Busiris* (2,705 tons) sunk by U-Boat about 200 miles W.N.W. from Alexandria.

Russian troops routed Turco-German rebel detachment between Teheran—Hamadan, in Sultan Bulak Pass.

Gen. Aylmer to command Tigris line.

December 10.

Captains Boy-Ed and von Papen recalled from U.S.

December 10 (continued).

Ypres salient heavily shelled.

Italian success on Bezzecca heights.

Russian fleet sank two Turkish gunboats, *Tash Kupru* and *Yozgad*, in Black Sea.

British withdrawal from Anzac and Suvla begun.

British at Kut repulsed more Turkish attacks.

December 11.

Belgian powder factory blown up at Havre.

Gen. von Falkenhayn declined to entertain Gen. von Conrad's proposal for joint Austro-German offensive against Italy, on ground that German troops were needed elsewhere.

Bulgarians attacked Anglo-French at Furka and lost 8,000 men.

Greece to keep only one division at Salonika.

Gallipoli casualties to date=25,000 dead, 75,000 wounded, 96,000 sick, 12,000 missing.

Arabs routed near Mersa Matruh (W. Egypt).

Kut garrison repulsed more Turkish attacks.

Russians occupied Hamadan (Persia).

*December 12.

Close of Derby Recruiting Campaign.

British s.s. *Southgarth* bombed by German aircraft off La Panne; missed.

British raid at Neuve Chapelle.

Bulgarians entered Doiran, Gevgeli, and Struga (Macedonia).

Turkish attacks at Kut-el-Amara repulsed.

December 13.

French destroyed last German bridge at St. Mihiel.

Allied troops withdrawn across Greek frontier. Salonika being fortified.

S.S. *Cawdor Castle* (6,243 tons) warded off U-Boat by gunfire in Mediterranean.

British force defeated 1,200 Arabs west of Mersa Matruh (W. Egypt).

December 14.

British reply to German ¦ *Baralong* Memorandum.

German seaplane destroyed off Belgian coast by Flight Sub-Lieut. Graham.

Gen. Smith-Dorrien to command in E. Africa.

December 15.

British Northern Blockade Squadron intercepted and sent to Kirkwall two neutral ships, steaming at high speed at night without lights on December 15 and 16, evidently intending to evade blockade.

Sir J. French retired from command of Army in France and Flanders; Sir D. Haig to succeed. Sir J. French appointed to command at home.

German aeroplane raid on Verdun.

Germans repulsed Russians near Lake Drisviaty (Dvinsk) and on Beresina R.

December 16.

Adm. Jerram, late China Station, relieved Adm. Warrender in command of 2nd Battle Squadron, Grand Fleet.

New Five Per Cent. Exchequer Bonds.

British trench raid near Armentières.

For List of Abbreviations see page iv.

December 17, 1915,

Seven German small cruisers and three T.B.D. Flotillas reconnoitred Skagerrak and Kattegat.

H.I.M.S. *Bremen* and German T.B.D. V191 sunk by British submarine in Baltic.

Lvov raided Rovno.

Russians repulsed Austrians on Strypa R. (Galicia).

Russians pursued rebels through Persian mountains towards Kermanshah.

British took Jang Mangas (Cameroons).

December 18.

Sir J. French's farewell to Army in France.

Slight British success at Kut (Tigris).

* December 19.

Sir D. Haig assumed command in France.

German gas attack at Ypres foiled.

Russian success near Lake Miadzol.

Withdrawal from Anzac and Suvla Bay (Gallipoli) successfully effected by Gen. Monro and Admiral Wemyss, with three casualties ; six guns lost : Turks deceived. (Movement completed by dawn 20th.)

Gounarist majority at Greek Elections.

December 20.

Adm. Bacon issued Memorandum for guidance of five 12-inch monitors and four M-class monitors which were placed across the Thames estuary from Clacton to Margate to assist in intercepting Zeppelins bound for London.

Commodore Tyrwhitt with Harwich Force swept for three days to Danish Coast.

La Panne, King Albert's H.Q., bombed by German aeroplanes.

Two British steamers torpedoed and sunk by U-Boat without warning off Boulogne ; 2 lost.

Haase resigned presidency of Socialist group in Reichstag ; Ebert succeeded.

Gen. Russky retired owing to ill-health.

Bulgarians and Greeks in collision at Koritza.

Persian rebels on Kermanshah road endeavouring to retreat towards Baghdad.

December 21.

Sir W. Robertson succeeded Sir A. Murray as Chief of Imperial General Staff ; latter to succeed Gen. Monro in the East ; and then Egypt ; Gen. Monro to succeed Sir D. Haig in command of First Army on W. Front.

French success at Hartmannsweilerkopf (Alsace) ; advance down far slopes ; 1,300 prisoners.

German Socialist split exhibited in Reichstag division on supplementary credits ; 20 Socialists, including Haase, voted in independent Minority against credits.

Austrian steamer carrying arms sunk by Italian T.B.D. in Adriatic.

Japanese s.s. *Yasaka Maru* sunk by U-Boat in Mediterranean.

Allies took Mangeles (Cameroons).

December 22.

Germans regained footing at Hartmannsweilerkopf (Alsace).

Gen. von Lüttwitz to command Xth (Prussian) Army Corps, vice Gen. von Emmich.

Turkish attack on Kut ; Turks penetrated fort, but driven out.

December 23.

H.M. T.B.D.s *Porpoise* and *Morning Star* hove to and badly damaged by heavy gale near Fair Island Channel, while escorting Russian ice-breaker to northward.

Further French success at Hartmannsweilerkopf (Alsace).

Turks besieging Kut reinforced from Gallipoli.

December 24.

British 3rd Light Cruiser Squadron from Rosyth swept down North Sea to Dogger and Little Fisher Bank.

French s.s. *Ville de la Ciotat* torpedoed by U-Boat in Mediterranean ; 80 lives lost.

British s.s. *Yeddo* (4,563 tons) sunk by U-Boat off Cape Matapan.

Russian offensive on Strypa R. (Galicia).

Reinforced Turks delivered furious assault on Kut-el-Amara ; repulsed.

December 25.

3,000 Arabs defeated at Mersa Matruh (W. Egypt).

Turks again repulsed at Kut Fort.

Prince Firman Fir ma, Persian Premier.

* December 26.

H.M. submarine E6 mined in North Sea.

Russian troops occupied Kashan and marched on Ispahan (Persia).

German ships sunk in Lake Tanganyika.

December 27.

H.M. monitor *Marshal Soult* (15-inch guns) bombarded Westende.

Heavy Russo - Austrian fighting on Bessarabia—Bukovina frontier.

H.M. T.B. 046 wrecked by heavy weather while in tow in E. Mediterranean.

December 28.

H.M. oiler *El Zorro* (5,989 tons) sunk by U-Boat 10 miles S. from Old Head of Kinsale.

S.S. *Huronian* (8,766 tons) torpedoed by U-Boat off Fastnet ; arrived Bantry Bay.

Cabinet and Compulsion.

Cabinet decided to redeem Prime Minister's " pledge " to married men under Derby Scheme.

Indian Corps left France.

Letts routed Germans on Courland Aa.

Russian success in Bukovina.

December 29.

More fighting round Chartorysk (Styr).

Austrian T.B.D.s *Triglav* and *Lika* sunk by Allied warships off Durazzo. French submarine *Monge* sunk by Austrian cruiser *Helgoland* ; T.B.D. *Fresnel* aground at mouth of Boyana.

French occupied Castellorizo Island.

Turks bombarded Kut liquorice factory.

December 30.

German aeroplane raid on Calais.

Germans exploded mines near Loos.

Near Hartmannsweilerkopf (Alsace) French captured Rehfelsen and Hirzstein.

Gen. von Falkenhayn, in conference with Adm. von Tirpitz and naval authorities at Berlin War Ministry, expressed himself as now in favour of unrestricted U-Boat warfare.

German Niemen Army renamed Eighth Army.

German aeroplanes bomb Salonika. German, Austrian, Turkish and Bulgarian Consuls arrested by Gen. Sarrail.

Gen. Monro left Mudros for Alexandria.

Sundays marked with Asterisk (*).

December 30, 1915 (*continued*).

P. & O. s.s. *Persia* (7,974 tons) sunk by U-Boat off Cape Martello, Crete ; 334 lost.

S.S. *Clan Macfarlane* (4,823 tons) sunk by U-Boat off C. Martello, Crete ; 52 lost.

British s.s. *Abelia* (3,650 tons) sunk by U-Boat off Gavdo Island.

December 31.

Cabinet and Compulsion.

Sir John Simon resigned.

H.M.S. *Natal* (13,550 tons) destroyed by nternal explosion in Cromarty Firth.

H.M.S. *Swift* joined Dover Patrol.

H.M. colliers *Satrap* and *Tynemouth* left Barry and Cardiff ; not since heard of.

Slight German success near Hulluch.

German counter-attack on Hirzstein.

Just before the turn of the year Gen. von Falkenhayn completed his Memorandum for the Kaiser advocating an assault on Verdun and immediate institution of un-restricted U-Boat warfare ; the first proposal was adopted ; the second was dropped, in deference to Herr von Bethmann-Hollweg's misgivings.

Russian offensive in S. Poland and Galicia ; Styr R. crossed near Chartorysk ; trenches on Strypa R. taken.

S.S. *Ionic* (12,332 tons) attacked by U-Boat with torpedo in Mediterranean ; missed.

January 1, 1916.

Russians drove Austrians across Styr N.W. of Chartorysk and took Khriask across river. S. of Chartorysk they took Kolki.

King Peter at Salonika.

British s.s *Glengyle* (9,395 tons), tor-pedoed by U-Boat, without warning, 240 miles E. by S. from Malta ; 10 lives lost.

Yaunde (Cameroons) occupied by British.

* January 2.

German raider *Möwe*, having passed up Norwegian coast and N. of Shetlands, laid mines between Cape Wrath and N. from Strathie Point.

French lost ground S. of Rehfelsen.

Turks shelled Kut-el-Amara (Tigris).

January 3.

Russian T.B.D. captured 11 Turkish sailing vessels in Black Sea.

January 4.

White Paper on *Baralong* case.

Lord Derby's Report ; 651,160 unstarred single men not offered themselves for service.

German attacks in Champagne.

Russian gain near Czernowitz (Buko-vina).

British s.s. *Coquet* captured by U-Boat and sunk with bombs 200 miles E. from Malta ; 17 lost ; 10 others captured by Arabs.

January 5.

Military Service Bill in Commons.

Battle Cruiser Fleet left Rosyth on three days cruise in Northern part of North Sea.

Russian offensive continues on Styr R. and Strypa R., and in Bukovina.

January 6.

H.M.S. *King Edward VII.* (16,350 tons), mined off N. Scotland while on passage from Scapa to Belfast. Mines here laid by *Möwe*.

H.M. submarine E17 wrecked off Texel.

Gen. Aylmer marched from Ali Gherbi to relieve Kut-el-Amara (Tigris).

January 7.

H.M.S. *Albemarle* left Scapa for Arch-angel.

German U-Boat Note to U.S. ; repara-tion offered for " damages caused by death or injuries to American citizens."

Russians took Chartorysk (Volhynia).

Allies repulsed Turkish attack at Helles.

Gen. Aylmer, marching on Kut, in touch with Turks near Sheikh Saad (Tigris).

January 8.

H.M.S. *Repulse* launched.

Struggle for Chartorysk (Volhynia).

Italian s.s. *Citta di Palermo* mined in Adriatic.

Gallipoli evacuated ; in Cape Helles zone one casualty ; 17 guns abandoned, operation completed 4 a.m. Jan. 9.

Gen. Aylmer defeated Turks near Sheikh Saad (Tigris).

* January 9.

H.M. submarine D7 left Blyth for ten days' cruise in Skagerrak.

Adm. von Pohl invalided ; Adm. Scheer Acting C.-in-C. High Sea Fleet.

German attack in Champagne repulsed.

Austrian assaults on Mt. Lovtchen (Montenegro), supported by warships.

Gen. Murray, C.-in-C. Mediterranean E.F., vice Gen. Monro.

Turkish retreat from Sheikh Saad (Tigris).

January 10.

Austrians took Mt. Lovtchen (Mon-tenegro).

Russian offensive in Caucasus.

Gen. Lake succeeded Gen. Nixon as C.-in-C. in Mesopotamia.

Gen. Aylmer halted at Sheikh Saad.

January 11.

British s.s. *Farringford* and s.s. *Cor-bridge* captured and sunk by German raider *Möwe* about 150 miles W. by N. from Cap Finisterre.

Austrians nearing Cettigne (Montenegro).

French landed at Corfu to prepare for Serbian Army ; Greek protest.

January 12.

H.M. oiler *Prudentia* sunk at Scapa in 80-mile gale ; one ammunition ship, one store-carrier, a tug and three trawlers ashore.

Allies blew up Demir Hissar bridge (Salonika Railway).

January 13.

H.M. collier *Dromonby* sunk by raider *Möwe* 220 miles W. of Lisbon. British s.s. *Author* and s.s. *Trader* captured and sunk 5 miles further West ; total : 10,700 tons.

German Naval Staff declared that if U-Boat campaign was to achieve success it must be waged ruthlessly.

Fall of Cettigne (Montenegro).

French submarine *Foucault* sank Aus-trian cruiser off Cattaro (Adriatic).

Gen. Aylmer defeated Turks at " Wadi position," near Orah (Tigris), 25 miles from Kut.

January 14.

German *Baralong* Note published ; British proposals rejected ; reprisals announced.

Turks reinforced German-led rebels at Kermanshah (Persia).

January 15, 1916.

British s.s. *Appam* (7,781 tons) captured by German raider *Möwe* off Madeira. British s.s. *Ariadne* sunk a few miles further East.

Adm. Scheer C.-in-C. High Sea Fleet ; Captain (later Rear-Adm.) von Trotha Chief of Staff.

First " Balkan Express " left Berlin.

German aeroplane raid on Dvinsk.

Russians routed Turko-German detachment at Kangavar (Persia) and took town.

Marshal von der Goltz inspected Turkish lines before Kut.

* January 16.

British s.s. *Clan Mactavish* (5,816 tons) captured and sunk by German raider *Möwe* 120 miles S. by W. from Funchal ; 17 lost.

Russian Caucasus offensive developing.

January 17.

Russians broke Caucasus line on 60-mile front, and drove Turks back on Erzrum.

Russian T.B.D. raid on Anatolian coast ; 163 vessels destroyed.

January 18.

H.M. submarine H6 wrecked at Schiermonnikoog on Dutch coast and interned.

Aeroplane raid on Dvinsk.

Kaiser and King Ferdinand at Nish.

Allied ships shelled Dedeagatch.

Germans evacuated Ebolowa—Akonolinga (Cameroons).

January 19.

War Council in London.

Russians resumed attack N.E. of Czernowitz (Bukovina).

Austro-Montenegrin negotiations broken off.

January 20.

Turkish Caucasus rout complete ; Russians took Hassan Kala.

Russians occupied Sultanabad (Persia).

January 21.

Russians shelled Deve Boyun Ridge (Erzrum).

Gen. Aylmer attacked Turks at Umm-el-Hanna, 20 miles from Kut ; relief force held up.

January 22.

British s.s. *Gemma* bombed by German aircraft off Deal ; missed.

British s.s. *Norseman* (9,542 tons) torpedoed by U-Boat in Salonika Bay ; beached.

Truce to bury dead at Umm-el-Hanna (Mesopotamia).

Gen. Townshend reported Kut could hold out 27 days.

* January 23.

British s.s. *Carlo* bombed by German aircraft in North Sea ; missed.

Aeroplane raid on Dover and E. Kent.

German gain near Neuville St. Vaast (Artois) ; French counter-attack and recovery.

Two French air squadrons bombed Metz.

Austrians occupied Skutari (Albania).

French air raid on Monastir—Gevgeli.

Gen. Wallace dispersed Senussi at Halazin, 25 miles from Mersa Matruh (W. Egypt).

January 24.

H.M. T.B.D. *Talisman* attacked by U-Boat off Blyth.

Military Service Bill passed.

German seaplane driven from Dover.

Germans bombarded Nieuport region ; infantry attack failed.

Fresh German attacks E. of Neuville (Artois).

January 25.

Germans again attacked near Neuville.

LZ77 raided Epernay.

Direct Vienna—Warsaw train service.

Austrians occupied S. Giovanni di Medua.

Gen. Townshend at Kut discovered hidden native stores ; able to hold out 84 days.

January 26.

Five British monitors bombarded German positions near Westende. Rear-Adm. de Marliave, commanding French Channel forces flew his flag in H.M. monitor *Lord Clive*.

British 1st Light Cruiser Squadron and 2nd Battle Cruiser Squadron, with T.B.D.s, left Rosyth for operations in Skagerrak.

Blockade Debate in Commons.

First Tank, " Mother," completed.

Germans driven back near Neuville.

Russians stormed Kangabazar (Erzrum).

Gen. Lake joined Gen. Aylmer at Umm-el-Hanna (Tigris).

January 27.

German attack N.W. of Loos repulsed.

" Spartakus " letters first circulated in Germany. Liebknecht presumed author.

Russian advance on Erzrum—Mush.

Floods at Kut.

January 28.

Clear channel swept from Cape Wrath to Scapa.

Germans failed against British at Carnoy (N. of Somme R.).

French lost Frise, but held Dompierre (S. of Somme).

Allies occupied Kara Burun (Salonika).

January 29.

First Tank trial at Hatfield.

Germans again failed at Dompierre.

*January 30.

LZ77 raided Paris ; 29 killed, 30 injured.

January 31.

H.M. M.L. 19 destroyed by fire at Harwich.

Zeppelin raid by L11, L13, L14, L15, L16, L17, L19, L20, and L21 over Suffolk and Midlands, including Walsall, Dewsbury, Tipton, Burton-on-Trent, Ilkeston, Derby, and Loughborough ; 70 killed, 113 injured.

Attempted raid on Paris ; airships turned back at Compiègne.

LZ85 raided Salonika.

February 1.

British s.s. *Appam* brought into Norfolk (Virginia) by German prize crew.

British s.s. *Franz Fischer* bombed and sunk by Zeppelin two miles S. from Kentish Knock ; 13, including master, killed.

British s.s. *Belle of France* (3,876 tons) sunk by U-Boat N.W. from Alexandria ; 19 lost.

M. Stuermer succeeded M. Goremykin as Russian Premier.

Sundays marked with Asterisk (*).

February 2, 1916.

Harwich 5th Light Cruiser Squadron at sea to intercept Zeppelins on return from E. coast.

Trawler *King Stephen* reported Zeppelin L19 wrecked North Sea.

Russian Bukovina offensive renewed.

February 3.

Russian progress on Dniester.

February 4.

LZ86 raided Dvinsk.

Cameroons refugees in Rio Muni.

February 5.

H.M.S. *Courageous* launched.

H.M. submarine D8 left Blyth for week's cruise off Norwegian coast.

＊February 6.

British s.s. *Flamenco* captured and sunk by German raider *Möwe* 310 miles N.E. by N. from Pernambuco.

British cruiser and French T.B.D. covering Serbian retreat engaged four Austrian T.B.D.s in Adriatic.

Turks defeated near Hamadan (Persia).

February 7.

Allies shelled Lille.

Fierce bombardment in Arras sector.

Gen. Brooking's force attacked by Arabs on Shatt-el-Hai (Mesopotamia).

February 8.

British s.s. *Westburn* captured by *Möwe* 530 miles N.N.E. from Pernambuco.

Germany notified neutrals that, after February 29, " enemy merchantmen carrying guns " would be treated by German naval forces as belligerents.

King George inspected Tank at Hatfield.

Germans entered French trenches W. of La Folie (Artois).

French cruiser *Amiral Charnier* sunk by U-Boat off Syria ; 1 survivor.

February 9.

British s.s. *Horace* captured and sunk by *Möwe* 610 miles N.N.E. from Pernambuco.

German seaplane raid on Margate and Broadstairs.

Russians crossed to W. bank of Dniester.

Gen. Brooking routed Arabs near Butani-yeh (Mesopotamia).

Gen. Smuts to command in E. Africa vice Gen. Smith-Dorrien.

German s.s. *Hedwig von Wissmann* sunk by British on Lake Tanganyika.

February 10.

Military Service Act operative.

Army Council thanked Mr. d'Eyncourt's Committee for evolving the Tank.

H.M. sloop *Arabis* sunk by German T.B.D. off Dogger Bank while operating with 10th Sloop Flotilla from the Humber, under Rear-Admiral of E. coast.

Battle Cruiser Fleet left Rosyth at night for the southward.

Harwich Force also put to sea ; and, later, Grand Fleet put out from Scapa.

Germany announced that from March 1 all armed merchantmen would be treated as belligerents.

Germany offered compensation for U.S. *Lusitania* victims.

February 11.

240,000 Canadians enlisted.

H.M.S. *Arethusa* mined in North Sea.

French recovery at Frise (Somme).

French success N.E. of Le Mesnil (Champagne).

Russians re-took Garbunovka (Dvinsk).

February 12.

H.M. store-carrier *Leicester* mined off Folkestone.

German Admiralty Staff Memorandum urging unrestricted U-Boat warfare.

German attacks at Pilkem, Steenstraate.

Fighting in Vimy sector.

French maintained gains at Le Mesnil (Champagne).

Russians took Kara Gobek N.E. of Erzrum.

Gen. Baratoff at Kermanshah.

British failed to reach Taveta (G.E. Africa).

＊February 13.

German attack on Soissons failed.

German success at Thaure-Somme Py.

Germans took trenches at Sept (Alsace).

Russians carried another Erzrum fort.

February 14.

British lost 600 yards of trench on the " Bluff " (S.E. of Ypres).

Further German attack on Soissons failed.

Austrian air raid on Milan.

Russians captured another Erzrum fort.

February 15.

U.S. rejected German claim to treat armed merchantmen as belligerents.

Russians captured inner Erzrum forts.

February 16.

French recovery near Tahure (Champagne).

Fall of Erzrum to Grand Duke Nicholas ; 13,000 Turks, 323 guns taken.

King's message to Kut Garrison.

Gen. Dobell reports conquest of Cameroons.

February 17.

Lusitania settlement deferred.

British s.s. *Demerara* (11,484 tons) chased by *Möwe* in N. Atlantic ; escaped.

British 3rd Cruiser Squadron with armed steamers *Dundee* and *Duke of Clarence* swept from Scapa down Norwegian coast ; two U-Boats sighted.

February 18.

H.M.S. *Malaya* joined 5th (*Queen Elizabeth*) Battle Squadron at Scapa.

Russians captured Mush and Akhlat ; 2,500 prisoners.

Russian ships destroyed bridges W. of Trebizond.

Mora, last Cameroons garrison, surrendered.

February 19.

German aeroplane bombed Kut.

Gen. Smuts at Mombasa.

＊February 20.

Four German seaplanes bombed Lowestoft and Walmer.

26 British aeroplanes raided Don behind German Flanders line.

German bombardment opened N. of Verdun.

For List of Abbreviations see page iv.

February 21, 1916.

Germans gained footing in British line in Givenchy Wood (Artois).

Battle of Verdun begun.

German attack from Brabant-sur-Meuse to Herbebois; Haumont Wood and Beaumont salient captured.

SLVII. raided Laneuveville.

LZ88 raided Châlons-s.-Marne.

LZ77 shot down at Revigny.

February 22.

H.M. submarines D7 and E30 proceeded to Skagerrak to stop iron ore trade from Narvik to Rotterdam.

British s.s. *Westburn* put into Teneriffe (Canary Is.) with German prize crew and 206 prisoners from ships sunk by raider *Möwe*.

German aeroplane raid on Dunkirk.

British recovery in Givenchy Wood.

LZ95 raided Vitry-le-François.

German progress at Verdun. French evacuated Haumont village, retook part of Beaumont salient; Bois de Caures evacuated.

Tsar reopened Duma in Petrograd.

February 23.

S.S. *Westburn* scuttled at Teneriffe.

Portuguese seized 36 German ships in Tagus.

Kaiser visited Wilhelmshaven.

Adm. von Pohl died in Berlin.

LZ87 raided Epinal.

At Verdun French evacuated Brabant, lost Beaumont, and withdrew from Samogneux—Ornes—Herbebois.

White Star s.s. *Olympic* (46,359 tons), missed by U-Boat torpedo in Mediterranean.

February 24.

French 1st and 20th Corps reinforced the line at Verdun.

French from E. of Champneuville to S. of Ornes before Verdun. Germans on Hill 344; lull in attack; Germans claimed 10,000 prisoners.

Russians, under Gen. Baratoff, captured Bidesurkh—Sakhne Passes (Persia); Turks retreat on Kermanshah.

February 25.

British s.s. *Saxon Prince* captured and sunk by *Möwe* 620 miles W. from Fastnet.

Gen. Pétain in command at Verdun.

Costly German attacks on Douaumont Plateau by 5th (Brandenburg) Division, repulsed from Douaumont village, but a few Germans reached old fort.

Germans captured Hill 344.

Russians beyond Erzrum took Ashkhala.

February 26.

Grand Fleet left Scapa for two days watching and exercise cruise in northern part of North Sea.

At Verdun struggle for Douaumont; Germans forced back from fort.

French air raid on Metz-Sablons.

French auxiliary *Provence II.* sunk by U-Boat in Mediterranean; nearly 1,000 lives lost.

Senussi defeated by S. Africans (Gen. Lukin) near Agagia (W. Egypt).

Russians captured Kermanshah (Persia).

*February 27.

Battle Cruiser Fleet joined Grand Fleet in North Sea; deployment practised.

P. & O. s.s. *Maloja* (12,431 tons) mined off Dover; 122 lives lost.

*February 27 (continued).

German attack N. of Ypres—Comines Canal repulsed.

German attack in Champagne.

French recovery at Fort Douaumont.

Germans reported capture of Champneuville and 15,000 prisoners; German attempts on Douaumont village, and Hill 255 repulsed.

Austrians captured Durazzo (Albania).

February 28.

German 1st Air Battle Squad. raided Verdun.

Douaumont fight continued; Germans took and lost village.

French E. of Verdun withdrew to Meuse Heights. German gain at Manheulles, S.E. of Verdun.

White Star s.s. *Olympic* (46,359 tons), missed by U-Boat torpedo in Mediterranean.

British s.s. *Masunda* shelled and sunk by U-Boat 106 miles S.W. from Cape Matapan.

British re-occupied Barani (W. Egypt).

February 29.

Trading with Enemy (Neutral Countries) Proclamation 1916.

Seaplane raided Broadstairs—Margate; fell into sea on return; picked up by French.

H.M. A.M.C. *Alcantara* fought German raider *Greif* in North Sea; *Greif* sunk by gunfire; *Alcantara* torpedoed. H.M.S. *Munster* rescued latter's crew; 209 survivors of former's complement of 306 picked up by H.M.S. *Comus* and A.M.C. *Andes*.

Chancellor von Bethmann-Hollweg, in a Memorandum to the Kaiser, expressed serious misgivings regarding danger of U.S. intervention, in event of German resort to unrestricted U-Boat warfare.

Germans entrenched on Poivre ridge, N. of Verdun; lull.

March 1.

Russian Press representatives visited Grand Fleet at Scapa.

Home Volunteer Force recognised.

M. Poincaré visited Verdun front.

H.M. sloop *Primula* sunk in E. Mediterranean by U35.

H.M. collier *Kilbride* sunk by U-Boat, 30 miles E. from Galita Is., Tunis.

Bulgarian raid at Matchukovo (Greece).

Russians N.E. of Bitlis (Caucasus).

March 2.

H.M.S. *Valiant* joined 5th (*Queen Elizabeth*) Battle Squadron at Scapa.

British steel helmets a success.

British recovered "International Trench," S.E. of Ypres.

Fight at Hohenzollern Redoubt (Loos).

German 1st Air Battle Squad. raided Verdun.

German guns active N. of Verdun: street fighting in Douaumont village; attack on Vaux repulsed.

Russians in Bitlis (Caucasus).

March 3.

French recovery at Douaumont (Verdun).

March 4.

H.M.S. *Renown* launched.

German raider *Möwe* at Kiel.

Douaumont (Verdun) bombarded; Germans failed E. of Poivre ridge.

Russians landed at Atina, 60 miles from Trebizond.

Sundays marked with Asterisk (*).

*March 5, 1916.

H.M. submarine D7 proceeded to Kattegat to intercept trade.

British 3rd Battle Squadron left Rosyth for cruise in centre of North Sea.

L11, L13, and L14 raided Hull, E. Riding, Lincoln, Leicester, Rutland, and Kent : 18 killed, 52 injured.

German 1st Air Battle Squad. raided Verdun.

Russians occupied Maprava, towards Trebizond.

British offensive in Kilimanjaro region.

March 6.

Grand Fleet on southerly sweep in North Sea.

Kaiser and Chancellor decided to postpone unrestricted U-Boat warfare, which Gen. von Falkenhayn and Adm. von Tirpitz advocated.

German attack to N.W. of Verdun ; Forges—Regnéville—Hill 265 carried.

LZ90 raided Bar-le-Duc.

March 7.

H.M. submarine E5 lost in North Sea.

Kaiser and Naval Staff decided that, for military reasons, the inauguration of unrestricted U-Boat warfare against England on April 1 was indispensable.

Germans captured Fresnes, S.E. of Verdun ; French recovery S. of Forges ; Germans repulsed near Douaumont.

Z XII. raided Stolpce.

Russians at Rizeh, nearing Trebizond.

Gen. Smuts advanced towards Kilimanjaro area (E. Africa).

March 8.

Adm. von Tirpitz, not having been invited to attend council of March 6 on U-Boat war, reported sick and was ordered by Kaiser to resign.

Germans failed at Vaux (Verdun).

Gen. Aylmer attacked Es Sinn position, 7 miles from Kut ; failed to take Dujailah Redoubt ; fell back.

March 9.

H.M. armed steamer *Fauvette* mined off E. Coast.

British s.s. *Harmatris* (6,387 tons) torpedoed by U-Boat quarter of a mile N.E. of Boulogne Breakwater.

Fresh German repulse at Vaux (Verdun).

Germany broke with Portugal.

Russian T.B.D. sunk by U-Boat off Varna.

Gen. Van Deventer occupied Taveta—Salaita (E. Africa).

March 10.

H.M.S. *Coquette* and T.B.D. No. 11 mined off E. Coast.

German surprise attack between Troyon—Berry-au-Bac (Aisne).

Germans recaptured Corbeaux Wood (Verdun) ; gained footing at Vaux.

German floating mines fished up at St. Mihiel (Meuse).

Germany declared war on Portugal.

Khalil Pasha, Turkish C.-in-C. in Irak and Governor of Baghdad invites Gen. Townshend to surrender.

March 11.

Battle Cruiser Fleet left Rosyth in support of light cruiser sweep off Norwegian coast.

March 11 (*continued*).

Russians occupied Karind (Persia).

Gen. Smuts defeated Germans W. of Taveta (E. Africa) ; Germans retreated towards Usambara Railway.

*March 12.

UB6 aground off Helvetsluis ; interned.

Adm. von Tirpitz tendered his resignation.

Gen. Gorringe in command Kut Relief Force, vice Gen. Aylmer.

March 13.

British occupied Moshi (E. Africa).

Gen. von Lettow's second relief ship arrived in E. Africa.

March 14.

H.M. submarine E30 proceeded to Kattegat to intercept contraband trade.

Harwich Light Cruiser Squadron at sea.

New German assault at Verdun ; attack repulsed between Béthincourt—Cumières ; gained footing on lower Mort Homme (main summit Hill 295).

Gen. Peyton reoccupied Sollum (W. Egypt).

March 15.

H.M.S. *Theseus* left Barry for Alexandrovsk (White Sea).

H.M.S. *Crescent* attacked by U-Boat S. of Hebrides.

French recovery on Mort Homme.

March 16.

British s.s. *Berwindvale* torpedoed and captured by U-Boat off Fastnet ; rescued.

Dutch Lloyd s.s. *Tubantia* (13,911 tons) (Amsterdam—Buenos Aires) sunk by U-Boat off Dutch coast.

Fresh German assaults on Mort Homme and Vaux (Verdun).

German IIIrd Army Corps withdrawn from Verdun front.

Gen. Roques, French War Minister, vice Gen. Galliéni.

Russian offensive in Lithuania.

Russians at Mamakhatun (Armenia).

Kut first line defences flooded.

March 17.

Adm. von Tirpitz's resignation accepted ; Adm. von Capelle new Secretary for Navy.

UC12 blown up by her own mines off Taranto.

LZ85 raided Salonika.

Crew of s.s. *Tara* rescued from Senussi at Bir Hakim (W. Egypt) by British Armoured Car Section under Duke of Westminster.

March 18.

All unmarried groups called up.

Dutch s.s. *Palembang* sunk by U-Boat in North Sea.

Allied airmen bombarded Zeebrugge.

French air raid on Mülhausen.

French destroyer *Renaudin* sunk by Austrian U-Boat in Adriatic.

Russian attack on Dvinsk front.

German aeroplane bombed Kut hospital.

*March 19.

H.M.S. *Hercules* completed six weeks turbine repairs at Scapa.

H.M.SS. *Calliope* and *Comus*, with four destroyers left for sweep off Norwegian coast ; *Calliope* put back to Rosyth, owing to serious fire in boiler-room.

For List of Abbreviations see page iv.

*March 19, 1916 (*continued*).

Four German seaplanes raided Deal, Dover, Margate and Ramsgate : 14 killed, 26 injured. One raider pursued and destroyed by Flight-Com. Bone.

Germans failed S. of Dvinsk.

Gen. A. Murray in command in Egypt, vice Gen. Maxwell.

Russians at Ispahan (Persia).

March 20.

Three German T.B.D.s chased back to Zeebrugge by four British T.B.D.s.

65 British, French, and Belgian aeroplanes bombed Zeebrugge—Houtlave.

Germans carried Avocourt Wood (Verdun) ; repulsed on Poivre heights.

Russian progress S. of Dvinsk.

British occupied Arusha (E. Africa).

March 21.

Germans bombarded Hill 304 (Verdun).

German Alpine Corps withdrawn from Macedonia.

German-Bulgar outposts driven in by French at Matchukovo, N. of Salonika.

Kilimanjaro area (E. Africa) conquered. Action at Kahe broken off by Gen. von Lettow. Germans blew up the *Königsberg* 6-inch gun which they had mounted against the British.

March 22.

British s.s. *Kelvinbank* (4,209 tons) torpedoed by U-Boat in Havre Roads.

German G.H.Q. ordered German military authorities at Roubaix immediately to make a levy of 2,000 workmen.

Germans gained at Haucourt (Verdun), threatened Mort Homme, but failed to reach Hill 304.

Turks bombarded Kut town.

March 23.

British raid on German trenches at Gommecourt in the new Souchez—Somme sector taken over from the French.

British s.s. *Minneapolis* (13,543 tons), torpedoed and sunk by U-Boat 195 miles E. of Malta.

P. & O. s.s. *Kaisar-i-Hind* (11,430 tons) missed by U-Boat torpedo in Mediterranean.

March 24.

S.S. *Sussex* (Folkestone—Dieppe) torpedoed with great loss of life.

H.M. submarine E24 lost in North Sea.

H.M. armed steamer *Marcella* sunk by collision in North Sea.

H.M.S. *Cleopatra*, flying broad pendant of Commodore Tyrwhitt, sailed with Harwich Force to carry out air attack on German Zeppelin base at Tondern. Adm. Beatty's Battle Cruiser Fleet left Rosyth in support.

Russians occupied Khizan, 35 miles S.E. of Bitlis (Caucasus).

March 25.

British seaplanes raided German airship sheds in Schleswig-Holstein, E. of Sylt ; three planes captured ; two convoying T.B.D.s, H.M.SS. *Medusa* and *Laverock* collided ; *Medusa* lost ; two German patrol vessels, *Otto Rudolf* and *Braunschweig*, sunk, German T.B.D. S22 mined, and G194 rammed and sunk by H.M.S. *Cleopatra* at about 10 p.m. Later, in disengaging herself, *Cleopatra* collided with H.M.S. *Undaunted*, which was damaged and towed to the Tyne for repairs.

Grand Fleet put to sea in heavy gale and now.

March 25 (*continued*).

German Governor of Lille invited local unemployed to " volunteer " for agricultural and other work outside the city.

*March 26.

British cruiser forces, supported later in the day by 5th Battle Squadron, covered return of H.M.S. *Undaunted* across North Sea to the Tyne in heavy weather.

Fighting round Hohenzollern Redoubt (Loos) ; British success.

Russian offensive in Lithuania continued.

March 27.

British Fleets returned to port.

H.M. T.B.D. *Michael* damaged by collision with another T.B.D. off Noss Head.

Allied War Council in Paris.

British success at St. Eloi (Ypres) ; first and second line trenches on 600-yard front captured.

Italian centre forced back N.W. of Gorizia.

Russians 30 miles from Trebizond.

March 28.

H.M. collier *Rio Tiete* sunk by U-Boat W. of Ushant.

Conservatives in Reichstag moved immediate inauguration of unrestricted U-Boat warfare. Adm. von Capelle pointed out that not enough U-Boats were available.

Fighting at St. Eloi continued.

Germans repulsed at Haucourt-Malancourt (Verdun).

Italian recovery at Gorizia.

March 29.

Grand Fleet put to sea for battle exercises.

At Verdun French regained S.E. horn of Avocourt Wood and Avocourt redoubt ; German counter repulsed. Germans reached Malancourt.

Gen. Shuvaieff Russian War Minister, vice Gen. Polivanoff.

LZ86 raided Minsk.

March 30.

LZ81 and LZ88 over East Coast.

Fresh attacks on Fort Douaumont (Verdun) repulsed ; German pressure on Malancourt.

More German floating mines in Meuse at St. Mihiel.

March 31.

169,066 Australians embarked to date.

Five Zeppelins (including LZ87, LZ90, and LZ93) dropped 90 bombs in Lincoln, Essex, and Suffolk : 48 killed, 64 injured. One Zeppelin attacked at 9,000 ft. and bombed by Lieut. Brandon, R.F.C. ; another, L15, hit by gunfire, fell into sea off Kentish Knock ; crew of 17 captured.

H.M. oiler *Goldmouth* and s.s. *Achilles* (7,043 tons) sunk by U-Boat off Ushant.

French evacuate Malancourt (Verdun). Germans repulsed at Mort Homme, but gain footing in Vaux.

French Army motor-car service on Bar-le-Duc—Verdun road during March reached 6,000 lorries a day ; up to 90,000 men and 50,000 tons stores transported per week.

Franco-Russian H.S. *Portugal* announced torpedoed in Black Sea.

During March UB13 was lost from some unknown cause.

Sundays marked with Asterisk (*).

F

April 1, 1916.

L11 and L17 from Nordholz raided Durham and North Riding : 22 killed, 130 injured.

British s.s. *Ashburton* sunk by U-Boat off Ushant.

Germans repulsed between Douaumont—Vaux (Verdun).

＊April 2.

Six Zeppelins (including LZ88 and LZ90) raided London (sixth raid), E. Suffolk, Northumberland, and Scotland ; bombs on Edinburgh and Leith : 13 killed, 24 injured.

British 2nd Light Cruiser Squadron at sea to intercept returning Zeppelin raiders.

LZ93 raided Dunkirk.

German gain in Caillette Wood, between Douaumont—Vaux (Verdun).

German G.H.Q. advised the German Second, Third, Fifth, Sixth, and Seventh Army Commands of impending orders for organising slave labour in occupied districts, from which a first intalment of 50,000 workers was to be raised.

LZ86 raided Minsk.

British s.s. *Simla* (5,884 tons) sunk by U-Boat N.W. of Gozo.

British s.s. *Megantic* (14,878 tons) warded off U-Boat by gunfire in Mediterranean.

April 3.

H.M.S. *Devonshire* and two T.B.D.s in sweep from Rosyth to Norwegian coast intercepted one Swedish steamer.

British success at St. Eloi (Ypres).

Germans driven from N. edge of Caillette Wood and W. part of Vaux (Verdun).

H.M. collier *Sneaton* sunk by U-Boat N.N.E. from Cap de Garde, Tunis.

April 4.

L11 with L17 over Norfolk ; no damage.

German attack on French centre at Verdun failed ; French progress in Caillette Wood.

April 5.

British s.s. *Zent* (3,890 tons) sunk by U-Boat off Fastnet ; 49 lost.

Three British submarines left Blyth on an anti-U-Boat patrol of Shetlands—Heligoland line.

L11, L13, and L16 raided Durham and Yorkshire : one person killed, 9 injured.

UB26 sunk off Havre by Anglo-French Flotilla.

Germans at Verdun won Haucourt; failed against Béthincourt.

German floating mines exploded in Meuse at St. Mihiel.

British s.s. *Chantala* (4,951 tons) sunk by U-Boat off Cape Bergut ; 9 lost.

Turkish positions 20 miles from Kut taken by Gen. Gorringe ; Turks retired to Falahiyah—Sanna-i-Yat positions; Falahiyah carried.

April 6.

H.M.S. *Roxburgh* and two T.B.D.s swept down Norwegian coast.

Germans won crater at St. Eloi.

Germans penetrated at Hill 304 (Verdun).

Kut Relief Force held up at Sanna-i-Yat.

British s.s. *Yonne* (4,039 tons) sunk by U-Boat off Shershel, Algeria.

British took Lol Kissale (E. Africa).

April 7.

British s.s. *Braunton* (4,575 tons) sunk by U-Boat off Beachy Head.

Germans repulsed at Hill 304 (Verdun).

April 8.

French evacuated Béthincourt salien (Verdun).

H.M. collier *Zafra* (3,578 tons) sunk b; U-Boat N. from Oran.

＊April 9.

British s.s. *Eastern City* and s.s. *Glenal mond* sunk by U-Boat off Ushant.

Great German assault at Verdun ; ad vanced Mort Homme trench entered.

Gen. Pétain's famous Order of the Da; to Verdun Army : " *Courage, on les aura !* "

Second British attack failed at Sanna-i Yat

April 10.

British s.s. *Margam Abbey* (4,471 tons sunk by U-Boat S.W. from Lizard.

British s.s. *Silksworth Hall* (4,777 tons sunk by U-Boat off Corton Light ; 3 lost.

British s.s. *Robert Adamson* (2,978 tons sunk by U-Boat off Shipwash Light.

British retook crater at St. Eloi.

German Alpine Corps from Macedonia reinforced in Champagne.

German gain on Mort Homme (Verdun)

Portuguese occupied Kionga (E. Africa)

April 11.

Count Bernstorff, having advised Berlir that President Wilson deplored *Sussex* inci dent, which was calculated to impede his pro posed peace action, Herr von Jagow replied that Germany was at one with U.S. in hoping for return of peace.

German Sixth Army H.Q. transmitted tc Lille commandant orders for forcible levy of workers.

British repelled attack at La Boisselle (Albert).

Germans repulsed between Douaumont—Vaux (Verdun).

Italian success on Adamello Range (Tren tino).

British s.s. *Angus* (3,619 tons) sunk by U-Boat off Valencia.

April 12.

H.M. seaplane carrier *Campania* returned to Scapa from Liverpool fitted with " flying off " deck and experimental kite-balloon.

German attack on British trenches or Ypres—Pilkem road.

Germans repulsed on left bank of Meuse.

British s.s. *Orlock Head* sunk by U-Boat off Barcelona.

British advance on S. bank of Tigris opposite Sanna-i-Yat.

Gen. Van Deventer occupied Umbugwe (Köthersheim, E. Africa).

April 13.

British s.s. *Chic* (3,037 tons) sunk by U-Boat off Fastnet ; 9 lost.

Australian reconnaissance in Sinai.

British occupied Ufiome (E. Africa).

April 14.

Sir Roger Casement left Wilhelmshaven in U-Boat for Ireland.

British s.s. *Shenandoah* (3,886 tons) mined off Folkestone Gate.

British air-raid on Constantinople—Adrianople by three naval aeroplanes under Squad.-Comm. J. R. W. Smyth-Pigott.

April 15.

309,000 Canadians enlisted to date.

British s.s. *Fairport* (3,838 tons) sunk by U-Boat off Bishop Rock.

April 15, 1916 (*continued*).

French at Douaumont (Verdun) occupied trenches ; 200 prisoners.

Gen. von Falkenhausen appointed first commander of German Coast Defence forces.

British food aeroplanes reached Kut.

*April 16.

British s.s. *Harrovian* (4,309 tons) sunk by U-Boat off Bishop Rock.

British s.v. *Cardonia* (2,169 tons) sunk by U-Boat off Fastnet.

British raid S. of Béthune—La Bassée road.

Russians landed at Platana, W. of Trebizond.

Further fighting on Tigris.

April 17.

Germans repulsed between Meuse—Douaumont (Verdun).

Prussian Guard Reserve Corps reconstituted on E. front.

Fall of Trebizond to Grand Duke Nicholas.

British carried Beit Aiessa position near Kut ; Turkish counter-attack.

Fighting at Kondoa Irangi (E. Africa).

April 18.

U.S. *Sussex* Note to Germany.

Bulgarians raided Greek frontier.

April 19.

Mr. Wilson in Congress on U-Boat policy.

German gains at St. Eloi and on Ypres—Langemarck road.

German attacks at Les Eparges (Woevre).

Death of Marshal von der Goltz in Mesopotamia.

British occupied Kondoa Irangi (E. Africa)

April 20.

H.M.S. *Glorious* launched.

German auxiliary *Aud* and U-Boat with Sir Roger Casement arrived at night off Kerry and landed arms and munitions at Tralee.

British s.s. *Sabbia* (2,802 tons) mined and sunk off May Island.

British s.s. *Cairngowan* (4,017 tons) sunk by U-Boat off Fastnet.

British s.s. *Whitgift* (4,397 tons) sunk by U-Boat off Ushant ; 32 lost.

Germans repulsed at Les Eparges.

First Russian contingent for W. Front (8,000 men) at Marseilles.

April 21.

Sir Roger Casement landed from U-Boat on Tralee shore ; captured ; German auxiliary *Aud* scuttled.

British s.s. *Feliciana* (4,283 tons) sunk by U-Boat off Fastnet.

Grand Fleet put to sea and move to vicinity of Horn Reef, in order to detain High Sea Fleet in North Sea, while Russian Baltic minefields were being relaid.

British recaptured ground on Ypres—Langemarck road lost on 19th.

French airman from Salonika bombed Sofia.

April 22.

Grand Fleet's sweep interrupted by thick fog off Little Fisher Bank. During evening H.M.SS. *Australia* and *New Zealand* were damaged by collision and sent back to their bases ; later three T.B.D.s also damaged

April 22 (*continued*).

by collision ; during night H.M.S. *Neptune* considerably damaged by collision with neutral steamer.

By order of German Commandant of Lille, 64th Reserve Infantry Regiment began at 5 a.m. forcible impressment of workers for deportation in daily batches of 1,400—men and women in equal numbers.

*April 23.

Irish " Republic " proclaimed in Dublin by Countess Markievicz.

UC3 destroyed by mined nets in southern North Sea.

British s.s. *Parisiana* and s.s. *Ribston* sunk by U-Boat off Ushant (7,800 tons).

French progress at Caurettes Wood (Verdun).

Turco-German attack at Duweidar (Sinai) repulsed ; British at Katiyeh withdrew.

Third British attack on Sanna-i-Yat.

April 24.

Dublin Rebellion ; armed Sinn Feiners occupied Stephen's Green ; seized Post Office, City Hall, etc.

Grand Fleet returned to base during day, fuelled, and during evening put to sea for another southward sweep.

Three Zeppelins raided Norfolk, Lincoln, Cambridge, and Suffolk.

German aeroplane driven off at Dover.

LZ93 raided Gravelines.

UB3 destroyed by H.M. drifter *Gleaner* of the Sea with bombs 25 miles off Walcheren.

British mine-net barrage stretched along Belgian coast. H.M. monitor *General Wolfe*, while supporting this operation, was straddled by Tirpitz (Ostend) Battery with four salvoes at 32,000 yards range.

Allied ships bombarded Zeebrugge.

H.M. T.B.D. *Melpomene* hit by shell from one of German Zeebrugge shore batteries at 16,000 yards range.

High Sea Fleet, with eight airships put out at 10 a.m. to support cruiser raid on East Anglian coast. H.I.M.S. *Seydlitz* mined at 2 p.m. ; returned to port.

Relief ship *Julnar* failed to reach Kut.

April 25.

Martial law in Dublin ; garrison, reinforced from Belfast and England, drove rebels from City Hall.

LZ87, LZ88, LZ93, LZ97 and six naval airships raided London (7th raid), E. Suffolk, Essex, and Kent.

German battle-cruiser squadron off Lowestoft for about half an hour, engaged by local naval forces : 25 casualties.

Adm. Jellicoe informed by Admiralty at 4.20 a.m. that German ships were shelling Lowestoft proceeded southward at full speed ; Adm. Beatty, with Battle Cruiser Fleet, well to S.E. in direction of Terschelling, just missed cutting off Germans from their base.

H.M. trawler *King Stephen* sunk by German T.B.D. G41 in North Sea.

H.M. submarine E22 sunk by UB18 in North Sea.

U-Boats ordered to resume operations according to Prize Law.

LZ81 raided Etaples.

April 26.

Dublin Rebellion in hand ; Liberty Hall destroyed by gunfire from H.M.S. *Helga* and occupied by military ; cordon of troops round centre of city.

Sundays marked with Asterisk (*).

April 26, 1916 (continued).

LZ87 raided Margate.

LZ93 raided French Channel ports.

SL VII. raided Dünamünde.

German aeroplane raid on Dvinsk.

Anzacs reoccupied Katiyeh (Sinai).

Gen. Townshend and Khalil Pasha met on Tigris to discuss eventual surrender of Kut.

April 27.

Martial law in Ireland.

Fire in Sackville Street, Dublin.

German gas attack S. of Hulluch.

UC5 captured off Essex coast by H.M.S. *Firedrake.* This submarine was later moored in the Thames and shown to the public.

H.M.S. *Russell* (14,000 tons) mined off Malta.

H.M. sloop *Nasturtium* mined in Mediterranean.

LZ86 raided Rieshiza.

April 28.

British trench-raid near Double Crassier (Loos).

German attack at Dvinsk.

LZ86 raided Dvinsk railways.

SL VII. raided Wenden (Livonia).

British auxiliary yacht *Ægusa* sunk off Malta.

April 29.

Irish Rebellion broken; three leaders—Pearse, Connolly, and MacDonagh surrendered.

British 3rd Battle Squadron left Scapa to be based on Sheerness, as additional guard against coast raids.

British s.s. *Teal* sunk by U-Boat two miles E. from Seaham Harbour.

Crown Prince of Bavaria, commander Sixth Army, in special order thanked press-gangs for successful work at Lille, Roubaix, and Tourcoing (22-iv.-16).

Further gas attacks N. of Loos defeated.

French gain N. of Mort Homme and Cumières (Verdun).

Italian success on Adamello (Trentino).

British s.s. *City of Lucknow* (3,677 tons) torpedoed by U-Boat 60 miles E. from Malta.

Russian reverse S. of Dvinsk.

Fall of Kut announced after 143 days' siege; Gen. Townshend's force (2,970 British, 6,000 Indians) surrendered.

✳ April 30.

End of Dublin Rebellion; De Valera surrendered.

During April U 10 was mined off Zeebrugge.

German attack from Messines Ridge smashed by artillery.

May 1.

Surrenders at Cork, etc. Lord French reported Dublin quiet.

Belgian Coast Patrol instituted (10-x.-16).

Germans repulsed E. of Ypres and N. of Albert.

Gen. Nivelle in command at Verdun, vice Gen. Pétain to command French centre Army Group.

French took trenches S.E. of Douaumont Fort (Verdun).

Karl Liebknecht arrested in Berlin for attempting to induce soldiers at Potsdam Railway Station not to return to the front.

May 2.

Grand Fleet left its bases to cover air operation off Horn Reef and detain High Sea Fleet in North Sea.

May 2 (continued).

Five Zeppelins (including L20 and LZ98) raided Yorkshire, Northumberland, and Scotland; about 100 bombs dropped: 9 killed 30 injured.

French troops occupied Florina, S. of Monastir.

May 3.

Mr. Birrell resigned; three Irish rebel leaders shot.

New Military Service Bill; compulsory principle for married men.

Nine British submarines in position of Horn Reef, Vyl Light, and Terschelling H.M. minelayers *Abdiel* and *Princess Margaret* laid mines S. of Vyl Light and N. of West Frisian Is.

Aeroplane raid on Deal; 4 injured.

L20 wrecked off Stavanger, Norway.

French push at Verdun; positions N.W of Mort Homme taken.

Z XII. raided Luninetz.

LZ86 raided Minsk railways.

May 4.

Fourth phase of U-Boat war: Germany in reply to U.S. *Sussex* Note, undertook that U-Boats should observe rules of cruiser warfare, in expectation that U.S. would secure mitigation of British blockade.

Four more Irish rebels shot.

British 1st Light Cruiser Squadron from Rosyth, with 16 T.B.D.s convoying seaplane carriers *Vindex* and *Engadine* arrived at dawn N. of Horn Reef for attack on Tondern Zeppelin base; only one seaplane reached objective; others damaged by sea. Battle Cruiser Fleet and Grand Fleet in support.

Zeppelin L7 shot down by H.M.SS *Galatea* and *Phaeton* off Schleswig, and sunk by H.M. submarine E31.

French submarine *Bernouille* sank Austrian T.B.D. in Adriatic.

LZ85 destroyed by Allied Fleet over Salonika Harbour.

Italians landed at Mersa Moresa (Cyrenaica).

May 5.

" Major " John McBride, Irish rebel shot.

German gain at Hill 304 (Verdun).

May 6.

Countess Markievicz condemned to death by court-martial for her part in Irish Rebellion; sentence commuted to penal servitude for life.

Germans bombarded Hill 304 (Verdun)

Belgians occupied Kigali, Ruanda, S.W of Victoria Nyanza.

✳ May 7.

Belgian Coast Barrage completed.

Violent German attacks at Hill 304 and Fort Douaumont (Verdun).

May 8.

U.S. reply to German Note.

Four more Irish rebels shot.

White Star s.s. *Cymric* (13,370 tons torpedoed by U-Boat 140 miles W.N.W. from Fastnet; 5 lost.

Anzacs in France.

Further German attacks on Hill 304 (Verdun) repulsed.

Turkish air raid on Port Said.

German rally in E. Africa; Belgian advance into Ruanda; Germans attacked Nhika (P.E. Africa).

May 9, 1916.

Russians reached Kasr-i-Shirin, 110 miles from Baghdad.

May 10.

British 4th Light Cruiser Squadron during sweep off Norwegian coast intercepted one neutral steamer with iron ore for Lübeck.

German assault on French lines defending Hill 287 (Verdun) ; French counter-attack at Mort Homme.

Germans repulsed at Kondoa Irangi (E. Africa).

May 11.

Mr. Asquith proceeded to Dublin.

De Valera sentenced to death ; sentence commuted to penal servitude for life.

Germans carried 500 yards of British trenches N.E. of Vermelles ; part regained.

German attack W. of Vaux pond.

British occupied Umbulu (E. Africa).

May 12.

Two more Irish rebels shot.

Attacks on French centre at Verdun.

Gen. Townshend left Baghdad for Constantinople.

Belgians reported in Kigali (G.E. Africa).

Further German attack on Nhika (P.E. Africa) repulsed.

May 13.

British attacked at Ploegsteert Wood (Ypres) ; Germans driven back.

German attacks repulsed W. of Hill 304, and N.E. of Mort Homme (Verdun).

British s.s. *Eretria* (3,464 tons) mined 15 miles S.S.W. from Ile D'Yeu, Bay of Biscay.

H.M. monitor M30 sunk in action off Smyrna.

Turks at Ashkala, W. of Erzrum forced back Russian centre.

*May 14.

German attacks at Hohenzollern Redoubt—Hulluch (Loos).

Austrian bombardment in Trentino.

Russians on Persian border at Revanduz, on road to Mosul.

May 15.

Sir Roger Casement charged with high treason at Bow-street.

British exploded mines and occupied 250 yards of trench on Vimy Ridge.

Austrian assault in Trentino ; Italian centre retired.

British force (Col. Kelly) advanced on El Fasher, capital of Sultan of Darfur.

May 16.

British T.B.D.s and monitors engaged German T.B.D.s off Belgian coast ; Germans withdrew.

Austrian gains in Trentino, at Rovereto, and on Folgaria Plateau ; attempt to storm Zugna Torta, S. of Rovereto.

H.M. Fleet Messenger *Clifford* sunk by U-Boat off Crete.

Anzacs stormed Turkish camp at Bayoud (Sinai).

Russians at Mamakhatun, W. of Erzrum.

May 17.

New Air Board under Lord Curzon.

Germans captured crater on Vimy Ridge.

Italian rally at Zugna Torta.

May 18.

French repulsed attack on Avocourt Wood—Hill 304 (Verdun).

Italians evacuated Zugna Torta (Trentino).

British raid on El Arish (Sinai).

H.M.ML. 40 destroyed by fire, Suez Canal.

May 19.

German seaplanes raid Kent coast ; Dover bombed. One raider brought down by British naval patrol off Belgian coast

German 1st Air Squad. raided Dunkirk. British s.s. *Seattle* (5,113 tons) bombed and damaged in dock.

Further German attack on Avocourt Wood—Hill 304 (Verdun) ; Germans took work S. of Hill 287.

Italians lost Monte Toraro—Spitz Tonezza (Trentino).

Turks evacuated Beit Aeissa (Tigris) ; Dujailar Redoubt carried by Gen. Gorringe.

May 20.

German 1st and 3rd Air Squads. raided Dunkirk. British s.s. *Lord Strathcona* (7,335 tons) bombed and damaged in dock.

Five German divisions assaulted Mort Homme (Verdun) ; summit Hill 295 taken.

Italians evacuated Armentera ridge (Trentino).

Gen. Lake reported S. bank of Tigris as far as Shatt-el-Hai free of Turks.

Gen. Baratoff's Cossacks in touch with British at Ali Gharbi (Tigris).

*May 21.

British Summer Time Act in force.

German 1st Air Squad. raided Dunkirk. Two British steamers hit ; slight damage.

Germans carried 1,500 yards of British trench at Vimy Ridge.

French took trenches between Avocourt Wood—Meuse ; repelled attacks on W. slopes of Mort Homme (Verdun).

Turkish air raid on Port Said.

May 22.

H.M. submarine E30, on patrol with H.M. submarine D7 in Kattegat, sank one German merchant steamer off the Kullen.

German 1st and 3rd Air Squads. raided Dunkirk.

French 5th Division (Gen. Mangin) at Verdun carried German trenches on 2,000 yards front Thiaumont Farm—Douaumont Fort ; and entered fort.

May 23.

Mr. Asquith moved £300,000,000 credit.

H.M. minelayer *Biarritz* laid first of a series of anti-U-Boat minefields in Moray Firth.

U-Boats in position off E. Coast in support of forthcoming sortie by High Sea Fleet. U43 and U44 off Scapa ; U66 E. of Orkneys ; U47 off Kinnaird Head ; U24, U32, U51, U52, U63, and U70 off Firth of Forth ; UB22 off Flamborough Head ; UB21 off the Humber ; U67 N. of Terschelling.

German counter at Thiaumont—Douaumont (Verdun) repulsed. Germans gained Cumières.

Italians fell back between Astico—Brenta R. (Trentino).

British occupied El Fasher, Darfur (Sudan).

May 24, 1916.
New Military Service Bill passed.
H.M. submarine E18 lost in the Baltic.
Great battle at Verdun; two armies engaged on whole front; Germans again took Douaumont ruins; French regained part of Cumières.
Italians in Trentino on S. Posina Ridge and E. of Val d'Assa on Sette Communi Plateau.
British occupied Lembeni (G.E. Africa).

May 25.
New Military Service Act in force.
King George's Message to Nation announced that voluntary system yielded 5,041,000 men; Derby scheme 2,829,263, including 1,150,000 single men.
Great German attack at Verdun between Haudromont Wood—Thiaumont Farm.
Strong Austrian pressure in Trentino.
Gen. Smuts occupied Same, on Usambara Railway.

May 26.
U.S. Note on Allied searching of neutral mails.
British s.s. El Argentino (6,809 tons) and s.s. Denewood mined off Southwold and Aldeburgh.
French at Verdun recovered between Haudromont Wood—Thiaumont Farm. German attack between Avocourt Wood—Mort Homme repulsed.
Italians driven from heights E. of Val d'Assa (Trentino).
Bulgaro-Germans occupied Fort Rupel on Greek frontier; Kavala threatened; excitement in Greece.

May 27.
U74 sunk by H.M. trawlers Searanger, Oku, and Rodino by gunfire off Aberdeenshire coast.
Death of Gen. Galliéni.
French gain S.W. of Mort Homme.
Austrians on Sette Communi Plateau.
H.M. collier Trunkby sunk by U-Boat 50 miles S. by E. from Port Mahon, Minorca.

✶May 28.
German Alpine Corps from Champagne on Verdun front.
Austrian offensive continued, especially N. of Asiago.
Italian T.B.D. sank Austrian transport at Trieste.
British s.s. Lady Ninian (4,297 tons) sunk by U-Boat off Algiers.

May 29.
German attacks on Hill 304 (Verdun) repulsed; N.W. of Cumières Germans gained some trenches.
Italians evacuated Asiago and Arsiero.
British s.s. Elmgrove, s.s. Southgarth, and s.s. Baron Vernon sunk by U-Boat off Algiers.

May 30.
H.M. fleetsweeper Gentian attacked and missed by U-Boat 40 miles E. of Pentland Firth.
Grand Fleet put out for one of its periodical sweeps in North Sea. Battle Cruiser Fleet and 5th Battle Squadron proceeded to appointed position in advance of main force.
French at Verdun abandoned Béthincourt—Cumières road between Mort Homme—Cumières; evacuated Caurettes Wood; with-

May 30 (continued).
drew towards Chattancourt; drove Germans back to Cumières.
Violent Austrian assaults in Trentino.
British s.s. Dale Garth, s.s. Julia Park, and s.s. Baron Tweedmouth sunk by U-Boat off Algeria; three days total: over 20,000 tons.
Turks recovered Mamakhatun (Armenia).
German trenches at Pangani (G.E. Africa) carried by Gen. Smuts; Germans retired to Mkomazi. Gen. Northey announced to be at Neu Langenburg.

May 31.
The Battle of Jutland.
Battle Cruiser Fleet (1st and 2nd Squadrons)—H.M.SS. Lion (F.F. Adm. Beatty), Princess Royal (F. Adm. Brock), Tiger, Queen Mary, New Zealand (F. Adm. Pakenham) and Indefatigable—supported by 5th Battle Squadron—H.M.SS. Barham (F. Adm. Evan-Thomas), Warspite, Valiant and Malaya—in advance of Main Battle Fleet, by 2 p.m. in Lat. 56°47' N., Long. 4°40' E., in North Sea.
2.00 p.m.—Adm. Beatty turned N.E. to meet Adm. Jellicoe at appointed position, Lat. 57°45' N., Long. 4°15' E.
2.20 p.m.—British light forces ahead of Battle Cruiser Fleet sighted German ships to E.S.E. Adm. Beatty turned S.S.E., course for Horn Reef, to intercept.
2.35 p.m.—Adm. Beatty altered to E. and N.E., towards heavy smoke visible E.N.E. Seaplane carrier Engadine sent up seaplane scout; first such reconnaissance in action.
3.31 p.m.—Adm. Beatty sighted German Battle Cruiser Squadron — H.I.M.SS. Lützow (F. Adm. Hipper), Derfflinger, Seydlitz, Moltke, and Von der Tann—steering E.N.E.
Battle Cruiser Fleet, on line of bearing, closed German Squadron from 23,000 yards on E.S.E. course at 25 knots; 5th Battle Squadron, 10,000 yards astern, conformed.

BATTLE CRUISER ACTION.
3.48 p.m.—Both battle cruiser forces opened fire almost simultaneously at about 18,500 yards. Action on E.S.E. to S.S.E. course.
4.00 p.m.—Range about 16,000 yards.
4.06 p.m.—Indefatigable hit by salvo from Von der Tann; magazine exploded; ship sunk by another salvo.
4.08 p.m.—British 5th Battle Squadron in action at 19,000—20,000 yards; German Light Cruiser Squadron driven off to eastward.
4.15 p.m.—Destroyer action; two German T.B.D.s sunk; Nestor and Nomad disabled; sunk later by German Battle Fleet.
4.26 p.m.—Queen Mary hit by salvo from Derfflinger; magazine exploded; ship sunk.
4.42 p.m.—Adm. Beatty (now in Lat. 56°33½' N., Long. 5°49' E.), sighted German High Sea Fleet, under Adm. Scheer (F.F. Friedrich der Grosse), led by 3rd (König) Squadron, steering northwards.
British ships in succession turned 16 points to starboard; German battle cruisers followed suit, taking station ahead by High Sea Fleet.
At time of this turn to northward Adm. Beatty and Adm. Jellicoe with Main Battle Fleet were over 50 miles apart and closing at about 45 miles per hour.

May 31, 1916 (*continued*).

4.45 p.m. Battle cruiser action renewed on northerly course, with *Barham* and *Valiant* supporting Battle Cruiser Fleet ; *Warspite* and *Malaya* engaged at 19,000 yards German 1st and 3rd High Sea Squadrons.

5.00 p.m.—British Battle Cruiser Fleet outdistancing German ships on northerly run.

5.20 p.m.—German battle cruisers ordered "to give chase."

5.35 p.m.—Adm. Beatty altered from N.N.E. to N.E. to conform to signalled course of British Main Fleet.

5.42 p.m.—British battle cruisers again in touch with German ships. *Lion* fired 15 salvoes during next 10 minutes.

6.00 p.m.—Adm. Beatty sighted Main Fleet. Adm. Jellicoe (F.F. *Iron Duke*) in Lat. 57°11′ N., Long. 5°39′ E., his main force having maintained since 4 p.m. a "fleet speed" of 20 knots, on a course S.E. by S., with Battle Fleet in divisions line ahead disposed abeam to starboard.

6.02 p.m.—Fleet speed reduced to 18 knots ; subsequently reduced to 14 knots to allow Battle Cruisers to pass ahead.

MAIN DAYLIGHT ACTION.

6.16 p.m.—Upon Adm. Beatty's report giving High Sea Fleet's position, Adm. Jellicoe signalled Battle Fleet to form line of battle on port wing column ; course S.E. by E.

At this point German battle cruisers sank *Defence* (F. Adm. Arbuthnot) and damaged *Warrior*, of Adm. Jellicoe's advanced cruiser line, which shortly after 6.5 p.m. had crossed *Lion's* bows from port to starboard in order to finish off *Wiesbaden*, one of German light cruisers under their fire. Disabled *Warrior* passed astern of 5th Battle Squadron (turning to port to form astern of 6th Division) just as *Warspite's* helm jammed ; this mishap compelled latter to continue her turn, brought her under heavy fire, but enabled *Warrior* to draw clear.

Hereabouts, the 3rd Battle Cruiser Squadron — *Invincible* (F. Adm. Hood), *Inflexible* and *Indomitable*—(detached by Adm. Jellicoe at 4 p.m. in support of Adm. Beatty), came up from the eastward, where with *Canterbury* and *Chester* it had engaged German light-cruiser screen in a sharp encounter in which T.B.D. *Shark* was sunk. Upon sighting *Lion*, Adm. Hood at 6.16 p.m. took station ahead of Battle Cruiser Fleet and engaged German battle cruisers at 8,600 yards. Soon after 6.30 p.m. *Invincible*, under repeated salvoes, notably from *Derfflinger*, blew up and sank ; but Adm. Hood's arrival in commanding position on bow of German Fleet caused latter to make large turn to starboard, his squadron being probably mistaken for British Battle Fleet.

6.31 p.m.—*Iron Duke* engaged leading ship of *König* Squadron at 12,000 yards ; on starboard wing *Marlborough* (F. Adm. Burney) had already opened fire at 6.17 p.m. on ship of *Kaiser* class at 13,000 yards.

6.33 p.m.—Fleet speed increased to 17 knots. Action now joined, but impeded by mist and smoke.

At head of German Battle Cruiser line *Lützow* hauled away badly damaged ; *Derfflinger* ceased fire.

6.38 p.m.—British deployment completed.

May 31 (*continued*).

6.45 p.m.—*Lion* once more leading Battle Cruiser Fleet at head of British battle line in following formation :

1st Div. *King George V.* (F. Adm. Jerram)
2nd Div. *Orion* .. .. (F. Adm. Leveson)
3rd Div. *Iron Duke* .. (F. Adm. Jellicoe)
4th Div. *Benbow* .. (F. Adm. Sturdee)
5th Div. *Colossus* .. (F. Adm. Gaunt)
6th Div. *Marlborough* . (F. Adm. Burney)

6.50 p.m.—British Fleet altered course to S., by divisions, to close German Fleet.

Adm. Hipper left *Lützow*, which fell out on fire and with heavy list ; not until about 9 p.m. was he able to transfer his flag to *Moltke*. Meanwhile *Derfflinger* led German battle cruisers.

6.54 p.m.—*Marlborough* torpedoed, but continued in action.

7.00 p.m.—Adm. Jellicoe ordered 2nd Battle Squadron to take station ahead of *Iron Duke ;* 1st Battle Squadron to form astern.

During next half-hour British ships held their targets under intermittent but effective fire, at ranges varying from 15,000 yards in van to 8,500 yards in rear. German Fleet turning westward.

7.05 p.m.—British line, after closing three points to starboard, turned away to avoid torpedo attack. German T.B.D. V48 sunk by gunfire.

7.15 p.m.—Adm. Scheer, drawing off his main force, ordered his already battered battle cruisers to "close the enemy."

7.25 p.m.—Another German torpedo attack successfully dealt with by British light forces.

7.33 p.m.—British Fleet back on S. by W. course.

7.37 p.m.—German battle cruisers broke off action ; *Derfflinger* on fire.

7.40 p.m.—Adm. Beatty reported German position to westward.

7.41 p.m.—German Fleet no longer in sight from *Iron Duke ;* British Battle Fleet altered course, by divisions, three points more to starboard (*i.e.* to S.W.).

7.50 p.m.—German T.B.D. S35 sunk by British 12th Flotilla.

7.59 p.m.—British Fleet altered to W., by divisions, on sighting isolated German ships, which gradually turned away.

8.25 p.m.—British Battle Cruiser Fleet in effective touch with German ships for a few minutes.

8.30 p.m.—British Fleet, after turn by divisions to S.W., again in single line.

8.38 p.m.—*Falmouth* last British ship in touch with German Fleet.

NIGHT ACTION.

9.00 p.m.—British Fleet, after altering by divisions to S., formed divisions in line ahead disposed abeam to port, with columns one mile apart ; destroyers five miles astern of Battle Fleet.

9.32 p.m.—Mine-laying flotilla leader *Abdiel* laid minefield 15 miles from Vyl Light.

10.00 p.m.—*Iron Duke* in Lat. 56°22′ N., Long. 5°47′ E. ; course S. ; speed 17 knots. Fleet order from W. to E. now :

Battle Cruiser Fleet ;
    2nd Battle Squadron ;
    4th Battle Squadron ;
    1st Battle Squadron ;
    5th Battle Squadron ;
2nd Light Cruiser Squadron astern of 5th Battle Squadron ;

Sundays marked with Asterisk (*).

May 31, 1916 (*continued*).

4th Light Cruiser Squadron ahead of Battle Fleet ;

11th, 4th, 12th, 9th, 10th, and 13th Flotillas from W. to E. astern of Battle Fleet.

10.04—British flotillas, after dropping astern, repelled attack by *Hamburg* and *Elbing*.

10.20 p.m.—British 2nd Light Cruiser Squadron engaged ships of German 4th Scouting Group ; German light cruiser *Frauenlob* sunk ; British cruisers *Southampton* and *Dublin* damaged.

11.30 p.m.—British 4th Flotilla engaged German cruisers ; *Tipperary* sunk ; *Broke* damaged, rammed *Sparrowhawk*, which was later abandoned.

German light cruisers *Rostock* and *Elbing*, on port wing of 1st High Sea Squadron, at this period attempted to cross line to starboard, in order to escape torpedo attack ; *Rostock* torpedoed ; *Elbing* collided with battleship *Posen* ; both cruisers later blown up.

MIDNIGHT.—During this period remainder of 4th Flotilla twice engaged German battleships ; *Fortune* and *Ardent* sunk German battleship *Pommern* sunk, probably in this action.

At this stage also, probably, British cruiser *Black Prince* sunk by *Thüringen* and *Ostfriesland*, of 1st High Sea Squadron.

0.30 a.m.—British T.B.D. *Turbulent* rammed and sunk by German large vessel, which also damaged *Petard* by gunfire.

1.45 a.m.—German battle cruiser *Lützow* now abandoned ; crew taken off by German T.B.D.s ; ship sunk by torpedo.

2.00 a.m.—British 12th Flotilla attacked German battleships at about 3,000 yards. Disabled *Marlborough*, unable to maintain fleet speed, sent back to base under escort ; Adm. Burney's flag transferred to *Revenge*.

2.35 a.m.—British T.B.D. *Moresby*, 13th Flotilla, attacked four *Deutschland* battleships.

2.47 a.m.—Dawn. British Fleet (battle cruisers in Lat. 55° N., Long. 6° E. (approximately), altered course to N., and formed single line ahead.

During successive phases of Jutland Battle Grand Fleet steamed following distances :

3.48 — 6.17 p.m. Battle Cruisers.. 64 miles
6.17 — 9.00 p.m. Battle Cruisers.. 57 miles
6.17 — 9.00 p.m. Battle Fleet .. 47 miles
9 p.m.—2.00 a.m. Grand Fleet .. 85 miles

Ships sunk in Jutland Battle :
British : Battle Cruisers—*Queen Mary*, *Indefatigable* and *Invincible* ; Cruisers—*Defence*, *Warrior* and *Black Prince* ; T.B.D.s—*Ardent*, *Fortune*, *Nestor*, *Nomad*, *Shark*, *Sparrowhawk*, *Tipperary* and *Turbulent*. German : Battleship — *Pommern* ; Battle Cruiser—*Lützow* ; Light Cruisers—*Elbing*, *Frauenlob*, *Rostock* and *Wiesbaden* ; T.B.D.s—S35, V4, V27, V29 and V48.

Casualties in Jutland battle :

	Killed	Wounded
British	.. 6,014	.. 674
German	.. 2,400	.. 400

Three Jutland V.C.s :
Cmdr. E. B. S. Bingham (*Nestor*), Cmdr. Loftus Jones (*Shark*), Boy Jack Cornwall (*Chester*).

[*For Continuation see June 1 and 2.*]

First British J class submarine completed at Devonport during May.

French progress at Mort Homme.

May 31 (*continued*).

Italian withdrawal at Posina-Asiago.

Anzac raid at Bir Salmana (Sinai).

During May UB15 lost in Mediterranean

During May Germans completed the Tauroggen-Radzivilischki railway.

June 1.

Grand Fleet in North Sea (see 31-v.-16).

3.44 a.m.—Battle Fleet altered course, by divisions, to westward, where Zeppelin reported.

3.50 a.m.—L11 which had been sent up with L13, L17, L22, and L24 about midnight to reconnoitre, sighted and fired at.

4.45 a.m.—Battle Fleet in Lat. 55°29' N. Long. 6°02' E.

5.15 a.m.—Battle Cruiser Fleet joined Main Fleet in search for German ships reported by *Dublin*.

5.30 a.m.—*Ostfriesland* mined W. of List.

5.48 a.m.—Battle Cruisers in Lat. 55°45' N. Long. 6°16' E., steering S.E., and later S. at 18 knots.

6.00 a.m.—Battle Fleet altered course to S.E. ; at 17 knots.

7.00 a.m.—Harwich Force, now at sea, ordered to screen *Marlborough*, which, later, was attacked and missed by U46.

7.15 a.m.—Battle Fleet again turned northward.

7.30 a.m.—Battle Cruisers turned N.E. and later, to N.

8.00 a.m.—*Warrior* abandoned.

8.15 a.m.—Battle Fleet in Lat. 55°54' N. Long. 6°10' E., steering N. at 17 knots at 8.52 Fleet turned S.W.

10.00 a.m.—Battle Cruisers again in sight ahead of Battle Fleet, course altered to N. by W.

Noon.—Battle Fleet in Lat. 56°20' N., Long 6°25' E., returning to base.

Adm. Scheer, in F.F. *Friedrich der Grosse* arrived in Wilhelmshaven Roads at 1 p.m. remainder of High Sea Fleet followed during the day.

French first line at Verdun penetrated between Douaumont-Vaux Pond.

Heavy Austrian attack on Italian left centre, Monte Pasubio—S. of Arsiero.

British s.s. *Dewsland* and s.s. *Salmonpool* sunk by U-Boat off Algeria.

June 2.

Grand Fleet arrived at its bases, fuelled and was reported ready for sea at four hour notice at 9.45 p.m.

Disabled *Marlborough* reached Humber at 8 a.m *Warspite* had returned independently to Rosyth. *Broke* reached Tyne *Acasta* and *Onslow* were towed into port.

Bulk of damaged British ships repaired by first week in July ; *Chester* complete July 29 ; *Marlborough* first week in August.

Adm. Scheer reported to Kaiser that High Sea Fleet would be out of dockyard hands by mid-August ; but *Seydlitz* was not ready by that date, while *Derfflinger* took six months to repair. *Seydlitz*, *Ostfriesland* and *Helgoland* were repaired at Wilhelmshaven *Grosser Kurfürst*, *Markgraf*, and *Moltke* were sent to Hamburg ; *König* and *Derfflinger* were to Kiel.

Heavy German attack between Hooge and Ypres-Roulers railway ; British trenches entered on 3,000 yards front to depth of 700 yards in direction of Zillebeke. Gen. Mercer killed ; Gen. Williams wounded and captured.

French recovery S. of Caurettes Wood (Verdun) ; German progress in Caillette

June 2, 1916 (*continued*).
Wood, S. of Vaux Pond, and at Damloup ;
Germans broke in N. of Vaux Fort.
Anglo-Belgian success near Bismarcks-
burg (G. E. Africa).

June 3.
King George's message to the Fleet.
British s.s. *Golconda*, (5,874 tons), sunk
by U-Boat off Aldeburgh ; 19 lost.
Canadian counter-attack at Ypres
recovered much captured ground.
German attack N. of Fricourt repulsed.
Germans failed to turn French positions
at Vaux (Verdun).
Austrian Trentino offensive held.
Russian bombardment on Southern front.
State of siege at Salonika.
Gen. Townshend at Constantinople.

*June 4.
Further German attacks at Vaux.
Austrian attacks fails S. of the Posina.
German aeroplane raid on Dubno.
Great Russian offensive ; Gen. Brusiloff's
four armies advanced from Pripet R. to
Rumanian frontier ; 13,000 prisoners.

June 5.
Battle Cruiser Fleet reorganised.
Lord Kitchener and Staff lost in H.M.S.
Hampshire ; mined off Orkneys on way to
Russia. Germans later credited U80 with
mining this area during Jutland Battle.
Kaiser visited Wilhelmshaven.
Further German assaults repulsed be-
tween Vaux—Damloup (Verdun).
German attacks failed between Krevo—
Smorgon (Vilna).
Russian offensive proceeding ; another
12,000 prisoners.
French T.B.D. *Fantassin* sunk in collision
off Corfu.

June 6.
German gains at Hooge (Ypres).
Russians took Lutsk and cross Ikva—
Styr line ; 15,000 more prisoners.
Allies' pacific blockade of Greece.

June 7.
Germans stormed Vaux Fort (Verdun),
after heroic defence by Major Raynal.
Austrian attacks failed S. and S.W. of
Asiago.

June 8.
British patrol action off Zeebrugge ;
German T.B.D.s chased back to port.
German attacks repulsed E. and W. of
Thiaumont Farm (Verdun).
Italians abandoned Monte Castelgonberto
(Sette Communi).
Russians took Butchatch (E. Galicia) ;
crossed Strypa R. ; 13,000 more prisoners.
British at Salonika, Butkovo—Tachinos,
on Struma R.
Gen. Hannyngton reached Mazinde (E.
Africa) ; Col. Murray occupied Bismarckburg.
Belgians at Usumbura (Lake Tanganyika).

June 9.
M. Briand, Gens. Joffre and Roques in
London.
German attacks failed W. and S.W. of
Hill 304 (Verdun).
Italians lost Monte Lemerle.
Italian transport *Principe Umberto* sunk
by U-Boat in Adriatic.

June 9 (*continued*).
Russians took 5,000 more prisoners.
Gen. Hannyngton occupied Mombo (G.E.
Africa). British naval forces at Ukerewe
(Victoria Nyanza).

June 10.
Italian Ministry resigned.
Russians took Dubno (Volhynia) ; Gen.
Lechitsky progressed towards Czernowitz ;
35,000 more prisoners.
Gen. Hoskins at Kualamo (E. Africa).

*June 11.
British trawlers *Onward*, *Era*, and *Nellie
Nutton* sunk in action with U-Boats in North
Sea.
German raid N. of Bruges (Champagne).
German attacks repulsed W. of Vaux
and at Thiaumont (Verdun).
German attacks failed near Krevo (Vilna).
Russians took 7,000 more prisoners ;
progress towards Czernowitz. Austrian
centre firm at Tarnopol.

June 12.
Germans penetrated advanced French
positions on Hill 321, four miles from Verdun.
Italian counter-offensive in Lagarina
Valley and on Posina-Astico front.
Russian advance on Kovel ; Torchin, 14
miles W. of Lutsk, taken ; Dniester line
forced at Zaleshchyki ; Horodenka taken ;
1,000 more prisoners.
Anti-Entente riots in Athens.
British occupied Wilhelmsthal, Usambara
(E. Africa).

June 13.
Canadians recaptured old Zillebeke posi-
tions lost on June 2.
Russians in Volhynia, 25 miles W. of
Lutsk, took Kozin ; another 6,000 prisoners
taken. In E. Galicia they took Sniatin.
British air raid on Turkish camps and
aerodrome at El Arish and Bir Mazar (Sinai).
Great Arab rising led by Sherif Hussein
of Mecca, King of the Hedjaz, and his son
Emir Feisal. Mecca, Medina, and Jeddah
attacked. Arabs repulsed at Medina, but
penetrated into Mecca and Jeddah.
Sir P. Sykes and British column entered
Kerman (S. Persia).
Gen. von. Lettow wounded near Kondoa.

June 14.
King George visited Grand Fleet.
British 1st Light Cruiser Squadron, with
T.B.D.s, left for the Naze, thence back to
Rosyth.
Allied Economic Conference in Paris.
Italians captured Austrian trenches E. of
Monfalcone (Isonzo).
Russian flotilla attacked German convoy
in Baltic ; two German T.B.D.s and one
auxiliary cruiser, *Hermann*, sunk.
Russian attacks in Lutsk salient ; 31,000
more prisoners.

June 15.
King George at Scapa addressed officers
and men of Grand Fleet on board Adm.
Jellicoe's Flagship, *Iron Duke*.
French carried trench on S. slopes of
Mort Homme (Verdun) ; Germans repulsed
at Caillette Wood.
Austrian attack on Monte Pau, S.W. of
Asiago, failed.
Signor Boselli formed new Italian
Ministry ; Baron Sonnino Foreign Minister.

Sundays marked with Asterisk (*).

June 15, 1916 (*continued*).
Russian attack on Austrian centre in E. Galicia ; 14,000 more prisoners.
Gen. Hannyngton took Korogwe (E. Africa).

June 16.
German attacks repulsed W. of Hill 304 (Verdun).
Italian progress in Trentino.
British s.s. *Gafsa* shelled and sunk by U-Boat 80 miles S.W. by S. from Genoa.
German counter-attack on Styr—Stockod line S.W. of Kolki, failed.

June 17.
Germans repulsed at Mort Homme— Thiaumont—Hill 320 (Verdun). French carried trenches on Hill 321.
Gen. Lechitsky in Czernowitz. Russian cavalry entered Radziviloff, 12 miles N.E. of Brody.

*June 18.
H.M.S. *Eden* sunk in the Channel.
Germans repulsed N. of Hill 321 (Verdun).
Death of Gen. von Moltke.
Further Russian successes in Lutsk salient. Desperate German counter-attacks round Svidniki. Russians forced to retire from Stockhod.
Arabs masters of Jeddah ; 1,000 Turk prisoners.
Germans defeated at Pongwe (E. Africa).
British s.s. *Beachy* (4,718 tons) sunk by U-Boat off Port Mahon.

June 19.
H.M. submarine G4, on patrol in Kattegat, sank by gunfire German s.s. *Ems*, on passage from Christiana to Lübeck with oil, zinc and copper.
Germans repulsed N.W. of Hill 321 (Verdun).
Fighting in Lutsk salient ; Austrians resisting round Lokatchy. Russians across Sereth R. (Bukovina).
Raid on Turkish aerodrome at El Arish.

June 20.
Germans penetrated Russian trenches at Smorgon (Vilna) ; driven out.

June 21.
Corton Light Vessel, four miles N.E. by E. from Lowestoft, mined ; five lives lost.
German attacks on Mort Homme (Verdun) and W. and S. of Vaux Fort ; French advanced positions penetrated.
Russians at Radautz, S. of Czernowitz.
U35 at Cartagena with autograph letter from Kaiser to King of Spain.
Italian auxiliary *Citta di Messina* and French T.B.D. *Fourché* torpedoed in Otranto Straits.
Allied Note to Greece : Demobilisation, new Government, fresh elections, and dismissal of anti-Entente officials demanded ; demands accepted ; Skouloudis Ministry resigned ; M. Zaimis formed new Cabinet.
Arabs masters of Mecca.

June 22.
H.M. submarine-minelayer E41 laid first mines from a British submarine in Heligoland Bight.
German attack at Givenchy ; British trenches seized on narrow front.
French recovery in Fumin—Chenois woods (Verdun). Germans failed at Hill 321.

June 22 (*continued*).
Russians occupied Kuty.
Bulgarians crossed Mesta R. ; Greeks evacuated Fort Nea Petra.

June 23.
G.E.R. s.s. *Brussels* (Capt. Fryatt) captured by German T.B. and taken into Zeebrugge ; sixth encounter.
" Merchant " U-Boat *Deutschland* (Capt. König) left Heligoland for U.S.
German attacks in Champagne.
Germans at Verdun occupied Hills 320 and 321, Thiaumont Work and Fleury.
Russians took Kimpolung and cleared Bukovina.

June 24.
British guns active on whole W. front.
During this week before Somme Battle 70 raids were carried out on British W. Front, and gas was discharged at over 40 points.
French counter-attack at Verdun ; progress at Fleury.
LZ87 scouted over Baltic.
Germans defeated on Lukigura R. (E. Africa).

*June 25.
H.M.SS. *Comus* and *Constance*, from Scapa, swept down Norwegian coast.
British bombarded Lens.
R.F.C. destroyed nine German observation balloons on W. Front.
German attempt at Verdun to advance W. of Thiaumont Work ; French recovery between Fumin—Chenois woods.
Italian advance ; Asiago, Priafora, and Cengio Mountains retaken ; Arsiero threatened.
Russians repulsed attacks W. of Sokal (Volhynia).

June 26.
British guns active on W. front.
French gains at Verdun near Thiaumont Work ; German attacks at Fleury and W. of Hill 304.
Italians reoccupied Arsiero—Posina.

June 27.
British reconnaissances from La Bassée Canal to Somme line.
German aeroplane raid on Dvinsk.
Furious fighting on Kovel road (Volhynia).
Further Italian progress in Trentino.

June 28.
French grenade attack N. of Hill 321 (Verdun) and in outskirts of Thiaumont Work ; German attacks failed.
Strikes in Berlin and Brunswick munition works.
Gen. Lechitsky defeated Austrians on 25-mile front E. of Kolomea (E. Galicia) ; 10,000 prisoners.

June 29.
Sir Roger Casement sentenced to death for high treason.
British activity all along line in France.
Russians at Kolomea (E. Galicia).

June 30.
Chancellor Bethmann-Hollweg at Wilhelmshaven informed Adm. Scheer that he was opposed to unrestricted U-Boat warfare, which might place Germany's fate in the hands of a single U-Boat commander.
French retook Thiaumont Fort (Verdun)

For List of Abbreviations see page iv.

July 1, 1916.

British naval 12-inch gun mounted at Adenkerke, about 27,000 yards from Tirpitz Battery, fired first round.

Between January—July 1916 British strength Western Front rose from 450,000 to 660,000 bayonets and sabres.

First phase of Somme Battle.

Battle of Somme : Great Franco-British advance N. and S. of Somme R. ; British Fourth Army (Gen. Rawlinson) and part of Third Army (Gen. Allenby) attacked on 20-mile front, Maricourt-Gommecourt, and broke into German forward defences on 16-mile front towards Bapaume. Montauban and Mametz captured ; Fricourt threatened ; footing gained in Leipzig Redoubt ; at Thiepval and N. of Ancre attack held up ; Gommecourt, Serre, and Grandcourt reached, but not held ; French under Gen. Foch attacked from British right to five miles S. of Somme R. towards Péronne ; captured outskirts of Hardecourt and Curlu, and took Frise, Dompierre, Béquicourt, Bussu, and Fay.

Russian progress towards Stanislau.

Turks claim recapture of Kermanshah.

*July 2.

Somme Battle : Gen. Gough in command from La Boiselle to Serre ; Gen. Rawlinson to push home British right attack.

Allied advance on Somme continued ; British took Fricourt and progressed near La Boiselle ; French took Curlu and Herbecourt ; prisoners 9,500 to date.

N. of Pripet Marshes Russians on offensive at Smorgon and Baranovitchi. Austro-German progress in Lutsk salient.

British s.s. *Rockcliffe* sunk by U-Boat in Black Sea.

Gen. Smuts reported British occupation of Bukoba—Karagwa, W. of Victoria Nyanza.

July 3.

In Somme Battle British captured La Boiselle ; French took Chapitre Wood, Feuillères, Buscourt and Flaucourt, on road to Péronne, and Assevillers farther S. ; total prisoners 12,300.

Germans took and lost Damloup Work (Verdun).

German Settlement Law, providing for capitalisation of military pensions for purchase of homesteads, especially in Baltic provinces.

Gen. Evert pierced Hindenburg's front at Baranovitchi ; over 4,000 prisoners.

Belgians defeated Germans at Biramulo. E. of Usumbura (E. Africa).

July 4.

Admiralty approved proceedings of Grand Fleet in Jutland Battle.

H.M. sloop *Rosemary* torpedoed by U-Boat in North Sea ; towed into Humber.

On Somme further French advance on S. face of salient ; French took Belloy-en-Santerre, Estrées, Sormont Farm beyond Buscourt ; their line to S. conforming. British took Bernafay Woods to E. of Montauban, and Caterpillar Wood to the N. ; unsuccessful German counter-attacks at Thiepval.

Russian success in Lutsk salient. N. of Lutsk Russian offensive on Styra—Stokhod line. In E. Galicia, advancing from Kolomea, Russians cut railway from Hungary between Delatyn—Körösmezö.

Turco-German Suez Canal force formed.

July 5.

British s.s. *Lestris* captured by German T.B. and U-Boat between Maas Light and Schouwenbank ; taken into Zeebrugge.

French won Hem, N. of Somme R. ; consolidated at Estrées—Belloy. British won more ground on Thiepval slopes and reached outskirts of Contalmaison.

H.I.M.SS. *Goeben* and *Breslau* bombarded Russian Black Sea ports and sank H.S. *Ypered.*

July 6.

Sir E. Grey raised to Peerage. Mr. Lloyd George War Secretary ; Lord Derby Under-Secretary.

H.M. submarine E26 lost in North Sea.

UC10 destroyed by H.M. motor-boat *Salmon*, by depth-charge in North Sea.

British on Somme carried a trench on 1,000 yard front E. of La Boiselle and defeated German counter-attack S.W. of Thiepval.

Great battle N. of Lutsk salient on Styr—Stokhod line. Gen. von Linsingen lost 8,000 prisoners. Russians advanced along Sarny-Kovel Railway ; Count Bothmer in E. Galicia retreated to Koropieo R. ; Russians took 10,000 prisoners.

July 7.

U77 lost in North Sea.

British began second stage of Somme advance : 500 yards forward on 2,000 yard front E. of La Boiselle ; trenches carried at Fricourt ; Prussian Guard beaten E. of Contalmaison ; part of Leipzig Redoubt carried ; footing gained in Ovillers outskirts.

N. of Lutsk salient Russians reached line Gorodok—Manievitche—Zogarovka and approached Stokhod R.

Tanga, terminus of the Usambara Railway, occupied by British naval forces.

July 8.

" Merchant " U-Boat *Deutschland* at Baltimore.

Declaration of London rescinded.

British s.s. *Pendennis* captured by U-Boat in North Sea and taken to Germany.

British 12-inch gun at Adenkerke fired 21 rounds at Tirpitz Battery (Ostend) ; target found on seventh round fired, or third round spotted.

British on Somme entered Ovillers and Trônes Wood. French took Hardecourt.

Russian pursuit along Sarny-Kovel railway. Gen. Lechitsky at Delatyn (E. Galicia).

Russians carried Turkish positions W. of Erzrum.

Russo-Japanese Agreement published.

*July 9.

German aeroplane raid over North Foreland and Dover.

British 12-inch gun at Adenkerke fired 39 rounds at Tirpitz Battery (Ostend) ; target found at third round.

N. of Somme R. British captured Maltz Horn Farm, between Hardecourt—Trônes Wood.

Gen. Foch advanced S. of Somme R. along Bray — Péronne Road and took Biaches, W. of Péronne ; French in outskirts of Barleux and in Belloy-en-Santerre ; progress at La Maisonette Farm.

Four British drifters surprised by Austrian cruiser *Novara* in Adriatic ; *Astrum Spei* and *Clavis* sunk.

Russians won more crossings on the Stokhod R.

Fighting at Sanna-i-Yat (Tigris).

Sundays marked with Asterisk (*).

July 10, 1916.
British s.s. *Calypso* torpedoed by U-Boat, without warning, in North Sea ; 30 lives lost.
In Somme Battle British held Contal-maison and all except N. border of Mametz Wood ; progress E. of Ovillers—La Boiselle ; German counter-attacks in Trônes Wood.
French captured Hill 97 and La Maison-nette Farm.
Italian T.B.D. *Impetuoso* torpedoed by Austrian U17 in Adriatic.
German resistance on Stokhod R.

July 11.
Three British trawlers of Peterhead Patrol sunk by gunfire of four U-Boats off Aberdeen.
U-Boat bombarded Seaham Harbour.
Sir D. Haig reported completion of capture of first German defence system on Somme along 14,000 yard front ; 7,500 prisoners in 10 days' fighting, with 26 field guns. British held all but N. end of Trônes Wood.
German attack at Verdun from Fleury to Chenois ; Fleury village captured ; footing gained in Damloup battery and Fumin Wood. French regained part of ground.
Gen. Maude to command Tigris column, vice Gen. Gorringe.

July 12.
H.M.S. *Galatea* attacked and missed by U-Boat torpedo off Aberdeen coast.
British light forces from Rosyth swept up Norwegian coast and back.
On Somme : British held Mametz Wood ; progress in Trônes Wood.
German gain before Verdun.
Fierce fighting on Strypa R. Russians took 2,000 prisoners.
Russian progress towards Erzinjan (Armenia) ; Turks 20-30 miles W. of Erzrum.

July 13.
U.S. naval authorities pronounced " Merchant " U-Boat *Deutschland* not a warship.
H.M. armed steamer *Duke of Cornwall* missed by two U-Boat torpedoes, while boarding a ship S.E. of Pentland Skerries.
August Bank Holiday suspended.
Equipment Conference at War Office.
In Somme Battle : S. Trônes Wood consolidated by British.
Heavy fighting in Austrian centre near Butchatch (E. Galicia) ; Russians took 12,000 prisoners.

July 14.
U51 torpedoed and destroyed by H.M. submarine H5 in mouth of Jade R.
British attacked second Somme line and carried it on four-mile front. Longueval, Bazentin-le-Grand and le-Petit village, cemetery, and wood, and whole Trônes Wood taken. British cavalry charged—7th Dragoon Guards and Deccan Horse—near Bois des Foureaux (High Wood).
German counter-attack at Baranovitchi.
Gen. Crewe captured Muanza (Victoria Nyanza).

July 15.
British advance on second Somme line continued ; Delville Wood taken and held by South Africans ; Arrow Head Copse, Waterlot Farm, and outskirts of Pozières captured, and further progress made in Foureaux Wood ; over 2,000 more prisoners, making total over 10,000 since July 1.
H.M. submarine H3 lost in Adriatic.

July 15 (*continued*).
Gen. Sakharoff broke S.W. face of Lutsk salient opposite Vladimir—Volynsk—Brody on 12-mile front ; 13,000 prisoners.
Grand Duke Nicholas captured Baiburt on Erzrum –Trebizond road.

*July 16.
British N. of Somme captured German second-line positions on 1,500-yard front N.W. of Bazentin-le-Petit Wood ; part of Ovillers garrison surrendered ; British withdrew from Foureaux (High Wood).
Russian success near Kemmern (Riga).
British s.s. *Euphorbia* and s.s. *Wilton Hall* sunk by U-Boat off Algiers.
British s.s. *Virginia* sunk by U-Boat off Cape Matapan.

July 17.
Grand Fleet proceeded on three days cruise for battle exercises N. and E. of Shetlands.
British light forces from Rosyth swept up Norwegian coast and back.
British N. of Somme completed capture of Ovillers and advanced towards Pozières and Martinpuich. S. of Somme German counter-attacks at Biaches and La Maison-nette Farm repulsed.
British s.s. *Rosemoor* sunk by U-Boat off Algiers.

July 18.
Second Phase of Somme Battle.
Germans at this date had 138 battalions engaged in and behind line N. of Somme, as compared with 62 at beginning of battle.
N. of Somme German counter-attacks against Longueval and Delville Wood ; both partly recaptured.
British s.s. *Llongwen* sunk by U-Boat off Algiers.

July 19.
Successful British raid near Armentières.
New German First Army formed on Somme out of N. Wing of Second Army, under Gen. F. von Below.
Gallwitz Army Group formed on the Somme.
N. of Somme heavy fighting on Longueval—Delville Wood front ; most of the ground recaptured. British advanced S. of Thiepval and E. of Leipzig Redoubt. French took trenches S. of Estrées.
French gain at Thiaumont—Fleury.

July 20.
British 12-inch gun at Adenkerke fired 11 rounds at Tirpitz Battery (Ostend).
N. of Somme British advanced 1,000 yards N. of Bazentin—Longueval line ; Bois de Foureaux (High Wood) again penetrated
French advanced between Hardecourt and Somme ; S. of river German first line between Berleux—Soyécourt, and Estrées—Vermand Ovillers carried ; 3,000 prisoners.
British s.s. *Grangemoor*, s.s. *Karmia* and s.s. *Yzer* sunk by U-Boat off Algiers.
Gen. Sakharoff defeated Austrians on S.W. face of Lutsk salient ; 4,000 prisoners.
Russian advance on Erzinjan (Armenia) Gumishkhaneh taken.

July 21.
British light forces from Rosyth swept towards Horn Reef.
British 12-inch gun at Adenkerke fired seven rounds at Tirpitz Battery (Ostend).

July 21, 1916 (continued).

British later in the year mounted a second 12-inch 50-ton gun near Adenkerke position, and also a third six miles in rear.

N. of Somme British withdrew from Bois de Foureaux (High Wood). German attack on Leipzig Redoubt repulsed.

S. of river German counter-attack at Soyécourt.

Successful Italian attack in Fassa Alps.

British s.s. *Wolff* sunk by U-Boat off Algiers.

M. Sazonoff, Russian Foreign Minister, resigns.

Lutsk Battle continued; Germans driven over Styr R. ; 14,000 prisoners.

Irak Group, German and Turco-Persian mixed force, began operations in Persia.

July 22.

N. of Somme British attacked along Pozières—Guillemont front; severe street fighting at Pozières.

French gained at Fleury (Verdun).

Italian progress.

British s.s. *Knutsford* and s.s. *Olive* sunk by U-Boat off Cape Corbelin (Algeria).

British occupied waterholes at Tissa Kiva Meda (E. Africa).

*July 23.

British put to flight three German T.B.D.s near mouth of Scheldt.

British seaplane patrolling off Zeebrugge shot down by U-Boat and captured by German T.B.D.

N. of Somme greater part of Pozières taken by British.

British s.s. *Badminton* sunk by U-Boat off Algerian coast.

British occupied Pangani (E. Africa).

July 24.

British light forces from Rosyth swept up Norwegian coast and back.

N. of Somme Pozières fighting continued; German counter-attacks repulsed. S. of river French progress S. of Estrées and N. of Vermand Ovillers.

French took a redoubt at Thiaumont.

Gen. Sakharoff attacked 12 miles from Brody (Galicia); German advanced lines penetrated.

Serbians drove Bulgarians back on Greek frontier.

July 25.

N. of Somme British approached Hill 160, N. of Pozières; German attacks repulsed. Pozières completely in British hands.

Gen. Sakharoff defeated Gen. von Linsingen on Slonuvka R. Austrians evacuating Brody.

Fall of Erzinjan (Armenia) to Gen. Yudenitch.

July 26.

H.M.S. *Yarmouth* missed by U-Boat torpedo in North Sea.

British 2nd Light Cruiser Squadron, with T.B.D.s, proceeded westward of Little Fisher Bank, thence swept to the Naze on look-out for Zeppelin.

British s.s. *Eskimo* (3,326 tons), captured and taken to Germany by German auxiliary cruiser off Risoer, in Norwegian territorial waters; crew, except one, made prisoners.

N. of Somme British carried a trench N. of Pozières—Bazentin-le-Petit. S. of river.

July 26 (continued).

French progress at Estrées; fighting at Soyécourt.

French progress at Thiaumont Work, N. of Verdun.

Gen. Sakharoff progressed towards Brody.

July 27.

Capt. Charles Fryatt, commander of G.E.R. s.s. *Brussels*, court-martialled and shot at Bruges by German authorities in Belgium for alleged attempt to ram U33 (see 28-iii.-15).

N. of Somme British recovered nearly all of lost portion of Delville Wood; fighting at Longueval, where orchard recovered. Thiepval threatened.

LZ88 scouted over Baltic.

Russians broke German first line W. of Lutsk ; 9,000 prisoners.

SL X. raided Sebastopol.

Belgians took Kigoma, Lake Tanganyika.

July 28.

Zeppelin raid on Lincoln and Norfolk.

British N. of Somme recaptured whole Delville Wood; last German positions at Longueval taken; progress near Pozières.

German 1st Independent Aeroplane Squad. raided Paris.

Fall of Brody (Galicia) to Russians. Renewed Russian offensive on Stokhod. Crossings forced near Kashovka and Gulevitche ; 4,000 prisoners.

H.M. auxiliary *Majestic II.* sprang a leak and sank near Oran.

July 29.

H.M.S. *Chester* completed repairs after Jutland at Hull.

British s.s. *Fordingham* bombed and missed by German aircraft off Bridlington.

Two German Air Squads. raided Dvinsk.

In three days' battle for Brody Russians took over 20,000 prisoners ; German line before Kovel—Vladimir—Volhynsk broken.

British reach Central Railway at Dodoma (E. Africa).

*July 30.

Anglo-French advance E. from Delville Wood to Somme ; British entered Guillemont, but withdrew. French reached outskirts of Maurepas beyond Combles-Péronne railway and captured and held Monacu Farm.

Hindenburg C.-in-C. from Baltic to Dniester ; his Army front to include Prince Leopold and Linsingen Groups, and Second Austro-Hungarian Army.

On Stokhod Russian captures totalled 49 guns and 9,000 prisoners.

Russian troops at Salonika.

UB44 destroyed by H.M. drifters *Quarry Knowe* and *Garrigill* with nets and depth-charges in Otranto Straits.

British occupied section of Central Railway at Kikombo (E. Africa).

July 31.

During 12 months ended July 31, 16 German shipbuilding yards delivered 65 U-Boats of 32,959 tons.

Zeppelin raid on Norfolk, Suffolk, Cambridge, Lincoln, Nottingham, and Kent.

Italians cleared Val Cismon.

Austrians fell back S. of Brody.

Force of 18,000 Turks under Gen. Kress von Kressenstein entrenched at Oghratina—Mageibra (Sinai).

British occupied Saranda and Kilimatinde on Central Railway (E. Africa).

Sundays marked with Asterisk (*).

August 1, 1916.

"Merchant" U-Boat *Deutschland* left U.S. for Germany.

British light forces from Rosyth swept down Norwegian coast and back.

Duke Albrecht of Wurtemberg and Crown Prince Rupprecht, commanding German Fourth and Sixth Armies, created Field Marshals.

S. of Somme French gained between Estrées—Belloy-en-Santerre.

German attack at Verdun W. and S. of Thiaumont work repulsed; French counter-offensive.

British occupied Sadani (E. Africa).

August 2.

Zeppelin raid on Norfolk, E. Suffolk, and Kent.

British aeroplanes raided St. Denis Westrem aerodrome and Brussels Zeppelin sheds.

N. of Somme French captured strongly fortified work between Hem—Monacu Farm.

French successes at Verdun, S. of Fleury; German trenches carried; 800 prisoners.

Italian battleship *Leonardo da Vinci* destroyed by explosion at Taranto.

Russians on Sitovitche—Yanovka line (Stokhod).

Ujiji, German port on Lake Tanganyika, taken by Belgians. German vessel, *Graf von Götzen*, destroyed by Belgian gunboat *Netta*.

August 3.

H.M.S. *Marlborough's* departure from the Tyne delayed by mines laid off the Longstone.

Four British C class submarines left the Nore in tow for Archangel bound for Baltic.

Sir Roger Casement hanged.

British gains N. of Bazentin-le-Petit.

French at Verdun retook Fleury; progressed towards Thiaumont; 1,750 prisoners to date.

Russians 20 miles E. of Kovel.

H.M. minesweeper *Clacton* sunk by U-Boat at Chai Aghizi.

Turks advance between Katia and Hamisah (Sinai).

Belgians occupied Ujiji, Lake Tanganyika.

August 4.

H.M. submarine K1 (2,650 tons) commissioned.

H.M.S. *Cleopatra* mined off Thornton Ridge, reached Nore for repairs.

N. of Somme British advanced against German second line N. and W. of Pozières, gaining trench near Mouquet Farm and crest of ridge above Courcelette and Martinpuich.

Germans took and lost Fleury (Verdun).

British s.s. *Favonian* and s.s. *Tottenham* sunk by U-Boat off Marseilles.

Italians won and lost Hills 85 and 121 E. of Monfalcone (Isonzo).

Gen. Sakharoff in Galicia progressed.

Turkish attack E. of Suez Canal near Romani defeated; 2,500 prisoners taken.

August 5.

Gen. Sakharoff made progress W. of Brody; 3,000 prisoners.

British s.s. *Mount Coniston* sunk by U-Boat off Meda Is. (Spain).

British pursued Turks in Suez Canal area.

✻August 6.

N. of Somme further British progress at Pozières towards Martinpuich.

✻August 6 (*continued*).

Great Italian offensive on Isonzo; after terrific bombardment Italians took Sabotino ridge, Hill 188, Podgora ridge and town (including Monte Calvario), Monte San Michele ridge and Hill 85 E. of Monfalcone.

Gen. Sakharoff progressed S. of Brody.

Turks counter-attacked in Armenia.

August 7.

N. of Somme British attacked Guillemont; French carried German trenches at Hem between Wood—Somme R.

French progress S. of Thiaumont Work and at Fleury (Verdun).

Italian Isonzo offensive continued.

Gen. Lechitsky 12 miles from Stanislau; 2,000 prisoners.

British s.s. *Newburn* and s.s. *Trident* sunk by U-Boat off Dragonera Is., Majorca.

August 8.

King George visited Somme front.

N. of Somme British continued against Guillemont; S.W. of village line advanced 400 yards.

French advanced E. of Hill 139, N. of Hardecourt, and seized wood N. of Hem.

Germans gained and lost Thiaumont Work.

British s.s. *Imperial* sunk by U-Boat off Marseilles.

Italians crossed Isonzo.

Gen. Lechitsky 6 miles from Stanislau; 7,400 prisoners.

Turks retired from Oghratina (Sinai) to Birel Abd.

British occupied Mhonda, Nguru Hill (G.E. Africa).

August 9.

Zeppelin raid on Northumberland, Durham, Yorkshire (particularly Hull), and Norfolk: 10 killed, 16 wounded.

N. of Somme British gained 200 yards on 600-yard front, N.W. of Pozières.

German counter-attack N. of Hem Wood repulsed.

British s.s. *Antiope* sunk by U-Boat off Marseilles.

H.M. submarine B10 sunk by aircraft bomb at Venice.

Fall of Gorizia to Italians, who crossed Isonzo, pursued Austrians, occupied Rosenthal—Vertoibica line; 12,000 prisoners to date.

Russians 2 miles from Stanislau.

French bombarded Doiran (Serbo-Greek frontier).

Turkish counter-attack at Birel Abd (Sinai) repulsed.

British reached Matamondo, Nguru Hill (E. Africa).

August 10.

H.M.S. *Blonde* ashore on Lowther Rock, Pentland Firth, in thick weather; towed off damaged next day.

N. of Somme Germans repulsed between Mouquet Farm—Pozières.

Fall of Stanislau to Gen. Lechitsky, who advanced on Halicz. Gen. Sakharoff across Sereth R. towards Lemberg—Odessa railway.

Italian attack on Carso.

Gen. von Winckler to command Eleventh Army in Macedonia, vice Gen. von Gallwitz.

Allied offensive on Salonika front. Doiran bombarded and Hill 227 captured by French.

Russians evacuated Hamadan.

For List of Abbreviations see page iv.

August 11, 1916.

British air raid on Brussels—Namur airship sheds and Belgian railways.

On Somme British advanced N. of Bazentin-le-Petit.

Italians on the Carso crossed Vallone, advanced E. of Doberdo.

First Italian contingent at Salonika.

Turks routed near Bir el Bayud (Sinai). Kress von Kressenstein abandoned Bir el Abd, retired to El Arish. "Second invasion of Egypt" failed.

British defeat Germans at Matamondo (G.E. Africa).

August 12.

British 4th Light Cruiser Squadron from Scapa proceeded towards Udsire Light, where it met convoy of ten British merchant ships from Baltic which were escorted across North Sea to Rattray Head.

Seaplane raid on Dover : 7 injured.

French penetrated 1,000 yards into German third line from Somme R. to Hardecourt on 4-mile front; took S. part of Maurepas and cemetery; 1,000 prisoners. British advance N.W. of Pozières 400 yards deep on mile front.

Italian Carso progress.

Gen. Shtcherbatcheff advanced against Austrian centre in Galicia; Count Bothmer fell back on Bug—Zlota Lipa.

Russian recovery in Armenia.

British reached Ruhungu, Nguru Hills; occupied Mpapua (E. Africa).

*August 13.

H.M.S. *Lassoo* mined near Maas Light.

S. of Somme French progressed S.W. of Estrées; N. of river Germans entered part of captured trenches W. of Pozières.

Russians captured Mariampol (Galicia). Italian advance E. of Isonzo.

August 14.

Artillery activity N. and S. of Somme.

LZ88 scouted over Baltic.

Russians in Galicia crossing Zlota Lipa—Bistritza.

Italian Carso advance: Austrian lines W. of San Grado—Mt. Pecinka and 1,400 prisoners taken.

H.M. special service ship *Remembrance* sunk by U-Boat in Mediterranean.

August 15.

H.M.S. *Furious* launched.

H.M. armed steamers *Dundee* and *King Orry*, disguised as merchantmen, left Scapa for operations off Norwegian coast, supported by H.M.S. *Constance* and T.B.D.s ; one Norwegian steamer, with magnetic iron ore for Rotterdam, intercepted.

King George returned to England after visiting Army in France.

Gen. Brusiloff on Zlota Lipa S. of Brzezany; Gen. Lechitsky at Solotvina in Yablonitza Pass (Carpathians). Russian captures from beginning of offensive, 358,000 prisoners.

French took "Tortoise Hill," near Doiran (Salonika).

Gen. Smuts through Nguru Hills (E. Africa); Bagamoyo occupied by naval forces.

August 16.

French advance on Somme; mile of trenches taken, Guillemont—Maurepas road reached ; German positions E. of Maurepas—

August 16 (*continued*).

Cléry road taken on 2,000-yard front. British in outskirts of Guillemont.

British success at Kidete (E. Africa).

August 17.

On Somme British captured trench N.W. of Bazentin. German counter-attacks repulsed N.W. of Pozières.

British s.s. *Swedish Prince* sunk by U-Boat, 12 miles N.W. from Pantelleria.

Bulgarian move on Kavala ; British in contact at Doldjeli ; Serbs in contact S.E. of Florina.

British auxiliary yacht *Zaida* sunk by U-Boat in Alexandretta Gulf.

August 18.

Grand Fleet put out for sweep in southern waters; H.M.S. *Iron Duke* attacked and missed by U-Boat torpedo.

High Sea Fleet (3rd and 1st High Sea Squadrons, with battleships *Bayern, Grosser Kurfürst,* and *Markgraf* acting together with two surviving battle cruisers *Moltke* and *Von der Tann*) left Jade R. at 8 p.m. to carry out a raid on Sunderland, covered by High Sea and Flanders U-Boats and eight airships.

German Chancellor, with Kaiser's approval, instructed Count Bernstorff, ambassador at Washington, that Germany would gladly accept President Wilson's good offices in promoting peace conference among belligerents.

Great British advance N. of Somme on 11-mile front, Thiepval—Guillemont, and towards Ginchy ; ridge summit gained in several places. Leipzig Redoubt carried. French took more of Maurepas and Calvary Hill, and extended E. of Maurepas—Cléry road. German line shortened at Guillemont—Maurepas.

French progress at Thiaumont (Verdun).

Bulgarians occupied Florina (Greece) ; Serbians back on Ostrovo Lake.

Gen. Smuts' forces crossed Wami R. at Dakawa (E. Africa).

August 19.

H.M. submarine E23 in Heligoland Bight unsuccessfully attacked H.I.M.S. *Derfflinger* at 3.13 a.m., but twice, at 5 and 7.20 a.m., torpedoed H.I.M.S. *Westfalen*, which returned to the Jade.

Grand Fleet at dawn concentrated near "Long Forties," steering southward, with Battle Cruiser Fleet 30 miles ahead. At 5.55 a.m. H.M.S. *Nottingham*, in advance of battle cruisers, attacked by U52 and hit by two torpedoes and at 6.26 a.m. by a third ; crew taken off ; ship sank at 7.10 a.m. From 8.24 a.m. Zeppelins were reported : L11, L13, L21, L22, L24, L30, L31, and L32 strung out across North Sea. At 10.10 a.m. H.M. submarine E23, on patrol in Heligoland Bight, reported ships of High Sea Fleet steering west. German ships, however, turned back early in the day, and at 3.56 p.m. Adm. Jellicoe ordered Grand Fleet, which had been manœuvring to intercept, to return. On return passage H.M.S. *Falmouth*, hit by four torpedoes by U66 and U63, sank near Flamborough Head. At 6 p.m. Adm. Beatty reported German U-Boat screen extending N.E. for about 25 miles from Lat. 54.19 N., Long. 1.0 E. At 7.30 p.m. Commodore Tyrwhitt with Harwich Force, also abandoned pursuit.

Germans repulsed at Fleury (Verdun).

Russian advance on Stokhod R.

Bulgaro-Serb fight at Florina.

Sundays marked with Asterisk (*).

＊August 20. 1916.
Serb success in Moglena sector. British and French in action along Macedonian front.

August 21.
UC7 torpedoed and destroyed by H.M. submarine E54 off Schouwen Bank Light.
N. of Somme British within 1,000 yards of Thiepval ; they established themselves outside Mouquet Farm and penetrated Guillemont.
French progress N. of river near Cléry and S. of river E. of Soyécourt and S.W. of Estrées.
King of Italy visited Gorizia.
Russian T.B.D. mined in Riga Gulf.

August 22.
H.M. submarine E16 lost in North Sea.
British repulsed counter-attacks S. of Thiepval.
French success N. of Maurepas.
Russians S. of Jablonitza Pass.
Italian successes in Dolomites.
Serb progress in Moglena.
Gen. Van Deventer captured Killossa on Central Railway (G.E. Africa).

August 23.
LZ97 and LZ98 over E. Suffolk.
" Merchant " U-Boat *Deutschland* back in Germany.
Karl Liebknecht sent to penal servitude for his May-Day activity in Berlin.
N. of Somme British gained another 200 yards of trench S. of Thiepval. German counter on Guillemont station repulsed.
Italian gain in Fassa Alps.
Russians in Caucasus recaptured Mush ; defeated Turks at Rayat (Turco-Persian frontier) ; 2,300 prisoners.
British advance on Mrogoro (E. Africa).

August 24.
H.M.SS. *Warspite* and *Valiant* collided during night in Scapa Flow; both ships damaged and docked.
On Somme : French captured all Maurepas. Further British advance towards Thiepval, across Leipzig salient, and on E. and N.E. edges of Delville Wood towards Ginchy.
Germans evacuated Mrogoro (Central Railway) (E. Africa).

August 25.
Zeppelin raid on London (8th), E. Suffolk, Essex, and Kent : 9 killed, 40 injured.
H.M. armed steamer *Duke of Albany* sunk by U-Boat in North Sea.
Bulgarians in Kavala (E. Greece).
Russian Troops on Salonika front.

August 26.
On Somme British took another 200 yards of trench N. of Bazentin-le-Petit.
Serb progress in Ostrovo district.
Bulgarians at Kavala bombarded by British fleet.
Gen. Moschopoulos, Greek Chief of Staff, vice Gen. Dousmanis.
British at Mrogoro (E. Africa).

＊August 27.
N. of Somme British progress N.W. of Ginchy.
Russian advance towards Halicz (Galicia).
Italy declared war on Germany.
Rumania declared war on Austria-Hungary.

＊August 27 (*continued*).
Bulgarian thrust E. of Struma R. Gree
Fourth Army Corps surrendered to Germans sent to Görlitz.
M. Venizelos appealed to Greek peoplo t defend national honour.

August 28.
Bavarian Crown Prince's (Western) Arm Group formed.
Gallwitz (Somme) Army Group dissolvec
Gen. von Heeringen to command Germa Coast Defence, vice Gen. von Falkenhausei who took over Sixth Army.
Gen. von Schubert to command Germa Seventh Army, vice Gen. von Heeringen.
Italians captured Mte. Cauriol.
Germany declared war on Rumania.
Mackensen to command new Germa Army Group against Rumania.
LZ101 raided Bukarest.
Rumanians crossed Transylvanian fror tier ; in contact with Austrians in tł passes.

August 29.
British captures on W. Front since July 266 officers, 15,203 men, 86 guns, 160 machir guns.
Fall of Gen. von Falkenhayn ; Marsh Hindenburg appointed Chief of Staff ar Gen. Ludendorff Chief-Quartermaster.
Prince Leopold of Bavaria C.-in-C. c E. Front.
Russian success on Zlota Lipa.
Austrian retreat in Transylvania befo Rumanians, who took Petroseny, Brasso, ar Kezdi Vasarhely.

August 30.
H.M. submarine E43 sailed for Katteg to operate against a German decoy trawler.
German High Command discussed b again postponed unrestricted U-Boat war c the ground that Holland and Denmai might be provoked.
Two months of Somme Battle ende German attempts near Guillemont ar Foureaux Wood defeated. British captur small salient S. of Martinpuich.
Russian progress in Jablonitza Pass.
Russian troops in Dobrudja.
Turkey declared war on Rumania.
Venizelist revolt at Salonika.

August 31.
SL XI. tried to reach London.
H.M.S. *Abdiel*, from Scapa, laid min at night off Horn Reef.
Kaiser again held war council at Ples decision as to unrestricted U-Boat war be deferred until Rumanian campai; developed.
N. of Somme German attack rou High (Foureaux) Wood and Ginchy ; ε vanced British trench reached at two poin
Germans during August completed Shav Mitau railway.
German attacks at Vladimir Volyr (Volhynia). Fighting at Halicz (Galicie over 15,000 prisoners taken on all Russi fronts.
Ottoman 15th Corps now on Aust: German South Army front.
British s.s. *Duart* sunk by U-Boat Algerian coast.

September 1.
N. of Somme British recovery Foureaux Wood—Ginchy.
Austrians retired at Orsova (Danube).

For List of Abbreviations see page iv.

September 1, 1916 (*continued*).

Bulgaria declared war on Rumania.

Bulgarians crossed Dobrudja border.

September battle in Carpathians begun.

Allied naval demonstration off Piræus.

H.M. collier *Swift Wings* sunk by U-Boat off Cape Bengut, Algeria.

September 2.

British s.s. *Kelvinia* (5,039 tons) mined off Caldy Is., Bristol Channel.

Russian success N. of Jablonitza Pass.

Bulgarian offensive in Dobrudja.

Allied Note to Greece; control of posts and telegraphs demanded: Central agents to be expelled; four German steamers at Piræus seized.

British s.s. *Strathallen* sunk by U-Boat 20 miles N.E. from Philippeville.

*September 3.

Thirteen Zeppelins (including LZ90, LZ97, LZ98, and SL XI.) raided London (9th raid), E. Riding, Lincs, Nottingham, Norfolk, Suffolk, Cambridge, Hunts, Essex, Herts, Beds, and Kent; one airship destroyed at Cuffley (Enfield) by Lieut. Robinson, R.F.C. (awarded V.C.). Casualties, 4 killed, 12 injured.

German military and naval council at Pless decided to leave question of unrestricted U-Boat warfare to discretion of Supreme Command.

Great Anglo-French Somme attack: British took part of Mouquet Farm and all Guillemont; Ginchy gained and lost; French attacked from Maurepas, took Le Forest and trenches N. of it to Combles, and, farther S., Cléry, on Péronne road; over 2,000 prisoners.

German attempt to break Vaux-Chapître (Verdun) defences. French progress E. and N.W. of Fleury.

Russians before Brzezany, and 12 miles S. of Halicz (Galicia).

Rumanians took Orsova (Danube).

September 4.

British 2nd Battle Cruiser Squadron and 2nd Light Cruiser Squadron from Rosyth swept towards the Naze, to southward of Little Fisher Bank, and back.

On Somme: From Mouquet Farm to junction with French all German second line in British hands; Wedge Wood captured, footing gained in Leuze Wood. French pressed on E. of Le Forest; 500 more prisoners. French attacked S. of Somme on 12-mile front, from Barleux to S. of Chaulnes; took Soyécourt, Chilly, part of Vermandovillers, and Chaulnes Wood; 2,700 prisoners.

French gained more ground N. of Fleury.

Russians on Gnila Lipa opposite Halicz.

LZ86 and LZ101 raided Bukarest.

Russo-Rumanians and Bulgaro-Germans in contact in Dobrudja; latter captured Dobritch, Boltchik, and Kavarna; fighting at Tutrakan.

Dar-es-Salaam (E. Africa) surrendered to British naval forces.

September 5.

On Somme: British extended 1,500 yards E. of Guillemont: held Leuze Wood—Falfemont Farm, and Ginchy outskirts.

French advanced E. of Le Forest; stormed Hôpital Farm, occupied part of Marrières Wood, and progressed E. of Cléry. Advance continued S. of river.

Struggle for Halicz continued.

September 6.

British s.s. *Torridge* (5,036 tons) sunk by U-Boat, 40 miles S.W. from Start Point.

British s.s. *Strathtay* (4,428 tons) sunk by U-Boat off Pontusval, Finisterre.

N. of Somme: Leuze Wood cleared.

S. of Somme: French took most of Berny, part of Deniécourt, and approached Chaulnes Station.

LZ88 raided Runö (Riga Gulf).

Bulgarians took Tutrakan (Dobrudja).

New German Ninth Army formed, including Alpine Corps, under Gen. von Falkenhayn, for Rumanian campaign.

September 7.

S. of Somme further French success round Deniécourt.

Russians attacking Halicz.

Rumanian advance N.W. of Petroseny.

Action at Kisaki (G.E. Africa).

September 8.

H.M. monitors *Marshal Soult, Lord Clive* and *General Wolfe* bombarded Belgian coast.

Three British motor-boats lost and s.s. *Achaia* torpedoed outside Oran.

H.M. collier *Butetown* and s.s. *Llangorse* sunk by U-Boat off Cape Matapan.

Fighting at Dobritch (Dobrudja). Rumanians bombarding Vidin, Lom Palanka, and Rahova on the Danube.

September 9.

H.M. monitors *Prince Rupert* and *Prince Eugène* bombarded Belgian coast.

N. of Somme British captured Ginchy and ground between it and Leuze Wood.

German G.H.Q. transferred from Charleville to Pless.

Rumanians took Toplitza (Transylvania).

*September 10.

British s.s. *Lexie* sunk by U-Boat off Ushant.

German counter failed N. of Somme round Ginchy—Mouquet Farm.

H.M. ML. 149 destroyed by fire at Taranto.

Rumanians bombarded Rustchuk.

Austrians evacuated Hermannstadt (Transylvania).

Bulgaro-Germans took Silistria.

British forces crossed Struma R., drove Bulgarians from villages E. of river, occupying Yeni Keui, which they abandoned later.

British at Kidodi, on Ruaha R., barred German retreat from Mrogoro (E. Africa).

Action at Dutumi (G.E. Africa).

September 11.

H.M. monitors *Marshal Soult, Prince Rupert* and *Lord Clive* bombarded Belgian coast.

Russian advance in Carpathians; Kapul Mt., N. of Kirlibaba Pass, captured.

M. Zaimis, Greek Premier, resigned.

September 12.

H.M. monitors *Erebus, Terror, Sir John Moore,* and *General Craufurd* bombarded Belgian coast.

Great French advance N. of Somme from S. of Combles to the river; Hill 145, Marrières Wood, and all German trench system up to Bapaume—Péronne road taken; road cut from S. of Rancourt to S. of Bouchavesnes; Brioche, Bouchavesnes and Hill 76, N. of Péronne, carried; 1,500 prisoners.

Sundays marked with Asterisk (*).

September 13, 1916.

H.M. monitor *Terror*, F. Adm. Bacon, off Zeebrugge ; H.M. monitors *Erebus, Marshal Soult, Sir John Moore, Prince Rupert* and *General Wolfe* bombarded Belgian coast.

N. of Somme French advance across Bapaume—Péronne road; Bois l'Abbé Farm carried ; German third line taken, and trench system S. of Le Priez Farm, S.E. of Combles ; 2,300 prisoners to date.

September 14.

British s.s. *Counsellor* mined off Galley Head.

N. of Somme British stormed German trenches S.E. of Thiepval on 1,000-yard front, including " Wunderwerk." French carried Le Priez Farm.

Fresh Italian advance in Carso ; positions captured E. of Vallone ; over 2,000 prisoners.

H.M. collier *Inververbie* and ML. 230, ML. 253, and ML. 255 sunk by U-Boat off Cape Rizzuto (Italy).

Rumanians retired on Kara Orman— Cuzgun (Dobrudja) ; advanced in Transylvania, crossed Aluta R., E. of Hermannstadt, N.W. of Brasso.

British at Doiran stormed " Machine Guns Knob," N. of Machukovo, but withdrew.

September 15.

H.M. monitors *Lord Clive* and *Terror* bombarded Belgian coast.

Third phase of Somme Battle.

First British Tanks in action.

British Somme advance on 6-mile front, N. of Albert—Bapaume road—Bouleaux Wood, to depth of 2,000-3,000 yards ; Flers, Martinpuich, Courcelette, all High Wood, most of Bouleaux Wood taken. Over 4,000 prisoners.

French captured trenches S. of Rancourt, and a system N. of Le Priez Farm. S. of Somme French advanced E. of Deniécourt and N.E. of Berny.

Italians captured San Grado (Carso).

French submarine *Foucault* bombed by Austrian seaplane in Adriatic.

Austrian counter in Transylvania.

Allies carried heights overlooking Florina.

Gen. Smuts' columns S. of Uluguru Hills, effected junction near Kissaki (E. Africa).

September 16.

N. of Somme British gains at Courcelette extended on 1,000-yard front ; Danube trench and strong work at Mouquet Farm taken.

Further Italian gains in Carso.

Russian attacks N. of Halicz ; nearly 4,000 prisoners.

Russo-Rumanians retired on Rahova— Tuzla (Dobrudja).

M. Kalogeropoulos Greek Premier.

H.M. submarine E12 sank Turkish munition ship in Burgas Bay.

⁎September 17.

U53 left Heligoland for U.S., there to await " merchant " U-Boat *Bremen*.

French attacked S. of Somme R. ; took Vermandovillers—Berny ; progress between Berny—Deniécourt.

British s.s. *Dewa* and s.s. *Lord Tredegar* sunk by U-Boat E. of Malta.

September 18.

H.M.S. *Renown* left Fairfield yard.

N. of Somme : British progress N.W. of Combles, where " Quadrilateral " captured,

September 18 (*continued*).

N. of Martinpuich and E. of Courcelette, French captured Deniécourt ; over 1,600 prisoners.

Heavy fighting at Merisov (Transylvania).

Franco-Russian troops took Florina.

Serbians won summit of Kaymaktchalan.

September 19.

British success S. of Arras.

Four British C class submarines arrived at Kronstadt.

Bulgaro-Germans held on Rahova—Tuzla line (Dobrudja).

Allied blockade of Greece.

Belgians at Tabora (G.F. Africa).

September 20.

H.M. collier *Etton* mined in entrance to White Sea.

British light forces from Rosyth swept to Norwegian coast and back.

Grand Fleet left Scapa for battle exercises between Orkneys and Shetlands and Norwegian coast.

U53, bound for U.S., passed N. of Shetlands.

German counter against French on Somme failed.

French success S. of Thiaumont Work and in E. part of Vaux—Chapitre Wood (Verdun).

First number of German revolutionary periodical *Spartakus* issued.

Italian advance E. of Gorizia and in Carso.

Rumanians evacuated Petroseny.

Lull in Dobrudja.

German 1st Air Squad. raided Tchernavoda.

British s.s. *Persic* (12,042 tons) attacked and missed by U-Boat torpedo in Mediterranean.

September 21.

H.M.S. *Repulse*, new battle cruiser (25,500 tons, six 15-inch guns), joined Grand Fleet at Scapa.

N. of Somme British progress on mile front at Martinpuich—Flers ; two trench lines taken.

September 22.

British s.s. *Colchester* captured by German T.B.s in North Sea and taken to Zeebrugge.

British s.s. *Kennett* sunk by U-Boat in Baltic.

German seaplane over Dover.

LZ97 raided Boulogne.

Germans repulsed W. of Mouquet Farm. French nearer Combles.

Austrians reached Vulcan Pass (Transylvania).

September 23.

New floating dock for light cruisers and T.B.D.s arrived at Invergordon from the Tyne.

Zeppelin raid by about 12 airships on London (10th raid), Lincs, Notts, Norfolk, and Kent ; L32 and L33 brought down in Essex ; one in flames by aeroplane at Great Bursted, and one, crew of which surrendered, by gunfire near Mersea Island : 40 killed, 130 injured.

British s.s. *Dresden* and s.s. *Pearl* sunk by U-Boat off the Nab.

Italians captured two peaks in Fassa Alps.

September 23, 1916 (*continued*).

Serbians drove back Bulgarians 300 yards on Kaymaktchalan plateau.

British s.s. *Charterhouse* sunk by U-Boat off Formentera.

*September 24.

H.M. monitor *Terror* bombarded Zeebrugge.

Krupp's Essen works bombed by French airmen, Capt. de Beauchamps and Lieut. Daucourt.

LZ81 raided Bukarest.

Austrians moving on Roter Turm Pass (Transylvania).

Mackensen in Dobrudja 15 miles behind Rasova—Tuzla line.

Venizelist Revolution in Crete.

British s.s. *Bronwen* sunk by U-Boat off Dragonera Is.

September 25.

German Chancellor informed Count Bernstorff, Ambassador at Washington, that unrestricted U-Boat warfare was contemplated, in order to relieve Somme front and bring England to her knees.

Seven Zeppelins raided Lancs, Yorks, and Lincs ; 43 killed, 31 injured (16 casualties at Bolton).

LZ98 raided Boulogne.

British Somme advance : Lesbœufs—Morval captured ; communications with Combles practically severed. Germans abandoned Bouleaux Wood. French took Rancourt—Le Priez Farm ; advanced to outskirts of Frégicourt ; carried Hill 120 N.E. and Hill 130 S.E. of Bouchavesnes.

Austro-Germans near Roter Turm Pass (Transylvania).

LZ101 and 1st Air Squad. raided Bukarest.

Rumanian progress in Dobrudja.

M. Venizelos left Athens for Crete and Salonika to head Nationalist movement.

September 26.

H.M. armed yacht *Conqueror II.*, one patrol trawler and two British steamers torpedoed by U-Boats in Fair Island Channel,

British light forces from Rosyth swept to southward of German North Sea minefield.

N. of Somme British attacked Thiepval, penetrated village and carried Zollern Redoubt—Mouquet Farm ; French and British together captured Combles ; British stormed Gueudecourt ; their cavalry pursued. French took Frégicourt and advanced to edge of St. Pierre Vaast Wood. French attack S. of Somme.

Austrians carried W. side of Roter Turm Pass (Transylvania).

LZ81 and 1st Air Squad. raided Bukarest.

H.M. auxiliary *Stirling Castle* sunk by explosion off Malta.

British s.s. *Boddam*, s.s. *Newby* and s.s. *Mathe* sunk by U-Boat E. of Barcelona.

September 27.

N. of Somme British completed capture of Thiepval, carried parts of Schwaben and Stuff Redoubts, and advanced N. of Flers on 1,000-yard front E. of Eaucourt l'Abbaye.

French extended their gains E. and S.E. of Rancourt and entered St. Pierre Vaast Wood.

German attack repulsed at Thiaumont Fleury (Verdun).

German attacks W. of Lutsk (Volhynia).

German 1st Air Squad. raided Bukarest.

British s.s. *Rallus* and s.s. *Secondo* sunk by U-Boat off Dragonera Is.

September 28.

N. of Somme British took Thiepval cemetery and most of Schwaben Redoubt ; advanced N. and N.E. of Courcelette and at Martinpuich—Gueudecourt. French progress at Frégicourt—Morval.

September 29.

Gen. Elles to command Tanks in France.

British gained Destremont Farm, S.W. of Le Sars.

Greek Provisional Government under M. Venizelos at Salonika.

September 30.

H.M. submarine G12, returning from patrol off Horn Reef, engaged U-Boat by gunfire, but failed to score.

H.M.S. *Lion*, with Battle Cruiser Fleet, swept towards the Naze and proceeded to Scapa.

Gen. Estienne to command French Tanks.

N. of Somme British held remainder of ridge N. of Thiepval, except part of Schwaben Redoubt.

German High Command during September decided to prepare Siegfried position (Arras—Aisne R.).

New Russian move on Lemberg ; fighting S.W. of Brody and N.E. of Halicz ; over 4,000 prisoners.

Von Falkenhayn failed to cross Danube at Korabia (Rumania).

German 1st Air Squad. raided Bukarest.

Great Serb success at Kaymaktchalan (Macedonia). British seized part of Bulgarian Struma line.

*October 1.

German High Command was informed that Kaiser had ordered Count Bernstorff to induce President Wilson to promote peace.

Zeppelin raid on London (11th), Lincs, Norfolk, Cambs, Northants, Herts. One airship down in flames at Potter's Bar : one killed, one injured. Lieuts. Brandon and Tempest awarded D.S.O.

LZ98 raided Etaples.

Fresh British Somme attack on 3,000 yard front ; Eaucourt l'Abbaye taken.

German counter repulsed S. of Brzezany (Galicia).

Mackensen's centre and right repulsed in Dobrudja. Rumanian division across Danube at Rahova (Rustchuk).

October 2.

H.M. collier *Lotusmere* sunk by U43 48 miles N.N.E. from Teriderski Lighthouse.

British 1st Battle Squadron left Scapa for two days cruise to eastward.

Germans N. of Somme regained footing in Eaucourt l'Abbaye.

Russian success S. of Brzezany (Galicia) ; furious fighting ; 5,000 prisoners in three days ; attacks W. of Lutsk.

Rumanian rally S. of Roter Turm Pass, Rumanians crossed Danube at Rahova.

Bulgarian counter on Struma line defeated.

Bulgarian retreat towards Monastir. Allies advancing from Florina.

Italians occupied Albanian ports.

French minesweeper *Rigel* torpedoed by U35 in Mediterranean.

British s.s. *Huntsfall* sunk by U-Boat off Skyro.

Sundays marked with Asterisk (*).

October 3, 1916.

N. of Somme British recapture Eaucourt l'Abbaye.

H.M. submarine E19 (Cmdr. Cromie) sinks German merchantman in Baltic.

German Twelfth Army dissolved.

Rumanian success in Dobrudja, and between Hermannstadt—Brasso (Transylvania).

First Battle of Monastir : Serbs reach Kenali.

British across Struma take Yeni Keui.

Athens Cabinet resigns.

October 4.

H.M. collier *J. Y. Short* sunk by U-Boat 80 miles from Vardö.

British s.s. *Brantingham* sunk by U-Boat in Arctic Ocean ; 24 lives lost.

French advance E. of Morval ; nine guns taken.

Rumanians captured 13 guns in Dobrudja ; withdrew from Rahova, across Danube. Fogaras evacuated.

Serbs E. of Monastir ; 90 sq. miles of Serb territory regained.

H.M.T. *Franconia* (18,150 tons) torpedoed by U-Boat, without warning, 195 miles E. from Malta ; 12 lives lost.

French auxiliary *Gallia* sunk in Mediterranean by U35.

October 5.

On Somme : British advance N.E. of Eaucourt l'Abbaye.

Gen. Sakharoff attacked Austrian Gen. Boehm-Ermolli between Brody—Tarnopol on 25-mile front.

LZ101 raided Ciulnita.

Rumanian retreat towards Brasso and in the Fogaras—Vladeni sector.

October 6.

British s.s. *Hyndford* warded off U-Boat by gunfire in Arctic Sea.

In connexion with new U-Boat cruiser campaign Chancellor informed High Command that unrestricted warfare was Kaiser's concern as commander-in-chief, but that it impinged also on foreign political sphere.

N. of Somme British captured mill between Le Sars—Eaucourt l'Abbaye.

Reichstag Centre Party relieved Chancellor in advance of all political liability if High Command should advocate unrestricted U-Boat warfare.

Further British progress towards Seres (Macedonia).

October 7.

U53 at Newport (Rhode Is.).

Battle Cruiser Fleet from Scapa swept towards the Naze and to S.W. of Little Fisher Bank to examine neutral trawlers.

Two British light cruisers left Scapa to meet at sea British airships from Longside near Peterhead, for joint exercises.

N. of Somme British took Le Sars in advance from Albert—Bapaume road— Lesbœufs ; progress 600-1,000 yards between Gueudecourt—Lesbœufs. German attack on Schwaben Redoubt failed. French progress at Morval—Bouchavesnes.

Rumanians retired on Predeal—Orsova ; Brasso and Szekeley Udvarhely recaptured by Austro-Germans.

October 7 (*continued*).

British advance between Struma R. and Demir Hissar—Seres railway (Macedonia).

⁑October 8.

U53 torpedoed eight vessels off Nantucket Light and started back on return to Germany.

Spanish schooner *Virgen del Socorro*, chartered by fugitive German war prisoners from Cameroons who had been interned in Spain, left Vigo in attempt to reach German waters, with 13 German officers and men.

British 2nd Battle Squadron left Scapa for two days cruise to eastward.

On Somme : British progress N. of Courcelette—Warlencourt road. French progress to Sailly, across Bapaume—Péronne road.

Falkenhayn's Transylvanian offensive progressed ; Törzburg taken. Germans took Danube Is., N.W. of Sistovo.

French at Kishovo in advance on Monastir.

M. Lambros Greek Premier.

October 9.

Kaiser sent reminder to Mr. Gerard, U.S. ambassador to Berlin (now in U.S.), that in April, at Charleville, he had held out prospect of early peace action by President Wilson.

British s.s. *Astoria* sunk by U-Boat N.W. of Vardö ; 17 lives lost.

Italian success at Mt. Pasubio (Trentino).

Further Rumanian retreat.

Italians at Premeli (Yoyusa R.).

Serbs crossed Tcherna, E. of Monastir.

M. Venizelos at Salonika.

October 10.

British s.s. *Gardepee* sunk by U-Boat 70 miles N.N.E. from North Cape.

H.M. submarine E19 sank German s.s. *Lulea* in Baltic.

Belgian Coast Patrol suspended. During the period 1-v.-16 the day Patrol was out for 144 out of 163 days, and the submarines patrolled on 112 nights. German aircraft attacked the Patrol 28 times ; 12 U-Boats were attacked and 9 actions with German T.B.D.s were fought by the Patrol. H.M. monitor *Prince Rupert* on one occasion was shelled and straddled by Knocke Battery at 34,000 yards range.

S. of Somme French progress at Berny— Chaulnes ; Bovent, outskirts of Ablaincourt, most of Chaulnes Wood carried.

Great Italian success in Carso.

Rumanian Second Army resisting S. of Brasso ; Gen. Avaresco in command. Austro-Germans on frontier ridge of Törzburg Pass.

Gen. Otto von Below to command German forces in Macedonia.

French carried first Bulgarian (Macedonian) lines on heights W. of Ghevgeli ; British cavalry 2 miles from Seres.

Allies demanded surrender of whole Greek Fleet, except 3 ships.

H.M. oiler *Elax* sunk by U-Boat off Cape Matapan.

October 11.

British s.s. *Iolo* sunk by U-Boat 153 miles N. from Vardö.

H.M. submarine E19 sank Hamburg s.s. *Walter Leonhardt*, *Gutrure*, *Director*

October 11, 1916 (*continued*).

Rippenhagen and *Nicomedia*, mostly ore-laden, in Baltic. S.S. *Nike* sent with prize crew to Reval.

Italians defeated Austrian counter in Carso, continued advance; 1,700 more prisoners.

British s.s. *Crosshill* (5,002 tons) sunk by U-Boat 60 miles W. from Malta.

Serbs gained footing in Brod (Monastir).

October 12.

N. of Somme British attacked heights in front of Bapaume—Péronne road; progress W. of Le Transloy; French continued W. of Sailly-Saillisel.

Mauser works at Oberndorf bombed by Franco-British air squadron.

Further Italian progress in Carso.

Fighting in Transylvanian passes; Germans at Predeal, where Rumanians held frontier ridge.

October 13.

H.M.S. *Fearless* and three British submarines left Scapa for Alexandrovsk to operate against U-Boats in White Sea.

Norway prohibited belligerent submarines from using her waters.

Adm. Nepenin, Russian C.-in-C. in Baltic, vice Adm. Kanin.

Further Italian advance on Isonzo front.

Rumanian retreat in Törzburg Pass; invaders 6 miles within Rumanian territory. Austrians repulsed in Predeal—Vulcan Passes and Oitoz Valley.

British s.s. *Welsh Prince* sunk by U-Boat off Cape Matapan.

October 14.

H.M.S. *Glorious* commissioned.

N. of Somme British progress at Schwaben Redoubt. French progressed S. of river, W. of Belloy-en-Santerre took Genermont.

Austrians on Predeal frontier ridge.

*October 15.

N. of Somme British progress at Stuff Redoubt. French in outskirts of Sailly-Saillisel.

Russian successes at Yablonitza and Kirlibaba (Carpathians).

Germans attacked Russo-Rumanian Army junction at Dorna Watra.

October 16.

On Somme : French progress at Sailly-Saillisel.

Germans captured Gyimes Pass (Transylvania); Falkenhayn held in Törzburg Pass ; slight German progress at Dorna Watra.

October 17.

British light forces from Rosyth swept down to Little Fisher Bank and back.

Baron Burian, Austro-Hungarian Foreign Minister, visited German G.H.Q. at Pless and suggested to Chancellor von Bethmann-Hollweg that Central Powers should intimate readiness to discuss peace on terms.

Fight for Rumanian passes ; invaders checked in Gyimes Pass.

Serbs took Brod, towards Monastir.

Allied troops landed at Athens.

Italian T.B.D. torpedoed in Adriatic.

October 18.

H.M. collier *Ethel Duncan* sunk by U-Boat 40 miles W.N.W. from Noop Heap, Orkneys.

Anglo-French Somme advance ; British progress N. of Gueudecourt and towards Butte de Warlencourt ; French took Sailly-Saillisel ; S. of river they captured whole La Maisonnette Château—Biaches front.

H.M. submarine E9 (Cmdr. Horton) sank German s.s. *Soderham*, of Hamburg, and s.s. *Pernambuco* (Lulea-Stettin), with 3,500 tons iron ore, in Baltic.

Rumanian success in Gyimes Pass and S. of Törzburg Pass.

Greek National Defence Cabinet at Salonika.

October 19.

British cruisers swept for two days down Norwegian coast.

British s.s. *Alaunia* (13,405 tons) mined off Royal Sovereign Light.

On Somme : Slight British progress at Butte de Warlencourt ; total prisoners since July 1 = 28,918. French took Saillisel.

H.M. submarine E9 sank German steamers *Johannes Russ* and *Dal Alfven* in Baltic.

H.M. submarine E38 torpedoed H.I.M.S. *München* in Heligoland Bight ; *München* towed back damaged.

Austrian attacks at Pasubio (Trentino) repulsed.

German attack on Gnila Lipa (Galicia).

New offensive by Mackensen in Dobrudja.

Rumanians fighting 12 miles within Gyimes Pass ; invaders repelled at Oitoz Pass.

October 20.

German Submarine Note to Norway.

British s.s. *Cabotia* sunk by U-Boat, 120 miles W.N.W. from Tory Is. ; 32 lives lost.

British s.s. *Barbara* sunk by U-Boat off Isle of Wight.

British s.s. *Midland* sunk by U-Boat off Ushant.

N. of Somme German attacks on Schwaben and Stuff Redoubts defeated.

Falkenhayn within Törzburg Pass ; Rumanians withdrew in Buzau Pass.

Rumanians lost Tuzla (Dobrudja).

Heavy fighting at Dorna Watra.

Russian battleship *Imperatritsa Maria* blown up at Sebastopol.

October 21.

On Somme : British attack on 5,000-yard front between Schwaben Redoubt—Le Sars ; line advanced 300-500 yards ; Stuff Redoubt and Regina Trench carried. French gained footing in Chaulnes Woods ; repulsed attacks on Sailly-Saillisel.

H.M. oiler *Clearfield* left Invergordon for Hampton Roads ; not since heard of.

Count Stürgkh Austrian Premier, shot in Vienna by Friedrich Adler.

Mackensen successful in Dobrudja ; Russo-Rumanian retreat ; German cut trans-Dobrudja railway.

Invaders in Predeal Pass.

*October 22.

British 4th and 5th Battle Squadrons left Scapa for two days watching and exercise cruise to eastward.

German aeroplane over Sheerness.

Sundays marked with Asterisk (*).

*October 22, 1916 (*continued*).

On Somme: French gained Ridge 128, W. of Sailly-Saillisel.

Rumanians evacuated Constanza.

German progress in Predeal Pass.

British s.s. *Cluden* and s.s. *W. Harkess* sunk by U-boat off Cape Tenez, Algeria.

October 23.

Aeroplane bombed Margate: 2 injured.

H.M.S. *Genista* torpedoed in North Sea.

On Somme: British attack E. of Lesbœufs—Gueudecourt.

Austrians at Predeal (Transylvania).

Germano-Bulgars at Constanza; Rumanians withdrew N. of Dobrudja railway.

LZ97 raided Bukarest.

October 24.

Four British steamers chased by U-Boat in Channel; two warded off attack by gunfire; two rescued, one of which already captured by German submarine.

French victory at Verdun; German line pierced on 5-mile front to a depth of 2 miles; Douaumont—Thiaumont retaken; 3,500 prisoners.

Vulcan Pass (Transylvania) captured by invaders; violent fighting in Törzburg--Predeal Passes; Rumanian successes at Roter Turm—Oitoz Passes.

Germans pressing on Tchernavoda (Dobrudja).

LZ101 raided Fetesti.

October 25.

British s.s. *City of Edinburgh* (6,255 tons) warded off U-Boat by gunfire in Channel.

Further French gains at Verdun; 1,000 more prisoners.

Chancellor had audience of Kaiser on eventual peace action, which was approved.

Austrians took Predeal town.

Tchernavoda (Dobrudja) fell to Germans; Rumanians retired north.

Italians from Albania in touch with Allied Macedonian left.

October 26.

H.M. collier *Oola* sunk by U-Boat 22 miles N.E. by N. from North Cape.

British submarine proceeded to Skagerrak to operate against German decoy vessels.

H.M. merchant cruiser *Kildonan Castle* of 10th Northern Blockade Squadron, attacked and missed by two U-Boat torpedoes off Iceland.

T.B.D. action in Channel; H.M.S. *Flirt* lost; H.M.S. *Nubian* torpedoed and grounded; empty British transport *Queen* sunk. Two German T.B.D.s believed sunk on way back.

British s.s. *Rowanmore* (10,320 tons) sunk by U-Boat 128 miles W.N.W. from Fastnet; master made prisoner.

British s.s. *Rappahannock* sunk by U-Boat off Scilly Is.; 37 lives lost.

On Somme: German attack on Stuff Redoubt driven off.

German attacks at Verdun repulsed; prisoners increased to 5,000.

Rumanians repulsed violent attack Törzburg Pass; further retreat in Vulcan Pass (Transylvania).

German pressure in Dobrudja weakening; Rumanians 25 miles N. of Tchernavoda—Constanza Railway.

October 27.

Six British drifters sunk by German T.B.D.s in Dover Straits.

Russian reverse in Dorna Watra sector.

Rumanian success in Uzal Valley; 90 prisoners; Rumanian counter-attack in Törzburg Pass; 300 prisoners; and in Jiul Valley (Vulcan Pass); 450 prisoners.

October 28.

H.M.S. *Courageous* commissioned.

British light forces from Rosyth proceeded on two days reconnaissance to S. of German North Sea minefield.

U53 reached Heligoland on return from U.S.

Australian Referendum: majority against conscription.

British s.s. *Marina* sunk by U-Boat off Fastnet.

H.S. *Galeka* (6,772 tons) mined off Cap la Hogue.

On Somme: British progress N.E. of Lesbœufs.

French carried quarry N.E. of Douaumont (Verdun) and recovered Fumin Wood.

Capt. Boelke, German airman, killed in air collision on W Front.

Austro-German advance S. of Roter Turm Pass.

French recovered Gardilovo toward Monastir.

*October 29.

N. of Somme: French carried trench system N.W. of Sailly-Saillisel. S. of Somme Germans penetrated La Maisonnette Château.

Rumanian pressure in Jiul Valley (Transylvania); 1,022 prisoners to date; slight German progress in Aluta Valley.

Three British steamers sunk by U-Boat off Cape Trafalgar and Cape St. Vincent.

October 30.

British s.s. *Mantola* (8,253 tons), mined in North Sea; arrived London.

Gen. Shtcherbatcheff forced back N. of Halicz; Russian progress W. of Lutsk.

Rumanian pursuit of invaders in Vulcan Pass (Transylvania).

UB45 lost by accident in Black Sea.

Gen. Northey defeated Germans at Lupembe (E. Africa).

October 31.

Battle Cruiser Fleet left Rosyth on three days observation and exercise cruise in central and northern parts of North Sea.

Kaiser wrote to Chancellor that as ruler responsible to God he felt strong enough to perform the " moral deed " of proposing peace.

German War Munitions Office instituted under Gen. Groener.

Gen. Shtcherbatcheff heavily engaged N. of Halicz.

Further Rumanian progress in Jiul Valley; invaders checked in Törzburg Pass; Austrian success in Predeal Pass (Transylvania).

British success on Struma; three more villages captured; 300 prisoners.

UB7 lost during October in Black Sea.

November 1.

" Merchant " U-Boat *Deutschland* again in U.S.

Two British steamers warded off U-Boat by gunfire in Arctic Sea.

For List of Abbreviations see page iv.

November 1, 1916 (continued).

Adm. Jellicoe landed from H.M.S. *Iron Duke* at Cromarty and proceeded to London to confer with Mr. Balfour on U-Boat menace.

British s.s. *Seatonia* sunk by U-Boat 80 miles N.W. from Fastnet.

French T.B. 300 mined off Havre.

Dutch s.s. *Oldambt*, being taken by German prize crew into Zeebrugge, cut out by British scouting craft ; five German T.B.D.s engaged and put to flight.

British Somme operations since mid-October yielded 31,132 prisoners to date.

North of Somme : Anglo-French advance N.E. of Lesbœufs towards Péronne road.

Germans evacuated Fort Vaux (Verdun).

Great Italian advance in Carso ; heights E. of Gorizia cleared ; Austrian N. sector broken ; 4,700 prisoners.

Italian T.B.D. raid on Pola.

Kaiser communicated to Emperor Francis Joseph his view of proposed peace offer (17-x.-16).

LZ97 raided Bukarest.

Austro-German pressure in Transylvanian passes ; Rumanians holding in Vulcan Pass. Russian Gen. Sakharoff to command in Dobrudja.

November 2.

U56 destroyed by Russian patrol vessels off Vardö.

British 2nd Battle Squadron left Scapa for two days cruise eastward of Shetlands.

N. of Somme : British captured trench E. of Gueudecourt.

S. of Somme : French raid W. of Lancourt, 8 miles S. of Chilly.

French occupied Vaux Fort (Verdun).

Italian Carso offensive proceeding ; heights above Kostanjevica taken ; 3,498 more prisoners. Austrian counter-attack.

Violent Austrian attacks at Predeal ; Rumanian success in Vulcan Pass.

Russian fleet bombarded Constanza.

November 3.

H.M. oiler *Ponus* wrecked in Falmouth Bay.

H.M. submarine E19 sank German s.s. *Ruomi* of Hamburg in Baltic.

H.M.S. *Botha* and H.M.S. *Faulknor* with T.B.D. forces from Scapa and Cromarty, supported by 1st Light Cruiser Squadron, swept up Norwegian coast.

French on outskirts of Vaux village (Verdun).

Italians nearing Kostanjevica (Carso).

November 4.

U20, which sank *Lusitania*, aground off Jutland ; destroyed by her own crew.

H.I.M.SS. *Grosser Kurfürst* and *Kronprinz* torpedoed and damaged by H.M. submarine J1 off Jutland in supporting German forces engaged in salving U20 and U30. As former could not be refloated, she was blown up by her crew.

French occupied Damloup Work ; now holding all former main defences of Verdun.

Russian fleet again bombarded Constanza.

✳November 5.

Adm. Jellicoe returned to Grand Fleet from London.

On Somme : French recaptured most of Saillisel ; attacked St. Pierre Vaast Wood. British progress on 1,000-yard front near Butte de Warlencourt ; attacked Le Transloy ; part of gains lost.

November 5 (continued).

French took all Vaux village (Verdun).

Germany and Austria - Hungary proclaimed an " Independent State of Poland," with an " hereditary Monarchy and Constitution."

German success W. of Predeal, and S.E. of Roter Turm Pass.

Hindenburg and Ludendorff agreed to proposed German peace offer, provided that German " National Service " programme first became law.

British on Struma front took Nevolien.

November 6.

On Somme : Further French advance in St. Pierre Vaast Wood ; 600 more prisoners.

Russian success S. of Dorna Watra.

Fierce fighting S. of Roter Turm Pass, 12 miles within Rumanian frontier.

P. & O. s.s. *Arabia* (7,933 tons) sunk by U-Boat W. by S. from Cape Matapan.

British operations on Wadai border ; Ali Dinar, ex-Sultan of Darfur, killed.

November 7.

President Wilson re-elected in U.S.

French success S. of Somme R. ; advance N. of Chaulnes ; Ablaincourt—Pressoire, and approaches to Gomiécourt taken. N. of river, British progress E. of Butte de Warlencourt ; N. of Ancre ; German attack W. of Beaumont-Hamel repulsed.

H.M. submarine E19 torpedoed and sank H.I.M.S. *Ancona* in Baltic.

November 8.

On Somme : Hand-to-hand fight at Saillisel.

Kaiser at Pless approved Chancellor's draft of joint terms upon which Austro-German peace action would proceed.

Falkenhayn progressed in Roter Turm Pass (Transylvania) ; penetrated 15 miles within Rumanian frontier N. of Rymnik.

Russo-Rumanian counter in Dobrudja.

November 9.

H.M. minesweeper *Fair Maid* mined near Cross Sand Buoy.

First British 500lb. bomb dropped by Short seaplane on Ostend-Zeebrugge.

Air battle N.E. of Bapaume : 30 British machines routed 40 Germans ; brought down 6 ; 4 British machines lost.

Portuguese Army ready to leave for W. front.

German success against Russian centre near Baranovitchi.

Russo-Rumanians at Dumarea, W. of Tchernavoda.

November 10.

Allied aeroplanes attacked harbour works and U-Boat shelters at Ostend—Zeebrugge.

On Somme : French captured trenches N.E. of Lesbœufs ; and repulsed attack at Saillisel ; German attack near Deniécourt repulsed.

German naval raid W. of Reval.

Austro-German advance in Jiul Valley.

Serb progress towards Monastir.

November 11.

Two British steamers sunk by U-Boat off Ushant.

British s.s. *City of Cairo* (7,672 tons) warded off U-Boat by gunfire off Cape Ortegal.

On Somme : French progress at Saillisel. German attack S.E. of Berny repulsed.

Sundays marked with Asterisk (*).

November 11, 1916 (*continued*).
British took Farmers Road, near Regina Trench.
Rumanian stand S. of Roter Turm Pass.
Allied recovery in Dobrudja.

#**November 12.**
British s.s. *Lady Carrington* sunk by U-Boat, 98 miles N. by W. from Cape Ortegal.
On Somme : French completed recapture of Saillisel.
Rumanians gave ground within frontier at Roter Turm Pass (Transylvania).
Serb progress towards Monastir ; Iven captured ; over 1,000 prisoners, 16 guns.

November 13.
British s.s. *Corinth* sunk by U-Boat off Flamborough Head.
Two British steamers sunk by U-Boat between 15 and 20 miles from Beachy Head.
Ancre Battle : New British attack N. and S. of Ancre R. ; German first-line defences penetrated on 5-mile front ; Beaumont-Hamel—St. Pierre Division stormed ; 3,300 prisoners.
German progress in Roter Turm—Vulcan Passes (Transylvania).

November 14.
British steamer sunk by U-Boat about 20 miles S. from Littlehampton.
Three British steamers attacked and chased by U-Boat off Ushant ; rescued.
Ostend gasworks hit during raid by 23 British aeroplanes.
Ancre Battle : British advance continued ; Beaucourt taken ; over 5,000 prisoners. British local advance E. of Butte de Warlencourt.
M. Miliukoff in Duma inveighed against the Rasputin—Stuermer *régime* and the dark forces behind the Russian Throne.
Rumanians retreating in Roter Turm—Vulcan Passes.
German 1st Air Squad. raided Bukarest.
Further Serb success on Tcherna R. ; 3,000 prisoners in four days ; Allies captured Kenali defences ; Bulgars fell back 5 miles S. of Monastir.
French auxiliary *Burdigala* mined in Mediterranean.

November 15.
H.M.S. *Fearless* left Alexandrovsk on return to Scapa.
British s.s. *Lake Michigan* (9,288 tons), and *St. Leonards* mined off Brest and Harvre ; reached port.
British aeroplanes bombed Ostend—Zeebrugge.
German counter-attacks N. of Chaulnes defeated.
Falkenhayn progressed in Rumanian passes ; German heavy guns through Törzburg Pass ; 20 miles within frontier at Roter Turm Pass and 25 miles at Vulcan Pass.
Serb advance on Tcherna R. continued.

November 16.
British steamer mined about ten miles W. by S. from Beachy Head.
British s.s. *Trevarrack* sunk off Guernsey.
Ancre Battle : Further British advance E. of Beaucourt ; some ground lost E. of Butte de Warlencourt ; over 6,000 prisoners since November 13.
Rumanians still retreating in Roter Turm Pass ; severe fighting in Törzburg, Vulcan, and Predeal Passes.
Herr von Kühlmann German Ambassador to the Porte, vice Count Wolff-Metternich.

November 17.
British s.s. *Monmouth* mined off Cherbourg ; towed in.
British naval aeroplanes raided Ostend—Zeebrugge.
Ancre Battle : British advance N.E. of Beaumont-Hamel and N. of Beaucourt.
French airman, Capt. de Beauchamps, bombed Munich ; crossed Alps ; landed N. of Venice.

November 18.
H.M. merchant cruiser *Otway*, of 10th Northern Blockade Squadron, intercepted Norwegian s.s. *Older*, in charge of German U-Boat prize crew ; steamer brought into Stornoway.
Ancre Battle : British reached outskirts of Grandcourt.
Total British captures in Somme Battle since July 1 : Over 38,000 prisoners, including 800 officers ; 29 heavy guns, 96 field guns and howitzers, 136 trench mortars, 514 machine-guns.
Falkenhayn broke Rumanian front in Jiul Valley ; reached Orsova-Craiova Railway.

*****November 19.**
Fall of Monastir to Gen. Sarrail's forces ; Serbs advanced beyond and took seven villages E. and N.E. of the town.
Falkenhayn extended S. of Vulcan—Roter Turm Passes, approached Craiova.
Admiral du Fournet demanded departure of Central Ministers from Athens and surrender of military material.
German defeat at Lupembe (E. Africa).

November 20.
German 1st Air Squad. raided Bukarest.

November 21.
Death of Emperor Francis Joseph.
Accession of Emperor Charles.
Fall of Craiova to Falkenhayn.
Fighting N. of Monastir.
British H.S. *Britannic* (48,158 tons) mined in Ægean ; 21 lives lost.

November 22.
H.M. submarine E30 lost in North Sea.
Adm. Scheer visited G.H.Q., Pless.
Herr Zimmermann German Foreign Secretary vice Herr von Jagow.
Fighting at Orsova (Danube).
German 1st Air Squad. raided Bukarest.
Fierce fighting N. of Monastir.

November 23.
Six German T.B.D.s raided N. end of Downs, where they were driven off by Ramsgate drifter night-patrol.
Mackensen crossed Danube at Sistovo and took Simnitza ; Rumanians fell back on Aluta ; Turnu Severir held by Germans.
Allied progress N. of Monastir.
H.S. *Braemar Castle* (6,318 tons) mined in Ægean ; beached.

November 24.
Grand Fleet put to sea for cruise in northern waters.
National Service Bill in Reichstag.
Admiral du Fournet's ultimatum to Greece ; 10 mountain batteries demanded by Dec. 1 ; other material by Dec. 15.

November 25.
Gen. von Lüttwitz to command IIIrd Prussian Army Corps vice Gen. von Lochow.
Mackensen joined Falkenhayn ; Upper Aluta line turned.
Rumanian Orsova garrison cut off.

*November 26, 1916.
German naval raid on Lowestoft ; armed trawler *Narval* sunk.
French battleship *Suffren* sunk by U-Boat off Lisbon.
Mackensen 50 miles from Bukarest ; Gen. von Delmensingen captured Rymnik.
Serbs captured Hill 1,050 (N. of Monastir).
Admiral du Fournet interviewed King Constantine at Athens.

November 27.
Adm. Jellicoe met Mr. Balfour at Rosyth and accepted appointment as First Sea Lord.
Zeppelin raid on Durham, Yorks, Staffs, and Cheshire ; 100 bombs dropped : 4 killed, 37 injured. One airship brought down off Durham coast by airman, one damaged by gunfire and brought down off Norfolk Coast by airmen.
Rumanian retreat ; Giurgiu (Danube) and Curtea de Arges captured ; Aluta line abandoned.
Germans took Slatina.
Further Serb advance in Macedonia.
British s.s. *City of Birmingham* (7,498 tons) sunk by U-Boat off Malta.
H.M. collier *Reapwell* sunk by U-Boat 148 miles N.W. by N. from Alexandria.

November 28.
Adm. Jellicoe issued Farewell Order to Grand Fleet.
First aeroplane raid on London (12th air raid) ; 10 injured. Raider brought down in France.
Naval aeroplanes bombed Zeebrugge.
Russian success E. of Jablonitza Pass and in Kirlibaba region.
Mackensen 17 miles from Bukarest.
British s.s. *Megantic* (14,878 tons) chased by U-Boat in Mediterranean ; escaped.

November 29.
Admiral Jellicoe First Sea Lord, vice Admiral Jackson ; Admiral Beatty C-in-C. Grand Fleet.
Falkenhayn at Pitesti—Campolung.
British s.s. *Luciston* mined off Dellamara Point, Malta.
British s.s. *Minnewaska* (14,317 tons) mined in Suda Bay.

November 30.
UB19 engaged and sunk off Portland Bill by H.M.S. *Penshurst* (Q7).
Germans nearing Bukarest.
UC15 was lost during November in Black Sea.

December 1.
Mr. Lloyd George urged Mr. Asquith to establish small War Cabinet.
H.M. submarine E37 lost in North Sea.
Gen. von Lochow, ex-IIIrd Army Corps, in acting command of Fifth Army, vice German Crown Prince.
Arges battle begun before Bukarest.
Admiral du Fournet landed troops at Piræus ; after some fighting Allies withdrew ; King Constantine offered six batteries instead of 10 demanded.

December 2.
British s.s. *Voltaire* (8,618 tons) captured and sunk by German raider *Möwe* 650 miles W. from Fastnet.

December 2 (*continued*)
British s.s. *Umona* warded off U-Boat by gunfire in Arctic Sea.
M. Trepoff, new Russian Premier, announced in Duma that Allies acknowledged Russia's title to Constantinople.
M. Purishkevitch in Duma joined in denunciation of "dark forces" behind Russian Throne.
Slight Russian gain N. of Rumanian frontier.
German progress in Rumania ; heavy fighting in Arges Valley ; Rumanians retired along Pitesti—Bukarest railway.
Serious crisis in Greece.
British s.s. *Istrar* sunk by U-Boat about 120 miles N.N.W. from Alexandria.

*December 3.
Mr. Asquith accepted reconstruction.
H.M. special service ship *Perugia* sunk by U-Boat in Genoa Gulf.
British s.s. *Lucellum* (5,184 tons) torpedoed by U-Boat in Mediterranean ; arrived Villefranche.
U-Boats bombarded Funchal (Madeira).
French gunboat *Surprise* torpedoed by U38.
German victory on Arges R. ; Tirgovistea taken ; First Rumanian Army defeated and driven beyond Titu ; Rumanian Army S.W. of Bukarest driven back ; furious fighting in Dobrudja.
Serb advance N.E. of Monastir.

December 4.
UC19 sunk in Dover Straits by H.M.S. *Llewellyn* with depth-charges.
Hindenburg "National Service" programme became law, under administration of Gen. Groener
Germans advancing towards Ploesti, centre of Rumanian oil fields.
Rumanians blew up Bukarest arsenal.
Further Serb gains N.E. of Monastir.
British s.s. *Caledonia* (9,223 tons) sunk by U-Boat 125 miles E. by S. from Malta.

December 5.
Mr. Asquith resigned, following resignation of Mr. Lloyd George, who had failed to carry his point with the Premier, and threatened resignation of Unionist leaders ; King sent for Mr. Bonar Law.
Admiral Burney and Captain Halsey Second and Fourth Sea Lords.
Russians on commanding height in Jablonitza Pass.
Germans outside Bukarest.
German 1st Air Squad. raided Bukarest.
Serb success N.E. of Monastir against Prussian Guard Chasseurs.
Athens terrorism ; Venizelists murdered.

December 6.
Mr. Bonar Law declined to form Ministry ; Mr. Lloyd George accepted.
British s.s. *Mount Temple* (9,792 tons) captured and sunk by German raider *Möwe* 620 miles W. from Fastnet.
UB29 sunk off Bishop Rock Lighthouse, Scilly Is., by H.M.S. *Ariel* with high explosive sweeps.
Slight German gain at Hill 304 (Verdun).
Bukarest fell to Mackensen ; Ploesti taken ; oil wells first destroyed by Allies.
Rumanian Government at Jassy.
More outrages in Athens.

December 7.
British s.s. *Conch* (5,620 tons) sunk by U-Boat off Anvil Point ; 28 lives lost.

Sundays marked with Asterisk (*).

December 7, 1916 (*continued*).

H.M.S. *Broke* (Cmdr. E. R. G. R. Evans) joined Dover Patrol.

French T.B.D. *Yatagan* sunk in Channel.

French recovery at Hill 304 (Verdun)

Renewed Russian offensive in Carpathians.

Germans on Bukarest—Ploesti line barred Rumanian retreat from Predeal. Orsova division surrendered at Caracal.

Blockade of Greece from Dec. 8 until outrages on Allies in Athens compensated.

December 8.

British s.s. *King George* sunk by *Möwe* 700 miles E. from Cape Race.

H.M. trawler *Dagon* torpedoed by U-Boat off Royal Sovereign Light; the only trawler so lost in Dover area during war.

Hindenburg secured Kaiser's assent to text of Army Order to be issued with German peace offer, calling upon the German troops in the field not to relax their efforts.

Murman Railway (from ice-free port of Romanoff to Petrograd) announced open.

Bulgarians crossed Danube E. of Bukarest.

December 9.

British s.s. *Cambrian Range* sunk by *Möwe* 610 miles from Cape Race.

British s.s. *Strathalbyn* mined off Cherbourg Breakwater.

Rumanians pressed back E. of Ploesti.

*December 10.

British s.s. *Georgic* (10,077 tons) sunk by *Möwe* 590 miles from Cape Race.

Russian advance in Kirlibaba region, and in Trotus Valley.

Rumanian recovery E. of Ploesti.

Wireless messages intercepted between King Constantine and Berlin.

December 11.

British s.s. *Yarrowdale* captured by *Möwe* 540 miles from Cape Race and taken to Germany.

Mr. Lloyd George, Lord Curzon, Lord Milner, and Mr. Henderson to form new War Cabinet; Mr. Bonar Law to lead Commons; Lord Derby, War Secretary; Sir E. Carson, First Lord of Admiralty; Mr. Balfour, Foreign Secretary; Mr. Chamberlain, India; Dr. Addison, Munitions; Lord Devonport, Food Controller; Lord Robert Cecil, Blockade.

M. Briand reconstructed French Ministry with smaller War Council. Gen. Lyautey War Minister.

British air raids on Zeebrugge.

Germans 20 miles east of Ploesti.

Italian battleship *Regina Margherita* mined off Avlona (Albania).

Allied Note to Greece; complete demobilisation, restoration of Allied control of posts, telegraphs, and railways, and release of Venizelists demanded.

December 12.

British s.s. *St. Theodore* captured by *Möwe* 520 miles W. from Flores; converted into raider (30-xii.-16); sunk 12-ii.-17.

German Peace Proposals: Chancellor announced in Reichstag that the Central Powers had made overtures through neutral Governments.

Gen. Joffre, French Generalissimo, became technical military adviser to new French War Committee; Gen. Nivelle assumed command on W. Front. Vice-

December 12 (*continued*).

Admiral Gauchet succeeded Admiral Fournet in command of Allied Fleets Mediterranean.

British s.s. *St. Ursula* (5,011 tons) su by U-Boat off Malta.

Fighting N. of Monastir.

Venizelist troops landed at Hermopc (Syra, Ægean).

December 13.

Kaiser, in speech to troops at Mülhause explained bearing of German peace offer.

Austrian Cabinet of Dr. von Kör resigned; Dr. von Spitzmüller succeeded.

Rumania, S. of Bukarest—Tchernavc line in Mackensen's hands.

British s.s. *Bretwalda* sunk by U-Boat Malta.

British resumed offensive towards Kt advanced through Es Sinn position to Hai and bombarded Sanna-i-Yat, on other bank Tigris.

December 14.

Mr. Bonar Law, referring to Germ peace proposals, reiterated Mr. Asquit statement: "The Allies require that th shall be adequate reparation for the past a adequate security for the future."

M. Pokrovsky, Russian Foreign Ministe

British s.s. *Caledonia* (7,572 to1 mined off Marseilles; reached port.

British s.s. *Russian* (8,825 tons) and Westminster sunk by U-Boat about 200 mi E. by S. from Malta; 43 lives lost.

Allied ultimatum to Greece; all Gre troops to leave Thessaly.

British naval aeroplanes bombarc Kuleli—Burgas bridge, S. of Adrianople.

December 15.

French Victory at Verdun; German fro broken to depth of 2 miles; Poivre Rid Vacherauville, Louvemont, and Hardaumc —Bezonvaux Works taken with 7,5 prisoners.

Germans at Buzan (Rumania).

British naval aeroplanes bombed Razlo' (Serbia).

Greece accepted Allied Ultimatum.

British outposts 1,200 yards from Tig S. of Kut.

Gen. Smuts gained ground N.W. Kibata (E. Africa).

December 16.

French extended at Verdun; gain Bezonvaux village, and progressed in B des Caurières; nearly 10,000 prisoners, guns.

German pursuit in Wallachia a Dobrudja.

UB46 mined at Dardanelles.

*December 17.

British s.s. *Pascal* (5,587 tons) sunk U-Boat off Casquets.

Gen. von der Marwitz in command German Second Army, vice Gen. von Gallwi who took over Fifth Army from Germ Crown Prince.

German counter-attack at Verd French now claimed 11,300 prisoners, 115 gu 107 machine-guns.

U20 destroyed in Straits of Otranto H.M. drifter *Fisher Girl* with nets and dep charges.

For List of Abbreviations see page iv.

*December 17, 1916 (*continued*).

Germans approaching Braila ; Russo-Rumanians retired in Dobrudja.

Greek Government issued warrant against M. Venizelos for treason.

December 18.

German "Peace" Note at Foreign Office.

Mr. Lloyd George on German peace offer and new Government's war policy ; formal reply to German Note to be given in full accord with Allies, who had each "separately and independently arrived at identical conclusions " ; "restitution, reparation, and a guarantee against repetition" demanded. Goverment decided to recognise agents of M. Venizelos, to call an Imperial Conference, to take over shipping and mining, and to institute National Service.

British s.s. *Dramatist* (5,415 tons) sunk by *Möwe* 490 miles S.W. from Flores.

British s.s. *Flimston* (5,751 tons) sunk by U-Boat off Ushant.

French retook Chambrettes Farm (Verdun).

Russians checked Germans 30 miles from Braila.

December 19.

Mackensen 25 miles from Braila ; German Ninth Army held up.

December 20.

President Wilson suggested belligerents should intimate views as to peace terms.

Gen. Ludendorff urged upon Chancellor that, in view of Mr. Lloyd George's speech, unrestricted U-Boat warfare could no longer be delayed.

British s.s. *Hildawell* mined in North Sea ; 22 lives lost.

British s.s. *Itonus* (5,340 tons) sunk by U-Boat off Malta.

Activity at Monastir ; German reinforcements.

British advance to right bank of Tigris, S.E. of Kut.

December 21.

H.M.SS. *Hoste* and *Negro* lost by collision in North Sea.

Russian withdrawal in Dobrudja.

Allied Note to Greece ; prohibition of reservists' meetings, control of telegraphs, posts and railways, release of imprisoned Venizelists and inquiry into Athens disturbances demanded.

H.M. oiler *Murex* sunk by U-Boat off Port Said.

British occupied El Arish (Sinai).

British air raid on Bargela, new Turkish base, 19 miles W. of Kut.

Adm. von Holtzendorff, Chief of German Admiralty Staff, drew up Memorandum urging immediate unrestricted U-Boat warfare, on the ground that England could thereby be brought to her knees within five months.

December 22.

King's Message proroguing Parliament : " the vigorous prosecution of the war must be our sole endeavour."

Swiss Peace Note to belligerents.

Count Czernin Austro-Hungarian Foreign Minister vice Count Burian.

Five-day Austro-German attack on Rimnic Sarat (Wallachia) begins.

December 23.

British s.s. *Bertrand* and s.s. *William Middleton* attacked by U-Boat in Bristol Channel ; rescued.

December 23 (*continued*).

Hindenburg in Berlin urged Chancellor to expedite inauguration of unrestricted U-Boat warfare.

Russo-Rumanians in Dobrudja withdrawing across Danube.

British s.s. *Thistleban* sunk by U-Boat off Alexandria.

British captured Bir el Magdhaba (Sinai) ; 1,350 prisoners, guns, and stores taken.

*December 24.

British s.s. *Paul Paix* mined in Bristol Channel ; towed into port.

Chancellor maintained his view that unrestricted U-Boat warfare was an act of foreign policy for which he was responsible.

Germans clearing Dobrudja ; took Tulcea and attacked Macin bridgehead covering crossing to Braila ; further Allied retreat in Wallachia.

December 25.

Dominion Premiers invited to "Special War Conference of the Empire."

British 9.2 inch Battery on Belgian coast completed.

Tsar's order to his troops : " Time not yet come for conclusion of peace."

Germans held before Braila.

LZ101 raided Galatz.

December 26.

German reply to American Peace Note ; immediate meeting of delegates suggested.

German High Command again urged Chancellor not to allow any political considerations to delay so vital a military measure as unrestricted U-Boat warfare.

Gen. Joffre created Marshal of France.

British airmen bombed Dillingen and French airmen bombed Neunkirchen and Hagondangen.

Fierce struggle in Wallachia.

December 27.

Fall of Rimnic Sarat (Wallachia) to Austro-Germans.

Austro-German offensive on borders of Moldavia.

French battleship *Gaulois* sunk by U-Boat in Ægean.

British airmen destroyed Chikaldir Bridge on Baghdad Railway.

December 28.

British s.s. *Suffolk* (7,573 tons) mined in the Channel ; arrived Portsmouth.

Heavy fighting in Oitoz Pass.

December 29.

H.M. minesweeper *Ludlow* and s.s. *Zoroaster* mined off Shipwash Light.

Sir D. Haig's Somme Battle Dispatch.

German attack N.W. of Verdun repulsed.

Scandinavian Peace Note to belligerents.

Russian Duma prorogued.

Monk Rasputin murdered in Petrograd at the Palace of Prince Yussupoff.

December 30.

British s.s. *St. Theodore* (12-xii.-16), after conversion into raider by *Möwe*, captured and sank British sailing vessel *Jean* 60 miles E. from St. Paul Rocks.

British s.s. *Aspenleaf* mined in the Channel ; towed into port.

Sundays marked with Asterisk (*).

December 30, 1916 (*continued*).

Allies negatived German proposals, which were described as lacking substance and precision, less an offer of peace than a war manœuvre.

German advance towards Braila.

＃December 31.

British pilot cutter *Protector* mined off entrance to the Tyne ; 19 lives lost.

British s.s. *City of Oran* warded off U-Boat by gunfire in Channel.

Sir D. Haig promoted Field-Marshal.

Two German attacks in Champagne repulsed.

Germans repulsed near Braila.

Further Allied Note to Greece again demanding reparation for events of Dec. 1 and 2.

January 1, 1917.

German raid at Ypres.

German attack at Verdun failed.

Further German success in Dobrudja.

Cunard s.s. *Ivernia* (14,278 tons) sunk by U-Boat in Mediterranean. Crew and over 2,000 troops rescued by H.M. T.B.D. *Rifleman* and two trawlers.

British carried German lines S. of Uluguru Hills (E. Africa).

January 2.

Lord Cowdray chairman Air Board, vice Lord Curzon.

British repulsed German raid E. of Vermelles.

Two British steamers chased by U-Boat in Bay of Biscay ; escaped.

January 3.

German gains in Milcovu Valley (Rumania).

Russo-Rumanians lost Jijila (Dobrudja).

Russian success in S. Bukovina.

Russian battleship *Peresviet* mined near Port Said.

January 4.

British raids near Wytschaete and N.E. of Arras.

Russo-Rumanian position before Braila pierced. Germans entered Macin.

Gen. Smuts' forces occupied German camp on Tshogowali R. (E. Africa).

Capt. F. C. Selous, D.S.O., 25th Royal Fusiliers, killed in action at Beho-Beho (E. Africa).

January 5.

Mr. Lloyd George and Lord Milner at Rome Conference.

British s.s. *Allie* sunk by U-Boat off Ile de Ré.

British s.s. *Eastgate* captured by U-Boat in Bay of Biscay ; rescued.

Raid on British trenches S. of Loos repulsed.

On Somme : British raids near Beaumont-Hamel ; two outposts captured.

Fall of Braila; Allies evacuated Dobrudja.

Khadairi Bend operations, E. of Kut, begun.

British on N. bank of Rufiji R. (E. Africa).

January 6.

British raid S.E. of Arras towards Tilloy.

Germans N.W. of Braila advanced to Sereth R. and organised defences of N. Dobrudja.

＃January 7.

German Foreign Secretary Zimmermann asks Count Bernstorff how unrestricted U-Boat war could be conducted without provoking breach with U.S.A.

British s.s *Radnorshire* sunk by German raider *Möwe* 110 miles E. from Pernambuco.

British s.v. *Brenda* sunk by U-Boat ten miles S.W. from Beachy Head.

British raid near Armentières.

Russian advance 4 miles W. of Riga.

January 8.

Ypres heavily shelled.

Unsuccessful German attempts S.E. of Souchez.

Prince Golitzin Russian Premier vice M. Trepoff.

Russian gains held near Riga ; attacks developing at Riga—Jacobstadt (Dvina).

Fall of Focsani (Rumania) ; nearly 5,400 prisoners claimed by Germans.

New Allied Note to Greece ; 48 hours time-limit.

January 9.

H.M. collier *Minieh* (3,806 tons) sunk by German raider *Möwe* 170 miles E.N.E. from Pernambuco.

British s.s. *Gladys Royle* (3,268 tons) sunk by German raider *Seeadler* 120 miles S.W. from Santa Maria, Azores.

British s.s. *Alexandrian* attacked by U-Boat off Fastnet ; beached Berehaven.

British s.s. *Excellent* sunk by U-Boat N.W. Noop Head, Orkneys.

Kaiser and Chancellor von Bethmann-Hollweg at War Council at Pless G.H.Q., assented to institution of unrestricted U-Boat warfare on February 1, on the strength of an Admiralty Staff pledge that this would bring England to her knees by next harvest.

Kaiser's Order to Admiralty Staff :—

"*I command that unrestricted U-Boat warfare shall be instituted with the utmost energy on February 1. You are forthwith to make all necessary preparations, but in such a way that this design does not become prematurely apparent to the enemy and to neutrals. The material plan of operations is to be submitted to me.*"

Artillery activity on Ancre R. ; British seized trench section E. of Beaumont-Hamel ; 140 prisoners. British raid opposite Hulluch.

Further Russian gain between Tirul Marsh—Aa R. (Riga) ; 32 guns taken.

British s.s. *Baynesk* (3,286 tons) sunk by U-Boat 130 miles N.W. Alexandria.

Anzacs and Imperial Camel Corps captured strong Turkish position at Rafa, 30 miles N.E. of El Arish ; 1,600 prisoners.

Indian Division captured 1,000 yards of trench in Mesopotamia ; Sanna-i-Yat bombarded.

January 10.

British s.s. *Netherby Hall* (4,461 tons) sunk by German raider *Möwe* 300 miles E. by N. from Pernambuco.

British s.s. *Lundy Island* sunk by German raider *Seeadler* 190 miles S.E. from Santa Maria, Azores.

Count Bernstorff telegraphed to Berlin F.O. that unrestricted U-Boat war would render rupture with U.S. inevitable.

Allied reply to President Wilson's Note (21-xii.-16) published : Terms included compensation to Belgium, Serbia, and Montenegro ; evacuation of invaded territories of France, Russia, and Rumania ; reorganisation of Europe on basis of nationality ; and

January 10, 1917 (*continued*).
eviction of Turks from Europe ; no extinction of Germanic peoples.

Gen. Nivelle transferred French G.H.Q. to Beauvais, from Chantilly, where it had been established since 30-xi.-14.

Russians drove Austro-Germans back across Putna R. (Rumania).

Qualified Greek acceptance of Allied demands (8-i.-17).

Turkish trenches on right bank Tigris, in loop N.E. of Kut taken ; British cavalry occupied Hai.

January 11.
British 7th Division carried 1,200 yards of trenches on spur E. and N.E. of Beaumont Hamel.

H.M.S. *Cornwallis* (14,000 tons) sunk by U-Boat off Malta.

H.M. seaplane-carrier *Ben-my-Chree* (3,888 tons) sunk by gunfire in Castellorizzo harbour (Asia Minor).

January 12.
British s.s. *Auchencraig* (3,916 tons) sunk by U-Boat off Ushant ; 4 lost.

British s.s. *Brentwood* mined off Whitby.

German counter in Riga district failed.

Mihalea on Lower Sereth R. (Rumania) stormed by Turks ; Russian success at Radulesti ; Rumanian success in Casin Valley.

January 13.
British s.s *Amazon* (10,000 tons) attacked by U-Boat with torpedo off Cape Finisterre ; missed.

British raids W. of Wytschaete and at Armentières—Neuve Chapelle.

Germans in British post N.W. of Serre.

U.S. and Dutch Ministers left Rumania.

Rebels advancing on Zuara (W. of Tripoli), defeated by Italians.

S. bank of Tigris E. of Kut-el-Amara by this date nearly clear of Turks.

* January 14.
H.M.S. *Penshurst* (Q7), Capt. F. H. Grenfell, R.N., engaged and sank UB37 in Channel.

British raid E. of Loos.

Germans again checked in Moldavia.

Japanese battle-cruiser *Tsukuba* blown up in Yokosuka Harbour.

January 15.
First meeting of Inter-Allied Executive in London for allocation of neutral tonnage to Britain, France, and Italy.

Gen. Smuts to represent S. Africa at Imperial War Conference.

British s.s. *Port Nicholson* (8,418 tons) mined off Dunkirk ; 2 lost.

Brisk fight between Aisne—Argonne.

Rumanian advance S.W. of Pralea.

British s.s *Garfield* sunk by U-Boat 60 miles N.E. Alexandria.

January 16.
Kaiser, having read Count Bernstorff's telegram of Jan. 10, instructed his Chancellor that the Pless decision of Jan. 9 would be carried out regardless of U.S.

German Chancellor confidentially informed Count Bernstorff of Pless decision on Jan. 9, and intimated that Germany was ready to risk breach with U.S.

British raid in Lens region.

January 16 (*continued*).
Gen. Bieliaeff Russian War Minister, vice Gen. Shuvaieff.

Two Turkish ships reported sunk by Russian submarine near Bosporus.

Mackensen checked on Sereth R. (Rumania).

Italian advance S. of Lake Ochrida (Macedonia).

Greece accepted Allied demands (8-i.-17)

January 17.
Mr. Balfour's covering Note to Allied reply to President Wilson published.

British occupied German posts N. of Beaucourt on 600-yard front.

British raid in Loos region.

German aeroplane raid on Dvinsk.

Rumanian success in Moldavia.

January 18.
British s.s. *Manchester Inventor* (4,247 tons) sunk by U-Boat about 50 miles N.W. from Fastnet.

January 19.
London (Silvertown) munition-factory explosion ; 69 killed.

H.M. submarine E36 lost in North Sea.

British s.s. *Nailsea Court* (3,295 tons) sunk by U-Boat off Skelligs.

British s.s. *Tremeadow* (2,653 tons) sunk by U-Boat off Ushant.

Successful British raid at St. Eloi.

Last German effort against Rumanian Sereth line ; Nanesti taken.

January 20.
British s.s. *Bulgarian* (2,515 tons) sunk by U-Boat in Atlantic ; 14 lost.

British s.s. *Neuquen* (3,583 tons) sunk by U-Boat off Skelligs ; 18 lost.

British s.s. *Planudes* mined in North Sea ; 11 lost.

British raid at Neuve Chapelle.

Joint Austro-German conference in Vienna decided Austria should join in unrestricted U-Boat warfare.

British air raid on Baghdad.

Hai salient operations begun.

Gen. Hoskins to command in E. Africa vice Gen. Smuts, designated to attend Imperial War Cabinet.

Progress on Rufiji R. (E. Africa).

* January 21.
British raid at Loos.

German raid N. of Arras.

January 22.
President Wilson in Message to U.S. Senate deprecated peace based on victory of either belligerent group.

Allied naval conference at Admiralty in London on Mediterranean policy.

British s.s. *Trevean* (3,081 tons) sunk by U-Boat off Fastnet.

French sailing ship *Anna* sunk by U53 in English Channel.

German raid N.E. of Ploegsteert Wood.

German attack at Verdun driven off.

Sixteen British naval aeroplanes bombarded Burbach furnaces (Sarre).

German attacks on Riga front driven off.

LZ 97 raided Kishineff.

Bulgarians crossed arm of Danube opposite Tulcea.

January 23.
Col. House, in New York, informed Count Bernstorff of President Wilson's desire

January 23, 1917 (*continued*).

to promote peace on basis of his Message of day before.

H.M. A.M.C. *Laurentic* (14,892 tons) mined off Irish coast.

British s.s. *Clan Shaw* (3,943 tons) mined off the Tay ; 2 lost.

German T.B.D. division encountered in North Sea by British light forces ; one German T.B.D. sunk, others scattered. Another T.B.D. action off Schouwen Bank ; H.M.S. *Simoon* torpedoed (sunk by British ships) ; 47 lives lost ; battered German T.B.D. V69 put into Ymuiden with many casualties.

Two German attempts between Armentières—Ploegstreet.

British raid at Neuville.

Russians lost ground W. of Riga.

Bulgarians at Tulcea driven across Danube by Russians ; 337 prisoners.

Germans in Rumania now held on Galatz—Focsani (Sereth) line.

January 24.

German and British raids on W. front.

French raids on Somme and in Woevre.

Gen. von Quast to command Prussian Guard Corps, vice Gen. von Plettenberg.

German progress along Aa W. and S.W. of Riga.

German force (39 Europeans, 250 natives) surrendered in S. of G.E. Africa.

January 25.

German T.B.D. bombarded Southwold.

British raids at Hulluch.

Heavy German attack at Verdun repulsed.

British attack S.W. of Kut and W. of Hai R. ; 1,100 yards of first line and considerable second-line trench gained ; not all held.

January 26.

U76 sunk by Russian trawlers in Arctic.

New British minefield off Jutland.

British raids at Loos—Vermelles.

German attacks at Riga broken.

British carried whole second-line on Hai near Kut ; severe Turkish losses.

British s.s. *Matheran* (7,654 tons) mined off Dassen Is., Cape of Good Hope ; 1 lost.

January 27.

British s.s *Artist* (3,570 tons) sunk by U-Boat off the Smalls ; 35 lost.

British s.s *Ava* (5,076 tons) sunk by U-Boat off S. Ireland ; 92 lost.

British success near Le Transloy, on right of Somme front ; 350 prisoners.

German Crown Prince promoted General of the Infantry, on Kaiser's Birthday.

Russians penetrated on 3,000-yard front Austrian line on Kimpolung—Jakobeny road, at junction of Bukovina—Transylvania—Rumania ; over 1,000 prisoners.

* January 28.

H.M. T.B. 24 wrecked off Dover Breakwater.

Spanish s.s. *Nueva Montana*, with ore for Newcastle, sunk by U53 off Ushant.

British raids near Neuville—Festubert—Armentières.

French patrol actions in Champagne and Alsace.

Russian raid S. of Brzezany.

Turkish 15th Army Corps in Galicia.

LZ98 raided Petrograd.

British holding all Turkish first and second lines S.W. of Kut and right bank of Tigris on 4,300-yard front, and 600 yards of third and fourth lines.

January 29.

Herr von Bethmann-Hollweg instructed Count Bernstorff to communicate in Washington the terms on which Germany might have made peace in December, 1916, and to say that, while Germany welcomed President Wilson's intimation (23-i.-17), it was too late to revoke U-Boat orders.

Spanish s.s. *Algorta*, with ore for Stockton, sunk by U53 off Ushant.

British raids near Butte de Warlencourt and I'. of Souchez.

Lord Milner in Petrograd for Allied Conference.

January 30.

German attacks between Soissons—Reims failed.

Fighting at Hill 304 (Verdun).

LZ98 raided Petrograd.

German assaults at Riga between Tirul Swamp—Aa R. ; Russians retired at one point.

Further Russian success near Jakobeny.

January 31.

Count Bernstorff at Washington ordered at 10 a.m., "sabotage" of German ships in U.S. ports, in anticipation of rupture.

Germany announced "unrestricted naval warfare" from Feb. 1 ; all sea traffic to be prevented in wide zones round Britain, France, Italy, and in E. Mediterranean. U.S. to have access to Falmouth with one steamer per week, and a Dutch paddle steamer to ply between Flushing—Southwold. German Chancellor explained and justified policy.

Germans claimed 440,000 tons sunk during January, last month of restricted U-Boat war. British estimate = 324,016 tons.

During the two years immediately preceding the unrestricted U-Boat campaign 27 per cent. of vessels sunk by submarine were sunk without warning.

F.O. statement that Germany intended to sink British hospital ships ; allegations that they were used for transport of troops and munitions denied ; reprisals threatened.

Norwegian s.s *Hickla* sunk by U53 off Lizard.

British s.s. *Foyle* warded off U53 by gunfire at entrance to Channel.

Commodore G. M. Paine to be Fifth Sea Lord and Chief of Naval Air Service.

British raid S.E. of Neuville. German attacks near Beaucourt and Serre failed.

Russian recovery near Riga.

Russians took 1,000 prisoners in Bukovina.

During January the Amanus Tunnel (Baghdad Railway) was completed for traffic.

February 1.

U.S. resented German " blockade " proposals.

Unrestricted U-Boat war : campaign begun.

British s.s. *Essonite* (589 tons) sunk by U-Boat off Trevose Head ; 10 lost.

British smacks *I'll Try* (Skipper Thomas Crisp) and *Boy Alfred* (Skipper Wharton, D.S.C.) engaged two U-Boats off Lowestoft ; one U-Boat presumed sunk by gunfire (see 15-viii.-17).

R.M. Labour Corps formed.

British raid N.E. of Gueudecourt.

Germans penetrated Russian line 15 miles S. of Halicz ; repulsed.

Further British success at Kut ; last trench line but one E. of Tigris-Hai junction taken.

February 2, 1917.

Lord Devonport, British Food Controller, asked for voluntary restriction of consumption.

British s.s. *Lux* (2,621 tons) sunk by U53 westward of Ushant ; 29 lost.

British airmen from Dunkirk dropped bombs on German T.B.D.s and U-Boats ice-bound in Bruges Docks.

Mekran Mission returned to Chahbar.

February 3.

U.S. broke with Germany ; Count Bernstorff given his passports and Mr. Gerard recalled from Berlin.

German auxiliary cruisers interned in U.S. Navy yard seized ; four Hamburg-Amerika liners placed under Panama Canal Zone authorities.

British s.s. *Port Adelaide* (8,000 tons), *Hollinside* and *Eavestone*, and s.v. *Belford* sunk by U-Boat W.S.W. of Fastnet.

U.S. s.s. *Housatonic* sunk by U53 off Scilly Is., U60 in company.

Three British (Short) seaplanes dropped eighteen 112lb. bombs on German ships ice-bound in Bruges Docks.

British line E. of Beaucourt advanced 500 yards on 1,200-yard front.

Three lines of Turkish trenches W. of Hai—Tigris junction captured by British.

*February 4.

President Wilson invited all neutrals to follow U.S. example and break with Germany.

German ships interned at Manila disabled by their crews ; 17 German merchantmen taken over by U.S. naval authorities.

British s.s. *Palmleaf* (5,489 tons), *Floridian* (4,777 tons) and *Turino* (4,241 tons) sunk by U-Boat off Fastnet.

British s.s. *Ghazee* (5,084 tons) sunk by U-Boat off Galley Head.

One French and one Russian schooner sunk by U53 off Scilly Is. ; U83 in company.

German counter-attacks failed at Beaucourt. British gain on S. slopes of Serre.

Preliminary order issued for German withdrawal in Arras—Aisne R. sector on to Siegfried position (16-iii.-17).

Senussi defeated at Girba (W. Egypt) by British armoured car column under Gen. Hodgson.

British near Kut holding all left bank of Hai ; Turks fell back to liquorice factory.

February 5.

U.S. Shipping Board took over all ships on American Register.

Switzerland declined to follow U.S. in breaking with Germany.

Three British steamers, totalling over 11,000 tons, sunk by U-Boat off Fastnet.

British s.s. *Argyllshire* (12,097 tons) torpedoed by U-Boat off Start Point ; reached port.

Swedish s.s. *Bravalla* sunk by U53 off Scilly Is.

Tsar called conference to discuss future of Poland.

British dispersed Senussi, occupied Siwa (W. Egypt).

February 6.

British s.s. *Crown Point* (5,218 tons) sunk by U-Boat off Scilly Is. ; 7 lost.

Mr. N. Chamberlain's National Service Scheme.

Indian Registration Ordinance.

British on Ancre occupied ground between Grandcourt—Stuff Redoubt.

February 6 (*continued*).

Dahra Bend operations, W. of Kut, begun.

British s.s. *Tyndareus* (11,000 tons) mined off Cape Agulhas, Cape Colony,

February 7.

British s.s. *California* (8,669 tons), *Vedamore* (6,330 tons), *Saxonian* (4,855 tons) and *Gravina* (1,242 tons) sunk by U-Boat off Fastnet ; 74 lost.

Two British steamers sunk by U-Boat off Whitby ; 16 lost.

On Ancre : British took Grandcourt and Baillescourt Farm.

February 8.

B.I. s.s. *Mantola* (8,253 tons) sunk by U-Boat in Atlantic ; 7 lost.

H.M.S. *Gurkha* mined off Dungeness.

H.M.S. *Liberty* rammed and sank UC46 in Dover Straits.

H.M.S. *Thrasher* engaged and sank UC39 in North Sea.

U-Boat shelled coast off mouth of Adour R.

On Somme : British reached top of Sailly-Saillisel ridge (Hill 153) ; further progress from Grandcourt ; successful raid S. of Bouchavesnes.

February 9.

British raids near Ypres and Vermelles.

Attempted German raids near Armentières.

Austrian attack E. of Gorizia.

February 10.

British s.s. *Japanese Prince* (4,876 tons) sunk by U-Boat off Bishop Rock.

British s.s. *San Fraterno* (9,587 tons) mined off Firth of Forth ; beached.

British took trenches S. of Serre Hill.

Gen. Maude's troops carried trenches W. of Kut and liquorice factory.

*February 11.

Cunard s.s. *Lycia* (2,715 tons) sunk by U-Boat N.E. from S. Bishop.

H.I.M. T.B.D. V69 left Ymuiden after repairs (22-i.-17).

British advance along Beaucourt road ; 600 yards of trench taken ; German attempts near Serre frustrated.

Italian line re-established E. of Gorizia.

Archduke Frederick retired.

Germans crossed frozen Dniester S. of Halicz ; repulsed.

Turks hemmed in on Tigris W. of Kut.

February 12.

President Wilson refused to reopen with Germany until U-Boat order of Jan. 31 withdrawn.

White Star s.s. *Afric* (12,000) sunk by U-Boat off Eddystone.

British s.s. *Pinna* (6,288 tons) torpedoed by U-Boat off S. Bishop ; beached.

British raids E. of Ypres, at Neuville and Souchez.

German raid near Pys frustrated.

British s.s. *Cilicia* (3,750 tons) mined off Dassen Is., Cape of Good Hope.

February 13.

Submarine debate in House of Lords.

German attacks S. of Serre repulsed.

February 14.

Count Bernstorff sailed from U.S.

Seven British steamers and one sailing ship sunk by U-Boats.

Sundays marked with Asterisk (*).

February 14, 1917 (*continued*).

British s.s. *Millicent Knight* (3,563 tons) attacked with bombs by German aircraft in the Downs.

German raids near Messines and Loos beaten off. French raid at Compiègne.

German raid near Zloczow (Galicia); Russian line penetrated.

February 15.

British s.s. *Brecknockshire* (8,423 tons) and *French Prince* (4,766 tons) sunk by German raider *Möwe* 490 miles E.N.E. from Cape Frio, Brazil.

White Star s.s. *Celtic* (20,904 tons) mined in Irish Sea; arrived Liverpool.

German assault between Tahure—Massiges (Champagne); French line penetrated between Maisons de Champagne—Butte du Mesnil; Hill 185 captured; over 800 prisoners.

Russian line at Zloczow re-established.

Talaat Pasha, in his first speech in Turkish Chamber as Grand Vizier, proclaimed equality for all peoples in Ottoman Empire.

Gen. Maude cleared Turks from Dahra bend (Tigris); nearly 2,000 prisoners.

February 16.

British s.s. *Eddie* (2,652 tons) sunk by German raider *Möwe* 550 miles N.E. from Cape Frio, Brazil.

British War Loan: over £1,000,000,000 new money.

LZ107, fitted with observation "basket," raided Boulogne.

French success at Amertzwiller (Alsace).

February 17.

H.M.S. *Farnborough* (Q5), Capt. Gordon Campbell, R.N., sank U83 S.W. of Ireland.

British s.s. *Iolo* (3,840 tons) sunk by U-Boat off Fastnet; 2 lost.

Two British steamers sunk by U-Boat off Portland Bill; 11 lost.

British s.s. *Okement* (4,349 tons) sunk by U-Boat off Malta; 11 lost.

Further British advance on Ancre; position covering Miraumont—Petit Miraumont captured on 2,500-yard front; progress N. of Baillescourt Farm.

Russian success S.W. of Ocna, Trotus Valley (Moldavia).

British attack on Sanna-i-Yat failed.

British s.s. *Worcestershire* (7,175 tons) mined ten miles S.W. from Colombo; 2 lost.

✻February 18.

P. & O. s.s. *Berrima* (11,137 tons) torpedoed by U-Boat in Channel; towed into Portland.

German assaults on lost Ancre positions defeated; 773 prisoners in two days.

Italians and French in touch in S. Albania; Greece cut off from Central Powers.

February 19.

British s.v. *Pinmore* (2,431 tons) sunk by German raider *Seeadler* 540 miles N.E. from St. Paul Rocks.

H.M. special-service ship *Lady Olive* sunk by U-Boat in English Channel.

British advanced post near Le Transloy rushed.

German G.H.Q. transferred from Pless to Kreuznach.

February 20.

British raids S.W. of Ypres and S. of Armentières.

British thrust N.E. of Gueudecourt.

February 20 (*continued*).

British s.s. *Rosalie* (4,237 tons) sunk by U-Boat off Algerian coast; 21 lost.

Turkish detachments reported captured at Bir el Hassana and Nakhl (Sinai).

February 21.

New British blockade order.

Sir E. Carson on U-Boat menace.

Austrian attacks in S. Bukovina failed.

H.M. fleet messenger *Princess Alberta* (1,596 tons) sunk by mine on passage from Stavros to Mudros.

British s.s. *Wathfield* (3,012 tons) sunk by U-Boat off Cape Carbon, Algeria; 18 lost.

British s.s. *Perseus* (6,728 tons) mined 11 miles W. from Colombo; 3 lost.

February 22.

Seven Dutch ships torpedoed outside Falmouth by U21; three sunk.

U84 heavily engaged by British T.B.D., driven back damaged to German home port.

German raids near Vermelles—Neuve Chapelle failed.

Gen. Maude again attacked at Sanna-i-Yat; two trench lines taken.

February 23.

UC32 blown up by her own mines off Sunderland.

British s.s. *Grenadier* sunk by U-Boat off Shipwash Light; 8 lost.

British s.s. *Belgier* (4,588 tons) and *Iser* (2,160 tons) sunk by U-Boat off Belle Ile 1 lost.

British s.s. *Katherine* (2,926 tons) sunk by German raider *Möwe* N.E. from St. Paul Rocks.

British s.s. *Trojan Prince* (3,196 tons) sunk by U-Boat off Cape Shershel, Algeria 2 lost.

British s.s. *Longhirst* (3,053 tons) sunk by U-Boat off Cape Bon, Tunis; 2 lost.

British captured trench positions near Gueudecourt; slight advance on Ancre near Petit Miraumont. British raids near Souchez.

Gen. Maude crossed Tigris at Shumran Bend, above Kut; third and fourth Sanna-i-Yat lines taken.

February 24.

British s.s. *Falcon* (2,244 tons) sunk by U-Boat off Fastnet.

White Star s.s. *Megantic* (14,878 tons) attacked by U-Boat with torpedo in Mediterranean; missed.

British s.s. *Dorothy* (3,806 tons) sunk by U-Boat off Pantellaria; 6 lost.

German retreat on Ancre; British followed and occupied Petit Miraumont.

Fall of Kut-el-Amara to Gen. Maude Sanna-i-Yat evacuated; Turks retreated along Baghdad road; over 1,700 prisoners and much war material taken.

✻ February 25.

Cunard s.s. *Laconia* (18,000 tons) torpedoed 160 miles N.W. from Fastnet; lost; some American casualties.

British s.s. *Huntsman* (7,460 tons) and *Aries* (3,071 tons) sunk by U-Boat off Fastnet; 2 lost.

British s.s. *Algiers* (2,361 tons) sunk by U-Boat off Owers Light; 8 lost.

German T.B.D. raid on Broadstairs Margate; 2 deaths. British T.B.D. engaged German T.B.D.s in Channel.

Duke Albrecht of Wurtemberg's Army Group formed on W. Front.

*February 25, 1917 (*continued*).

Gen. Sixt von Armin, IVth Corps, promoted to command German Fourth Army.

Gen. von Kraewel to command IVth Corps vice Gen. von Armin.

German retirement on Ancre, 2-3 miles deep on 11-mile front ; British occupied Serre Miraumont, Pys, Luisenhof Farm, Beauregard dovecote, and Warlencourt—Eaucourt, and advanced towards Irles.

LZ101 raided Jassy (Rumania).

British pursuit 15 miles W. of Kut.

British advance on Baghdad begun.

February 26.

President Wilson asked Congress for power to arm U.S. merchantmen.

British s.v. *British Yeoman* (1,953 tons) sunk by German raider *Seeadler* 230 miles N.W. from St. Paul Rocks.

British s.s. *Burnby* (3,665 tons) sunk by U-Boat N. from Cape Falcone.

British s.s. *Clan Farquhar* (5,858 tons) sunk by U-Boat N. from Ben Ghazi ; 49 lost.

British Ancre advance ; Le Barque occupied. British line now opposite Roye.

Fighting 30 miles W. of Kut ; H.M.S. *Firefly* recaptured.

February 27.

President Wilson intimated that he deemed the sinking of s.s. *Laconia* the "overt act" for which he had been waiting.

British s.s. *Tritonia* (4,445 tons) sunk by U-Boat off Tearagh Island ; 2 lost.

British s.s. *Brodmore* (4,071 tons) sunk by U-Boat off Marsa Susa.

Further British advance towards Bapaume ; Ligny, Gommecourt, and W. and N. outskirts of Puisieux-au-Mont occupied.

Local strikes in Petrograd.

Austrian success near Dorna Watra, S. Bukovina.

German 1st Air Squad. raided Salonika.

Turkish rout along Baghdad road through Azizieh continued.

H.M. oiler *Turritella* (5,528 tons) captured by raider *Wolf* 600 miles W. from Minikoi ; scuttled, Indian Ocean : 4-iii.-17.

February 28.

First month of unrestricted U-Boat war ended. Germans claimed 781,500 tons sunk ; admitted two U Boats lost. British estimate = 500,573 tons.

During February 6 U-Boats, 45 UB-Boats and 3 "Merchant" U-Boats were ordered.

During February the Folkestone-Grisnez Mine Barrage was planned.

British nearer Bapaume ; Thilloy captured ; remainder of Puisieux-au-Mont taken ; advance 1,000 yards E. of Gommecourt ; trench captured on Saily-Saillisel ridge.

French gunboat *Cassini* torpedoed by U-Boat in Mediterranean.

Russian recovery in Bukovina.

British captures since Tigris crossed : 4,300 prisoners, 28 guns.

March 1.

German plot in U.S. disclosed ; German Foreign Secretary, Zimmermann, attempted to negotiate alliance with Mexico, who should induce Japan to join in attack on America.

Capt. Dreyer to be Director of Naval Ordnance.

H.M.S. *Pheasant* mined off Orkneys.

Elder Dempster s.s. *Drina* (11,483 tons) sunk by U-Boat off Skokham Is. ; 15 lost.

H.M.S. *Laverock* on patrol in Channel hit by torpedo that did not explode.

March 1 (*continued*).

H.M. submarine C19 (no gun armament) attacked and attempted to ram U-Boat off N. Hinder ; missed.

German T.B.D.s from Zeebrugge attacked Broadstairs.

British s.s. *Munificent* (3,270 tons) sunk by U-Boat off Cape Gris Nez ; 3 lost.

Two British steamers and six fishing craft sunk by U-Boat between Boulogne-Havre.

H.S. *Glenart Castle* (6,807 tons) mined in Channel ; towed in.

German Ancre retreat : N. of Miraumont British line advanced 600 yards on 2,500-yard front ; 2,133 prisoners in Feb. ; 11 villages recaptured.

Emperor Charles relieved Baron Conrad von Hötzendorf of his post as Austrian Chief of General Staff and appointed him commander in Tirol. Gen. von Arz new Chief of Staff.

British s.s. *Junna* (4,152 tons), for Calcutta, sunk by German raider *Wolf* 650 miles W. from Minikoi.

March 2.

Two British sailing vessels sunk by U-Boat S.S.W. from Dungeness.

British advance on Ancre beyond Warlencourt—Puisieux.

Russians retook Hamadan (Persia).

March 3.

British s.s. *Kincardine* (4,108 tons) sunk by U-Boat off Tearagh Is.

British s.s. *Newstead* (2,836 tons) and *Sagamore* (5,197 tons) sunk by U-Boat about 150 miles W. from Fastnet ; 67 lost.

British s.s. *Craigendoran* (2,789 tons) sunk by U-boat off Cape Sigli, Algeria ; 3 lost.

British s.s. *River Forth* (4,421 tons) sunk by U-Boat off Malta ; 2 lost.

On Ancre : German retreat over 5 miles to depth of ¼ mile E. of Gommecourt and N. of Puisieux.

Gen. Birdwood's 1st Anzac Corps at Ligny-Thilloy.

\# March 4.

President Wilson's armed neutrality resolution obstructed in Senate.

British s.s. *Rhodanthe* (3,061 tons) sunk by German raider *Möwe* 330 miles S.S.W. from St. Vincent, C.V.

British War Office conference decided formation of nine battalions of 72 Tanks each, with 352 Tanks as first reinforcement ; 1,000 Tanks in all.

On Ancre : further German retreat on 2-mile front E. of Gommecourt ; British took front and support trenches at Bouchavesnes.

German attack at Verdun on 2-mile front between Bezonvaux—Fosses Wood ; foothold gained N. of Caurières Wood.

Bread riots in Petrograd.

German 1st Air Squad. raided Salonika.

March 5.

H.M. submarine C19 attacked and attempted to ram U-Boat off N. Hinder ; missed.

H.I.M.S.S. *Kronprinz* and *Grosser Kurfürst* damaged by collision during squadron practice in Heligoland Bight ; docked for several weeks ; High Sea Fleet paralysed.

Austria-Hungary in Note to U.S. associated herself with German U-Boat policy.

On Ancre : Further British progress S. of Bucquoy—Achiet-le-Petit. German counter-attack near Bouchavesnes failed.

Sundays marked with Asterisk (*).

March 5, 1917 (*continued*).

French recovery at Verdun.

Turks abandoned strong position W. of Shalal (Sinai).

British cavalry at Lajj, 9 miles from Ctesiphon, 27 miles from Baghdad.

Russians attacked Turks between Hamadan—Kermanshah.

March 6.

Two British steamers sunk by U-Boat off the Fastnet ; 23 lost.

On Ancre : British advance N.W. of Irles and N. of Puisieux.

Petrograd food riots : shops plundered.

Gen. Maude's cavalry 6 miles from Diala, 14 miles from Baghdad.

Turks retiring on Kangavar (Persia).

March 7.

British s.s. *Westwick* (5,694 tons) mined off Roche Point.

Kaiser promised Prussian Franchise reform.

Tsar left Tsarskoe Selo for G.H.Q. at Mohileff.

Street demonstrations in Petrograd.

March 8.

On Ancre : Slight British advance.

French in Champagne recovered most of Butte du Mesnil—Maisons de Champagne salient ; 136 prisoners.

Death of Count Zeppelin.

Petrograd rationing order.

Austro-Germans took Rumanian positions between Trotus—Uzal Valley (Moldavia).

British s.s. *Georgian* (5,088 tons) sunk by U-Boat off Cape Sidero ; 5 lost.

Dardanelles Commission Interim Report.

Gen. Maude crossed Tigris S. of Diala.

March 9.

British s.s. *Eastpoint* (5,234 tons) sunk by U-Boat off Eddystone.

French took over 200 prisoners near the Caurières Wood (Verdun).

First mass demonstrations in Petrograd : police resisted.

Gen. Maude forced passage of Diala (Tigris).

March 10.

British s.s. *Otaki* (9,575 tons) and *Esmeraldas* (4,678 tons) sunk by German raider *Möwe* 420 miles W. from Lisbon.

H.M. submarine G13 torpedoed and sank UC43 N.W. of Muckle Flugga Lighthouse.

British s.s. *San Eduardo* (6,225 tons) torpedoed by U-Boat off Stornoway ; reached port.

British advance on Ancre ; Irles taken by 2nd and 18th Divisions ; 292 prisoners.

Petrograd rioters shot ; general cessation of work ; outbreak in Moscow.

Adm. Nepenin shot by Russian revolutionary sailors at Helsingfors.

Turks broken before Baghdad ; Gen. Maude advancing.

Baghdad railway station occupied by part of Gen. Cobbe's force.

✻March 11.

British s.s. *Horngarth* (3,609 tons) sunk by German raider *Seeadler* 220 miles E.N.E. from St. Paul Rocks.

✻March 11 (*continued*).

Cunard s.s. *Folia* (6,705 tons), New Yor for Bristol, sunk by U-Boat off Irish coast.

Gen. von Boehn to command Germa Seventh Army on the Aisne vice Gen. vo Schubert.

Barricades in Petrograd ; many regiment going over.

Second battle of Monastir begun.

Fall of Baghdad to Gen. Maude ; Britis pursued Turks and occupied Kazimain, N. o the city.

British s.s. *Wordsworth* (3,509 tons) sunk by German raider *Wolf* 680 miles E. from Mahe, Seychelles.

March 12.

Revolution in Russia following on Army' refusal to deal with food rioters in Petrogra and proroguing of the Duma, which, headed by M. Rodzianko, called upon Tsar for repre sentative Government ; practically all troop with revolutionaries, who stormed Fortress o Peter and Paul ; Cabinet resigned, and Duma failing reply from Tsar, elected Provisiona Government, and declared itself in per manent session ; arrest of ex-Ministers ordered.

H.M. submarine E49 mined off Shetlands.

H.M.S. Q19 sank U85 in Wester Channel.

H.M.S. *Medea* sank UC18 in North Se with explosive sweeps.

Slight British advance on the Bouch avesnes ridge.

French progress in Champagne ; Hill 18 regained.

British advance 1,000 yards on 3,500 yard front in Doiran sector. Italian ad vance E. of Monastir.

March 13.

Fighting in Petrograd : Admiralty and Winter Palace in hands of revolutionaries now holding the whole city ; MM. Shtcheg lovitoff, Stürmer, Protopopoff, and Goremy kin, Archbishop Pitirim, and others arrested Tsar appointed Gen. Ivanoff military dictato to deal with rising, but latter failed to reach capital.

Tsar left Mohileff but, unable to reach either Moscow or Petrograd, all lines being blocked, diverted his train to Pskoff.

British s.s *Demeterton* (6,048 tons) sunk by German raider *Möwe* 730 miles E. by N. from Cape Race.

British s.s. *Norwegian* (6,327 tons) sunk off Seven Heads ; 5 lost.

H.M.S. *Meteor* mined ; reached Dover.

H.M. special service ship *Warner* sunk by U-Boat off W. Ireland.

Germans abandoned forward crest of Bapaume Ridge on 3½-mile front (Le Transloy —Loupart) ; fell back on Rocquigny— Bapaume—Ablainzeville. British in Loupart Wood and Grévillers, 1½ miles from Bapaume ; progress E. and N.E. of Gommecourt.

French gain at St. Mihiel.

British 30 miles beyond Baghdad.

Russians occupied Kermanshah (Persia).

China broke with Germany.

March 14.

British s.s. *Governor* (5,524 tons) sunk by German raider *Möwe* 930 miles W. from Fastnet ; 4 lost.

British s.s. *Bray Head* (3,077 tons) sunk by U-Boat N.W. from Fastnet ; 21 lost.

Orient s.s. *Orsova* (12,036 tons) torpedoed by U-Boat off Eddystone ; reached port.

Gen. Lyautey, French War Minster, resigned.

March 14, 1917 *(continued)*.

Germans retiring N. and S. of Somme R. abandoned trenches near St. Pierre Vaast Wood.

British advance towards Achiet-le-Petit and Essarts.

Count Bernstorff returned to Germany.

Russian Provisional Government : Prince George Lvoff, Premier ; MM. Miliukoff (Foreign Affairs), Gutchkoff (War), Shingareff (Finance), and Kerensky (Justice). Moscow adhered to Provisional Government.

Revolutionary outbreak at Kronstadt.

Gen. Maude's troops at Bakuba, 35 miles N.E. of Baghdad.

March 15.

H.M.S. *Foyle* mined in Dover Straits.

British s.s. *Frimaire* (1,778 tons) sunk by U-Boat off Belle Ile ; 12 lost.

British progress on 2½-mile front between St. Pierre Vaast Wood—Saillisel.

Tsar at Pskoff abdicated for himself and son, and transferred his rights to his brother, Grand Duke Michael Alexandrovitch.

Massacre of Russian naval officers at Kronstadt.

Turkish position at Mushaidie, 20 miles N. of Baghdad, captured by British.

March 16.

British s.s. *Norma Pratt* (4,416 tons), sunk by U-Boat 150 miles W. from Bishop Rock.

British s.s. *Narragansett* (9,196 tons) sunk by U-Boat off S.W. Ireland ; 46 lost.

H.M.S. *Achilles* and armed boarding steamer *Dundee* intercepted and sank German raider *Leopard*, converted s.s. *Yarrowdale* 31-xii.-16), outward bound under Norwegian style of *Rena*.

German aeroplane raid on Kent, particularly Margate.

Zeppelin raid over Kent and Sussex. No casualties. On return flight the five German naval airships that took part in this raid were overtaken by fresh winds, with the result that L40 and L41 alone reached their shed at Ahlhorn, while L35 came down at Dresden, L42 at Jüterbog, and L39 was destroyed by French guns over Compiègne on following morning.

German withdrawal in Arras-Aisne R. sector begun.

British advance on Somme ; Moslain Wood and all St. Pierre Vaast Wood, except N.E. corner, occupied.

Tsar left Pskoff for Mohileff.

Grand Duke Michael accepted Russian succession if decision ratified by Constituent Assembly. Provisional Government appointed Gen. Alexeieff to succeed Grand Duke Michael as C.-in-C. and Gen. Korniloff commander in Petrograd.

Kronstadt massacre continued.

Turkish Sixth Army engaged by Russians near Kaerind (Persia).

March 17.

H.M. sloop *Mignonette* mined off S.W. Ireland.

British s.s. *Antony* (6,446 tons) sunk by U-Boat W. from Coningbeg Light ; 55 lost.

Aeroplane raid over Kent ; no casualties.

M. Briand's Cabinet resigned.

German withdrawal in the West along 90-mile front followed by Allied advance ; British advanced from Arras to Roye road and took Bapaume, Chaulnes, and 13 villages . and S. of Somme : French further S.

March 17 *(continued)*.

advanced between Andéchy—Oise R. ; Roye, Lassigny, and many villages retaken.

Russians occupied Kaerind, 150 miles from Baghdad.

* **March 18.**

Brig.-Gen. J. B. White to command Canadian Forestry Corps.

Three U.S. steamers sunk by U-Boat.

H.M. sloop *Alyssum* mined off S.W. Ireland.

German T.B.D. raid on Kent coast ; Ramsgate shelled. H.M.S. *Paragon* torpedoed ; another T.B.D. *Llewellyn* damaged ; reached Dover.

British s.s. *Greypoint* sunk by German T.B.D. two miles S.E. from Broadstairs Landing. *Greypoint* was the only merchant vessel sunk or hit by German T.B.D.s in their raids in the Channel and Downs.

Fall of Péronne and Mont St. Quentin to British, who took over 60 villages in two days. W. bank of Somme occupied from Péronne to Epénancourt ; further N. Beugny— Ytres line reached ; Beaureins, S. of Arras, taken. Somme bridge repaired at Brie.

Anglo-French cavalry entered Nesle.

French advance between Avre R.— Aisne R. on 37½ mile front ; Noyon and many villages taken.

German attack on Mort Homme— Avocourt front (Verdun) ; trenches and prisoners taken.

Russians took Harunabad, 20 miles S.E. of Kermanshah (Persia).

March 19.

British s.s. *Alnwick Castle* (5,900 tons) sunk by U-Boat W. by S. from Bishop Rock ; 40 lost.

German retreat on Cambrai—St. Quentin —La Fère—Noyon continued ; French took Chauny and Ham ; over 170 villages taken by Allies in three days. British on Somme line from Canizy to Péronne ; N. of Péronne on line Bussu—Barastre—Velu—St. Léger— Beaureins. Cavalry in touch with Germans at Nurlu, Bertincourt, Noreuil and Henin-sur-Cojeul.

M. Ribot's new French Cabinet ; with M. Painlevé, War Minister ; Adm. Lacaze, Marine ; M. Thomas, Munitions ; M. Thierry, Finance ; and M. Maginot, Colonies, as War Committee.

French Dreadnought *Danton* torpedoed off Sardinia.

M. Miliukoff notified Allied representatives in Petrograd of the end of Tsarism in Russia.

Gen. Maude's troops occupied Feluja (Euphrates).

March 20.

President Wilson summoned special sitting of Congress for April 2 " to receive a communication by the Executive on grave questions of national policy."

Allied progress towards Cambrai—St. Quentin along 80-mile front ; British S. of Germaine — Haucourt — Nurlu — Bus — Morchies ; Germans pivoting near Arras ; French occupied Jussy—Tergnier ; their cavalry within 5 miles of St. Quentin. Between Somme and Oise they reached Guiscard and further S. the Ailette line.

Tsar arrested at Mohileff.

LZ101 raided Mudros.

British s.s. *Danubian* (5,064 tons) mined 11 miles S. by W. from Asses Ears, Aden ; reached port.

Sundays marked with Asterisk (*).

March 21, 1917.

Imperial War Conference in London.

U.S. s.s. *Healdton*, Philadelphia for Rotterdam sunk by U-Boat ; 21 lost.

British H.S. *Asturias* (12,000 tons) torpedoed by U-Boat off Start Point ; beached ; 35 lost.

On Somme front British took Beaumetz-les-Cambrai, close up to Hindenburg line. French S. of St. Quentin forced Crozat Canal.

March 22.

British s.s. *Rotorua* (11,140 tons) sunk by U-Boat E. from Start Point.

German raider *Möwe* returned to Kiel after four months' cruise, during which she sank or captured 27 ships of 123,444 tons.

German resistance increasing ; heavy fighting on French left between St. Quentin—La Fère and on Crozat Canal. French progress N. of Soissons and across Ailette R.

Ex-Tsar prisoner at Tsarskoe Selo.

March 23.

H.M.S. *Laforey* mined in Channel.

British s.s. *Maine* (3,616 tons) sunk by U-Boat off Start Point.

British s.s. *Clan Macmillan* (4,525 tons) sunk by U-Boat off Newhaven.

British s.s. *Eptalofos* (4,431 tons) sunk by U-Boat N.W. from Malta ; master, two officers, four engineers, and one gunner made prisoners.

Fighting on British front between Arras and Bapaume—Cambrai road.

French defeated Germans between St. Quentin—La Fère.

Germans flooded Oise Valley ; La Fère under water ; further French advance on Crozat Canal.

Gen. Alexeieff reported great German concentration on Riga—Dvinsk front.

Rumanian set-back S. of Trotus Valley.

March 24.

British at Roisel, 7 miles E. of Péronne.

French advance to W. bank of Oise between St. Quentin—La Fère ; further advance on eastern bank of Ailette.

Russian Provisional Government recognised by Great Britain, France, and United States.

*March 25.

German T.B.D.s bombarded Dunkirk.

French advance towards St. Quentin ; progress S. of Oise in Lower Coucy Forest ; further progress S. of Somme.

British s.s. *Berbera* (4,352 tons) sunk by U-Boat E. from Catania.

British s.s. *Vellore* (4,926 tons) sunk by U-Boat N.W. from Alexandria.

March 26.

H.M.S. *Myrmidon* mined in Channel.

British s.s. *Ledbury* (3,046 tons) sunk by U-Boat off Ben Ghazi.

British took Lagnicourt, 6 miles N.E. of Bapaume.

French took Coucy-le-Château and Folembray ; progress N. of Soissons at Vrégny.

Russians yielded at Baranovitchi.

Slight Austrian progress S. of Gorizia.

French gains W. of Monastir ; total 2,000 prisoners.

First stage of Gaza battle ; Ali Muntar position taken by Gen. Dobell's Eastern Force.

March 27.

British s.s. *Glenogle* (7,682 tons) sunk U-Boat S.W. from Fastnet.

British auxiliary barque *Neath* (5, tons) sunk by U-Boat S.E. from Fastnet.

British s.s. *Kelvinhead* (3,063 to mined off Liverpool Bar Light.

Cunard s.s. *Thracia* (2,891 tons), w ore from Bilbao for Ardrossan, sunk by Boat N. from Belle Ile ; 36 lost.

British approaching Hindenburg took Longavesnes, Liéramont, Equanco Villers, and Saulcourt, near Roisel ; cav cleared Villers Faucon.

French progress between La Fère—La all Lower Coucy Forest held.

" Vienna Document " drawn up by F von Bethmann-Hollweg and Count Czerni

Gen. Dobell's force, after abandoning recovering Gaza positions captured the before, finally compelled to retire.

March 28.

Three British ships sunk by U-Boat S. Arklow Light Vessel ; lightship also boar and sunk by U-Boat.

British s.s. *Gafsa* (3,974 tons) sunk U-Boat off Kinsale Head.

British s.s. *Snowdon Range* (4,662 t sunk by U-Boat off Bardsey Is.

British s.s. *Cannizaro* (6,133 tons) s by U-Boat S.S.W. from Fastnet.

British advance on Bapaume—Cam road beyond Beaumetz ; gains near (silles.

German success W. of Maisons de Ch pagne.

French recovery at Avocourt Wor Hill 304 (Verdun).

March 29.

British s.s. *Crispin* (3,965 tons) *Lincolnshire* (3,965 tons) sunk by U-boa Waterford.

British ss. *Mascota* captured and sun German T.B.D. 8 miles E. from Lowest crew prisoners.

German outpost-leader *Bismarck* m and sunk in Heligoland Bight.

British at Neuville Bourjonval, 7 S.E. of Bapaume.

Socialists in Reichstag voted ag Government on Emergency Budget.

British s.s *Khiva* (8,947 tons) atta by U-Boat with torpedo in Mediterran missed.

March 30.

H.S. *Gloucester Castle* (7,999 tons) pedoed in mid-Channel ; towed in.

British progress towards Cam Ruyaulcourt Fins, Sorel, Heudicourt, M ville, Vermand, and Soyécourt taken.

French advance N.E. of Soissons Margival—Vrégny.

Russian Provisional Government anteed Polish independence.

British s.v. *Dee* sunk by German r *Wolf* 410 miles W. by S. from Cape Leer

March 31.

Second month of unrestricted U-war ended. Germans claimed 885,000 sunk ; admitted six U-Boats lost.

British estimate = 555,991 tons.

During March the torpedo becam general weapon of the U-Boat campai

During March the coal-trade bet England and France was brought convoy.

For List of Abbreviations see page iv.

March 31, 1917 (*continued*).

Cunard s.s. *Valacia* (6,526 tons) torpedoed by U-Boat off Eddystone ; towed into Plymouth.

British s.s *Queen Louise* (4,879 tons) torpedoed by U-Boat in Channel ; reached Havre.

Great British advance N.E. of St. Quentin ; Jeancourt, Hervilly, Herbecourt, Vendelles taken.

Prince Sixte of Bourbon communicated to President Poincaré in Paris Emperor Charles's first " peace letter."

British s.s. *Brodness* (5,736 tons) sunk by U-Boat W.N.W. from Port Anzio.

Gen. Maude's troops at Deli Abbas, 13 miles S.W. of Kizil Robat ; Deitawa—Sindia, 35 miles N. of Baghdad, occupied.

* April 1.

British advance towards Hindenburg line : Savy, 4 miles from St. Quentin, taken, and Epéhy—Peizières on Bapaume—Péronne railway ; 1,239 prisoners in March, 4,600 since beginning of year.

French progress between Ailette R. and Laon road.

British s.s. *Kasenga* (4,652 tons) sunk by U-Boat off Cape Palos, Spain.

British s.s. *Warren* (3,709 tons) sunk by U-Boat S.W. from Civita Vecchia.

British s.s. *Zambesi* (3,759 tons) sunk by U-Boat off Alexandria.

April 2.

President Wilson asked Congress to declare that a state of war existed with Germany, who was warring against all mankind.

U.S. armed liner *Aztec* torpedoed off French coast.

H.M. monitor *Marshal Ney* fitted with 6-inch guns detailed for defence of the Downs.

British approaching St. Quentin ; Francilly—Selency, Selency, and Holnon taken. N. of Bapaume—Cambrai road they carry in front of Hindenburg Line—Doignies, Louveral, Lagnicourt, Noveuil, Longatte, Ecoust—St. Mein, Croisilles and Henin-sur-Cojeul.

British now close up to Hindenburg Line all the way from N. of St. Quentin to Arras, on the general line Selency—Jeancourt — Epehy — Ruyalcourt — Doignies — Mercatel—Beaureins.

British s.s. *Britannia* (3,129 tons) sunk by U-Boat W.N.W. from Pantellaria.

British and Russians (Gen. Baratoff's orce) in touch on Diala R., S.W. of Khanikin.

April 3.

French closing in on St. Quentin took Dallon, Giffécourt, and Cerizy. N. of Soissons they seized outskirts of Laffaux and Vauzeny.

Germans bombarded Reims ; 2,000 shells a city.

Germans carried Stokhod bridgehead ; many Russian prisoners.

British s.s. *Cloughton* (4,221 tons) mined, and *Oberon* (5,142 tons) torpedoed in Mediterranean ; both reached port.

British s.s. *Ardgask* (4,542 tons) sunk by U-Boat off Cape Rosello, Sicily.

April 4.

U.S. Senate passed war resolution.

British s.s. *Hunstanton* (4,504 tons) sunk by U-Boat off Scilly Is.

British airmen bombed Zeebrugge.

British carried Metz-en-Couture, towards Cambrai.

Further French progress towards St. Quentin ; N.E. of Dallon French took Grugies, and further S.W. Urvillers and Moy-sur-Oise.

French G.H.Q. at Compiègne.

British s.s. *City of Paris* (9,239 tons) sunk by U-Boat S.E. from Cap d'Antibes ; 122 lost.

British s.s. *Margit* (2,490 tons) sunk by U-Boat off Cape Matapan.

Russians occupied Khanikin (Mesopotamia).

April 5.

British s.s. *Canadian* (9,309 tons) sunk by U-Boat W. from Fastnet.

British s.s. *Benheather* (4,701 tons) sunk by U-Boat W.N.W. from Fastnet.

British s.s. *Calliope* (3,829 tons) sunk by U-Boat off Ustica.

H.M. submarine C7 sank UC68 off Schouwen Bank, Flanders coast.

German aeroplane bombed Ramsgate ; no casualties.

British naval aeroplanes from Dunkirk dropped four 520-lb. bombs and thirty-one 65-lb. bombs on Zeebrugge, driving about ten German T.B.D.s out to sea from shelter of the Mole.

Great air battles in France.

British advance between Cambrai—St. Quentin ; Ronssoy and Lempire taken.

April 6.

U.S. declared war on Germany.

British s.s. *Powhatan* (6,117 tons) sunk by U-Boat off N. Rona Is.

British s.s. *Rosalind* (6,535 tons) sunk by U-Boat off Fastnet.

British s.s. *Spithead* (4,697 tons) sunk by U-Boat N.W. from Damietta Light.

More air battles in France ; 28 British machines missing and 49 German machines driven down in two days.

French bombardment opened, preliminary to Second Aisne Battle (April 16).

Germans bombarded Reims.

April 7.

Cuba declared war on Germany.

H.M.S. *Jason* mined off W. Scotland

British s.s *Lapland* (18,565 tons) mined off Liverpool Bar Light ; reached port ; 2 lost.

German T.B.D. G88 torpedoed by British submarine off Zeebrugge.

British naval aeroplanes from Dunkirk dropped two 550lb. bombs, one 264lb. bomb, one 100lb. bomb, and twenty-nine 65lb. bombs on German seaplane base at Zeebrugge.

British 2 miles from St. Quentin.

Kaiser promised Prussian Franchise Reform " after the war."

Two British steamers sunk by U-Boat off Sardinia.

* April 8.

Austria broke with U.S.

Panama to assist U.S. in defence of Canal.

Two British steamers sunk by U-Boat westward of Ushant.

April 8, 1917 (*continued*).

British s.s. *Torrington* (5,597 tons) sunk by U-Boat; position not known; 34 lost.

British First Army allotted eight Tanks Third Army 40 Tanks, and Fifth Army 12 Tanks on front of attack before Arras.

British progress in Mesopotamia; left bank of Shatt-el-Adhaim captured; Belad station (Baghdad—Samara railway) occupied.

April 9.

Brazil and Bolivia broke with Germany.

Battle of Arras and Vimy. Great British attack N. and S. of Arras from Givenchy-en-Gohelle to Croisilles. Advance on 12-mile front to depth of 3,000 yards; La Folie Farm and Wood, and whole of Vimy Ridge, except Hill 145, won by Gen. Byng's Canadian Corps, of Gen. Horne's First Army. Thelus, Athies, St. Laurent Fampoux, Blangy, Feuchy, Railway Triangle, Hyderabad Redoubt, Observation Ridge, Tilloy-les-Mofflaines, "The Harp Position," Telegraph Hill, and Neuville-Vitasse taken. Nearly 6,000 prisoners by noon. Farther S. Boursies, Hermies, and Deniécourt carried on Bapaume —Cambrai road; Havrincourt Wood penetrated. N. of St. Quentin Fresnoy-le-Petit, Pontru, and Le Verguier taken.

Gen. Maude occupied Harbe, 4 miles N. of Belad.

April 10.

H.S. *Salta* mined off Havre; 79 missing.

H.M.S. P26 mined in Channel.

Arras Battle: British progress; Hill 145, last Vimy height held by Germans, Farbus and Farbus Wood taken; outskirts of Monchy-le-Preux reached; Louverval towards Cambrai, taken; over 11,000 prisoners to date.

British s.s. *Dalton* (3,486 tons) sunk by U-Boat off Cape Matapan.

April 11.

British s.s. *Branksome Hall* (4,262 tons) torpedoed by U-Boat in Channel; towed in.

British s.s. *Duchess of Cornwall* (1,706 tons) sunk by U-Boat off Cape Barfleur; 23 lost.

Arras Battle: British took Monchy-le-Preux and La Bergère; Tanks penetrated Bullecourt, S.E. of Croisilles, but British later evacuated.

French advance resumed N. and N.E. of Soissons.

Activity in Champagne and Woevre.

British s.s. *Imperial Transport* (4,648 tons) sunk by U-Boat off Alexandria. Two other British steamers sunk in Mediterranean.

British defeated Turks near Deltawa, and chased them back to Deli Abbas (Mesopotamia).

April 12.

British s.s. *Toro* (3,066 tons) sunk by U-Boat off Ushant; 14 lost.

British s.s. *Lismore* (1,305 tons) sunk by U-Boat off Havre; 5 lost.

Arras Battle: British offensive northwards; advance on either side of the Souchez R. towards Lens—two hills "The Pimple "— Bois-en-Hache won; S. of the Scarpe "The Egg" position, Wancourt and Heninel tormed with aid of Tanks; heights on W. bank of Cojeul gained; further S. an attack on 9-mile front from Metz-en-Couture to Hargicourt won Gouzeaucourt, Gauche Wood—Sart Farm.

April 12 (*continued*).

Gen. F. von Below, German Seco Army, transferred his H.Q. from Cambra Réthel.

Count Czernin in Memorandum Emperor Charles appealed to him to h warning of Russian Revolution and m peace betimes, especially in view of T entry into war and U-Boat failure.

British s.s. *Glencliffe* (3,673 tons) su by U-Boat off Tabarca Is., Spain.

British s.s. *Kildale* (3,830 tons) sunk U-Boat off Pantellaria.

April 13.

Allied Naval Conference at Washingt U.S. warships ordered to co-operate W. Atlantic Patrol; six T.B.D.s European waters; America's first act of w

British s.s. *Lime Branch* (5,379 to torpedoed by U-Boat off Ushant; reacl port.

British s.s. *Kariba* (3,697 tons) sunk U-Boat off Ushant; 13 lost.

British s.s. *Argyll* (3,547 tons) sunk U-Boat off Bishop Rock; 22 lost.

British s.s. *Bandon* (1,456 tons) sunk U-Boat off Mine Head, S. Ireland; 28 lost

British s.s. *Strathcona* (1,881 tons) su by U-Boat off Ronaldshay; 9 lost.

Arras Battle: British fighting on mile front from Loos to W. of Cambi Angres, Bailleul, Willerval, Petit Vi Vimy, and Givenchy-en-Gohelle in D plain; farther S. Fayet, outside St. Quen carried; total prisoners 13,000.

French attack on 5-mile front S. of Quentin.

M.L.534 destroyed by fire at Taranto.

British s.s. *Zara* (1,331 tons) sunk U-Boat off Heliso Is.; 27 lost.

First All-Russian Soviet Congress: R lution against annexations and indemnities.

April 14.

Arras Battle: British nearer Le Double Crassier (near Loos), Liévin, Cité St. Pierre, N.W. of Lens, taken. S. Scarpe, Gricourt, outside St. Quentin, sei

Great French artillery activity N. Aisne and in E. Champagne.

Anglo-French aeroplanes bombed Freik as reprisal for attacks on British hosp ships.

British s.s. *Hermione* (4,011 tons) mi off Coningbeg Light.

British s.s *Patagonier* (3,832 tons) s by U35 W. from Gibraltar.

＊April 15.

Arras Battle: Further British adva towards Lens: Riaumont Wood tal German counter-attack astride Bapaum Cambrai road before Quéant failed, ex temporarily at Lagnicourt. Villaret, N of St. Quentin, taken.

French bombardment on Aisne.

French War Mission to U.S. (M. Vivi Marshal Joffre, Adm. Chocheprat and Mar de Chambrun) left Paris.

British s.s. *Cairndhu* (4,019 tons) s by U-Boat off Beachy Head; 11 lost.

British s.s. *Cameronia* (10,963 tons) s by U-Boat E. from Malta; 11 lost.

B.I. s.s. *Mashobra* (8,236 tons) sunk Austrian U-Boat S.W. from Cape Matap

British s.s. *Arcadian* (8,939 tons) sunl U-Boat N.E. from Milo; 35 lost.

Turks, retreating before Gen. Ma reached Jebel Hamrin, whence they starte April 9.

For List of Abbreviations see page iv.

April 16, 1917.

Second Aisne Battle: Great French attack under Gen. Nivelle on Soissons—Reims front; German first positions carried between Soissons—Craonne, including Mt. Sapin, Le Balcon, Hurtebise Farm, part of Chavonne, and W. and S. slopes of Les Grinons; German second positions carried between Craonne—S. of Juvincourt, including Bois des Buttes; and, farther S. towards Reims advance reached W. outskirts of Beméricourt, and Loivre and Coucy captured, the latter by the Russian contingent. Over 10,000 prisoners.

British advanced beyond Epéhy towards Le Catelet, between Cambrai—St. Quentin. Round Lens they entered suburb of Cité St. Edouard. Arras offensive slacker, but pressure maintained during Aisne battle.

First French Tanks (including eight Schneider companies) in action on French Fifth Army front, Chemin-des-Dames.

Food strikes in Berlin.

Gen. Maude within 15 miles of Samarra.

British s.s. *Queen Mary* (5,658 tons) and *Towergate* (3,697 tons) sunk by U-Boat N.W. from Fastnet.

April 17.

British s.s. *Winifredian* (10,422 tons) mined in North Sea; *Nirvava* (6,021 tons) mined in Channel; *Gisella* mined off Lewis Is.; all reached port.

British s.s. *Kish* (4,928 tons) and *Cairnhill* (4,981 tons) sunk by U-Boat N.W. from Fastnet; 6 lost.

British s.s. *Clan Sutherland* torpedoed by U-Boat in Channel; beached; 12 lost.

British H.SS. *Donegal* and *Lanfranc* (6,287 tons) sunk in Channel by U-Boats without warning; 75 drowned, including 16 Germans.

British s.s. *Brisbane River* (4,989 tons), *Corfu* (3,695 tons) and *Fernmoor* (3,098 tons) sunk by U35 and another U-Boat W. from Gibraltar; 3 lost.

British progress N. of Gouzeaucourt.

Second Aisne Battle: French attack extended E. into Champagne to beyond Auberive, which was taken; advance on 7-mile front from Prunay, carrying heights S. of Moronvilliers (Battle of Moronvilliers).

Second stage of Gaza Battle: British advanced from Wadi-Ghuzzeh (Palestine), captured Turkish first positions on 6½-mile front; Tanks in action; attack held.

April 18.

U.S. Emergency Fleet Corporation established with capital of £10,000,000 by U.S. Shipping Board.

British gains at Loos-Fampoux; Villers-Guislain, 12 miles S. of Cambrai, taken.

Aisne Battle: French progress; Vrégny salient reduced by capture of Nanteuil-la-Fosse and of Chavonne, Chivy, Vailly, Ostel, Braye-en-Laonnois, Metz Farm, and outskirts of Courtecon, Bois des Boches and Ville-aux-Bois, S.E. of Craonne taken.

On Moronvilliers (Champagne) front French reached summits of Mont Haut, but failed to hold.

British s.s. *Trekieve* (3,087 tons) sunk by U35 W. from Gibraltar; 3 lost.

Gen. Maude annihilated 18th Turkish A. C. covering Istabulat station, 12 miles S.E. of Samarra; 1,217 prisoners.

April 19.

UC30 mined in North Sea.

Six German seaplanes attacked British mine-net division guarding N. Goodwin Nets.

April 19 (*continued*).

One German machine attacked drifters with a torpedo; first use of this device; torpedo missed.

Aisne Battle: French further reduced Vrégny salient; on West, Laffaux—Condé Fort taken, on East, Jouy—Aizy; Germans driven back on Chemin-des-Dames. German withdrawal to Siegfried zone completed.

French progress E. of Reims, S.W. of Moronvilliers.

Mr. Lloyd George, M. Ribot, and Baron Sonnino conferred at St. Jean de Maurienne.

British s.s. *Limeleaf* (7,339 tons) torpedoed by U-Boat in Channel; towed in.

British s.s. *Sowwell* (3,781 tons) sunk by U35 W. by S. from Gibraltar; 21 lost.

April 20.

U.S. broke with Turkey.

H.M.S. *Heather*, Q16, fought her second U-Boat action off Irish coast during April.

British s.s. *Malakand* (7,653 tons) sunk by U-Boat W. of Bishop Rock.

German T.B.D.s shelled Calais.

British at Gonnelieu, 8 miles S.W. of Cambrai.

Aisne Battle: French across W. end of Chemin-des-Dames; 19,000 prisoners to date; advance N. of Sancy on Vrégny Plateau.

At Moronvilliers French reached Mont Teton summit.

British s.s. *Lowdale* (2,660 tons) and *Nentmoor* (3,535 tons) sunk by U35 and another U-Boat W. of Gibraltar.

British s.s. *Lcasowe Castle* (9,737 tons) torpedoed by U-Boat W. from Gibraltar; reached port.

British s.s. *San Hilario* (10,157 tons), *Torr Head* (5,911 tons), *Portloe* (3,187 tons) and *Emma* (2,520 tons) sunk by U-Boat westward of Fastnet.

April 21.

British s.s. *Telena*, (4,778 tons), *Diadem* (4,307 tons) and *Pontiac* (1,698 tons) sunk by U-Boat westward of Fastnet.

British s.s. *Sebek* (4,601 tons) sunk by U-Boat N.W. from Tory Island.

Six German T.B.D.s attempted raid on Dover; G85 rammed and sunk by H.M.S. *Broke*; G42 sunk by H.M.S. *Swift*.

Slight British progress towards Lens and E. of Fampoux.

Further French progress N. of Sancy between Aisne and Chemin-des-Dames.

Turks evacuated Istabulat. Gen. Maude attacked 6 miles farther towards Samarra.

✳April 22.

H.M. Q22 (s.v. with auxiliary power) engaged and possibly sank U-Boat about 30 miles S. of Kinsale Head.

British s.s. *Dykland* (4,291 tons) sunk by U-Boat W. from Fastnet.

British s.s. *Karroo* (6,127 tons) attacked by U-Boat with two torpedoes and gunfire W. from Scilly Is.; missed; rescued.

M.L.431 destroyed by fire at Poole.

British s.s. *Capenor* (2,536 tons) mined at entrance to La Pallice Roads.

Gen. von Falkenhausen Governor-General of Belgium, vice Gen. von Bissing, deceased.

Gen. Otto von Below in command of German Sixth (Lille) Army vice Gen. von Falkenhausen.

British progress E. of Havrincourt Wood; part of Trescault taken.

Sundays marked with Asterisk (*).

*April 22, 1917 (*continued*).
German counter-attacks at Moronvilliers E. of Reims, defeated.
Gen. von Hutier assumed command of German Eighth (Riga) Army.

April 23.
Mr. Balfour in Washington.
H.M. T.B. 24 sunk in Dover Harbour : raised.
Three British seaplanes attacked 5 German T.B.D.s off Belgian coast : one believed sunk.
Arras Battle resumed : Great British advance along Scarpe R. on a 12,000-yard front ; Gavrelle—Guémappe taken ; about 2,000 prisoners ; farther S. remainder of Trescault and most of Havrincourt Wood taken ; farther S. again St. Quentin Canal near Vendhuille reached.
Aisne Battle : Fierce fighting on Craonne Ridge ; French improved towards Juvincourt.
Gen. Maude occupied Samarra Station.

April 24.
British s.s. *Thistleard* (4,136 tons) sunk by U-Boat W.N.W. from Tory Island.
British s.s. *Abosso* (7,782 tons) sunk by U-Boat W. by N. from Fastnet ; 65 lost.
British s.s. *Anglesea* (4,534 tons) and *Ferndene* (3,770 tons) sunk by U-Boat W. of Bishop Rock ; 9 lost.
British s.s. *Kenilworth* (2,735 tons) sunk by mine off Brest.
Further British advance between Sensée R.—Monchy ; Bilhem, N.E. of Trescault, carried ; great German losses before Gavrelle.
LZ101 raided Mudros.
British troops attacked on right bank of Shatt-el-Adhim ; Turkish retreat to Jebel Hamrin.

April 25.
British s.s. *Swanmore* (6,373 tons), *Stephanotis* (4,060 tons). *Vauxhall* (3,629 tons) and *Hesperides* (3,393 tons) sunk by U-Boat westward of Fastnet ; 18 lost.
H.M.T. *Ballarat* (P. & O., 11,120 tons), escorted by H.M. T.B.D. *Phœnix*, sunk by U-Boat S. by W. from Wolf Rock, while bound up Channel with Australian drafts ; all landed.
White Star s.s. *Baltic* (23,876 tons) attacked by U-Boat with torpedo off W. Ireland ; missed.
German T.B.D. flotilla bombarded Dunkirk ; French T.B.D. *Etandard* sunk.
LZ97 raided Avlona.
British advance at Doiran.

April 26.
Adm. Jellicoe telegraphed to Adm. de Chair at Washington to inform U.S. Navy Department that during week before 55 British ships of approximately 180,000 tons had been sunk, and to urge U.S. authorities to concentrate on vital question of defeating U-Boat menace.
White Star s.s. *Baltic* (23,876 tons) attacked by U-Boat with torpedo off S. Ireland ; missed.
British s.s. *Harflete* (4,814 tons), *Manchester Citizen* (4,251 tons) and *Rio Lages* (3,591 tons) sunk by U-Boat N.W. from Fastnet.

April 26 (*continued*).
German attack on Gavrelle repulsed with great loss ; British took positions each side of Scarpe between Roeux—Gavrelle.
German counter-attacks on Chemin-des Dames repulsed.
British s.v. *Monitor* sunk by U-Boat off Cap d'Antibes.
British s.s. *Chertsey* (3,264 tons) sunk by U-Boat off Algiers.

April 27.
Mr. Page, U.S. Ambassador in London wired to Washington urging dispatch of 30 or more T.B.D.s to European Waters to relieve U-Boat pressure.
British s.s. *Beemah* (4,750 tons) sunk by U-Boat off Bishop Rock.
British s.s. *Dromore* (4,398 tons) and *Dunmore Head* (2,293 tons) sunk by U-Boat off Tory Island.
German T.B.D.s shelled Ramsgate Raiders engaged by H.M. monitor *Marshal Ney* and by 6-inch shore batteries.
British s.s. *Glencluny* (4,812 tons) and *Karuma* (2,995 tons) sunk by U-Boat off Cape Sigli, Algeria.

April 28.
U.S. Congress passed Conscription Bills.
British s.s. *Jose de Larrinaga* (5,017 tons) and s.v. *Port Jackson* (2,309 tons) sunk westward of Fastnet ; 26 lost.
P. & O. s.s. *Medina* (12,350 tons) sunk by U-Boat off Start Point ; 6 lost.
British s.s. *Teakwood* (5,315 tons) sunk by U-Boat S.W. from Sapienza Is.
British s.s. *Pontiac* (3,345 tons) sunk by U-Boat N.E. from Marsa Susa.
Herr Helfferich in Reichstag claimed over 1,600,000 tons of shipping, of which over 1,000,000 British, sunk in first two months of unlimited U-Boat warfare. He adjured Germans to hold out, since the U-Boat grip was at England's throat.
New British thrust E. of Vimy Ridge against Oppy line ; Arleux taken by Canadians
French since April 19 claimed 20,780 prisoners.

*April 29.
British s.s. *Daleby* (3,628 tons) sunk by U-Boat N.W. from Fastnet ; 25 lost.
British s.s. *Ikbal* (5,434 tons) and *Comedian* (4,889 tons) sunk by U-Boat W. by S. from Bishop Rock ; 3 lost.
British s.s. *Karonga* (4,665 tons) sunk by U-Boat in Messina Strait ; 18 lost.
Gen. Pétain Chief of Staff to Gen. Nivelle
Further progress towards Oppy line ; trench system S. of it taken on mile front.

April 30.
Third month of unrestricted U-Boat war ended. Germans claimed 1,091,000 tons sunk : admitted 2 U-Boats lost.
British estimate = 870,359 tons.
During April the trade between Scandinavia and British North Sea ports was brought under convoy.
U93 engaged in St. George's Channel by H.M. Q. schooner *Prize*, Lieut. Sanders, R.N.R. ; submarine damaged, forced to dive ; German commander and two of crew taken prisoners.
U62 reported having captured commander of H.M. Q12.

April 30, 1917 (*continued*).

British s.s. *Gretaston* (3,395 tons) sunk by U-Boat in Atlantic ; 29 lost.

Two British steamers sunk by U-Boat westward of Fastnet ; 21 lost.

H.M. sloop *Tulip* sunk by U-Boat in Atlantic.

Zierikzee, at mouth of Scheldt, bombed by aeroplane, 3 people killed.

Moronvilliers (E. of Reims) fighting resumed : French advanced ; took crest of Mont Perthois.

Gen. Maude defeated 13th Turkish A.C. at Shatt-el-Adhaim gorge, in Jebel Ham.

Turks announced that Russians had evacuated Mush (Armenia).

May 1.

H.M. submarine E54 torpedoed and sank U81 about 150 miles S.W. from Valentia Is.

H.M. collier *Gena* torpedoed and sunk by German seaplane off Southwold.

British s.s. *Bagdale* (3,045 tons) sunk by U-Boat off Creac'h Point, Ushant ; 23 lost.

British s.s. *British Sun* (5,565 tons) sunk by U-Boat E.S.E. from Malta.

Sir D. Haig announced 19,343 German prisoners, including 393 officers, taken on British W. Front in April, and 257 guns, 227 trench mortars, and 470 machine guns.

Russian Provisional Government pledged itself to continue war to " decisive victory."

May 2.

British s.s. *San Melito* (10,160 tons) chased by U-Boat off Orkneys ; repulsed attack by gunfire.

H.M.S. *Derwent* mined in Channel ; 62 missing.

British s.s. *Camerata* (3,723 tons) torpedoed by U-Boat in Mediterranean ; beached.

H.M. C.M.B.s 2, 7, 10, and 13, from Dover engaged four German T.B.D.s off Ostend : two C.M.B.s put out of action.

French active at Moronvilliers, E. of Reims.

May 3.

E. of Arras, another great battle on 12-mile front ; British won ground, especially on the wings. Fresnoy carried by Canadians and Hindenburg line penetrated E. of Bullecourt. Cherisy and Roeux entered, but later abandoned.

Russian Note to Allies confirming intention to continue war.

British s.s. *Palm Branch* (3,891 tons) attacked by U-Boat in Arctic Sea ; repulsed by gunfire.

British s.s. *Ussa* (2,066 tons) mined off Cherbourg.

First six U.S. T.B.D.s at Queenstown, where they were placed under Adm. Bayly.

May 4.

Adm. Jellicoe to be Chief of reconstituted Naval (War) Staff ; Adm. Oliver Deputy-Chief ; and Adm. Duff Assistant Chief.

British s.s. *Dilar de Larrinaga* (4,136 tons) sunk by U-Boat off Tuskar Light ; 20 lost.

British ss. *Maidan* (8,205 tons) chased by U-Boat in St. George's Channel ; repelled attack by gunfire.

Allied conference in Paris decided to give immediate effect to the British plan of

May 4 (*continued*).

a Northern offensive, involving abandonment of Gen. Nivelle's plan.

Further British progress E. of Bullecourt and near St. Quentin—Hargicourt.

Aisne attack renewed : French took Craonne and first-line trenches N.W. of Reims on 4,000-yard front between Berry-au-Bac—Brimont.

French progress at Moronvilliers (E. of Reims) ; over 1,000 prisoners.

Count Bernstorff received by Kaiser at German G.H.Q., Kreuznach, six weeks after his return from Washington.

British s.s. *Transylvania* (14,315 tons) sunk by U-Boat off Cape Vado, Gulf of Genoa ; 12 lost. Japanese Mediterranean T.B.D.s assisted in saving the 4,000 soldiers and nurses on board.

May 5.

Mr. Balfour addressed U.S. Congress.

H.M. sloop *Lavender* sunk by UC75 in English Channel.

Cunard s.s. *Feltria* (5,254 tons), New York to Avonmouth, sunk by U-Boat S.E. from Mine Head ; 45 lost.

British s.s. *Talawa* (3,834 tons) torpedoed by U-Boat in Mediterranean ; beached.

British s.s. *Harmattan* (4,792 tons) mined off Cape Rosa, Algeria ; 36 lost.

Fierce fighting on British front ; part of German first line, near Lens, taken.

On Aisne : Great French advance on nearly 20-mile front ; Craonne ridge summit won with Chemin-des-Dames ; over 6,000 prisoners ; great progress near Laffaux, where Hill 157 and Laffaux Mill captured.

Petrograd Soviet Council by small majority passed vote of confidence in Russian Provisional Government.

Venizelists, with French troops, attacked Bulgarian Macedonian trenches on 3-mile front.

* May 6.

British s.s. *Adansi* (2,644 tons) sunk by U-Boat off Fastnet.

Mr. Lloyd George, Lord Robert Cecil, Gen. Robertson, and Adm. Jellicoe at War Conference in Paris.

On Aisne : French took Chevreux, N.E. of Craonne. Craonne—Reims battle ended.

Germans escaped from Rufiji Valley (E. Africa), reached Kitunda *en route* for Tabora.

May 7.

German aeroplane dropped four bombs in N.E. London ; 1 killed ; 2 injured.

German repulse near Lens.

Australians widened their hold on Hindenburg line between Bullecourt—Quéant ; footing gained in S.E. corner of Bullecourt.

French extended S. of Sapigneul.

British s.s. *Polamhall* (4,010 tons) sunk by U-Boat W.S.W. from Bishop Rock.

British s.s. *Kinross* (4,120 tons) sunk by U-Boat E. from Wolf Rock.

British s.s. *Repton* (2,881 tons) sunk by U-Boat off Cape Matapan.

British s.s. *Griqua* (3,344 tons) torpedoed by U-Boat in Mediterranean ; beached.

May 8.

British s.s. *San Patricio* (9,712 tons) torpedoed by U-Boat in Bristol Channel ; arrived.

Germans recaptured Fresnoy at heavy cost.

Sundays marked with Asterisk (*).

May 8, 1917 (*continued*).

French N.E. of Craonne, carried German line on 1,200-yard front; 200 prisoners; slight French gains S. of Berry-au-Bac and E. of Reims.

Director of Intelligence at German G.H.Q. to direct military side of propaganda service.

Liberia broke with Germany.

May 9.

H.M.S. *Milne* rammed and sank UC26 off the Thames.

German outpost ship *Mettelkamp* mined and sunk N. of Borkum.

U93, which had put to sea on April 13, returned to Heligoland, having sunk up to April 30 some 27,000 tons (see 30-iv.-17).

British air squadrons from Dunkirk dropped over 9,000lb. of bombs on Bruges, Zeebrugge and Ostend.

French on Aisne repulsed German attacks.

Chancellor von Bethmann - Hollweg, replying to Count Czernin's Memorandum of 12-iv.-17, which was communicated by Emperor Charles to the Kaiser, expressed confidence in outcome of U-Boat campaign.

Petrograd Soviet Committee advocated international Socialist peace conference.

British attack N. of Salonika between Vardar R.—Lake Doiran; 500-yard advance on 2-mile front; Serbs and Russians engaged in Monastir sector.

May 10.

H.I.M.S. *Hindenburg* commissioned.

UC76 blown up while shipping mines in Heligoland Harbour; commander killed.

Eleven German T.B.D.s chased back into Zeebrugge by British scouting force from Harwich under Commodore Tyrwhitt.

French repulsed attack (Aisne) at Chevreux, and advanced N. of Sancy.

Gen. Korniloff resigned Petrograd command and went to the front.

French and Venizelists gained ground at Liumnitza (Macedonia).

May 11.

British s.s. *Calchas* (6,748 tons) and *Barrister* (3,679 tons) sunk by U-Boat off Irish coast.

British s.s. *Hindoo* (4,915 tons) torpedoed by U-Boat in Mediterranean; beached.

U93, towed by H.I.M. T.B.D. V163, reached Wilhelmshaven.

German minesweeper sunk off Horn Reef.

British took Cavalry Farm, astride Arras —Cambrai road, Roeux cemetery and chemical works.

May 12.

Voluntary "groups" for men up to 50 to be formed in U.K.

H.M. oiler *San Onofre* (9,717 tons) sunk by U-Boat 64 miles N.W. from Skelligs; 1 lost.

British s.s. *Galicia* (5,922 tons) mined off Teignmouth.

British s.s. *Wirral* (4,207 tons) sunk by U-Boat off Utvaer Is., Norway; 1 lost.

British s.s. *Zanoni* (3,851 tons) sunk by U-Boat off Cape Oropesa; 1 lost.

British s.s. *Locksley Hall* (3,635 tons) and *Egyptian Prince* (3,117 tons) sunk by U-Boat S.E. from Malta; 6 lost.

British naval and air forces bombarded Zeebrugge.

British took most of Bullecourt; progress round Roeux.

Artillery activity on Italian eastern front.

＊May 13.

British s.s. *Jessmore* (3,911 tons) sunk by U-Boat off Fastnet.

M. Gutchkoff, Russian Minister of War and Marine, resigned.

Russian detachments across Dialah towards Kifri (Mesopotamia) retired.

May 14.

Adm. Jellicoe Chief of Naval Staff. Sir E. Geddes Admiralty Controller for building, armament, and munitions, with honorary and temporary rank of Vice-Admiral.

British s.s. *Lewisham* (2,810) torpedoed by U-Boat off Fastnet; 24 lost.

British s.s. *Arlington Court* (4,346 tons) torpedoed by U-Boat off S.W. Ireland; towed in.

British s.s. *Volga* (4,404 tons) torpedoed by U-Boat in Mediterranean; beached.

H.M. submarine C6 attacked U-Boat off Hinder Light and pursued it by use of hydrophones; U-Boat escaped.

L22 destroyed by British naval forces in North Sea while scouting in company with L23.

U59 and German minesweeper *Fulda* mined and sunk in Heligoland Bight.

British took Roeux; line advanced N. of Gavrelle.

10th Isonzo Battle: Italian attack N. and S. of Gorizia and in N. Carso.

British progress on 5,000-yard front at Doiran.

May 15.

L16 and L37 sent up to scout over North Sea, compelled to return by dense fog.

German outpost vessel *Heinrich Rathjen* mined while trying to communicate with U59 sunk in Heligoland Bight.

Gen. Pétain French C.-in-C. vice Gen. Nivelle. Gen. Foch Chief of Staff vice Gen. Pétain. French G.H.Q. at Compiègne.

German success W. of Bullecourt. Stubborn fighting round Roeux; heavy German losses.

French line penetrated E. of Fort Malmaison (Aisne).

Italian offensive continued; progress in Plava area, on Mte. Santo, and heights E. of Gorizia; 3,375 prisoners.

Austrian light forces sank 14 British drifters in Adriatic; driven off by H.M.SS. *Dartmouth* and *Bristol*, and Franco-Italian T.B.D.s; *Dartmouth* hit by torpedo; Italian airmen disabled one cruiser off Cattaro.

French T.B.D. *Boutefeu* mined in Otranto Straits.

British s.s. *Tung Shan* (3,999 tons) sunk by U-Boat off Cape San Antonio.

British s.s. *Pancras* (4,436 tons) torpedoed by U-Boat in Mediterranean; beached; refloated.

Gens. Brusiloff and Gurko asked to resign.

May 16.

U.S. Representatives passed amended Conscription Bill.

British s.s. *Middlesex* (8,364 tons) sunk by U-Boat N.W. from Tory Island.

British s.s. *Highland Corrie* (7,583 tons) sunk by U-Boat off Owers Light; 5 lost.

British s.s. *Pagenturm* (5,000 tons) sunk by U-Boat off Beachy Head; 4 lost.

British s.s. *Kilmaho* sunk by U-Boat off Lizard; 21 lost.

H.I.M. T.B S27 mined and sunk in the Bight while convoying U86 to westward.

H.I.M. minesweeper M14 and T.B. 78 mined and sunk in trying to locate lost U59.

May 16, 1917 (*continued*).

H.I.M.S. *Kaiser* at Kiel for repairs.

German 3rd High Sea Squadron in Baltic.

Austrian counter on Isonzo defeated.

Coalition in Russia under Prince Lvoff ; M. Kerensky War Minister ; M. Tereshtchenko Foreign Minister, for M. Miliukoff, who resigned. Five Socialists included.

Major-Gen. Van Deventer to command in E. Africa vice Major-Gen. Hoskins.

May 17.

U.S. Senate passed amended Conscription Bill.

U.S. T.B.D. flotilla in British waters.

Admiralty Convoy Committee formed.

H.M.S. *Glen* destroyed UB39 by gunfire off Isle of Wight.

H.M.S. *Setter* sunk by collision in North Sea.

British steamer sunk by German T.B.D.s off North Hinder ; 11 lost.

U86 left port for Flamborough Head.

London and W. Riding Territorials completed capture of Bullecourt on Hindenburg line, before which the Australians had maintained themselves for a fortnight.

German assaults at Laffaux and N.W. of Braye defeated by French, who advanced E. of Craonne.

Austrian defeat on Isonzo ; Italians reached W. slopes of Mte. Santo ; 6,432 prisoners to date.

Rumanian T.B. *Smeul* capsized and sunk in Black Sea.

May 18.

President Wilson signed Conscription Act, authorising him to raise 500,000 men by selective drafts of men between 21 and 30 inclusive—to raise U.S. Regular Army to full strength by voluntary enlistment and National Guard by voluntary enlistment, and, if necessary, by selective draft ; to maintain all these forces by draft and to decree National Registration of all men between ages of 21 and 30 inclusive. A special clause made it illegal to sell intoxicating liquor to any officer or man in uniform.

British s.s. *Llandrindod* (3,841 tons) sunk by U-Boat N.W. from Fastnet.

British s.s. *Penhale* (3,712 tons) sunk by U-Boat off Tearaght Is.

British s.s. *Camberwell* (4,078 tons) mined off Dunnose Head.

British s.s. *Mary Baird* (1,830 tons) mined off Pendeen Cove ; 7 lost.

British s.s. *Elford* (1,739 tons) mined off Nab Light.

British s.s. *Millicent Knight* (3,563 tons) sunk by U-Boat eastward of Malta.

Italians on summit of Mte. Vodice.

May 19.

President Wilson decided to send U.S division to France under Gen. Pershing.

British s.s. *Farnham* (3,102 tons) sunk by U-Boat off Fastnet ; 17 lost.

White Star s.s. *Celtic* (20,904 tons) attacked by U-Boat with torpedo off S.W. Ireland ; missed.

British s.s. *Mardinian* (3,322 tons) sunk by U-Boat off Tabarca Is.

British s.s. *Mordenwood* (3,125 tons) sunk by U-Boat off Cape Matapan ; 21 lost.

Fierce fighting on Mte. Vodice ; Austrian prisoners to date over 7,000.

New Russian Coalition Government declared against separate peace.

＊ May 20.

British attacked between Bullecourt—Fontaine-les-Croisilles ; and established themselves in Hindenburg Line on mile front.

French Aisne — Champagne offensive begun April 16, ended with German attempts on Chemin-des-Dames, and with French success at Moronvilliers, E. of Reims ; 1,000 prisoners ; Mte. Cornillet taken.

Further Italian gains on Vodice and S. of Gorizia.

H.M. special service ship *Lady Patricia* sunk by U-Boat in Atlantic.

H.M. seaplane 8663 bombed and sank UC36 E.N.E. of N. Hinder Light.

British s.s. *Tycho* (3,216 tons) and *Porthkerry* (1,920 tons) sunk by U-Boat off Beachy Head ; 22 lost.

British s.s. *Birchgrove* (2,821 tons) attacked by German seaplanes in North Sea with torpedoes and machine-gun ; missed.

British s.s. *Caspian* (3,606 tons) sunk by U-Boat off Cape Cervera, Spain ; 25 lost.

Central Soviet Committee formed to control Government in Russia.

May 21.

British progress between Bullecourt—Fontaine ; all Siegfried Line now captured, except 2,000 yards W. of Bullecourt.

Austrian attacks in Dolomites failed.

British s.s. *Jupiter* (2,124 tons) sunk by U-Boat off Beachy Head ; 19 lost.

British s.s. *City of Corinth* (5,870 tons) sunk by U-Boat off the Lizard.

British s.s. *Ampleforth* (3,873 tons) sunk by U-Boat off Gozo ; 4 lost.

British s.s. *Don Diego* (3,632 tons) sunk by U-Boat off Linosa ; 5 lost.

May 22.

British s.s. *Lanthorn* (2,299 tons) sunk by U-Boat off Whitby.

On Aisne : French assault about Craonne ; three trench lines carried E. of Chevreux.

Count Tisza, Hungarian Premier, resigned.

Major Wintgens, commander of German party escaping from Rufiji (E. Africa), captured by Belgians.

May 23.

L40, L42, L43, L44 (Flag of German Airship Commodore Capt. Strasser), and L45 raided Harwich and E. Anglia ; 3 killed, 16 injured.

L43 struck by lightning on return voyage to Nordholz ; undamaged.

Great Italian advance in S. Carso from Kostanjevica to the sea ; Hudi Log, Jamiano, Hill 92, E. of Pietra Rossa, carried ; over 9,000 prisoners.

British s.s. *Chicago City* (2,324 tons) torpedoed by U-Boat off S. Ireland ; towed in ; beached ; 2 lost.

British s.s. *Elmmoor* (3,744 tons) sunk by U-Boat off Syracuse.

British s.s. *England* (3,798 tons) sunk by U-Boat off Cape Bon ; 3 lost.

May 24.

First homeward-bound Atlantic convoy started.

British s.s. *Jersey City* (4,670 tons) sunk by U-Boat N.W. from Flannan Islands.

British s.s. *Belgian* (3,657 tons) sunk by U-Boat westward of Fastnet ; 2 lost.

British s.s. *Madura* (4,484 tons) attacked by U-Boat with two torpedoes at entrance to Channel ; one missed, other failed to explode.

Further Italian gains in Carso ; heavy fighting ; 10,245 prisoners in two days.

Sundays marked with Asterisk (*).

May 24, 1917 (*continued*).

British monitors shelled Austrian lines from Trieste Gulf.

UC24 sunk off Cattaro by French submarine *Circe*.

Gen. Sarrail suspended Allied offensive on Salonika Front.

May 25.

Raid by 17 German aeroplanes on Folkestone ; 95 killed and 192 injured ; 3 aeroplanes brought down on return journey by R.N.A.S. from Dunkirk.

H.M. oiler *Oakleaf* sunk by U-Boat 64 miles N.W. from Butt of Lewis.

British s.s. *Sjaelland* (1,405 tons) sunk by U-Boat off Start Point.

British s.s. *Kohinur* (2,265 tons) sunk by U-Boat N. from Alexandria ; 37 lost.

Gen. Ilse to command XVth (Prussian) Corps, vice Gen. von Deimling.

Further Italian progress in S. Carso ; nearly 23,000 prisoners in two weeks.

May 26.

H.M. A.M.C. *Hilary* (6,239 tons) sunk by U-Boat in Atlantic.

H.S. *Dover Castle* (8,271 tons) torpedoed by U-Boat N. from Bona in Mediterranean ; 7 missing.

B.I. s.s. *Umaria* (5,317 tons) sunk by U-Boat S. by W. from Policaster (Italy) ; 5 lost.

British s.s. *Holmesbank* (3,051 tons) sunk by U-Boat N.W. from Alexandria.

Italians took and lost Kostanjevica.

* May 27.

Italians before third Austrian line ; San Giovanni won ; Timavo R. crossed ; fighting E. of Gorizia. Austrians claimed 13,000 prisoners since opening of offensive.

British s.s. *Dartmoor* (2,870 tons) sunk by U-Boat S.E. from Fastnet ; 25 lost.

British s.s. *Boldwell* (3,118 tons) sunk by U-Boat off Linosa ; 3 lost.

May 28.

Gen. Pershing sailed from New York.

British s.s. *Antinoe* (2,396 tons) and *Limerick* (6,827 tons) sunk by U-Boat W. by S. from Bishop Rock ; 29 lost.

MM. Ribot, Cambon, Painléve, and Gen. Foch conferred with War Cabinet in London.

French Socialists decided to attend Stockholm Conference.

Italian gain near Medeazza ; Austrian attacks E. of Hudi Log and at Vodice repulsed.

Polish congress at Cracow resolved that Poland must be united and independent and have access to sea.

May 29.

British s.s. *Clan Murray* (4,835 tons) sunk by U-Boat W. by S. from Fastnet ; 64 lost.

British s.s. *Oswego* (5,793 tons) and *Ashleaf* (5,768 tons) sunk by U-Boat W. from Bishop Rock.

H.M.S. *Matchless* brought into Dover in sinking condition after collision.

Mr. Henderson on special mission to Russia.

May 30.

H.M.S. *Mastiff* ashore at Shakespeare Cliff ; refloated.

Fierce fighting on Moronvilliers Ridge, E. of Reims ; Germans occupied some trenches on Mont Haut.

May 30 (*continued*).

German bid for Lithuanian sympathies by institution of Lithuanian "national" council.

May 31.

Fourth month of unrestricted U-Boat war ended. Germans claimed 869,000 tons sunk ; admitted 7 U-Boats lost. British estimate = 589,754 tons.

British s.s. *Hanley* (3,331 tons) and *Bathurst* (2,821 tons) sunk by U-Boat W. from Bishop Rock.

British s.s. *Rosebank* (3,837 tons) sunk by U-Boat N. from Ben Ghazi ; 2 lost.

French aeroplanes bombed Zeebrugge U-Boat base and Ghistelles aerodrome.

French recovery E. of Reims.

Gen. Sukhomlinoff, ex-Russian War Minister, found guilty of neglect to supply Army with munitions at beginning of war.

Austrian Reichsrath's first meeting since outbreak of war ; Emperor Charles promised constitutional reforms after the war.

June 1.

British naval aeroplanes dropped over 5 tons of explosives on Ostend—Zeebrugge—Bruges.

British took 3,412 German prisoners in May, 1917 ; total on W. Front 76,067 since war began.

Slight German gain on French front near Laffaux.

French Government declined to grant passports to French Socialists for Stockholm.

British s.s. *Cavina* (6,539 tons) sunk by U-Boat W. by S. from Fastnet.

British s.s. *Kingstonian* (6,564 tons) ashore near Cape Granitola, Sicily, attacked by U-Boat with torpedo ; missed.

June 2.

Canadian attack S. of Souchez R. ; progress S. of Lens ; violent artillery fire, especially at Wytschaete (Ypres).

French summary of Allied spoils in spring offensive : over 52,000 prisoners, including over 1,000 officers, 446 heavy and field guns, and 1,000 machine guns.

British s.s. *Hollington* (4,221 tons) sunk by U-Boat off Faeroe Is. ; 30 lost.

British s.s. *Tonawanda* (3,421 tons) torpedoed by U-Boat in Channel.

H.M.T. *Cameronian* sunk by U-Boat N.W· from Alexandria ; 11 lost.

Brazilian neutrality revoked in war between Germany and U.S. German ships in Brazil ports taken over.

British s.s. *Wairuna* (3,947 tons) sunk by German raider *Wolf* off Sunday Is., Kermadec Is., S. Pacific. This British steamer was chased and challenged at sea by the German raider's seaplane.

*June 3.

British s.s. *San Lorenzo* (9,607 tons) torpedoed by U-Boat off N.W. Ireland ; reached port.

British s.s. *Merioneth* (3,004 tons) sunk by U-Boat N.W. from Tromsö.

Heavy bombardment of German air camps at St. Denis, Vyfweegn, Ghistelles, Zeebrugge, and Bruges.

German recovery S. of Souchez.

French aeroplanes bombed Treves as reprisal for bombardment of Bar-le-Duc.

Albanian independence, under Italian protection, proclaimed.

#June 3, 1917 (*continued*).

Austrian T.B.D. *Wildfang* torpedoed by Italian submarine in Adriatic.

British s.s. *Greenbank* (3,881 tons) and *Islandmore* (3,046 tons) sunk by U-Boat off Cape Falcon, Algeria.

British s.s. *Dockleaf* (5,311 tons) mined in Mediterranean, reached port.

Russian appeal to all nations to conclude peace without annexations or indemnities.

June 4.

British s.s. *Southland* (11,899 tons) and *City of Baroda* (5,541 tons) sunk by U-Boat N.W. from Tory Is.; 10 lost.

British s.s. *Phemius* (6,699 tons) sunk by U-Boat N.W. from Eagle Island.

British s.s. *Manchester Trader* (3,398 tons) sunk by U-Boat S.E. from Pantellaria.

Gen. Brusiloff Russian C.-in-C. vice Gen. Alexeieff, resigned.

Bolshevist rule at Kronstadt.

June 5.

Nearly 10,000,000 on U.S. Register.

Aeroplane raid over Essex and Kent; 13 killed, 34 injured. Returning raiders intercepted off Ostend by British Dunkirk patrols; 2 out of 16 machines destroyed, 2 sent down out of control.

Adm. Bacon's monitors *Erebus* and *Terror* bombarded Ostend docks and works. Tirpitz, Hindenburg, and new 15-inch Jacobsenessen batteries replied.

British s.s. *Manchester Miller* (4,234 tons) sunk by U-Boat N.W. from Fastnet; 8 lost.

British s.s. *Kallundborg* (1,590 tons) sunk by U-Boat S.S.W. from Toulon.

German T.B.D. S20 sunk by British off Belgian coast.

British gain S. of Souchez R.; attack S. of Scarpe R.; progress on Greenland Hill.

Gen. von Falkenhayn relinquished command of German Ninth Army in Rumania.

June 6.

Lord Northcliffe to succeed Mr. Balfour as head of British Mission to U.S.

Nieuwmunster aerodrome bombed by British naval aeroplanes.

M. Jonnart, Allied plenipotentiary, arrived in Greece.

British s.s. *Parthenia* (5,160 tons) sunk by U-Boat W. by N. from Bishop Rock; 3 lost.

British s.s. *Mitra* (5,592 tons) torpedoed by U-Boat in Mediterranean; reached port.

June 7.

First Stage of Flanders Battle.

Messines Battle: Great British victory between Ypres—Armentières; Messines Ridge carried; Oosttaverne captured; German defences on 9-mile front around St. Eloi. Wytschaete, Messines stormed; over 5,000 prisoners; 19 mines exploded before attack.

German attempt on French Chemin-des-Dames positions.

H.M.S. *Pargust*, Q ship (Capt. Gordon Campbell, R.N., V.C.), sank UC29 S.W. of Ireland.

British s.s. *Ikalis* (4,329 tons) and *Jonathan Holt* sunk by U-Boat N.W. from Fastnet.

British s.s. *Cranmore* (3,157 tons) torpedoed by U-Boat off W. Ireland; beached.

British s.s. *Oldfield Grange* (4,653 tons) and *Mahopac* (2,216 tons) torpedoed by U-Boat in Channel; both beached.

June 7 (*continued*).

British s.s. *Sir Francis* (1,991 tons) sunk by U-Boat off Scarborough; 10 lost.

British s.s. *Errington Court* (4,461 tons) mined in Mediterranean; beached.

Russian Council of Peasants' Delegates appealed to Army to defend the country.

June 8.

Gen. Pershing, American C.-in-C., arrived in London.

German counter-attacks at Messines beaten off; total 6,400 prisoners.

British s.s. *Manchester Engineer* (4,465 tons) chased by U-Boat in Arctic Sea; rescued.

British s.s. *Enidwen* (3,594 tons), *Orator* (3,563 tons), and *Saragossa* (3,541 tons) sunk by U-Boat N.W. from Fastnet; 5 lost.

British s.s. *Russian Prince* (4,158 tons) torpedoed by U-Boat off S.W. Ireland; reached port.

British s.s. *Huntstrick* (8,151 tons) and *Isle of Jura* (3,809 tons) sunk by U-Boat off Cape Spartel; 17 lost.

M.L.540 and M.L.541 lost in s.s. *Huntstrick*, torpedoed by U-Boat off Tangier.

Italians occupied Yanina (Epirus).

June 9.

British s.s. *Baron Cawdor* (4,316 tons). *Haulwen* (4,032 tons) and *Appledore* (3,843 tons) sunk by U-Boat westward of Fastnet; 7 lost.

British s.s. *Egyptiana* (3,818 tons) sunk by U-Boat W.S.W. from Scillies.

British s.s. *Harbury* (4,572 tons) sunk by U-Boat W. from Ushant; 12 lost.

White Star s.s. *Ceramic* (18,481 tons) attacked by U-Boat with torpedo at entrance to Channel; missed.

Russian Government refused unlimited armistice proposed by German Commander on Eastern Front.

#June 10.

President Wilson's Message to Russian Provisional Government defining U.S. war aims.

British s.s. *Perla* (5,355 tons) and *Marie Elsie* (2,615 tons) sunk by U-Boat N.W. from Cape Teriberski, Lapland; 7 lost.

British s.s. *Ribera* (3,511 tons) sunk by U-Boat off Cape Wrath.

British s.s. *Bay State* (6,583 tons), *Scottish Hero* (2,205 tons) and *Galicia* (1,400 tons) sunk by U-Boat westward of Fastnet.

British s.s. *Anglian* (5,532 tons) sunk by U-Boat S.W. from Bishop Rock.

British s.s. *Dulwich* (1,460 tons) mined off Shipwash Light; 5 lost.

Admiralty reported all large shipping removed from Ostend Harbour, apparently as effect of bombardment.

Fighting between Adige—Brenta; Italians won Agnello Pass and most of Mte. Ortigara.

Germans in Lukuledi estuary (E. Africa) driven into interior.

June 11.

British s.s. *Knight Commander* (7,241 tons) torpedoed by U-Boat in Atlantic; towed in.

British s.s. *Polyxena* (5,737 tons), *Teviotdale* (3,847 tons) and *City of Perth* (3,427 tons) sunk by U-Boat W. of Fastnet; 16 lost.

British s.s. *South Point* (4,258 tons) sunk by U-Boat S.W. from Bishop Rock.

Sundays marked with Asterisk (*).

June 11, 1917 (*continued*).

Cunard s.s. *Ausonia* (8,153 tons), Montreal to Avonmouth, torpedoed by U-Boat off S. Ireland ; reached port.

British s.s. *Benha* (1,878 tons) sunk by U-Boat N.E. from Marsa Susa.

British s.s. *City of Exeter* (9,373 tons) mined off Bombay ; reached port.

Two German seaplanes brought down in Channel by British drifter which attacked a squadron of five.

British advance on S. wing of new front E. of Messines-Wytschaete Ridge ; trench system near La Poterie Farm captured on mile front ; progress towards Warneton.

British reply to Russian Note of May 3.

M. Jonnart, Allied Plenipotentiary in Greece, demanded King Constantine's abdication.

June 12.

H.M. trawler *Sea King* destroyed UC66 by depth-charges off Lizard.

British s.s. *Amakura* (2,316 tons) sunk by U-Boat N.W. from Tory Island ; 2 lost.

British s.s. *Coronado* (6,539 tons) torpedoed by U-Boat off S. Ireland ; reached port.

British s.s. *Haverford* (11,635 tons) attacked by U-Boat with torpedo off S. Ireland ; missed.

Further British advance towards Warneton on 2-mile front ; Gapaard taken.

Russian Soviet Council replied to letter from Mr. Henderson and MM. Thomas and Vandervelde, explaining scope of proposed international Socialist conference.

King Constantine abdicated in favour of second son Alexander. French force at Corinth ; Franco-British at Larissa (Thessaly).

British sailors took Turkish fortress of Saliff on Arabian Red Sea shore.

June 13.

Daylight raid by 15 Gothas on London (14th raid), Margate and Essex ; 162 killed, 432 injured. One raider down.

British s.s. *Kelvinbank* (4,072 tons) sunk by U-Boat N. from Cape Wrath ; 16 lost.

British s.s. *Darius* (3,426 tons) sunk by U-Boat S.W. from Fastnet ; 15 lost.

British s.s. *St. Andrews* (3,613 tons) sunk by U-Boat off Cape Spartivento ; 3 lost.

Sir D. Haig reported 7,342 prisoners since June 7.

Gen. Pershing in France.

Austrian reverse in Trentino.

June 14.

British naval forces destroyed Zeppelin L43 in North Sea.

Germans yielding E. of Messines Ridge, towards Armentières and E. of Gapaard. Infantry Hill, E. of Monchy, stormed by British.

Mr. Root and U.S. Mission in Petrograd.

H.M. A.M.C. *Avenger* (15,000 tons) sunk by U-Boat in N. Atlantic.

Transport s.s. *Basi*, with 3,400 tons of ammunition ashore at Le Touquet ; towed to Boulogne.

British s.s. *Carthaginian* (4,444 tons) mined off Innistrahul Light.

British s.s. *Kankakee* (3,718 tons) torpedoed by German seaplane off Sunk Light ; 3 lost.

British s.s. *Canto* (1,243 tons) attacked by German seaplanes with three torpedoes and machine-gun ; missed.

British s.s. *New Zealand Transport* (4,481 tons) sunk by U-Boat in Ægean ; 3 lost.

June 14 (*continued*).

British s.s. *Lowther Castle* (4,439 tons) mined in Mediterranean ; reached port.

June 15.

H.M. special service ship *Zylpha* sunk by U-Boat off S.W. Ireland.

British s.s. *Westonby* (3,795 tons) sunk by U-Boat S.W. from Fastnet.

British s.s. *Wapello* (5,576 tons) sunk by U-Boat off Owers Light ; 2 lost.

British s.s. *Addah* (4,397 tons) sunk by U-Boat off Penmarch ; 9 lost.

British s.s. *Pasha* (5,930 tons) sunk by U-Boat in S. entrance to Messina Straits ; 3 lost.

British s.s. *Elvaston* (4,130 tons) torpedoed by U-Boat in Mediterranean ; reached port ; 3 lost.

Release of Irish Rebellion prisoners announced.

Lord Rhondda Food Controller, vice Lord Devonport.

British airmen from Dunkirk, in new 375 h.-p. Rolls-Royce D.H.4 machine, reconnoitred and photographed, unescorted, Antwerp and Hoboken docks.

British naval aeroplanes bombed St. Denis Westrem aerodrome (Ghent).

British captured further section of Hindenburg line N.W. of Bullecourt.

Italians captured strong position on Corno Cavento with garrison and guns.

June 16.

British s.s. *Jessie* (2,256 tons) sunk by U-Boat W. from Bishop Rock.

British s.s. *Fallodon* (3,016 tons) torpedoed by U-Boat off S. Ireland ; towed in.

Fighting round Bullecourt.

Russian Duma resolved against separate peace.

British withdrew on left bank of Struma R. (Macedonia) owing to advent of malaria.

Allied blockade of Greece suspended.

*June 17.

Adm. Sims, U.S.N., hoisted his flag at Queenstown, in temporary absence of Adm. Bayly (on leave).

British s.s. *Fornebo* (4,259 tons) sunk by U-Boat off Cape Wrath.

British s.s. *Lizzie Westoll* (2,855 tons) sunk by U-Boat N.W. from Fastnet.

British s.s. *Tyne* (2,909 tons) sunk by U-Boat off the Lizard.

British s.s. *Stanhope* (2,854 tons) sunk by U-Boat off Start Point ; 22 lost.

British s.s. *Claveresk* (3,829 tons) attacked by U-Boat with torpedo off Casablanca ; missed.

P. & O. s.s. *Kaisar-i-Hind* (11,430 tons) attacked by U-Boat with torpedo W. from Gibraltar ; missed.

L42, prevented by weather from raiding London, bombed Dover.

L44, L45, and L48, also unable to reach London, bombed Suffolk area. L48 brought down in flames by R.F.C.

Portuguese troops reported by Sir D. Haig in action on W. Front.

Germans took part of Hurtebise salient.

Italians rectified Carso front.

June 18.

British s.s. *Buffalo* (4,106 tons) sunk by U-Boat N.W. from Cape Wrath.

British s.s. *Queen Adelaide* (4,965 tons) sunk by U-Boat N.N.E. from St. Kilda.

British s.s. *Elele* (6,557 tons), *English*

June 18, 1917 (*continued*).

Monarch (4,947 tons) and *Thistledhu* (4,032 tons) sunk by U-Boat N.W. from Fastnet.

P. & O. s.s. *Palma* (7,632 tons), New York to Liverpool, attacked by two U-Boats 300 miles off Irish coast; three torpedoes fired; missed; U-Boats stalled off by gunfire; ship rescued by U.S. T.B.D. and British auxiliary.

Fighting at Infantry Hill. French captured salient between Mont Cornillet—Mont Blond (Champagne).

Herr Hoffman, Swiss Foreign Minister, who had forwarded German proposals to Herr Grimm in Petrograd, resigned.

German air-raid on Dvinsk.

June 19.

King George abolished foreign titles in British Royal family, and conferred British peerages upon the Tecks and Battenbergs.

British s.s. *Great City* (5,525 tons) torpedoed by U-Boat off Scilly Is.; towed in.

British s.s. *Batoum* (4,054 tons) and *Brookby* (3,679 tons) sunk by U-Boat off Fastnet; 1 lost.

British s.s. *Penpol* (2,061 tons) captured by U-Boat in Gulf of Bothnia and taken to Germany.

H.M. CMB.1 sunk in action off Ostend.

Minor fighting on Arras front; slight British gains S. of Cojeul R. and N. of Souchez R.; recovery at Infantry Hill.

Italian success in Trentino.

French submarine *Ariane* sunk by U-Boat off Tunis.

June 20.

Mr. Daniels, U.S. Navy Secretary, in response to Mr. Page's dispatch of 27-iv.-17, agreed to send 32 U.S. T.B.D.s to European waters.

H.M. sloop *Salvia* sunk by U-Boat off W. Ireland.

British s.s. *Ruperra* (4,232 tons) sunk by U-Boat off Pantellaria.

Russian Black Sea Fleet mutiny. Adm. Koltchak arrested and forced to resign.

German attacks N. of Souchez R.

Germans in French trench near Vauxaillon.

Italians blew up a mountain spur, W. of Ampezzo Valley (Carnia); Austrian garrison destroyed.

June 21.

British s.s. *Ortona* (5,524 tons) and *Lord Roberts* (4,166 tons) sunk by U-Boat off Fastnet.

French recovery near Vauxaillon.

German attack on Teton crest, Moronvilliers, failed.

June 22.

British s.s. *Melford Hall* (6,339 tons) sunk by U-Boat off Tory Island.

British s.s. *Miami* (3,762 tons) sunk by U-Boat off Fastnet.

German gain in assault on French N. of Braye-en-Laonnois.

June 23.

Intense artillery activity on W. Front towards Flanders coast.

Greek political conference to establish national government under M. Venizelos.

British s.s. *Osmanieh* (4,041 tons) attacked by U-Boat with two torpedoes in Mediterranean; missed.

*June 24.

H.M.S. *Tartar* mined; reached Dover.

British s.s. *Sylvanian* (4,858 tons) sunk by U-Boat off Tory Island; 2 lost.

British s.s. *Clan Davidson* (6,486 tons), *Saxon Monarch* (4,828 tons), *Crown of Arragon* (4,500 tons) and *South Wales* (3,668 tons) sunk by U-Boat W. and S.W. from Scilly Is.; 17 lost in all.

British s.s. *Don Arturo* (3,680 tons) sunk by U-Boat in Atlantic; 34 lost.

British s.s. *Cestrian* (8,912 tons) sunk by U-Boat off Skyro; 3 lost.

P. & O. s.s. *Mongolia* (9,505 tons) sunk off Bombay by mine laid by German raider *Wolf*; 24 lost.

British progress on 2,500-yard front E. of Souchez R., S.W. of Lens; numerous British raids.

Fighting near Vauxaillon; French gain.

British s.s. *Meggie* (1,802 tons) captured by U-Boat in Gulf of Bothnia; taken to Germany.

Ukraine Rada proclaimed autonomy.

M. Zaimis, Greek Premier, resigned.

June 25.

British gains S. of Scarpe R. near Fontaine.

French on Craonne Ridge N.W. of Hurtebise Farm, took stronghold known as "Dragon's Cave"; 300 prisoners.

Dr. Michahelles, German Minister at Christiania, recalled, after discovery of German bomb plot in Norway.

M. Venizelos in Athens.

British s.s. *Anatolia* (3,847 tons) mined off Genoa.

British s.s. *Southern* (5,694 tons) mined in Mediterranean; beached.

June 26.

U.S. First Division at St. Nazaire.

British progress S.W. of Lens; enemy positions astride Souchez R. on 2-mile front, including La Coulotte, taken.

M. Venizelos formed Cabinet.

British s.s. *Haverford* (11,635 tons) torpedoed by U-Boat off W. Scotland; beached; 8 lost.

British s.s. *Birdoswald* (4,013 tons) sunk by U-Boat off Tarragona.

June 27.

Mesopotamia Commission Report.

Vincent-Bingley Report on failure of Mesopotamia medical service.

British s.s. *Armadale* (6,153 tons) and *Baron Ogilvy* (4,570 tons) sunk by U-Boat off Tory Island.

Cunard s.s. *Ultonia* (10,402 tons), inward bound, sunk by U-Boat 350 miles W. from Land's End; crew rescued by Q. Boat; 1 lost.

French cruiser *Kléber* mined off Brest.

Dunkirk bombarded by German 15-inch gun at Leugenboom; 55 shells fired at 24 miles range.

British Dominion Battery 12-inch naval gun at Adenkerke retaliated by firing on Ostend.

German attack near Fontaine, S. of Scarpe R., defeated.

Hindenburg wrote to the Kaiser urging that moral of German people must be raised, but that this task seemed beyond the present Chancellor.

June 28.

British s.s. *Northfield* (2,099 tons) torpedoed by U-Boat in Channel; reached port.

Sundays marked with Asterisk (*).

June 28, 1917 (*continued*).

British progress on 2-mile front across Souchez R. towards Lens ; Avion entered ; German forward positions on 2,000-yard front S. and W. of Oppy taken ; 247 prisoners.

Heavy German attacks on Aisne front beaten off.

Germans penetrated French first-line defences W. of Hill 304 (Verdun).

June 29.

H.M. special service ship *Bayard* sunk by collision in English Channel.

Germans gained footing in French salient near Cerny, W. of Craonne.

French recovery at Hill 304 (Verdun) ; slight German progress W. of Mort Homme.

Gen. Allenby to command in Egypt and Palestine, vice Gen. Murray. Gen. Byng in command of British Third Army on W. Front, vice Gen. Allenby. Gen. Currie in command of Canadian Corps, vice Gen. Byng.

June 30.

H.M.S. *Cheerful* mined off Shetlands.

British s.s. *Fairmuir* chased by U-Boat in Arctic Sea ; escaped.

British s.s. *Ilston* (2,426 tons) sunk by U-Boat off Lizard ; 6 lost.

British s.s. *Haigh Hall* (4,809 tons) sunk by U-Boat off Malta.

Fifth month of unrestricted U-Boat war ended. Germans claimed 1,016,000 tons sunk ; admitted 3 U-Boats lost.

British estimate = 675,154 tons.

During June 95 U-Boats were ordered.

UB36 lost during June ; cause unknown.

British progress S. and S.W. of Lens ; German defences on ½-mile front captured.

U.S. Naval Air Contingent, first American force in France, reached Bordeaux during June.

German gain across Ailles-Paissy road.

Italians evacuated Agnella border pass.

Greece broke with Central Powers.

Action at Lutende, (G. E. Africa).

German troops driven from Nyasaland border to Rovuma border by Anglo-Portuguese.

*July 1.

H.M.S. *Cossack* damaged by explosion of depth-charge after collision ; towed into Dover.

British s.s. *Don Emilio* (3,651 tons) sunk by U-Boat off W. Shetland ; 1 lost.

British s.s. *Demerara* (11,484 tons) torpedoed by U-Boat in Bay of Biscay ; beached ; 1 lost.

French recovery at Ailles—Paissy.

Russian "Red" Army under Gen. Brusiloff attacked on 20-mile front about Brzezany (Galicia) ; three trench lines carried and Tseniovka crossed ; 10,000 prisoners. M. Kerensky at front.

July 2.

H.M.S. *Zubian* joined Dover Patrol.

British s.s. *Thirlby* (2,009 tons) sunk by U-Boat off Fastnet ; 2 lost.

British set-back at Lens.

Germans failed at Avocourt—Hill 304 (Verdun).

German "Asia Corps" formed.

Russian progress around Brzezany ; 6,300 more prisoners. Turkish 15th Corps still fighting in Galicia.

July 3.

British s.s. *Matador* (3,642 tons) sunk by U-Boat off Fastnet ; 2 lost.

July 3 (*continued*).

British s.s. *Mongara* (8,205 tons) sun by U-Boat off Messina Breakwater.

British s.s. *City of Cambridge* (3,84 tons) sunk by U-Boat off Jidjelli.

German attack at Jouy—Craonne, N. Aisne R., beaten back with great loss.

Further Russian attack on Brzezany heights round Zboroff captured ; artiller activity increasing towards Stokhod R.

July 4.

U-Boat attack in force on U.S. Atlanti transports beaten off by U.S. T.B.D.s ; a least one U-Boat destroyed.

Raid on Suffolk and Essex (Harwich by 12 to 14 German aeroplanes ; 17 killed, 3 injured. Two raiders brought down in flame and third damaged S.E. of Ostend by Britis naval aircraft from Dunkirk.

British s.s. *Hurstside* (3,149 tons) sun by U-Boat off Cape Wrath.

British s.s. *Goathland* (3,044 tons) sun by U-Boat off Belle Ile ; 21 lost.

H.M. sloop *Aster* mined in Mediterranean

H.M. special service ship *Mona* blow up to avoid capture off Cape Passaro (Medi terranean).

July 5.

British s.s. *Cuyahoga* (4,586 tons) sun by U-Boat off Tory Island.

British s.s. *Edurna* (4,735 tons), tor pedoed by U-Boat in Mediterranean, arrived.

British advance on 600-yard front, S.W of Hollebeke.

Reichstag assembled in order to vot supplementary war credit of 15,000,000,00 marks.

Further fighting at Brzezany (Galicia).

July 6.

Canadian Commons passed Conscriptio Bill.

British s.s. *Ariadne Christine* (3,550 tons and *Wabasha* (5,864 tons) torpedoed by U Boat in Channel ; first beached, second arrived ; 2 lost.

H.M.S. *Itchen* torpedoed in North Sea.

British s.s. *Cumberland* (9,471 tons sunk by mine laid overnight by German raider *Wolf* off Gabo Is., on Sydney-Melbourne route.

Hindenburg and Ludendorff arrived in Berlin, in order to urge Kaiser to dismiss Chancellor, whom they considered no longer able to cope with home discontent.

Russian attack in Galicia extending towards Stanislau ; 1,000 more prisoners or Brzezany front.

July 7.

Great German daylight raid on London and Margate by 24 aeroplanes (including German 3rd Air Squad.) ; 57 killed and 19 injured ; G.P.O. bombed ; four raiders down on return journey, one at Thames mouth two at sea 40 miles from E. coast, and fourth off Scheldt R. ; two British pilots and one observer killed, one observer injured ; two British machines destroyed, two crashed.

British s.s. *Condesa* (8,557 tons) sunk by U-Boat W. from Bishop Rock.

British s.s. *Bellucia* (4,368 tons) sunk by U-Boat off Lizard ; 4 lost.

British s.s. *Tarquah* (3,859 tons) sunk by U-Boat off Bull Rock.

Slight British advance E. of Wytschaete

French aeroplanes bombed Treves Coblenz, Ludwigshafen, and Essen as reprisa for German raids on Nancy and Epernay.

July 7, 1917 (*continued*).

British s.s. *Wilberforce* (3,074 tons) sunk by U-Boat off Cape Gata.

British s.s. *Southina* (3,506 tons) sunk by U-Boat off Cape Sigli, Algeria.

Gen. von Falkenhayn in command of new Yildirim Army Group in Turkey.

*July 8.

U.S. embargo on food, metals, and coal.

British s.s. *Obuasi* (4,416 tons) and *Valetta* (5,871 tons) sunk by U-Boat N.W. from Fastnet ; 2 lost.

British s.s. *Pegu* (6,348 tons) mined off Galley Head ; 1 lost.

British s.s. *Vendée* mined in mouth of Gironde R.

German attack across Soissons—Laon road ; local gain near Braye-en-Laonnois.

Gen. Korniloff broke Austrian front W. of Stanislau, S. of Halicz ; over 7,000 prisoners. Russian cavalry crossed Bistritza and pursued Austrians 8 miles to Lukwa R.

July 9.

Secret House of Commons sitting on London air raid.

H.M.S. *Vanguard* (19,250 tons) blown up at Scapa by internal explosion ; 97 survivors.

British s.s. *Prince Abbas* (2,030 tons) sunk by U-Boat off Fair Is. ; 2 lost.

British s.s. *Hartley, Haslingden, Beatrice,* and *Jarrix* attacked by German seaplanes with torpedoes in North Sea ; missed.

British armed trawler *Iceland* destroyed two German seaplanes in North Sea.

British Messines line advanced E. of Oosttaverne.

Germans beaten off E. of Hurtebise. French recovery at Braye-en-Laonnois.

German military propaganda service created, for "enlightenment" of Army at the front.

Gen. Korniloff 5 miles S.W. of Halicz ; Austro-Germans behind Lomnica R. ; 1,000 more prisoners.

British airmen over Constantinople bombed H.I.M.S. *Goeben* and Turkish War Office.

Russians reported their evacuation of Khanikin, &c. (Mesopotamia).

July 10.

Intense artillery fight on Belgian coast ; German marines attacked E. of Yser mouth and won ground on 1,400-yard front ; two British platoons surrounded, fought to last man ; opposite Lombartzyde Germans penetrated British advanced positions, but driven out.

Kaiser in Berlin refused Chancellor's offer to resign.

Gen. Korniloff took Halicz.

H.M. Q schooner *Glen* engaged and probably sank U-Boat about 40 miles S.W. of Weymouth.

British s.s. *Seang Choon* (5,807 tons) and *King David* (3,680 tons) sunk by U-Boat off Fastnet ; 21 lost.

British s.s. *Garmoyle* (1,229 tons) sunk by U-Boat off Mine Head ; 20 lost.

British s.s. *Flamma* (1,920 tons) mined in North Sea ; beached.

July 11.

U.S. Emergency Fleet Corporation authorised to construct, purchase and requisition vessels.

British s.s. *Kioto* (6,182 tons) and *Muirfield* (3,086 tons) sunk by U-Boat westward of Fastnet ; 2 lost.

July 11 (*continued*).

British s.s. *Anglo-Patagonian* (5,017 tons) sunk by U-Boat off Les Sables d'Olonne ; 4 lost.

British s.s. *Grosvenor* attacked with bombs by German aircraft in Dunkirk Harbour ; missed.

British naval aeroplanes from Dunkirk dropped over 6½ tons of bombs on Bruges Docks.

British Carnac Battery (naval 9·2-inch guns) bombarded by Hindenburg 15-inch and Tirpitz Batteries at Ostend.

Slight German progress E. of Monchy.

Kaiser promised equal franchise for next Prussian elections.

Gen. Korniloff 17 miles from Stanislau.

British column from Feluja (Euphrates) engaged Turkish force upstream and inflicted considerable loss.

July 12.

British s.s. *Castleton* (2,395 tons) sunk by U-Boat S.W. from Bishop Rock.

H.M.S. *Patriot* sank U69 in North Sea.

Mesopotamia debate ; Mr. Chamberlain resigned from India Office.

Hindenburg and Ludendorff telegraphed from Kreuznach G.H.Q. their joint resignation to Kaiser in Berlin.

Gen. Korniloff advanced towards Dolina.

King of Hedjaz, having defeated Turks, master of country between Akaba and Hedjaz railway.

July 13.

U.S. called up 678,000 men.

Hindenburg and Ludendorff summoned to Berlin ; Kaiser decided to dismiss Chancellor von Bethmann-Hollweg ; Count Hertling declined to succeed ; Herr Georg Michaelis appointed.

Russian progress around Kalush (Galicia) ; 1,600 more prisoners.

July 14.

King and Queen returned to London after 10 days in France.

British s.s. *Calliope* (2,883 tons) sunk by U-Boat in Atlantic ; 27 lost.

British s.s. *Exford* (5,886 tons) sunk by U-Boat off Ushant ; 6 lost.

Germans attacked Chemin-des-Dames, W. of Craonne ; won two trench lines in Cerny salient, but failed to hold.

French at Moronvilliers gained Mont Haut—Le Teton ; 360 prisoners.

Esthonian Diet met at Reval.

British raid near Gaza (Syria).

*July 15.

British s.s. *Mariston* (2,908 tons) and s.v. *Dudhope* (2,086 tons) sunk by U-Boat W. from Fastnet ; 28 lost.

British s.s. *Torcello* (2,929 tons) sunk by U-Boat S.W. from Bishop Rock ; 1 lost.

British s.s. *Trelissick* (4,168 tons) sunk by U-Boat off Ushant.

British s.s. *Westmeath* (9,179 tons) torpedoed by U-Boat in Channel ; arrived.

German assault on Mont Haut defeated.

Italian raid near Versic (Carso) ; 275 prisoners.

German reinforcements in Galicia.

Four Russian Cadet Ministers resigned, as protest against Government's Ukrainian policy.

July 16, 1917.

British s.s. *Tamele* (3,932 tons) and *Ribston* (3,372 tons) sunk by U-Boat westward from Fastnet ; 26 lost.

British s.s. *Valentia* (3,242 tons) sunk by U-Boat off Bishop Rock ; 3 lost.

British s.s. *Henry R. James* (3,146 tons) mined off Ile de Bas ; 24 lost.

British s.s. *Khephren* (2,774 tons) sunk by U-Boat E. from Malta.

British s.s. *Firfield* (4,029 tons) sunk by U-Boat off Cape Papas, Nikaria.

Six German steamers intercepted off Dutch coast by British naval forces ; four captured and two driven ashore by gunfire.

German attacks on Moronvilliers Ridge.

Russian withdrawal in Galicia.

Disorder in Petrograd due to disbandment of recalcitrant regiments ; mutiny engineered by Bolshevists under Lenin.

July 17.

Royal House assumed name of Windsor.

Sir E. Carson entered War Cabinet ; Sir E. Geddes First Lord ; Dr. Addison Minister of Reconstruction ; Mr. Churchill Munitions ; Mr. Montagu India vice Mr. Chamberlain.

British s.s. *Haworth* (4,456 tons) sunk by U-Boat W. from Fastnet.

P. & O. s.s. *Kaisar-i-Hind* (11,430 tons) attacked by U-Boat with torpedo S.W. of Scilly Is. ; missed.

French completed recovery on Hill 304 (Verdun) ; 425 prisoners.

Continued disorder in Petrograd ; mutineers from Kronstadt arrived.

July 18.

British s.s. *City of Canton* (6,692 tons) warded off U-Boat attack by gunfire off N.W. Scotland.

German attacks near St. Quentin and at Avocourt Wood (Verdun) defeated.

Petrograd revolt crushed.

Fight on Russian front for Novica.

July 19.

German attack S. of Lombartzyde.

German attacks near St. Quentin and between Craonne—Hurtebise defeated.

Chancellor Michaelis declared for victor's peace and inviolability of German territory.

Under influence of urgent representations by Count Czernin to German Centre and Socialists, Reichstag adopted Resolution in favour of peace without annexations or indemnities.

German counter-attack (supported by 1st and 2nd Prussian Guard Divisions and four other Divisions from Argonne) on Russian front ; Russian positions E. of Zloczow pierced as result of insubordination among rank and file.

British s.s. *Bramham* (1,978 tons) mined off Lizard ; 1 lost.

H.M. collier *Clan McLachlan* (4,729 tons) sunk by collision near Gibraltar.

British s.s. *Eloby* (6,545 tons) sunk by U-Boat S.E. from Malta ; 56 lost.

Two Turkish cavalry regiments driven back at Beersheba (Palestine).

German main position attacked at Narongombe, S.W. of Kilwa (E. Africa) ; Germans retire to Mbemkuru Valley.

July 20.

British s.s. *Fluent* (3,660 tons) mined off Anvil Point.

P. & O. s.s. *Salsette* (5,842 tons) sunk by U-Boat off Portland Bill ; 15 lost.

July 20 (*continued*).

British s.s. *City of Florence* (5,399 tons) sunk by U-Boat off Ushant.

Breach in Russian front growing ; German progress towards Tarnopol ; retreat stayed in Brzezany—Halicz sector.

Soviet rule at Nijni Novgorod.

Successful British raid at Gaza (Syria).

July 21.

H.M. submarine C34 sunk by U52 off Shetlands.

British s.s. *Coniston Water* (3,738 tons) sunk by U-Boat off Butt of Lewis.

British s.s. *African Prince* (4,916 tons) and *Ramillies* (2,935 tons), and s.v. *Harold* sunk by U-Boat off Tory Is. ; 13 lost.

British s.s. *Paddington* (5,084 tons) and *Dafila* (1,754 tons) sunk by U-Boat off Fastnet ; 31 lost.

White Star s.s. *Ceramic* (18,481 tons) chased by U-Boat in Bristol Channel ; rescued.

British s.s. *Trelyon* (3,099 tons) mined and wrecked off Scarborough.

German Government's plan for " nationalising " Courland and Lithuania developed.

Russian retreat on Sereth R. ; Germans in Tarnopol suburbs.

*July 22.

Aeroplane raid on Essex and Suffolk (Harwich and Felixstowe), with 15-21 machines of German 3rd Air Squad. ; 13 killed, 26 injured ; German formation broken up and attack driven off ; one raider brought down near Belgian coast by R.F.C. patrol.

Furious artillery battles in Flanders and along Chemin-des-Dames ; Crown Prince's attack on ridge heavily repulsed, though Germans on California Plateau (Craonne).

Prince Lvoff resigned. M. Kerensky Russian Premier and War Minister.

Russians took offensive near Krevo, E. of Vilna ; penetrated German positions 2 miles deep ; 1,000 prisoners ; further success jeopardised by indiscipline.

Siam at war with Germany.

British s.s. *Cotovia* (4,020 tons) sunk by mine off Auskerry.

British s.s. *Rota* (2,171 tons) sunk by U-Boat off Berry Head ; 5 lost.

July 23.

Russian retreat on 150-mile front ; fall of Halicz, Stanislau evacuated ; Germans across Sereth, S. of Tarnopol. Russian operations at Dvinsk and Smorgon followed by voluntary withdrawal.

Russo-Rumanian successes in Susitza—Putna valleys ; 2,000 prisoners, 57 guns.

M.L.474 destroyed by fire after being struck by Turkish shell near Chios.

H.M. A.M.C. *Otway* (12,000 tons) sunk by U-Boat in N. Atlantic.

British s.s. *Ashleigh* (6,985 tons) and *Huelva* (4,867 tons) sunk by U-Boat S.W. from Fastnet.

July 24.

Canadian Conscription Bill passed.

French recovery about Craonne.

Fall of Stanislau and Tarnopol to Austro-Germans.

Herr von Kühlmann retired from German Embassy at Constantinople.

British s.s. *Blake* (3,740 tons) sunk by U-Boat off Cape Wrath ; 5 lost.

British s.s. *Zermatt* (3,767 tons) and *Brumaire* (2,324 tons) sunk by U-Boat off Ushant ; 5 lost.

July 25, 1917.

British s.s. *Oakleaf* (8,106 tons) sunk by U-Boat off Butt of Lewis.

British s.s. *Purley* (4,500 tons) and *Peninsula* (1,384 tons) sunk by U-Boat off Fastnet ; 1 lost.

British s.s. *Monkstone* (3,097 tons) sunk by U-Boat off Scilly Is. ; 1 lost.

British s.s. *Rustington* (3,071 tons) sunk by U-Boat off Ushant.

Adm. Bacon with Adm. Ronarc'h in H.M.S. *Broke*, superintended relaying of 12-mile net-barrage off Belgian coast in one and a half hours.

Artillery battle in Flanders.

Fighting on California Plateau (Craonne) ; French repelled counter-attacks.

Gen. Ludendorff issued from German G.H.Q. a confidential instruction warning against spread of " political propaganda " in the Army and ordaining a special inquisition into all letters from the front.

Russian retreat pivoting on Trembowla.

Russian Provisional Government revived death penalty in army.

July 26.

H.M.S. *Ariadne* (11,000 tons), minelayer, sunk by U-Boat off Beachy Head.

UC61 stranded off Cape Gris Nez ; captured by Belgian cavalry.

British s.s. *Ludgate* (3,708 tons) mined off Galley Head ; 24 lost.

British s.s. *Carmarthen* (4,262 tons) sunk by U-Boat off Lizard.

British s.s. *Somerset* (8,710 tons) sunk by U-Boat off Ushant.

P. & O. s.s. *Mooltan* (9,723 tons) sunk by U-Boat off Cape Serrat ; 2 lost.

Paris Balkan Conference ended.

Fall of Kolomea.

July 27.

British s.s. *Candia* (6,482 tons) sunk by U-Boat off Owers Light ; 1 lost.

H.M.A.T. *Cambrian* stranded on N. Goodwin refloated.

H.M. monitors *Erebus, Terror*, and *Marshal Soult* took up Belgian coast patrol.

German attacks on Craonne and Moronvilliers ridges.

German 4th Air Squad. raided Paris.

Rumanian advance towards Kezdi—Vasarhely.

July 28.

558,858 voluntary enlistments in U.S.

Germans reached the Russian frontier on both sides of Husiatyn.

Rumanians 10 miles from old positions on 20-mile front ; 3,000 prisoners.

British s.s. *Whitehall* (3,158 tons) sunk by U-Boat off Fastnet ; 1 lost.

British s.s. *Glenstrae* (4,718 tons) sunk by U-Boat off Bishop Rock ; 1 lost.

*July 29.

British s.s. *Adalia* (3,847 tons) sunk by U-Boat off Muckle Flugga ; 1 lost.

UB20 bombed and destroyed in North Sea by H.M. seaplanes 8662 and 8676.

UB27 rammed and depth-charged by H.M.S. *Halcyon* in North Sea.

Flanders artillery battle more intense.

German 4th Air Squad. raided Paris.

Gen. Ludendorff issued from German G.H.Q. detailed programme for patriotic propaganda in the Army.

*July 29 (*continued*).

Germans across Galician border ; bitter Russian resistance S. of Dniester ; retirement in Bukovina.

Rumanian offensive continued.

British s.s. *Manchester Commerce* (4,144 tons) sunk by U-Boat off Cape Spartel ; 1 lost.

P. & O. s.s. *Okhla* (5,288 tons) sunk by mine laid by German raider *Wolf* off Bombay ; 9 lost.

Action at Narumgombe (G. E. Africa).

July 30.

First U.S. Conscript drafted.

British s.s. *Manchester Inventor* (4,112 tons) sunk by U-Boat off Muckle Flugga.

German military engineers in Belgium restored and completed Canal du Centre, near Mons.

French success on 1,600-yard front S. of La Royère (Aisne) ; 210 prisoners.

Fall of Zaleszczyki—Sniatyn.

British s.s. *Shimosa* (4,221 tons) sunk by U-Boat off Eagle Is. ; 17 lost.

British s.s. *Ganges* (4,177) tons sunk by U-Boat off Cape Spartel ; 1 lost.

July 31.

Second stage of Flanders battle.

Great Allied attack around Ypres on 15-mile front ; British advanced from Lys Valley N. beyond Ypres to Yser Canal, to depth of over 2 miles, taking Pilken, St. Julien, Frezenberg, and Westhoek, and S. of Ypres—Menin road, Hollebeke—La Basse Ville ; French forced passage of Yser Canal took Steenstraate—Bixschoote. Over 6,000 prisoners taken by British.

H.M. escort ship *Quernmore* (7,302 tons) sunk by U-Boat 160 miles from Tory Island.

British s.s. *Belgian Prince* (4,765 tons) sunk by U44 (Lt.-Comdr. P. Wagenfuhr), N.W. from Tory Island ; crew of 39 lined up on submarine's deck and drowned by submergence of boat ; master made prisoner.

British s.s. *Orubian* (3,876 tons) sunk by U-Boat N.W. from Eagle Is. ; 1 lost.

British s.s. *Snowdonian* (3,870 tons) sunk by U-Boat off Santa Maria Azores.

During July the British homeward trade from Gibraltar was brought under convoy.

Sixth month of unrestricted U-Boat war ended. Germans claimed 811,000 tons sunk ; admitted 7 U-Boats lost.

During first six months of unrestricted campaign, number of U-Boats at sea averaged 47 per month ; tonnage claimed sunk averaged about 900,000 tons per month ; U-Boats admitted lost averaged 4·5 per month.

U-Boat tonnage built during 12 months ended 31·vii·-17 = 101 boats of 56,453 tons.

German attacks on Russian line near Brody.

During July LZ120 was credited with a 101 hour non-stop flight over the Baltic.

August 1.

At Ypres : Counter-attacks on new British line ; St. Julien and some ground along Ypres—Roulers railway lost ; latter recovered. British line advanced near Zillebeke—Zandvoorde road ; French won fresh ground on W. bank of Yser Canal.

German advance near Russian frontier at Zbrucz R., and in Bukovina towards Czernowitz ; footing gained in Bessarabia.

Gen. Korniloff Russian C.-in-C., vice Gen. Brusiloff.

German Government had by this date reached understanding with Ukrainian separatists.

Sundays marked with Asterisk (*).

August 1, 1917 (*continued*).

British s.s. *Karina* (4,222 tons) sunk by U-Boat off Waterford coast ; 11 lost.

British s.s. *Laertes* (4,187 tons) sunk by U-Boat off Prawle Point ; 14 lost.

British s.s. *Llandudno* (4,187 tons) sunk by U-Boat off Porquerolles Is. ; 1 lost.

August 2.

German raider *Seeadler* wrecked on Lord Howe Is. (Pacific).

U.S. Senate by 65 to 20 adopted National Prohibition Amendment to Constitution.

British s.s. *Newlyn* (4,019 tons) sunk by U-Boat off Prawle Point ; 4 lost.

British s.s. *Beechpark* (4,763 tons) sunk by U-Boat S. from Scilly Is.

Adm. Lacaze, French Minister of Marine, resigned.

German attack on Infantry Hill, E. of Monchy ; front-line trenches taken.

Russian retreat : Germans on Podolian frontier. Kimpolung (Bukovina) taken.

H.M. fleet messenger *Ermine* (1,777 tons) sunk by mine or U-Boat in Ægean.

August 3.

British retook St. Julien ; recovery at Infantry Hill.

Czernowitz (Bukovina) fell to Germans.

Heavy fighting near Lindi (G.E. Africa), and up Lukuledi R.

August 4.

UC44 blown up by her own mines off Waterford.

British s.s. *British Monarch* (5,749 tons) mined off Porquerolles.

British s.s. *Cairnstrath* (2,128 tons) sunk by U-Boat S.S.W. from Ile du Pilier ; 22 lost.

British s.s. *Countess of Mar* (2,234 tons) sunk by U-Boat off Bayonne ; 20 lost.

German progress E. of Czernowitz (Bukovina).

*August 5.

U.S. National Guard (about 300,000 men) passed into Federal Service.

British s.s. *Kathleen* (3,915 tons) sunk by U-Boat off Skelligs ; 1 lost.

Russians E. of Czernowitz, but fell back.

August 6.

Adm. Wemyss Second Sea Lord.

British s.s. *Argalia* (4,641 tons) sunk by U-Boat N.W. from Tory Is. ; 3 lost.

Slight British progress W. and S.W. of Lens.

Herr von Kühlmann German Foreign Secretary vice Herr Zimmermann.

Russian National Ministry under M. Kerensky.

Mackensen's Army stormed Russo-Rumanian positions N. of Focsani ; 1,300 prisoners.

British s.s. *Matunga* (1,608 tons) sunk by German raider *Wolf* 300 miles from Riche Island, New Guinea.

August 7.

H.M. special service ship *Bracondale* sunk by U-Boat in Atlantic.

British s.s. *Port Curtis* (4,710 tons) sunk by U-Boat W. from Penmarch.

British s.s. *Iran* (6,250 tons) sunk by U-Boat off Santa Maria, Azores.

Russian counter on Galician frontier.

German progress N. of Focsani (Moldavia).

August 8.

H.M.S. *Dunraven*, Q ship (Capt. Gordo Campbell, V.C., R.N.) attacked and set o fire by U-Boat off Ushant after an actio described by Adm. Jellicoe as "perha the finest feat performed by decoy shi during the war"; survivors rescued T.B.D.s; ship taken in tow in sinkir condition (see : 10-viii.-17).

French gain N.W. of Bixschoote.

Bolshevist and Social Revolutionary co ference under Lenin in Petrograd.

Russians pressed back S. of Kimpolung

Mackensen progressed N.W. of Focsan reached Susitza R. ; over 3,000 prisoners three days ; Russo-Rumanians retired Trotus Valley.

Activity on Salonika front.

British s.s. *Llanishen* (3,837 tons) sur by U-Boat off Cape de Creus, Gulf of Lyon 2 lost.

August 9.

H.M.S. *Recruit II.* mined in North Sea

Further French gain near Bixschoote.

Mackensen across Susitza R. on wic front ; Rumanian railways and rear of arn in mountains threatened.

British s.s. *Canara* (6,012 tons) torpedo by U-Boat in Mediterranean ; towed in ; lost.

August 10.

British Labour Party Conference decid to send delegates to a "consultative conference at Stockholm.

H.M. special service ship *Dunraven*, to pedoed by U-Boat on August 8, sank in to at entrance to Channel.

British s.s. *War Patrol* (2,045 tons) sur by mine off Penmarch ; 13 lost.

British advanced E. of Ypres on 2-mi front ; remainder of Westhoek and tl Ridge captured ; Glencorse Wood enterec 240 prisoners. French crossed Steenbeek.

Further Russo-Rumanian retirement Trotus Valley.

British s.s. *City of Athens* (5,604 ton sunk 20 miles N.W. from Cape Town by mir laid by German raider *Wolf* ; 19 lost.

August 11.

Mr. Henderson resigned from Cabine owing to Government view of his attitu at Labour Party Conference ; Mr. Barnes succeed him in War Cabinet.

British gain near Ypres—Staden railwa British back in Glencorse Wood.

Russo-Rumanians retired in Trot Valley ; counter-attack at Focsani ; 1,2 prisoners ; but Allies evacuated Maracesti Furceni ; Germans claimed 6,500 prisoners.

Rumanian Royal Family leaving Jassy

British s.s. *Lynorta* (3,684 tons) sunk l U-Boat N.W. Tory Is. ; 2 lost.

British s.s. *Sonnie* (2,642 tons) sunk l U-Boat off Le Four Light ; 11 lost.

*August 12.

Twenty German aeroplanes (3rd A Squad.) raided Essex and Kent (Southend ar Margate) ; 32 killed, 46 injured. One Got destroyed during raiders' return to Belgi coast.

U44 rammed and sunk by H.M.S. *Orac* off Norwegian coast, S. of Bergen.

Russian T.B.D. *Burakoff* mined in Balti Russian resistance on Zbrucz R.

Rumanian offensive in Trotus highland further retirement in the Focsani sector.

British s.s. *Roanoke* (4,803 tons) sunk l U-Boat off Butt of Lewis.

For List of Abbreviations see page iv.

August 13, 1917.

H.M. sloop *Bergamot* sunk by U-Boat in Atlantic.

British s.s. *Camito* (6,611 tons) mined off N.W. Ireland; reached port.

British s.s. *Akassa* (3,919 tons) sunk by U-Boat off Galley Head; 7 lost.

British s.s. *Turakina* (9,920 tons) sunk by U-Boat W.S.W. from Bishop Rock; 2 lost.

British s.s. *Maston* (3,881 tons) sunk by U-Boat off Cape Spartivento; 2 lost.

British Government refused passports for Stockholm Conference.

Rumanian progress in Trotus Valley.

August 14.

British progress on Steenbeek.

Peace proposals by Pope published.

China declared war on Germany—Austria.

August 15.

Sir D. Haig attacked from N.W. outskirts of Lens—Bois Hugo, N.E. of Loos; Hill 70 and Cité Ste. Elizabeth—Cité St. Emile—Cité St. Laurent taken; 896 prisoners.

Ex-Tsar sent to Tobolsk.

Mackensen progressed on Sereth R.

H.M. armed fishing craft *Nelson* and *Ethel and Millie* sunk by U-Boat off E. Coast of England, after gallant action in which former's skipper, Thomas Crisp, D.S.C., R.N.R., was mortally wounded.

British s.s. *Hylas* (4,240 tons) sunk by U-Boat E. from Butt of Lewis.

British s.s. *Brodstone* (4,927 tons) sunk by U-Boat off Ushant; 5 lost.

August 16.

Ypres Battle : Second Assault.

British attack S.E. and E. of Ypres, from Glencorse Wood—Langemarck; latter taken; 1,800 prisoners. French across Steenbeek. German " pill-boxes " were first encountered in this phase of the Flanders battle; and hereabouts also Germans first applied their system of holding lightly the forward trench lines.

German counter at Lens beaten back.

British s.s. *Palatine* (2,110 tons) sunk by U-Boat off Canna Island.

British s.s. *Athenia* (8,668 tons) sunk by U-Boat N. from Inishtrahull; 15 lost.

White Star s.s. *Delphic* (8,273 tons) sunk by U-Boat S.W. from Bishop Rock; 5 lost.

British s.s. *Manchester Engineer* (4,465 tons) sunk by U-Boat off Flamborough Head.

T.B.D. action in German Bight; German T.B.D. and two minesweepers badly damaged.

H.M. special service ship *Bradford City* sunk by U-Boat in Messina Straits.

Rumanians repulsed Germans near Ocna, in Susitza Valley and near Focsani.

China at war with Germany.

August 17.

British s.s. *Edina* sunk by U-Boat off Store Dimon, Faroë.

French gains E. of Bixschoote.

Heavy fighting in Trotus Pass.

August 18.

Kaiser, following upon a mutiny in H.I.M.SS. *Prinz Regent Luitpold* and *Friedrich der Grosse*, arrived at Wilhelmshaven and visited Heligoland in Adm. Scheer's new F.F. *Baden*. This was Kaiser's first sea-trip during the war.

German 3rd Air Squad. tried to reach E. coast.

British s.s. *Rosario* (1,821 tons) sunk by U-Boat in Atlantic; 20 lost.

August 18 (continued).

UB32 bombed and sunk by H.M. seaplane 9680 off Cape Barfleur.

British s.s. *Politania* (3,133 tons) sunk by U-Boat off Cape Sigli.

Attacks on Canadian positions N.W. of Lens defeated.

Action at Narunju (G. E. Africa).

*August 19.

11th Italian attack on Isonzo front; Austrian first line from Plava to the sea carried; N. of Plava Isonzo crossed.

Germans on outskirts of Ocna (Trotus Valley); Rumanians still resisting; Mackensen in Focsani region.

British s.s. *Gartness* (2,422 tons) sunk by U-Boat off Malta; 13 lost.

August 20.

Slight British advance N. of Bixschoote

French attack at Verdun on 11-mile front by Gen. Guillaumat's Second Army. German defences carried to depth of 2,000 yards; Avocourt Wood, two summits of Mort Homme, Corbeaux Wood, Cumières Wood, Talou Hill, Champneuville, Hills 344 and 240, and Mormont Farm won; 4,000 prisoners.

Italian advance; furious fighting in Carso and before Mte. Hermada; Austrian line between Korite—Selo penetrated; progress on Bainsizza Plateau; over 10,000 prisoners to date.

German offensive on Riga front; owing to indiscipline Russians retired.

British s.s. *Bulysses* (6,127 tons) sunk by U-Boat N.W. from Butt of Lewis.

British s.s. *Claverley* (3,829 tons) sunk by U-Boat off Eddystone; 10 lost.

British s.s. *Elswick Lodge* (3,558 tons) sunk by U-Boat off Ushant; 4 lost.

British s.s. *Edernian* (3,588 tons) sunk by U-Boat off Southwold; 14 lost.

H.M. submarine E47 lost in North Sea.

August 21.

One or two Zeppelins on Yorkshire coast driven off; no damage.

British naval forces brought down Zeppelin off Jutland.

H.M. monitor *Erebus* bombarded Ostend Dockyard.

Canadians carried positions W. and N.W. of Lens on 2,000-yard front.

French progress at Verdun; Oie Hill, Regnéville, Samogneux, and fortifications around Hill 344 taken; over 5,000 prisoners to date.

Italian progress; over 13,000 prisoners.

British s.s. *Devonian* (10,435 tons) and *Roscommon* (8,238 tons) sunk by U-Boat N.W. from Tory Island.

Cunard s.s. *Volodia* (5,689 tons) sunk by U-Boat off Ushant; 10 lost.

UC41 depth-charged by H.M. trawlers *Jacinth* and *Chikara* off Firth of Tay.

British s.s. *Goodwood* (3,086 tons) sunk by U-Boat off Cape Bon.

August 22.

Ten aeroplanes of German 3rd Air Squad. raided Margate, Ramsgate and Dover; 12 killed, 25 injured; three raiders brought down and five of German supporting squadron lost.

Dover C.M.B.s sent to Zeebrugge to fire torpedoes on inner side of Mole, where German T.B.D.s moored.

Total German prisoners now in British hands, 102,218; Germans holding about 43,000. British (including Indian) prisoners.

Sundays marked with Asterisk (*).

August 22, 1917 (*continued*).

British line advanced 500 yards on mile front near Ypres—Menin road ; farther N. advance of 800 yard on 4,000-yard front.

Lens invested S., W., and N.

Italian progress on Bainsizza Plateau and farther S. ; over 16,000 prisoners to date.

German activity on Dvina, 10 miles S. of Riga ; Russian line withdrawn.

French auxiliary *Golo II.* torpedoed near Corfu.

British s.s. *Verdi* (7,120 tons) sunk by U-Boat N.W. from Eagle Island ; 6 lost.

August 23.

British s.s. *Boniface* (3,799 tons) sunk by U-Boat off Aran Is. ; 1 lost.

German 1st Air Squad. raided Dunkirk.

Canadians in Green Crassier, S. of Lens.

Italians carried fresh positions ; over 20,000 prisoners.

Sukhomlinoff trial began in Petrograd.

August 24.

British forced back at Ypres—Menin road ; fierce fighting in Inverness Copse—Glencorse Woods.

French success at Verdun ; Hill 304 and Camard Wood taken ; S. bank of Forges Brook reached.

Italians captured Mte. Santo.

British s.s. *Heatherside* (2,767 tons) sunk by U-Boat in Atlantic ; 27 lost.

British s.s. *Springhill* (1,507 tons) mined off Scarborough ; 5 lost.

British s.s. *Penelope* sunk by U-Boat in Baltic.

British s.s. *Kilwinning* (3,071 tons) sunk by U-Boat off Malta.

August 25.

British s.s. *Sycamore* (6,550 tons) sunk by U-Boat off Tory Is. ; 11 lost.

B.I. s.s. *Malda* (7,896 tons) and British s.s. *Nascent* (4,969 tons) sunk by U-Boat off Bishop Rock ; 70 lost.

Second stage of Flanders battle ended.

All-Russia Conference at Moscow.

*August 26.

British success E. of Hargicourt ; German line driven in half a mile on mile front.

French attack on left bank of Meuse, N. of Verdun, between Mormont Farm—Chaume Wood ; Fosse and Beaumont Woods taken ; over 1,000 prisoners.

Italian line through Siroka Njivo—Jelenik—Kobelik, to Mte. Santo ; 23,000 prisoners to date.

German progress E. of Czernowitz.

British s.s. *Durango* (3,008 tons) sunk by U-Boat off Barra Head.

British s.s. *Kenmore* (3,919 tons) sunk by U-Boat off Inishtrahull ; 5 lost.

British s.s. *Assyria* (6,370 tons) sunk by U-Boat off Tory Is.

British s.s. *Marmion* (4,066 tons) sunk by U-Boat off Ushant ; 17 lost.

British s.s. *Titian* (4,170 tons) sunk by U-Boat off Malta.

British s.s. *Hathor* (3,823 tons) sunk by U-Boat off Cape Tedles, Algeria.

British s.s. *Bhamo* (5,244 tons) damaged by mine laid by German raider *Wolf* off Cape Agulhas, Cape Colony ; reached port.

August 27.

British progress E. and S.E. of Lange-marck.

August 27 (*continued*).

Turkish Report on Armenian "Conspiracies" published.

British s.s. *Nairn* (3,627 tons) sunk by U-Boat off Ben Ghazi.

August 28.

Canadian Conscription Act signed.

British s.s. *Hidalgo* (4,271 tons) and *Whitecourt* (3,680 tons) sunk by U-Boat N.N.E. from North Cape ; 15 lost.

Furious fighting on Bainsizza Plateau against powerful Austrian line ; 1,000 more prisoners taken on heights E. of Gorizia.

Moscow Conference ended ; Gen. Kornilov on dangers of military position.

Russian division in Focsani region broke.

August 29.

President Wilson's reply to Pope's Peace Note.

British s.v. *Cooroy* (2,470 tons) sunk by U-Boat off Waterford coast.

British s.s. *Lynburn* mined off Arklow Light ; 8 lost.

British s.s. *Treloske* (3,071 tons) sunk by U-Boat off Cape Finisterre ; 1 lost.

British s.s. *Vronwen* (5,714 tons) sunk by U-Boat off Gozo ; 1 lost.

British s.s. *Cliftower* (3,509 tons) torpedoed by U-Boat in Mediterranean ; towed in.

August 30.

British s.s. *Noya* (4,282 tons) sunk by U-Boat S.W. from Lizard ; 1 lost.

British s.s. *Eastern Prince* (2,885 tons) sunk by U-Boat.

British advance E. of St. Janshoek.

German Airship Commodore, Capt. Strasser, invested with Pour le Mérite Order by Adm. Scheer at Ahlhorn, S. of Oldenburg.

Mgr. Pacelli, Papal Nuncio at Munich, transmitted to German Chancellor in Berlin a copy of an Anglo-French communication addressed to the Vatican with a view to eliciting German intentions regarding Belgium (see 24-ix.-17).

Italian progress on N. slopes of Mte. St. Gabriele and N. of Hermada.

Germans active in Riga Gulf.

Serb progress in Dobropolie—Moglen sector (Macedonia).

British advance on 800-yard front in Palestine.

August 31.

London Aircraft Defence Area formed during August.

French progress on mile front N.W. of Hurtebise.

German "Fatherland Party" founded during August.

Russo-Rumanians repelled German attacks in Focsani region.

During August the Otranto Mine Barrage was begun.

Allies driving Germans in E. Africa towards Mahenge.

British s.s. *Westbury* (3,097 tons) sunk by U-Boat off Fastnet.

British s.s. *Miniota* (6,422 tons) sunk by U-Boat off Start Point ; 3 lost.

September 1.

British light forces sank four German minesweepers off Jutland.

British loss and recovery near Havrincourt.

Italian pressure on Mte. St. Gabriele.

September 1, 1917 (*continued*).

German Eighth Army (Gen. von Hutier), including 1st and 2nd Prussian Guard Divisions from Galicia, forced Dvina at Uexküll, 18 miles above Riga.

*September 2.

U28 lost off North Cape.

British s.s. *Olive Branch* (4,649 tons) sunk by U-Boat off North Cape ; 1 lost.

British s.s. *Rytonhall* (4,203 tons) sunk by U-Boat off Ushant.

British s.s. *Wentworth* (3,828 tons) sunk by U-Boat off Belle Ile ; 1 lost.

German aeroplanes over E. Kent ; Dover bombed ; one killed, 6 injured.

Italian progress in Brestovica Valley.

Riga evacuated by Russians.

German surrender at Kakera (E. Africa).

September 3.

German 3rd Air Squad. raided Kent ; 132 killed, 96 injured, of whom 131 killed and 90 injured were in uniform, mainly naval ratings at Sheerness—Chatham.

German 1st Air Squad. raided Calais—Dunkirk.

British s.s. *Orangemoor* (4,134 tons) bombed and damaged by German aircraft in Dunkirk Harbour.

Fall of Riga ; German warships in Riga Gulf shelled villages S. of Pernau.

British s.s. *Treverbyn* (4,163 tons) sunk by mine off S. Uist ; 27 lost.

British s.s. *Ragnhild* (1,495 tons) sunk by U-Boat off Flamborough Head ; 15 lost.

British s.s. *La Negra* (8,312 tons) sunk by U-Boat off Start Point ; 4 lost.

September 4.

Blackpool Trade Union Congress against Stockholm Conference.

U-Boats shelled Scarborough ; 3 killed, 5 injured.

About 20 German aeroplanes of 3rd Air Squad. raided London (16th raid) and Home Counties at night ; 19 killed, 71 injured ; one machine brought down off Sheerness.

Heavy fighting N.E. of Gorizia ; Italian gain round Mte. St. Gabriele ; 1,600 prisoners.

Germans across Livonian Aa. N.E. of Riga.

September 5.

British s.s. *Echunga* (6,285 tons) sunk by U-Boat off Ushant ; 9 lost.

British s.s. *San Dunstano* (6,220 tons) torpedoed by U-Boat in Channel ; reached port.

More fighting N.E. of Gorizia and in S. Carso ; 700 more prisoners by Italians.

Russian retreat N. and E. of Riga ; Dvina line lost up to Friedrichstadt ; Germans claimed 7,500 prisoners.

September 6.

Sir E. Geddes First Lord of Admiralty vice Sir E. Carson.

Adm. Wemyss Deputy First Sea Lord.

British progress N. of Frezenberg (Ypres) and N.W. of Lens.

H.M. collier *Clan Ferguson* (4,808 tons) sunk by U-Boat 15 miles off Cape Spartel.

September 7.

British lost ground N. of Frezenberg.

Italian pressure N.E. of Gorizia ; over 30,000 prisoners to date.

Russian retreat on Riga-Pskoff road.

Count Bernstorff to be German Ambassador to the Porte vice Herr von Kühlmann.

British s.s. *Hunsbridge* (3,424 tons) sunk by U-Boat off Cape Spartel ; 3 lost.

British s.s. *Brodmead* (5,646 tons) torpedoed by U-Boat W. from Gibraltar ; reached port ; 12 lost.

British s.s. *Myrmidon* (4,965 tons) torpedoed by U-Boat in Mediterranean ; beached ; 2 lost.

British s.s. *Minnehaha* (13,714 tons) sunk by U-Boat S.E. from Fastnet ; 43 lost.

September 8.

U.S. Government disclosed that German diplomatic agent at Buenos Aires had transmitted to Berlin through Swedish colleague sailings of Argentine ships, and recommended they be either spared or " sunk without trace."

British s.s. *Newholm* (3,399 tons) mined off Start Point ; 20 lost.

British monitor carried out night bombardment of Middelkerke, with aeroplane spotting between moon and target.

French assault N. of Verdun, E. of Meuse, between Caurières—Chaumes Woods ; latter captured ; 800 prisoners.

M. Kerensky dismissed Gen. Korniloff, who marched on Petrograd.

*September 9.

British s.s. *Tuscarora* (7,106 tons) torpedoed by U-Boat in Atlantic ; reached port ; 3 lost.

UC93 interned at Cadiz.

M. Ribot failed to form Cabinet ; M. Painlevé called.

British captured 600 yards of trench S.E. of Hargicourt.

Gen. von Quast, Prussian Guard Corps, in command of Sixth Army, vice Gen. O. von Below, to command new German Fourteenth Army against Italy.

Austrian counter-attacks at Mte. St. Gabriele repulsed.

September 10.

Distilling stopped in U.S.

UC42 blown up by her own mines outside Cork Harbour.

British s.s. *Ionna* (3,459 tons) torpedoed by U-Boat in Bristol Channel ; reached port.

Five small British sailing-craft captured and sunk by U-Boat off Cornish Coast ; 4 lost.

M. Kerensky virtual dictator ; Gen. Korniloff's advance-guard at Gatchina.

Austrian attack in S. Carso defeated.

Allied pressure in Ochrida region (Macedonia) ; 150 prisoners.

September 11.

Swedish Government statement on German use of Swedish diplomatic channels between Berlin and Buenos Aires.

British s.s. *Vienna* (4,170 tons) sunk by U-Boat off Ushant ; 25 lost.

British s.s. *Emdleton* (5,377 tons) sunk by U-Boat off Cape Spartel.

British s.s. *Urd* (3,049 tons) sunk by U-Boat off Cape Palos, Spain ; 3 lost.

Crown Council in Berlin.

September 11, 1917 (*continued*).

M. Kerensky Russian Generalissimo.

Russian stand S. of Riga—Wenden road.

Success on Rumanian front S. of Radautz.

September 12.

Argentine Government handed passports to Count Luxburg, German Minister at Buenos Aires.

U45 torpedoed and sunk by H.M. submarine D7 off N. Ireland.

British naval airmen bombed Zeebrugge.

M. Painlevé Premier and War Minister.

Polish "Council of Regency" appointed by Austro-German patent.

Allied progress round Lake Ochrida.

British s.s. *Gibraltar* (3,803 tons) sunk by U-Boat S.E. from Cap de Creus, Gulf of Lyons : 4 lost.

September 13.

Mr. Lansing published letter in which German Minister to Mexico suggested to Herr Zimmermann a German decoration for the Swedish Chargé d'Affaires in Mexico, who had been acting as German agent.

German attacks on Langemarck positions.

Gen. Korniloff failed ; Gen. Alexeieff negotiated with him ; Gen. Krimoff, Korniloff's commander against Petrograd, committed suicide.

Russians holding at Segewold (Livonia).

Germans withdrew from Husiatyn.

British s.s. *Bengali* (5,684 tons) torpedoed by U-Boat in Mediterranean ; reached port ; 1 lost.

September 14.

Gen. Korniloff surrendered to Gen. Alexeieff.

British progress E. of Westhoek.

British s.s. *Chulmleigh* (4,911 tons) sunk by U-Boat off Cape Salon, Spain.

September 15.

British s.s. *Santaren* (4,256 tons) and *Rollesby* (3,955 tons) sunk by U-Boat off Muckle Flugga.

British s.s. *Idomeneus* (6,692 tons) torpedoed by U-Boat off W. Scotland ; beached ; 4 lost.

British naval aircraft attacked German shipping between Ostend—Blankenberghe ; German T.B.D. hit and trawler sunk.

British took strong point N. of Inverness Copse ; great air activity on W. front.

Italian gains S.E. of Bainsizza Plateau.

German Fourteenth Army (including German Alpine Corps, German Chasseur Division, 5th Brandenburg Division, and Austrian "Edelweiss" Division) concentrating on Isonzo front.

Russia a republic ; Government entrusted to Council of Five under M. Kerensky.

✳**September 16.**

H.M. submarine G9 accidentally sunk in North Sea.

British s.s. *Arabis* (3,928 tons) sunk by U-Boat off Ushant ; 20 lost.

Heavy air fighting on W. Front. Stuttgart, Colmar, &c., bombed by Allies.

German Crown Prince attacked in Apremont Forest ; no headway.

September 17.

H.M.S. *Stonecrop*, Q ship, engaged and probably sank U-Boat off S.W. Ireland.

September 17 (*continued*).

British s.s. *Queen Amelie* (4,278 tons sunk by U-Boat off Muckle Flugga.

Gen. von Falkenhayn completed his concentration in Palestine.

September 18.

Artillery activity in Ypres sector.

Italians took 200 prisoners in Val Sugana

British s.s. *Joseph Chamberlain* (3,709 tons) sunk by U-Boat off Muckle Flugga ; 18 lost.

H.M. special service ship *Glenfoyle* sunk by U-Boat in Atlantic.

H.M.S. *Contest* sunk by U-Boat in Channel.

British s.s. *Polar Prince* (3,611 tons) and *Arendal* (1,387 tons) sunk by U-Boat off Cape Spartel.

British s.s. *Port Kembla* (4,700 tons) sunk off Cape Farewell, New Zealand, by mine laid by German raider *Wolf*.

September 19.

Great artillery activity on both sides of Ypres sector.

On Aisne Germans gained and lost footing in salient near Froidemont Farm.

German reply to Papal Note ; no reference to Belgium.

German attacks E. of Riga checked by Lettish battalions.

British s.s. *Saint Ronald* (4,387 tons) sunk by U-Boat N.N.W. from Tory Is. ; 24 lost.

British s.s. *Etal Manor* (1,875 tons) sunk by U-Boat off Waterford coast ; 6 lost.

September 20.

Third stage of Flanders Battle.

Great British attack E. of Ypres, along Ypres—Menin road ; Inverness Copse, Glencorse Wood, Veldhoek, and part of Polygon Wood taken ; 2,000 prisoners.

German attack S.E. of Cerny (Aisne).

Gen. Alexeieff resigned as Chief of Staff to Kerensky.

British s.s. *Fabian* (2,246 tons) sunk by U-Boat off Cape Spartel ; 3 lost.

British s.s. *Kurdistan* (3,720 tons) sunk by U-Boat off Pantellaria.

September 21.

At Ypres : counter-attacks on new British positions repulsed ; British advance between Langemarck—Hollebeke ; positions won S. of Tower Hamlets ; over 3,000 prisoners.

Russians retired from the Jacobstadt bridgehead, 70 miles up Dvina from Riga ; over 1,000 prisoners claimed by Germans.

Kieff congress of Russian border peoples votes for federation.

Germans in E. Africa driven from direction of Kilwa to Mbemkuru R. ; the group towards Lindi pressed by British and Belgian forces.

H.M. submarine C17 lay off Zeebrugge to register tidal curves on Belgian coast.

September 22.

British s.s. *Greleen* (2,286 tons) sunk by U-Boat off Berry Head ; 19 lost.

British monitors shelled Ostend. H.M.S. *Terror* scored three hits on dockyard and damaged floating dock. After this bombardment Germans gave up Ostend as sea base.

Three German seaplanes destroyed by British naval aeroplane patrol.

For List of Abbreviations see page iv.

September 22, 1917 (*continued*).

H.M. seaplane *America*, operating from Dunkirk, bombed and destroyed UC72 N.E. of E. Hinder Bank.

✻September 23.

British s.s. *Hornsund* (3,046 tons) sunk by U-Boat off Scarborough ; 1 lost.

U.S. Tank Corps established.

LZ103 raided French Channel ports.

Germans repulsed S. of Pskoff road.

September 24.

Zeppelin raid on Lincs and Yorks ; 3 injured.

German 3rd Air Squad. raided London, Kent and Essex ; 21 killed, 70 injured. Dunkirk also raided. One raider brought down at Ghistelles.

Germans repulsed N. of Bois de Chaume (Verdun).

Chancellor Michaelis replied to Mgr. Pacelli's letter of 30-viii.-17, but evaded precisions regarding Belgium.

British s.s. *Boynton* (2,578 tons) sunk by U-Boat off Cape Cornwall ; 23 lost.

September 25.

German 3rd Air Squad. raided London (19th raid) and Kent ; 9 killed, 23 injured.

German 1st Air Squad. raided Boulogne—Calais—Dunkirk. This was the first of a series of determinded raids on the British Depôt Aerodrome, which was ultimately wrecked.

British s.s. *Polescar* (5,832 tons) bombed and damaged by German aircraft in Dunkirk Harbour ; 2 lost.

LZ103 raided French Channel ports.

Adm. Jellicoe visited Dover Patrol, and, with Adm. Mayo (C.-in-C. U.S. Atlantic Fleet) and Adm. Bacon, witnessed bombardment of Ostend by H.M. monitor *Terror*. The three admirals proceeded from Dunkirk in H.M.S. *Broke*, in which Adm. Mayo's flag was hoisted. This was first occasion in which a U.S. admiral was under fire in a British warship.

At Ypres : Germans penetrate British lines between Tower Hamlets—Polygon Wood ; ejected.

German attacks repulsed between Fosses --Chaume Wood (Verdun).

German Kilwa (E. Africa) column broken up ; fresh Allied attacks on Lindi column.

September 26.

At Ypres : New British advance on 6-mile front from Tower Hamlets Ridge to E. of St. Julien ; Tower Hamlets spur, rest of Polygon Wood, and Zonnebeke taken ; advance towards Passchendaele ; over 1,000 prisoners to date.

British s.s. *San Zeferino* (6,430 tons) torpedoed by U-Boat in St. George's Channel ; reached port ; 3 lost.

British s.s. *Port Victor* (7,280 tons) torpedoed by U-Boat in English Channel ; reached port.

Russian T.B.D. *Okhotnik* mined in Baltic.

September 27.

British s.s. *Greltoria* (5,143 tons) sunk by U-Boat off Flamborough Head.

UC21 mined N.E. of N. Foreland.

H.M. CMB8 sunk off Belgian coast to avoid capture.

Allied naval aircraft bombed St. Denis Westrem aerodrome (Ghent).

September 27 (*continued*).

At Ypres : powerful German counter-attacks on new British positions repulsed ; total 1,600 prisoners.

German attacks repulsed in Aisne and Argonne.

British s.s. *Swan River* (4,724 tons) sunk by U-Boat off Oran.

September 28.

UC6 bombed and destroyed by H.M. seaplane 8676 E. of Sunk Light.

About 20 German aeroplanes of 3rd Air Squad. raid Home Counties ; driven off from London ; one reported down in Thames Estuary, and second off coast. No casualties.

As result of successive German raids on Dunkirk, British Aircraft Depot at St. Pol was practically demolished and had to be decentralised.

Gen. Maude defeats Turks at Ramadie (Euphrates) ; 3,455 prisoners, including Turkish commander, Ahmed Bey ; 13 guns.

September 29.

Raid on London by three groups of aeroplanes of German 3rd Air Squad. : broken up by anti-aircraft fire ; only two or three machines penetrated ; 14 killed, 87 injured.

British s.s. *Kildonan* (2,118 tons) sunk by U-Boat off Pendeen Light ; 14 lost.

H.M.SS. *Tirade* and *Sylvia*, on convoy-duty off Lerwick, destroyed UC55 ; crew 29, of whom 19 rescued.

✻September 30.

German 3rd Air Squad. raided London, Kent and Essex ; about 10 aeroplanes penetrated outer defences ; four or five raiders reached London ; 14 killed, 38 injured.

During September R.N.A.S. from Dunkirk dropped 86 tons of bombs on Ostend, Zeebrugge, &c. ; 18 German aircraft were destroyed and 43 driven down.

Three German attacks in Ypres sector defeated.

Austrians repulsed on Bainsizza Plateau : Italians took over 3,000 prisoners in three days.

British s.s. *Drake* (2,267 tons) and *Heron* sunk by U-Boat off Ushant ; 22 lost.

British s.s. *Midlothian* (1,321 tons) sunk by U-Boat S. from Cape Greco, Cyprus.

October 1.

U36 and U106 destroyed in North Sea by British T.B.D.s and other light craft.

German 3rd Air Squad. raided London with four groups of machines ; a few penetrated defences and bombed S.W. district. Kent and Essex visited ; 11 killed, 41 injured.

LZ103 raided French Channel ports.

Powerful German attacks from Ypres-Menin road to Polygon Wood ; two British posts captured at S.E. end of wood.

Russian advance S. of Riga—Pskoff railway.

British s.s. *Normanton* (3,862 tons) and *Mersario* (3,847 tons) sunk by U-Boat W. by N. from Cape Spartel ; 3 lost.

German force of 200 surrendered N. of Central Railway, E. Africa ; severe fighting at Lindi.

Sundays marked with Asterisk (*).*

October 2, 1917.

H.M.S. *Drake* (14,000 tons) sunk by U-Boat in North Channel.

British s.s. *Lugano* (3,810 tons) sunk by mine off Rathlin Is.

German gain N. of Hill 344 (Verdun).

Marshal Hindenburg's 70th birthday.

Austrian attack on W. slopes of San Gabriele repulsed.

Count Czernin at Budapest on the need for a new world.

British s.s. *Nuceria* (4,702 tons) and *Almora* (4,385 tons) sunk by U-Boat off Cape Spartel; 2 lost.

October 3.

British s.s. *Hurst* (4,718 tons) sunk by U-Boat off Skokham Island.

British s.s. *Memling* (7,307 tons) sunk by U-Boat in Laberildut Channel, near Brest.

Germans repulsed between Tower Hamlets—Polygon Wood.

October 4.

At Ypres: Great British victory in front of Passchendaele Ridge on 8-mile front from railway N. of Langemarck and Tower Hamlets Ridge on Ypres—Menin road. Part of Poelcappelle, Broodseinde, and Becelaere heights taken; over 3,000 prisoners; Germans regained ground in Reutelbeek valley, S.E. of Polygon Wood.

October 5.

Chilwell munitions works blown up.

UB41 blown up off Scarborough.

British s.s. *Toledo* (1,159 tons) destroyed in Baltic to avoid capture.

Nearly 4,500 German prisoners in Passchendaele fighting.

German attack N. of Hill 344 (Verdun).

Austrian T.B. No. 11 surrendered to Italians near Ancona.

British s.s. *Forestmoor* (2,844 tons) sunk by U-Boat off Cape Spartel; 22 lost.

British s.s. *Bontnewydd* (3,296 tons) sunk by U-Boat N.N.E. from Marsa Susa; 3 lost.

October 6.

Uruguay and Peru broke with Germany.

At Ypres: British raid S.E. of Broodseinde; nearly 5,000 prisoners to date.

Russian success S. of Czernowitz.

British s.s. *Civilian* (7,871 tons) sunk by U-Boat N. from Alexandria; 2 lost.

British s.s. *Bedale* (2,116 tons) sunk by U-Boat off Mine Head; 3 lost.

British s.s. *Le Coq* (3,419 tons) mined in Bay of Biscay; towed in.

✻October 7.

UC93, interned at Cadiz, " escaped."

British s.s. *Aylevarroo* sunk by U-Boat off S. Ireland; 20 lost.

At Ypres: German attack S. of Reutel and E. of Polygon Wood failed.

M. Kerensky's Coalition Government.

October 8.

British s.s. *Memphian* (6,305 tons) and *Greldon* (3,322 tons) sunk by U-Boat E.N.E. from N. Arklow Light; 60 lost.

British s.s. *Richard de Larrinaga* (5,591 tons) sunk by U-Boat off Ballycottin Is.; 35 lost.

October 9.

At Ypres: Franco-British attack between Passchendaele Ridge—Houthulst Forest; St.

October 9 (*continued*).

Jean, Mangelaere, Veldhoek, and Koeku taken with rest of Poelcappelle; over 1,00 prisoners.

H.M. A.M.C. *Champagne* (5,360 tons) sun by U-Boat in Atlantic.

British s.s. *Peshawur* (7,634 tons) sun by U-Boat off Ballyquintin Point, Co. Down 11 lost.

British s.s. *Main* sunk by U-Boat : Luce Bay; 12 lost.

British s.s. *Poldown* (1,370 tons) sunk U-Boat off Trevoce Head; 18 lost.

Adm. von Capelle announced in Reichst mutiny in German Navy; attacked Indepe dent Socialists (see 18-viii.-17).

October 10.

At Ypres: German counter-attacks con pelled British retirement between Poelca pelle—Wallemolen; French extended Corverbeek valley; over 2,000 prisoners date.

H.M escort ship *Bostonian* (5,736 ton sunk by U-Boat 34 miles S.E. Start Point.

British s.s. *Gowrie* (1,031 tons) sunk U-Boat off Cherbourg.

October 11.

British Government stopped commerci cable communication with Holland un Dutch Government stopped German miner traffic through Holland into Belgium.

At Ypres: Attacks on French positions Germans repulsed in Champagne.

H.I.M.S. *Moltke* (F. Adm. Schmidt) ar 3rd and 4th High Sea Squadrons assemble in Danzig Bay, in support of German exped tion to Baltic Is. now mustered at Libau 19 transports, protected by Adm. Reuter light cruisers and T.B.D. flotillas.

British s.s. *Rhodesia* (4,313 tons) sunk U-Boat off Coningbeg Light; 4 lost.

British s.s. *Baychattan* (3,758 tons) sun by U-Boat off Prawle Point.

British s.s. *Mira* (3,700 tons) sunk mine off Beachy Head.

British s.s. *Cayo Bonito* (3,427 tons) sun by U-Boat off Genoa; 6 lost.

October 12.

Sir R. Borden's Canadian Coalition.

At Ypres: British attack on 6-mi front along Passchendaele Ridge to Houthul Forest; some objectives gained; bad weath impeded; nearly 1,000 prisoners.

German attack at Hurtebise—Chevreu (Aisne) gained temporary footing in advance line.

Germans occupied most of Oesel Is. (Rig Gulf); naval forces in support. In suppor ing these operations H.I.M.SS. *Bayern* an *Grosser Kurfürst* were damaged by mines.

British s.s. *Cape Corso* (3,890 tons) to pedoed by U-Boat in Bristol Channel owed in; 13 lost.

October 13.

First draft under Canadian Conscriptio Law. Total 439,806 voluntary enlistments.

Germans took Arensburg (Oesel Is).

British s.s. *Alavi* (3,627 tons) sunk U-Boat off Cape Palos; 13 lost.

✻October 14.

Naval action between Oesel—Dagö Is Russian T.B.D. *Grom* captured and or Russian gunboat sunk.

British s.s. *Semantha* (2,847 tons) sun by U-Boat off Cape St. John, Crete; 32 lost

October 15, 1917.

British 1st Division (Gen. Strickland) withdrawn from Le Clipon, between Calais—Dunkirk, where it had been awaiting for several months an opportunity of carrying out Adm. Bacon's scheme for landing on Belgian coast.

British s.s. *San Nazario* (10,064 tons) torpedoed by U-Boat off Scilly Is. ; reached port.

German progress in Oesel Is. ; Russian garrison partly escape ; 3,500 prisoners claimed ; German warships land detachments in Runö—Abrö Is.

British s.s. *White Head* (1,172 tons) sunk by U-Boat off Suda Bay ; 23 lost.

Gens. von Lettow-Vorbeck and Wahle in four days' engagement at Mahiwa (G. E. Africa).

October 16.

U.S. T.B.D. torpedoed ; reached port ; one killed, 5 wounded.

Adm. Moore to be controller of Mechanical Warfare (Tanks) Department vice Col. Stern.

Whole Oesel Is. now in German hands ; Germans claimed 10,000 prisoners ; civil evacuation of Reval.

October 17.

H.M. T.B.D.s *Mary Rose* and *Strongbow*, convoying 12 Scandinavian merchantmen, attacked by two fast German light cruisers, *Brummer* and *Bremse*, between Shetland—Norway and sunk with nine of convoy.

Baltic Battle : Germans pressed Russian naval forces back to Moon Sound ; Russian battleship *Slava* lost ; two German trawlers destroyed by fire, and two T.B.s blown up in Russian minefield.

U.S. transport *Antilles*, homeward bound, torpedoed by U-Boat in Atlantic.

British s.s. *Polvena* (4,750 tons) and *Manchuria* (2,997 tons) sunk by U-Boat off Ushant ; 29 lost.

British s.s. *California* (5,629 tons) sunk by U-Boat off Cape Villano ; 4 lost.

H.S. *Goorkha* (6,335 tons) mined in Mediterranean ; reached port.

October 18.

German attack failed on Vauclere Plateau. Germans captured Moon Is. ; 5,000 prisoners claimed.

October 19.

Raid by 11 airships on London, Midlands, and E. counties ; one drifted over London with engines shut off, dropped three bombs ; 36 killed, 55 injured. On return journey strong N.E. wind sprang up and many of the airships drifted over France ; three brought down (at Saint-Clément, Serqueux, and Sisteron) and two lost in the Mediterranean. Six returned.

U.S. announced conditional supplies to Holland and Scandinavia.

H.M. A.M.C. *Orama* (12,927 tons) sunk by U-Boat in Atlantic.

H.M. submarine E45 destroyed UC79 in North Sea.

Dunkirk bombarded by German T.B.D.s. H.M. monitor *Terror* torpedoed by German T.B.D.s and stranded N. of Dunkirk ; after temporary repairs at Dunkirk, brought to Dover floating on her lower messdeck ; later towed to Portsmouth stern first for repairs.

British s.s. *Waikawa* (5,666 tons) sunk by U-Boat off Start Point.

October 19 (continued).

British s.s. *Australdale* (4,379 tons) sunk by U-Boat off Cape Villano ; 27 lost.

British s.s. *War Clover* (5,174 tons) sunk by U-Boat off Pantellaria ; 14 lost.

British s.s. *Good Hope* (3,618 tons) and *Elsiston* (2,908 tons) sunk by U-Boat E. by S. of Malta ; 1 lost.

British s.s. *Pera* (7,635 tons) sunk by U-Boat off Marsa Susa ; 1 lost.

Germans captured Dagö Is. ; 1,200 prisoners claimed.

October 20.

Baltic Battle : Germans took Schilden Is. ; four Russian vessels ashore. British submarine sank German transport and torpedoed German Dreadnought.

British s.s. *Ionian* (8,268 tons) sunk by U-Boat off St. Govan's Head ; 7 lost.

British s.s. *Colorado* (7,165 tons) sunk by U-Boat off Start Point ; 4 lost.

British s.s. *Collegian* (7,520 tons) sunk by U-Boat off Alexandria.

*October 21.

H.M.S. *Marmion* sunk by collision in North Sea.

German troops on Russian mainland at Verder, opposite Moon Is.

British s.s. *Gryfevale* (4,437 tons) chased by U-Boat off Cape Blanco ; ran ashore.

Skirmish at Lukuledi (G.E. Africa).

October 22.

Anglo-French advance on either side of the Ypres—Staden railway, 1,000 yards deep, from N. of Mangelaere to E. of Poelcappelle ; 200 prisoners ; Germans recapture part of Houthulst Forest.

French assault on Laffaux salient (S.W. of Laon) ; one German division succumbed to French gas attack ; Chavignon gained ; Germans retired on Oise-Aisne Canal.

British s.s. *Zillah* (3,788 tons) sunk by U-Boat off Kildin Is., Murman Coast ; 18 lost.

Germans withdrew on wide front between Riga Gulf—Dvina R.

October 23.

Battle of La Malmaison.

Great French victory across the Soissons—Laon road, on ridge dividing Aisne—Ailette valleys, on 6-mile front from Vaux-aillon ; German positions penetrated over 2 miles deep ; Allemant, Vaudesson, Chavignon, and Malmaison Fort taken ; Germans driven down towards Ailette ; 7,500 prisoners and 25 guns from eight divisions.

Austro-German bombardment of Italian positions from Mte. Rombon to N. Bainsizza Plateau around Tolmino.

Order in Council whereby First Sea Lord as Chief of Naval Staff was made responsible to First Lord of Admiralty.

UC16 destroyed by H.M.S. *Melampus*, S.E. of Selsea Bill.

British s.s. *Seistan* (4,238 tons) and *Tredegar Hall* (3,764 tons) sunk by U-Boat off Flamborough Head ; 8 lost.

British s.s. *Lepanto* (6,389 tons) torpedoed by U-Boat in Channel ; reached port ; 2 lost.

October 24.

French on Aisne took total 8,000 prisoners ; no German counter.

Great Austro-German attack on Isonzo front ; Second Italian Army defeated on 20-mile front between Plezzo — Tolmino ;

October 24, 1917 (*continued*).
attack led by German A.C. in Caporetto sector ; 10,000 prisoners claimed.

British s.s. *Euston* (2,841 tons) sunk by U-Boat off Cape Matapan ; 1 lost.

British s.s. *Ilderton* (3,125 tons) sunk by U-Boat off Kildin Is., Murman Coast.

H.M. submarine C32 ashore and blown up in the Baltic.

October 25.
Further French advance on Aisne : Pargny—Filain and Pinon—Pinon Forest ; 800 prisoners ; German retreat across Oise-Aisne Canal ; over 11,000 prisoners and 120 guns captured to date.

Fall of Italian Boselli Cabinet.

Italians preparing to evacuate Bainsizza Plateau ; Mte. Matajur S.W. of Caporetto captured ; Germans claimed 30,000 prisoners.

British cavalry captured three villages S. of Seres, Struma Front.

British s.s. *Ness* (3,050 tons) and *Sheaf Blade* (2,378 tons) sunk by U-Boat off Cape de Gata ; 4 lost.

British s.s. *Wearside* (3,560 tons) mined off Sunk Light.

October 26.
Anglo-French attacks N., N.E., and E. of Ypres ; British advance on main ridge towards Passchendaele and between Passchendaele — Poelcappelle ; progress towards Gheluvelt ; French attacked between St. Jansbeck—Corverbeek R. ; took Dvaeibank.

Austro-German progress on Isonzo ; Italian left wing on Julian front penetrated ; invaders debouching into plains ; Bainsizza Plateau evacuated ; 60,000 prisoners, 500 guns claimed.

Interned German gunboat *Eber* set on fire and sunk by Germans at Bahia.

British s.s. *Sapele* (4,366 tons) sunk by U-Boat off Tory Is. ; 3 lost.

October 27.
Fall of Cividale to Austro-Germans entering Friuli Plain ; 80,000 prisoners claimed.

H.M. T.B.D.s *Botha* and *Mentor*, with French T.B.D.s *Capitaine Mehl* and *Magon* engaged and drove off three large German T.B.D.s on Belgian Patrol line.

First U.S. troops in Western line.

French advance 2,000 yards on 4,000-yard front on both sides Ypres—Dixmude road ; Aschhoop, Merckem, Kippe taken ; 200 prisoners.

Germans evacuated Werder Peninsula.

British bombardment of Gaza.

✳**October 28.**
H.M. monitor *Erebus* hit in the " blister," amidships, by German electrically controlled motor-boat, off Belgian coast. This was second such attack on the Patrol. On first occasion the boat was sunk by H.M. monitor M24 ; on third and last occasion the boat was sunk by H.M. T.B.D. *North Star*.

British s.s. *Baron Balfour* (3,991 tons) sunk by U-Boat N. from Sem Is., Murman Coast.

German assault at Verdun gained footing N. of Caurières Wood.

Gorizia fell ; Italians retiring on Tagliamento R. ; 100,000 prisoners, 700 guns claimed.

Signor Orlando, Italian Premier.

British s.s. *Ferrona* (4,591 tons) sunk by U-Boat off Valencia ; 1 lost.

October 29.
Aeroplane raid on Essex ; no casualties.

Brussels Municipal Council successfully resisted German attempts to impart a Flemish bias to the city administration.

Fall of Udine to Austro-Germans.

Progress in Ploecken region.

British s.s. *Namur* (6,701 tons) sunk by U-Boat off Gibraltar ; 1 lost.

October 30.
German 3rd Air Squad. raided Calais and Sheerness.

Canadians reached outskirts of Passchendaele ; progress in Poelcappelle district ; nearly 200 prisoners.

Italian retreat to Tagliamento continued ; rearguard actions.

Chancellor Michaelis resigned.

British and French warships joined in bombardment of Gaza.

October 31.
German 3rd Air Squad., 30 aeroplanes in seven groups, attacked London, Kent and Essex at night ; about three machines penetrated defences ; 10 killed and 22 injured.

Aeroplane over Dover ; no casualties.

UC13 lost and UC14 mined off Zeebrugge during October ; while UC62 was lost in North Sea ; cause unknown.

During October the 8th Brigade R.F.C. was formed to operate from the Nancy area against German chemical and iron industries (8-vi.-18).

By October 700 Mark IV. Tanks had been delivered in France.

Italians behind Tagliamento ; 60,000 more prisoners claimed.

Gen. Allenby took Beersheba ; 1,800 prisoners, 15 guns.

During October a " through " convoy from England to Port Said was started.

H.M. sloop *Begonia* probably sunk by U-Boat during October in Atlantic.

British s.s. *Cambric* (3,403 tons) sunk by U-Boat off Cape Shershel ; 24 lost.

British s.s. *Phare* (1,282 tons) sunk by U-Boat off Scarborough ; 14 lost.

November 1.
UC63 sunk by H.M. submarine E52 in Dover Straits.

German retreat at Chemin-des-Dames on 12-mile front ; French occupy Courtecon, Cerny, Ailles, and Chevreux ; patrols reach Ailette R.

Count Hertling German Chancellor vice Herr Michaelis.

Gen. Allenby carried W. and S.W. defences of Gaza on 5,000-yard front ; 444 prisoners ; progress N. of Beersheba.

British s.s. *Margam Abbey* (4,367 tons) torpedoed by U-Boat in Mediterranean ; beached ; 2 lost.

November 2.
H.M. CMB11 lost in Dover Straits ; on fire after collision.

British s.s. *Cape Finisterre* (4,380 tons) sunk by U-Boat off Manacles Buoy ; 35 lost.

British s.s. *Branksome Hall* (4,262 tons) torpedoed by U-Boat in Channel ; beached.

British naval raid in Kattegat, between Anholt Is.—Cape Kullen ; German auxiliary *Marie* and 10 patrol craft sunk.

German auxiliary *Kronprinz Wilhelm* destroyed by British 15th T.B.D. Flotilla in the Sound.

French occupied all Chemin-des-Dames ; reached Ailette R. on 12-mile front.

November 2, 1917 (continued).
Pressure on Italian Tagliamento line.
Battle of Gaza continued.
Turks encountered 85 miles up Tigris;
retreat on Tekrit.
American-Japanese Agreement regarding
China.

November 3.
UC65 torpedoed and sunk by H.M. submarine C15 in English Channel.
British s.s. *Atlantian* (9,399 tons) torpedoed by U-Boat in Irish Channel; reached
port.
Austro-German attack in Giudicaria zone
repulsed; arrival of French troops in Italy.

* November 4.
Mr. Lloyd George, M. Painlevé, Gens.
Smuts and Robertson proceeded to Italy.
Austro-Germans forced Tagliamento N. of
Pinzano; 6,000 prisoners claimed. Arrival
of British troops in Italy announced.
British s.s. *Antaeus* (3,061 tons) sunk by
U-Boat off Cape Bon.
British s.s. *Border Knight* (3,724 tons)
sunk by U-Boat off Lizard; 1 lost.

November 5.
British s.s. *Clan Cumming* (4,808 tons)
torpedoed by U-Boat in English Channel;
towed in; 13 lost.
British s.s. *Amberton* (4,556 tons) tor-
pedoed by U-Boat in Mediterranean; beached.
Italian retreat from Tagliamento on
Piave.
Gen. Maude defeated Turks on Tigris
before Tekrit, 100 miles from Baghdad.

November 6.
Canadians won Passchendaele, Goudberg,
and Mosselmarkt; over 400 prisoners.
Italians withdrawing from Tagliamento
reach Livenza R.
H.M. special service ship *Peveril* sunk by
U-Boat outside Straits of Gibraltar.
Gen. Allenby's troops captured Turkish
lines on Wadi Khuweilfeh—Wadi Sheria,
11 miles N. of Beersheba.
Gen. Maude occupied Tekrit (Tigris).

November 7.
Italians retiring from Piave; Germans
claimed 250,000 prisoners, 2,300 guns to date.
Lenin's *coup d'état* in Petrograd.
Fall of Gaza to Gen. Allenby; Anglo-
French warships off Palestine coast; British
pressing on to Wadi Hesi, 8 miles N. of Gaza.

November 8.
Col. House arrived in London.
Petrograd Soviet Congress decided on
peace proposals to Central Powers.
Gen. Maude withdrawing from Tekrit;
Turks withdrew 30—50 miles northward on
Mosul road.

November 9.
Allied Conference at Rapallo created
Supreme Allied Political Council for W.
Front, assisted by permanent Military
Committee, consisting of Gens. Foch, Cadorna,
and Wilson.
Gen. Diaz Italian C.-in-C. vice Gen.
Cadorna.
Gen. Fayolle in command of French
troops in Italy.
Italians on Piave; Austro-German descent
in Trentino, taking Asiago ruins.

November 9 (continued).
Turks evacuated Wadi Hesi—Ascalon;
retreated on Hebron—Jerusalem; lose 70 guns;
10,000 casualties.
British s.s. *Ardglamis* (4,540 tons) sunk by
U-Boat off Cape Spartel.
British s.s. *Ballogie* (1,207 tons) sunk
by U-Boat off Filey; 13 lost.

November 10.
British s.s. *Appleleaf* (5,891 tons) mined
in North Sea; towed in.
British gains N.W. of Passchendaele.
Germans repulsed at Chaume Wood
(Verdun) and Hartmannsweilerkopf (Alsace).
Gen. Plumer in command of British forces
in Italy.
Austro-German attacks on Upper Piave;
Belluno occupied.

* November 11.
Austro-German attacks from Asiago
Plateau in rear of Italian positions on Piave
defeated.
Turks on Jerusalem—Hebron line.
Total, 5,894 prisoners to date.
H.M. monitor, M15, and H.M.S. *Staunch*
sunk by U-Boat off Palestine coast S. of Gaza.
British s.s. *Southgate* (3,661 tons) mined
in Mediterranean; reached port.

November 12.
Mr. Lloyd George in Paris on necessity
for Allied War Council, to want of which he
attributed Serbian, Rumanian, and Italian
disasters.
Germans established bridgehead across
Lower Piave at Zenson, 20 miles N.E. of
Venice; Italians evacuated Fonzaso and part
of Val Sugana, overlooking Brenta.
British s.s. *Barbary* (4,185 tons) sunk by
U-Boat N.W. from Port Said; 3 lost.

November 13.
Fall of Painlevé Government.
Austro-German groups across Piave at
Grisolera, 20 miles N.E. of Venice; checked
on Veccia Piave.
Kerensky's forces defeated at Tsarskoe
Selo.
Gen. Allenby drove Turks from Wadi
Sukereir, 12 miles N. of Ascalon; they retired
on Wadi Surar, 8 miles S. of Joppa. Junction
of Beersheba—Damascus and Jerusalem lines
taken; over 1,500 prisoners.
UC51 sunk by H.M.S. *Firedrake* in North
Sea.
British s.s. *Carlo* (3,040 tons) and *Ard-
more* (1,304 tons) sunk by U-Boat off Coning-
beg Light; 21 lost.
British s.s. *Australbush* (4,398 tons) sunk
by U-Boat off Eddystone; 2 lost.
British s.s. *Axminster* (1,905 tons) sunk
by U-Boat off Pakefield Gat; 3 lost.

November 14.
Attempts on Italian lines from Trentino
to Middle Piave repulsed.
British s.s. *Trowbridge* (3,172 tons) sunk
by U-Boat off Cape de Gata.
British s.s. *Prophet* (3,230 tons) sunk by
U-Boat off Antikithera Island.
Kerensky escaped from Gatchina.
Gen. von Lettow-Vorbeck prepared to
leave his temporary " capital " at Chivata and
to retire towards Kitangari (G. E. Africa).

November 15.
U.S. auxiliary *Alcedo* torpedoed by U-Boat
in Bay of Biscay.

Sundays marked with Asterisk (*).

November 15, 1917 (*continued*).

British s.s. *Garron Head* (1,933 tons) mined N.E. from Bayonne ; 28 lost.

British s.s. *Gasconia* (3,801 tons) and *Kyno* (3,034 tons) sunk by U-Boat off Cape Shershel ; 8 lost.

British captures on all fronts since beginning of war, 166,000 prisoners, over 800 guns. Since July 1, 1916, British had taken 101,534 prisoners on W. Front.

Italian resistance on Piave stiffening ; retreat in Val Sugana.

Bolshevists proclaimed right of Russian peoples to self-determination.

Gen. Allenby 3 miles from Joppa ; over 9,000 prisoners since October 31.

British occupied Chivata (G. E. Africa).

November 16.

M. Clemenceau formed French Ministry.

Great Austro-German attack on 20-mile front from Lower Alps—Querro (Piave) ; Mte. Prasalon taken ; Italians retired towards Mte. Grappa guarding Venetian Plain ; Germans crossed Lower Piave at Folina—Fagare ; dispersed at Folina ; fighting at Zenson ; Italians took over 1,000 prisoners.

November 17.

North Sea skirmish ; German scouting forces, under Adm. Reuter in H.I.M.S. *Königsberg*, with *Kaiser* and *Kaiserin* in support, chased from Horn Reef—Terschelling line to within 30 miles of Heligoland by British cruiser force including H.M.S. *Repulse* (F. Adm. Phillimore). The two German battleships came into action, followed by battle cruisers *Hindenburg* and *Moltke* ; but Germans withdrew with loss of patrol-boat *Kedingen*, while the *Königsberg* was set on fire, and a third German vessel was also damaged.

Italians destroyed Austrian detachments which crossed Piave at Fagare.

Gen. Allenby's forces at Joppa ; Turks retiring parallel to Auja R., 4 miles N.

British s.s. *Clan Maccorquodale* (6,517 tons) sunk by U-Boat N.W. from Alexandria.

British s.s. *Croxteth Hall* (5,872 tons) sunk 25 miles W. from Bombay by mine laid by German raider *Wolf* ; 9 lost.

U58 sunk by U.S. T.B.D.s *Fanning* and *Nicholson* off S. Ireland.

UB18 mined off Start Point.

British s.s. *Western Coast* sunk by U-Boat off Eddystone ; 17 lost.

British s.s. *Abaris* and *David Lloyd George* torpedoed in Channel.

＊November 18.

H.M. submarine K1 (2,650 tons) sunk by collision in North Sea.

H.M.S. P57 rammed and destroyed UC47 in North Sea.

Austrians took Quero (Upper Piave) and Mte. Cornella ; Italian counter-attack on Asiago Plateau ; over 200 prisoners.

Austrians claimed capture of bridgehead 12 miles from Avlona (Albania).

H.M. sloop *Candytuft* sunk by U-Boat in Mediterranean.

British s.s. *Huntsgulf* (3,185 tons) torpedoed by U-Boat in Mediterranean ; reached port.

Gen. Allenby's cavalry occupied Beit-ur-et-Tahta, 12 miles S.W. of Jerusalem.

Death of Gen. Maude in Mesopotamia.

Surrender of 262 German soldiers, 700 Askaris S.E. of Chivata (G. E. Africa). Gen. von Lettow at Kitangari.

November 19.

British s.s. *Aparima* (5,704 tons) sunk by U-Boat off Anvil Point ; 56 lost.

British s.s. *Farn* (4,393 tons) sunk by U-Boat off Start Point.

British s.s. *Clangula* (1,754 tons) sunk by U-Boat off Hartland Point ; 15 lost.

British s.s. *Jutland* sunk by U-Boat off Ushant ; 26 lost.

U.S. T.B.D. *Chauncey* sunk in collision near Gibraltar ; 21 lives lost.

Mr. Lloyd George defended his Allied Council scheme and his Paris speech ; he announced five U-Boats destroyed on the 17th.

Gen. Elles's Special Order to British Tank Corps before Cambrai Battle.

Frenchsu ccess at Chaume Wood (Verdun).

British in Judean Highlands. Kuryet el-Enab carried, 6 miles W. of Jerusalem.

November 20.

British War Cabinet and U.S. Mission conferred at Downing-street.

British attack at Cambrai.

Hindenburg line broken on 10-mile front facing Cambrai, by Third Army (Gen. Byng), to a depth of 4-5 miles ; no artillery preparation ; Tanks cut passages through wire ; Bonavis, Lateaux Wood, La Vacquerie, Welsh Ridge, Ribécourt, Couillet Wood Flesquières, Havrincourt, Marcoing, Neuf Wood, Graincourt, and Anneux taken advance to within 5 miles of Cambrai Auxiliary thrusts near Bullecourt—Epéhy.

Austrian assaults on Mte. Pertica, N.W. of Mte. Grappa, repulsed.

Soviet peace offer to Central Powers.

M. Golubovitch elected first President of independent Ukraine.

November 21.

British gained ground on E. bank of Scheldt Canal ; Noyelles, Cantaing, part of Bourlon Wood, and Moeuvres taken ; Fontaine Notre Dame, 4,000 yards from Cambrai, entered ; 8,000 prisoners to date.

French carried salient S. of Juvincourt (Craonne Plateau) ; 400 prisoners.

Austro-Germans took Mte. Fontana Secca between Brenta—Piave.

Gen. Dukhonin, Russian C.-in-C., refusing to offer armistice to Germans, superseded by Bolshevist Ensign Krilenko.

Gen. Allenby took Nebi Samwil Ridge (Mizpah), 5 miles from Jerusalem.

German surrender in Kitangari Valley (E. Africa). Gen. von Lettow marching S. reached Rovuma R. with reorganised forces.

British s.s. *Aros Castle* (4,460 tons) sunk by U-Boat W. by S. from Bishop Rock ; lost.

British s.s. *Breynton* (4,240 tons) torpedoed by U-Boat in St. George's Channel reached port.

German extension of barred shipping zone.

LZ103 raided French Channel ports.

November 22.

British advance towards Zandvoorde S.E. of Ypres.

Germans retook Fontaine Notre Dame.

British s.s. *King Idwal* (3,631 tons) sunk by U-Boat off Buchan Ness ; 1 lost.

British s.s. *Hartland* (4,785 tons) and *Redbridge* (3,834 tons) torpedoed by U-Boat in St. George's Channel ; both reached port 2 lost.

British s.s. *Kohistan* (4,732 tons) sunk by U-Boat off Marittimo.

For List of Abbreviations see page iv.

November 22, 1917 (*continued*).
Russians announced 1,600 Turks surrendered near Diala R. (Mesopotamia).
British captured Turkish post at Tabir, 15 miles from Aden.

November 23.
British s.s. *La Blanca* (7,779 tons) sunk by U-Boat off Berry Head ; 2 lost.
British s.s. *Westlands* (3,112 tons) sunk by U-Boat off Ile de Vierge.
Further British advance W. of Cambrai ; Canadians gained important spur between Mœuvres—Quéant.
Allied Military Missions at Russian G.H.Q. protested against any breach of the Pact of London, 5.-ix.-14.

November 24.
U48 (725 tons, 43 crew) destroyed off Goodwins by H.M.S. *Gipsy* and five H.M. drifters ; 19 survivors. Dover Salvage Corps boarded the wrecked submarine in Deal lifeboat and secured some of her papers.
British s.s. *Dunrobin* (3,617 tons), *Sabia* (2,807 tons) and *Nyassa* (2,579 tons) sunk by U-Boat off Lizard ; 42 lost.
British took nearly all Bourlon Wood and village W. of Cambrai ; over 100 guns to date.
Gen. Marshall to succeed the late Gen. Maude in Mesopotamia.

* November 25.
British s.s. *Ostpreussen* (1,779 tons) mined off Shipwash Light ; 1 lost.
British s.s. *Oriflamme* (3,764 tons) mined off Nab Light.
Germans recovered part of Bourlon ; 9,774 prisoners to date.
French attack at Samogneux (Verdun).
Austro-Germans repulsed between Brenta—Piave. Italians took 200 prisoners near Mte. Grappa.
Austrians forced Osum R. (Albania) ; driven back by Italians.
British s.s. *Karema* (5,285 tons) sunk by U-Boat off Cape de Gata ; 3 lost.
British s.s. *Ovid* (4,159 tons) sunk by U-Boat off Suda Bay ; 2 lost.
Gen. Allenby's mounted troops at Ain Karim, 3½ miles N. of Jerusalem.
Gen. von Lettow crossed Rovuma R. from G. E. into P. E. Africa, at Ngomano, where Germans captured local Portuguese post.

November 26.
Lord Rothermere President of Air Council.
British s.s. *Crenella* (7,035 tons) torpedoed by U-Boat off S.W. Ireland ; reached port.
French carried strong point N. of Hill 344 (Verdun).
Austro-Germans repulsed E. of San Marino (Brenta). Offensive checked ; Italian front hardening ; guns and reserves flowing up.

November 27.
British s.s. *Almond Branch* (3,461 tons) and *Eastfield* (2,145 tons) sunk by U-Boat off Dodman Point ; 2 lost.
British s.s. *Bleamoor* (3,755 tons) sunk by U-Boat off Berry Head ; 8 lost.
British advance towards Bourlon—Fontaine Notre Dame ; 500 prisoners.
Russian T.B.D. *Dyelnyi* mined in Baltic.

November 27 (*continued*).
British s.s. *Thornhill* (3,848 tons) and *Glenbridge* (3,845 tons) torpedoed by U-Boat in Mediterranean ; both beached ; 1 lost.
Capt. Tafel, with 3,500 Germans and native troops, surrendered near Nevale (E. Africa).

November 28.
British s.s. *Apapa* (7,832 tons) sunk by U-Boat off Lynas Point ; 77 lost.
British s.s. *Jane Radcliffe* (4,074 tons) sunk by U-Boat off Antimilo.
Attack on Belgian positions near Aschhoop repulsed.
Petrograd Soviet by wireless intimated to Central Powers its readiness to negotiate armistice and peace.

November 29.
Allied Conference opened.
Lord Lansdowne's letter to *Daily Telegraph* declaring war had lasted too long, and suggesting restatement of British war aims.
ML52 destroyed by fire at Sandown.
UB61 mined off Terschelling.
British advance W. of Bourlon Wood.
Count Hertling in Reichstag announced Germany prepared to treat with Bolshevists.
British monitor destroyed bridge on Piave.

November 30.
November was the month of smallest British shipping losses since institution of unrestricted U-Boat warfare ; of 51 ships sunk, 10 were mined ; largest number lost in English Channel, where 14 were sunk by U-Boat and 7 were mined.
British s.s. *Derbent* (3,178 tons) sunk by U-Boat off Lynas Point.
British s.s. *Kalibia* (4,930 tons) sunk by U-Boat off Lizard ; 25 lost.
UC57 lost in Baltic during November ; cause unknown.
During November the British and U.S. Navies agreed jointly to lay the Northern Barrage from Scotland to Norway, and 100,000 new type mines were ordered (8-vi.-18).
German counter at Cambrai.
Strong German attacks, under Gen. von der Marwitz, on new British line before Cambrai ; six or seven divisions attacking from Crèvecœur — Vendhuille penetrated British positions as far as La Vacquerie—Gonnelieu—Gouzeaucourt, and took Lateau Wood, S. of Masnières ; La Vacquerie regained ; Germans driven back from Gouzeaucourt and ridge E. of village ; from Masnières northwards British positions intact ; many Germans killed ; Germans claimed 4,000 prisoners, 60 guns.
Austro-Germans reached Tagliamento.
L59 during November credited itself with a non-stop 96-hour flight from Yamboli (Bulgaria) to Khartum, where it was recalled by wireless, although it had started out for G. E. Africa with 14 tons of stores for Gen. von Lettow.

December 1.
British s.s. *Molesey* (3,218 tons) sunk by U-Boat off Brighton Light.
British s.s. *Euphorbia* (3,109 tons) and *Rydal Hall* (3,314 tons) sunk by U-Boat off Royal Sovereign Light ; 37 lost.
British s.s. *Helenus* (7,555 tons) torpedoed by U-Boat in English Channel ; reached port.
British recovered Gonnelieu ; withdrew from Masnières salient ; 11,551 prisoners ; 138 guns to date.

Sundays marked with Asterisk (*).

December 1, 1917 (*continued*).

G. E. Africa reported by Gen. van Deventer clear of enemy ; Gen. von Lettow-Vorbeck across Rovuma in Mozambique.

*December 2.

UB81 mined off Isle of Wight.

British s.s. *Kintuck* (4,639 tons) sunk by U-Boat off Godrevy Light ; 1 lost.

British s.s. *Berwick Law* (4,680 tons) sunk by U-Boat off Cape Tenez ; 1 lost.

British took 120 prisoners N. of Passchendaele.

Russian (Bolshevist) parlementaires proceeded, via Dvinsk, to German Eastern H.Q. at Brest-Litovsk.

First suspension of hostilities on E. Front in Gen. von Linsingen's sector.

Germans at Nangwale (P. E. Africa).

December 3.

British gains S.W. of Polygon Wood.

Slight British withdrawal at La Vacquerie and E. of Marcoing ; Germans claimed 6,000 prisoners, 100 guns to date.

Bolshevist troops under Krilenko secured surrender of Russian General Staff at Mohileff ; Gen. Dukhonin, C.-in-C., murdered ; Gen. Korniloff escaped.

Turks driven by Russians from hills N. of Deli Abbas ; they retired up Kifri road towards Jebel Hamrin.

British s.s. *Livonia* (1,879 tons) sunk by U-Boat off Start Point ; 23 lost.

British s.s. *Dowlais* (3,016 tons) sunk by U-Boat off Cap de Fer ; 26 lost.

December 4.

President Wilson's Message to Congress : " Our object is to win the war."

Supreme Allied Naval Council formed.

Gen. Weygand to represent France on Versailles Council. Gen. Foch to remain Chief of Staff.

German attacks on salient from Mte. Sisemol, near Asiago, towards Brenta R. ; Mts. Badeneche—Tondarecar stormed.

Russian Duma occupied by Red Guard.

Gen. Marshall took Salkaltutan Pass on Deli Abbas—Kifri road.

British s.s. *Forfar* (3,827 tons) sunk by U-Boat off Lizard ; 3 lost.

British s.s. *Brigitta* (2,084 tons) mined off Nab Light ; 2 lost.

British s.s. *Milton* (3,267 tons) torpedoed by U-Boat in St. George's Channel ; reached port ; 1 lost.

British s.s. *Manchester Mariner* (4,106 tons) mined in English Channel ; saved by mine defence.

December 5.

U-Boat Office established in Berlin as separate Department, under Adm. Ritter von Mann. During December 120 U-Boats were ordered.

British s.s. *Greenwich* (2,938 tons) sunk by U-Boat off Planier Is.

British evacuated Bourlon Wood at night without casualties and without German knowledge.

Austrian progress in Asiago salient ; Mts. Zomo and Castelgomberto stormed ; 11,000 prisoners, 60 guns claimed.

Russo-German Armistice for Dec. 7.

Gen. Marshall across Nahrin R. drove Turks out of Kara Tepe.

December 6.

Early morning raid by 25 aeroplanes (German 3rd Bomb. Squad.) ; five or six reached London (25th raid) ; 8 killed, 2 injured. Two raiders down. Kent and Essex visited.

U.S. T.B.D. *Jacob Jones* torpedoed o entrance to the Channel.

UC69 rammed and sunk by U96 off Cap Barfleur.

British s.s. *Ilvington Court* (4,217 ton sunk by U-Boat off Shershel ; 8 lost.

British s.s. *Asaba* sunk by U-Boat o Lizard ; 16 lost.

German attacks round La Vacquerie.

Lisbon rising. New Provisional Govern ment, under Dr. Sidonio Paes, reaffirme solidarity with Allies.

Austrians captured Mt. Sisemol, E. Asiago ; attempts in Val Frenzela failed 15,000 prisoners claimed to date.

Trotsky in Petrograd notified Allie representatives of armistice on E. front.

December 7.

U.S. at war with Austria.

H.M.S. *Hornet* in collision ; towed 1 Dover.

British s.s. *Earl of Elgin* (4,448 tons) sun by U-Boat off Carnarvon Bay Light ; 18 los

German trenches captured N. of L Vacquerie and British line improved.

Armistice on Russian Front.

Gen. Allenby's occupation of Hebron.

December 8.

During the four weeks ended on this da R.N.A.S. anti-U-Boat patrols covered 91,00 miles and sighted 17 U-Boats, of which 1 were attacked.

During the same period British airshi covered 50,000 miles and sighted 6 U-Boat of which 5 were attacked.

H.M. armed steamer *Grive* torpedoed i North Sea ; foundered on December 24.

British s.s. *Maindy Bridge* (3,653 ton sunk by U-Boat off Sunderland ; 2 lost.

British s.s. *Lampada* (2,220 tons) sun by U-Boat off Whitby ; 5 lost.

British s.s. *Consols* (3,756 tons) sunk 1 U-Boat off Cape Bon ; 3 lost.

British s.s. *Chyebassa* (6,249 tons) to pedoed by U-Boat in Mediterranean ; reache port.

Gen. Allenby's advance from Bethlehei passing Jerusalem on E., and cutting Jer salem—Jericho road, while further N. 1 cut the Schechem road ; Jerusalem isolated.

*December 9.

Fall of Jerusalem to Gen. Allenby.

British s.s. *Venetia* (3,596 tons) sunk 1 U-Boat off Whitby Rock buoy.

British s.s. *Nyanza* (6,695 tons) an *Sedbergh* (4,230 tons) torpedoed by U-Boa in English Channel ; both arrived ; 50 lost.

British s.s. *War Tune* (2,045 tons) sun by U-Boat off Black Head ; 1 lost.

Italians torpedoed two Austrian battl ships of the *Monarch* type in Trieste ; on the *Wien*, sunk.

Central Powers and Rumania signe armistice agreement at Focsani.

Lenin Government announced Cossac rising under Gens. Kaledin and Korniloff o Don, and under Gen. Dutoff in Urals.

December 10.

Panama declared war on Austria.

U75 mined off Terschelling.

UB75 mined off Flamborough Head.

December 10, 1917 (*continued*).

British s.s. *Aureole* (3,998 tons) mined off W. Scotland ; reached port.

Gen. Dubail's official indictment of M. Caillaux.

German post E. of Boursies (Cambrai) carried.

Armistice on Rumanian front.

December 11.

Gen. Allenby entered Jerusalem.

Cuba declared war on Austria.

British s.s. *Oldfield Grange* (4,653 tons) sunk by U-Boat off Tory Island.

British non-rigid airship, with crew of five, believed destroyed by German seaplane in North Sea.

British aeroplanes raided country between Metz and Rhine ; bombed Pirmasens Junction.

British s.s. *D. A. Gordon* (2,301 tons) and *Minorca* (1,145 tons) sunk by U-Boat off Cape Huertas ; 16 lost.

British s.s. *Persier* (3,874 tons) sunk by U-Boat off Cape Spartivento ; 1 lost.

Russian Constituent Assembly met in Petrograd ; boycotted by Bolshevists.

December 12.

Five convoyed neutral vessels and one British vessel with escort of two T.B.D.s and four trawlers attacked on Lerwick—Bergen route by four German T.B.D.s, G101, G103, G104, and V106 ; H.M.S. *Pellew* disabled ; H.M.S. *Partridge*, trawlers, and convoy sunk.

H.M.SS. *Shannon* and *Minotaur*, with four T.B.D.s, at sea to westward, and 3rd Light Cruiser Squadron at sea to southward and eastward of convoy, failed to intercept raiders, owing especially to short daylight hours.

H.M.S. *Wolverine* sunk in collision off Irish coast.

British s.s. *Leonatus* (2,099 tons) mined off Kirkadister Light.

British s.s. *Cordova* (2,284 tons) sunk by German T.B.D. in North Sea.

Two trawlers and two neutral vessels sunk off the Tyne by German T.B.D.s.

President Bernardino Machado exiled from Portugal.

Funchal (Madeira) shelled by U-Boats.

German attack on mile front between Bullecourt—Quéant ; small British salient captured.

Gen. von Kirchbach to command German Eighth (Riga) Army, vice-Gen. von Hutier.

Gen. Allenby reported advance between Joppa — Jerusalem and Budrus — Sheikh Obeid ; Rahid, N. of Midieh, captured.

December 13.

Sir E. Geddes stated Germany building U-Boats faster than she was losing them ; Britain losing shipping faster than she could build.

H.M. armed steamer *Stephen Furness* sunk by U-Boat in Irish Sea.

British s.s. *Arnewood* (2,259 tons) mined off Skye.

British s.s. *Garthwaite* (5,690 tons) sunk by U-Boat off Whitby ; 14 lost.

British captured post S. of Villers-Guislain ; improved near Bullecourt.

Austrian attack on Mte. Grappa defeated. French batteries in action.

Russian Constituent Assembly dispersed by Bolshevists.

Gen. Allenby extended N.E. of Jerusalem.

December 14.

British s.s. *Volnay* (4,610 tons) mined off Manacles.

British s.s. *Coila* (4,135 tons) sunk by U-Boat off Valencia ; 3 lost.

Germans entered British front trench on 300-yard front near Polderhoek Chateau (Ypres) ; part regained.

Austrians gained Col Caprile, one of Valstagna defences.

French cruiser *Châteaurenault* sunk in Ionian Sea by UC38, which was destroyed.

December 15.

Allied War Council at Versailles established.

Russo-German armistice signed at Brest-Litovsk for one month from December 17.

Separation of Church and State in Russia.

Gen. Guillaumat to command at Salonika, vice Gen. Sarrail.

Gen. Allenby advanced 2,500 yards on 5-mile front N.E. of Ludd.

British s.s. *Bernard* (3,682 tons) sunk by U-Boat off Bishop Rock ; 1 lost.

British s.s. *Sachem* (5,354 tons) torpedoed by U-Boat in English Channel ; reached port

*December 16.

H.M. sloop *Arbutus* sunk by U-Boat off Bristol Channel.

British s.s. *Bristol City* (2,511 tons) sunk by U-Boat in Atlantic ; 30 lost.

British s.s. *Formby* (1,282 tons) sunk by U-Boat in Irish Sea ; 15 lost.

British s.s. *Foylemore* (3,831 tons) sunk by U-Boat off Lizard.

Italian recovery on Col Caprile.

December 17.

U.S. submarine. F1 sunk in collision with F3.

Russo-German armistice.

Bolshevist ultimatum to Ukraine.

Germans at Chirumba (P. E. Africa).

December 18.

Canadian elections with large Unionist and Conscription majority.

German 3rd Bomb. Squad. raided E. coast ; five machines reached London ; Kent and Essex visited : 14 killed, 85 injured. One raider brought down by gunfire off Kent coast ; another believed destroyed in Channel.

Austrian attacks E. of Brenta R. from Col Caprile to Mte. Pertica ; Austrians captured Mte. Asolone ; over 2,000 prisoners claimed.

Kaiser in council at Kreuznach approved terms to Russia.

Gen. Eichhorn, commanding German Tenth (Dvinsk) Army promoted Field-Marshal.

Rostoff in Gen. Kaledin's hands.

Gen. Allenby holding high ground E. of Abu Dis, 2 miles S.E. of Jerusalem.

British s.s. *Coningbeg* (1,279 tons) sunk by U-Boat in Irish Sea ; 15 lost.

British s.s. *Riversdale* (2,805 tons) sunk by U-Boat off Prawle Point ; 1 lost.

December 19.

UB56 mined in Folkestone Barrage.

U-Boat sighted, engaged, and chased off by H.M. armed motor trawler *Take Care* in Start Bay

Cunard s.s. *Vinovia* (7,046 tons) sunk by U-Boat off Wolf Rock ; 9 lost.

British s.s. *Alice Marie* (2,210 tons) sunk by U-Boat off Start Point.

British s.s. *Trevelyan* (3,066 tons) torpedoed by U-Boat in English Channel ; beached.

Sundays marked with Asterisk (*).

December 19, 1917 (*continued*).

Fighting on Piave; Italians recaptured part of Mte. Asolone.

Ukrainian Republic demanded recognition. Ukraine forces mobilised under Gen. Shtcherbatcheff.

December 20.

Mr. Lloyd George stated Russian collapse and Italian defeat had imposed fresh obligations upon Great Britain.

Second Australian Referendum showed 165,000 anti-conscription majority; increase of over 100,000 on 1916 figures.

Germans captured post E. of Messines.

Gen. Gröner to command XXVth (Prussian) Reserve Corps on W. Front.

Austro-German delegates arrived at Brest-Litovsk (German Eastern H.Q.) for peace conference with Bolshevists. Chief delegates: Herr von Kühlmann (Germany), Count Czernin (Austria) and M. Joffe (Russia).

British s.s. *Polvarth* (3,146 tons) sunk by U-Boat off Ushant; 2 lost.

British s.s. *Fiscus* (4,782 tons) and *Waverley* (3,853 tons) sunk by U-Boat off Cape Ivi, Algeria; 23 lost.

December 21.

British s.s. *City of Lucknow* (8,293 tons) sunk by U-Boat N.E. from Cani Rocks.

Italians recaptured whole Mte. Asolone.

Gen. Allenby crossed Auja R.; seized high ground near coast; advanced E., up Damascus railway, and along Jerusalem—Jericho road.

December 22.

German 3rd Bomb. Squad. attacked Kentish coast; one machine over land; forced down; crew captured; no casualties.

Germans drove in British posts on 700-yard front near Ypres—Staden railway.

Peace negotiations, under presidency of Herr von Kühlmann, opened at Brest-Litovsk between Soviet Russia and four Central and confederate Powers.

Canadian Prohibition Order for Dec. 31.

British s.s. *Clan Cameron* (3,595 tons) sunk by U-Boat off Portland Bill.

British s.s. *Mabel Baird* (2,500 tons) sunk by U-Boat off Lizard; 5 lost.

British s.s. *Colemere* (2,120 tons) sunk by U-Boat off the Smalls; 4 lost.

British s.s. *Hunsbrook* (4,463 tons) torpedoed by U-Boat in Bristol Channel; towed in; 3 lost.

∗December 23.

H.M.SS. *Surprise, Tornado* and *Torrent* mined off Dutch coast.

British s.s. *Grantley Hall* (4,008 tons) mined off Orfordness.

British s.s. *Dunedin* (4,796 tons) mined in Mediterranean; towed in.

Austrians nearer Valstagna; 9,000 prisoners claimed.

December 24.

British s.s. *Elmleaf* (5,948 tons) torpedoed by U-Boat off N.W. Scotland; reached port.

British s.s. *Luciston* (2,877 tons) torpedoed by U-Boat in English Channel; beached.

British s.s. *Canova* (4,637 tons) sunk by U-Boat off Mine Head; 7 lost.

British s.s. *Daybreak* (3,238 tons) sunk by U-Boat off South Rock; 21 lost.

British s.s. *Turnbridge* (2,874 tons) sunk by U-Boat off Cape Ivi; 1 lost.

December 24 (*continued*).

British s.s. *Argo* (3,071 tons) sunk U-Boat off Cape Tenez, Algeria.

At Brest-Litovsk Austro-Germans out with Bulgarians.

December 25.

H.M.S. *Penshurst* (Q7) sunk by U-F off Bristol Channel.

H.M.S. P56 rammed and depth-char U87 in the Channel.

British s.s. *Agberi* (4,821 tons) sunk U-Boat off Bardsey Island.

British s.s. *Hyacinthus* (5,756 tons) pedoed by U-Boat in English Chan reached port.

British s.s. *Cliftondale* (3,811 tons) s by U-Boat off Cape Tenez, Algeria; 3 los

British s.s. *Umballa* (5,310 tons) sunk U-Boat off Cape Scalea, Gulf of Policas 15 lost.

Austrians reached Sasso.

At Brest-Litovsk: Austro-Germ sought to pledge Bolshevists to secure Ent adhesion to Soviet peace principles wi ten days.

British forces pursued across boundar G. E. African frontiers; patrols 40 miles of Rovuma R.

December 26.

Adm. Wemyss First Sea Lord

Adm. Jellicoe created Viscount (of Scapa).

British s.s. *Benito* (4,712 tons) and *genna* (5,772) sunk by U-Boat off Dod Point.

German attacks at Caurières W N. of Verdun, repulsed.

Special negotiations begun at Brest.

Attacks on British lines N. of Jerusa

December 27.

British s.s. *Adela* sunk by U-Boat off Skerries, Anglesea; 24 lost.

Gen. von Hutier in command of German Eighteenth Army formed on the C

British counter on Jerusalem front p trated Turkish lines 4,000 yards on 9- front. Germans among prisoners.

Deadlock at Brest on question of occu territories.

Germans retreating before British fo into Mozambique captured Portuguese pos Mt. M'Kula.

December 28.

British s.s. *Santa Amalia* (4,306 t and *Maxton* (5,094 tons) sunk by U-F off Malin Head; 44 lost.

British s.s. *Lord Derby* (3,757 t sunk by U-Boat off St. Ann's Head; 3 l

British s.s. *Chirripo* (4,050 tons) sunk mine off Black Head, Belfast.

British s.s. *Alfred H. Read* (457 t sunk by mine at entrance to Mersey; 39 l

British s.s. *Robert Eggleton* (2,274 t sunk by U-Boat off Bardsey Island; 1 los

British s.s. *Fallodon* (3,012 tons) sunk U-Boat off St. Catharine's; 1 lost.

British s.s. *Clara* (2,425 tons) sunk U-Boat off the Runnelstone.

Labour Conference accepted War A Memorandum.

After inconclusive discussion of fut of Russian occupied territories, Brest ference adjourned until January 5.

Esthonia proclaimed independence.

Gen. Allenby progressed N. of Jerusal Ramah—Beitunia captured; 130 prisor

For List of Abbreviations see page iv.

December 29, 1917.

Adm. Keyes to command at Dover vice Adm. Bacon, superseded.

British s.s. *Ennismore* (1,409 tons) sunk by U-Boat off Girdleness; 10 lost.

British s.s. *Inverness* torpedoed by U-Boat in North Sea; reached port.

Gen. Allenby advanced another 3 miles; took Shechem road; further advance on Jericho road and N.W. of Beth Horon.

* December 30.

German attacks S. of Cambrai on 2-mile front gained lodgment in two small salients; British recovery.

H.M.S. *Attack* torpedoed off Alexandria.

British s.s. *Aragon* (9,588 tons) sunk by U-Boat off Alexandria.

British s.s. *Zone* (3,914 tons) sunk by U-Boat off St. Ives.

British s.s. *Hercules* (1,295 tons) sunk by U-Boat off Whitby; 12 lost.

December 31.

Canadian Prohibition Order in force.

British s.s. *Westville* (3,207 tons) sunk by U-Boat off St. Catherine's.

During December four U.S. battleships under Adm. Rodman (F. *New York*) arrived in British waters and were incorporated in Grand Fleet as Sixth Battle Squadron.

During the year 1917 hydrophones were so perfected that the supply of the general service portable type was increased from 2,750 on July 31 to 3,680 on Dec. 31, and of the directional type from 500 to 1,950.

By the end of 1917 over 4,400 British merchant ships had received a defensive gun armament, as compared with 1,420 on Jan. 1, and 3,000 on July 1. Of the 2,180 new guns mounted in 1917 only 190 were less than 12-pounders.

During the whole of 1917 R.N.A.S. anti-U-Boat aeroplane patrols sighted 135 U-Boats, of which 85 were attacked; while British airships sighted 26 and attacked 15 U-Boats.

During the fourth quarter of 1917 nearly 10,400 British mines were laid in Heligoland Bight and Dover Straits, as compared with 18,600 laid in the Bight and off U.K. coasts during first three quarters.

During 1917 British Auxiliary Patrols increased from 2,500 craft to 3,084, including 1,230 on E. Coast and 824 in the Channel.

During 1917 the average number of mines swept up per month by British minesweepers was 355, as compared with 178 per month in 1916; in April 515 mines were swept up and only 188 in December.

H.M. fleet messenger *Osmanieh* (4,041 tons) mined off Alexandria.

January 1, 1918.

Rear-Adm. Roger Keyes (Dover) given acting rank of Vice-Admiral.

British s.s. *Genesee* (2,892 tons) torpedoed by U-Boat in North Sea; reached port.

British during December took on W. Front: 1,018 German prisoners, including 12 officers, four guns, three trench mortars, 103 machine-guns.

Position-warfare in Flanders and Artois until April 30.

Position-warfare in Champagne until mid-July.

Position-warfare in Upper Alsace until Armistice.

Gallwitz Army Group formed at Verdun.

Middlesex Regiment's raid on British Piave front.

January 1 (*continued*).

British s.s. *Sandon Hall* (5,134 tons) sunk by U-Boat off Linosa.

British s.s. *Egyptian Transport* (4,648 tons) torpedoed by U-Boat in Mediterranean; beached; 5 lost.

January 2.

British s.s. *Kingsley* (633 tons) engaged and warded off U-Boat by gunfire in English Channel; 5 lives lost in action.

British s.s. *Gallier* (4,592 tons) sunk by U-Boat off Wolf Rock.

Kaiser in Berlin discussed with Hindenburg and Ludendorff new frontier with Russia. German G.H.Q. urged speedy decisions at Brest-Litovsk.

Bolshevists denounced German Brest-Litovsk conditions as annexationist; Poland and Lithuania must settle their own future; Germany must withdraw from occupied provinces to permit referendum.

January 3.

H.M. collier *Birchwood* (2,756 tons) sunk by U-Boat E. of Blackwater Light vessel.

H.M. collier *Gartland* (2,613 tons) sunk by U-Boat E.S.E. of Owers Light vessel.

H.M. colliers *Steelville* (3,649 tons) and *Allanton* (4,253 tons) sunk by U-Boat N. of Cape Bon.

British advance S. of Lens.

Severe German losses in attack on French trenches near Anspach (Upper Alsace).

French air raids on Rombach, Metz-Sablons, Conflans, and Arnaville.

Bolshevists proposed transfer of peace negotiations from Brest-Litovsk to Stockholm.

January 4.

H.S. *Rewa* (7,300 tons) sunk by U-Boat off Hartland Point; 4 lost.

British s.s. *Iolanthe* (3,081 tons) sunk by U-Boat off Portland Bill.

British s.s. *Glenarm Head* (3,908 tons) sunk by U-Boat off Brighton Light; 2 lost.

British s.s. *Birtley* (1,438 tons) sunk by U-Boat off Flamborough Head; 18 lost.

Naval air raid on Ghistelles (Belgium).

Allied air raids on Denain (N. of Cambrai), Menin, and Roulers railway station.

Four British posts pressed back near Canal du Nord (Cambrai).

Herr von Kühlmann and Count Czernin back at Brest-Litovsk.

Austrian retirement in Tomba sector.

Gen. Allenby reported British line N. of Jerusalem advanced over a mile.

January 5.

Mr. Lloyd George on war aims after conference with Mr. Asquith, Viscount Grey, and Labour Party.

German attack on British position E. of Bullecourt failed.

British s.s. *Knightsgarth* (2,889 tons) sunk by U-Boat off Rathlin Island; 2 lost.

British s.s. *Rose Marie* (2,220 tons) sunk by U-Boat off N. Arklow Light; 1 lost.

British s.s. *War Baron* (5,730 tons) sunk by U-Boat off Godrevy Light; 2 lost.

British s.s. *Rio Claro* (3,687 tons) sunk by U-Boat in Rapallo Bay.

British s.s. *Hong Moh* (3,910 tons) damaged by mine off S.E. coast of Arabia.

* January 6.

British s.s. *Spenser* (4,186 tons) and *Halberdier* (1,049 tons) sunk by U-Boat off Bardsey Island; 5 lost.

Sundays marked with Asterisk (*).

*January 6, 1918 (*continued*).

British s.s. *Gascony* (3,132 tons) sunk by U-Boat off Owers Light.

British s.s. *Arca* (4,839 tons) torpedoed by U-Boat in English Channel ; reached port.

At Brest-Litovsk Austro-German delegates negotiated with Ukrainians.

Austrian attacks before Avlona (Albania).

Arab raid on Hedjaz Railway 20 miles S. of Maan.

Gen. Dunsterville left Karachi for Basra and Baghdad.

January 7.

Successful French raid near Seicheprey (Woevre).

Trotsky arrived at Brest-Litovsk as chief Soviet delegate.

British s.s. *Arab* (4,191 tons) sunk by U-Boat off Cape Serrat, Tunis ; 21 lost.

Fighting at junction of Lawambula R.—Lujenda R. (Mozambique) ; Germans defeated in Mwembe area.

January 8.

President Wilson's " 14 Points " Message to Congress declared for open diplomacy, free seas, no economic barriers, reduced armaments, and territorial settlement on lines similar to those laid down by Mr. Lloyd George (see 5-i.-18). " Treatment accorded to Russia by her sister-nations will be the acid-test of their goodwill."

Sir G Buchanan returned to England from Petrograd.

U.S. Tank School at Langres.

Preliminary proceedings at Brest-Litovsk. Talaat Pasha arrived.

January 9.

H.M.S. *Racoon* wrecked off Ireland ; all hands lost.

Sir D. Haig's dispatches covering operations in 1917 to eve of Battle of Cambrai published.

UB69 destroyed by H.M.S. *Cyclamen* with explosive paravanes 12 miles N.W. from Cape Bon.

British s.s. *Bayvoe* (2,979 tons) sunk by U-Boat off Iles de Glenan ; 4 lost.

At Brest-Litovsk Central Powers refused to transfer negotiations to Stockholm, and intimated that, failing any Allied response, their offer on 25-xii.-17 to negotiate a " no-annexation, no indemnity " peace had lapsed.

January 10.

Position-warfare in Vosges and Lorraine until Armistice.

Austrians abandoned some positions near Piave mouth.

British s.s. *Cardiff* (2,808 tons) sunk by U-Boat in Bay of Biscay ; 8 lost.

British s.v. *W. C. McKay* sunk by U-Boat off Azores ; 6 lost.

Trotsky agreed to continue negotiations at Brest-Litovsk. Ukraine to be represented.

January 11.

Adm. Bacon, commanding Dover Patrol, transferred to Munitions Ministry.

Brest-Litovsk conference discussed territorial questions and representation of Russian Border States.

Three British columns (from Rovuma R., Lake Nyasa, and coast), with Portuguese, pursuing German forces escaped into Mozambique.

January 12.

H.M.SS. *Narbrough* and *Opal* wrecked off Orkneys ; 1 survivor.

German attack at Chaume Wood (Verdun) fails.

Count Hertling addressed to German G.H.Q. a detailed memorandum on the functions of the military in political decisions

At Brest-Litovsk German military delegate, Gen. Hoffmann, delivered an arrogant speech and was congratulated by Gen. Ludendorff from Kreuznach.

British column at Port Amelia (P. E Africa).

* January 13.

British s.s. *Rapallo* (3,811 tons) sunk by U-Boat off Cape Peloro, Sicily ; 1 lost.

January 14.

Sir A. Geddes introduced new Man Power Bill in Commons ; 420,000-450,000 men wanted from munition factories, shipbuilding works, etc. ; age limit unchanged ; no compulsion for Ireland.

Yarmouth bombarded by German T.B.D.s ; 4 killed, 8 injured ; s.s. *Horshan* damaged.

H.M. submarine G8 lost in North Sea.

M. Caillaux arrested in Paris.

British air raid on Karlsruhe.

Italian advance E. of Brenta Valley.

January 15.

Cambrai Inquiry : British War Cabinet satisfied that Higher Command was not surprised ; deprecated public discussion of " breakdown which undoubtedly occurred " (see 20-xi.-17).

British s.s. *Spital* (4,718 tons) sunk by U-Boat off St. Anthony Point.

British s.s. *War Song* (2,535 tons) sunk by U-Boat off Ile de Sein ; 16 lost.

ML278 wrecked on Dunkirk Pier.

U.S. First Army Corps formed on W Front, under Gen. Liggett (Neufchateau) with control of 1st, 2nd, 26th, and 42nd Divisions.

Austrian strikes spreading.

Count Czernin at Brest-Litovsk received urgent appeals from Vienna to conclude an early " bread-peace."

Soviet Government's order for arrest of King of Rumania, and for his removal to Petrograd.

January 16.

U.S. documents in Caillaux Case ; Count Bernstorff's reports on M. Caillaux's visit to S. America in 1915.

Political mass-strike in Vienna.

January 17.

British s.s. *War Thistle* (5,166 tons) torpedoed by U-Boat in English Channel ; reached port.

British s.s. *Kingsdyke* (1,710 tons) sunk by U-Boat off Cape Barfleur ; 16 lost.

British s.s. *Messidor* (3,883 tons) torpedoed by U-Boat in Bay of Biscay ; reached port.

British s.s. *Windsor Hall* (3,693 tons) sunk by U-Boat off Alexandria ; 27 lost.

Vienna Government sought to obtain temporary supplies from Germany.

January 18.

H.M. tug *Blackcock* wrecked in White Sea

Constituent Assembly in Petrograd refused to submit to Bolshevist dictation.

British advance on 4-mile front near Durah, 12 miles N. of Jerusalem.

January 19, 1918.

Gen. **H.** Lawrence to be Chief of Staff to Sir D. Haig vice Gen. L. Kiggell.

H.M. submarine H10 lost in North Sea.

UB22 sunk by mine in North Sea.

Two German T.B.D.s mined off Jutland.

Petrograd Bolshevists dissolved Constituent Assembly.

British s.s. *Trocas* (4,129 tons) sunk by U-Boat off Skyros Light ; 24 lost.

* January 20.

Gen. Gough's Fifth Army front on British right in France prolonged 28 miles by relief of Gen. Humbert's French Third Army down to Barisis. British now held 125 miles of active front. Gen. Humbert halted about Montdidier.

Naval action off Imbros ; H.I.M.SS. *Goeben* and *Breslau* emerged from Dardanelles, sank H.M. monitor *Raglan* (6,150 tons) and monitor M28 ; S. of Imbros *Breslau* manœuvred by H.M. T.B.D.s *Lizard* and *Tigress* into minefield and sunk ; *Goeben* escaped, but struck mine, and was beached at Nagara Point, where naval aircraft attacked her .

H.M. armed steamer *Louvain* sunk by U-Boat in Mediterranean ; 224 lost.

H.M. escortship *Mechanician* (9,000 tons) sunk by U-Boat off St. Catherine's Point.

British s.s. *Harmonides* (3,521 tons) torpedoed by U-Boat in English Channel ; reached port.

British s.s. *Queen Margaret* (4,972 tons) mined in English Channel, reached port.

H.I.M. T.B.D.s A73 and A77 mined in Heligoland Bight.

Delegates left Brest-Litovsk to confer with their governments.

January 21.

Sir E. Carson resigned from War Cabinet.

British s.s. *Teelin Head* (1,718 tons) sunk by U-Boat off Owers Light ; 13 lost.

British s.s. *West Wales* (4,331 tons) sunk by U-Boat S.E. from Malta ; 2 lost.

Austrian political strike ended ; Count Czernin again repudiated annexationist aims.

British in contact with part of von Lettow-Vorbeck's force 50 miles from coast (E. Africa).

January 22.

British s.s. *Serrana* (3,677 tons) sunk by U-Boat off St. Catherine's ; 5 lost.

British s.s. *Greatham* (2,338 tons) sunk by U-Boat off Dartmouth ; 7 lost.

British s.s. *Admiral Cochrane* (6,565 tons) and *Corton* (3,405 tons) torpedoed by U-Boat in English Channel ; towed in.

British s.s. *Anglo-Canadian* (4,239 tons) and *Manchester Spinner* (4,247 tons) sunk by U-Boat off Malta ; 3 lost.

Emperor Charles held council in Vienna to hear Count Czernin's report on Brest negotiations.

January 23.

White Star s.s. *Justicia* (32,234 tons) attacked by U-Boat with torpedo in Irish Channel ; missed.

British Public Meals Order.

German gain and loss at Nieuport.

German Fourteenth (Italian) Army Command lapsed.

British s.s. *Birkhall* (4,541 tons) sunk by U-Boat off Cape d'Oro, Ægean ; 2 lost.

January 23 (*continued*).

Trotsky notified all foreign countries that German peace condition constituted " a demand for a most monstrous annexation."

January 24.

Counts Hertling and Czernin replied to Mr. Wilson and Mr. Lloyd George on war aims.

January 25.

U.S. auxiliary *Guinevere* wrecked on French coast.

British s.s. *Normandy* sunk by U-Boat off Cape La Hague ; 14 lost.

British s.s. *Eastlands* (3,113 tons) sunk by U-Boat off Ile de Vièrge ; 1 lost.

German raid E. of Loos.

Allied air raids on Mannheim, Treves, Thionville, and Saarbrücken.

Fighting between Bolshevist Red Guards and Finnish troops.

January 26.

U84 rammed and destroyed by H.M.S. P62 in approach to Irish Channel.

U109 destroyed by gunfire by H.M. drifter *Beryl III.* in Eastern Channel.

UB35 depth-charged and destroyed by H.M.S. *Leven* in Dover Straits.

British s.s. *Manhattan* (8,115 tons) torpedoed by U-Boat in English Channel ; reached port.

Boulogne, Dunkirk and Calais raided by German 3rd Bombing Squadron.

Petrograd Soviet declared war on Kieff Rada.

Hedjaz Arabs under Emir Feisul defeated Turks near Tafile.

* January 27.

Cunard s.s. *Andania* (13,405 tons) sunk by U-Boat N.N.E. from Rathlin Island ; 7 lost.

Allied air raid on Treves.

H.I.M.S. *Goeben* refloated and towed to Constantinople.

Gen. Dunsterville left Baghdad on his special mission to Baku.

January 28.

Air raid on London by 15 aeroplanes (German 3rd Bombing Squadron) in three groups ; about five machines penetrated defences ; later one other machine reached London ; 67 killed, 166 injured ; about 70 British airmen up ; one raider down in flames in Essex.

UB63 depth-charged and destroyed by H.M. trawlers *W. S. Bailey* and *Fort George* in North Sea.

H.M.S. *Hazard* sunk by collision in Channel.

M. Malvy indicted before High Court of French Senate.

Helsingfors captured by Red Guards.

Strikes in Berlin, Hamburg, Kiel, &c.

Italian attack between Asiago R.—Brenta Valley ; Col del Rosso taken ; 1,500 prisoners.

Austro-German delegates returned to Brest-Litovsk.

H.M. submarine E14 sunk in action in Dardanelles.

January 29.

British s.s. *Ethelinda* (3,257 tons) sunk by U-Boat N.W. from Skerries, Anglesea ; 26 lost.

January 29, 1918 (*continued*).

British s.s. *Butetown* (1,829 tons) sunk by U-Boat off Dodman Point ; 2 lost.

Aeroplane raid on London, Kent, and Essex ; 10 killed ; 10 injured.

British Naval air raid on Coolkerke aerodrome, N. of Bruges.

British s.s. *Geo* (3,048 tons) sunk by U-Boat off Cape Peloro, Sicily ; 16 lost.

Italian progress ; Mte. di Val Bella taken ; total 2,600 prisoners.

Trotsky returnd to Brest-Litovsk.

Helsingfors seized by Red Guards.

January 30.

Adm. Bronti to command Brazilian Fleet for service in European waters.

Versailles Council's third meeting.

German aeroplane raid on Paris ; 26 persons killed, 192 injured ; one raider down.

German strikes spread to Munich, &c ; intensified state of siege declared in Berlin ; *Vorwärts* suppressed.

Plenary sitting at Brest ; Soviet hopes raised by Berlin and Vienna outbreaks.

British s.s. *Maizer* (7,293 tons) sunk by U-Boat off Cape Ferrat.

British s.s. *Minnetonka* (13,528 tons) sunk by U-Boat E.N.E. from Malta ; 4 lost.

British line advanced near Anutieh, 12 miles N. of Jerusalem.

January 31.

Canadian War-Time Prohibition in force.

H.M. submarine E50 lost in North Sea.

H.M. submarines K4 and K17 (2,650 tons) sunk in collision in North Sea.

British s.s. *Towneley* (2,476 tons) sunk by U-Boat off Trevose Head ; 6 lost.

U95 lost in January ; cause unknown.

During January the German airship Fleet was reduced to 9 by disastrous fire at Ahlhorn (Oldenburg), which destroyed four Zeppelins and one Schütte-Lanz, and all the sheds except one.

Berlin riots suppressed ; Herr Dittmann, Independent Socialist Leader, arrested.

Austrians repulsed at Mte. di Val Bella.

February 1.

Sir E. Geddes stated Britain now sinking U-Boats as fast as Germany could build.

British s.s. *Cavallo* (2,086 tons) and s.v. *Kindly Light* sunk by U-Boat off Trevose Head ; 3 lost.

British s.s. *Arrino* (4,484 tons) sunk by U-Boat off Ile de Vièrge.

Sir D. Haig reports 171 German prisoners in January.

Germans behind Siegfried Line and in Artois prepare for grand assault on 21-iii.-18.

German Seventeenth Army formed in Thiérache under Gen. von Below, ex-Fourteenth Army.

Berlin strikes settled.

Central Powers recognised Ukraine Republic.

Greek troops mutinied at Lamia ; mutiny suppressed ; MM. Skouloudis and Lambros and other adherents of ex-King Constantine arrested.

British s.s. *Glenamoy* (7,269 tons) torpedoed by U-Boat in Mediterranean ; reached port.

February 2.

British s.s. *Jaffa* (1,383 tons) sunk by U-Boat off Owers Light ; 10 lost.

British s.s. *Avanti* (2,128 tons) sunk by U-Boat off St. Alban's Head ; 22 lost.

February 2 (*continued*).

British s.s. *Celia* (5,004 tons) and *New minster Abbey* (3,114 tons) sunk by U-Boat off Cape de Creus.

German raid on British line at Poelcapelle.

At Brest-Litovsk duel of words between Petrograd and Kieff delegates.

⋕ February 3.

Versailles Council's decision announced vigorous prosecution of war.

U.S. War Secretary stated U.S. troop now on actual battle-front in France.

British s.s. *Sofie* sunk by U-Boat in Bristol Channel ; 8 lost.

British s.s. *Lofoten* sunk by U-Boat off Start Point ; 17 lost.

British s.s. *Aboukir* (3,660 tons) sunk by U-Boat off Cape de Creus.

British occupied Utarika, Lujenda Valley, Mozambique ; Germans retreated eastward.

February 4.

UC50 depth-charged and destroyed by H.M.S. *Zubian* off Dungeness.

Cunard s.s. *Aurania* (13,936 tons) sunk by U-Boat off Inishtrahull ; 8 lost.

British s.s. *Treveal* (4,160 tons) sunk by U-Boat off Skerries, Anglesey ; 33 lost.

British s.s. *Standish Hall* (3,996 tons) sunk by U-Boat off Alexandria.

British s.s. *Sardinia* (6,580 tons) and *General Church* (6,600 tons) torpedoed by U-Boat in Mediterranean ; reached port.

Trial of Bolo Pasha begun in Paris.

Herr von Kühlmann and Count Czernin in Berlin to confer with G.H.Q.

German Nineteenth Army formed, under Gen. von Bothmer, ex-Southern Army disbanded.

Gen. Kaledin renounced headship of Don Cossacks in favour of Gen. Alexeieff.

February 5.

Cunard s.s. *Tuscania* (14,348 tons), with U.S. troops, torpedoed by U-Boat off Irish coast ; 166 missing.

British s.s. *Cresswell* (2,829 tons) sunk by U-Boat off Kish Light.

British s.s. *Mexico City* (5,087 tons) sunk by U-Boat off S. Stack, Holyhead ; 29 lost.

British s.s. *Glenartney* (7,263 tons) sunk by U-Boat off Cape Bon ; 2 lost.

French air raid on Saarbrücken.

Austro-German Brest delegates conferred in Berlin with Gen. Ludendorff, who urged immediate decisions.

February 6.

British s.s. *Westmoreland* (9,512 tons) torpedoed by U-Boat in Bristol Channel ; lost.

German raider *Wolf*, homeward bound in Denmark Strait.

Austro-German delegates returned Brest-Litovsk.

Germany gave Rumania four days within which to enter into peace negotiations.

Bratiano Cabinet resigned

February 7.

British s.s. *Beaumaris* (2,372 tons) sunk by U-Boat off the Longslips.

British s.s. *Sturton* (4,406 tons) sunk by U-Boat off Porquerolles Island.

Kaiser ordered Herr von Kühlmann terminate negotiations at Brest and to demand Russian Baltic Provinces.

February 8, 1918.

Lord Jellicoe hoped U-Boats would be killed by about August.

H.M.S. *Boxer* sunk by collision in Channel.

U38 mined in Folkestone Barrage.

British s.s. *Basuta* (2,876 tons) sunk by U-Boat off Lizard ; 1 lost.

Gen. Giardina Italian member of Versailles Committee vice Gen. Cadorna.

French repulsed German attacks N. of Chemin-des-Dames and in Woevre.

British s.s. *Artesia* (2,762 tons) sunk by U-Boat E. by N. from Madeira ; 1 lost.

British s.s. *Cimbrier* (3,905 tons) torpedoed by U-Boat in Mediterranean ; reached port.

February 9.

Embargo on Dutch commercial cables provisionally raised.

At Brest-Litovsk Central Powers signed separate peace with Ukraine, providing for export of 1,000,000 tons of surplus foodstuffs in return for concession of Kholm territory.

Gen. Averescu formed Rumanian Cabinet.

British s.s. *Lydie* (2,559 tons) sunk by U-Boat off Manacles ; 2 lost.

British s.s. *Antenor* (5,319 tons) torpedoed by U-Boat in Mediterranean ; reached port.

*February 10.

Soviet Russia out of the war ; army to demobilise. Trotsky evaded formal treaty with Central Powers.

Lord Beaverbrook Minister of Propaganda, vice Sir E. Carson.

Australian raid near Warneton (Messines).

Austrian attacks at Asiago defeated.

British s.s. *Romford* (3,035 tons) sunk by U-Boat off Cape Carthage ; 28 lost.

February 11.

President Wilson in Congress stated that no general peace should be obtained by separate negotiations.

H.M. special service ship *Westphalia* (1,467 tons) sunk by U-Boat in Irish Sea.

British s.s. *Baku Standard* (3,708 tons) sunk by U-Boat off Tod Head ; 24 lost.

British s.s. *Merton Hall* (4,327 tons) sunk by U-Boat off Ushant ; 57 lost.

French air raid on Metz.

Berlin announced 31 air raids in Germany during January : 14 casualties.

Austrian defeat about Frenzela Gorge ; attempted landing at Zenson loop of Piave prevented.

Trotsky intimated Russia would neither fight nor negotiate.

February 12.

Mr. Lloyd George indicated change in military situation owing to enormous German reinforcements, and stated that Versailles decisions were unanimous.

U89 rammed and sunk by H.M.S. *Roxburgh* off N. Ireland.

H.M. mine-carrier *Eleanor* (1,980 tons) sunk by U-Boat off St. Catherine's Point ; 34 lost.

British s.s. *Polo* (2,915 tons) sunk by U-Boat off St. Catherine's Point ; 3 lost.

Canadian raids near Hargicourt—Lens.

French air raids on Thionville, Conflans, Chambley, and Metz-Sablons.

Germans bombed Nancy.

British air raid on Offenburg.

Austrian attack in Col Caprile area defeated.

U-Boat officially reported sunk by Japanese T.B.D. in Mediterranean.

February 13.

British s.s. *Lackawanna* (4,125 tons) torpedoed by U-Boat in North Sea ; reached port.

French, after artillery preparation, in which U.S. batteries participated, won German salient between Tahure—Butte du Mesnil (Champagne) on 1,500-yard front ; penetrate German third line ; 177 prisoners.

Gen. Alexeieff defeated by Bolshevists ; Gen. Kaledin committed suicide.

Ludendorff at Homburg promised the Kaiser a German victory in coming offensive.

French submarine *Bernouilli* lost in Adriatic.

February 14.

British s.s. *Saga* (1,143 tons) sunk by U-Boat off Sunderland.

British s.s. *Atlas* (3,090 tons) sunk by U-Boat off Hartlepool.

British s.s. *Carlisle Castle* (4,325 tons) and *War Monarch* (7,887 tons) sunk by U-Boat off Royal Sovereign Light.

British s.s. *Ventmoor* (3,456 tons) sunk by U-Boat off Skyros ; 21 lost.

Canadian raid at Lens.

Bolo Pasha condemned to death.

Gen. Allenby advanced 2 miles on 6-mile front at Mukhmas, E. of Jerusalem—Shechem road.

February 15.

Dover shelled by U-Boat : 1 child killed, 7 persons wounded.

German 2nd (Heinecke) T.B.D. Flotilla, from the Bight, raided Folkestone-Gris Nez Barrage ; one British Admiralty trawler and seven drifters sunk ; raiders chased by Dover T.B.D. Patrol, made for Zeebrugge, outside which H.I.M. T.B.D. G102 ran on a mine and was damaged.

Spread of Bolshevist domination in Finland.

British s.s. *San Rito* (3,310 tons) sunk by U-Boat off Chios ; 3 lost.

February 16.

Gen. Sir Henry Wilson Chief of Imperial General Staff, vice Gen. Robertson.

Air raid on London by six German aeroplanes ; one penetrated defences : 12 killed, 6 injured.

Raid on Dover beaten off ; one German machine destroyed.

British s.s. *Pikepool* (3,683 tons) torpedoed by U-Boat in English Channel ; reached port.

U.S. Army Supply Services at Tours.

*February 17.

Air raid on London by six or seven machines ; one penetrated defences ; 21 killed, 32 injured.

British s.s. *Northville* (2,472 tons) sunk by U-Boat off Berry Head.

British s.s. *Pinewood* (2,219 tons) sunk by U-Boat off Mine Head ; 2 lost.

British airmen bombed railway at Conflans.

German G.H.Q. announced Russian armistice expired on Feb. 18.

Gen. Dunsterville at Enzeli.

February 18.

Air raid on London ; no machine penetrated defences. No casualties.

British raid in Houthulst Forest.

German attempt near Tahure (Champagne) defeated.

Sundays marked with Asterisk (*).

February 18, 1918 (continued).
British airmen bombed Treves and Thionville twice within 36 hours ; two machines missing.

Hostilities resumed in Russia ; German army crossed Dvina, occupied Dvinsk—Lutsk ; German advance on Kovel.

Russians evacuated Armenia.

Turks at Platana, 8 miles from Trebizond.

February 19.
British s.s. *Beacon Light* (2,768 tons) sunk by U-Boat S.E. from Butt of Lewis ; 33 lost.

British s.s. *Glencarron* (5,117 tons) and *Philadelphian* (5,165 tons) sunk by U-Boat S.E. from Lizard ; 4 lost.

British s.s. *Barrowmore* (3,832 tons) sunk by U-Boat N.W. from Bishop Rock ; 25 lost.

British s.s. *Commonwealth* (3,353 tons) sunk by U-Boat off Flamborough Head ; 14 lost.

British s.s. *Athenic* (4,078 tons) torpedoed by U-Boat in North Sea ; towed in.

Mr. Lloyd George defended Versailles arrangements and Government action with regard to Gen. Robertson.

Gen. Rawlinson appointed to Versailles.

German armies advanced from Riga to Volhynia into heart of Russia ; 2,500 prisoners, several hundred guns taken.

Gen. Allenby advanced 2 miles on 15-mile front towards Jericho.

U-Boat officially reported sunk by Japanese T.B.D. in Mediterranean.

February 20.
French raid in Lorraine, E. of Nancy ; 525 prisoners.

German advance towards Reval, Petrograd, Moscow, and Kieff ; 9,000 prisoners to date.

Bolshevists ready to negotiate.

British s.s. *Djerv* (1,527 tons) sunk by U-Boat off Skerries, Anglesea ; 2 lost.

British s.s. *Huntsmoor* (4,927 tons) sunk by U-Boat off Owers Light ; 20 lost.

British s.s. *Balgray* (3,603 tons) sunk by U-Boat off Dellimara Point, Malta.

Gen. Allenby within 4 miles of Jericho ; advance N. of Jerusalem on 4-mile front up Shechem road.

Gen. Marshall advanced up Euphrates and occupied Khan Aby Rayat, 14 miles N. of Ramadie ; patrols within 10 miles of Hit.

Gen. Dunsterville returned from Enzeli to Hamadan, his H.Q. until 1-vi.-18.

February 21.
German terms to Russia : Poland, Baltic Provinces, Lithuania, Ukraine, and Finland to be surrendered ; army to be demobilised and warships, including those of Entente, to be disarmed or interned ; commercial Treaty of 1904 to be resumed ; German forces 50 miles from Petrograd and 60 miles from Reval ; Hapsal and Minsk occupied.

Turks reconquering Armenia ; 50 miles behind former Russian front.

Fall of Jericho to Gen. Allenby. Australian Mounted Brigade entered the city. British established on Jordan, threatening Hedjaz railway.

British s.s. *Rio Verde* (4,025 tons) sunk by U-Boat off Mull of Galloway ; 20 lost.

British s.s. *Cheviot Range* (3,691 tons) sunk by U-Boat S. from Lizard ; 27 lost.

February 22.
British s.s. *Haileybury* (2,888 tons) sunk by U-Boat S.E. from the Maidens ; 2 lost.

February 22 (continued).
German raid on British line on Ypres—Staden railway.

Germans at Walk (Baltic Provinces).

February 23.
British s.s. *Remus* (1,079 tons) sunk by U-Boat S.W. from Copinsay, Orkney ; 5 lost.

British s.s. *British Viscount* (3,287 tons) sunk by U-Boat off Skerries, Anglesey ; 6 lost.

British s.s. *Birchleaf* (5,873 tons) torpedoed by U-Boat in Irish Channel ; beached ; 3 lost ; master taken prisoner.

Franco-American raid over Ailette R.

German armies nearing Reval and Kieff.

Turks N. of Jericho and beyond Jordan ; holding bridgehead giving access to Hedjaz railway.

＊February 24.
Inter-Allied Labour Conference at Westminster published memorandum on War Aims.

British s.s. *Renfrew* (3,830 tons) sunk by U-Boat off St. Anne's Head ; 40 lost.

British s.s. *Nyanza* (6,695 tons) torpedoed by U-Boat in English Channel ; towed into Newhaven ; 4 lost.

German raider *Wolf* at Kiel after 15 months' cruise ; 11 vessels presumably sunk by *Wolf* in Indian and Pacific Oceans.

Esthonian Republic proclaimed.

Germans took Dorpat ; 3,000 prisoners reached Zhitomir.

Turks recaptured Trebizond.

February 25.
First London Ration Order.

UB17 depth-charged and destroyed by H.M.SS. *Onslow* and *Polyanthus* and H.M. trawlers *Wimpole*, *Robert Preston*, and *John Pasco*.

British s.s. *Rubio* (2,395 tons) mined off Shipwash Light.

British s.s. *Appalachee* (3,767 tons) torpedoed by U-Boat off N. Ireland ; towed in.

German North Corps took Reval.

German Ukraine campaign continued.

Gen. Liman von Sanders succeeded Gen. von Falkenhayn in the Yildirim command (see 9-vii.-17).

February 26.
H.S. *Glenart Castle* (6,824 tons), outward bound, sunk in Bristol Channel ; of 200 on board, 38 survived.

British s.s. *Tideria* (4,880 tons) sunk by U-Boat off Black Head.

British s.s. *Dalewood* (2,420 tons) sunk by U-Boat off Isle of Man ; 19 lost.

British s.s. *Berwen* (3,752 tons) mined in North Sea ; towed in.

British s.s. *Greavesash* (1,263 tons) and *Romny* (1,024 tons) sunk by U-Boat off Cape Barfleur ; 17 lost.

British s.s. *Eumalus* (6,696 tons) sunk by U-Boat off Ile de Vièrge.

British s.s. *Maltby* (3,977 tons) sunk by U-Boat S.W. from Pantellaria ; 5 lost.

British patrols reached Dead Sea.

February 27.
Germans at Wesenberg (Esthonia).

Count Czernin met King Ferdinand of Rumania at Rasaciuni station and urged acceptance of Austro-German terms.

British s.s. *Machaon* (6,738 tons) sunk by U-Boat N.E. from Cani Rocks, Tunis.

For List of Abbreviations see page iv.

February 27, 1918 (*continued*).

British s.s. *Kerman* (4,397 tons) and *Marconi* (7,402 tons) torpedoed by U-Boat in Mediterranean ; reached port ; 2 lost.

British s.s. *Princess Irma* (1,520 tons), *Kirkham Abbey* (1,166 tons) and *Lady Carmichael* (tug) attacked by German aircraft with bombs and machine-gun off Hook of Holland ; tug slightly damaged.

February 28.

During February the Channel Train Ferry Service was opened.

Germans took Rieshitza.

Austrians invaded Ukraine.

Gen. Brooking at Ana, Euphrates.

March 1,

H.M. A.M.C. *Calgarian* (17,515 tons) torpedoed by U-boat off Irish coast.

British s.s. *Penvearn* (3,710 tons) sunk by U-Boat off S. Stack ; 21 lost.

German T.B.D. and two minesweepers mined off Vlieland.

British on W. Front during February took 312 prisoners.

British raid S. of Armentières ; many German raids in Flanders, particularly on Portuguese front near Neuve Chapelle.

Germans attacked at the Butte du Mesnil ; gained footing in positions captured by French on Feb. 13.

Germans entered Kieff and Gomel.

March 2.

Germany informed Sweden she proposed to use Aaland Islands as base for German expedition to Finland ; 15 German warships reported off Gothland.

British s.s. *Carmelite* (2,583 tons) sunk by U-Boat off Calf of Man ; 2 lost.

British s.s. *Rockpool* (4,502 tons) sunk by U-Boat off Eagle Island.

British s.s. *Kenmare* (1,330 tons) sunk by U-Boat off Skerries, Anglesey ; 29 lost.

Germans took Zhmerinka.

Soviet delegates returned to Brest.

Rumania agreed to negotiate.

*March 3.

German attacks on Belgians near Nieuport defeated.

British raid at Warneton.

German attempts near Lens and N. and S. of St. Quentin.

German military movements in Great Russia ended ; over 60,000 prisoners, 2,600 guns claimed since beginning of operations.

Soviet Russia signed Peace of Brest-Litovsk with four Central and confederate Powers.

Germans demanded surrender of Ardahan, Kars, and Batum. Bolshevists accepted German terms.

Gen. Allenby advanced 3,000 yards on 3-mile front between Jerusalem—Schechem.

British s.s. *Romeo* (1,730 tons) sunk by U-Boat off Mull of Galloway ; 29 lost.

British s.s. *Northfield* (2,099 tons) sunk by U-Boat off Lundy Island ; 15 lost.

March 4.

Australian raid at Warneton.

French raid near Les Eparges (Woevre).

Germans reached Narva.

Rumania accepted Central terms: cession of Dobrudja to Bulgaria, readjustment of frontier between Rumania and Hungary.

British s.s. *Clan Macpherson* (4,779 tons) sunk by U-Boat off Cape Serrat ; 18 lost.

March 4 (*continued*).

British s.s. *Roxburgh* (4,630 tons) sunk by U-Boat off Cape St. John, Crete ; 6 lost.

British s.s. *Clan Graham* (5,213 tons) torpedoed by U-Boat in Mediterranean ; reached port ; 3 lost.

British s.s. *Castle Eden* (1,949 tons) sunk by U-Boat off Inistrahull ; 1 lost.

British s.s. *British Princess* (7,034 tons) torpedoed by U-Boat off N. Ireland ; reached port ; 1 lost.

March 5.

Belgian counter-attack N. of Pervyse ; 100 prisoners, seven machine guns.

German Expedition to Finland, escorted by H.I.M.SS. *Westfalen* (F. Adm. Meurer), *Rheinland* and, later, *Posen*, with attendant craft, arrived off Eckerö, Aaland Islands.

Germans formally occupied Livonia and Esthonia.

Preliminary Treaty between Rumania and Central Powers concluded at Buftea.

British s.s. *Kosseir* (1,855 tons) attacked by aircraft in Mediterranean.

Sir E. Geddes on falling off in ship building.

British s.s. *Uskmoor* (3,189 tons) sunk by U-Boat off Prawle Point.

British s.s. *Estrella* (1,740 tons) mined off Shipwash Light ; 20 lost.

British s.s. *Clan Mackenzie* (6,544 tons) torpedoed by U-Boat in Channel ; reached port ; 6 lost.

March 6.

H.M. submarine H5 sunk by collision in Irish Sea.

Inter-Allied Committee for Chemical Warfare supplies formed.

British s.s. *Kalgan* (1,862 tons) sunk by U-Boat off Yafa, Syria ; 1 lost.

March 7.

Air raid on London (moonless night) ; two out of seven or eight raiders penetrated defences : 23 killed, 39 injured.

British s.s. *Tarbetness* (3,018 tons) sunk by U-Boat off Carnarvon Light.

British s.s. *Cliffside* (4,969 tons) torpedoed by U-Boat in English Channel ; beached.

German raid N.W. of La Bassée.

Peace between Germany and Finland.

Gen. Allenby advanced 3 miles on 18-mile front across Jerusalem—Schechem road.

March 8.

German gain S. of Houthulst Forest ; counter-attack drove Germans behind original line. German attack near Polderhoek Château S. of Ypres.

Aeroplane raid on Paris by German 1st, 5th, and 7th Bombing Squadrons ; one Gotha down.

British s.s. *Corsham* (2,760 tons) sunk by U-Boat off Tees R. ; 9 lost.

British s.s. *Madeline* (2,890 tons) sunk by U-Boat off Pendeen ; 3 lost.

British s.s. *Saba* (4,257 tons) mined in English Channel ; reached port.

British s.s. *Ayr* (3,050 tons) and *Uganda* (4,315 tons) sunk by U-Boat off Linosa ; 1 lost.

British s.s. *Mitra* (5,592 tons) torpedoed by U-Boat in Mediterranean ; reached port.

Four-day battle for Tel-el-Sur (Palestine).

Sundays marked with Asterisk (*).

March 9, 1918.

U.S. Navy commissioned by British Admiralty to lay oil pipe-line from Clyde to Forth (see 11-vii.-18 and 9-xi.-18).

German raid on Portuguese near Neuve Chapelle ; counter-attack penetrated German second line.

British s.s. *Silverdale* (3,835 tons) sunk by U-Boat off Cani Rocks, Tunis.

British airmen on Italian Front during period from 10-xi.-17 to date brought down 64 Austro-German aeroplanes and 9 balloons ; 12 British machines and 3 balloons lost.

Gen. Allenby's troops forced Auja R. on British right ; in centre Tel-el-Sur mountain barrier overcome ; fighting in Robbers' Valley, 12 miles from Schechem.

Gen. Marshall occupied Hit (Euphrates).

✳March 10.

H.S. *Guildford Castle* (8,036 tons), homeward bound from E. Africa, torpedoed in Bristol Channel ; reached port.

UB58 mined in Folkestone Barrage.

French Shipping Requisition.

Gen. the Earl of Cavan in command of British Forces in Italy, vice Gen. Plumer, who returned to France.

British s.s. *Chagres* (5,288 tons) sunk by U-Boat off Cape Drepano, Crete ; 1 lost.

Turks retreating from Hit occupied Khan Baghdadie on Aleppo road.

March 11.

German 1st and 7th Bombing Squadrons raid Paris ; four raiders down ; 34 killed, 79 injured, and 66 suffocated in panic in underground refuges.

UB54 depth-charged and destroyed by H.M.SS. *Sturgeon, Thruster,* and *Retriever* in North Sea.

French submarine *Diane* lost in Channel.

Australian raids near Messines.

German raids at Passchendaele Ridge, near Armentières, and against Portuguese, near Laventie, defeated.

British s.s. *Nellore's* sixth escape from U-Boat.

British s.s. *Stolt-Nielsen* (5,684 tons) sunk by U-Boat off Dellimara Point, Malta.

British advance astride the Jerusalem—Schechem road.

Turks retook Erzrum after stern Armenian defence.

March 12.

Three Zeppelins raided Yorks ; Hull bombed ; one killed.

British s.s. *Savan* (4,264 tons) and *Clarissa Radcliffe* (5,754 tons) torpedoed by U-Boat in English Channel ; reached port.

Germans repulsed at Vaudesincourt. E. of Reims.

Germans landed at Abo (Finland).

Germans reached Odessa.

French T.B. 333 sunk by collision in W. Mediterranean.

British three-mile advance on 11-mile front on Palestine coast ; five villages taken.

Japanese and Chinese volunteers in fight with Bolshevists at Blagovestchensk (Amur) ; 11 Japanese casualties.

March 13.

Raid by Zeppelin on Durham ; Hartlepool bombed ; 8 killed and 39 injured.

British s.s. *Crayford* (1,209 tons) sunk by U-Boat off Skudenes ; 1 lost.

British s.s. *Tweed* (1,025 tons) sunk by U-Boat off St. Catherine's Point ; 7 lost.

March 13 (*continued*).

German strong point S.E. of Polygo Wood carried ; Australian raid near Ypres–Comines Canal.

Allied air raids on Coblenz and Freiburg

Petrograd being evacuated. U.S. Embass removed to Vologda.

March 14.

French recovery on Moronvilliers Ridg (Reims).

Moscow Soviet Congress ratified Bres Treaty.

Germans took Bakhmatch.

British s.s. *Comrie Castle* (5,173 ton torpedoed by U-Boat in English Channel beached ; 9 lost.

British s.s. *Ardandearg* (3,237 tons) sun by U-Boat off Malta ; 2 lost.

B.I. s.s. *Umta* (5,422 tons) torpedoed b U-Boat in Mediterranean ; reached Naples c 17-iii.-18 ; 8 lost.

British in Jordan Valley secure groun overlooking Jericho—Schechem road, 3 mile N. of Wadi Auja.

March 15.

H.M. submarine D3 accidentally sunl in Channel.

U110 depth-charged and destroyed b H.M.SS. *Moresby* and *Michael* off N. Irelanc

R.M.S.P. s.s. *Amazon* (10,037 tons) sun by U-Boat off Malin Head.

British s.s. *Armonia* (5,226 tons) sunk b U-Boat off Porquerolles Is., Toulon ; 7 los

British s.s. *Clan Macdougall* (4,710 ton sunk by U-Boat off Cape Carbonara, Sa dinia ; 33 lost.

March 16.

French raids near Cheppy—Malancou (Verdun) ; 160 prisoners. Germans pen trate French trenches at Samogneux—Bea mont—Bezonvaux ; 200 prisoners claimed.

British air raid on Zweibrücken.

H.M. oiler *Oilfield* (4,000 tons) sunk k U-Boat 15 miles N.W. from Cape Wrath.

British s.s. *Author* (5,596 tons) slightl damaged by U-Boat torpedo in Englis Channel.

H.M. collier *Ellaston* sunk by U-Boat 180 miles W. by S. from Palma (Canary Is.).

✳March 17.

British s.s. *Sea Gull* (976 tons) sunk k U-Boat off Lynas Point ; 20 lost.

British s.s. *Ivydene* (3,541 tons) sunk k U-Boat off Cape Bugaroni, Algeria ; 1 lost.

British s.s. *Waihemo* (4,283 tons) sur by U-Boat in Gulf of Athens.

Germans took Nikolaieff, Black Sea.

March 18.

British s.s. *Bayyitano* (3,073 tons) sur by U-Boat off Lyme Regis ; 2 lost.

British s.s. *Grainton* (6,042 tons) to pedoed by U-Boat in Irish Sea ; reache port.

Holland accepted Allied terms for use Dutch shipping in U.S. and Entente ports exchange for food.

British and Portuguese raids on Arme tières and Cambrai fronts.

French raid near Reims.

British air raid on Mannheim ; 38 rai into Germany since October ; 448 tons explosives dropped.

German G.H.Q. moved forward from S to Avesnes.

March 18, 1918 (*continued*).

Entente Note on German crimes against Russia ; Russo-German treaty not recognised.

British s.s. *Saldanha* (4,594 tons) sunk by U-Boat off Algiers ; 6 lost.

British s.s. *John H. Barry* (3,083 tons) sunk by U-Boat off Cape Bugaroni, Algeria ; 3 lost.

March 19.

British s.s. *Burnstone* (2,340 tons) sunk by U-Boat off Farn Islands ; 5 lost.

British s.s. *Luxor* (3,571 tons) sunk by U-Boat off St. Catherine's Point.

Mr. Baker, U.S. War Secretary, inspected 1st and 42nd Divisions on W. Front.

H.M. A.M.C. *Montagna* torpedoed by U-Boat in Western Channel.

German attacks near Souain (Champagne) defeated ; at Bois Brulé (Woevre) ; Germans gained and lost foothold in French trenches.

British gain in foothills overlooking Plain of Sharon.

March 20.

President Wilson authorised seizure of Dutch ships in U.S. ports.

Sir E. Geddes stated world tonnage from beginning of war to end of 1917 fallen by 8 per cent. net ; British tonnage by 20 per cent. net ; total tonnage sunk in first year of unrestricted U-Boat warfare 6,000,000, against German claims of 9,500,000.

Lord Pirrie Controller-General of Merchant Shipbuilding.

British s.s. *Kassanga* (3,015 tons) sunk by U-Boat off Arklow Light.

British s.s. *Custodian* (9,214 tons) torpedoed by U-Boat in Irish Channel ; reached port.

British s.s. *Boorara* (6,570 tons) torpedoed in Channel ; reached port ; 5 lost.

Calais and Dunkirk raided by German Third Bombing Squadron.

Mr. Baker, U.S. War Secretary, inspected 2nd U.S. Division on W. Front.

German armies, after three months' preparations, in position for new Western offensive ; final council at German G.H.Q. Avesnes. Over 40 German divisions transferred from E. to W. front.

H.M. oiler *Samoset* (5,251 tons) and s.s. *St. Dimitrios* (3,359 tons) and *Yochow* (2,127 tons) sunk by U-Boat 50 miles N.E. from Port Said ; 53 lost.

British s.s. *Lord Ormonde* (3,914 tons) torpedoed by U-Boat in Mediterranean ; reached port.

March 21.

The Kaiser-Battle.

German Offensive began. First Assault : Second Somme Battle : German Seventeenth, Second, and Eighteenth Armies (Gens. O. von Below, von der Marwitz, and von Hutier, under joint direction of German and Bavarian Crown Princes) attacked British Third and Fourth Armies on 50-mile front between Scarpe—Oise. British defences penetrated ; 40 out of 60 German divisions identified. Germans took Bullecourt, Noreuil, Longatte, Ecoust St. Mein, Doignies, Lagnicourt, Louverval, Roussoy, Hargicourt. Villeret, Templeux, and Maissliny. S. of St. Quentin they occupied Essigny, Benay, and Quessy. Fine British resistance, especially at Epéhy and Le Verguier, which remained untaken, and round Lagnicourt.

March 21 (*continued*).

British s.s. *Ikeda* (6,311 tons) sunk by U-Boat off Brighton Light.

British s.s. *Begonia* (3,070 tons) sunk by U-Boat off Wolf Rock.

H.M. T.B.D.s *Botha* and *Morris* and French T.B.D.s *Mehl*, *Magon*, and *Bouclier* sank two German T.B.D.s in North Sea : later, in action with five German T.B.D.s, which bombarded Dunkirk, sank one, possibly two. Raiders chased back to Zeebrugge by British C.M.B. and R.N.A.S. squadron.

British monitors bombarded Ostend.

Capt. Marshall, British Political Officer at Nejef, murdered.

March 22.

Somme Battle : Germans broke through British positions W. and S.W. of St. Quentin ; endeavoured to turn British right ; forced Crozat Canal at Jussy—Quessy—La Montagne ; took Tergnier. British stand at Fontaine-les-Clercs. N. from St. Quentin Germans took Holmon Wood, Caulaincourt, Le Verguier, Roisel, St. Emilie, Villers Faucon, Epéhy, and St. Léger. British retired to Somme line; abandoned Flesquières salient, W. of Cambrai. Germans claimed 16,000 prisoners, 200 guns.

Kaiser conferred on Hindenburg the Iron Cross with Golden Rays ; this unique distinction bestowed only on Blücher after Waterloo.

H.M. sloop *Gaillardia* mined in North Sea ; 68 lost.

British s.s. *Polleon* (1,155 tons) sunk by U-Boat off the Tyne ; 4 lost.

British s.s. *Trinidad* (2,592 tons) sunk by U-Boat off Codling Light ; 39 lost.

H.M.T. *Chupra* (6,175 tons) slightly damaged in action E. from Azores with U-Boat, which fired 40 rounds.

Gen. Allenby crossed Jordan, advanced towards the Hedjaz Railway.

March 23.

Somme Battle : Fall of Ham to Germans ; British in new positions S. and W. of St. Quentin ; new German efforts to turn British right defeated at Jussy ; Germans seized Aubigny, Brouchy, and Ollezy.

French in action on British right ; took over part of British line ; Germans claimed 25,000 prisoners and 400 guns to date. British line at end of day from N. to S. : Boyelles—Beugny—Bertincourt—Bus—Péronne — St. Epenancourt—Pargny—Bethencourt — Voyennes—S. of Ham—S. of Tergnier.

Gen. Fayolle organising line of resistance with Gen. Humbert's Third Army covering Noyon and Oise R., while Gen. Debeney's First Army covered Roye—Moreuil.

Paris shelled for seven hours at 20-minute intervals by long-range gun at Crépy. near Laon, about 70 miles off ; aeroplane raid.

British s.s. *Etonian* (6,515 tons) sunk by U-Boat off Old Head of Kinsale ; 7 lost.

British s.s. *Meline* (6,970 tons) torpedoed by U-Boat in North Sea ; reached port.

British s.s. *Sequoya* (5,263 tons) torpedoed by U-Boat in English Channel ; reached port.

British airmen raided Bruges docks.

Boulogne raided by German 3rd Bombing Squadron.

H.M. T.B.D. *Arno* sunk by collision off Dardanelles.

British s.s. *Demodocus* (6,689 tons) torpedoed by U-Boat in Mediterranean ; reached port ; 6 lost.

Sundays marked with Asterisk (*).

March 23, 1918 (*continued*).
British **s.s.** *Shadwell* (4,091 tons) torpedoed by U-Boat in Mediterranean ; reached port ; 13 lost.
B.I. **s.s.** *Morvada* (8,193 tons), in convoy through Mediterranean, attacked by U-Boat with torpedo ; torpedo deflected by gunfire.

＊March 24.
Somme Battle : Fall of Péronne and Bapaume to Germans. Gallant stand by S. Africans in Marrières Wood, which they lost. Further S. Germans took Nesle, Guiscard, and Chauny ; 30,000 prisoners and 300 guns claimed to date. Allies now on general line Boyelles—Sapignies—Ligny, Le Sars—Bazentin, Montauban—Herr—Biaches — Epenancourt—W. of Nesle—W. of Guiscard.
German attack E. of Lunéville defeated.
Paris again bombarded by " Big Bertha," long range gun ; 27 shells.
British air raid on Cologne.
Italian mining-vessel *Partenope* sunk by U-Boat off Bizerta.
British s.s. *Anchoria* (5,430 tons) torpedoed by U-Boat off N. Ireland ; reached port.
British s.s. *Anteros* (4,241 tons) sunk by U-Boat off S. Stack ; 2 lost.
British s.s. *War Knight* (7,951 tons) mined after collision in English Channel ; on fire ; beached ; 32 lost.
Gen. Allenby 11 miles E. of Jordan.

March 25.
M. Clemenceau, Lord Milner, Gens. Haig, Wilson and Pétain at Doullens decided to appoint Gen. Foch Allied C.-in-C.
Somme Battle : Heavy fighting between Péronne—Bapaume ; Germans reached, near Maricourt, their original July, 1916, line ; 45,000 prisoners, 600 guns claimed to date. French (Gen. Pellé) evacuated Noyon. Allies by end of day on general line Puisieux—Beaucourt—line of the Ancre to E. of Albert—Braye — Frise — Hattencourt — Liancourt—W. of Noyon.
Gen. Grant organised and later transferred to Gen. Carey a " mixed " force collected for defence of British line S. of Somme.
Paris again bombarded by long-range gun ; one gun burst ; crew killed.
British s.s. *Warturm* (4,965 tons) torpedoed by U-Boat in Mediterranean ; 2 lost.
British took Es Salt ; progress towards Hedjaz Railway at Amman.
Japan and China agreed to co-operate in resisting hostile influences likely to endanger peace in Far East.

March 26.
Boulogne, Dunkirk, Calais raided by German 3rd Bombing Squadron.
Somme Battle : Fighting N. of Somme died down ; British line through Sailly-le-Sec, Albert, Beaumont Hamel, Puisieux, Ayette, Boiry, Henin, and Wancourt to Scarpe R. Heavy German attacks S. of Somme ; Roye, Chaulnes, Hattencourt, Liancourt, Estrées, and Bray lost ; in S.W. corner of front Germans, aiming at Montdidier, took Le Quesnoy and reached Erches, but British clung to Andechy on flank and held up advance. British, French, and Americans in action ; French reinforcements arrived. Germans claimed 963 guns and 100 Tanks.
First British Whippet Tanks in action at Mailly-Maillet.
Preliminaries of Rumanian Treaty initialled.

March 26 (*continued*).
Gen. Allenby's cavalry approached A٢ man, Hedjaz Railway.
Gen. Marshall defeated Turkish Army Khan Baghdadie ; 3,000 prisoners.
H.M. mine-carrier *Lady Cory-Wright* su٢ by U-Boat off the Lizard ; 39 lost.
U61 depth-charged and destroyed H.M.S. P51 in approach to Irish Channel.
British s.s. *British Star* (6,888 tons) t٢ pedoed by U-Boat in North Sea ; reach٢ port.

March 27.
Somme Battle : British line held N. Somme, but Albert lost ; N. of Ancre Ablain٢ ville and Ayette taken by Germans ; Germa٢ aiming at Amiens crossed to S. bank of Som٢ between Cerisy—Chipilly and force Briti٢ out of Proyart, Frameviller, and Morcou٢ further S. they took Lassigny, Andech٢ Davenescourt, and Montdidier. Allied li٢ now ran W. of Ablainzeville and Ayette٢ Beaucourt—W. of Albert—Bouzencourt٢ Harbonnières—Rosières—Arvillers—S.W. Montdidier—W. of Lassigny.
H.M.S. *Kale* mined in North Sea.
British s.s. *Allendale* (2,153 tons) su٢ by U-Boat off the Lizard ; 1 lost.
British s.v. *Watauga* sunk by U-Boat ٢ by N. from Lisbon ; 5 lost.

March 28.
H.M. T.B.D.s *Abdiel*, *Legion*, *Telemach٢ Vanquisher*, *Ariel*, and *Ferret* swept i٢ Heligoland Bight, destroyed three Germ٢ armed trawlers and captured 72 officers a٢ men.
Gen. Rawlinson in command of Brit٢ forces S. of Somme ; Gen. Gough to organ٢ new British defence lines.
German attack in Scarpe Valley E. Arras towards Vimy Ridge repulsed w٢ heavy loss. Germans claimed 70,000 prisone٢ 1,100 guns to date. Germans beaten S. of Scarpe in Bucquoy sector ; furth٢ German progress towards Amiens as far٢ Hamel. French progress in Montdidier sect٢
Gen. Pershing at Clermont offered G٢ Foch of all available U.S. forces.
Fighting at El-Kafr (Palestine).
British s.s. *Inkosi* (3,661 tons) sunk٢ U-Boat off Mull of Galloway ; 3 lost.
British s.s. *Dryden* (5,839 tons) mined٢ R. Mersey ; reached port.
H.M. armed steamer *Tithonus* sunk٢ U-Boat in North Sea.

March 29.
German progress between Albert—A٢ R., 11 miles from Amiens.
Good Friday. Long-range bombardme٢ of Paris ; shell hit church of St. Gerv٢ crowded with worshippers during servi٢ About 75 killed, 90 injured.
Gen. Pershing telegraphed to U.S. W٢ Department that he had " made all our ٢ sources available, and our Divisions will used if and when needed."
British troops from Montello (Pia٢ sector relieved Italians between Asiago a٢ Canove.
Germans occupied Poltava.
British s.s. *T. R. Thompson* (3,538 to٢ sunk by U-Boat seven miles S. from Ne٢ haven ; 33 lost.

March 30.
King George returned from W. Front٢
Mr. Lloyd George announced Gen. Foc٢ appointment to co-ordinate action of Alli٢ Armies in France.

March 30, 1918 (*continued*).

Fighting N. of Somme at Boiry—Boyelles ; Germans repulsed with loss ; near Serre British took 230 prisoners. Between Somme R.—Avre R. Germans took and lost Demuin. French retook Moreuil ; 700 prisoners.

*March 31.

Germans, after 10 days' battle called by Kaiser the " greatest in history," claimed 75,000 prisoners, about 1,000 guns.

French progress at Moreuil—Lassigny ; advance near Orvillers ; 200 prisoners.

German Bug Army disbanded.

Marshal von Eichhorn assumed command of German Kieff Army Group.

British retired from Amman-Es Salt.

White Star s.s. *Celtic* (20,904 tons) torpedoed by U-Boat in Irish Channel ; reached port ; 6 lost.

British s.s. *Conargo* (4,312 tons) sunk by U-Boat off Calf of Man ; 9 lost.

British s.s. *Excellence Pleske* (2,059 tons) sunk by U-Boat off Dungeness ; 13 lost.

British s.s. *Alcinous* (6,743 tons) torpedoed by U-Boat in English Channel ; reached port.

April 1

R.N.A.S. and R.F.C. amalgamated in R.A.F.

H.M.S. *Falcon* sunk by collision in North Sea.

British s.s. *Ardglass* (4,617 tons) sunk by U-Boat off the Maidens ; 6 lost.

U.S. battalions to be brigaded with French and British units so long as necessary.

British took prisoners near Hébuterne and between Avre R.—Luce R. French and British successes near Moreuil—Hangard ; French retained Grivesnes, 5 miles N.W. of Montdidier.

Gen. Marshall now 250 miles from Aleppo.

April 2.

British took Ayette, between Arras—Albert ; 192 prisoners. French widen salient N. of Le Plémont ; 60 prisoners.

Count Czernin in Vienna describes the import of Austrian overtures to France.

Germans at Ekaterinoslav.

British s.s. *Solway Queen* sunk by U-Boat off Black Head, Wigton ; 11 lost.

April 3.

German Balite (12th Landwehr) Division landed at Hangö (S. Finland), where Russian submarines AG11, 12, 13, and 15 had previously been destroyed ; gunboat *Bobyr* was captured. Finnish White Guards took Tammerfors.

H.M. submarines E1, E8, E9, E19, C26, C27, C35, destroyed at Helsingfors to avoid capture.

April 4.

Great German assault (20 divisions) along roads leading to Amiens ; advance either side of Moreuil ; slight British retirement near Hamel—Vaire Wood ; French surrendered Morisel—Mailly—Raineval, but advanced N. of Orvillers Sorel. Germans claimed 90,000 prisoners, 1,300 guns to date.

Failure of this day's assault compelled German G.H.Q. to abandon all further idea of taking Amiens.

H.M.S. *Bittern* sunk by collision in Channel.

April 5.

Strong German attacks from Somme N. beyond Bucquoy ; little success, heavy losses ; E. of Hébuterne British took 200 prisoners. French recovery between Moreuil—Montdidier.

Japanese and British Marines at Vladivostok ; Adm. Kato in command.

British s.s. *Cyrene* (2,904 tons) sunk by U-Boat off Bardsey Island ; 24 lost.

British s.s. *Clam* (3,552 tons) torpedoed by U-Boat in Irish Channel ; reached port.

April 6.

British retook Aveluy Wood, N. of Albert ; 140 prisoners. French withdrew near Chauny. Germans claimed 1,400 prisoners.

During first week in April British 52nd Division transferred from Palestine to W. Front ; its place taken by 7th (Meerut) Division from Mesopotamia.

Turks, after occupation of Ardahan, moved on Batum.

British s.s. *Headcliffe* (3,654 tons) repelled U-Boat attack by gunfire off Gambia R.

ML421 wrecked in Seaford Bay.

*April 7.

British s.s. *Boscastle* (2,346 tons) sunk by U-Boat off Strumble Head ; 18 lost.

British s.s. *Port Campbell* (6,230 tons) sunk by U-Boat W.S.W. from Bishop Rock.

British s.s. *Cadillac* (11,106 tons) and *Knight Templar* (7,175 tons) torpedoed by U-Boat W. and S.W. from Scilly Islands ; reached port.

British s.s. *Highland Brigade* (5,669 tons) sunk by U-Boat off St. Catherine's Point.

French withdrew between Oise—Coucy Forest ; Germans claimed Pierremand—Folembray and 2,000 prisoners.

Arabs under Emir Feisul occupied Kerak, Turkish headquarters E. of Dead Sea.

British s.s. *Eboe* (4,866 tons) attacked by U-Boat by gunfire off Sierra Leone ; escaped.

April 8.

British Front northward to Armentières heavily bombarded.

French retired S. of Oise from Lower Coucy Forest—Coucy le Château.

Germans entered Kharkoff.

British s.s. *Tainui* (9,965 tons) torpedoed by U-Boat in English Channel ; reached port.

British s.s. *Bengali* (5,684 tons) sunk by U-Boat off Alexandria.

April 9.

New British Military Service Bill.

The German Offensive. Second Assault : The Battle of the Lys.

German attack between Armentières—La Bassée on Anglo-Portuguese front of nearly 10 miles ; line penetrated about Neuve Chapelle—Fauquissart, and through Richebourg—Laventie. Allies retired on Lys between Estaires—Bac St. Maur. Givenchy entered, but Germans expelled. Attack on French near Hangard (Amiens) defeated. .

Portuguese sector of front attacked was held by Portuguese 2nd Division, under Gen. Gomes da Costa ; under the onslaught of eight German divisions, Portuguese lost 317 officers and 7,000 men.

Gen. Foch at Montreuil. As Lys Battle developed, he ordered on April 12 Gen. Robillot's 2nd Cavalry Corps to proceed from

April 9, 1918 (*continued*).
Aumale to Steenwoorde, and two French infantry Divisions were also transferred N. to Flanders Heights. This new group was placed under Gen. de Mitry.

M. Clemenceau, in reply to Count Czernin's speech of 2-iv.-18, disclosed Emperor Charles's peace-letter of 31-iii.-17, and its acknowledgment of French title to Alsace-Lorraine.

Bessarabian Diet voted union with Rumania.

British s.s. *Sunik* (5,017 tons) torpedoed by U-Boat in Mediterranean ; beached.

Gen. Allenby advanced 2,500 yards between coast and Jerusalem—Schechem road. Since declaration of independence by King of Hedjaz Arabs had cleared Red Sea coast for 800 miles and accounted for 40,000 Turkish troops.

April 10.
Fighting spread to Messines Ridge ; British pressed back to top of ridge and Ploegsteert in the S. ; in Armentières sector Germans crossed Lys between Estaires—Bac St. Maur ; 6,000 prisoners, 100 guns claimed.

Count Czernin branded M. Clemenceau's statement of 9-iv.-18 as a lie.

Germans at Bielgorod.

Turkish offensive in Palestine N.E. of Joppa ; British recovery.

British s.s. *Westfield* (3,453 tons) sunk by U-Boat off Bishop Rock.

British s.s. *Henley* (3,249 tons) sunk by U-Boat off the Lizard ; 6 lost.

British s.s. *Paul Paix* (4,196 tons) torpedoed by U-Boat in English Channel ; reached port.

British s.s. *Airedale* (3,044 tons) torpedoed by U-Boat in Mediterranean ; beached.

British s.s. *Warwickshire* (8,012 tons) torpedoed by U-Boat in Mediterranean ; reached port.

British s.s. *Burutu* (3,902 tons) attacked by U-Boat with torpedo and gun off Monrovia ; attack resisted by gunfire ; 2 lost.

U-Boat shelled Monrovia (Liberia).

April 11.
Sir D. Haig's Army Order :
" . . . With our backs to the wall, and believing in the justice of our cause, each one of us must fight on to the end."

Second German attack on Messines Ridge heavily defeated at Wytschaete—Hollebeke ; in centre Germans pushed on from Lys towards Bailleul ; Armentières evacuated, where Germans reported capture of garrison of 3,000 men ; British forced back at Estaires—Steenwerck, and behind Lys, surrendered Merville, and gave ground in Ploegsteert region ; German attempt to force Lawe, covering Béthune, heavily defeated. Germans claimed 20,000 prisoners, over 200 guns in Northern battle to date.

ML356 sunk after collision off Dover.

British s.s. *Myrtle Branch* (3,741 tons) sunk by U-Boat off Inishtrahull ; 15 lost.

UB33 mined in Folkestone Barrage.

H.I.M.S. *Rheinland* (18,900 tons), Aaland Is. to Danzig, aground off Lagskär Point ; lightened of 6,400 tons ; floated after fifteen weeks ; towed to Kiel ; disabled for remainder of war.

British s.s. *Highland Prince* (3,390 tons) sunk by U-Boat off Cape Bon ; 3 lost.

British s.s. *Kingstonian* (6,564 tons) torpedoed by U-Boat in Mediterranean ; beached ; 1 lost.

April 11 (*continued*).
Turkish attacks near Ghoraniyeh brid E. of Jordan and near Schechem road repuls

One of Gen. Northey's columns heav engaged N.E. of Mozambique ; severe Gern losses.

April 12.
Last effective Zeppelin raid on Engla Lincs, Lancs, and Warwick attacked ; 7 kill 20 injured. Total number of airship rai 51. Total airship casualties : 556 killed, 1,357 injured, of whom 498 and 1,236 civilia 171 women, 110 children killed ; 431 wom 218 children injured

German Army airships not used for ra on England since August, 1917. Navy ships claimed 47 raids on England ; total tons of bombs dropped, of which 45 t dropped on London.

Air raid on Paris : 26 killed, 72 injur British s.s. *Luis* (4,284 tons) sunk U-Boat off St. Catherine's Point ; 4 lost.

H.M. CMB18A sunk by collision Belgian coast

H.M. CMB33A sunk in action off Osten Germans gained ground towards Baille enter Neuve Eglise, and again penetra Messines ; in centre they forced Lawe R.

British s.s. *Autolycus* (5,806 tons) *a Moyune* (4,935 tons) sunk by U-Boat Cape Palos, Spain.

April 13.
Germans driven from Neuve Egli attacks at Meteren—Wulverghem defeatec German Baltic Division, supported German naval squadron, occupied Helsingfc Fall of Batum to Turks.

Hedjef murderers surrendered.

During second week in April Brit 74th Division transferred from Palestine W. Front ; its place taken by 3rd (Lahc Division.

British s.s. *Harewood* (4,150 tons) su by U-Boat W. by S. from Lisbon ; 2 lost.

British s.s. *Bassam* (3,040 tons) cha by U-Boat off Sierra Leone ; escaped.

＊April 14.
Gen. Foch's appointment as Allied C. C. in France announced.

German attacks repulsed, especially Merville—Bailleul : 150 prisoners. Brit evacuated Neuve Eglise.

Emperor Charles telegraphed to Kai that in his peace-letter of 31-iii.-17, he wr precisely the contrary of what M. Clemenc made him say regarding Alsace-Lorraine, a that the Austrian guns on W. front dem strated his loyalty.

British s.s. *Marstonmoor* (2,744 to sunk by U-Boat off Cape Wrath.

British s.s. *Cheford* (2,995 tons) sunk U-Boat off Bardey Island.

British s.s. *Santa Isabel* (2,023 tons) su by U-Boat about 15 miles W. from C Verde ; 1 lost.

April 15.
British s.s. *Pomeranian* (4,241 tons) su by U-Boat off Portland Bill ; 55 lost.

British s.s. *Tanfield* (4,538 tons) *City of Winchester* (7,981 tons) torpedoed U-Boat in English Channel ; reached port

British warships sank 10 German traw in Kattegat.

April 15, 1918 (*continued*).

Fall of Bailleul and Wulverghem to German Fourth Army now reinforced by Alpine Corps; German attacks near Wytschaete.

Count Czernin's resignation announced, following M. Clemenceau's publication of Emperor Charles's letter admitting "just claims of France to Alsace-Lorraine." Count Burian succeeded at Ballplatz.

German operations against 2nd Polish Corps.

April 16.

Gen. Goethals U.S. Director of Purchase, Storage, and Traffic.

Dutch Government announced intention of sending convoy to E. Indies.

British s.s. *Hungerford* (5,811 tons) sunk by U-Boat off Owers Light; 8 lost.

British s.s. *Lake Michigan* (9,288 tons) sunk by U-Boat off Eagle Island; 1 lost.

British s.s. *Ladoga* (1,917 tons) sunk by U-Boat off S. Arklow Light; 29 lost.

Germans seized and lost Wytschaete—Meteren. British withdrew in Passchendaele area. French co-operated on North front.

Allied advance on Struma (Salonika front).

B.I. s.s. *Nirpura* (7,640 tons) sunk by U-Boat off Cape Roca.

April 17.

Fighting near Bixschoote; Belgians took 700 prisoners.

British withdrew from Wytschaete—Meteren.

Bolo Pasha shot at Vincennes.

Dr. Trumbitch visited Gen. Diaz at Italian G.H.Q.

UB82 destroyed by H.M. drifters *Light*, *Pilot Me*, and *Young Fred* off N. Ireland.

British s.s. *Bamse* torpedoed by U-Boat off Portland Bill; 4 lost.

April 18.

British Military Service Bill passed.

Lord Milner War Secretary. Lord Derby, vice Lord Bertie, Ambassador to France. Mr. Chamberlain joined War Cabinet.

Heavy German attacks on 11-mile front around Givenchy defeated; 200 prisoners. French attack in Avre Valley, E. of Amiens; 500 prisoners; progress to outskirts of Castel.

Signor Orlando announced in Rome that Italian troops had been sent to French front.

B.I. s.s. *Itria* sunk by collision while in convoy in Mediterranean.

Allies withdrew from captured Struma villages (Salonika).

Enver Pasha visited Batum.

British s.s. *Runswick* (3,060 tons) sunk by U-Boat off Trevose Head.

British s.s. *Pentyrch* (3,312 tons) sunk by U-Boat off Brighton Light; 1 lost.

April 19.

Advanced trenches at Givenchy—Festubert recovered.

U.S. troops N.W. of Toul lost and regained Seicheprey; heavy German losses.

Germans formally occupied Crimea and remained until Armistice.

British s.s. *War Helmet* (8,184 tons) sunk by U-Boat off Owers Light.

British s.s. *Lord Charlemont* (3,209 tons) sunk by U-Boat off Alboran Island; 8 lost.

April 20.

British s.s. *Florrieston* (3,366 tons) and *Lowther Grange* (3,926 tons) sunk by U-Boat off S. Stack; 19 lost.

April 20 (*continued*).

British and German light forces engaged in Heligoland Bight; German T.B.D. hit.

German attack N.E. of Ypres frustrated.

*April 21.

Capt. M. von Richthofen, first of the great German Aerial Chaser Formations ("Circus"), with 80 victims to his name, killed on W. Front.

King George's Message to munition workers; all losses of guns and expenditure of munitions during Western battle made good.

German G.H.Q. proposed to Chancellor Hertling German occupation of Dutch Zeeland province, ostensibly in order to counteract Allied air reconnaissances. Chancellor vetoed proposal.

German attack at Mesnil, N. of Albert, repulsed.

British s.s. *Normandiet* (1,843 tons) sunk by U-Boat off Calf of Man; 19 lost.

British s.s. *Landonia* (2,504 tons) sunk by U-Boat off Strumble Head; 21 lost.

British s.s. *Westergate* (1,760 tons) sunk by U-Boat off Start Point; 24 lost.

British s.s. *Lompoc* (7,270 tons) torpedoed by U-Boat in North Sea; reached port.

British s.s. *Bellview* (3,567 tons) sunk by U-Boat off Cape Bon.

UB71 destroyed by ML413 in W. Mediterranean.

April 22.

British advance near Robecq; 120 prisoners.

Two British T.B.D.s engaged five Austrian T.B.D.s in Adriatic; latter escaped to Durazzo.

UB55 mined in Folkestone Barrage.

British s.s. *Eric Calvert* (1,862 tons) sunk by U-Boat off St. Anthony Point; 2 lost.

British s.s. *Dronning Maud* (2,663 tons) sunk by U-Boat off Cape Sigli, Algeria; 1 lost.

British s.s. *Welbeck Hall* (5,643 tons) and Egyptian s.v. *Mashalla* sunk by U-Boat off Port Said.

April 23.

St. George's Day.

Naval raid on Zeebrugge—Ostend by forces under Vice-Adm. Keyes; after intensive bombardment by monitors, H.M.SS. *Vindictive* (Capt. Carpenter), *Iris*, and *Daffodil* ran alongside Mole at Zeebrugge; storming parties landed; three obsolete cruisers, H.M.SS. *Iphigenia*, *Intrepid*, and *Thetis* filled with concrete entered harbour; *Iphigenia* and *Intrepid* successfully sunk at entrance of Bruges Canal; obsolete submarine C3 run against Zeebrugge Mole and blown up. At Ostend two block ships, H.M.SS. *Brilliant* and *Sirius*, run ashore.

H.M.S. *North Star* sunk in action at Zeebrugge.

ML110 and ML424 lost in action off Zeebrugge.

Adm. Scheer (F.F. *Baden*) sallied out with High Sea Fleet and Adm. Hipper's Battle Cruisers for a raid on the British and Norwegian convoy line.

Sir D. Haig reported 102 German divisions used against British since March 21, many two or three times.

Germans repulsed E. of Robecq, and N.E. of Bailleul.

First Tank duel on W. Front. Near Cachy one British male and two female Tanks attacked three large German Tanks; two

April 23, 1918 *(continued)*.
femeles destroyed; male knocked out one
opponent, routed two others.

Austro-German agreement with Ukraine
whereby Central Powers assumed collection
of foodstuffs in S. Russia.

Guatemala at war with Germany.

April 24.

Fresh German attacks in Amiens sector on
8-mile front from N. of Villers-Bretonneux
to W. bank of Avre; British retired from
Villers-Bretonneux; German attacks in Avre
Valley failed.

Arabs occupied 53 miles of Hedjaz railway
S. of Maan.

Germans in Mozambique retired to
Lurio R.

British s.s. *Agnete* (1,127 tons) sunk by
U-Boat off Start Point; 12 lost.

H.M. submarine E45 laid mines between
Heligoland and Ruter Gat.

German High Sea Fleet turned for home
40 sea-miles W.S.W. from Stavanger, with
H.I.M.S. *Moltke* disabled by engine trouble
in tow of *Oldenburg*.

April 25.

British regained Villers-Bretonneux; over
600 prisoners. Heavy German attacks from
N. of Bailleul to Wytschaete region, especially
before Mont Kemmel; British withdrew;
Germans claimed 6,500 prisoners.

Mr. Balfour, from F.O., instructed
British Minister at The Hague to inform Dutch
Government that Great Britain did not recog-
nise " right of convoy."

Lord Rothermere resigned Air Ministry.

U104 sunk by H.M.S. *Jessamine* off S.
Ireland.

Disabled German battle cruiser *Moltke*
torpedoed and damaged amidships by H.M.
submarine E24 off Horn Reef; *Moltke* proceeded to Jade, together with remainder of
High Sea Fleet. This was last German Fleet
sortie.

German minesweeper M67 mined and
sunk in the Bight.

H.M. minesweeper *St. Seiriol* mined off
Shipwash Lights.

H.M. sloop *Cowslip* sunk by U-Boat off
Cape Spartel.

H.M. TB90 capsized and sunk off
Gibraltar.

H.M. special service ship *Willow Branch*
sunk by U-Boat probably off W. coast of
Africa, E. of Cape Verde.

April 26.

Germans captured Kemmel hill and village
and Dranoutre; Allies pressed back towards
Locre, but stood at La Clytte—Scherpenberg;
four attacks on Locre defeated, and at Voormezeele. More fighting on the Amiens front;
900 German prisoners.

British s.s. *Llwyngwair* (1,304 tons) sunk
by U-Boat off Seaham Harbour; 8 lost.

British s.s. *Gresham* (3,774 tons) sunk by
U-Boat off Strumble Head.

Sir William Weir British Air Minister.

April 27.

Germans took and lost Voormezeele.

British s.s. *Romany* (3,983 tons) sunk by
U-Boat off Cape Spartivento, Sardinia.

British s.s. *Upada* (5,257 tons) torpedoed
by U-Boat in Mediterranean; reached port
1 lost.

Turks in Kars, where they plundered the
town and destroyed the Russian 1878 memorial.

 # April 28.

British s.s. *Upcerne* (2,984 tons) sunk l
U-Boat off Coquet Island; 16 lost.

British s.s. *Oronsa* (8,075 tons) sunk l
U-boat off Bardsey Island; 3 lost.

H.M. CMB39B accidentally burnt ;
Dunkirk.

French submarine *Prairial* lost by coll
sion off Havre.

Germans reached Taganrog.

British occupied Kifri.

April 29.

British F.O. notified of Dutch Gover
ment's intention to send convoy to E. Indi
about mid-June.

Mr. Ian Macpherson, M.P., Vice-Preside
Army Council.

Maj.-Gen. Harington Deputy Chief Ir
perial Gen. Staff.

German defeat on 10-mile front
Meteren—Vormezeele; 13 divisions repuls
with heavy loss; three British divisions ho
N. sector; French recovery at Scherpenberg
Mont Rouge.

British s.s. *Australia* (3,687 tons) sun
by U-Boat off Dungeness; 5 lost.

British s.s. *Broderick* (4,321 tons) sur
by U-Boat off Hastings.

British s.s. *Ella Sayer* (2,549 tons) sur
by U-Boat off Royal Sovereign Light; 2 los

British s.s. *Kut Sang* (4,895 tons) sur
by U-Boat off Cape Palos, Spain; 59 lost.

British s.s. *Kingstonian* (6,564 ton
ashore in Carloforte Roadstead; total wrec

White Guards took Viborg.

Gen. Skoropadsky Hetman at Kieff.

April 30.

Fighting in Noyon sector.

Germans after March-April assaults on \
Front claimed 130,000 prisoners, 1,600 guns

UB85 destroyed by H.M. drifter *Coreops*
in Irish Sea.

British s.s. *Kafue* (6,044 tons) sunk l
U-Boat off Mull of Galloway; 1 lost.

British s.s. *Isleworth* (2,871 tons) sun
by U-Boat 3 miles S.W. from Ventnor Pie
29 lost.

British s.s. *Umbra* (2,042 tons) sunk l
U-Boat off Royal Sovereign Light; 20 lost.

British s.s. *Conway* (4,003 tons) sunk l
U-Boat off Cape Palos, Spain.

Gen. Allenby's advance towards Hedj
railway, S. of Es Salt; 260 prisoners; p
gress near Jerusalem—Schechem road; Ar
forces took 550 prisoners on Hedjaz railw
near Maan.

Gen. Marshall reached Tauk R.; to
1,800 prisoners.

May 1.

British took 5,241 German prisoners
W. Front in April (1,661 in March).

At the beginning of May British Arr
in France mustered 45 effective Division
2 were in line with reduced cadres; 8 h
been temporarily written off as fighting uni

Americans on Amiens front near Mo
didier.

Germans established military dictatorsl
in Ukraine; Marshal Eichhorn ordered pe
antry to sow the land.

Germans at Sebastopol.

British s.s. *Matiana* (5,313 tons) sunk
U-Boat on Keith Reef.

British s.s. *Canonesa* (5,583 tons) t
pedoed by U-Boat in English Chann
reached port; 8 lost.

May 1, 1918 (continued).

Tsar removed by Bolshevists from Tobolsk to Ekaterinburg: Imperial Family arrived three weeks later.

British s.s. *Era* (2,379 tons) sunk by U-Boat off Cape Tenez ; 12 lost.

Australians captured Es Salt, half-way between Jordan R.—Hedjaz Railway ; 350 prisoners. Turks surprised Australian mounted brigade near Jisr-ed-Damieh ford and compelled them to fall back ; nine guns abandoned.

May 2.

UB31 destroyed by H.M. drifters *Lord Leitrim* and *Ocean Roamer* in southern North Sea.

UC78 destroyed by H.M. drifters *Mary* and *Our Friend* in Eastern Channel.

British s.s. *Medora* (5,135 tons) sunk by U-Boat off Mull of Galloway.

British s.s. *Girdleness* (3,018 tons) sunk by U-Boat off Trevose Head ; 2 lost.

British s.s. *Franklyn* (4,919 tons) sunk by U-Boat off Port Mahon.

British s.s. *Flawyl* (3,592 tons) sunk by U-Boat off Pantellaria ; 1 lost.

Heavy bombs dropped by R.N.A.S. on Zeebrugge lock gates.

French attacked at Hailles—Castel ; seized Hill 82 and wood skirting Avre R. ; over 100 prisoners.

Germans entered Donetz region W. of Don R.

Turkish attempt on Gen. Allenby's positions at Es Salt repulsed ; 314 prisoners.

May 3.

British minor success near Hinges, S.W. of Locre ; 40 prisoners.

Austrian Reichsrath adjourned ; Dr. von Seidler, Premier, announced Parliamentary Government impossible ; Bohemia to be divided into national districts.

Serbs captured advanced Bulgarian positions in Dobropolie (Macedonia).

British s.s. *Pancras* (4,436 tons) torpedoed by U-Boat in Mediterranean ; reached port ; 2 lost.

British withdrew from Es Salt behind Jordan ; 900 prisoners taken, including 43 Germans ; Arab forces damaged Hedjaz Railway N. of Maan.

May 4.

British s.s. *Polbrae* (1,087 tons) sunk by U-Boat off Sharpnose, N. Devon ; 2 lost.

Austrians seized German foodstuffs in transit from Rumania and Ukraine.

* May 5.

Lord French to be Lord-Lieutenant of Ireland.

Australians advanced 1,200 yards at Morlancourt—Sailly-le-Sec, between Ancre R.—Somme R. ; 200 prisoners.

H.M. sloop *Rhododendron* sunk by U-Boat in North Sea.

British s.s. *Clan Ross* (5,971 tons) torpedoed by U-Boat in Mediterranean ; reached port ; 9 lost.

Gen. von Lettow defeated by part of Gen. Northey's column 15 miles W. of Nanungu, 160 miles S. of Lake Nyassa.

May 6.

British s.s. *Leeds City* (4,298 tons) sunk by U-Boat off Skulmartin Light.

British s.s. *Sandhurst* (3,034 tons) sunk by U-Boat off Corsewall Point ; 20 lost.

March 8 (continued).

Russian ships bombarded Mariupol (Sea of Azoff) occupied by Germans.

May 7.

Peace signed at Bukarest between Rumania and the Central Powers. Dobrudja as far as the Danube ceded, Bulgaria regained territory lost by treaty of 1913, Rumania to renounce all claim to compensation for damage done by invading armies, including requisitions (a sum of about £50,000,000). Oil concessions and many other economic advantages obtained by Central Powers.

Gen. Maurice's letter to the Press imputing misstatements to British Ministers in regard to the military position.

H.M. CMB10 accidentally burnt at Dover.

British s.s. *Nantes* (1,580 tons) sunk by U-Boat off Fair Island ; 22 lost.

Gen. Marshall's troops entered Kirkuk, 110 miles S.E. of Mosul.

May 8.

German attack at La Clytte—Voormezeele ; British centre dented ; French advance S. of La Clytte.

Gen. J. W. McAndrew, Chief of Staff to Gen. Pershing at U.S. G.H.Q., Chaumont, vice Gen. Harbord, appointed to command 4th U.S. (Marine) Infantry Brigade.

Germans occupied Rostoff-on-Don.

British s.s. *Quito* (3,358 tons) torpedoed by U-Boat in Irish Channel ; reached port.

British s.s. *Dux* (1,349 tons) sunk by U-Boat off Godrevy Light.

British s.s. *Ingleside* (3,736 tons) sunk by U-Boat off Algiers ; 11 lost.

UB70 destroyed by H.M.S. *Basilisk* in W. Mediterranean.

May 9.

Mr. Asquith's motion to refer Gen. Maurice's charges defeated by 293 votes to 106 in House of Commons.

UB78 rammed and sunk by H.M.T. *Queen Alexandra* in English Channel.

British s.s. *Baron Ailsa* (1,836 tons) sunk by U-Boat off the Smalls ; 10 lost.

British s.s. *Wileysike* (2,501 tons) sunk by U-Boat off St. Ann's Head ; 4 lost.

Germans defeated at Voormezeele—La Clytte near Ridge Wood ; Allied set-back and recovery N. of Kemmel ; fighting at Bucquoy and near Albert ; French surprise attack at Grivesnes. N.W. of Montdidier ; 258 prisoners.

Italians stormed Mte. Carlno (Vallarsa).

May 10.

Mr. Baker, U.S. War Secretary, announced that the estimate of 500,000 U.S. troops to be dispatched to France early this year had already been surpassed.

UB16 sunk by H.M. submarine E34 off Orfordness.

British s.s. *Amplegarth* (3,707 tons) mined off Dover Harbour.

H.M.S. *Vindictive*, filled with concrete, sunk as block-ship at Ostend.

ML254 sunk off Ostend to avoid capture.

British s.s. *Itinda* (5,251 tons) sunk by U-Boat off Marsa Susa ; 1 lost.

British s.s. *Szechuen* (1,862 tons) sunk by U-Boat off Port Said ; 9 lost.

French improve N. of Kemmel village.

May 11.

New German U-Boat cruiser U154 sunk by British Atlantic escort submarine E35 off Cape St. Vincent after two hours' action.

Sundays marked with Asterisk (*).

May 11, 1918 (*continued*).

W. of Avre Valley French defeated German attack ; 100 prisoners.

Marshal Mackensen C.-in-C. of Austro-German Army of occupation in Rumania.

British s.v. *Massouda* sunk by U-Boat off Marsa Matruth.

British advance on Baghdad—Mosul road ; Turks driven over Lesser Zab, 70 miles from Mosul ; 30 more prisoners, two guns.

Turks and Kurds across Persian frontier at Ushnu—Suj Bulak.

* May 12.

U103 rammed and sunk by White Star R.M.S. *Olympic* (46,359 tons) in English Channel.

UB72 torpedoed and destroyed by H.M. submarine D4 in English Channel.

British s.s. *Haslingden* (1,934 tons) sunk by U-Boat off Seaham Harbour ; 11 lost.

British s.s. *Inniscarra* (1,412 tons) sunk by U-Boat off Ballycottin Island ; 28 lost.

British s.s. *Benlawers* (3,949 tons) mined in Irish Channel ; reached port ; 5 lost.

Italian T.B.D.s sank Austrian transport off Durazzo.

British s.s. *Vimeira* (5,884 tons) sunk by U-Boat off Lampedusa.

British s.s. *Omrah* (8,130 tons) sunk by U-Boat off Cape Spartivento ; 1 lost.

Emperor Charles arrived at Spa, in order to apologise to Kaiser for deception in peace-letter affair, and to discuss basis of an Austro-German " League of Arms."

Arabs N. and S. of Maan took 264 Turkish prisoners and demolished part of Hedjaz railway.

May 13.

British s.s. *Esperanza de Larrinaga* (4,981 tons) torpedoed by U-Boat off N. Ireland ; reached port ; 1 lost.

Fighting near Robecq—Merville—Kemmel ; Germans at Kleine Vierstraat repulsed by French.

H.M. fleet messenger *Chesterfield* sunk by U-Boat off Malta.

May 14.

Enemy fails against Australians S.W. of Morlancourt. French gain S. of Hailles, Avre Valley ; 70 prisoners.

H.M.S. *Phœnix* sunk by U-Boat in Adriatic.

British s.s. *Woolston* (2,986 tons) sunk by U-Boat off Syracuse Harbour ; 19 lost.

May 15.

British s.s. *Pennyworth* (5,388 tons) torpedoed by U-Boat in English Channel ; reached port ; 1 lost.

British s.s. *War Grange* (3,100 tons) torpedoed by U-Boat in Bristol Channel ; beached ; 5 lost.

French progress N. of Kemmel.

Paris *Bonnet Rouge* trial ended ; Duval sentenced to death.

Agreement announced between Entente, Japan, and China for preservation of peace in Far East and against German penetration.

May 16.

British s.s. *Tartary* (4,181 tons) sunk ┤ U-Boat off Skulmartin Light.

British s.s. *Tagona* (2,004 tons) sunk ┤ U-Boat off Trevose Head ; 8 lost.

H.M. collier *Heron Bridge* sunk by U-Bo 320 miles E. by N. from San Miguel (Azore

British s.s. *Llancarvan* (4,740 tons) su┤ by U-Boat 370 miles E. by N. from S┤ Miguel (Azores).

UC35 sunk by French patrol vessel Ail off Sardinia.

May 17.

German-Irish plot ; 150 Sinn Feine including de Valera, Count Plunkett, Count Markievicz, Arthur Griffith, &c., arrested.

Franco-Italian 12-mile advance on ┤ mile front W. of Koritza.

British s.s. *Mavisbrook* (3,152 tons) su┤ by U-Boat off Cape de Gata ; 18 lost.

British s.s. *Sculptor* (4,874 tons) t┤ pedoed by U-Boat off Oran ; beache┤ wrecked ; 7 lost.

British s.s. *Elswick Grange* (3,926 to┤ torpedoed by U-Boat in Mediterranea┤ reached port ; 1 lost.

May 18.

Australians captured post W. of Morla court and raided Ville-sur-Ancre, N.W. Morlancourt ; 381 prisoners.

First British daylight air raid on Cologn all machines returned safely.

British s.s. *Hurunui* (10,644 tons) su┤ by U-Boat S.W. from Lizard ; 1 lost.

British s.s. *Denbigh Hall* (4,943 tons) a┤ *Scholar* (1,635 tons) sunk by U-Boat W.S.┤ from Bishop Rock ; 2 lost.

U39, damaged by bombs from Fren seaplane, towed into Cartagena harbour another U-Boat ; interned.

British s.s. *Chesterfield* (1,013 tons) su┤ by U-Boat N.E. from Malta ; 4 lost.

British s.s. *Media* (5,437 tons) torpedo┤ by U-Boat in Mediterranean ; reached por┤

French T.B.D. *Catapulte* sunk by collisi┤ off Bizerta.

* May 19.

Thirty-second and last · air raid London (German 3rd Bombing Squadro┤ in which some new large Gothas participate┤ five raiders destroyed, two others believ┤ fallen in flames into the sea ; 49 killed, 1 injured.

German airmen bombed large group British hospitals at Etaples, far outsi┤ battle area in France ; 300 casualties.

Ville-sur-Ancre taken by 2nd Australi Division ; 400 prisoners.

Italians stormed advanced positions Capo Sile, N.E. corner of Venetian Lagoo┤

British s.s. *Snowdon* (3,189 tons) sunk ┤ U-Boat off Malta ; 2 lost.

British s.s. *Saxilby* (3,630 tons) torpedo┤ by U-Boat in Mediterranean ; reached por┤

Nanungu, German H.Q. in Mozambiq┤ occupied by Gen. Edwards.

May 20.

British s.s. *Manchester Importer* (4,0┤ tons) torpedoed by U-Boat in English Chann┤ reached port.

For List of Abbreviations see page iv.

May 20, 1918 (*continued*).

French advance E. and N.E. of Locre; objectives reached on 2½-mile front; over 500 prisoners.

Successful British operation N.W. of Merville; 30 prisoners.

May 21.

Two Gotha squadrons tried to raid Paris; three persons killed; one raider down.

Since German offensive on March 21, 1,000 German aeroplanes had by this date been destroyed or driven down.

British air raid on Mannheim.

British s.s. *Chatham* (3,592 tons) sunk by U-Boat off Cape Matapan.

British troops at Fathah, 45 miles above Tekrit (Tigris).

May 22.

British air raids on Zeebrugge; German T.B.D. sunk by bomb.

British air raid on Liége railway junctions.

German air raid on Paris by about 30 machines; one penetrated defences; one person killed, 12 injured.

Foreign Affairs Committee of Federal Council met in Berlin.

Gen. Edwards in contact with Von Lettow between Nanungu — Mahua and drove him westwards. Governor Schnee lost his baggage in hasty retirement.

May 23.

Mr. Lloyd George at Edinburgh; Allies sinking U-Boats faster than enemy can build them, and building merchantmen faster than Germans can sink them.

H.M. A.M.C. *Moldavia* (9,500 tons) sunk by U-Boat in Channel; 56 U.S troops killed by explosion.

British s.s. *Skaraas* (1,625 tons) sunk by U-Boat off Black Head; 19 lost.

British s.s. *Innisfallen* (1,405 tons) sunk by U-Boat off Kish Light.

H.M. submarine E56 attacked with bombs by German seaplane off South Dogger Bank.

UB52 torpedoed and destroyed by H.M. submarine H4 between Brindisi and Avlona.

May 24.

British Government Paper on connexion between Sinn Fein and Germany.

British s.v. *Ruth Hickman* sunk by U-Boat N.W. from Graciosa (Azores).

British s.s. *Elysia* (6,397 tons) torpedoed by U-Boat in Mediterranean; reached port; 13 lost.

May 25.

British s.s. *Rathlin Head* (7,378 tons) torpedoed by U-Boat off S.W. Ireland; reached port; 3 lost.

British s.s. *Anne* (4,083 tons) torpedoed by U-Boat in Channel; reached port; 1 lost.

Italian attack N. of Adamello, between Lake Garda and Swiss frontier.

*May 26.

UB74 depth-charged and destroyed by H.M. armed yacht *Lorna* in English Channel.

British s.s. *Kyarra* (6,953 tons) sunk by U-Boat off Anvil Point; 6 lost.

British s.s. *Princess Royal* (1,986 tons) sunk by U-Boat off St. Agnes Head; 19 lost.

*May 26 (*continued*).

Italians took Monticello Pass (Adamello); 870 prisoners, 12 guns; and stormed Austrian positions at Capo Sile; 440 prisoners.

British s.s. *Leasowe Castle* (9,737 tons) sunk by U-Boat off Alexandria; 9 lost.

May 27.

The German Offensive. Third Assault: Battle of the Aisne.

Great German attack (28 divisions of Seventh and First Armies, under Gens. von Boehn and F. von Below) on Aisne front between Soissons—Reims; along Chemin-des-Dames French held; Germans pressed on towards Aisne Valley, reached Pont Archy, 5 miles from start. British between Craonnelle—Bermericourt attacked; British right held, left pressed back to second line. Chemin-des-Dames lost; Germans across Aisne R. on 18-mile front between Vailly—Berry-au-Bac, advanced towards Vesle R.

Smaller attack launched at Locre—Voormezeele, S. of Ypres, repulsed by French; German gains only near Dickebusch Lake.

Long-range bombardment of Paris.

British s.s. *Cairnross* (4,016 tons) and *Merionethshire* (4,308 tons) sunk by U-Boat N.W. from Flores (Azores).

British s.s. *Uganda* (5,431 tons) sunk by U-Boat N.E. from Algiers.

May 28.

Allies recovered S. of Ypres; retook trenches E. of Dickebusch Lake.

Great battle continued on Aisne—Vesle plateaux; Germans forced Vesle R., 12 miles from start. Allies held on Vrégny plateau—St. Thierry heights. Germans claim 15,000 prisoners.

U.S. 1st Division carried German salient at Cantigny, N.W. of Montdidier.

Armenia declared her independence.

German troops in Mozambique driven S. across Lurio R.

May 29.

Germans extended to Vrégny plateau; Soissons taken; progress towards Reims and S. of Vesle R. towards Marne R.; 25,000 prisoners claimed to date.

British s.s. *Begum* (4,646 tons) and *Carlton* (5,262 tons) sunk by U-Boat W. by S. from Bishop Rock; 15 lost.

British s.s. *Missir* sunk by U-Boat off Alexandria; 34 lost.

British s.s. *Antinous* (3,682 tons) torpedoed by U-Boat in Mediterranean; reached port.

May 30.

Germans held at outlets from Soissons; in centre they reached Fère-en-Tardenois: Allies firm around Reims; 35,000 prisoners claimed by Germans to date.

Kaiser viewed battlefield from Chemin des Dames.

Germans arranged for British not to bomb Cologne on Corpus Christi day, but themselves raided Paris with 1st and 4th Bombing Squadrons.

Ten British vessels sunk by U-Boat off Calf of Man.

UC49 depth-charged and destroyed by H.M.S. *Fairy* and H.M.T. *Bombadier* in North Sea.

Arrival of 23 U.S. flying boats and personnel at Killingholme, originally designed

May 30, 1918 (continued).

as base for attacks on Heligoland area ; ultimately the American planes were diverted to
anti-U-Boat work on E. Coast.

Cunard s.s. *Ausonia* (8,153 tons) sunk by
U-Boat W. by S. from Fastnet ; 48 lost.

British s.s. *Waneta* sunk by U-Boat off
Kinsale Head ; 8 lost.

British s.s. *War Panther* (5,260 tons)
torpedoed by U-Boat in English Channel ;
reached port.

British s.s. *Asiatic Prince* (2,887 tons)
sunk by U-Boat off Malta.

British s.s. *Aymeric* (4.363 tons) sunk by
U-Boat off Cape Matapan.

Greek success W. of Vardar R., near
Serbian border ; 1,500 Bulgaro - German
prisoners.

May 31.

Germans reached Marne R. on 10-mile
front at Château-Thierry—Dormans ; French
Soissons—Noyon salient flattened ; 45,000
prisoners, 400 guns claimed to date.

U.S. 3rd Division, Gen. Dickman, at
disposal of French High Command in Château-
Thierry sector.

H.M. T.B.D. *Fairy* (380 tons) sunk after
ramming and destroying UC75 in North Sea.

UB119 lost in May ; cause unknown.

Dutch official statement published in-
timating that commandant of proposed E.
Indian convoy would "not tolerate any
examination of the convoyed ships."

U.S. transport *President Lincoln* sunk.

British s.s. *Galileo* (6,287 tons) torpedoed
by U-Boat in English Channel ; beached.

Fire at Stambul : £T520,000 damage.

June 1.

Germans held between Oise—Marne in
direction of Paris ; progress down Ourcq
Valley to edge of Villers-Cotterets Forest,
40 miles from Paris. At Reims French lost
and retook Fort de La Pompelle ; 200 prisoners.

Bavarian Crown Prince wrote to Chancellor Hertling that he was sceptical of German
victory, and that Germany should content
herself with her gains in the East.

Krupp's Essen works now staffed to
maximum war strength of 75,000 men and
23,000 women, as compared with 35,000 men
and 200 women on 1.-viii.-14.

British cavalry withdrawn from Kirkuk
(Mesopotamia).

Gen. Dunsterville's Mission at Kasvin.

Massacre of Armenians by Tartars at
Katherinenfeld (S. of Tiflis).

*June 2.

U.S. 2nd Division in position on French
Sixth Army front.

Germans checked ; French counter-
attack between Ourcq R.—Marne R. ; local
progress. German attack on Chtâeau-Thierry
road broken S.E. of Bouresches.

British s.s. *Dunaff Head* (5,877 tons) attacked by U-Boat at entrance to the Clyde ;
torpedo missed.

June 3.

German attacks between Soissons—
Noyon. Choisy Hill retaken by French for
fifth time ; Germans checked between Aisne R.
—Ourcq R., but captured Pernant. French
regained Faverolles, S.E. of Villers-Cotterets ;
S. of Ourcq R. Germans took Veuilly-La-
Poterie.

June 3 (continued).

British s.s. *Glaucus* (5,295 tons) sunk b
U-Boat off Cape Granitola (Sicily) ; 2 lost.

British s.s. *Nora* (3,933 tons) sunk b
U-Boat S.E. from Malta ; 1 lost.

British s.s. *Antiope* (3,004 tons) tor
pedoed by U-Boat in North Sea ; reache
port.

June 4.

U-Boats off U.S. coast.

British s.s. *Cento* (3,708 tons) torpedoe
by U-Boat in North Sea ; reached port.

British s.s. *Strombus* (6,163 tons) tor
pedoed by U-Boat in Mediterranean ; reache
port.

Supreme War Council intimated tha
Allies " will baffle enemy's purpose and i
due course bring him to defeat."

German efforts slackening ; German
penetrated Retz Forest in front of Viller
Cotterets ; repulsed.

Turco-Armenian peace convention signe
at Batum.

June 5.

Second U.S. Registration.

Gen. Robertson in temporary comman
Home Forces.

Germans failed at Longpont, N. edge
Retz Forest ; attempt to cross Oise nea
Vingré, N. of Aisne, defeated ; 150 prisoner

Chancellor Hertling replied to Bavaria
Crown Prince's letter of 1.-vi.-18, that hop
of collapse of one of Western Powers shoul
not yet be abandoned.

British s.s. *Harpathian* (4,588 tons) sun
by U-Boat off Cape Henry, Virginia, U.S.A.

British s.s. *Polwell* (2,013 tons) sunk b
U-Boat off Rockabill.

H.M. armed steamer *Snaefell* sunk b
U-Boat in Mediterranean.

British s.s. *Archbank* (3,767 tons) an
Menzaleh (1,859 tons) sunk by U-Boat E.S.E
from Malta ; 11 lost.

June 6.

H.S. *Koningin Regentes*, in company wit
s.s. *Sindoro* carrying British delegates t
Hague Prisoners' Conference, sunk, presun
ably by U-Boat torpedo.

British s.s. *Huntsland* (2,871 tons) sun
by U-Boat off Havre.

Allied reactions increasing ; N. of Aisn
R. Le Port taken.

Gotha raid on Paris.

Paris Defence Committee ; Gen. Guillat
mat Military Governor vice Gen. Dubail.

June 7.

Mr. Balfour formally notified Dutc
Minister in London that Great Britain coul
not abandon the right of visit and search.

British s.s. *Diana* (1,119 tons) sunk b
U-Boat off Flamborough Head.

British s.s. *Hogarth* (1,231 tons) sunk b
U-Boat off the Longstone ; 26 lost.

Between Marne R.—Reims British r
gained Bligny ; Franco - Americans retoo
Veuilly-La-Poterie.

Turco-German Caucasus expedition ; 15t
Bavarian Chasseurs battalions participate
until Armistice.

June 8.

Gen. Franchet d'Espérey to be Allie
C.-in-C. at Salonika vice Gen. Guillaumat.

First American mines laid on Norther
Barrage ; 3,385 mines laid in 3½ hours. Th

June 8, 1918 (*continued*).

Americans laid a total of 56,570 mines on the Barrage, 80 per cent. of the whole. Their best performance was to lay 5,520 mines in 3 hours 50 minutes.

British Independent Force, R.A.F., formed from the original 8th Brigade R.F.C. operating from Nancy area ; strength raised from 3 to 10 Squadrons—5 for day bombing, 4 for night bombing, and one for reconnaissance, escort, &c.

British s.s. *Saima* (1,147 tons) and *Hunsgrove* (3,063 tons) sunk by U-Boat off Trevose Head ; 19 lost.

Gen. Allenby progressed near Tabor.

Gen. Bitcherakoff left Kasvin for Enzeli.

*June 9.

Battle of Noyon : New German offensive (Eighteenth Army, Gen. von Hutier) on 22-mile front at Montdidier—Noyon ; French back on left and about 5 miles in centre, but firm on right ; principal German progress along Matz Valley.

Three British steamers unsuccessfully attacked by U-Boat in St. George's Channel.

British s.s. *Vandalia* (7,333 tons) sunk by U-Boat off the Smalls.

British s.s. *Moidart* (1,303 tons) sunk by U-Boat off Lyme Regis ; 15 lost.

Two Austrian Dreadnoughts, *Szent Istvan* and *Prinz Eugen*, torpedoed by Com. Luigi Rizzo, Italian Navy, off Dalmatian coast ; Austrians admitted loss of former.

H.M. collier *Clan Forbes* sunk by U-Boat 115 miles W.N.W. from Alexandria.

British s.s. *Pandit* (5,917 tons) and *Tewfikieh* (2,490 tons) sunk by U-Boat W.N.W. from Alexandria ; 11 lost.

German High Command requested Enver Pasha to withdraw Turkish forces from all Caucasus territories other than Kars, Batum, and Ardahan.

June 10.

Mr. Baker, U.S. War Secretary, stated that over 700,000 U.S. troops had already been sent to France.

U.S. 2nd Division carried part of Belleau Wood.

Stubborn French resistance at Montdidier—Noyon. Germans in centre swept forward on 6-mile front to Aronde Valley ; driven back by French counter-attacks ; on right French back to Ribécourt ; Germans claimed 8,000 prisoners.

Australian advance S. of Morlancourt, between Ancre R.—Somme R., on 2,500-yard front ; 300 prisoners.

H.M. auxiliary *Lowtyne* (3,231 tons) sunk by U-Boat off Whitby.

ML64 destroyed by fire in Granton Harbour.

British s.s. *Borg* (2,111 tons) and *Mountby* (3,263 tons) sunk by U-Boat off the Lizard ; 24 lost.

British s.s. *Brodholme* (5,747 tons) torpedoed by U-Boat in Mediterranean; beached ; 4 lost.

June 11.

French counter on 7-mile front, Rubescourt—St. Maur, regained Belloy ; over 1,000 prisoners, several guns. Germans claimed 10,000 prisoners to date in new offensive.

Count Burian in Berlin adhered to Austro-Polish solution.

British s.s. *Lorle* (2,686 tons) sunk by U-Boat off the Lizard ; 19 lost.

British s.s. *Bona* (2,694 tons) sunk by a U-Boat off Beer Head.

June 12.

British s.s. *Kennington* (1,526 tons) sunk by U-Boat off Flamborough Head ; 4 lost.

French gain on left near Belloy—St. Maur ; 400 more prisoners ; on right Germans crossed Matz R., entered and lost Melicocq. French abandoned Choisy salient. New German attack towards Compiègne.

British s.s. *Kul* (1,095 tons) sunk by U-Boat off Wolf Rock ; 4 lost.

British s.s. *Penhallow* (4,318 tons) sunk by U-Boat off Cape Caxine (Algiers) ; 1 lost.

Gen. Bitcherakoff, with his Cossacks and one squadron 14th Hussars, fought battle of Mandjil Bridge against Kuchik Khan's Jangali levies led by German Capt. von Passchen.

British column in Mozambique drove Gen. von Lettow across Ligonya R.

June 13.

Dutch Government acquiesced in British conditions respecting proposed convoy to E. Indies.

Paris raided by German 1st and 4th Bombing Squadrons.

On Villers-Cotterets front Germans checked after 2 miles ; they claimed 15,000 prisoners, 150 guns.

Americans N.W. of Château Thierry completed capture of Belleau Wood.

U.S. airmen's first single-handed raid ; Dommary Baroncourt Station, N.W. of Metz bombed.

Austrian attack at Tonale Pass defeated.

H.M. A.M.C. *Patia* (6,000 tons) sunk by U-Boat in Bristol Channel.

British s.s. *Kalo* (1,957 tons) sunk by U-Boat off Flamborough Head ; 3 lost.

June 14.

Gen. Dubail to be Grand Chancellor of the Legion of Honour.

Standstill in German Western attack.

Turks claimed Tabriz.

June 15.

British night operations N. of Béthune ; German forward positions on 2-mile front gained ; nearly 200 prisoners. S. of Aisne R., French seized Cœuvres-et-Valsery ; 130 prisoners.

Gen. Degoutte, French 21st Army Corps, to command Sixth Army on the Marne.

German air raid on Paris.

Germans at this date claimed 208,000 prisoners and 2,500 guns on W. Front.

Kaiser at German G.H.Q. celebrated 30th anniversary of his accession by speech, challenging Anglo-Saxon ideals to a last mortal combat with Prusso-German ideals.

Austrian offensive with 60 divisions from Asiago plateau to the sea ; British line (23rd Division on the right, 48th Division on the left) on plateau bent back but restored ; on Grappa front Austrians gained footing in front-line positions ; ejected. Austrians crossed Piave R. in Montello sector and between Fagare—Musile. Italians took 3,000 prisoners, Austrians claimed 10,000.

Conrad's Tirol Army Group broken.

British s.s. *Kieldrecht* (1,284 tons) sunk by U-Boat off Flamborough Head.

British s.s. *Cairnmona* (4,666 tons) torpedoed by U-Boat in North Sea ; reached port ; 3 lost.

*June 16.

British s.s. *Melanie* (2,996 tons) sunk by U-Boat off Robin Hood Bay ; 5 lost.

Austrians held except from Montello sector along Piave R., where they gained

*June 16, 1918 (*continued*).

part of Montello crest; Capo Sile, N.E. corner of Venetian Lagoons taken.

Gen. von Lettow reached Alto Moloque (P. E. Africa).

June 17.

Last German air raid on England; aeroplane attack on Kent; no casualties.

Total number of air raids was 108, 51 by airships and 57 by aeroplanes. Casualties caused by aeroplanes were 857 killed, 2,050 njured; 619 killed, 1,620 injured were civilians; 195 women, 142 children killed; 585 women, 324 children injured. For airship casualties see 12-iv.-18.

Total air raid casualties: 1,413 killed (795 men—499 civilians and 296 military—366 women, and 252 children); 3,407 injured (1,849 men—1,328 civilians and 521 military—1,016 women, 542 children).

French local operations near Hautebraye, N.W. of Soissons; 370 prisoners.

Italian counter-attacks from Montello to the sea repulsed; Austrians endeavouring to establish new openings on Piave R.; in Grappa region Allies gained ground.

Partial strike in Vienna following reduction of bread ration.

British s.s. *Kandy* (4,921 tons) torpedoed by U-Boat in Mediterranean; reached port.

U64 destroyed by H.M.SS. *Lychnis* and *Partridge II.* in W. Mediterranean.

Cavalry reconnaissance E. of Jordan R.

June 18.

Germans repulsed before Reims.

Gen. von Mudra relieved Gen. F. von Below in command of German First (Reims) Army.

Austrian attempts to cross Piave R. repulsed; river in flood, many bridges washed away. Italians retook Capo Sile; over 9,000 prisoners to date.

M. Malinoff Bulgarian Premier vice M. Radoslavoff.

Cunard s.s. *Dwinsk* (8,173 tons) sunk by U-Boat about 400 miles N.E. by N. from Bermuda; 24 lost.

British s.s. *Norfolk Coast* sunk by U-Boat off Flamborough Head; 8 lost.

Russian battleship *Svobodnaya Rossiya* (ex-*Ekaterina II.*) torpedoed by Russian T.B.D. *Kertch* in Black Sea.

Germans landed at Poti, N. of Batum.

Gen. von Lettow moving S. in Mozambique, nearing coast.

June 19.

Fight between British naval squadron and German seaplanes N. of Heligoland Bight; one seaplane destroyed by gun-fire.

Franco-American War Affairs organised under direction of M. André Tardieu.

Paris raided by German 1st and 4th Bombing Squadrons.

Position-warfare between Meuse—Moselle until September.

Counter-revolution reported in W. Siberia; Bolshevists overthrown.

Four-hour action from 5 a.m. fought by British fishing convoy headed by *Conan Doyle* with three-gun U-Boat N.W. from Orkneys.

June 20.

UC64 mined in Folkestone Barrage.

Italians regained initiative; furious fighting from Montello to the sea; Austrian lines on Montello thrown back.

June 20 (*continued*).

Italians recovered about half their losses, including Fagare and Zenson sectors; several hundred prisoners; most of Montello retaken; 400 prisoners; Austrian line at Cortellazzo, Piave Mouth, carried; 200 prisoners.

June 21.

British s.s. *Montebello* (4,324 tons) sunk by U-Boat off Ushant; 41 lost.

Austrian attempts to recover initiative in Grappa and Montello regions defeated. Italians enlarged Cavazuccherina bridgehead; 150 prisoners.

June 22.

British raided German trenches at Bucquoy; Tanks for first time engaged in night action.

Austrian retreat across Piave R. begun; floods preventing communication.

German occupation of Ukraine until Armistice.

British s.s. *Rhea* (1,308 tons) mined off Etaples.

*June 23.

Successful British operation on Lys front, S.W. of Meteren; 50 prisoners.

Austrians defeated; pursued by Italians, they crossed Piave in disorder; Montello, and all right bank of Piave, except at Musile, recovered; 4,000 prisoners; total Italian captures 16,000 to date.

British s.s. *London* (1,706 tons) sunk by U-Boat off Whitby.

June 24.

U.S. Senate ratified Reciprocal Conscription Treaty with Great Britain.

German Foreign Secretary von Kühlmann in Reichstag declared that "purely military termination of war is improbable."

Remaining Austrians on right bank of Piave disposed of; 1,000 prisoners. Italian progress in Grappa region; 1,300 prisoners; total 20,000 to date.

June 25.

U.S. Second Army Corps formed under Gen. Read, H.Q. at Fruges.

U.S. Marine Brigade's success in Belleau Wood, S.W. of Château Thierry; 264 prisoners (30-iv.-18).

British air raid on Karlsruhe.

Italians took Capo Sile bridgehead; 509 prisoners.

British s.s. *Orissa* (5,358 tons) sunk by U-Boat off Skerryvore; 6 lost.

British s.s. *African Transport* (4,482 tons) sunk by U-Boat off Whitby; 3 lost.

British s.s. *Atlantian* (9,399 tons) sunk by U-Boat off Eagle Island.

June 26.

M. Kerensky at London Labour Conference.

British took German strong point W. of Vieux Berquin.

Gotha raid on Paris; no casualties.

UC11 mined E. from Harwich.

British s.s. *Tortuguero* (4,175 tons) sunk by U-Boat off Eagle Island; 12 lost.

British s.s. *Raranga* (10,040 tons) torpedoed by U-Boat in English Channel; reached port.

British s.s. *Wimmera* (3,022 tons) mined and sunk off Hooper's Point, New Zealand; 16 lost.

June 27, 1918.

H.S. *Llandovery Castle* (11,423 tons) sunk by U-Boat 120 miles from Irish coast; 146 lost.

Four British T.B.D.s, patrolling off Belgian Coast, engaged eight German T.B.D.s, which later were reinforced by three more destroyers. Action broken off.

British s.s. *Keelung* (6,672 tons) sunk by U-Boat off Ushant; 6 lost.

Forty-fifth air raid on Paris; 11 killed, 14 injured.

June 28.

French penetrated Lavertine Valley between Aisne R.—Villers-Cotterets Forest; over 1,000 prisoners. British advanced nearly one mile E. of Nieppe Forest on 3½-mile front; over 300 prisoners.

U.S. War Department authorised organisation of Chemical Warfare Service.

H.M. submarine D6 sunk by U-Boat off N. Ireland.

British s.s. *Sunnixa* (1,913 tons) sunk by U-Boat off Sunderland; 2 lost.

British s.s. *Queen* (4,956 tons) sunk by U-Boat off Cape Villano; 20 lost.

June 29.

U.S. Army Appropriations Bill passed.

British s.s. *Herdis* (1,157 tons) and *Florentia* (3,680 tons) sunk by U-Boat off Robin Hood Bay; 3 lost.

French S. of Ourcq R. carried hill crest between Mosloy—Passy-en-Valois; half-mile advance on nearly 2-mile front.

Italians recovered Mte. di Val Bella (Asiago plateau); 800 prisoners. Five miles farther E. strong post taken at Sasso Rosso.

Czecho-Slovaks under Gen. Diterichs in control at Vladivostok.

*June 30.

During quarter ended June 30 world's tonnage began to show a net gain of 100,000 tons per month.

British s.s. *Wilton* (4,281 tons) torpedoed by U-Boat in English Channel; reached port.

British s.s. *Origen* (3,545 tons) sunk by U-Boat off Ushant; 1 lost.

British action N.W. of Albert; over 50 prisoners. French took 200 more prisoners between Ourcq R.—Marne R.

Ten French Armies now grouped under Gens. Fayolle, Maistre, and Castelnau; on left, First (Debeney) on Avre, Third (Humbert) to Nouvron, Tenth (Mangin) to Ourcq R., Sixth (Degoutte) to Marne R.; in centre, Ninth (Mitry) on Marne R., Fifth (Berthelot) W. of Reims, Fourth (Gouraud) E. of Reims; on right, Second (Hirschauer), Eighth (Gérard), and Seventh (Boissoudez).

Gen. Degoutte's order in honour of U.S. Marine Brigade's gallantry on 25-vi.-18 at Belleau Wood; this wood thenceforth to be styled in Army Orders "Marine Brigade Wood."

German G.H.Q. at this date were counting upon "victory," with the aid of 200,000 men from Austria, Ukraine, Palestine, etc.

Italians captured Col del Rosso; 2,000 prisoners.

H.M. submarine E21 torpedoed and sank an Austrian ammunition transport inshore close to Piana, Dalmatian coast.

July 1.

U.S. 2nd Division carried Vaux, near Château-Thierry; 450 prisoners. Farther N. French took St. Pierre Aigle.

July 1 (*continued*).

By July British effective Divisions in France had risen from 45 to 52.

During June British Independent Air Force carried out 74 raids on Germany.

British air raid on Mannheim.

British air raid on Cattaro.

Hindenburg and Ludendorff declared that, in view of Kühlmann's speech on 24-vi.-18, they could no longer work with him.

Mackensen Army Group in Rumania dissolved.

Col. Bitcherakoff left Enzeli for Alyat, S. of Baku.

U.S. transport *Corrington* torpedoed.

British s.s. *Charing Cross* (2,534 tons) sunk by U-Boat off Flamborough Head.

British s.s. *Westnoor* (4,329 tons) sunk by U-Boat about 200 miles N.W. from Casablanca; 2 lost.

Gen. von Lettow crossed Likungo R. (P. E. Africa).

July 2.

President Wilson announced that over 1,000,000 Americans had sailed for France.

Capt. F. C. Dreyer, R.N., Director of Naval Ordnance, appointed to new post of Director of Naval Artillery and Torpedoes, Naval Staff.

B.I. s.s. *Shirala* (5,306 tons) sunk by U-Boat off Owers Light; 8 lost.

British s.s. *Royal Sceptre* (3,838 tons) torpedoed by U-Boat in English Channel; reached port.

Kaiser and Chancellor at Spa vetoed Admiralty Staff proposal to enlarge the field for the new U-Boat cruisers by declaring submarine blockade of E. coast of America.

French advance near Moulin - sous - Touvent, N. of Aisne R.; 457 prisoners.

Americans took 100 more prisoners at Belleau—Vaux.

Italians captured important points on Grappa; 600 more prisoners. Heavy blow to Austrians in Piave Delta; over 1,900 prisoners.

Gen. von Lettow attacked Anglo-Portuguese force at Namacurra (P. E. Africa).

July 3.

Death of Lord Rhondda.

French advance between Autrèches—Moulin-sous-Touvent; over 1,000 prisoners.

Germans in Finland prepared to advance on Murman Railway.

Sultan of Turkey dead.

Gen. Bitcherakoff sailed from Enzeli for Alyat, 35 miles S.W. from Baku.

July 4.

President Wilson's address to Diplomatic Corps at Washington's tomb.

English-speaking Union founded.

American troops for first time in action brigaded with British on W. front.

Australian Corps (Gen. Monash) and Americans (of Gen. Bell's 33rd U.S. Division) captured Hamel, S. of Somme R.; over 1,500 prisoners. Of the 60 Tanks (Mark V.) engaged 55 came out undamaged.

U.S. First Army Corps regrouped, to include 1st, 2nd, 3rd, 4th, 26th, and 28th Divisions.

Italians took 419 more prisoners in Piave Delta.

British s.s. *Merida* (5,951 tons) torpedoed by U-Boat in Mediterranean; reached port; 1 lost.

Sundays marked with Asterisk (*).

July 5, 1918.

Australian front advanced 2,000 yards N.E. of Villers-Bretonneux.

Gen. von Lettow re-crossed Likungo R. (P. E. Africa), and drew off in N.E. direction.

British motor-vessel *Vera Elizabeth* sunk by U-Boat off Sydero, Faeroe Islands.

July 6.

Piave Delta cleared ; invaders back over New Piave. Since June 15 Italians had taken some 24,000 prisoners. Progress N. of Mte. Grappa ; 51 prisoners.

Franco-Italian offensive in S. Albania between coast—Tomorica Valley ; over 1,000 prisoners.

H.M. submarine C25 attacked by five German seaplanes with bombs and machine-guns off Harwich ; commander and five men killed.

British s.s. *Huntscraft* (5,113 tons) torpedoed by U-Boat in English Channel ; reached port ; 6 lost.

British s.s. *Port Hardy* (6,533 tons) sunk by U-Boat off Cape Spartel ; 7 lost.

British s.s. *Bertrand* (3,613 tons) sunk by U-Boat off Cape Bon, Tunis.

Count Mirbach, German Envoy at Moscow, murdered.

*July 7.

British s.s. *Ben Lomond* (2,814 tons) sunk by U-Boat off Daunt's Rock ; 23 lost.

German airmen bombed Belgian hospital near La Panne (Yser) ; over 50 girls killed.

Australians again advanced on 3,000-yard front in hills each side of Somme R.

July 8.

French thrust S. of Aisne, E. of Villers-Cotterets, on 2-mile front ; 370 prisoners.

Kaiser at Spa dismissed Herr von Kühlmann.

Italians forced Vojusa, N. of Avlona (Albania). British monitors co-operated.

Czecho-Slovaks at Irkutsk.

British s.s. *Mars* (3,550 tons) sunk by U-Boat off Bishop Rock.

British s.s. *Chicago* (7,709 tons) and *War Crocus* (5,296 tons) sunk by U-Boat off Flamborough Head ; 3 lost.

July 9.

Mr. J. R. Clynes Food Controller.

H.M. CMB2 accidentally burnt in Portsmouth Harbour.

Adm. von Hintze, German Foreign Secretary, vice Herr von Kühlmann.

July 10.

French took Courcy, N. of Ourcq R.

Italians at Berat ; French took 250 more prisoners near Tomorica R.

Baron Kress von Kressenstein, German Commissioner at Tiflis, telegraphed to Berlin appealing to Central Powers to intervene on behalf of Armenians who were threatened with extinction.

Gen. Horvath's new Siberian Government.

UB65 lost off Cape Clear.

British s.v. *Charles Theriault* set on fire by U-Boat in Atlantic ; towed in.

July 11.

U.S. supply ship *Westover* torpedoed.

P. & O. s.s. *Nellore's* ninth encounter with U-Boat ; escaped.

Work begun on oil pipe-line between Clyde and Forth.

Australian raid near Merris ; 150 prisoners.

July 12.

French took Castel—Auchin Farm, N.W of Montdidier ; over 500 prisoners. Longpont, near Villers-Cotterets Forest, regained

Austrians fell back in Albania ; over 2,200 prisoners to date.

Allied force on Murman coast.

Japanese battleship *Kawachi* blown up in Tokuyama Bay ; 500 lost.

July 13.

British 22nd Corps transferred to Ardre sector of French front.

British s.s. *Plawsworth* (4,724 tons) sunk by U-Boat off Bishop Rock ; 1 lost.

British s.s. *Badagri* (2,956 tons) sunk by U-Boat off Cape St. Vincent.

British s.s. *Imber* (2,154 tons) torpedoed by U-Boat in Mediterranean ; reached port.

Turkish attacks on British positions covering Jordan passages and N. of Jericho ; E. of Jordan Turks routed by Indian Lancers ; N. of Jericho British positions penetrated but restored ; 510 prisoners, including 350 Germans.

*July 14.

British advance E. of Dickebusch Lake on 2,000-yard front near Ridge Wood ; 328 prisoners.

Czecho-Slovaks captured Kazan.

French s.s. *Djemnah* sunk by U-Boat in Mediterranean ; 442 lost.

British s.s. *Branksome Hall* (4,262 tons) and *Waitemata* (5,432 tons) sunk by U-Boat off Marsa Susa.

Gen. Allenby's positions on both sides of Jordan attacked ; on W. position restored by Australian Light Horse Brigade ; on E. by the charge of another cavalry Brigade, including Jodhpur Lancers.

Gen. von Lettow at Ociva (P. E. Africa).

July 15.

The German Offensive. Fifth Aassult

Second Battle of the Marne.

German attack (with Third, First, and Seventh Armies) opened on 50-mile front E. and W. of Reims ; on E. between Prunay—Massiges Germans held in battle positions by Gen. Gouraud's Fourth Army, including U.S. 42nd Division ; on W. between Coulommes—Fossoy Germans advanced 2 to 3 miles. Marne crossed at Fossoy, &c. ; Americans retired, but recover ; 1,000 prisoners.

H.M.T. *Barunga* (7,484 tons) sunk off Bishop Rock.

July 16.

Ex-Tsar Nicholas II. murdered by Bolshevists at Ekaterinburg.

French held Germans E. of Reims, but slightly back at Prunay ; W. of Reims Germans progressed up Marne R. to Reuil, towards Epernay, and between Marne—Reims. Americans recovered N. of St. Agnan—La Chapelle. Germans claimed 13,000 prisoners.

Adm. von. Holtzendorff again sought to induce Chancellor Hertling to consent to U-Boat blockade of E. coast of America.

Marshal Conrad von Hötzendorf relieved of Trentino command and retired with title of Count and rank of " Colonel of all the Guards."

H.M. sloop *Anchusa* sunk by U-Boat off N. Ireland.

British s.s. *Southborough* (3,709 tons) sunk by U-Boat off Scarborough ; 30 lost.

July 16, 1918 (continued).

Italian T.B.D. *Garibaldino* sunk by collision.

British s.s. *War Swallow* (5,216 tons) sunk by U-Boat S.W. from Malta ; 7 lost.

July 17.

Australians advanced 600 yards, E. of Villers-Bretonneux on 2,000-yard front.

Germans progressed towards Epernay (held by Gen. de Mitry's Ninth Army), reached Montvoisin—Chêne la Reine ; latter regained ; between Marne—Reims they reached Nanteuil—Pourcy, but driven out by Italians. E. of Reims Germans defeated S. of Prunay. Germans claimed 18,000 prisoners to date.

Cunard s.s. *Carpathia* (13,603 tons) sunk by U-Boat W. by N. from Bishop Rock ; 5 lost.

British s.s. *Harlseywood* (2,701 tons) torpedoed by U-Boat in Bristol Channel ; beached.

July 18.

The Allied Offensive. First Assault : Battle of Tardenois.

Gen. Foch's great counter-stroke on 27-mile front at Fontenoy—Belleau, W. of Soissons—Château-Thierry. French Tenth Army (Gen. Mangin), including 1st and 2nd U.S. Divisions, with 20th Corps, reached Mont de Paris, one mile from Soissons and Crise Valley for 5 miles E. of Buzancy ; maximum penetration 8 miles ; 5,000 prisoners, 30 guns. S. of this Franco-Americans (Gen. Degoutte) advanced 3 to 5 miles. S. of Marne R. Germans reached St. Agnan heights. Gen. Gouraud retook Prunay.

In French Tenth Army area 223 out of 324 Tanks were engaged.

July 19.

British 9th Division retook Meteren, Lys front ; 350 prisoners.

Franco - American progress towards Soissons — Château - Thierry road ; 16,000 prisoners, 50 guns to date. S. of Marne R. Allies retook Montvoisin ; 400 prisoners, four guns. Germans claimed 20,000 prisoners since July 15.

U.S. cruiser *San Diego* mined off Fire Is.

White Star s.s. *Justicia* (32,234 tons) inward bound in convoy, attacked and hit with four torpedoes by UB64, about 20 miles W. by N. from Skerryvore.

UB110 rammed, depth-charged and destroyed by H.M.S. *Garry* and ML263 N.E. from Whitby.

Tondern (Schleswig-Holstein) bombed by British airmen, escorted by detachment of Grand Fleet, including H.M.S. *Furious* as aircraft-carrier ; two Zeppelins believed destroyed ; four British machines failed to return ; three landed in Danish territory.

H.M. CMB50 sunk in Heligoland Bight to avoid capture.

British s.s. *Polpero* (3,365 tons) torpedoed by U-Boat in Mediterranean ; reached port ; 3 lost.

July 20.

Germans recrossed Marne R. ; 20,000 prisoners, 400 guns to Allies to date.

H.M. submarine E34 lost in North Sea.

White Star s.s. *Justicia* (32,324 tons) again torpedoed and this time sunk by U54 off N. Ireland.

UB124 sunk by H.M. T.B.D. *Marne*.

July 20 (continued).

British s.s. *Gemini* (2,128 tons) sunk by U-Boat off Godrevy Light ; 2 lost.

British s.s. *Orfordness* (2,790 tons) sunk by U-Boat off Newquay ; 2 lost.

British s.s. *Kosseir* (1,855 tons) sunk by U-Boat off Alexandria ; 39 lost.

Gen. Dunsterville's Hants and Gurkha force at Resht defeated Jangali attack.

*July 21.

French retook Château-Thierry ; reached Soissons—Château-Thierry road along almost whole length. Between Marne R.—Reims British co-operating with French and Italians, took Bois de Courton, pushed down Ardre Valley, took Marfaux (which they lost) and Coitrin ; 1,500 more prisoners.

U-Boat sank three coal barges and tug off Cape Cod.

British s.s. *Mongolian* (4,892 tons) sunk by U-Boat off Filey Brig ; 36 lost.

British s.s. *Upada* (5,257 tons) torpedoed by U-Boat in Mediterranean ; reached port ; 3 lost.

July 22.

Allies crossed Marne R. at Chassins—Passy, near Dormans ; Germans retreated 5-6 miles beyond Château-Thierry, between Ourcq R.—Marne R. Franco-Americans reached Bezu—Epieds ; British between Marne R.—Reims took 200 prisoners. E. of Reims Gen. Gouraud reoccupied old positions.

Gen. Rogers Q.M.G. U.S. Army at Tours.

Allies over half-way between Berat—Elbasan (Albania) ; 3,000-4,000 prisoners.

British s.s. *Eurylochus* (5,723 tons) chased by U-Boat off Madeira ; escaped.

Gen. von Lettow crossed Namirue R. (P. E. Africa).

July 23.

French advanced on 2-mile front N. of Ourcq R., across Soissons—Château-Thierry road ; reached outskirts of Taux ; S. of Ourcq R. advanced towards Fère-en-Tardenois. Between Marne R.—Reims British again carried Marfaux ; 300 more prisoners. Between Montdidier—Amiens French (supported by 36 British Tanks) advanced 2 miles on 4-mile front towards Avre Valley ; took Mailly-Raineval, Sauvillers, Aubvillers ; 1,850 prisoners, four guns.

H.M. A.M.C. *Marmora* (10,500 tons) sunk by U-Boat off S. Ireland.

British s.s. *Anna Sofie* (2,577 tons) sunk by U-Boat off Trevose Head ; 1 lost.

British s.s. *Boorara* (6,570 tons) torpedoed by U-Boat in North Sea ; reached port.

British s.s. *Messidor* (3,883 tons) sunk by U-Boat off Port Mahon ; 1 lost.

British convoy for Assyrians of Urmia district reached Sain Kala.

July 24.

Allied progress N. of Château-Thierry towards Fère-en-Tardenois, to line Oulchy-le-Château—Jaulgonne ; also along Marne R. in Fère Forest ; five guns taken. British advance N. of Ardre R., between Vrigny—Ste. Euphraise.

German-Ukrainian Treaty ratified.

Baron von Hussarek Austrian Premier vice Dr. von Seidler.

H.M.S. *Pincher* wrecked on Seven Stones.

British s.s. *Defender* (8,520 tons) torpedoed by U-Boat off S. Ireland ; reached port.

British s.s. *Rutherglen* (4,214 tons) sunk by U-Boat off Port Mahon.

July 25, 1918.

First shipment of U.S. 14-inch naval guns reached St. Nazaire ; first gun in position on W. Front about a month later ; five of these guns fired in all 782 rounds at targets about Longuyon, Mengiennes, Montmédy, Laon, Mortiers, Terguier, &c.

Allied advance of about one mile ; Fère Forest—La Croix Rouge Farm won ; later Oulchy-le-Château—Villemontoire taken.

Czecho-Slovaks at Simbirsk (Volga).

British s.s. *Magellan* (3,642 tons) torpedoed by U-Boat off Cape Serrat ; 1 lost.

British s.s. *Indore* (7,300 tons) torpedoed by U-Boat off N. Ireland ; beached ; 2 lost.

Five British steamers, including s.s. *Melita* (13,967 tons) unsuccessfully attacked by U-Boats in Atlantic ; attacks repelled by gunfire.

British s.s. *Blairhall* (2,549 tons) sunk by U-Boat off Sunderland ; 1 lost.

July 26.

Germans yielding on Marne R. towards Epernay ; Reuil recovered. By nightfall general German retreat started in this direction, subsequently extending to Ardre R. and Ourcq R.

Anti-Bolshevist *coup* at Baku.

July 27.

German retreat spreading ; cavalry and Tanks pursuing. French took 200 prisoners at Mont-sans-Nom, E. of Reims.

1,250,000 Americans embarked for France by this date.

British s.s. *Kirkham Abbey* (1,166 tons) sunk by U-Boat off Winterton ; 8 lost.

British s.s. *Subadar* (4,911 tons) sunk by U-Boat off Cape Roca ; 3 lost.

✳July 28.

Adm. Scheer summoned to Spa to relieve Adm. von Holtzendorff as Chief of German Naval Staff.

Adm. Hipper to be C.-in-C. High Sea Fleet, vice Adm. Scheer.

French Air " Ace " records to this date : Lieut. Fonck 66 ; Lieut. Nungesser 44 ; Lieut. Madon 41 German machines brought down.

Since German retreat began Allies advanced 4 miles on 20-mile front. Ourcq R. forced ; Fère-en-Tardenois taken.

Gen. Rawlinson's Fourth (British) Army and Gen. Debeney's First (French) Army placed under Sir D. Haig for second Allied assault.

British s.s. *Hyperia* (3,908 tons) sunk by U-Boat off Port Said ; 7 lost.

July 29.

French carried German positions N.E. of Oulchy-le-Château ; Grand Rozoy taken ; 450 prisoners ; they surrounded Buzancy ; 200 prisoners. Bitter fighting between Fère-en-Tardenois—Ste. Euphrasie. Allies won Sergy. Australian advance at Morlancourt on 2-mile front ; 143 prisoners.

Hindenburg telegraphed to Enver Pasha, desiring " as a Christian " that Turkish Government should immediately permit return of 500,000 starving Armenian refugees to their homes in the Caucasus.

British s.s. *Rio Pallaresa* (4,034 tons) sunk by U-Boat E.N.E. from Malta ; 2 lost.

July 30.

H.M. special service ship *Stockforce* (732 tons) sunk by U-Boat in English Channel,

July 30 (*continued*).

after action in which submarine was destroyed by Q. ship's gunfire.

British s.s. *Bayronto* (6,045 tons) torpedoed by U-Boat in English Channel reached port ; 2 lost.

British s.s. *War Deer* (5,323 tons) torpedoed by U-Boat in North Sea ; reached port.

Australians captured Merris, on Meteren front ; 169 prisoners.

Bitter German resistance ; Allies straightened on E. wing ; took Romigny—St. Gemm in centre.

Marshal Eichhorn assassinated at Kieff

July 31.

UB108 lost in July ; cause unknown.

U-Boat tonnage built during 12 month ended 31-vii.-18 = 99 boats of total 68,67 tons.

During July there embarked for V Front 306,185 U.S. troops, as compared wit 278,800 in June, 246,000 in May, 118,50 in April, and 84,000 in March.

Americans, after hard fight, took Seringe Gen. Harbord in charge of U.S. Suppl Services at Tours vice Gen. Kernan.

August 1.

Anglo-French progress N. of Ourcq R ridge between Ourcq R.—Aisne R. carried 2-mile advance along Fère road ; 600 prisoner Farther E. Cierges won ; 100 prisoners.

Modyugski Island, Archangel, capture by Allied warships.

Armenian Parliament opened at Erivan

August 2.

Fall of Soissons following rapid Germa retreat ; Allies held Crise line ; farther they took Arcy—Coulanges ; E. of th Gueux—Thillois ; over 6 mile advance places ; over 50 villages regained.

H.M. T.B.D.s *Ariel* and *Vehement* min in North Sea.

British s.s. *Malvina* (1,244 tons) sunk b U-Boat off Flamborough Head ; 14 lost.

Adm. Scheer Chief of German Admiral Staff, vice Adm. von Holtzendorff, retir and promoted Grand Admiral.

French submarine *Floréal* lost by collisi in Ægean.

Allied landing at Archangel.

Japan, in concert with U.S., decided land troops at Vladivostok.

August 3.

Germans across Vesle R. ; Allied advan on 30-mile front to Fismes ; Americans outskirts. Germans withdraw behind Anc R. ; Hamel—Dernancourt abandoned.

Gen. Bullard, H.Q. Coulanges, in co mand of U.S. Third Army Corps (e " French " 38th Corps), with 32nd U. Division in line, 28th in support, and 3 in reserve, advancing towards the Vesle.

H.S. *Warilda* (7,713 tons) torpedoed a sunk by U-Boat off Owers Light ; 112 wound drowned.

UB53 mined in Otranto Barrage.

Enver Pasha replies to Hindenbur appeal of 29-vii.-18 that on military groun he could not permit return of all 500,000 A menian refugees to the Caucasus, since th were in league with the British.

British landing at Vladivostok.

✳August 4.

Battle of Tardenois ended with relief Paris, recovery of Château-Thierry a

*August 4, 1918 (*continued*).

Soissons, and Allied capture of 35,000 prisoners, 700 guns.

French reached Vesle, E. of Fismes, which was taken by Americans. U.S. Third Army Corps H.Q. at Coulanges. E. of Soissons Allies across Aisne R., Germans withdraw on right bank of Avre, between Montdidier—Moreuil on 10-mile front.

British Mission at Enzeli.

British s.v. *Nelson* sunk by U-boat off Shelburne, N.S.

British s.s. *Clan Macnab* (4,675 tons) sunk by U-boat off Pendeen Light ; 22 lost.

British s.s. *Waipara* (6,994 tons) torpedoed by U-Boat in English Channel ; reached port ; 1 lost.

August 5.

Last airship attempt on England :

Five airships off E. Anglian coast ; no bombs dropped ; L70, Germany's most modern airship (with the German airship Commodore, Capt. Strasser, on board), brought down in flames 40 miles from land.

Lull on Vesle front.

Long-range bombardment of Paris resumed.

British s.s. *Luz Blanca* (4,868 tons) sunk by U-Boat about 25 miles S.W. from Outer Gas Buoy, Halifax, N.S. ; 2 lost.

British s.s. *Freshfield* (3,445 tons) sunk by U-boat off Cape Colonne, Italy ; 3 lost.

British s.s. *Polescar* (5,832 tons) and *Tuscan Prince* (5,275 tons) torpedoed by U-Boat in English Channel ; reached port ; 2 lost.

British Consulate at Moscow raided by Bolshevists.

August 6.

Gen. Foch to be Marshal of France.

Gen. Pétain received Military Medal.

Gen. von Bolhn to command new Army Group (2nd, 18th, and 9th German Armies) on Ancre-Oise front.

German attack S. of Morlancourt ; part of Australian gains retaken.

French Senate condemned M. Malvy to five years' banishment.

British s.s. *Bencleuch* (4,159 tons) attacked by U-Boat off Cape Hatteras.

British s.s. *Highland Harris* (6,032 tons) sunk by U-Boat off Eagle Island ; 24 lost.

British s.s. *Biruta* (1,732 tons) sunk by U-Boat off Calais ; 12 lost.

H.M.S. *Comet* sunk by U-Boat in Mediterranean.

British s.s. *Clan Macneil* (3,939 tons) sunk by U-Boat off Alexandria.

August 7.

Franco-Americans across Vesle R. between Braine—Fismes. German attacks between Oise—Aisne, near Vailly—Tracy-le-Val repulsed. N. of Reims French advance between Réthel—Laon railways.

French cruiser *Dupetit-Thouars* torpedoed by U-Boat in N. Atlantic.

British s.s. *Clan Macvey* (5,815 tons) attacked by U-Boat in English Channel ; torpedo missed.

August 8.

The Allied Offensive. Second Assault : The Battle of Amiens.

" The Black Day of the German Army."
--Ludendorff, in his " War Memoirs."

Sir D. Haig attacked on 15-mile front E. of Amiens with Fourth British Army (Gen.

August 8 (*continued*).

Rawlinson), including Canadian, Australian, and 3rd British Corps, and First French Army (Gen. Débeney). British reached objectives N. and S. of Somme R. French attacked from Braches and crossed Avre ; 100 guns, 7,000 prisoners by 3 p.m. Advance at one point 7 miles deep.

Germans styled the Ancre—Avre Battle the " Tank-Battle." Whole of British Tank Corps, less one brigade, engaged ; out of 435 machines assembled 430 went forward. On second day 145, and on third day 67 were in action.

Kaiser at Spa entertained Archduke William, Austrian " Pretender " to Ukraine.

Gen. Count Kirchbach in command of German Kieff Army Group, vice Marshal Eichhorn, murdered 30-vii.-17.

British s.s. *Clan Macvey* (5,815 tons) sunk by U-Boat about ½ mile from Anvil Point ; 7 lost.

British s.s. *Portwood* (2,241 tons) torpedoed by U-Boat in English Channel ; reached port ; 3 lost.

August 9.

On Lys Germans evacuated more positions won in April offensive. British advanced mile from W. of Merville to Locon.

Anglo-French progress N. and S. of Somme R. N. of river Germans momentarily regained Chipilly. British advanced S. of Somme, took Mebaricourt and Rosières—Lihons, within 2 miles of Chaulnes. Farther S. French took Pierrepont ; over 4-mile advance to Arvillers ; 24,000 prisoners, over 200 guns. Gen. Humbert's French Third Army struck S.E. on German flank below Montdidier.

Americans took Fismettes (Vesle) ; 100 prisoners.

Austrian 1st Division (Gen. Metzger) on Verdun front ; Austrian 35th Division in Woevre.

Last long-range bombardment of Paris. During whole period since March 23, 168 shells fired. Total casualties : 196 killed, 417 wounded.

Gabriele d'Annunzio's flight over Vienna.

British s.s. *Glenlee* (4,915 tons) sunk by U-Boat off Owers Light ; 1 lost.

British s.s. *Anselma de Larrinaga* (4,090 tons) torpedoed by U-Boat in English Channel ; reached port.

August 10.

French carried Montdidier ; progress in three days' fighting over 12 miles along Amiens—Roye road. Hallu, on Roye—Chaulnes railway, captured.

British s.s. *Madame Renee* sunk by U-Boat off Scarborough ; 10 lost.

*August 11.

Fight between British naval light forces and aircraft reconnoitring W. Frisian coast and German aircraft. German airship down in flames. H.M. CMBS 40, 42, and 47 sunk.

Stiff fighting at Lihons ; German attacks repulsed. French advance S. and S.W. of Roye ; Les Loges, S.E. of Tilloloy, and Carnoy Farm, before Lassigny *massif*, taken.

German G.H.Q. issued General Order noting that at Amiens the Second Army had been surprised by massed Tank attack.

Crown Prince Boris of Bulgaria at Spa.

First Japanese troops at Vladivostok.

Gen. von Lettow's forces, after reconnoitring to the coast at Angoche (P. E.

*August 11, 1918 (*continued*).

Africa), turned sharp southward at Chalau and from Metil they turned W. to Ili.

British s.s. *City of Adelaide* (8,389 tons) sunk by U-Boat E.N.E. from Malta ; 4 lost.

British s.s. *Penistone* (4,139 tons) sunk by U-Boat S.W. from Nantucket Island ; 1 lost.

August 12.

British progress near Roye road, E. of Fouquescourt, and on S. bank of Somme.

Herr Helfferich, Count Mirbach's successor at Moscow, reported to Kaiser at Spa that he had transferred seat of German mission in Soviet Russia to Pskoff.

British raids on Jerusalem—Schechem road ; 600 Turkish casualties.

British s.s. *Anhui* (2,209 tons) sunk by U-Boat off Cape Greco, Cyprus ; 4 lost.

August 13.

King George returned to England from nine days' visit to W. Front.

French holding most of Lassigny *massif ;* severe fight for Bois des Loges ; French took Belval, 2 miles S. of Lassigny. Since Aug. 8 : 675 guns counted and 28,000 prisoners. Since July 18 : 70,000-80,000 prisoners.

Hindenburg, Ludendorff, Chancellor Hertling, Foreign Secretary Hintze conferred at Spa and agreed that war could no longer be ended by military means.

Czecho-Slovaks recognised as Allies.

British s.s. *City of Brisbane* (7,094 tons) sunk by U-Boat off Newhaven.

August 14.

Germans evacuating Ancre positions in Hébuterne sector ; Beaumont Hamel, Serre, Puisieux, Bucquoy abandoned. French progressed N. and E. of Lassigny *massif* to E. of Belval ; on Oise R. they took Ribécourt.

Kaiser at Spa conferred with Crown Prince, generals and ministers, and instructed Adm. von Hintze to invoke mediation of Queen of Netherlands.

Gen. von Lettow pursued in P. E. Africa about 60 miles inland from coast at Angoche.

British s.s. *Wallsend* (2,697 tons) sunk by U-Boat off Robin Hood Bay.

UB57 mined off Zeebrugge.

August 15.

French completed capture of Lassigny *massif*. Since Aug. 8 : 33,000-34,000 prisoners, 600-700 guns.

British troops crossed Ancre ; progress between Beaucourt-sur-Ancre—Puisieux.

German air raid on Paris suburbs.

Emperor Charles, Count Burian, and Gen. von Arz conferred at Spa with Kaiser, Hertling, Hindenburg and Ludendorff ; need for peace agreed ; neutral mediation to be preferred.

British troops now holding road from Baghdad through Persia, to Enzeli, whence detachments sent to Baku and to E. shore of Caspian.

H.M.SS. *Scott* and *Ulleswater* sunk by U-Boat in North Sea.

August 16.

German repulse by British at Dammery. Anglo-French progress towards Fresnoy-les-Roye—Fransart. French progress W. of Roye and in Loges Wood.

Gen. Otani, commanding Allied expedition at Vladivostok.

August 16 (*continued*).

Sir Chas. Eliot British High Commission in Siberia.

British s.s. *Lackawanna* (4,125 ton attacked E. of New York by U-Boat wit two torpedoes and gunfire ; torpedoes missed and steamer escaped, after replying wit her own gun.

British s.s. *Mirlo* (6,978 tons) sunk b U-Boat about ½ mile S. by E. from Wimb Shoal Buoy, Cape Hatteras ; 9 lost.

British s.s. *Escrick* (4,151 tons) sunk b U-Boat off Cape Finisterre ; 1 lost.

August 17.

Allies within 1,000 yards of Roye. Frenc carried Canny-sur-Matz ; progress betwee Oise—Aisne.

British s.s. *Eros* (1,122 tons) sunk b U-Boat off Filey Brig ; 7 lost.

British s.s. *Denebola* (1,481 tons) sun by U-Boat off Gurnard Head ; 2 lost.

British s.s. *Zinal* (4,037 tons) sunk b U-Boat N.E. from Terceira (Azores) ; 2 los

Laibach Slav congress opened.

Gen. Dunsterville arrived in s.s. *Presider Kruger* at Baku, whither he had been precede by 39th Brigade from Baghdad.

*August 18.

British advance on 4 miles front betwee Vieux Berquin—Bailleul ; Oultersteene taken 676 prisoners. French advance in angl between Oise—Aisne on 10-mile front betwee Tracy-le-Val—Nouvron-Vingre.

Kaiser left Spa for Homburg, wher German Empress had suffered a heart attack

August 19.

French attacked N. of Oise R. betwee Noyon—Lassigny ; Le Hamel taken. Britis advanced on 6-mile front opposite Mervill which they enter.

British s.s. *Charity* (1,735 tons) torpedoe by U-Boat in Bristol Channel ; reached port

British s.s. *Idaho* (3,023 tons) sunk b U-Boat off Cape Villano ; 11 lost.

British s.s. *Marie Suzanne* (3,106 tons sunk by U-Boat off Mudros.

British s.s. *Umvolosi* (2,980 tons) mine in Indian Ocean ; reached port.

Bolshevist raid at Gradekovo (Vladivos tok—Kharbin railway).

August 20.

The Battle of the Ailette.

Gen. Mangin advanced 3 miles betwee Oise—Aisne ; over 8,000 prisoners. Lombra reached.

Prince Eitel Friedrich, Kaiser's second son, in command of 1st Prussian Guard Divi sion on German Ninth Army (Oise—Aisne front.

Three British fishing vessels captured b U-Boat off Cape Canso, N.S. ; two sunk third, *Triumph* (239 tons), converted int German raider.

British s.s. *Boltonhall* (3,535 tons) sunk by U-Boat off Bardsey Island ; 5 lost.

French submarine *Circé* torpedoed b Austrian U-Boat off Cattaro.

Baron Kress von Kressenstein telegraphed final appeal to Berlin to intervene on behal of Armenia ; otherwise, he said, responsibility for extinction of this ancient Christian people would fall upon Central Powers.

August 21.

The Battle of Bapaume.

Gen. Byng's Third Army, with 28(Tanks, attacked on 10-mile front N. of Ancre

August 21, 1918 (*continued*).

R. ; Beaucourt, Bucquoy, Ablainzeville, Moyenneville reached in first stage ; Achiet-le-Petit, Courcelles in second. Gen. Humbert at Lassigny. S. of Oise R. Gen. Mangin advanced to Cuts, Camelin, Pontoise, out-flanking Noyon. Nearer Soissons, French captured Laval.

British air-raids on Frankfurt, Cologne, Mannheim, and Treves.

Adm. von Hintze informed Reichstag party leaders of German Government's efforts to secure peace.

British s.v. *Pasadena* sunk by U-Boat S.S.E. from Cape Canso, N.S.

British s.s. *Thespis* (4,343 tons) attacked by U-Boat E. from New York ; torpedo missed ; steamer escaped.

British s.s. *Diomed* (7,523 tons) sunk by U-Boat E.S.E. from Nantucket Island ; 2 lost.

British s.s. *Boscawen* (1,936 tons) sunk by U-Boat off Bardsey Island ; 1 lost.

August 22.

New British stroke between Ancre R.—Somme R. on over 6-mile front from N. of Bray to Albert ; German counter-attack N. of Bray drove back advanced British troops. Since 21-viii.-18 over 5,000 prisoners. Gen. Mangin progressed S. of Oise R. to Quierzy ; St. Aubin—Pommières taken.

British s.v. *Abbasieh* sunk by U-Boat off Alexandria.

ML403 blown up in Runswick Bay while endeavouring to salve German torpedo.

British s.s. *Palmella* (1,352 tons) sunk by U-Boat off S. Stack ; 28 lost.

August 23.

Main attack in Bapaume Battle by British Third and Fourth Armies, supported by about 100 Tanks.

British engaged on 30-mile front from Mercatel, 5 miles S. of Arras, to Lihons ; on left, Gomiécourt, Ervillers, Hamelincourt, Boyelles, Boiry-Bacquerelle taken ; on left centre Achiet-le-Grand, Bihucourt, and ridge overlooking Irles carried ; S. of Somme R. Herleville, Chuignes, Chuignolles taken by Australian Corps. German lines penetrated over 2 miles deep ; thousands of prisoners. Bray taken by Australians at midnight. Gen. Mangin holding Oise—Ailette line as far as Coucy-le-Château railway.

British s.s. *Australian Transport* (4,784 tons) sunk by U-Boat off Marittimo ; 1 lost.

August 24.

British occupied more high ground S.E. of Albert ; Thiepval Ridge carried ; La Boisselle, Ovillers, Mouquet Farm, Thiepval, Grandcourt taken ; Miraumont outflanked ; Loupart Wood—Biefvillers carried ; Bapaume outskirts reached at Avesnes ; on extreme left St. Leger—Henin-sur-Cojeul captured.

U.S. 301st Heavy (Tank) Battalion left Wool for France, where it fought with British Tank Corps.

Adm. von Hintze advised Baron von Kress that Berlin Government had exhausted its diplomatic resources on behalf of Armenia and that further action must wait upon developments elsewhere (see 20-viii.-18).

British s.s. *Delphinula* (5,238 tons) torpedoed by U-Boat in Mediterranean ; reached port.

Gen von Lettow crossed Upper Likungo R. (P. E. Africa).

Third U.S. Registration.

August 24 (*continued*).

British s.s. *Flavia* (9,291 tons) sunk by U-Boat off Tory Island ; 1 lost.

British s.s. *Virent* (3,771 tons) sunk by U-Boat off the Smalls.

British s.s. *Auckland Castle* (1,084 tons) sunk by U-Boat off Farn Island ; 12 lost.

*August 25.

Neuville Vitasse—Favreuil carried, and whole Albert—Bapaume road, with Martin-puich, Le Sars, Warlencourt, Le Barque, Mametz, Mametz Wood ; 17,000 prisoners.

British s.s. *Erik* and four British fishing vessels captured and sunk by U-Boat off St. Pierre and Little Miquelon, N.F.L. ; a fifth captured by converted decoy-trawler *Triumph*.

U-Boat (number unknown) sighted, depth-charged and destroyed by H.M.S. *Medea* 3 miles E. from Whitby.

Austrians claimed recapture of Berat (Albania).

British s.s. *Willingtonia* (3,228 tons) sunk by U-Boat off Marittimo ; 4 lost.

Gen. von Lettow now marching N. on Regone (P. E. Africa).

August 26.

The Battle of the Scarpe.

British attack spread northwards along both banks of Scarpe ; N. of river German first line carried S. of Gavrelle ; Roeux outskirts reached ; S. of river Orange Hill, Wancourt, Monchy taken. High ground between Croisilles—Heninel captured ; below this Bazentin-le-Grand, and Suzanne—Cappy (Somme).

U.S. 339th Infantry Regiment and other American details embarked at Newcastle for Archangel, to co-operate with Anglo-French forces there.

U-Boat captured and sank British s.v. *Gloaming* off St. Pierre, N.F.L.

U.S. auxiliary *Tampa* torpedoed in Channel.

Austrians retook Berat.

British Baku Force attacked by Turks.

August 27.

British advanced along whole front ; took Fontaine-les-Cappy (S. of Somme R.), Ver-mandovillers, Longueval, Delville Wood, Bernafay Wood, Beugnatre (N.E. of Bapaume), Fontaine-les-Croisilles, Chérisy, Vis-en-Artois, Sart Woods (between Scarpe R.—Sensée R.) ; above Scarpe R., Roeux, Green-land Hill, Gavrelle. Roye fell to Gen. Debeney.

U.S. Senate passed Man Power Bill.

British s.s. *Ant Cassar* (3,544 tons) sunk by U-Boat off Strumble Head.

German-Russian Supplementary Treaty, on basis of which Germans hoped to establish German-Turkish-Ukrainian-Russian under standing.

August 28.

German retreat on most of front from Scarpe R. to above Aisne ; S. of Scarpe Canadians took Boiry—Notre Dame—Pelves ; farther S. Croisilles taken ; on N. bank of Somme Hardecourt—Curlu carried. French took Chaulnes—Nesle, and in Noyon sector Pont l'Evêque, Suzoy, Vaucherelles, Por-quericourt.

UC.70 depth-charged and destroyed by H.M.S. *Ouse* in North Sea.

British s.s. *Lompoc* (7,270 tons) torpedoed by U-Boat in North Sea ; reached port ; 1 lost.

August 28, 1918 (*continued*).

British s.s. *Giralda* (1,100 tons) sunk by U-Boat off Whitby ; 6 lost.

August 29,

Fall of Bapaume and Noyon to British and French respectively. British fighting on line Combles, Morval, Beaulencourt, Frémicourt ; S. of Somme R. they took most of ground up to bed of river at Péronne, with Hem on N. bank. Gen. Mangin's centre over Ailette R.

U.S. Senate passed clause in Food Production Bill to effect that U.S. should be entirely "dry" from July 1, 1919, until demobilisation completed.

UB109 mined in Folkestone Barrage.

H.M. escort ship *Puruni* wrecked off Mayere Is., Grenadines, W. Indies.

Dutch Minister in Berln ihad by this date expressed readiness, in accordance with Adm. von Hintze's appeal, to invoke good offices of his Government in favour of mediation.

August 30.

British entered Bailleul.

Canadians took Haucourt, N. of junction of Hindenburg and Quéant—Drocourt lines. London and W. Lancs troops took and lost Bullecourt—Heudecourt. British cross Somme S. and W. of Péronne. French crossed Canal du Nord ; entered Chevilly ; seized Mont St. Siméon, E. of Noyon.

U.S. 64th Infantry ("The Terrible") Brigade stormed Juvigny.

Gen. Pershing (G.H.Q. Ligny) in command of U.S. First Army Sector, on 50-mile front from Port-sur-Seille, E. of Moselle, to Châtillon-sous-les-Côtes, E. of Verdun, with following forces in line for attack on St. Mihiel salient : U.S. 1st Corps, Gen. Liggett (H.Q. Saizerais) ; U.S. 4th Corps, Gen. Dickman (H.Q. Toul) ; French 2nd Colonial Corps, Gen. Blondlat (H.Q. Ernécourt) ; U.S. 5th Corps, Gen. Cameron (H.Q. Ancemont) ; with 2,900 guns.

Count Burian notified Berlin Government of Austrian intention to take independent peace action.

Gen. von Lettow engaged at Lioma (P. E. Africa).

Two British fishing vessels sunk by U-Boat off St. John's, N.F.L.

August 31.

Germans abandoned Kemmel—Steenwerck.

Australians took Mont St. Quentin, above Péronne. French advanced N. of Noyon ; took Campagne on E. bank of Canal du Nord. Gen. Mangin progressed above Soissons, carried Juvigny, Crécy-au-Mont, Leury, Crouy.

Capt. Cromie, R.N. murdered by Bolshevists at British Embassy, Petrograd.

Anglo-Russian Baku Force attacked by Turks.

President Wilson signed U.S. Man Power Bill.

British s.s. *Milwaukee* (17,323 tons) sunk by U-Boat S.W. from Fastnet ; 1 lost.

UB12 mined in North Sea during August.

✳September 1.

On Lys front Neuve Eglise captured.

Fall of Péronne ; Sailly-Saillisel taken ; on left, British took Bouchavesnes—Rancourt and reached W. edge of St. Pierre Vaast Wood ; 2,000 prisoners. Bullecourt—Heude-

✳September 1 (*continued*).

court retaken, with Beaulencourt and high ground at Mœuvres.

This day closed second stage of British offensive. First stage freed Amiens ; second stage turned Somme line. In ten days 2⅓ British Divisions had beaten 35 German Divisions, taking 34,000 prisoners, 270 guns

Fresh Turkish attack at Baku.

British preliminary assault on Vardar R

British s.s. *Baron Minto* (4,537 tons torpedoed by U-Boat in Mediterranean reached port.

Gen. von Lettow's E. African force reduced to 176 whites and 1,487 native troops

British s.s. *Actor* (6,082 tons) torpedoed by U-Boat in Irish Channel ; reached port.

British s.s. *City of Glasgow* (6,545 tons) and *Mesaba* (6,833 tons) sunk by U-Boat off Tuskar Rock ; 32 lost.

September 2.

British Offensive. Third Stage : Wotan position stormed.

Drocourt—Quéant line breached by Canadians of Gen. Horne's First Army and 17th Corps of Gen. Byng's Third Army on 6-mile front from Etaing to neighbourhood of Quéant ; Dury and, later, Cagnicourt—Villers taken ; Le Transloy—St. Pierre Vaast Wood captured ; 18,000 prisoners. Gen Mangin took Neuilly—Terny Sorny.

Hindenburg on anniversary of Sedan (1870) warned German Army and people against enemy propaganda.

British s.s. *Ariadne Christine* (3,550 tons mined in Arctic Ocean ; towed in.

British s.s. *San Andres* (3,314 tons) sun by U-Boat N.W. from Port Said.

Czechs and Semenoff's Cossacks in touch

September 3.

Germans evacuated Lens.

Fall of Drocourt ; English, Scottish, an Naval troops, under Gen. Fergusson, through Quéant—Pronville defences, and advanced on Inchy—Mœuvres ; later Baralle, Ruman court, Lécluse, behind Drocourt—Quéan line, taken. S. of Péronne French across Somme R. ; 1,400 prisoners.

During the fortnight from August 2 the British artillery on W. Front fired a daily average of over 11,000 tons of ammunition.

Count Hertling explained to Prussia Ministerial Council that Central Power could not risk making direct offer of peace but that every effort was being made t enlist neutral interest.

British s.s. *Highcliffe* (3,238 tons) sun by U-Boat off Tuskar Rock ; 1 lost.

September 4.

Ploegsteert and Hill 63 carried.

British in Mœuvres—Ecourt ; betwee Mœuvres—Péronne N. Zealanders too Ruyaulcourt and reached N. fringe of Havrin court Wood ; Manancourt—Etricourt carrie

British s.s. *Arum* (3,681 tons) sunk b U-Boat off Pantellaria.

British s.s. *War Firth* (3,112 tons) sun by U-Boat off the Lizard ; 11 lost.

September 5.

Gen. Humbert advanced towards S Quentin, from Noyon. N. of Vesle R. Frenc reached Aisne between Condé—Vieil—Arcy.

Hetman Skoropadski in Berlin.

Turks drove in Miane post betwee Kasvin—Tabriz.

Japanese at Khabarovsk.

September 6, 1918.

By the evening of this day the Lys salient had disappeared.

German retreat from Somme line from Péronne southwards. British advance on 12-mile front astride Amiens—St. Quentin road. Farther S. French N. of Oise R. took Ham—Chauny. Americans reached S. bank of Aisne at Condé—Villers.

Adm. von Hintze returned from Vienna to Berlin with information that Emperor Charles desired immediate peace.

Obozerskaya, 75 miles S. of Archangel, in Allied hands.

Gen. von Lettow engaged by K.A.R. column near Mt. Hulua (P. E. Africa).

British s.s. *Milly* (2,964 tons) sunk by U-Boat off Tintagell Head ; 2 lost.

September 7.

White Star s.s. *Persic* (12,042 tons) torpedoed by U-Boat N.W. Scilly Isles ; reached port.

British s.s. *Bellbank* (3,250 tons) sunk by U-Boat off Planier Island ; 1 lost.

British s.s. *Ruysdael* (3,478 tons) sunk by U-Boat off Ushant ; 12 lost.

Fighting on Armentières—Lens front.

*September 8.

H.M.S. *Nessus* sunk by collision in North Sea.

U.S. 3rd Corps relieved on Vesle by French 16th Corps and transferred to Souilly.

German G.H.Q. ordered that, for field signal purposes, messages concerning Tanks should have priority.

German resistance at Cambrai—St. Quentin.

French on Crozat Canal.

King of Bavaria at Sofia.

September 9.

N. of Havrincourt Wood British carried high ground overlooking Hindenburg line ; reached edge of Gouzeaucourt—Epéhy ; progress beyond Vermand. French across Crozat Canal.

Prince Frederick Charles of Hesse accepted offer of Finnish " Crown."

British s.s. *War Arabis* (5,183 tons) sunk by U-Boat off Cape Sigli, Algeria.

British s.s. *Policastra* (4,594 tons) torpedoed by U-Boat in Mediterranean ; reached port.

U92 mined in Northern Barrage.

British s.s. *Missanabie* (12,469 tons) sunk by U-Boat off Daunt's Rock ; 45 lost.

September 10.

UB83 depth-charged and destroyed by H.M.S. *Ophelia* in North Sea.

Adm. Scheer at G.H.Q., Spa.

Fighting in Siegfried positions continued.

September 11.

British between Cambrai—St. Quentin, took Attilly, Vermand, Vendelles. British captured Railway Triangle.

Adm. von Hintze, on return to Spa from visit to Vienna, instructed Berlin Foreign Office that Kaiser and G.H.Q. favour immediate appeal to Queen of Netherlands and that Germany's Allies should be advised.

New economic agreement for 1918-1919 signed at Kieff between Ukraine and Central Powers.

H.M. oiler *Tatarrax* sunk by explosion off Alexandria.

September 12.

The Battle of Havrincourt—Epéhy.

S.S. *Galway Castle* torpedoed.

British success on Cambrai front ; Trescault, Gouzeaucourt Wood, Havrincourt, Mœuvres taken ; 1,500 prisoners ; W. of St. Quentin British gained Holnon Wood ; French took Savy.

Battle of St. Mihiel.

Gen. Pershing attacked with First American Army St. Mihiel salient ; on S., on 12-mile front between Xivray—Fey-en-Haye, 5 mile advance in places ; Thiaucourt, Pannes, Nousard, Mt. Sec taken ; on W. of salient Combres carried ; 16,000 prisoners, 443 guns.

S.S. *Galway Castle* (7,988 tons) torpedoed and sunk by U-Boat S.W. from Fastnet ; 143 lost.

H.M. armed steamer *Sarnia* sunk by U-Boat in Mediterranean.

British s.s. *Chao Chow Fu* (1,909 tons), torpedoed by U-Boat in Mediterranean ; reached port.

September 13.

St. Mihiel salient flattened out.

Honved Division in Lorraine.

British 7th, 23rd, and 48th Divisions reduced from 13 to 10 battalions ; surplus battalions sent to France.

British s.s. *Buffalo* and *Setter* sunk by U-Boat off Corsewall Point ; 19 lost.

British s.s. *M. J. Craig* sunk by U-Boat off Black Head ; Belfast ; 4 lost.

September 14.

French carried Allemant—Laffaux Mill ; 2,500 prisoners.

During the six months from March 10 British airmen on Italian Front brought down 294 Austro-German aeroplanes and 9 balloons.

Austrian Peace Note ; concurrent German offer for Belgium to revert to neutrality ; old commercial treaties to be maintained, " Flemish " question to be dealt with, no indemnities, no reparation.

German Minister at Helsingfors communicated an offer that German troops should not attack in E. Karelia, provided Allies withdrew from N. Russia.

Allied bombardment of Bulgarian front from Doiran to Monastir.

U.S. men of 18-45 registered.

British s.s. *Neotsfield* (3,821 tons) sunk by U-Boat off Skulmartin Light.

British s.s. *Gibel-Hamam* (647 tons) sunk by U-Boat off Abbotsbury, Dorset ; 21 lost.

British s.v. *Aghios Nicolaos* captured and sunk by U-Boat off Paphos.

Turks (Caucasus-Islam Army) attacked at Baku ; British evacuated town and returned to Enzeli.

*September 15.

German retreat between Meuse—Moselle continued on 33-mile front from Bezonvaux, N.E. of Verdun, to Norroy, N. of Pont-à-Mousson ; Metz fortress guns in action. Further French advance E. of Vauxaillon ; Mt. des Singes taken ; 1,300 prisoners ; Vailly also taken.

Last German air raid on Paris ; two raiders down.

Franco-Serb offensive by Orient Army under Gen. Franchet d'Espérey and Marshal Mishitch, in Balkans against Bulgarians and German Eleventh Army (Gen. von Steuben).

British s.s. *Kendal Castle* (3,885 tons) sunk by U-Boat off Berry Head ; 18 lost.

Sundays marked with Asterisk (*).

September 16, 1918.

President Wilson's reply to Austria : U.S. " can and will entertain no proposal for a conference upon a matter concerning which it has made its position and purpose so plain."

Count Hertling explained to Conservative leader, Count Westarp, that Count Burian's peace step had prejudiced the appeal to Dutch mediation.

Franco-Serb advance on Dobropolje ; 16-mile front pierced in places to depth of 5 miles ; 4,000 prisoners, 30 guns.

Nuri Pasha entered Baku.

H.M.S. *Glatton* (5,700 tons), coast defence ship, blown up at Dover.

UB103 depth-charged and destroyed by H.M. airship SSZ1 and H.M. drifter *Young Crow* in Dover Straits.

British s.s. *Lord Stewart* (1,445 tons) sunk by U-Boat off Hopes Nose ; 1 lost.

British s.s. *Serula* (1,388 tons) sunk by U-Boat off Strumble Head ; 17 lost.

British s.s. *Ethel* (2,326 tons) sunk by U-Boat off Berry Head.

British s.s. *Acadian* (2,305 tons) and *Madryn* (2,244 tons) sunk by U-Boat off Trevose Head ; 25 lost.

British s.s. *Philomel* (3,050 tons) sunk by U-Boat off Glenan Island.

British s.s. *Tasman* (5,023 tons) and *Wellington* (5,600 tons) sunk by U-Boat off Cape Villano ; 19 lost.

September 17.

Franco-Serb progress in Macedonia on 22-mile front reached Tcherna R. ; advance in some places 12½ miles.

Egyptian s.v. *Cairo* sunk by U-Boat off Alexandria.

Gen von Lettow reached Mwembe (P. E. Africa).

British s.s. *Muriel* (1,831 tons) sunk by U-Boat off Peterhead.

British s.s. *Lavernock* (2,406 tons) sunk by U-Boat off Trevose Head ; 25 lost.

September 18.

Gen. Ludendorff at German G.H.Q. informed Adm. Scheer that abandonment of Flanders coast might eventually become necessary.

British Third and Fourth Armies attacked on 16-mile front at Holnon—Gouzeaucourt, stormed outer defences of Siegfried line, particularly before Le Verguier, Villeret, Hargicourt, and W. and S.W. of Bellicourt, on St. Quentin Canal ; Lempire taken ; 6,000 prisoners. French advanced about 2,000 yards on 6-mile front ; took Savy Wood—Fontaine-les-Clercs.

On this occasion British used dummy Tanks with great success.

At the close of these operations, in which 15 British Divisions defeated 20 German Divisions, and completed fourth stage of British offensive, British had taken nearly 12,000 prisoners and 100 guns.

Serb cavalry reached Poloshko (Tcherna R.) ; another cavalry force near Prilep ; Bulgarians in full retreat ; Anglo-Greek troops attacked W. and E. of Lake Doiran.

Japanese occupy Blagoveshtchensk.

British s.s. *Primo* (1,037 tons) sunk by U-Boat off Godrevy Light

British s.s. *John O. Scott* (1,235 tons) sunk by U-Boat off Trevose Head ; 18 lost.

September 19.

Great British attack in Palestine against Seventh, and Eighth Turkish Armies, reinforced by German special troops of " Asia Corps." Gen. Allenby struck on 16-

September 19 (*continued*).

mile front between Rafat and the sea infantry advanced 12 miles to Tul Keran railway junction ; cavalry advanced 22 mile to Liktera ; 8,000 prisoners.

British gain N. of Gauche Wood ; ove 10,000 prisoners to date. Mœuvres retaken

Serbs within 8 miles of Vardar R. and along Tcherna R. on left.

UB104 mined in Northern Barrage.

British s.s. *Barrister* (4,952 tons) sun by U-Boat off Chicken Rock, Isle of Man 30 lost.

September 20.

Gen. Allenby's advance in Palestine Nazareth, Afuleh, Beisan occupied by cavalry

French took Benay, S. of St. Quentin.

French submarine *Circé* sunk by L Boat off Cape Rodoni.

September 21.

Infantry advanced in Palestine to Be Dejan—Samaria—Bir Asur line ; cavalr operated southwards from Jenin—Beisan 18,000 prisoners, 120 guns to date.

British s.s. *Polesley* (4,221 tons) sunk b U-Boat off Pendeen Light ; 43 lost.

Franco-Serb armies passed Vozarci an Kavadar towards N. and reached Vardar F towards Negotin—Demir Kapu.

#September 22.

French Second Army relieved on Argonn front as far as La Harazée by Gen. Pershing Army, comprising : Gen. Dickman's 4t U.S. Corps at Port-sur-Seille ; Gen. Blondlat French 2nd Colonial Corps in Woevre Gen. Claudel's French 17th Corps i Verdun salient ; Gen. Bullard's 3rd U.! Corps extending thence to Malancourt ; Ge Cameron's 5th U.S. Corps to Vauquoi Gen. Liggett's 1st U.S. Corps to La Harazé where Gen. Gouraud's French Fourth Arm adjoined.

Bulgarian retreat on nearly 100-mi front, between Monastir—Lake Doira Allies took Ghevgeli (Vardar) ; Italians carrie Bobiste (Selechka Mts).

British s.s. *Gorsemore* (3,079 tons) sur by U-Boat off Cape Colonne, Italy.

Gen. Allenby reported Seventh and Eight Turkish Armies virtually ceased to exist 25,000 prisoners, 200 guns counted.

September 23.

Count Tisza, on a mission of inquiry int Southern Slav demands, estranged la sympathies for Monarchy by arrogant speec to local delegates at Serajevo, Bosnia.

French carried Prilep.

Fourth Turkish Army withdrawn towar Amman, Hedjaz railway, pursued by Coloni and Jewish troops, who reached Es Salt ; Hai —Acre occupied.

British s.s. *Aldershot* (2,177 tons) sunk l U-Boat off Dartmouth ; 1 lost.

British s.s. *Edlington* (3,864 tons) sur by U-Boat off Cape Passaro, Sicily.

September 24.

Kaiser visited Kiel U-Boat School ar expressed hope that U-Boats would still tu tide of war.

Anglo-French attack on 4-mile front : of Vermand towards St. Quentin. Briti progress near Selency ; 800 prisoners. Fren took Francilly-Selency ; over 500 prisoners.

German G.H.Q. informed Berlin Gover ment that armistice negotiations had becor inevitable.

For List of Abbreviations see page iv.

September 24, 1918 (continued).

Allied forces within 10 miles of Veles—Ishtip and Veles—Prilep roads; Vardar valley from Gradsko to Ghevgeli captured.

September 25.

British cavalry occupied Tiberias, Semakh, Ea Samrah on Sea of Galilee, and Amman, Hedjaz Railway; 45,000 prisoners, 265 guns to date.

British captured Selency.

Bulgaria proposed armistice; Gen. Franchet d'Espérey refused to suspend operations, but indicated conditions. Serbs captured Ishtip—Veles, cavalry pressed towards Uskub; Serb cavalry at Kochana, nearing Bulgarian frontier. British in Bulgaria opposite Kosturino, 6 miles S. of Strumnitza; over 10,000 prisoners, more than 200 guns.

Derbyshire Yeomanry, leading troops of British 16th Corps, were first Allied troops to enter Bulgaria.

U156 mined in Northern Barrage.

British s.s. Hebburn (1,938 tons) sunk by U-Boat off Mine Head; 6 lost.

September 26.

Battle of Champagne and Argonne.

Franco-American attack on 40-mile front from Mid-Champagne to the Meuse; French (Gen. Gouraud) advanced on left several miles; U.S. First Army (Gen. Pershing) advanced average 7 miles; Montfaucon—Varennes taken.

British troops, 16th Corps, at Strumnitza.

Bulgarian parlementaire, under white flag, in British lines.

September 27.

Battle of Cambrai—Hindenburg Line.

British First and Third Armies with 65 Tanks attacked before Cambrai; Hindenburg Line broken; Beaucamp, Flesquières, Graincourt taken; Canadians carried Bourlon—Bourlon Wood, Haynecourt; 10,000 prisoners.

Franco-American progress in Champagne; French crossed railway E. of Somme-Py; advance up to 6½ miles; 10,000 prisoners. Americans continued; 8,000 prisoners to date.

British s.s. Hatasu (3,193 tons) sunk by U-Boat off Oran; 2 lost.

French took Drushevo (Balkans).

Australian cavalry crossed Upper Jordan at Jisr Benat Yakub

Arabs in Deraa.

September 28.

Anglo-Belgian attack under King Albert on 23-mile front from near Dixmude to Ploegsteert; 4-mile advance took all Houthulst Forest; Wytschaete captured; 4,000 prisoners. British fleet co-operated off Belgian coast.

British before Cambrai took Gouzeaucourt, Marcoing, Sailly, Palluel.

Gen. Mangin advanced on Aisne R.; Germans withdrew to Ailette R.

In Champagne, French took Somme-Py and Maure; Americans reached Brieulles—Exermont.

German G.H.Q. demanded reconstruction of Berlin Government.

At Spa Hindenburg and Ludendorff agreed upon a German request for an armistice that would permit defence of Rhine line.

Bulgarian plenipotentiaries (MM. Liaptcheff and Radeff, with Gen. Lukoff) passed through British lines on way to Salonika.

Egyptian s.v. Benha sunk by U-Boat off Ras el Dabaa, W. from Alexandria.

Junction with Arabs near Deraa.

September 28 (continued).

Gen. von Lettow reached Upper Rovuma R. (P. E. Africa), and crossed back into G. E. Africa at Nagwamira.

British s.s. Baldersby (3,613 tons) sunk by U-Boat off Godling Light; 2 lost.

* September 29.

German Naval Corps ordered to prepare evacuation of Flanders U-Boat Base. The Corps had begun the day before its last battle on the coast, which it had held since 3-ix.-14 and defended with some 30 heavy guns (five 15-inch, four 12-inch, &c.), and many Q.F. batteries.

Anglo-Belgian progress of 4·6 miles; 6,000 prisoners; Dixmude, Passchendaele, Gheluvelt, Messines, &c., occupied; Roulers—Menin road reached.

British Fourth Army engaged on 12-mile front N. of St. Quentin.

British-American (2nd U.S. Corps) battle on 30-mile front from N. of Sensée R. to St. Quentin neighbourhood. British reached Cambrai outskirts; broke Hindenburg Line on 6-mile front between Cambrai — St. Quentin; 22,000 prisoners in three days.

During the three days crucial battle (September 27, 28, and 29) the British artillery fired nearly 65,000 tons of ammunition.

Gen. Mangin reached Ailette R.

At Spa German Foreign Secretary von Hintze informed Hindenburg and Ludendorff that he had not invoked Queen Wilhelmina's good offices, but favoured appeal to President Wilson. Kaiser concurred with Supreme Command in necessity for immediate action.

French cavalry at Uskub.

Bodies of Grand Duchess Elizabeth Feodorovna, Grand Duke Serge Michailovitch, and three other Grand Dukes murdered by Bolshevists found at Alapalvsk.

U.S. battleship Minnesota mined; reached port.

British s.s. Nyanza (4,053 tons) sunk by U-Boat off the Maidens; 13 lost.

British s.s. Libourne (1,219 tons) sunk by U-Boat off the Lizard; 3 lost.

ML247 wrecked off St. Ives.

UB115 destroyed by H.M.SS. Ouse and Star, with H.M. airship R29, in North Sea.

September 30.

Anglo-Belgian progress; Belgians fighting in Staden. British within 2 miles of Menin.

British in Cambrai outskirts; Blécourt, Masnières, Crèvecour, Villers-Guislain taken. Gap in Hindenburg Line enlarged by capture of Thorigny and Le Tronquoy.

Gen. Berthelot attacked between Vesle R.—Aisne R.

French carried Marfaux—Aure (Champagne).

Count Hertling and German Secretaries of State resigned. Kaiser and Hindenburg left Spa for Berlin.

Bulgaria surrendered on Allied terms.

French took Uskub.

Fall of Damascus.

H.M.S. Seagull sunk in collision in Firth of Clyde.

During September:
U102 mined in Northern Barrage;
UB127 mined in Northern Barrage;
UB113 probably lost in North Sea.

Before evacuating Flanders coast Germans destroyed: UB10, UB40, UB59, and UC4. Of the T.B.D.s, 24 returned to Wilhelms-

September 30, 1918 *(continued)*.

haven; 2 others were destroyed. Of the guns only 10 11-inch guns on railway mountings were retrieved; the remainder were blown up, including 5 15-inch, 4 12-inch, and a large number of 8-inch and 4-inch Q.F. guns.

During September German workshops turned out 774 torpedoes, four times as many as during whole of 1913. During war U-Boats alone fired about 5,000 torpedoes.

October 1.

Over 250,000 prisoners taken by Allies in France since July 15.

Belgian Army past Moorslede—Staden—Dixmude.

Fall of St. Quentin to French First Army; N. of St. Quentin British took Levergies—Estrées, and Vendhuile.

French progress between Vesle R.—Aisne R.

Gen. Gouraud advanced on 14-mile front in Champagne; took Birnaville, Condé, Autry, Vaux.

Naval, military, and industrial conference at Cologne on feasibility of new U-Boat programme.

In Austrian Chamber Baron von Hussarek proclaimed eleventh hour reconstruction of Dual Monarchy under federal auspices.

Italian advance in Albania; Berat taken.

German Eleventh (Balkan) Army reinforced by Prusso-Bavarian "Alpine Corps," &c.

British s.s. *Montfort* (6,578 tons) sunk by U-Boat W. by S. from Bishop Rock; 5 lost.

British s.s. *Bylands* (3,309 tons) sunk by U-Boat N.W. from Cape Villano.

October 2.

British took Ledeghem and crossed Lys R. between Wervicq—Comines. Germans withdrew from Armentières and Lens. British took Fleurbaix.

British broke Rumilly—Beaurevoir—Fonsomme line between Cambrai—St. Quentin.

Anglo-Italian warships attacked Durazzo; bombard base; sink two Austrian T.B.D.s.

H.M. oiler *Arca* (4,839 tons) sunk by U-Boat 40 miles N.W. from Tory Is.; 52 lost.

British s.s. *Bamse* (1,001 tons) and *Poljames* sunk by U-Boat off the Lizard; 24 lost.

B.I. s.s. *Nevasa* (9,071 tons), Glasgow to New York, attacked by heavy-gunned U-Boat off U.S. coast; escaped.

Two U-Boats presumed sunk by U.S. S.C.S. 215, 128 and 129.

October 3.

Franco-Belgian advance to Hooglede and Hooglede—Roulers road. British occupied Armentières.

N. of St. Quentin British Fourth Army attacked on 8-mile front, taking Sequehart; on left they took Ramicourt—Wiancourt, and N., Le Catelet—Gouy. S.E. of Le Catelet Australians broke Beaurevoir.—Fonsomme line.

French took Loivre, N.W. of Reims, and Challerange (Champagne).

Prince Max of Baden German Chancellor; Herr Solf at F.O.; Socialists accepted office.

October 3 *(continued)*.

Hindenburg attended Prince Max's first council in Berlin, and urged necessity for immediately ending the war.

British s.s. *Ariel* (3,428 tons) sunk by U-Boat off Cape Tenez.

British s.s. *Westwood* (1,968 tons) sunk by U-Boat off the Lizard; 1 lost.

British s.s. *Eupion* (3,575 tons) sunk by U-Boat off Loop Head; 11 lost.

October 4.

British advance on 20-mile front E. of Armentières—Lens; between Lens—Cambrai, N. of Scarpe R. and E. of Epinoy.

Franco-American advance between Reims—Verdun; French gained high ground N. and N.W. of Somme-Py; Americans advanced 2 miles on Varennes—Grand-Pré road.

German Note to President Wilson proposing Armistice.

Hindenburg returned to Spa.

King Ferdinand of Bulgaria abdicated in favour of Crown Prince Boris.

German Balkan units fighting Bulgarian rebels near Sofia.

British s.v. *Industrial* sunk by U-Boat off Nantucket Island.

H.M. submarine L10 (1,070 tons) sunk by German T.B.D.s in action in North Sea after herself sinking H.I.M. T.B.D. S33.

UB68 destroyed by H.M.S. *Snapdragon* and H.M. trawler *Cradosin* N.E. from Malta.

British s.s. *Oopack* (3,883 tons) sunk by U-Boat E. from Malta.

Egyptian s.v. *Kassid Karim* sunk by U-Boat off Alexandria.

Gen. von Lettow marching N. into G. E. Africa, W. of Songea.

October 5.

Further German Note to U.S.

British now holding main Hindenburg defences. During preceding nine days 30 British and 2 U.S. Divisions had beaten 39 German Divisions, taking 36,000 prisoners, 380 guns.

Germans retired from Scheldt Canal, which British Third Army crossed with its right and occupied Hindenburg Line to eastward.

German retreat in Champagne on 30-mile front to Suippes R.—Arnes R.; Moronvilliers Ridge—Brimont Fort captured.

British s.s. *Reventazon* (4,050 tons) sunk by U-Boat off Kassandra Point, Salonika Gulf; 15 lost.

Sir C. Eliot at Ekaterinburg.

*October 6.

British took Tresnoy, N. of Scarpe R.

French passed beyond Nogent l'Abesse—Arnes R. Germans behind Suippe R.; French crossed at Bertricourt.

Gen. Lord Cavan to command Tenth Italian Army, comprising 11th Italian and 14th British Corps.

Zahlek—Rayak, 30 N.W. of Damascus, occupied.

H.M. A.M.C. *Otranto* (12,000 tons) wrecked off Islay after collision.

October 7.

N. of Scarpe R. British gained Oppy—Biache St. Vaast.

N.E. of St. Quentin French took Remancourt.

French crossed Suippe R. at Pont Givart—Amenancourt; took Berry-au-Bac (Aisne).

October 7, 1918 (*continued*).

Spartacus Group conference at Gotha advocated formation of " Soviets " in Germany.

Italians captured Elbasan (Albania).

Talaat Ministry resigned.

Gen. Marshall ordered to attack Turkish Sixth Army covering Mosul.

October 8.

Second Battle of Le Cateau.

Great British attack by Third and Fourth Armies, assisted by Franco-Americans, on 21-mile front, Cambrai—St. Quentin, towards Le Cateau—Guise; in S. French took Essigny-le-Petit—Fontaine. Americans and British captured Beaurevoir—Masnières line, reached Cambrai—Guise road.

On British front 82 Tanks went into action : second recorded Tank duel took place this day ; German Tanks again routed.

Gen. Gouraud threatened Suippe line ; took Bazancourt ; entered Isles-sur-Suippe.

E. of Meuse R., Franco-American advance N. of Verdun.

British troops reach Beirut.

British s.s. *Thalia* (1,308 tons) sunk by U-Boat off Filey Brig ; 3 lost.

October 9.

Fall of Cambrai to Canadians of First Army. British Third and Fourth Armies, with British cavalry, defeated 23 German divisions between Cambrai—St. Quentin. Allies within 12 miles of Le Cateau. French advanced 5 miles E. of St. Quentin.

Italians at Elbasan.

President Wilson inquired in whose name Prince Max was speaking.

October 10.

British s.s. *Leinster* (2,646 tons) sunk by U-Boat off Kish Light, on Dublin—Holyhead route ; 176 lost.

British captured Le Cateau ; E. of Cambrai reached Solesmes-—Le Cateau road ; progress towards Douai between Lens—Scarpe R.

E. of St. Quentin French reached Oise line.

French passed Challerange ; took Grand-Pré station.

Gen. Milne to command Allied troops against Turkey.

October 11.

E. of Cambrai British won high ground at St. Aubert ; N. of Scarpe R. they advanced through the N. stretch of Drocourt—Quéant line.

German retreat between Soissons—Laon road and Grand-Pré ; Chemin des Dames, Suippe line, and main pass through Argonne evacuated. In Champagne on 37-mile front French at places penetrated over 6 miles.

Gen. Lord Cavan established near Treviso his H.Q. as commanded Tenth (Anglo-Italian) Army.

Baalbek (Syria) occupied.

October 12.

Prince Max informed President Wilson that he spoke in name of German people, and that German Army would evacuate occupied territories.

British in Douai outskirts and on Sensée Canal ; line extended up Selle R. to Haspres.

Gen. Pershing, while retaining supreme command of A.E.F., transferred command of

October 12 (*continued*).

U.S. First Army to Gen. Liggett ; Gen. Bullard to command new Second Army, with H.Q. at Toul.

Franco-Italian advance across Chemin-des-Dames.

Gen. Gouraud reached Vouziers.

Gen. O. von Below relieved Gen. von Mudra in command of German First Army, now withdrawn from Reims front.

Allies occupied Nish.

＊October 13.

President Wilson demanded German capitulation.

French (Gen. Mangin), occupied Laon—La Fère ; Germans retreating on nearly 100-mile front from Oise, E. of St. Quentin, to Argonne ; St. Gobain Forest evacuated, French occupied whole bend of Aisne and face Réthel.

Egyptian s.v. *Hamidieh* sunk by U-Boat N.W. from Alexandria.

Tripolis (Syria) occupied.

October 14.

Belgian, French (Gen. Degoutte), and British (Gen. Plumer) attack under King Albert on 28-mile front at Dixmude—Wervicq ; British Fleet co-operated. French carried Roulers, Belgians Iseghem ; farther N. Cortemarck Station captured.

Italians under Gen. Albricci took Sissonne, on Hunding Line.

Gen. Guillaumat to command French Fifth Army vice Gen. Berthelot, ordered back to Rumania.

Italians occupied Durazzo—Tirano.

British troops reached Irkutsk and left for Krasnoyarsk.

Gen. von Lettow reached Pangire (Jacobi) G. E. Africa.

British s.s. *Dundalk* (794 tons) sunk by U-Boat off Skerries, Anglesey ; 21 lost.

H.M. submarine J6 (1,900 tons) accidentally sunk in North Sea.

H.M. CMB71A missing off Belgian coast.

October 15.

Last German long-range bombardment of Dunkirk ; 2 women killed. In all during the war 7,514 bombs and projectiles were thrown into the town from land, sea, and air ; total 233 persons killed ; 336 injured. British D.S.C. and French Croix de Guerre were conferred on the town.

Allied progress in Flanders ; British took Menin ; Allies within a mile of Thourout.

S.W. of Lille British crossed Haute Deule Canal.

N. of Aisne R. French took Olizy and Termes near Grand-Pré.

German Federal Council resolved Constitutional changes whereby Reichstag invested with control over war and peace.

Cavalry occupied Homs.

October 16.

British Second Army captured Wervicq, Comines, Halluin, Wevelghem in Lys Valley, and part of Courtrai. Belgians and French take Ingelmünster—Lichtervelde, and outflank Thourout.

German reaction about Haussy.

H.M. collier *War Council* (5,875 tons) sunk by U-Boat W.S.W. from Cape Matapan.

Sundays marked with Asterisk (*).

October 16, 1918 (*continued*).
British s.s. *Pentwyn* (3,587 tons) sunk by U-Boat off the Smalls ; 1 lost.
UB90 engaged and sunk by H.M. submarine L12 off Danish coast.

October 17.
Fall of Ostend, Lille, and Douai.
Ostend evacuated. Adm. Keyes landed ; later King and Queen of Belgians visited town in H.M.S. *Termagant ;* and Belgian troops entered. Lille entered by British troops of Fifth Army. British across Haute Deule Canal, entered Douai.
Battle of the Selle.
Great Anglo-French attack southward from Le Cateau. N. of Oise R. 2 miles advance ; further N. Selle line forded by Tanks and part of Le Cateau carried.
Hungary separated from Austria.
Austria proclaimed a "Federation" of German-Austrians, Czechs, Ukrainians, and Yugo-Slavs.
Gen. von Lettow marches westward from Ubena to Kidugalla (G. E. Africa).
British s.s. *Bonvilston* (2,866 tons) sunk by U-Boat off Corsewall Point.

October 18.
Blankenberghe occupied ; Belgians close to Bruges ; French E. of Thielt towards Ghent. Gen. Plumer's Second Army advanced E. of Roubaix—Tourcoing. Gen. Horne's First Army completed conquest of Douai. Sensée R. crossed N. of Courtrai ; advance towards Denain. British-American offensive continued at Le Cateau—Bohain ; Wassigny—Ribeauville taken.
Provisional Czecho-Slovak Government in Paris recognised by Allies.
British entered Ubena (G.E. Africa), where they captured Gen. Wahle and other German sick.
British s.s. *Hunsdon* (2,899 tons) sunk by U-Boat off Strangford Light Buoy ; 1 lost.

October 19.
Belgians occupied Zeebrugge—Bruges. French (Gen. Degoutte) at Thielt. Gen. Debeney on Sambra—Oise Canal. British First Army captured Denain. French (Gen. Mangin) attack in German salient between Oise R.—Serre R. penetrated Hunding line on 3-mile front.
French nearing Widin (Danube).
British s.s. *Almerian* (3,030 tons) mined and sunk off Licata, Sicily.
UB123 mined in Northern Barrage.

*October 20.
Belgian coast cleared ; Germans in retreat from Dutch frontier to S. of Valenciennes. British Second Army 4 miles beyond Courtrai on Brussels road. British attack on Selle front at Denain—Le Cateau ; passage forced.
Sir D. Haig's message of thanks to Gen. Read for gallant services of U.S. 2nd Corps on Gen Rawlinson's Fourth Army front.
Hungarian troops mutinied in Val Sugana.
Gen. Townsend at Mitylene.
H.M. monitor M21 mined off Ostend.

October 21.
Germans on Lys Canal, Lys, Scheldt (Hermann) line. British Fifth Army reached Tournai outskirts ; progress towards Valenciennes.

October 21 (*continued*).
British 14th Corps (Gen. Babington) took over N. sector of Italian 11th Corps front from Salletuol to Pallanzon.
Karl Liebknecht released from prison.
German extreme Socialists began large purchases of arms with Russian money.
British s.s. *Moscow* (1,622 tons) scuttled by Bolshevists in Petrograd.
British s.s. *Saint Barchan* sunk by U-Boat off St. John's Point, Co. Down ; 8 lost.
ML561 mined off Ostend.

October 22.
British First Army entered W. suburbs of Valenciennes. Franco-Belgian attack on Lys Canal towards Ghent ; canal crossed ; 11,000 prisoners.
French (Gen. Mangin) advance on Serre front ; Chalandry—Grandloup captured.
Italian T.B.D. raid on San Giovanni di Medua.

October 23.
President Wilson's final reply to Germany ; willing to take up question of armistice, but extraordinary safeguards must be demanded.
British Third and Fourth Armies advanced 3-4 miles between Scheldt—Le Cateau on 20-mile front ; farther N. First Army, between Valenciennes—Tournai, took Bruay, Bleharies, Espain, towards Tournai.
French crossed Souche R.
Emperor Charles and Empress Zita visited Hungary.
Turkish retirement under British pressure in Mesopotamia towards Lesser Zab ; British within 4 miles of Kirkuk.

October 24.
British Third and Fourth Armies progressed between Scheldt R.—Sambre R. ; approached Landrecies—Mormal Forest ; in centre they arrived within a mile of Valenciennes-Metz railway.
Anglo-Italians, under Lord Cavan, gained footing on Grave di Papadopoli Is. in Piave R. In Grappa Italians took Mte. Solarolo ; French take Sisemol.
Hungarian troops mutinied at Fiume.
At Budapest Emperor Charles witnessed fall of Weckerle Cabinet.
Count Burian resigned.
Turks abandoned Fatha position (Tigris).

October 25.
British First Army N. of Valenciennes pushed through Raismes Forest into Condé loop of Scheldt. On S. Third Army gained 8 miles of Valenciennes—Avesnes railway Fourth Army co-operated on right.
French attack between Oise R.—Aisne R. on 25-mile front.
Berlin Government suppressed Hindenburg's order to the Army to fight on.
Anglo-Italian Army crossed Piave.
At Budapest Count Karolyi formed Hungarian National Council ; while Emperor Charles ordered Count Hadik to form new Ministry.
British entered Kirkuk and forced Lesser Zab.

October 26.
British took Artres—Famars, S. of Valenciennes ; farther S. they carried Englefontaine.
First French Army crossed Péron ; advanced between Sissonne—Château-Porcien

For List of Abbreviations see page iv.

October 26, 1918 (*continued*).

At Bellevue Castle in Berlin, Ludendorff tendered his resignation to Kaiser, who accepted. Hindenburg followed suit, but Kaiser urged him to remain.

Fall of Aleppo.

Turkish envoys arrived at Mudros; quartered in H.M.S. *Agamemnon*.

*October 27.

German retreat between Oise R.—Serre R. towards Hirson.

German reserves at Seraincourt bombed by 200 Allied aeroplanes.

Gen. de Castelnau in command of new group (Gen. Gérard's Eighth Army and Gen. Mangin's Tenth Army) for attack against Metz.

Gen. Gröner First Staff-Quartermaster to Hindenburg vice Gen. Ludendorff.

Professor Lammasch Austrian Premier; Count Julius Andrassy at Ballplatz.

Austria - Hungary sued for separate peace.

Czechs proclaimed their freedom.

Lord Cavan's Anglo-Italian Army now 2-3 miles beyond Piave R. Italian 18th Corps allotted to Tenth Army.

Italians captured Alessio (Albania).

Count Bernstorff resigned German Embassy to the Porte.

British 11th Cavalry Brigade in Mesopotamia in position in Huwaish Gorge blocking road to Mosul.

October 28.

Kaiser transfers to Reichstag his military and similar prerogatives.

Italians crossed Piave R., in Montello region.

Austria asks for Armistice.

Muslimieh Junction, N. of Aleppo, occupied.

British took Kalat Shergat (Tigris).

German U-Boats from Pola and Cattaro, 16 in number, set out on return voyage to German ports.

UB116 mined in entrance to Scapa Flow.

U78 sunk by H.M. submarine G2 in North Sea.

Insubordination in H.I.M.S. *Markgraf* on North Sea Station.

October 29.

H.M.S. *Ulysses* sunk by collision in Firth of Clyde.

On eve of final sortie into North Sea, German Battle Fleet assembled off Wilhelmshaven detained by mutiny in several ships.

French in outskirts of Guise.

Three Italian Armies progressed on 30-mile front; Tenth Army forced Monticano, N. of Oderzo; Twelfth Army carried Valdobbiadene and Mte. Cosen; Eighth Army (again including 18th Corps) captured Conegliano—Vittorio; Third Army across Lower Piave at San Dona di Piave—Zenson; 33,000 prisoners.

U.S. 332nd Infantry Regiment at Treviso at disposal of Gen. Diaz. This regiment was attached to Italian 31st Division, which had joined British 14th Corps.

Serbian cavalry reached Danube near Semendria.

Yugo-Slav independence proclaimed.

Italians at San Giovanni di Medua, Albania.

Gen. Milne on Maritza, with two British divisions, one French division, and 1st Hellenic division, ready to advance against Constantinople.

October 29 (*continued*).

Turks brought to battle 5 miles N. of Kalat Shergat; 1,000 prisoners.

October 30.

Kaiser left Berlin for W. Front.

German warships refused to sail further than Heligoland; Third High Sea Squadron passed to Kiel.

British entered Asiago.

Austrian defeat on Monticano and Livenza turned into a rout.

Austrian independence proclaimed.

Count Tisza murdered.

Hungarian Republic proclaimed. Count Karolyi given full powers to restore order.

Surrender of Ismail Hakki and Turkish Army on Tigris after six days' battle near Kalat Shergat; 7,000 prisoners.

Armistice with Turkey signed on board H.M.S. *Agamemnon* at Mudros : Passage for Allied Fleets through Bosporus to Black Sea; occupation of forts in Dardanelles and Bosporus necessary to secure their passage; immediate repatriation of all Allied prisoners.

October 31.

Spread of mutiny in German Navy; ships in Jade draw their fires.

Austrian Flagship *Viribus Unitis* torpedoed by Italians at Pola.

U47, U65, U72, U73, UB48, UB 129, UC25, UC34, UC53, and UC54 were destroyed by Germans at Pola and Cattaro during October to avoid surrender.

Italians entered Skutari.

Germans in Anatolia entrained for Constantinople. Lapse of Yildirim Command.

Gen. Lewin at Altun Keupri.

November 1.

British captures announced in October : 49,000 prisoners, 925 guns, 7,000 machine guns, 670 trench mortars.

Total Allied captures : 105,871 men, 2,472 officers, 2,064 guns, 13,639 machine guns, 1,193 trench mortars.

Allies at Audenarde.

The Battle of the Sambre.

British attacked Valenciennes; crossed Rhonelle R.; took Maresches—Aulnoy.

Franco-American advance from Vouziers —Olizy—Meuse; French took Rilly aux Oies, Semuy, Voncq, Falaise; Americans at St. Georges, Landreville, Chennery Bayonville, Cléry-le-Grand, &c.

Allied Conference at Versailles.

Royal Berkshire Regiment, 48th Division, pushing forward in Asiago sector, carried Monte Catz.

Ukrainians seized Lemberg.

British cavalry 12 miles S. of Mosul.

H.M. submarine G7 lost in North Sea.

November 2.

British (4th Canadian Division) entered Valenciennes; advanced to Marly, took Préseau—St. Hubert.

French reached Ardennes Canal; Americans at Buzancy, Cléry-le-Petit, Briquenay, Champigneulle.

French airman Lieut. Fonck brought down 6 German machines; total 75.

Hindenburg in a fresh "pastoral" appealed to all Germans to unite.

British 48th Division carried Monte Mosciagh, and by dark reached Vezzena, on Austrian soil, thus being first British force to enter enemy territory on W. Front.

Emperor Charles at Schönbrunn received Allied demand for capitulation.

Sundays marked with Asterisk (*).

November 2, 1918 (*continued*).

British s.s. *Murcia* (4,871 tons) sunk by U-Boat N. from Port Said ; 1 lost.

British s.s. *Surada* (5,324 tons) sunk by U-Boat in Port Said swept channel.

British s.s. *War Roach* (5,215 tons) torpedoed by U-Boat in Port Said swept channel ; reached port.

Gen. von Lettow, after forced marches, crossed from G. E. Africa into Rhodesia between Fife and Mwenzo.

＊November 3.

Allies at Ercloo ; nearing Ghent.

Germans fell back S. of Valenciennes and N. of Tournai.

Argonne cleared by Franco-Americans.

Americans took Halles, Brieulles-sur-Bar, Barricourt, &c.

German seamen's demonstration at Kiel.

Gen. Lord Cavan's Tenth Army on Tagliamento.

Italians occupied Trent.

Italians landed at Trieste and Lissa.

Emperor Charles signed order for cessation of hostilities and transferred chief command.

Ukrainians seized Czernowitz.

German Eleventh Army on Save—Danube line.

November 4.

Allied Offensive. Last Assault ; Battle of Sambre and Oise.

Decisive attack by British Fourth, Third, and First Armies on 30-mile front supported by 37 Tanks.

Great British advance on Valenciennes—Oisy line ; Fesmy, Catillon, La Folie, Landrecies, Locquignol, half Mormal Forest, Louvignies, Jolinetz, Herbignies, Le Quesnoy, Orsinval, Frasnoy, Reux-le-Bois, Preux-au-Sart, Bry, Eth, Wargnies-le-Grand, Wargnies-le-Petit, Sebourg, part of Rombies taken.

French on S. bank of Ardennes Canal.

Americans took Laneuville (Meuse), opposite Stenay, and crossed river ; U.S. 5th Division first across.

Versailles Conference settled Armistice terms.

Red Flag hoisted in all warships at Kiel, three officers shot in *König* for defending the ensign. Deputy Noske arrived.

U.S. 332nd Infantry Regiment received baptism of fire in brilliantly forcing Tagliamento.

Austrians accepted Armistice (3 p.m.).

H.M. patrol boat P12 sunk by collision in Channel.

November 5.

President Wilson informs German Government that Marshal Foch will receive accredited delegates and communicate Armistice terms.

The Grand Withdrawal of the German Armies in the West before the U.S. First Army ; the French Fourth, Fifth, Third, and First Armies ; and the British Fourth, Third, and First Armies.

German retreat on whole Scheldt—Meuse line. S. of Sambre—Oise Canal British take Prisches—Maroilles ; N. of Canal clear Mormal Forest ; nearing Bavai ; E. of Valenciennes they cross Belgian frontier ; take Roisin, Meaureau, Angreau ; held up at Angre and along Honelle R.

Last Tank action : 8 Whippets in support of Guards N. of Mormal Forest.

American advance towards Sedan.

November 5 (*continued*).

Bolshevist Envoy Joffe expelled fro Berlin.

General strike at Hamburg.

H.M. aircraft carrier *Campania* (18,0(tons) sunk by collision with H.M.S. *Reven* in Firth of Forth.

November 6.

Prime Minister announces in Commor that Versailles Conference has agreed Armi tice terms, and Germany has been referre to Marshal Foch.

German Armistice delegates, Herr Er berger, Count Oberndorff, Gen. von Günde Gen. von Winterfeld and Naval Capt. vc Selow, leave for front.

Kaiser arrives at Spa from Berlin.

British take Angre, cross Honelle R. take Quiévrechain—Baisieux and Aulnoyc.

French entered Guise ; cleared Nouvic Forest : took Vervins—Réthel.

Americans in W. outskirts of Sedan.

Bolshevist Envoy Joffe, before leavir Berlin, transfers 4,000,000 roubles to Germa Independent Socialist Cohn for revolutionar propaganda in Germany.

Directorate of Polish People's Republ formed.

Bavarian Chasseurs from Caucasus starte on four months' homeward march throug Ukraine.

Gen. von Lettow reaches Kajaml (Rhodesia).

November 7.

German Armistice delegates reache French lines in evening and proceeded t Château Francport.

British entered Bavai and crossed Scheld

Americans took portion of St. Mihiel o W. bank of Meuse.

U.S. Third Army H.Q. constituted unde Gen. Dickman, at Ligny-en-Barrois.

Gen. von Linsingen, commanding i Brandenburg, forbade formation of council on Soviet lines.

German Socialists demanded Kaiser' abdication by noon on following day.

Bavarian Republic proclaimed.

King of Bavaria escaped into Austria.

British s.s *Sarpedon* (4,393 tons) attacke by U-Boat in Mediterranean ; torpedo missed last officially recorded attack on Britis merchantman during the war.

November 8.

German Armistice delegates conducte to Rethondes Railway Station (Compiègn Forest), where Marshal Foch's special trai stood. Marshal presented Armistice term: Gen. Weygand, French Chief of Staff, attende with Adm. Wemyss, as Naval representative Reply in 72 hours, expiring 11 a.m. Frenc time on Monday, 11th. Erzberger asked fc immediate Armistice during negotiations Foch refused.

Gen. von Winterfeldt sent wireless messag announcing dispatch to Spa (German H.Q. of courier, Capt. Helldorf, and requestin facilities. Helldorf left in evening.

British occupied Avesnes—Hautmont reached Maubeuge outskirts. Across Scheld N.E. of Valenciennes they took Condé occupied part of Tournai.

French captured Mézières—Hirson.

Duke of Brunswick abdicated.

Kurt Eisner assumed control in Municl U34 destroyed by H.M.S. *Privet* (Q. 19 with ML155, ML373, near Gibraltar.

For List of Abbreviations see page iv.

November 9, 1918.

Belgians on Ghent—Terneuzen Canal.

British occupied Maubeuge (entered by Guards), Tournai, Peruwelz, Antoing, and N.E. of Tournai reached outskirts of Renaix.

Americans entered Stenay.

Capt. Helldorf, German courier carrying Armistice terms to Spa, held up by German bombardment along Capelle road. Arrangements made to take him in aeroplane, but at last moment firing ceased, and he proceeded.

At Spa, Kaiser, after Army's refusal to march against the revolutionaries, abdicated and decided to cross into Holland.

Revolution in Berlin; garrison mutinied; Prince Max transferred Chancellorship to Socialist leader Ebert. German Republic proclaimed by Scheidemann in Reichstag.

Saxony, Wurtemberg, &c., declared for Republic.

H.M.S. *Britannia* (16,350 tons) torpedoed by U-Boat off Cape Trafalgar.

Serbs crossed Danube N. of Semendria.

Rumanian ultimatum to Mackensen demanding German evacuation within 24 hours.

British 39th Brigade concentrating at Enzeli, with Russian and Armenian troops under Gen. Bitcharakhoff, for occupation of Baku. Nuri Pasha, Turkish commander in Caucasus warned to evacuate town by 17th.

Gen. von Lettow reached Kasama (Rhodesia), 100 miles S. of Abercorn.

✻November 10.

Belgians in Ghent; Canadians near Mons; French took Charleville—Rocroi, and approached Chimay; they crossed Meuse near Vrigné.

Americans in St. Mihiel salient captured St. Hilaire.

Kaiser took refuge in Holland.

Capt. Helldorf, German courier, reached German H.Q. at Spa at 10 a.m. with copy of Armistice terms; later, instructions to sign telephoned from Berlin to Spa; Helldorf returned with message.

German troops in Brussels hoisted Red Flag.

Joint Socialist Ministry in Berlin under Ebert and Haase.

Soviet councils assumed control in majority of German States.

H.M.S. *Shark* and French T.B.D. *Mangini* entered Dardanelles for Constantinople.

Mosul Vilayet in British hands; Turks withdrawn to Nisibin.

November 11.

At 2 a.m. courier Helldorf reached German delegates at Château Francport with Berlin decision; delegates immediately met Foch, and discussions on several points lasted till 5 a.m.

At 5 a.m. ARMISTICE signed at Rethondes Railway Station.

At 11 a.m. Armistice came into force and fighting ceased all along front.

General line reached by Allies on W. Front from N. to S.: Selzaete—Ghent—E. of Nederbrakel—Grammont—Lessines—Ghislenghien—Herchies—Jurbise — Boussoit — Erquelines — Sivry — Chimay — Rocroi — Mézières—Sedan—before Bazeilles—Mouzon —Stenay—Barlon—Louppy—Jametz—Damvillers—E. of Fresnes—E. of Thiaucourt—Nomény—Badonviller—W. of Senones—W. of Münster—Thann—W. of Altkirch—Swiss Frontier.

November 11 (*continued*).

At 8 p.m. Kaiser reached Amerongen Castle, Holland.

German Foreign Minister Solf entreated President Wilson to mitigate the Allied terms.

First German Army Soviet at Malines.

Canadians in morning captured Mons.

Death of Victor Adler.

Adm. Calthorpe to be British High Commissioner at Constantinople, with Rear-Adm. Webb as Assistant-Commissioner.

U157 interned in Norway.

November 12.

President Wilson prayed by Dr. Solf to hasten negotiations and save Germany from famine.

Mr. Hoover, U.S. Food Controller, urged continued economy in wheat and fats.

Dr. Addison, Minister of Reconstruction, outlined Government demobilisation policy, doles, &c.

Commodore S. S. Hall's message to officers and men of British Submarine Service congratulating them on having sunk 54 enemy warships and 274 other vessels.

Marshal Foch's Message to Allied Armies :—

"*Vous avez gagné la plus grande bataille de l'histoire et sauvé la cause la plus sacrée : La Liberté du Monde.*"

Hindenburg remained at head of German Army to lead troops home. Chancellor Ebert ordered Army to obey its officers.

German Republican programme.

Emperor Charles abdicated.

Mackensen retired through Hungary.

Gen. Pilsudski to form Warsaw Ministry.

Allied Fleet, with H.M.S. *Superb* (F. Adm. Calthorpe), in Dardanelles for Constantinople.

November 13.

President Wilson's conditional promise of food relief for Germany.

German light cruiser *Königsberg* brought to rendezvous off Rosyth Adm. Meurer and other German Fleet delegates to meet British Admiralty representatives and arrange execution of Armistice.

German Second Army disbanded.

Hindenburg transferred G.H.Q. to Cassel.

Prussian Republican Programme.

King of Bavaria abdicated.

Grand Duke of Baden abdicated.

Revolutionary disturbances in Holland; casualties in Amsterdam.

German troops in retreat began passing through Dutch Limburg.

Allied Fleet off Constantinople, 8 a.m.

Gen. van Deventer (E. Africa) summoned Gen. von Lettow to surrender in accordance with Armistice and proceed to Abercorn.

November 14.

Labour Party severed from Coalition.

Interned R.N.D. men left Holland for England.

Soviet programme in Saxony.

Grand Duke of Mecklenburg abdicated.

Swiss general strike collapsed.

Italian monitor, *A. Capellini*, capsized and sunk off Ancona.

November 15.

President Wilson again pressed by Dr. Solf to hasten food relief for Germany.

Bill entitling women to sit in Commons passed Lords.

British and German Naval delegates met at sea off Rosyth at 2.30 p.m. Adm.

November 15, 1918 (*continued*).

von Meurer visited Adm. Beatty in C.-in-c.'s cabin on board H.M.S. *Queen Elizabeth.*

Allied Armistice Missions at Spa.

M. Adolphe Max, Burgomaster of Brussels, returned from captivity in Germany.

Prussian Upper House abolished.

Professor Masaryk President, and Dr. Kramarzh Premier of Czecho-Slovakia.

November 16.

U.S. Government requested Dr. Solf to address himself to all Allies and not alone to President Wilson.

German Coast Defence H.Q. lapsed.

German Tenth Army in Lithuania.

Germans began to evacuate Ukraine.

British and Allied forces left Enzeli for Baku.

*November 17.

Sir R. Borden, Canadian Prime Minister, arrived in London to take part in Peace Conference.

Allied Armies began march to Rhine in accordance with Armistice in order named from N. to S. :—

Belgian Army.
British Second Army.
British Fourth Army.
U.S. Third Army.
French Tenth Army.
French Eighth Army.
French Fourth Army.
French Second Army.

U.S. 332nd Infantry with its battalions at Cormons, Cattaro, and Fiume.

Executive Committee of Berlin Workmen's and Soldiers' Councils claims political control.

Count Karolyi Hungarian Premier.

Anti-Hetman rising in Ukraine.

Remnants of German Asia Corps interned at Haida Pasha, Hadikoï, and Prinkipo.

British entered Baku, led by Gen. Thompson, and accompanied by ships flying British, French, Russian, and U.S.A. flags.

November 18.

President Wilson to attend Peace Conference.

Dr. Solf appealed to all Allies to mitigate terms.

Gen. von Beseler's Governor-Generalship of Warsaw terminated.

Italian Flotilla Leader, *C. Rossarol* mined off Pola.

Adm. Amet to be French High Commissioner at Constantinople.

Adm. Koltchak at request of Omsk Directorate assumed full power in Siberia.

November 19.

Total British casualties to date announced in Parliament :

Total, 3,049,991.

Killed and died : 37,876 officers ; 620,828 others.

Wounded : 92,664 officers : 1,939,478 others.

Missing (inc. prisoners) : 12,994 officers ; 347,051 others.

Also 19,000 deaths from various causes among troops not serving in any expeditionary force.

King George addressed Message to Empire on conclusion of war.

King and Queen of Belgians entered Antwerp.

November 19 (*continued*).

Belgian troops entered Brussels.

French entered Metz, under Gen. Pétain, created Marshal of France.

U.S. Second Army Corps at Le Mans, awaiting re-embarcation.

November 20.

Naval Censorship abolished.

First batch of 20 U-Boats surrendered to Rear-Adm. Tyrwhitt off Harwich at day-break.

Berlin Government apprised of shocking treatment of released prisoners ; failing satisfaction, this to be taken into account in arrangements for provisioning Germany.

November 21.

Main instalment of German High Sea Fleet under Rear-Adm. von Reuter surrendered for internment to Adm. Beatty off Firth of Forth, comprising :—

BATTLESHIPS.

Friederich der Grosse (F. Rear-Adm. von Reuter),
Bayern,
Grosser Kurfürst,
Kronprinz,
Markgraf,
Kaiser,
Kaiserin,
König Albert,
Prinzregent Luitpold.

BATTLECRUISERS.

Seydlitz (F. Comm. Taegert),
Moltke,
Derfflinger,
Hindenburg,
Von der Tann.

LIGHT-CRUISERS.

Karlsruhe II. (F. Comm. Harder),
Bremse,
Brummer,
Emden II.
Frankfurt,
Köln II.,
Nürnberg II.

These nine battleships, five battle cruisers, seven light cruisers, with 49 T.B.D.s passed through Grand Fleet, including ships of Dominions, France (Adm. Grasset), and U.S. (Adm. Sims). C.-in-C. Grand Fleet signalled : "The German flag is to be hauled down at 1557 (3.57 p.m.) to-day, Thursday, and is not to be hoisted again without permission."

German T.B.D. V30 mined on way over.

Second batch of U-Boats at Harwich ; 39 to date ; fortieth, U97, mined on way across.

First shipload of British prisoners from German ports left for England in Danish liner.

U.S. Third Army reached Luxembourg.

November 22.

Adm. von Reuter protested against Adm Beatty's order to haul down German flag and not hoist it again without permission.

Third batch of 20 U-Boats surrendered at Harwich.

H.M. submarine G11 wrecked of Howick.

King and Queen of Belgians made triumphal entry into Brussels.

Gen. Pershing entered Luxemburg.

For List of Abbreviations see page iv.

November 22, 1918 (*continued*).
Spartacist attack on Berlin Police Presidency.
Lettish Republic proclaimed at Riga.
Poles recovered Lemberg.

November 23.
U.S. war casualties : dead, 53,169 ; wounded, 179,625 ; prisoners, 2,163 ; missing, 11,160.
Mr. Hoover, U.S. Food Controller, in London to organise relief in Europe.
Adm. Beatty informed Adm. von Reuter that state of war still existed between Britain and Germany ; no enemy vessel therefore could fly national flag in British port.
U.S. advanced guard through Luxemburg on German frontier.
Amnesty in Prussia.
Provisional Government at Reval.

*November 24.
Twenty-eight more U-Boats at Harwich.
UC74 interned at Barcelona.
British Army on German frontier N. of Luxemburg.

November 25.
Parliament dissolved.
Unemployed grant in force.
U.S. anti-U-Boat Flotilla left Queenstown for home port.
Adm. Mayo, commanding U.S. Squadron in Europe, left England.
British minesweepers left to clear Baltic passage for British squadron to proceed to Kiel with inter-Allied Naval Commission under Adm. Browning to superintend execution of Armistice.
French, under Marshal Foch and Gen. de Castlenau, entered Strasbourg (Strassburg).
German States declared for German unity, pending Constituent Assembly's vote.
At Neustad (S. Austria) delegates from all Yugo-Slav States of late Dual Monarchy declared union with Serbia-Montenegro. King Peter offered Throne of new State. Prince Alexander remained Regent.
Gen. von Lettow, with 155 whites and 1,168 askaris, formally surrendered at Abercorn (Rhodesia) to Gen. van Deventer's representative, Gen. Edwards. German commander and officers retained swords and European rank and file retained their arms as far as Dar-es-Salaam.

November 26.
Bavarian Workmen's and Soldiers' Councils demanded trial of German war-criminals.

November 27.
U-Boats at Harwich now totalled 114 by arrival of 27 more.
U-Boat Programme :—
At the Armistice there were under construction : 440 U-Boats (including 137 large boats) ; projected : 330 U-Boats (including 117 large ones). Of these 360 were to be completed in 1919 ; and remaining 410 in 1920.
Last Germans left Belgium.
French armies on German frontier.
Allied squadron off Sebastopol. Russian ships in German hands, and four U-Boats surrendered.

November 28.
King and Prince of Wales welcomed in Paris.

November 28 (*continued*).
Kaiser at Amerongen signed formal abdication both as German Emperor and King of Prussia.
British light cruiser squadron at Copenhagen to superintend opening of Baltic.

November 29.
King George conferred Order of Merit on Marshal Foch.
Berlin Government decided to convene National Assembly for Feb. 16, 1919.
King of Wurtemberg abdicated.
Professor Masaryk, First President of new Czecho-Slovak Republic, arrived in London from New York.

November 30.
King George visited the Western front.
Belgians occupied German territory at Aix-la-Chapelle.

*December 1.
Adm. Beatty at Scapa on board U.S. battleship *New York* (F.Adm. Rodman), bade farewell to 6th (American) Battle Squadron of Grand Fleet.
By this date the following German submarines had been surrendered to British naval custody :—
U-Boats : 9, 19, 24, 30, 35, 43, 46, 52, 54, 55, 57, 60, 67, 70, 79, 86, 90, 91, 94, 96, 98, 100, 101, 105, 107, 108, 111, 112, 113, 114, 117, 118, 119, 120, 121, 123, 125, 126, 135, 139, 141, 160, 161, 162, 163, 164.
UA-Boats : 1.
UB-Boats : 21, 24, 25, 27, 28, 34, 60, 62, 64, 67, 73, 79, 80, 84, 86, 87, 89, 91, 92, 93, 94, 95, 96, 97, 98, 100, 101, 102, 106, 111, 112, 114, 118, 120, 121, 122, 125, 126, 131, 132, 142, 149, 150.
UC-Boats : 17, 31, 45, 58, 89, 92, 93, 94, 95, 96, 97, 98, 99, 100, 101, 102, 103, 104, 105.
U-Cruisers : 151, 152, 153, 155.
M. Clemenceau, Marshal Foch, Signor Orlando, and Baron Sonnino in London for preliminaries to Peace Conference ; Colonel House, U.S. representative, unable to attend owing to illness.
Americans entered Treves at 5.30 a.m. British Second Army (Gen. Plumer) crossed German frontier between Beho and Eupen and advanced towards Rhine.
Ultimatum from Marshal Foch to German Armistice Commission regarding delay in handing over locomotives.
German Crown Prince, now at Wieringen (Holland), also renounced his rights.
Krupp's Essen works reduced staff to 40,500 men and 6,400 women (see 1-vi.-18).
King and Queen of Rumania made official entry into Bukarest.
Rumanians of Transylvania voted unconditional union with Rumania.

December 2.
U-Cruiser 155 (ex-merchant U-Boat *Deutschland*) in tow of H.M. tug *Saucy* proceeded up the Thames.
Allied conference at Downing Street.
Attorney-General announced War Cabinet unanimously decided to press Holland for extradition of ex-Kaiser.
Scheldt question raised in Belgium.

December 3.
Downing Street Conference continued.
Allied Naval Armistice Commission left England for Wilhelmshaven.
British Naval force at Libau.

Sundays marked with Asterisk (*).

December 4, 1918.

President Wilson left in *George Washington* for Europe to take part in Peace Conference.

French and Italian representatives left London.

German battleship *König* and light cruiser *Dresden II.*, with one T.B.D., sent to Scapa to make up deficiencies in tale of surrendered ships.

British squadron with Adm. Browning and Allied Naval Armistice Commission arrived at Wilhelmshaven.

H.M.S. *Cassandra* mined in Baltic.

Centre party meeting at Cologne voted for Rhenish-Westphalian Republic.

December 5.

King of Belgians visited Paris.

Germans handed over 300,000,000 francs in gold exacted from Russia by Brest Treaty.

All Turkish warships and the German battle-cruiser *Goeben* now interned.

December 6.

President Masaryk of Czecho-Slovak Republic left London for Paris and Prague.

British cavalry entered Cologne at urgent request of local authorities, unable to suppress disorders.

December 7.

" British Day " celebrated in U.S.A.

President Masaryk received by President Poincaré in Paris.

Belgians reached Rhine at Crefeld.

British 28th Brigade, 9th Division, at Cologne.

Marshal Foch informed Germans that blockade must remain in force.

British Baltic squadron returned to Copenhagen from Libau.

*December 8.

King George and Prince of Wales at Ypres.

British 1st Cavalry Division reached Rhine on whole British front and secured crossings.

Naval Armistice Commission inspected German air stations at Borkum and Ahlhorn.

Caspian fight between British and Bolshevist armed vessels.

December 9.

King George visited Zeebrugge.

President Poincaré entered Strasbourg. and took possession in the name of France.

Naval Armistice Commission inspected flying stations at Bornholz and Heligoland.

German delegates for renewal of Armistice (Erzberger, Oberndorff, and Vanselow) left Berlin for Treves.

December 10.

King George returned to London

Emir Feisul, third son of King of Hedjaz, arrived in London as Arab delegate to Peace Conference.

President Poincaré and M. Clemenceau entered Mulhouse (Mülhausen).

Adm. Browning and Naval Armistice Commission inspected British merchantmen at Hamburg.

December 11.

Gen. Fergusson arrived at Cologne as Military Governor ; Union Jack hoisted over his H.Q. in Hotel Monopol.

Americans entered Coblenz.

French entered Mainz and restored order.

December 12.

Adm. Keyes presented with Freedom Dover.

Allied and German delegates met Treves to discuss Armistice renewal.

British cavalry crossed Rhine at Colog and occupied Armistice Bridgehead.

German Volunteer Defence Fo founded.

British Naval squadron at Reval; bo barded Bolshevist positions.

December 13.

Maharaja of Bikaner and Sir S. P. Sin Indian delegates to Peace Conference, arriv in England.

President Wilson landed at Brest.

British infantry, 2nd and Canad Corps, followed cavalry across Rhine Cologne—Bonn.

Americans crossed Rhine at Coblenz.

December 14.

British General Election ; Coalit majority.

Mr. J. W. Davis, new U.S. ambassad arrived in England.

U.S. battle squadron, after acting w Grand Fleet and escorting President Wil into Brest, sailed for home.

Armistice renewed at Treves till Jan. and eventually renewable until prelimin peace. Allies reserved right to occupy neut zone on right bank of Rhine ; deman 2,500,000 tons of cargo space lying in Germ ports ; and required battleship *Baden* inst of battle cruiser *Mackensen.*

British Naval squadron off Reval bo barded Bolshevist positions.

Ukraine Hetman overthrown at Kieff

Portuguese President assassinated Lisbon.

*December 15.

Bolshevists proclaimed Soviet Republic Esthonia.

December 16.

Gen. Botha arrived in London for Pe Conference.

President Wilson received Freedom Paris.

Deputy Leinert presided at Be Congress of German Workmen's and Soldie Councils.

December 17.

British occupation of Cologne Bridgehe complete.

U.S. troops in occupation of Cobl Bridghead.

December 18.

Adm. Browning's squadron left E for England.

Export of German money prohibited

December 19.

Sir D. Haig and his Army Commande Gens. Horne, First Army ; Plumer, Seco Army ; Byng, Third Army ; Rawlins Fourth Army ; and Birdwood, Fifth Arm with Lt.-Gen. H. A. Lawrence, Chief of St welcomed home to London.

Lord Milner's defence of British pol in Russia.

King of Italy visited Paris.

German National Assembly Electi fixed for Jan. 19, 1919.

For List of Abbreviations see page iv.

December 20, 1918.

H.M.S. *Coventry* left Copenhagen for Danzig.

British interned ships from Hamburg arrived in Tyne.

Spartacists raided Berlin *Vorwärts* office.

Serbo-Montonogrin Union.

December 21.

Prussian National Assembly Elections fixed for Jan. 26, 1919.

❋ December 22.

President Masaryk in Prague took oath to new Czecho-Slovak Republic.

December 23.

Sailors' riot in Berlin; Chancellery and Castle stables attacked.

December 24.

M. Pichon, French Foreign Minister, on Allied Russian policy.

Berlin riots continued.

Bolshevists took Perm.

December 25.

Hindenburg at Cassel issued manifesto on behalf of officers of German Army.

Revolutionaries occupied Berlin *Vorwärts* office.

December 26.

President Wilson arrived in England.

December 27.

President Wilson, Mr. Lloyd George, and Mr. Balfour conferred in London.

December 28.

President Wilson again conferred with British Ministers.

President Wilson at Guildhall on League of Nations.

Signor Bissolati resigned from Italian Cabinet on Jugo-Slav question.

H.M.S. *Calypso* credited with capture of two Bolshevist T.B.D.s, *Spartak* and *Avtroil*. one in act of bombarding lighthouse near Reval.

❋ December 29.

President Wilson visited Manchester.

M. Clemenceau in French Chamber asserted his faith in "Balance of Power" system, and continuance of alliance of British Empire, U.S., France and Italy. Mentioned "Freedom of Seas" conversation with Mr. Lloyd George, in which agreed nothing should make Britain unable again to come forward with her Fleet to help France and stated that he repeated this conversation to President Wilson, who concurred.

Independent Socialists, Haase, Dittmann, and Barth, withdrew from Berlin Government; Noske entered Ministry.

December 30.

Mr. Daniels, U.S. Navy Secretary, before House Naval Committee, declared, "if Versailles Conference did not result in general agreement, it was his firm conviction that U.S. must create "incomparably the greatest navy in the world.""

Dr. Solf, German Foreign Secretary, resigned.

December 30 (*continued*).

Spartacists transformed into German Communist Workers Party.

British detachment landed at Riga.

December 31.

President Wilson left England for Paris.

Mr. Balfour arrived in Paris and conferred with Colonel House.

Demobilisation and dissolution of German Landsturm.

Baku and Krasnovodak passed out of Gen. Marshall's command, being maintained via Batum, where British troops from Salonika had meanwhile arrived.

January 1, 1919.

The Times Red Cross Fund appeal closed: over £14,000,000 to date.

Strikes in Ruhr district.

British squadron left Riga.

January 2.

Bolshevists occupied Riga.

January 3.

President Wilson in Rome.

Independent Socialists retired from Prussian Government.

British Naval Mission at Danzig.

January 4.

Riga and Vilna occupied by Bolshevists.

❋ January 5.

"Spartacus" Week in Berlin.

January 6.

Ex-President Roosevelt died in U.S.

Liebknecht and Ledebour tried to set up Communist régime in Berlin.

President Masaryk at Prague called for better communications between Czecho-Slovakia and Allies.

Esthonia appealed to Britain for arms against Bolshevists.

January 7.

President Wilson returned to Paris from Rome.

British Baltic Squadron left Copenhagen for home.

Bremen Spartacist riots ended.

January 9.

Signor Orlando and Baron Sonnino arrived in Paris.

Inter-Allied Supreme Council of Supply and Relief formed under Mr. Hoover.

Riots in Westphalia and Saxony.

January 10.

Gen. Smuts's pamphlet on League of Nations.

Poles retook Lemberg from Ukrainians.

January 11.

Mr. Lloyd George and Mr. Bonar Law left for Paris with Sir R. Borden (Canada), Mr. Hughes (Australia), Gen. Botha (S. Africa), Sir W. F. Lloyd (Newfoundland), and Mr. Montague, Sir S. P. Sinha, and Maharajah of Bikaner (India).

Cuxhaven "Republic" proclaimed.

Bolshevists advanced from Vilna.

Sundays marked with Asterisk (❋).

*January 12, 1919.

Preliminary conference at Paris of principal Allied representatives sitting as Supreme War Council, with Mr. Wilson and Mr. Lansing, opened at 2.30 p.m. at Quai d'Orsay.

Hungarian National Council named Count Karolyi Provisional President of Hungarian Republic.

January 13.

U.S. House of Representatives voted £20,000,000 for European food relief.

Supreme War Council in Paris settled new Armistice terms and fixed first formal meeting of Peace Conference for Jan. 18.

Medina occupied in name of King of Hedjaz.

January 14.

Signor Orlando left Paris for Rome upon Signor Nitti's resignation from Cabinet.

Rioting at Dortmund.

January 15.

Paris Conference : British Empire, U.S., France, Italy, and Japan to have five delegates each ; Brazil, three ; Belgium, China, Greece, Poland, Portugal, Czecho-Slovakia, Rumania, and Serbia, 2 each ; Siam, Cuba, Guatemala, Haiti, Honduras, Liberia, Nicaragua, Panama, one each.

French Government notified of accession in Luxembourg of Princess Charlotte in room of Princess Adelaide.

Karl Liebknecht and Rosa Luxer.burg killed in Berlin.

January 16.

New Armistice Convention signed at Trèves.

M. Paderewski formed Warsaw Cabinet.

International Labour Conference at Berne.

Bolshevists repulsed at Merv.

January 17.

Japanese Delegation, with Baron Makino, in England for Paris Conference.

Paris Conference : Press regulations settled.

Serbia and Belgium accorded three delegates ; King of Hedjaz, two.

January 18.

Paris Conference : First formal meeting opened at 3.30 p.m. by President Poincaré.

M. Clemenceau permanent President of Conference.

*January 19.

New Zealand delegates, Mr. Massey and Sir J. Ward, in England.

Permanent Committee of Supreme Council of Supply and Relief held first meeting in Paris.

German National Assembly Elections : 163 Maj. Socialists ; 22 Min. Socialists ; 75 Democrats ; 21 German People's Party ; 88 Christian People's Party (centre) ; 42 German Nationalists ; 4 Bavarian Peasants' League ; 1 Schleswig-Holstein Rural Democrat ; 1 Brandenburger ; 4 German-Hanoverians. Total, 421 Deputies.

January 20.

Paris Conference : " Big Five " heard statement on Russia by M. Noulens, ex-French Ambassador at Petrograd.

January 20 *(continued).*

Council of Supply and Relief appro' Inter-Allied Commissions at Trieste, Bukar€ Constantinople and in Poland.

January 21.

Paris Conference : M. de Scaveni Danish Minister in Petrograd, heard.

January 22.

Paris Conference decided to send ci and military missions to Poland.

Proposal for meeting at Prinkipo Is., € of Marmora, between representatives of 1 various Russian factions and Allies approv by Conference ; invitations sent by wirele

January 23.

Entente mission at Teschen request Poles to evacuate territory disputed w Czecho-Slovakia.

January 24.

Supreme Council in Paris discuss strength of forces to be maintained on ' Front during Armistice.

Ukrainian and Esthonian represen tives in Paris state that their Governmei would refuse Prinkipo conference.

January 25.

Paris Conference : Second plenary sittii League of Nations resolution adopted President Wilson's motion.

Allied troops retired before Bolshevi: near Shenkursk (Archangel).

*January 26.

Prinkipo proposal described by Pet: grad *Red Gazette* as " Universal Surrender Bourgeoisie."

January 27.

" Red " Revolution in Finland.

Archangel Government rejected Prinki proposal.

January 28.

Paris Conference : German colonies d cussed.

January 29.

Paris Conference : Polish and Czech Slovak claims heard.

For German Pacific Is. President Wils suggested Australasian mandate.

January 30.

Paris Conference : Provisional arrang ment for German colonies and occupied ter tory in Asiatic Turkey.

Grand Dukes Nicholas Mikhailovitc Paul Alexandrovitch, George Mikhailovitc and Dmitri Constantinovitch shot in Peti grad.

Allied retirement near Tarasevo (Archa gel).

January 31.

Paris Conference : Allied delegates visit Teschen. Serb and Rumanian repi sentatives heard on Banat question.

*February 1.

Paris Conference : Czecho-Polish Tesche agreement.

For List of Abbreviations see page iv.

February 3, 1919.

Paris Conference : M. Venizelos on Greek claims.

League of Nations Committee held first meeting.

International Socialist Conference at Berne.

Bolshevists captured Kieff.

February 4.

Paris Conference : M. Venizelos on Greek interests in Asia Minor ; question referred to special committee.

February 6.

Paris Conference : Emir Feisul heard.

Soviet Government replied to Prinkipo proposal.

February 7.

League of Nations Committee completed first half of draft.

Allied success against Bolshevists near Kadish (Archangel).

*February 8.

Mr. Lloyd George returned from Paris for opening of Parliament.

" Russian Political Conference " under Prince Lvoff at Paris, representing Archangel, Ekaterinodar, and Omsk Governments, denied Bolshevist claim to represent Russia.

February 10.

Paris Conference : M. Klotz heard on work published by German General Staff in 1916 proving premeditated destruction of French industry.

Jugo-Slav offer to submit Adriatic dispute to President Wilson. Italy refused.

February 11.

Paris Conference : Belgian claims heard.

February 12.

Mr. Lloyd George in Parliament denied any suggestion of recognising Bolshevists.

Paris Supreme Council decided on terms of Armistice renewal.

February 13.

Paris Conference : Dr. Howard Bliss, President of American College, Beirut, and Chekri Ganem, President of Syrian National Committee heard.

February 14.

Paris Conference : Third Plenary Sitting. President Wilson read draft of League of Nations.

Terms of Armistice renewal until signing of Peace presented by Marshal Foch to Germans at Trèves.

*February 15.

Paris Conference : Lebanon deputation heard.

Bolshevist offensive in Esthonia.

February 16.

President Wilson left France for U.S.

New Armistice agreement signed at Trèves.

February 17.

Marshal Foch reported German acceptance of new Armistice conditions.

February 18.

Paris Conference : Yugo-Slavs heard.

February 19.

Attempt on M. Clemenceau in Paris by young anarchist Cottin.

February 20.

Soviet Government agreed to proposed visit of mission from Berne International Labour Conference.

Murder of Ameer Habibullah of Afghanistan.

February 21.

Paris Conference : Danish claims in Schleswig heard.

*February 22.

Truce between Poles and Ukrainians at Lemberg.

February 24.

President Wilson at Boston defended League of Nations.

Mr. J. T. O'Kelly, Sinn Fein " Envoy," in Paris.

Paris Conference : Albanian case heard.

Bolshevist Caspian flotilla surrendered to Allies.

February 25.

Paris Conference : Hungaro-Rumanian neutral zone.

February 26.

Paris Conference : Armenian claims heard.

February 27.

President Wilson at Washington discussed League of Nations with Congress Foreign Relations Committee.

M. Clemenceau returned to duty.

Britain recognised independence of Poland and Paderewski Government.

March 1.

Paris Conference : Marshal Foch on final Armistice terms.

March 3.

End of Lemberg truce ; Ukrainians bombarded town.

March 4.

President Wilson in New York on League of Nations before leaving for Europe.

Mr. Lodge's anti-League of Nations resolution in U.S. Senate.

Sundays marked with Asterisk (*).

March 5, 1919.
President Wilson sailed for Europe.
British Labour Party in England demanded abolition of conscription, and condemned League of Nations Covenant in existing form.
Paris Conference: Montenegrin case heard.

March 8.
Paris Conference: Interrupted Spa negotiations to be resumed at Brussels on 13th.
Belgian Commission's report on revision of 1839 Treaty.
Mr. Lloyd George received telegram from Gen. Plumer (British Army of Occupation) describing bad food conditions in W. Germany, and urging relief.
In Egypt Zaghlul Pasha and three other Nationalists arrested.

✴March 9.
Zaghlul Pasha and his three associates deported to Malta. Riots in Cairo.

March 12.
Gen. Allenby left Cairo for Paris.

March 13.
Spa negotiations resumed at Brussels.
Adm. Wemyss presented Allied terms regarding surrender of merchant fleet. Allies agreed to supply Germany with 300,000 tons of cereals and 70,000 tons of fats per month, if Germany deposited as guarantee £7,000,000 in gold in Bank of Belgium, and within 10 days, £11,000,000 more. German delegates accepted.

March 14.
President Wilson back in Paris.
Egyptian disorders more serious; number of troops killed by rioters.
Adm. Koltchak took Ufa from Bolshevists.

March 17.
M. Clemenceau received Esthonian, Lett, Lithuanian, and Ukrainian delegates, who asked recognition of independence and support against Bolshevists.

March 19.
Gen. Allenby arrived in Paris to advise on Syria and Palestine.
Letts captured Mitau from Bolshevists.

March 20.
M. Clemenceau, Mr. Lloyd George, President Wilson, M. Pichon, Mr. Balfour, and Gen. Allenby discussed Levant affairs.
Gen. Allenby left Paris for Egypt.
Poles relieved Lemberg.
League of Nations Select Committee heard neutral delegates.
Commission of International Labour Legislation adopted British Draft Convention.

March 21.
Paris Conference: Transport of Gen. Haller's Polish troops into Poland through Danzig discussed.
Second meeting of League of Nations Select Committee and neutral representatives.
Karolyi Government in Hungary resigned.
Gen. Allenby Special High Commissioner for Egypt and Sudan.

March 22.
Paris Conference: Polish Commission report.
First meeting of full League of Natior Commission since draft read on Feb. 1 Amendments discussed.
Soviet Government at Budapest; Be Kun Foreign Minister. Military allianc offered to Moscow Soviet accepted.

March 24.
Paris Conference: Council of Fou (President Wilson, Mr. Lloyd George, N Clemenceau, and Signor Orlando) to haste drawing up of Treaty.
Commission on International Labor Legislation approved report for full Co ference; annual meeting of representativ of States, employers, and employed recon mended; first meeting at Washington October.
Ex-Emperor Charles in Switzerland.

March 25.
Paris Conference: First meeting of Counc of Four.
Gen. Allenby back in Egypt. Situatic improving.

March 26.
Paris Conference: League of Natio Committee of Revision appointed: Lord I Cecil, M. Larnaude, M. Venizelos, and C House.
Gen. Noudant presented Note to Germa Armistice Commission demanding passa through Danzig for Gen. Haller's Poli troops.

March 28.
Paris Conference: Council of Four co cluded first survey of peace terms.
Germans refused landing of Polish troo at Danzig, but suggested Stettin, Königsber Memel, or Libau.

March 29.
Paris Conference: War responsibiliti Committee approved final report.

✴March 30.
Riots at Delhi in connexion wi "Passive Resistance" movement again Rowlatt Acts.

March 31.
Paris Conference: Council of Four co sulted Marshal Foch, Gens. Wilson, and Di on landing of Polish troops at Danzig.

April 1.
King of Belgians arrived in Paris I aeroplane.
Paris Conference: Council of Four decid to raise blockade as regards Poland, Esthoni German Austria, Turkey, Bulgaria, ar Czecho-Slovakia, and new territories occupi by Serbia and Rumania.
German Financial Delegation m Economic Council representatives at Villett
Bolshevist attacks on Archangel fro repulsed.
Gen. Allenby reported improvement Egypt.

For List of Abbreviations see page iv.

April 2, 1919,

King Albert conferred with Mr. Lloyd George in Paris.

Herr Erzberger at Spa to confer with Marshal Foch on Danzig question.

April 3.

Paris Conference : Council of Four considered Adriatic question.

Marshal Foch arrived at Spa.

Spain first neutral to notify desire to join League of Nations.

More bloodshed in Cairo.

April 4.

King Albert saw President Wilson in Paris.

Marshal Foch reported from Spa that Allies right to use Danzig for landing of Polish troops upheld, and further arrangements made to transport these troops by rail at German suggestion.

Gen. Smuts at Budapest.

April 5.

King Albert returned from Paris to Brussels by aeroplane.

Gen. Smuts left Budapest for Paris.

*April 6.

M. Paderewski arrives in Paris.

Allies evacuated Odessa.

April 7.

Grand Fleet disbanded.

Hungarian Soviet elections.

Gen. Allenby announced release of Zaghlul Pasha and his associates at Malta.

April 8.

Telegram signed by 200 M.P.s sent to Mr. Lloyd George in Paris urging firmness on indemnity question.

April 9.

In reply to M.P.s telegram Mr. Lloyd George said he means to stand by his pledges.

Another telegram, also signed by 200 M.P.s, urged British Delegation not to agree to any suggestion of recognising Moscow Government.

Advanced guard of British Relief Force left for N. Russia.

Sir Hussein Rushdi Pasha to form new Egyptian Cabinet.

April 10.

Paris Conference : League of Nations Committee accepted U.S. clause consecrating Monroe Doctrine. Japanese resolution on race equality vetoed.

Geneva to be seat of League of Nations.

April 11.

Paris Conference : Fourth Plenary Sitting. Draft Convention for International Labour Legislation approved.

League of Nations Commission completed revision of new draft.

Riots continued in India.

Egyptian Nationalist deputation left for Paris, picking up Zaghlul Pasha at Malta.

April 12.

Paris Conference : Council of Four considered Syria and Arabia.

April 16.

Mr. Lloyd George in House of Commons defended his action in Paris.

April 18.

Intimation to Germany to send plenipotentiaries to Versailles.

Mr. Gandhi advised suspension of Indian " Passive Resistance."

April 19.

German Government stated they would send two delegates on 25th to receive Treaty.

*April 20.

Allies advised Germany that plenipotentiaries must be sent.

Zaghlul Pasha in Paris.

April 21.

Germans agreed to send delegation headed by six plenipotentiaries to reach Versailles by 28th.

President Wilson withdrew from Adriatic discussion.

April 22.

Paris Conference : War Responsibility Commission's Report placed whole responsibility for war on Central Powers, and recommended trial of all persons guilty of offence against laws of war or humanity.

U.S. recognised British Protectorate in Egypt.

April 23.

Paris Conference : Following Adriatic statement by President Wilson, Italian Delegation decided to leave Paris.

April 24.

Signor Orlando left Paris.

April 25.

Paris Conference : First German Delegates at Versailles.

April 28.

Paris Conference : Fifth plenary sitting. Revised League of Nations Covenant approved ; Sir J. E. Drummond first Secretary-General.

Eighty German delegates at Versailles.

Allies evacuated Sebastopol.

April 29.

Count Brockdorff-Rantzau at Versailles.

Italian Chamber upheld Government by 382-40 votes.

April 30.

British Press Bureau closed.

Paris Conference : Shantung Agreement.

May 1.

German credentials presented at Versailles.

May 5.

Italian delegates to return to Paris.

Sundays marked with Asterisk (*).

May 6, 1919.

Paris Conference : Sixth Plenary Sitting. Treaty communicated to Allied delegates not concerned in drafting. Marshal Foch dissatisfied with guarantees for French security.

Council of Three disposed of German colonies.

Signor Orlando returned to Paris.

May 7.

Peace terms presented to Germans at Versailles. Written observations on whole Treaty to be presented within 15 days. Count Brockdorff-Rantzau declared that Germany refused to admit whole war guilt.

May 8.

Official summary of Peace terms published in England.

M. Paderewski left Paris for Warsaw.

Afghans across N.W. frontier.

May 9.

German Delegation at Versailles presented first two Notes on Treaty.

May 10.

Allies dismissed German Versailles Notes.

Fighting with Afghans on N.W. frontier.

May 12.

Paris Conference : Economic Council decided on blockade measures if Germany refused to sign.

May 13.

Germans at Versailles suggested Germany could provide sufficient coal to meet French demands without transfer of Saar.

British across Afghan frontier at Dakka fort.

May 14.

Baltic Committee met in Paris.

Dr. Renner and other Austrian Delegates at St. Germain.

Black Lists for Neutrals withdrawn.

May 15.

Paris Conference : Military terms for Austria discussed.

May 16.

Further German Note on Saar Valley.

Afghans attacked British at Dakka.

May 17.

Count Brockdorff-Rantzau left Versailles for Spa.

British captured and held hills W. of Dakka.

May 19.

Dutch-Belgian discussion of 1839 Treaty.

Count Brockdorff-Rantzau returned to Versailles from Spa with long German reply.

May 20.

Extension until 29th granted Germans to consider Treaty.

May 22.

German delegates left for Spa to deliberate with their Government.

May 23.

Bolshevists captured Merv (Trans-Caspia).

May 24.

German Saar proposal rejected.

British air raid on Kabul.

May 26.

Council of Four decided on conditions recognition of Adm. Koltchak.

May 27.

German counter proposals published i Berlin.

British Relief Force at Archangel.

May 28.

Ameer of Afghanistan requested armistice

May 29.

German counter proposals submitted t Allies.

May 30.

Council of Four considered Germa counter proposals.

June 2.

Draft Peace Treaty, still incomplete handed to Austrian delegation at St. Ger main.

June 3.

Dr. Renner left St. Germain for Vienna.

Viceroy of India replied to Afghan re quest for armistice.

June 4.

Bolshevists driving back Adm. Koltchak' left wing towards Ufa.

June 5.

Paris Conference : M. Paderewski hear on Polish frontiers.

June 6.

U.S. Senate's resolution of sympath with Irish " republicans."

June 7.

Dr. Renner returned to St. Germain fror Austria.

*June 8.

Count Brockdorff-Rantzau returned t Versailles.

June 9.

Bolshevists captured Ufa from Adm Koltchak.

June 10.

Knox Reservations in U.S. Senate.

First Austrian Note on Peace Draf presented.

June 12.

Turkish Peace Delegation in France.

Adm. Koltchak's reply to Allied Note 26-v.-19.

Gen. Denikin recognised Adm. Koltcha as supreme head of Russian Government.

June 14.

Afghan reply to Armistice terms receive at Peshawar.

June 16.

Paris Conference : Allied reply presente to Count Brockdorff-Rantzau, who left fo Weimar.

Adm. Koltchak in retreat.

June 17, 1919.
President Wilson left Paris for Brussels.
Austrian counter proposals presented.

June 20.
Count Brockdorff-Rantzau declined to sign; Scheidemann Cabinet resigns.

June 21.
German fleet at Scapa Flow scuttled by Adm. von Reuter.

* June 22.
New Bauer-Erzberger Government announced in National Assembly its willingness to sign.
New Nitti Cabinet in Rome.

June 23.
Herr von Haniel, in charge at Versailles, intimated Germany would sign.

June 24.
Belgium to receive priority in reparation from Germany.
Attempted counter-revolution in Budapest suppressed by Soviet.

June 25.
Allied Scapa Flow Note.

June 26.
British advance on Archangel front.

June 27.
Gen. Denikin took Kharkoff.

June 28.
PEACE SIGNED AT VERSAILLES, German plenipotentiaries : Herr Hermann Müller and Dr. Bell.
Last meeting of Council of Three.
Mr. Lloyd George and President Wilson signed Franco-British and Franco-American Treaties by which U.S. and Britain undertook to assist France in case of unprovoked German attack.

* June 29.
Mr. Lloyd George returned to England from Paris.
President Wilson left France for U.S.

July 1,
Bolshevists captured Perm from Adm. Koltchak.

July 2.
Peace proclaimed at St. James's Palace and in City.

* July 6.
National Peace Thanksgiving. King and Queen at St. Paul's.

July 7.
Mutiny on Archangel front.

July 8.
President Wilson back in U.S. prepared for Treaty campaign.

July 9.
Germany ratified Peace Treaty. Document signed by President Ebert and forwarded to Versailles by courier.

July 12.
Blockade of Germany raised.

July 19.
OFFICIAL PEACE DAY IN BRITISH EMPIRE.

* July 20.
Complete Austrian Peace Treaty handed to Dr. Renner at St. Germain.
Hungarians attacked Rumanians.

July 23.
Mutiny at Onega (Archangel).

July 26.
Bulgarian Peace Delegation in Paris.
Allied warning to Hungarian Soviet.
Conference with Afghans at Rawal Pindi.

July 31.
Gen. Rawlinson to co-ordinate British withdrawal from Archangel—Murmansk.

August 1,
Rumanians nearing Budapest.
Fall of Hungarian Soviet ; Bela Kun escaped to Austria, and interned.

* August 4.
Rumanians occupied Budapest.
Supreme Council raised blockade of Hungary.

August 5.
Austrian Treaty counter-proposals presented.
Rumanian C.-in-C. at Budapest presented ultimatum to Hungarian Government embodying armistice terms differing from those concluded in Nov., 1918, by Allies. Supreme Council refused to recognise.

August 6.
Fall of Hungarian Provisional Cabinet : Archduke Joseph " State Governor."

August 8.
Poles took Minsk from Bolshevists.
Peace with Afghanistan. No subsidy to New Ameer.

August 9.
Anglo-Persian Agreement signed at Teheran.

* August 18.
British motor-boat raid on Kronstadt.

August 22.
Supreme Council refused to countenance Archduke Joseph at head of Hungarian Government.

August 23.
Archduke Joseph resigned at Budapest.

September 2.
New Zealand ratified Versailles Treaty.
Allies replied to Austrian counter-proposals.

September 10.
Austrian Treaty signed at Saint-Germain.
Jugo-Slavs and Rumanians abstained.

September 12.
Canada and S. Africa ratified Versailles Treaty.
Gabriele d'Annunzio occupied Fiume with armed force and proclaimed annexation to Italy.

Sundays marked with Asterisk (*).

September 15, 1919.
Allies decided to evacuate Russia.

September 27.
Last British troops left Archangel.

October 2.
Australia ratified Peace Treaty.

October 7.
Italy ratified German and Austrian Treaties.

October 10.
King George ratified Versailles Treaty.

October 12.
British evacuation of N. Russia complete.

October 13.
France and Belgium ratified Versailles Treaty.

October 25.
Austria ratified St. Germain Treaty.

October 26.
Gen. Yudenitch failed before Petrograd.

November 11.
Armistice Anniversary in London : Two-minute homage to dead.

November 13.
Rumanians evacuated Budapest.

November 15.
Adm. Koltchak withdrew from Omsk to Irkutsk.

November 19.
U.S. Senate rejected Peace Treaty and adjourns.

November 26.
Bulgarian Treaty signed at Neuilly. Yugo-Slavs and Rumanians abstained.

December 5.
Yugo-Slavs signed Austrian and Bulgarian Treaties.

December 10.
Rumania signed Austrian and Bulgarian Treaties.

December 15.
Fiume Council declared for independence d'Annunzio remained.

January 10, 1920.
FORMAL RATIFICATION OF PEACE WITH GERMANY IN PARIS signed by M. Clemenceau, Mr. Lloyd George, Signor Nitti, Mr. Matsui, and German Baron von Lersner.   U.S. stood out.

January 12.
Bulgaria ratified treaty of Neuilly.

June 4.
Hungarian treaty signed (ratified November 13).

August 10.
Turkish treaty signed at Sevres.

APPENDICES.

APPENDIX I.

CASUALTIES IN THE WORLD-WAR 1914—1918.

Country.	Dead.	Missing, &c.	Wounded.	Totals.
America	107,284	4,912	191,000	303,196
Austria	687,534	855,283	2,500,000	4,042,817
Belgium	267,000	10,000	140,000	417,000
Britain	851,117	142,057	2,067,442	2,960,616
Bulgaria ..	101,224	10,825	1,152,399	1,264,448
France	1,039,600	245,900	2,560,000	3,845,500
Germany ..	1,600,000	721,000	4,064,000	6,385,000
Greece	15,000	45,000	40,000	100,000
Italy	462,391	569,216	953,886	4,385,487
Japan	300	3	907	1,210
Portugal ..	8,367			
Rumania ..	332,000	116,000	200,000	648,000
Russia	1,700,000	2,500,000	4,950,000	9,150,000
Serbia	707,343	100,000	350,000	1,157,343
Turkey	436,974	103,731	407,772	948,477

APPENDIX II.

GREAT BRITAIN'S SHARE IN VICTORY.

TOTAL BRITISH TROOPS.			CASUALTIES.		
			Approximate killed, died of wounds, died.	Approximate missing and prisoners.	Wounded.
British Isles	..	..	5,704,416	662,083	140,312	1,644,786
Canada	..	..	640,886	56,119	306	149,733
Australia ..	..	..	416,809	58,460	164	152,100
New Zealand	..	..	220,099	16,132	5	40,749
South Africa	..	..	136,070	6,928	33	11,444
India	..	..	1,401,350	47,746	871	65,126
Other Colonies	..	..	134,837	3,649	366	3,504
Total	..	..	8,654,467	851,117	142,057	2,067,442

BRITISH ARMY IN FRANCE, 1918.

—	Ration strength.	Combatant strength.	Rifle Strength.
March 11 ..	1,828,098	1,293,000	616,000
April 1 ..	1,667,701	1,131,124	528,617
Sept. 23 ..	1,752,829	1,200,181	493,306
Nov. 11 ..	1,731,578	1,164,790	461,748

U.S. ARMY IN FRANCE, 1918.

—	Ration strength.	Combatant strength.	Rifle strength.
March 11 ..	245,000	123,000	49,000
April 1 ..	319,000	214,000	51,000
Sept. 25 ..	1,641,000	1,195,000	341,000
Nov. 11 ..	1,924,000	1,160,000	322,000

COMPARISON OF CAPTURES.

The captures of prisoners and guns in France during the victorious offensive against the German army between July 18 and November 11 were as follows :

—	Prisoners.	Guns.
British Armies ..	200,000	2,540
French Armies ..	135,720	1,880
American Armies..	43,300	1,421
Belgian Armies ..	14,500	474

BRITISH IN OTHER THEATRES.

In addition, there were 80,000 British combatant troops in Italy who co-operated in the final defeat of the Austrian army at Vittorio Veneto, capturing 30,000 prisoners, and in the Eastern theatres of war, Palestine and Mesopotamia, where about 400,000 British troops on an average throughout 1918 were fighting, the complete defeat and destruction of the Turkish army was effected by the British alone, and a total of 85,000 prisoners taken.

APPENDIX III.

BRITISH OVERSEAS TRANSPORT.

SUMMARY OF PERSONNEL CARRIED.

End of :—	August 1915.	August 1916.	August 1917.	August 1918.
U.K. to France	1,224,257	3,154,743	5,705,190	9,337,395
France to U.K.	335,696	1,311,583	2,896,032	5,499,809
U.K. to Overseas	273,743	601,880	785,066	968,228
Overseas to U.K.	180,533	499,532	842,121	1,766,974
Overseas to Ports other than France	354,745	1,459,281	2,414,813	3,682,172
Coastwise Moves	158,414	182,485	217,471	235,471
Total..	2,517,388	7,209,224	12,860,693	21,490,049
Exchanged Prisoners ..	—	—	—	12,631

TOTAL TRANSPORT TO MARCH 2, 1919.

Personnel	Effectives			23,388,228	
	Non-Effectives			2,336,241	
	Prisoners			192,899	
	Animals			2,264,134	
	Vehicles			512,400	
Army Stores	British			47,992,839	Tons.
	Allied			4,964,811	,,

APPENDIX IV.

BRITISH NAVAL LOSSES.

A.—PERSONNEL.

Personnel.	Dead.	Wounded.	Missing.	Interned and Prisoners.	Total.
Officers	2,466	805	15	222	3,508
Men	30,895	4,378	32	953	36,258
Total	33,361	5,183	47	1,175	39,766

B.—SUMMARY OF WARSHIP LOSSES.

Class.	Period.					Total Number lost.	Total Displacement Tonnage lost GrossTonnage in italics is additional
	4 Aug. 1914 to 31 Dec. 1914.	1915.	1916.	1917.	1 Jan. 1918 to 11 Nov. 1918.		
	No.	No.	No.	No.	No.	No.	Tons.
Battleships	2	6	2	2	1	13	200,73
Battle Cruisers	—	—	3	—	—	3	63,00
Cruisers	6	2	4	1	—	13	158,30
Light Cruisers ..	3	—	3	—	6†	12†	46,25
Torpedo Gunboats ..	2	—	—	1	2	5	4,23
River Gunboats ..	—	2	—	—	—	2	—
Coast Defence Ships ..	—	—	—	—	1	1	5,70
Monitors	—	—	1	1	3	5	8,12
Sloops	—	—	4	10	4	18	22,63
Flotilla Leaders ..	—	—	2	—	1	3	5,20
Torpedo Boat Destroyers	1	8	14*	23	18	64*	52,04
Torpedo Boats	—	5	3	2	1	11	2,23
Submarines	4	10	12	7	21§	54§	43,64
Aircraft Carriers	1	—	—	1	1	3	27,48
Patrol Boats	—	—	—	1	1	2	1,22
Minelayers	—	1	—	1	—	2	{ 11,00 { 6,00
Armed Merchant Cruisers .	1	4	1	6	5	17	179,16
Armed Boarding Steamers	—	2	3	4	4	13	23,77
Coastal Motor Boats ..	—	—	—	3	10	13	8
Total—Nos.	20	40	52	63	79	254	—
Tons Displacement ..	124,172	119,890	190,378	103,785	113,682	—	651,907
Tons Gross	17,274	33,564	20,068	74,132	63,910	—	208,94

* Including Zulu and Nubian, damaged in action and afterwards made into one ship name Zubian (counted as one lost of 1,027 tons displacement).

† Six Light Cruisers sunk as blockships at Zeebrugge and Ostend.

‡ River Gunboats Comet and Shaitan, tonnage uncertain.

§ Including seven destroyed at Helsingfors to avoid capture.

THE TIMES DIARY AND INDEX OF THE WAR. 185

C.—ANALYSIS OF CAUSES OF LOSS.—WARSHIPS.

Class.	Action.	Submarine.	Mine.	Destruction to avoid Capture.	Used as Blockships.	Internal Explosion.	Collision.	Wrecked.	Accident.	Unknown.	Total.
Battleships	1	5	5	—	—	2	—	—	—	—	13
Battle Cruisers	3	—	—	—	—	—	—	—	—	—	3
Cruisers	5	5	1	—	—	1	—	1	—	—	13
Light Cruisers	1	3	2	—	6	—	—	—	—	—	12
Torpedo Gunboats	—	1	2	—	—	—	2	—	—	—	5
River Gunboats	—	—	—	—	—	—	—	2	—	—	2
Coast Defence Ship	—	—	—	—	—	1	—	—	—	—	1
Monitors	3	1	1	—	—	—	—	—	—	—	5
Sloops	1	11	5	—	—	—	—	—	—	1	18
Flotilla Leaders	1	1	—	—	—	—	1	—	—	—	3
Torpedo Boat Destroyers	16*	7	20	—	—	—	12	8	—	1	64*
Torpedo Boats	—	2	1	—	—	—	4	4	—	—	11
Submarines	3	4	4	9	1†	—	4	4	4	21	54
Aircraft Carriers	1	1	—	—	—	—	1	—	—	—	3
Patrol Boats	—	—	1	—	—	—	1	—	—	—	2
Minelayers	—	1	—	—	—	1	—	—	—	—	2
Armed Merchant Cruisers	1	11	1	—	—	—	—	2	—	2	17
Armed Boarding Steamers	1	9	1	—	—	—	1	1	—	—	13
Coastal Motor Boats	5	—	—	2	—	—	2	—	3	1	13
Total ..	42	62	44	11	7	5	28	22	7	26	254

* *Nubian* and *Zulu* counted as one.   † Blown up at Zeebrugge Mole.

D.—SUMMARY OF LOSSES OF AUXILIARY VESSELS.

Class.	4 Aug. 1914 to 31 Dec. 1914.	1915.	1916.	1917.	1 Jan. 1918 to 11 Nov. 1918.	Total Number lost.	Total Tonnage lost (Gross Tonnage in *italics*, Displacement Tonnage in ordinary type).
	No.	No.	No.	No.	No.	No.	Tons.
Hospital Ships ..	1	—	—	—	1	2	*15,199*
Frozen Meat Ship ..	—	—	—	—	1	1	*1,730*
Store Carriers ..	—	1	1	2	—	4	*4,779*
Ammunition Ship ..	—	1	—	—	—	1	*2,030*
Mine Carriers ..	—	—	—	—	2	2	*4,496*
Minesweepers ..	—	5	3	7	3	{ 5 / 13 }	3,990 / *7,758*
Auxiliary Patrol Paddlers.	—	—	2	—	—	2	*679*
Fleet Messengers..	—	3	1	4	1	9	*11,602*
Commissioned Escort Ships..	—	—	—	2	1	3	*22,082*
Miscellaneous	—	—	—	1	2	3	*4,698*
Colliers ..	2	33	38	115	56	244	*714,613*
Oilers ..	—	8	6	21	9	44	*216,445*
Special Service Ships ..	—	—	5	17	7	29	*35,760*
Tugs ..	—	3	—	1	10	14	*3,593*
Yachts ..	—	5	5	3	—	13	*7,179*
Whalers ..	—	—	—	—	2	2	*347*
Admiralty Trawlers	1	2	2	5	8	18	*4,719*
Hired Trawlers ..	13	50	58	86	39	246	*56,300*
Hired Drifters ..	2	13	40	42	33	130	*10,809*
Motor Launches..	—	—	6	7	11	24	*864*
Motor Boats ..	—	3	3	—	—	6	*61*
Total { Nos. ..	19	127	170	313	186	815	—
Tons Displacement.	—	—	810	1,620	1,560	—	3,990
Tons Gross. ..	*19,165*	*155,222*	*180,444*	*538,322*	*232,500*	—	*1,125,743**

* Excluding two Motor Boats and two Special Service Ships whose Tonnage is uncertain.

E.—ANALYSIS OF CAUSES OF LOSS.—AUXILIARY VESSELS.

Class.	Cause of Loss.									
	Action.	Submarine.	Mine.	Destruction to avoid Capture.	Fire.	Collision.	Wrecked.	Various.	Unknown.	Total.
Hospital Ships	—	1	—	—	—	—	1	—	—	:
Frozen Meat Ship	—	1	—	—	—	—	—	—	—	
Store Carriers	—	—	3	—	—	1	—	—	—	
Ammunition Ship	—	—	—	—	—	—	—	—	1	
Mine Carriers	—	2	—	—	—	—	—	—	—	:
Minesweepers	—	1	12	—	—	2	—	2	1	1:
Auxiliary Patrol Paddlers	—	—	—	—	—	—	—	2	—	
Fleet Messengers	—	6	2	—	—	—	—	1	—	:
Commissioned Escort Ships	—	3	—	—	—	—	—	—	—	:
Miscellaneous	—	2	—	—	—	—	1	—	—	:
Colliers	—	193	22	—	—	9	10	5	5	24·
Oilers	—	35	2	—	1	1	2	1	2	4·
Special Service Ships	—	22	2	1	1	2	—	1	—	2!
Tugs	1	1	—	—	—	2	9	1	—	1·
Yachts	1	2	4	—	1	2	2	1	—	1:
Whalers	—	—	1	—	—	—	1	—	—	:
Admiralty Trawlers	1	3	4	—	—	5	2	1	2	1:
Hired Trawlers	5	14	140	—	1	35	34	9	8	24·
Hired Drifters	32	3	32	—	3	33	11	8	8	13·
Motor Launches	3	—	1	—	8	1	4	7	—	2
Motor Boats	—	—	—	—	3	—	—	3	—	
Total	43	289	225	1	18	93	77	38	31	81

APPENDIX V.

Month.	A			B		
	No.	Gross Tonnage.	Lives lost.	No.	Gross Tonnage.	Lives lost.
1914.						
August	9	40,254	—	10	51,306	—
September	21	88,219	29	5	26,932	1
October	19	77,805	24	7	30,193	—
November	5	8,888	—	1	5,732	—
December	10	26,035	16	4	11,825	2
1915.						
January	11	32,054	21	2	3,613	—
February	14	36,372	30	14	51,475	13
March	23	71,479	161	38	108,033	2
April	11	22,453	38	10	41,870	10
May	19	84,025	1,208	19	117,591	—
June	31	83,198	81	20	87,979	—
July	20	52,847	28	19	88,886,	31
August	49	148,464	248	21	67,259	—
September	30	101,690	77	8	45,943	2
October	17	54,156	42	8	66,422	—
November	32	94,493	118	14	69,403	—
December	21	74,490	419	10	77,553	—
1916.						
January	16	62,288	64	16	70,429	—
February	26	75,860	291	12	138,050	—
March	26	99,089	73	14	54,038	—
April	43	141,193	131	13	60,738	—
May	20	64,521	14	15	55,172	2
June	16	36,976	64	12	53,867	—
July	28	82,432	69	7	23,609	—
August	23	43,354	8	15	47,667	—
September	42	104,572	20	29	122,933	—
October	49	176,248	197	33	134,023	1
November	49	168,809	100	40	181,891	4
December	58	182,292	186	46	203,340	1
1917.						
January	49	153,666	276	30	146,408	1
February	105	313,486	402	79	366,050	15
March	127	353,478	699	82	346,943	64
April	169	545,282	1,125	100	479,609	24
May	122	352,289	591	99	393,047	3
June	122	417,925	413	128	580,428	18
July	99	364,858	468	84	397,280	6
August	91	329,810	462	57	268,145	10
September	78	196,212	356	66	232,656	42
October	86	276,132	608	45	172,509	24
November	64	173,560	420	52	201,153	27
December	85	253,087	585	64	236,786	56
1918.						
January	57	179,973	291	52	97,833	24
February	69	226,896	697	56	192,721	12
March	82	199,458	510	85	342,141	95
April	72	215,543	489	65	277,984	6
May	60	192,436	407	75	241,369	59
June	51	162,990	469	40	183,206	12
July	37	165,449	202	54	208,228	18
August	41	145,721	217	55	202,744	7
September	48	136,859	521	35	148,151	—
October	25	59,229	318	18	85,196	—
To November 11	2	10,195	1	2	9,608	—
Total to Nov. 11, 1918	2,479	7,759,090	14,287	1,885	8,007,967	592

A.—Number and Gross Tonnage of British Merchant Vessels lost through Enemy action during each month since the outbreak of war.

B.—Number and Gross Tonnage of British Merchant Vessels damaged or molested by the Enemy during each month since the outbreak of war.

APPENDIX VI.

GERMAN NAVAL LOSSES.

A.—PERSONNEL.

Dead.	Fleet.	Marines.	Tsingtau.	Total.
Officers	946	328	10	1,284
Men	17,908	10,297	196	28,401
Total	18,854	10,625	206	29.685

B.—NUMBER OF SHIPS LOST.

Ship of the line 1	Large torpedo-boats 2
Battle cruiser.. 1	Small torpedo-boats 4
Armoured cruisers 6	Minesweepers 2
Light cruisers 17	Auxiliary cruisers .. .. ..
Gunboats 10	Fishing vessels, luggers, &c. .. 12
Destroyers 60	U-boats 20

C.—DETAILED U-BOAT LOSSES.

Year.	Number Lost.	Area where Lost.	Number Lost.
1914	5	Baltic	3
1915	19	North Sea, &c.	83
1916	25	Flanders Coast	72 + 4*
1917	66	Mediterranean	16 + 10*
1918	85	Black Sea	5
		(Interned)	7
Total	200	Total	200

* Blown up by own crews.

APPENDIX VII.

THE U-BOAT WAR.

TOTAL NUMBER OF 360 U-BOATS ENGAGED.

U-BOATS IN COMMISSION JULY, 1914.

Class.	Tons.	Speed.	
		Sur.	Sub.
U1-2A	—	—	—
U3-18	—	—	—
U19-28B	650	12	9

U-BOATS BUILT AND COMPLETED UP TO NOV., 1918.

Class.	Tons.	Radius.	Speed.		Armament.		
			Sur.	Sub.	Guns.	T.	M.
U29-30	675	9,800 miles at 8 knots	16·75	9·85	— —	4	—
U31-41c	685	9,000 ,, ,, 8 ,,	16·75	9·75	One 4·1 in. —	4	—
U43-50	725	11,250 ,, ,, 8 ,,	15·50	9·75	,, 4·1 in. —	6	—
U51-56	715	9,500 ,, ,, 8 ,,	17·00	9·50	,, 4·1 ,, One 3·4 in.	4	—
U57-62	768	11,400 ,, ,, 8 ,,	16·50	9·50	,, 4·1 ,, ,, 3·4 ,,	4	—
U63-65	810	9,200 ,, ,, 8 ,,	16·50	9·00	,, 4·1 ,, ,, —	4	—
U66-70	791	7,500 ,, ,, 8 ,,	17·00	10·60	,, 4·1 ,, —	5	—
U71-80D	755	8,000 ,, ,, 7 ,,	10·60	8·00	,, 4·1 ,, —	2	2
U81-86	808	11,250 ,, ,, 8 ,,	16·85	9·50	,, 4·1 ,, ,, 3·4 ,,	4	—
U87-92	757	11,500 ,, ,, 8 ,,	16·00	9·00	,, 4·1 ,, ,, 3·4 ,,	6	—
U93-98	857	8,500 ,, ,, 8 ,,	16·80	9·00	,, 4·1 ,, ,, 3·4 ,,	6	—
U99-104	750	10,500 ,, ,, 8 ,,	16·50	9·00	,, 4·1 ,, ,, 3·4 ,,	4	—
U105-114E	798	8,500 ,, ,, 8 ,,	16·50	9·40	,, 4·1 ,, ,, 3·4 ,,	6	—
U117-125	1,163	11,500 ,, ,, 8 ,,	15·00	7·50	,, 5·9 ,, —	4	2
U135-136F	1,175	10,000 ,, ,, 8 ,,	17·75	8·50	,, 5·9 ,, —	6	—
U139-141G	1,930	18,000 ,, ,, 8 ,,	15·80	8·00	Two 5·9 ,, —	6	—
U142	2,158	20,000 ,, ,, 8 ,,	18·00	8·00	,, 5·9 ,, —	6	—
U151-157H	1,510	25,000 ,, ,, 5·5 ,,	10·00	5·50	,, 5·9 ,, —	2	—
U160-163	821	8,500 ,, ,, 8 ,,	16·20	8·50	,, 4·1 ,, —	6	—
UA	270	950 ,, ,, 9·75,,	14·20	7·50	One 2·0 ,, —	3	—
UB1-17	127	1,500 ,, ,, 5 ,,	6·50	6·20	— —	2	—
UB18-47	272	7,000 ,, ,, 5 ,,	9·15	5·80	— ,, 3·4 ,,	2	—
UB48-149	516	9,000 ,, ,, 6 ,,	14·00	8·00	,, 4·1 ,, —	5	—
UC1-15	168	900 ,, ,, 5 ,,	6·50	5·67	— —	—	6
UC16-79	410	8,700 ,, ,, 7 ,,	12·00	7·45	— ,, 3·4 ,,	3	6
UC90-105	491	9,850 ,, ,, 7 ,,	11·50	6·60	,, 4·1 ,, —	3	6

A.—Ineffective ; used for training.
B.—U19 : first Diesel-engined boat.
C.—U31-41 : due for delivery Aug. 1, 1914 . U42 was to have been built by Fiat-San Giorgio.
D.—U71-80 : mine-boats.
E.—U117-125 : large mine-boats.
F.—U126-134, 137-138 : designed in 1916 as improved U93-98 type ; not completed.
G.—U139-141 : known as " U K." (cruiser) type.
H.—U151-157 : converted mercantile cruisers.

APPENDIX VIII.

BRITISH AIR-POWER.

A.—PERSONNEL.

	August, 1914.			December, 1916.		
	Officers.	Other Ranks.	Total.	Officers.	Other Ranks.	Total.
R.F.C.	147	1,097	1,244	5,982	51,915	57,897
R.N.A.S.	50	550	600	2,764	26,129	28,893
Royal Air Force	—	—	—	—	—	—
Total	—	—	1,844	—	—	86,790

	December, 1917.			October 1918.		
	Officers.	Other Ranks.	Total.	Officers.	Other Ranks.	Total.
R.F.C.	15,522	98,738	114,260	—	—	—
R.N.A.S.	4,765	43,050	47,815	—	—	—
Royal Air Force	—	—	—	27,906	263,842	291,748
Total	—	—	162,075	—	—	291,748

B.—MACHINES AND ENGINES ON CHARGE.

	August, 1914.		January, 1917.		January, 1918.		October, 1918.	
	Machines.	Engines.	Machines.	Engines.	Machines.	Engines.	Machines.	Engines.
R.F.C.	179	—	3,929	6,056	8,350	14,755	—	—
R.N.A.S.	93	—	1,567	3,672	2,741	6,902	—	—
R.A.F.	—	—	—	—	—	—	22,171	37,702
Total	272	—	5,496	9,728	11,091	21,657	22,171	37,702

C.—SQUADRONS MAINTAINED.

	Service.			Training (1 Training Depot Station reckoned as 3 Squadrons).		
	August, 1914.	October 31, 1918.	—	—	August, 1914.	October 31 1918.
Western Front	4 (R.F.C.)	84 & 5 flights	Home		1 (R.F.C.) 2 (R.N.A.S.)	174
Independent Force	—	10				
5th Group	—	3	Egypt		—	10
India	—	2	Canada		—	15
Italy	—	4				
Middle East	—	13				
Russia	—	$\frac{1}{3}$				
Home Defence	—	18				
Naval Units	1 (R.N.A.S.)	64				
Total	5	198½ & 5 flights	—		3	199

D.—RESULTS OF OPERATIONS IN THE AIR.

	July 1916, to Nov. 11, 1918.	January 1, 1918, to November 11, 1918.										
	Western Front.	Independent Force.	Home Forces.	5th Gr'p & Naval Units.	Italy.	Egypt.	Mesopotamia.	Salonika.	Palestine.	India (Aden).	Total.
Enemy aircraft accounted for, i.e., brought down or driven down	6,904	150	8	470	405	25	6	59	81	—	7,908
Our machines missing	2,484	111	—	114	44	9	13	8	24	—	2,810
Bombs dropped (tons)	6,402	540	—	662	59	43	25	130	74	30	7,945
Hours flown	889,526	11,784	—	39,102	25,206	7,022	7,862	13,417	21,848	579	1,016,346
Rounds fired at ground targets	10,382,182	353,257	—	—	222,704	50,937	107,563	193,354	735,550	7,527	11,858,137
Photographs taken ...	431,375	3,682	—	3,440	14,596	8,135	66,720	15,587	27,039	542	501,116
Enemy balloons brought down	258	—	—	—	—	—	—	—	—	—	258

NOTE.—Records are not available of results obtained by Expeditionary Force, Western Front, prior to July, 1916, or by 5th Group and Naval Units, or in Eastern Theatres prior to January, 1918. The absence of these records, however, will not materially affect the totals shown as regards enemy aircraft accounted for, our machines missing, or the weight of bombs dropped, owing to the comparatively recent growth in intensity of aerial fighting and the smaller number of aircraft engaged.

APPENDIX IX.

GERMAN AIRSHIP LOSSES.

NAVY.

Total Airships commissioned 61	
Total Airships lost :—	
Shot down, &c. .. .. 17 ⎫	
Stranded, &c. .. .. .. 28 ⎬ 51	
Scrapped, &c .. .. 6 ⎭	
Effective at end of War 10	

APPENDIX X.

AIR AND SEA RAIDS ON GREAT BRITAIN.

SUMMARY: AIR RAIDS AND BOMBARDMENTS.—December 16, 1914, to June 17, 1918.

	Civilian Casualties.								Sailors and Soldiers.		Total Casualties.
	Killed.				Injured.						
—	Men.	Women.	Children.	Total.	Men.	Women.	Children.	Total.	Killed.	Injured.	
Airship raids .. .	217	171	110	498	587	431	218	1,236	58	121	1,913
Aeroplane raids ..	282	195	142	619	741	585	324	1,650	238	400	2,907
Bombardments from sea	55	45	43	143	180	194	230	604	14	30	791
Totals	554	411	295	1,260	1,508	1,210	772	3,490	310	551	5,611

NUMBER OF AIR RAIDS.

1915		1916		1917		1918
20	....	22	....	6	....	3

APPENDIX XI.

British Guns on W. Front.	Total.
August, 1914 (medium and light)	486
August, 1918 (all calibres)	6,437

INDEX.

INDEX.

In each reference the first numeral indicates the Day of the Month, the second (Roman) the Month, and the third the Year. Thus, 12-viii.-15 denotes 12th August, 1915. Abbreviations : see List, page iv.

Aa R. — Germans driven beyond, 12-viii.-15; repulsed, 24-x.-15; 28-xii.-15; German progress, 24-i.-17; cross, 4-ix.-17

Aaland Islands — Germany informs Sweden of proposition to use as base, 2-iii.-18

"Abaris," s.s. — torpedoed, 17-xi.-17

Abbandan (Tigris) — assemblage of " Firefly " gunboat class begun, 24-viii.-15

Abbas Hilmi Pasha — deposed as Sultan of Egypt, 18-xii.-14

"Abbasieh," s.s. — sunk, 22-viii.-18

Abbeville — British G.H.Q. at, 8-x.-14

"Abdiel," H.M. minelayer — operations, 3-v.-16; in Jutland Battle, 31-v.-16; lays mines off Horn Reef, 31-viii.-16

"Abelia," s.s. — sunk, 30-xii.-15

Abercorn (N. Rhodesia) — German attacks fail, 5-ix.-14; German attacks, 28-vi.-15; besiege, 26-vii.-15; relieved, 1-viii.-15; von Lettow reaches Kasama, 9-xi.-18; ordered to surrender and proceed to, 13-xi.-18; surrenders, 25-xi.-18

Aberdeen — three trawlers sunk off, 11-vii.-16

Ablaincourt — outskirts carried, 10-x.-16; French take, 7-xi.-16

Ablain St. Nazaire — French progress, 14-iv.-15; 12-v.-15; 21-v.-15; captured, 28-v.-15

Ablainzeville — Germans at, 13-iii.-17; British reach, 21-viii.-18; taken by Germans, 27-iii.-18; Allied line W. of, 27-iii.-18

Abo — Germans land, 12-iii.-18

"Abosso," s.s. — sunk, 24-iv.-17

"Aboukir," H.M.S. — sunk, 22-ix.-14

"Aboukir," s.s. — sunk, 3-ii.-18

Abrö — German detachments landed, 15-x.-17

Absinthe — prohibited in France, 7-i.-15; 12-ii.-15

Abu Dis — British hold high ground E. of, 18-xii.-17

"Acadian," s.s. — sunk, 16-ix.-18

" A Capellini," Italian monitor — capsized and sunk, 14-xi.-18

"Acasta," H.M.S. — in Jutland Battle, 2-vi.16

Achi Baba — Allied attack, 4-vi.-15; Anglo-French advance, 12-vii.-15

Achiet-le-Grand — British carry, 23-viii.-18

Achiet-le-Petit — British progress south of, 5-iii.-17; advance towards, 14-iii.-17; reach, 21-viii.-18

"Achilles," H.M.S. — gun accident, 20-xi.-14; sinks German raider, 16-iii.-17; sunk, 31-iii.-16

Acre — occupied, 23-ix.-18

"Actor," s.s. — torpedoed, 1-ix.-18

"Adalia," s.s. — sunk, 29-vii.-17

Adamello — Italian successes, 11-iv.-16; 29-iv.-16; attack N. of, 25-v.-18; take Monticello Pass, 26-v.-18

"Adansi," s.s. — sunk, 6-v.-17

Ada Tsiganlia Island — Austrians occupy, 3-i.-15

"Addah," s.s. — sunk, 15-vi.-17

Addison, Dr. C. — Munitions Minister, 11-xii.-16; Minister of Reconstruction, 17-vii.-17; outlines demobilisation policy, 12-xi.-18

"Adela," s.s. — sunk, 27-xii.-17

Aden — British column moves out to Shaikh Othman, 3-vii.-15; British retire from Lahej towards, 5-vii.-15; Turkish forces driven back to Lahej from Shaikh Othman, 21-vii.-15; Turkish post at Tabir captured, 22-xi.-17

Adenkerke — naval 12-in. gun mounted; fires first round, 1-vii.-16; fires 39 rounds at Tirpitz Battery, 8-vii.-16; 9-vii.-16; 20-vii.-16; 21-vii.-16; two more guns mounted, 21-vii.-16; battery fires on Ostend, 27-vi.-17

"Adenwen," s.s. — captured by U29, 11-iii.-15

Adige R. — two bridges blown up, 24-v.-15; Italians advance, 1-vi.-15; fighting, 19-vi.-17

Adler, Friedrich — shoots Austrian Premier, 21-x.-16

Adler, Victor — death, 11-xi.-18

"Admiral Cochrane," s.s. — attacked by U-Boat, 22-i.-18

" Admiral Spaun," Austrian cruiser — bombards railway and coast round Viesti-Manfredonia, 25-v.-15

Admiralty: see under Navy (British)

Adour R. — coast off mouth shelled, 8-ii.-17

Adramyti Gulf — Turks bombarded, 3-iii.-15

Adrianople — air raid, 14-iv.-16

Adriatic — British naval orders to watch, 2-viii.-14; s.s. " Baron Gautsch " mined, 13-viii.-14; Italy given initiative, 10-v.-15; Austrian ships raid Italian coast, 24-v.-15; bombard Fano, 18-vi.-15; Italian T.B. sunk, 26-vi.-15; Austrian submarine U11 bombed, 1-vii.-15; Italians blockading E. coasts, 7-vii.-15; Austrian destroyers bombard coast towns, 23-vii.-15; Italian submarine " Nereide " sunk, 15-viii.-15; naval action between Anglo-French and Austrian ships, 6-ii.-16; British drifters surprised by " Novara "; " Astrum," and " Spei," " Clavis " sunk, 9-vii.-16; T.B.D.s engaged, 22-iv.-18

Italo-Yugo-Slav Dispute — Signor Bissolati resigns from Italian Cabinet on, 28-xii.-18; Council of Four consider, 3-iv.-19; Pres. Wilson withdraws from discussion, 21-iv.-19; Italian Delegation decides to leave Paris, 23-iv.19; leaves, 24-iv.-19; returns, 5-v.-19; 6-v.-19; Yugo-Slavs offer to submit matter to Pres. Wilson; Italy refused, 10-ii.-19

Aerial warfare:—

German fleets (continued) :—

Mlava, 10-viii.-14; Gumbinnen, 22-viii.-14; Nordenburg, 25-viii.-14; Insterburg, 9-ix.-14; — "Z.V.": raids Lodz, 11-viii.-14; Novo-Georgievsk, 22-viii.-11; Rypin, 25-viii.-14; Mlava, 27-viii.-14; — "Z.VI.": raids Liége, 5-viii.-14; — "Z.IX.": raids Antwerp, 24-viii.-14; Belgian Coast, 1-ix.-14; Ostend, 24-ix.-14; Boulogne, 26-ix.-14; — "Z.X.": raids Calais, 21-ii.-15; Paris, 20-iii.-15; — "Z.XII.": fitted with observation basket; raids . Calais, 17-iii.-15; 16-v.-15; raids Bialystok, 20-vii.-15; 5-viii.-15; 11-viii.-15; Malkin, 22-viii.-15; 2-viii.-15; Siedlce, 6-viii.-15; Vileika, 10-ix.-15; Lida, 13-ix.-15; Stolpce, 7-iii.-16; Luninetz, 3-v.-16; — "Z.XIX.": shot down, 25-i.-15

Casualties — one destroyed at Düsseldorf, 8-x.-14; one down in Alsace, 22-viii.-14; one damaged over Ostend, 17-v.-15; one destroyed between Ghent and Brussels, 7-vi.-15; one at Evere, 7-vi.-15; one off Kentish Knock; attack at, 9,000 ft., 31-iii.-16; one at Cuffley, 3-ix.-16; one near Mersea Island, 23-ix.-16; one destroyed at Potters Bar, 1-x.-16; one down off Durham; one off Norfolk, 27-xi.-16; one at Jutland, 21-viii.-17; three down over France, 19-x.-17; two in Mediterranean, 19-x.-17; four at Ahlhorn, 31-i.-18; two at Tondern, 19-vii.-18; one off Frisian coast, 11-viii.-18; statistics, see Appendix IX.

Observation basket — fitted to "ZXII.," 17-iii.-15; "L.Z.107," 16-ii.-17

Statistics: see Appendix IX.

Observation balloons — nine destroyed 25-vi.-16

Seaplanes — destroyed, 14-xii.-15; 22-ix.-17

Italian fleets — raids on Pola, 30-v.-15; 12-vii.-15

Raids on Great Britain — first raid (Dover), 24-xii.-14; first airship raid, 19-i.-15; last effective raid; synopsis, 12-iv.-18; last aeroplane raid, 12-vi.-18; last airship attempt, 5-viii.-18; total casualties; statistics of raids, 17-vi.-18; Appendix X.; — on Bedfordshire, 3-ix.-16; — Bolton, 25-ix.-16; — Braintree, 21-ii.-15; — Broadstairs, 9-ii.-16; 29-ii.-16; — Bury St. Edmunds, 30-iv.-15; — Cambridgeshire, 24-iv.-16; 3-vii.-16; 3-ix.-16; 1-x.-16; — Cheshire, 27-xi.-16; — Coggleshall, 21-ii.15; — Colchester, 21-ii.-15; — Deal, 19-iii.-16; 3-v.-16; — Dover, 24-xii.-14; 9-viii.-15; 23-i.-16; 24-i.-16; 19-iii.-16; 9-vii.-16; 9-viii.-16; 22-ix.-16; 17-vi.-17; 22-viii.-17; 2-ix.17; 31-x.-17; 16-ii.-18; — Durham, 15-vi.-15; 5-vi.-16; 9-viii.-16; 27-xi.-16; 13-iii.-18; — East Anglia, 23-v.-17; — East Coast, 30-iii.-16; 18-xii.-17; — Eastern Counties, 30-iii.-16; — Edinburgh, 2-iv.-16; — Essex, 16-iv.-15; 4-vi.-15; 12-viii.-15; 17-viii.-15; 11-ix.-15; 25-iv.-16; 3-ix.-16; 5-vi.-17; 13-vi.-17; 4-vii.-17; 22-vii.-17; 12-viii.-17; 24-i.-17; 30-ix.-17; 29-x.-17; 31-x.-17; 6-xii.-17; 18-xii.-17; — Faversham, 16-iv.-15; —Folkstone, 25-v.-17; — Foreland, North, 9-vii.-16; — Grimsby, 6-vi.-15; — Hartlepool, 13-iii.-18; — Harwich, 6-vi.-15; 12-vi.-15; 23-v.-17; 4-vii.-17; — Hertfordshire, 3-ix.-16; 1-x.-16; — Home Counties, 19-x.-15; — Hull, 6-vi.-15; 9-viii.-16; 12-iii.-18; — Huntingdonshire, 3-ix.-16; — Ipswich, 30-iv.-15; — Kent, 4-vi.-15; 23-i.-16; 5-iii.-16; 25-iv.-16; 19-v.-16; 31-vii.-16;

Aerial warfare:—

Raids on Great Britain (continued) :—

2-viii.-16; 25-viii.-16; 3-ix.-16; 16-iii.-17; 17-iii.-17; 5-iv.-17; 12-viii.-17; 2-ix.-17; 3-ix.-17; 24-ix.-17; 25-ix.-17; 30-ix.-17; 1-x.-17; 31-x.-17; 6-xii.-17; 18-xii.-17; 28-i.-18; 29-i.-18; — King's Lynn, 19-i.-15; — Lancashire, 25-ix.-16; 12-iv.-18; — Leith, 2-iv.-16; — Leyton and Leytonstone, 17-viii.-15; — Lincoln, 24-iv.-16; 28-vii.-16; 31-vii.-16; 3-ix.-16; 25-ix.-16; 1-x.-16; 24-ix.-17; 12-iv.-18; — London, 8-v.-15; 17-viii.-15; 7-ix.-15; 8-ix.-15; 13-x.-15; 25-iv.-16; 25-viii.-16; 1-ix.-16; 1-x.-16; 28-xi.-16; (first aeroplane); 13-vi.-17; 7-vii.-17; 4-ix.-17; 24-ix.-17; 25-ix.-17; 29-ix.-17; 30-ix.-17; 1-x.-17; 19-x.-17; 31-x.-17; 16-xii.-17; 22-xii.-17; 28-i.-18; 29-i.-18; 17-ii.-18; 18-ii.-18; 17-iii.-18; 19-v.-18; — Lowestoft, 20-ii.-16; — Margate, 9-ii.-16; 29-ii.-16; 19-iii.-16; 26-iv.-16; 23-x.-16; 13-vi.-17; 7-vii.-17; 22-viii.-17; — Midland Counties, 31-i.-16; 5-iii.-16; — Norfolk, 19-i.-15; 4-vi.-16; 24-iv.-16; 28-vi.-16; 31-vii.-16; 2-viii.-16; 9-viii.-16; 31-xi.-16; 1-x.-16; 27-xi.-16; — Northampton-shire, 1-x.-16; — Northumberland, 15-vi.-15; 2-iv.-16; 2-v.-16; 9-viii.-16; — Nottingham, 31-vii.-16; 3-ix.-16; — Ramsgate, 17-v.-15; 19-iii.-16; 5-iv.-17; 22-viii.-17; — Scotland, 2-iv.-16; 2-v.-16; — Sheerness, 25-xii.-14; 22-x.-16; 30-x.-17; — Sittingbourne, 16-iv.-15; — Snettisham, 19-i.-15; — statistics: see Appendix X.; — Southend, 10-v.-15; 26-v.-15; — Stafford-shire, 27-xi.-16; — Suffolk, 3-iv.-16; 3-vii.-15; 9-viii.-15; 12-viii.-15; 7-ix.-15; 12-ix.-15; 13-x.-15; 31-i.-16; 2-iv.-16; 24-iv.-16; 25-iv.-16; 31-vii.-16; 2-viii.-16; 23-viii.-16; 25-viii.-16; 3-ix.-16; 17-vi.-17; 4-vii.-17; 22-vii.-17; — Sussex, 16-iii.-17; — Tyne district, 14-iv.-15; — Walmer, 20-ii.-16; — Warwickshire, 12-iv.-18; — Yorkshire, 4-vi.-15; 6-vi.-15; 9-viii.-16; 5-iii.-16; 1-iv.-16; 5-iv.-16; 2-v.-16; 9-viii.-16; 3-ix.-16; 25-ix.-16; 27-xi.-16; 21-viii.-17; 24-ix.-17; 12-iii.-18; — Yarmouth, 19-i.-15.

Torpedo — first use, 19-iv.-17

Turkish fleets — raid Port Said, 21-v.-16

United States fleets — contingent reach Bordeaux, 30-vi.-17; first single-hand raid: on Dommary Baroncourt static, 13-vi.-18

Flying boats — 23 and personnel arrive Killingholme, 30-v.-18

Aerschot — Germans destroy, 19-viii.-14; bat ends, 17-ix.-14

"Africa," s.s. —sunk, 12-ii.-17

Afghans — cross N.W. frontier, 8-v.-19 fighting, 10-v.-19; British cross Afgh frontier at Dakkafort, 13-v.-19; Brit attacked at Dakka, 16-v.-19; capture a hold hills W. of, 17-v.-19; British air-r on Kabul, 24-v.-19; Ameer requests Arm tice, 28-v.-19; Indian Government's rep 3-vi.-19; reply to terms, 14-vi.-19; confere at Rawal Pindi, 26-vii.-19; signed, 8-viii.-

Africa, East — Germans repulsed on Ri Tsavo, 7-ix.-14; British shell Dar-es-Salaa 13-viii.-14; Germans take Taveta, 15-viii.-20-viii.-14; Gen. Stewart at Nairobi; G von Lettow at Moshi, 3-ix.-14; Dar-Salaam shelled, 2-i.-15; British raid Shir 8-i.-15; Mafia Islands occupied, 10-i.-British post at Jasin attacked, 18-i.-15; e renders, 19-i.-15; British blockade, 27-ii.-German reverse on Mara, 9-iii.-15; Li shelled, 20-iii.-15; action E. of Tav 29-iii.-15; Pangani shelled, 1-iv.-15; G mans defeated at Karunga, 6-iv.-fighting round Kilimanjaro, 24-iv.-

Allied Powers (continued) :--

Supply and Relief, Supreme Council of — formed under Mr. Hoover, 9-i.-19; Permanent Committee holds first meeting in Paris, 19-i.-19; approves inter-Allied commissions at Trieste, Bukarest, Constantinople, and in Poland, 20-i.-19; British food mission leaves for Trieste, 2-ii.-19; leaves for Warsaw, 4-ii.-19

War Council, Supreme — Mr. Lloyd George expresses need for, 12-xi.-17; defends scheme, 19-xi.-17; conference opens, 29-xi.-17; Gen. Weygand to represent France, 4-xii.-17; established, 15-xii.-17; third meeting, 30-i.-18; decision: vigorous prosecution of war, 3-ii.-18; Italian representative changed, 8-ii.-18; Mr. Lloyd George on decisions, 12-ii.-18; 19-ii.-18; intimate that Allies " will baffle enemy's purpose and in due course bring him to defeat," 4-vi.-18; meets in Paris, 12-i.-19; settles new Armistice terms and fixes first formal meeting of Peace Conference, 13-i.-19; discusses strength of forces to be maintained on W. front during Armistice, 24-i.-19; decides on terms of Armistice renewal, 12-ii.-19

" **Almerian,**" s.s. — mined, 19-x.-18

" **Almirante Latorre,**" Chilian battleship — purchased by Great Britain: renamed " Canada," 9-ix.-14

" **Almond Branch,**" s.s. — sunk, 27-xi.-17

" **Almora,**" s.s. — sunk, 2-x.-17

" **Alnwick Castle,**" s.s. — sunk, 19-iii.-17

Alsace — French enter Altkirch, 7-viii.-14; enter Mülhausen, 8-viii.-14; bring down Zeppelin, 22-viii.-14; French fall back, 26-viii.-14; occupy Aspach-le-Bas and Aspach-le-Haut, 2-xii.-14; near Altkirch, 3-xii.-14; advance near Cernay, 26-xii.-14; 3-i.-15; recover part of Steinbach, 31-xii.-14; 3-i.-15; recapture completed, 4-i.-15; progress N. Altkirch, 5-i.-15; 6-i.-15; take Burnhaupt-le-Haut, 7-i.-15; Germans regain, 8-i.-15; attack Hartmannsweilerkopf, 19-i.-15; heavy fighting, 20-i.-15; carry Hartmannsweilerkopf, 21-i.-15; struggle round, 22-i.-15; 23-i.-15; fog interferes with fighting, 25-i.-15; German success in Lauch Valley, 14-ii.-15; advance near Sulzern, 20-ii.-15; French attack on Hartmannsweilerkopf, 5-iii.-15; reach second line, 24-iii.-15; carry summit; Germans use liquid fire, 26-iii.-15; French fail, 12-iv.-15; advance along Fecht R., 19-iv.-15; Germans retake; French regain crest, 26-iv.-15; French advance in Fecht Valley, 16-vi.-15; Germans evacuate, 17-vi.-15; French enter Metzeral and bombard Münster, 19-vi.-15; French capture Sondernach, 22-vi.-15; German attacks at Metzeral repulsed, 27-vi.-15; French advance toward Münster along Fecht Valley, 20-vii.-15; German attacks near Metzeral, 22-vii.-15; French advance on Lingenkopf; second battle of Münster, 26-vii.-15; French success, 27-vii.-15; Germans attack at Lingenkopf and Barrenkopf, 2-viii.-15; Germans repulsed, 7-viii.-15; French take trenches between Sondernach and Landersbach, 27-viii.-15; progress at Hartmannsweilerkopf, 20-ix.-15; success at, 15-x.-15; fighting, 21-xii.-15; 22-xii.-15; 23-xii.-15; 30-xii.-15; 31-xii.-15; 2-i.-16; French patrol actions, 28-i.-17; French success at Amertzwiller, 16-ii.-17; Germans repulsed at Hartmannsweilerkopf, 10-xi.-17

Alsace, Upper — position warfare until Armistice: begun, 1-i.-18

Alsace-Lorraine — acknowledgment to French title contained in Emperor Charles's Peace-letter, 9-iv.-18; denial, 14-iv.-18

" **Alsatian,**" H.M.A.M.C. — commission 31-viii.-14; Adm. de Chair hoists flag 3-xii.-14

Altkirch — French enter, 7-viii.-14; fighti near, 3-xii.-14; French progress, 5-i.-1 6-i.-15; Allied line at Armistice, 11-xi.-18

Alto Moloqua — Germans reach, 16-vi.-18

Altun Keupri — Gen. Lewin at, 31-x.-18

Aluta R. — Rumanians cross, 14-ix.-1 Rumanians fall back on, 23-xi.-16; Up line turned, 25-xi.-16; slight German p gress, 29-x.-16

Alyat — Gen. Bitcherakoff leaves Enzeli f 1-vii.-18; 3-vii.-18

" **Alyssum,**" H.M.S. — mined, 18-iii.-17

Amade, Gen. d' (France) — Divisions und command falling back, 24-viii.-14; G Maunoury takes over position in Som Valley, 27-viii.-14; at Tenedos, 17-iii.-15

" **Amakura,**" s.s. — sunk, 12-vi.-17

" **Amalfi,**" Italian cruiser — sunk, 8-vii.-15

Amanus Tunnel — completed, 31-i.-17

Amarah — Turks surrender, 3-vi.-15; G Townshend leaves for, 25-viii.-15; arriv 28-viii.-15

" **Amazon,**" H.M.S. — shells Belgian coa 18-x.-14; hit off Westende, 20-x.-14

" **Amazon,**" s.s. — attacked, 13-i.-17; su 15-iii.-18

" **Amberton,**" s.s. — torpedoed, 5-xi.-17

Amenancourt — French cross Suippe, 7-x.-1

America — German blockade of East Coa proposal vetoed by Kaiser, 2-vii.-18

" **Ambuscade,**" H.M.S. — damaged in counter with H.I.M.S. " Hambur 16-xii.-14

Amerongen — Kaiser reaches Castle, 11-xi.- signs formal abdication, 28-xi.-18

Amertzwiller — French success, 16-ii.-17

Amet, Adm. (France) — appointed High Co missioner at Constantinople, 18-xi.-18

" **Amethyst,**" H.M.S. — damaged, 13-iii.-15

Amiens — 56 R.F.C. machines land 13-viii.-14; reached by Germans, 30-viii.- Germans aiming at, 27-iii.-18; progre 28-iii.-18; 29-iii.-18; great German assa along roads leading to, 4-iv.-18; failure assault compelled Germans to abandon i of taking, 4-iv.-18; French attacked ne Hangard, 9-iv.-18; attack in Avre Valley, of; 500 prisoners, 18-iv.-18; German atta in sector on 8-mile front, 24-iv.-18; fighti 26-iv.-18; Americans on front near Mo didier, 1-v.-18; French advance towards A Valley, 23-vii.-18; second assault of All offensive; battle, 8-viii.-18; British attack 15-mile front E. of, 8-viii.-18; progre 10-viii.-18

Amiens—St. Quentin road — British advance 12-mile front astride, 6-ix.-18

" **Amiral Charnier,**" French cruiser — su 8-ii.-16

" **Amiral Ganteaume,**" s.s. — torpedo 26-x.-14

Amman — British progress towards Hed Railway, 25-iii.-18; cavalry approachi 26-iii.-18; British retire, 31-iii.-18; T withdraw towards, 23-ix.-18; British occu 25-ix.-18

Ammunition: see Munitions

Ampezzo Valley — Italians blow up moun spur; Austrian garrison destroyed, 20-vi.-

" **Amphion,**" H.M.S. — at sinking of H.I.M " Königin Luise," 5-viii.-14; mined, 6-viii

" **Ampleforth,**" s.s. — sunk, 21-v.-17

" **Amplegarth,**" s.s. — mined, 10-v.-18

Amsterdam — Revolutionary disturban 13-xi.-18

Amur — Japanese and Chinese volunteers fight with Bolshevists, 12-iii.-19

Ana — British at, 28-ii.-18

Anafarta — slight advance, 9-viii.-15; fur attack fails, 10-viii.-15; 21-viii.-15

Anatolia — Russian Black Sea Fleet again bombards Heraclea, 15-iv.-15; portion of railway blown up, 21-viii.-15; Russian T.B.D.s raid coast: 163 vessels destroyed, 17-i.-16; Germans entrain for Constantinople, 31-x.-18

Anatolia, Western — Armenians deported, 12-viii.-15

" **Anatolia**," s.s. — mined, 25-vi.-17

Ancemont — H.Q. U.S. 5th Corps at, 30-viii.-18

" **Anchoria**," s.s. — torpedoed, 24-iii.-18

" **Anchusa**," H.M.S. — sunk, 16-vii.-18

Ancona — Italian monitor " A. Capellini " capsized and sunk, 14-xi.-18

" **Ancona**," H.I.M.S. — sunk, 7-xi.-16

" **Ancona**," s.s. — sunk, 7-xi.-15

Ancre R. — Germans attempt use of fireships N. of Albert, 3-ii.-15; British attack N. of held up, 1-vii.-16; battle, 13-xi.-16; 18-xi.-16; artillery activity, 9-i.-17; British occupy ground, 6-ii.-17; British take Grandcourt and Baillescourt Farm, 7-ii.-17; advance, 17-ii.-17; German assaults defeated, 18-ii.-17; British slight advance, 21-ii.-17; German retreat, 24-ii.-17; German retirement, 25-ii.-17; 1-iii.-17; 3-iii.-17; 4-iii.-17; British advance, 26-ii.-17; 2-iii.-17; 8-iii.-17; 10-iii.-17; Allies on line to E. of Albert, 25-iii.-18; Germans take villages N. of, 27-iii.-18; Germans withdrew behind, 3-viii.-18; new German Army Group formed on front, 6-viii.-18; Tanks in action, 8-viii.-18; Germans evacuate positions, 14-viii.-18; British cross; progress, 15-viii.-18; British attack on 10-mile front N. of, 21-viii.-18; new British stroke, 22-viii.-18

Ancre R.—Somme R. — Australian advance, 5-v.-18; 10-vi.-18

" **Andalusian**," s.s. — sunk, 12-iii.-15

" **Andania**," s.s. — attacked and chased, 3-xii.-15; sunk, 27-i.-18

Andéchy — French advance between Oise and, 17-iii.-17; British hold, 26-iii.-18; taken by Germans, 27-iii.-18

" **Andes**," H.M.A.M.C. — picks up survivors of German raider " Greif," 29-ii.-16

Andrassy, Count Julius (Hungary) — Foreign Minister, 27-x.-18

" **Anglesea**," s.s. — sunk, 24-iv.-17

Anglia, E. — German air raids, 23-v.-17; 5-viii.-18

" **Anglia**," H.S. — mined, 17-xi.-15

" **Anglian**," s.s. — sunk, 10-vi.-17

" **Anglo-Californian**," s.s. — attacked by U-Boat, 4 vii.-15

" **Anglo-Canadian**," s.s. — sunk, 22-i.-18

" **Anglo-Patagonian**," s.s. — sunk, 11-vii.-17

Angoche (P. E. Africa) — Germans reconnoitre, 11-viii.-18; Germans pursued, 14-viii.-18

Angola — Germans invade, 24-xii.-14

Angre — British held up, 5-xi.-18; taken, 6-xi.-18

Angreau — taken by British, 5-xi.-18

Angres — British take, 13-iv.-17

" **Angus**," s.s. — sunk, 11-iv.-16

" **Anhui**," s.s. — sunk, 12-viii.-18

" **Anna**," s.v. — sunk, 22-i.-17

" **Anna Sofie**," s.s. — sunk, 23-vii.-18

" **Anne**," s.s. — attacked by U-Boat, 25-v.-18

Anneux — taken by British, 20-xi.-17

Annunzio, Gabriele d' (Italy) — flies over Vienna, 9-viii.-18; occupies Fiume, 12-ix.-19; remains at, 15-xii.-19

" **Anselma de Larrinaga**," s.s. — torpedoed, 9-viii.-18

Anspach — Germans' severe losses in attack on French, 3-i.-18

" **Antaeus**," s.s. — sunk, 4-xi.-17

" **Ant Cassar**," s.s. — sunk, 27-viii.-18

" **Antenor**," s.s. — torpedoed, 9-ii.-18

" **Anteros**," s.s. — sunk, 24-iii.-18

" **Antilles**," U.S. Transport — torpedoed, 17-x.-17

" **Antilochus**," s.s. — attacked by U-Boat, 10-ix.-15

" **Antinoe**," s.s. — sunk, 28-v.-17

" **Antinous**," s.s. — attacked by U-Boat, 29-v.-18

" **Antiope**," s.s. — sunk, 9-viii.-16

" **Antiope**," s.s. — torpedoed, 3-vi.-18

Antoing — British occupy, 9-xi.-18

" **Antony**," s.s. — sunk, 17-iii.-17

" **Antrim**," H.M.S. — attacked by U-Boat, 9-x.-14

Antwerp — Belgian Government at, 17-viii.-14; raided by ZIX., 24-viii.-14; troops from Namur transferred, 30-viii.-14; German advance delayed by Belgians, 4-ix.-14; Belgians retire on, 17-ix.-14; besieged, 26-ix.-14; forts bombarded; siege begun, 27-ix.-14; attack continued, 28-ix.-14; waterworks destroyed, 30-ix.-14; forts fall, 1-x.-14; outer defences fall, 3-x.-14; evacuated; bombarded, 7-x.-14; inner forts fall, 8-x.-14; Germans enter, 9-x.-14; capitulates, 10-x.-14; Germans levy £20,000,000, 13-x.-14; despatches published, 4-xii.-14; British airmen reconnoitre, 15-vi.-17; King and Queen of the Belgians enter, 19-xi.-18

Anutieh — British line advanced near, 30-i.-18

Anzac — Colonial landing at, 25-iv.-15; reinforcements reach, 28-iv.-15; bombarded, 18-v.-15; Turkish attack repulsed, 19-v.-15; negotiations for truce to bury dead, 20-v.-15; arranged, 24-v.-15; Turkish attack repulsed, 30-vi.-15; new landing at Suvla Bay, 6-viii.-15; advance against Sari Bair ridge, 6-viii.-15; New Zealanders gain footing on Chanuk Bair crest, 8-viii.-15; Turks recover Chanuk Bair, 10-viii.-15; advance by British, 21-viii.-15; Australians repulse Turkish raid, 5-ix.-15; Turks attack, 4-xi.-15; British withdrawal, 10-xii.-15; successfully effected, 19-xii.-15

Anzacs — in France, 8-v.-16; 1st Corps at Ligny-Thilloy, 3-iii.-17; with Imperial Camel Corps take Turkish position at Rafa, 9-i.-17

" **Apapa**," s.s. — sunk, 28-xi.-17

" **Aparima**," s.s. — sunk, 19-xi.-17

Apia — New Zealand troops landed, 30-viii.-14

" **Apollo**," s.s. — sunk, 9-x.-15

" **Appalachee**," s.s. — torpedoed, 25-ii.-18

" **Appam**," s.s. — captured by German raider " Möwe," 15-i.-16; taken into Norfolk (U.S.), 1-ii.-16

" **Appledore**," s.s. — sunk, 9-vi.-17

" **Appleleaf**," s.s. — mined, 10-xi.-17

Apremont — French success, 29-xii.-14; French attacks, 16-ix.-17

" **Arab**," s.s. — sunk, 7-i.-18

Arabia — British force at Lahej attacked, 4-vii.-15; British retire from Lahej towards Aden, 5-vii.-15 Council of Four consider, 12-iv.-19

" **Arabia**," s.s. — sunk, 6-xi.-16

" **Arabian**," s.s. — sunk, 2-x.-15

" **Arabic**," s.s. — sunk, 19-viii.-15; German apology to U.S., 24-viii.-15

" **Arabis**," H.M.S. — sunk, 10-ii.-16

" **Arabis**," s.s. — sunk, 16-ix.-17

Arabs — rising against Turks, 13-vi.-16; 18-vi.-16; 21-vi.-16; raid Hedjaz Railway S. of Maan, 6-i.-18; damage Hedjaz Railway N. of Maan, 3-v.-18; demolish part of railway N. and S. of Maan: take 264 Turk prisoners, 12-v.-18

" **Aragon**," s.s. — sunk, 30-xii.-17

Arbuthnot, Adm. — transferred to 1st Cruiser Squadron, 15-i.-15

" **Arbutus**," H.M.S. — sunk, 16-xii.-17

" **Arca**," H.M. oiler — sunk, 2-x.-18

" **Arca**," s.s. — attacked by U-Boat, 6-i.-18

" **Arcadia**," s.s. — sunk, 15-iv.-17

Archangel — trade; protection arrangements, 17-xi.-15; Allied operations against Bolshevists: Modyngski Is. captured by Allied warships, 1-viii.-18; Allied landing, 2-viii.-18; American troops embark for, 26-viii.-18; retirement at Shenkursk, 25-i.-19; at Tarasevo, 30-i.-19; success at Kadish, 7-ii.-19; Bolshevists repulsed, 1-iv.-19; British Relief Force at, 27-v.-19; advance on front, 26-vi.-19; mutiny on front, 7-vii.-19; Gen. Rawlinson to co-ordinate British withdrawal, 31-vii.-19; last troops leave, 27-ix.-19

"**Archbank**," s.s. — sunk by U-Boat, 5-vi.-18

Archibald, James (U.S.). — discovered carrying documents compromising Dr. Dumba, 6-ix.-15; White Paper on, 22-ix.-15

Archibong — British at, 29-viii.-14

Arcy — taken by Allies, 2-viii.-18; French reach Aisne, 5-ix.-18

Ardahan — Russians destroy two Turkish Army Corps, 3-i.-15; Germans demand surrender; terms accepted, 3-iii.-18; Turks move on to Batum, 6-iv.-18; Turkish to remain in, 9-vi.-18

"**Ardandearg**," s.s. — sunk, 14-iii.-18

Ardennes Canal — French reach, 2-xi.-18; on S. bank, 4-xi.-18

"**Ardgask**," s.s. — sunk, 3-iv.-17

"**Ardglamis**," s.s. — sunk, 9-xi.-17

"**Ardglass**," s.s. — sunk, 1-iv.-18

Ardjiche — occupied, 17-v.-15

"**Ardmore**," s.s. — sunk, 13-xi.-17

Ardre — British 22nd Corps transferred to sector, 13-vii.-18; British push down Valley, 21-vii.-18; advance, 24-vii.-18; German retreat, 26-vii.-18

"**Arendal**," s.s. — sunk, 18-ix.-17

Arensburg — taken, 13-x.-17

"**Arethusa**," H.M.S. — commissioned as flagship to Commander Tyrrwhitt, 11-viii.-14; disabled in battle of Heligoland Bight, 28-viii.-14; assists in raid off Cuxhaven, 25-xii.-14; mined, 11-ii.-16

"**Argalia**," s.s. — sunk, 6-viii.-17

Argentine —

Shipping — sailings transmitted by German diplomatic agent to Berlin, 8-ix.-17; Swedish official statement, 11-ix.-17; German Minister handed passports, 12-ix.-17

Arges — battle, 1-xii.-16; 2-xii.-16; German victory, 3-xii.-16

Arges Valley — fighting in, 2-xii.-16

"**Argo**," s.s. — sunk, 24-xii.-17

Argonne — German successes, 15-x.-14; French recovery, 21-x.-14; French take Bagatelle; lost ground recovered, 29-xi.-14; Germans repulsed, 4-xii.-14; French success at Apremont, 29-xii.-14; German attack on Boureuilles, 3-i.-15; French attack near Courtechasse, 5-i.-15; Germans repulsed, 7-i.-15; heavy fighting at Fontaine Madame and St. Hubert, 22-i.-15; more fighting, 23-i.-15; Germans repulsed, 27-i.-15; French reverse near Fontaine Madame, 30-i.-15; Germans attack Bagatelle, 7-ii.-15; Germans attack in La Grurie Wood, 10-ii.-15; fail near Boureuilles, 5-iii.-15; fighting between Four de Paris and Bolante, 9-iii.-15; Germans attack at Bagatelle, 2-iv.-15; attack towards Vienne-le-Château, 20-vi.-15; Germans still attacking, 26-vi.-15; attacks at Bagatelle, 30-vi.-15; progress near Four de Paris; repulsed near Blanleuil, 2-vii.-15; Crown Prince's attack slackening, 4-vii.-15; Germans capture La Fille Morte Mill, 7-vii.-15; temporary gain at Vienne-le-Château at La Fille Morte, 13-vii.-15; repulsed, 15-vii.-15; French progress near Bagatelle, 22-vii.-15; Germans repulsed, 26-vii.-15; success at Hill 213, 2-viii.-15; attacks fail, 3-viii.-15; fierce fighting round Hill 213, 5-viii.-15; 6-viii.-15; Germans repulsed, 7-viii.-15; 11-viii.-15; violent artillery struggle, 29-viii.-15; heavy

Argonne (continued) :—

German attack repulsed, 8-ix.-15; offensive repulsed, 27-ix.-15; French mining success 12-xi.-15; fighting between Aisne and 15-i.-17; German attacks repulsed, 27-ix.-17 French relieved as far as La Harazée b U.S. Army, 22-ix.-18; battle, 26-ix.-18 Germans evacuate main pass, 11-x.-18 retreat on front from Oise to, 13-x.-18 cleared by Franco-Americans, 3-xi.-18

"**Argyll**," H.M.S. — attacked by U-Boat 20-vi.-15; wrecked, 28-x.-15

"**Argyll**," s.s. — sunk, 13-iv.-17

"**Argyllshire**," s.s. — attacked, 27-v.-15; torpedoed, 5-ii.-17

"**Ariadne**," H.I.M.S. — sunk, 28-viii.-14

"**Ariadne**," H.M. minelayer — sunk, 26-vii.-1

"**Ariadne**," s.s. — sunk, 15-i.-16

"**Ariadne Christine**," s.s. — torpedoed 6-vii.-17; mined, 2-ix.-18

"**Ariel**," s.s. — sunk, 3-x.-18

"**Aries**," H.M. Yacht — mined, 31-x.-15

"**Aries**," s.s. — sunk, 25-ii.-17

Arkhava — Turks repulsed, 12-x.-15

"**Arlanza**," H.M.A.M.C. — captured an released, 16-viii.-14; mined, 29-x.-15

Arleux — British take, 28-iv.-17

"**Arlington Court**," s.s. — sunk, 14-v.-17

"**Armadale**," s.s. — sunk, 27-vi.-17

Armenia (operations) — Russian success 10-xi.-14; Russians driven out of Kuprukeni 17-xii.-14; Turks reach Khorasan—Sarikamish, 25-xii.-14; withdraw from Sarikamish 28-xii.-14; defeated at Khorasan, 23-i.-15 counter-attack, 26-i.-15; defeated at Olti 4-iv.-15; besiege Van, 20-iv.-15; occupy Ardjiche, 17-v.-15; take Van, 19-v.-15 Russians at Alashgerd, 12-viii.-15; enter Van 16-viii.-15; progress towards Erzinjan 12-vii.-16; 20-vii.-16; Gumishkhanen taken 20-vii.-16; Erzinjan falls, 25-vii.-16; Turkish counter-attack, 6-viii.-16; Russians recover 12-viii.-16; Russians evacuate, 18-ii.-18 Turks re-conquering, 21-ii.-18

Armenia (political) — Russian orange book published, 9-ii.-15; Talaat Pasha informed Prince Hohenlohe that question " no longer exists," 31-viii.-15; Turkish report on " conspiracies " published, 27-viii.-17; Independence declared, 28-v.-18; peace convention with Turkey signed at Batum, 4-xi.-18; Parliament opened at Erivan, 1-viii.-18; claims heard by Peace Conference, 26-ii.-19

"**Armenian**," s.s. — sunk, 28-vi.-15

Armenians — Baron Kress von Kressenstein's appeals to Central Powers, 10-vii.-18; 20-viii.-18; Hindenburg telegraphs to Enver Pasha regarding return to home in Caucasus, 29-vii.-18; reply, 3-viii.-18; Adm. von Hintze's reply to Baron Kress von Kressenstein's appeal, 24-viii.-18

Deportations — from Constantinople, 25-iv.-15; Erzrum, 14-vi.-15; Sivas, 25-vi.-15; from Trebizond, 26-vi.-15; from Samsun, 27-vi.-15; from Cilicia, 27-vii.-15; from W. Anatolia, 12-viii.-15; from Konia, 16-viii.-15

Massacres — at Bitlis, 2-vii.-15; at Mush, 10-vii.-15; at Urfa, 19-viii.-15; reported, 25-viii.-15; 800,000 since May, 6-x.-15; at Katherinenfeld, 1-vi.-18

Armentara — Italians evacuate ridge, 20-v.-16

Armentières — German cavalry about, 6-x.-14; British nearing, 15-x.-14; British at, 18-x.-14; Germans bombard, 17-xii.-14; British trench raid, 16-xii.-15; 19-vii.-16; 7-i.-17; 13-i.-17; 28-i.-17; 20-ii.-17; German attempts between Ploegsteert and, 23-i.-17; German attempts near, 9-ii.-17; Germans yielding, 14-vi.-17; British raid S. of, 1-iii.-18; German raids defeated, 11-iii.-18; air raids on front, 18-iii.-18; British front heavily bombarded, 8-iv.-18; German attack, 9-iv.-18; cross Lys between

Armentières (continued) :—
Estaires—Bac St. Maur, 10-iv.-18; evacuated, 11-iv.-18; fighting on front, 7-ix.-18; Germans withdraw, 2-x.-18; British occupy, 3-x.-18; British advance E. of, 4-x.-18
Armentières—La Bassée — fighting, 15-xi.-15
Armin, Gen. Sixt von (Germany) — commands 4th (Prussian) Corps, 28-ix.-14; to command 4th Army, 25-ii.-17
Armlet Scheme: see under Army — Recruiting — Derby system
" Armonia," s.s. — sunk, 15-iii.-18
Army :—
Armies — **1st:** formation ordered; Gen. Haig to command, 25-xii.-14; Gen. Monro succeeds Sir D. Haig, 21-xii.-15; allotted 8 Tanks, 8-iv.-17; attacking Etaing—Quéant, 2-ix.-18; at battle of Cambrai, 27-ix.-18; attack on 30-mile front, 4-xi.-18; German withdrawl, 5-xi.-18; — **2nd:** formation ordered; Gen. Smith-Dorrien to command, 25-xii.-14; successes, 16-x.-18; march to Rhine begun, 17-xi.-18; crosses German frontier, 1-xii.-18; — **3rd:** attacks with 4th Army on 20-mile front in Somme Battle, 1-vii.-16; allotted 40 Tanks, 8-iv.-17; Gen. Byng commanding, 29-vi.-17; breaks Hindenburg line facing Cambrai, 20-xi.-17; attacked in Somme battle, 21-iii.-18; attack in battle of Bapaume, 21-viii.-18; 23-viii.-18; attack Etaing—Quéant, 2-ix.-18; cross Scheldt Canal; occupy Hindenburg line, 5-x.-18; attack on 30-mile front, 4-xi.-18; German withdrawal, 5-xi.-18; — **4th:** attacks on 20-mile front in Somme battle, 1-vii.-16; attacked in Somme battle, 21-iii.-18; placed under Sir D. Haig, 28-vii.-18; attacking in battle of Amiens, 8-viii.-18; in battle of Bapaume, 23-viii.-18; engaged N. of St. Quentin, 29-ix.-18; 3-x.-18; attack on 30-mile front, 4-xi.-18; German withdrawal, 5-xi.-18; march to Rhine begun, 17-xi.-18; — **5th:** allotted 12 Tanks, 8-iv.-17; prolongs front 28 miles to Barisis, 20-i.-18; enters Lille, 17-x.-18; — Lord Cavan's Army: on Tagliamento, 3-xi.-18
Brigades — **6th:** attacked by 2nd German Corps, 1-ix.-14; — **19th:** along Condé Canal, 22-viii.-14; in battle of Le Cateau, 26-viii.-14; joins 3rd Corps, 30-viii.-14; — **28th:** at Cologne, 7-xii.-18; — **39th:** concentrates at Enzeli, 9-xi.-18; proceeds to Baku, 17-viii.-18; — Northumberland Brigade: enters St. Julian for time, 26-iv.-15
Casualties: see under Casualties
Cavalry — Corps formed in France, 9-x.-14; — Gen. Allenby's Corps: on Wytschaete—Messines Ridge, 31-x.-14; — **1st** Division: secures Rhine crossings, 8-xii.-18; — **3rd** Division: landed at Zeebrugge; moved to Ostend, 8-x.-14; at Thourout, 11-x.-14; — **4th Brigade:** prolonged to Cambrai, 26-viii.-14 — **5th** Brigade: at Binche, 21-viii.-14; — **11th** Brigade: in Mesopotamia, 27-x.-18
Conscription: see Recruiting — Military Service Acts, below
Corps — **1st:** Gen. Haig commanding; at Maubeuge—Givry, 21-viii.-14; extended to Peissant, 22-viii.-14; attacked by artillery, 23-viii.-14; attacks towards Troyon—Courde-Soupir, 14-ix.-14; leaves Aisne for St. Omer, 11-x.-14; in Ypres Salient; relieved by French 9th Corps, 27-x.-14; casualties in first Ypres battle, 21-xi.-14; relieves Indians in Givenchy sector, 22-xii.-14; at Neuve Chapelle—Givenchy; attacks, 9-v.-15; — **2nd:** Gen. Smith-Dorrien takes over command, 17-viii.-14; at Maubeuge—Sars la Bruyères, 21-viii.-14; in battle of Le Cateau, 26-viii.-14; concentrates N.E. of

Army :—
Corps (continued) :—
Abbeville, 8-x.-14; on Neuve Chapelle front; relieved by Indian Corps, 28-x.-14; — **3rd:** Gen. Pulteney commanding; formed in France, 30-viii.-14; at Hazebrouck, 12-x.-14; captures L'Epinette, 12-iii.-15; in battle of Amiens, 8-viii.-18; — **4th:** formed, 10-x.-14; distributed, 27-x.-14; at Neuve Chapelle; repulses German counter-attacks, 12-iii.-15; — **14th:** in Italy, 6-x.-18; Italian 31st Division joins, 29-x.-18; — **16th:** enter Bulgaria, 25-ix.-18; at Strumnitza, 26-ix.-18; — **17th:** attack Etaing—Quéant, 2-ix.-18; — **22nd:** transferred to Arde sector, 13-vii.-18
Dispatches: see Dispatches
Divisions — effective: increased from 45 to 52 in France, 1-vii.-18; — **1st:** repulses German attack at Gheluvelt, 29-x.-14; broken by attack N. of Ypres-Menin Road, 31-x.-14; withdrawn from Le Clipon, 15-v.-17; — **2nd:** relieved by 51st Division, 19-v.-15; take Irles, 10-iii.-17; — **3rd:** holding salient round Mons, 22-viii.-14; attacked by German 1st Army, 23-viii.-14; — **4th:** arrives at Le Cateau, 25-viii.-14; in battle of Le Cateau, 26-viii.-14; joins 3rd Corps, 30-viii.-14; command: change, 21-ix.-14; — **5th:** position, 22-viii.-14; attacked by German 1st Army at Mons, 23-viii.-14; — **6th:** landed at St. Nazaire, 11-ix.-14; concentrated S. of Marne; proceeding to Aisne front, 14-ix.-14; — **7th:** landed at Zeebrugge, 7-x.-14; before Ostend, 8-x.-14; at Thielt, 12-x.-14; repulses German attack at Gheluvelt, 29-x.-14; Queen's Westminsters relieve Artists' Rifles, 1-xi.-14; attached to 1st Corps, 27-x.-14; progress toward Aubers, 13-iii.-15; relieved by Canadian Division, 19-v.-15; inspected by Gen. Joffre, 27-v.-15; commander, 27-v.-15; carry trenches Beaumont Hamel, 11-i.-17; reduced from 13 to 10 battalions; surplus sent to France, 13-ix.-18 — **9th:** retakes Meteren, 19-vii.-18; 28th Brigade at Cologne, 7-xii.-18; — **10th:** lands at Salonika, 5-x.-15; take Irles, 10-iii.-17; — **23rd:** on Asiago front; line bent but restored, 15-vi.-18; reduced from 13 to 10 battalions; surplus sent to France, 13-ix.-18; — **27th:** arrives at St. Omer, 23-xii.-14; — **42nd:** embarks at Southampton, 10-ix.-14; — **48th:** on Asiago front; line bent but restored, 15-vi.-18; reduced from 13 to 10 battalions; surplus sent to France, 13-ix.-18; pushes forward in Asiago sector, 1-ix.-18; carries Monte Mosciagh and reaches Vezzena, 2-xi.-18; — **51st** (Highland): relieves 2nd Division, 19-v.-15; — **52nd:** transferred to W. Front, 6-iv.-18; — **74th:** transferred to W. Front, 13-iv.18
Equipment — conference at War Office, 13-vii.-16
France and Flanders — expeditionary force: begins embarkation, 7-viii.-14; first troops at Boulogne, 9-viii.-14; force landed, 16-viii.-14; transfer from Aisne to left flank of Allied line proposed, 29-ix.-14; order issued, 1-x.-14 transfer begun, 3-x.-14; align on Gen. Muad'huy's left, 11-x.-14; completed, 19-x.-14; King's message, 9-xi.-14; withdrawn from Ypres to refit, 21-xi.-14; proposal to move to extreme left of line: not accepted by French, 9-xii.-14; amalgamation with Belgian Army proposed, 28-xii.-14; eleven new divisions; additional 17 miles taken over; Lord Kitchener's statement, 15-ix.-15; Sir J. French's farewell to, 18-xii.-15; Sir D. Haig assumes command, 19-xii.-15

Artois (continued) :—
22-ii.-16; position-warfare until April 30 begun, 1-i.-18; Germans prepare for March offensive, 1-ii.-18

Artres — taken, 26-x.-18

Artstetten — funeral of Archduke Ferdinand at, 4-vii. 14

Artuvin — Russians occupy, 6-iv.-15

" Arum," s.s. — sunk, 4-ix.-18

Arusha — occupied, 20-iii.-16

Arvilliers — Allies on line, 27-iii.-18; French advance, 9-viii.-18

Arz, Gen. von (Austria) — Kaiser decorates with Pour le Mérite order, 25-viii.-15; Chief of Staff, 1-iii.-17; confers with Kaiser at Spa, 15-viii.-18

" Asaba," s.s. — sunk, 6-xii.-17

" Asama," H.I.J.M.S. — keeps H.I.M.S. " Geier " under observation, 9-xi.-14

Ascalon — H.M.S. " Doris " raids, 15-xii.-14; Turks evacuate, 9-xi.-17; driven from Wadi Sukereir, 13-xi.-17

Aschhoop — taken by French, 27-x.-17; attack on Belgian positions repulsed, 28-xi.-17

" Ashburton," s.s. — sunk, 1-iv.-16

Ashkhala — Russians take, 25-ii.-16; Turks force back Russian centre, 13-v.-16

" Ashleaf," s.s. — sunk, 29-v.-17

" Ashleigh," s.s. — sunk, 23-vii.-17

" Asia Corps ": see under Germany (Army)

Asiago — Austrian offensive, 28-v.-16; Italians evacuate, 29-v.-16; withdrawal, 31-v.-16; Austrian attacks fail, 7-vi.-16; Italians re-take, 25-vi.-16; Austro-Germans take ruins, 9-xi.-17; attack from, 11-xi.-17; Italian counter-attack, 18-xi.-17; German attacks on salient from Mte. Sisemol towards Brenta R., 4-xii.-17; Austrians progress in salient, 5-xii.-17; Mte. Sisemol captured, 6-xii.-17; Austrian attacks defeated, 10-ii.-18; British troops relieve Italians, 29-iii.-18; British enter, 30-x.-18; pushing forward in sector, carry Monte Catz, 1-xi.-18

Asiago Plateau — Austrians attack with 60 divisions on front reaching to sea, 15-vi.-18; held : gains along Montello—Piave sector, 16-vi.-18; fighting continues, 17-vi.-18; 18-vi.-18; 19-vi.-18; Italian recovery, 20.vi. 18; 21-vi.-18; Austrians begin Piave retreat, 22-vi.-18; continued in disorder, 23-vi.-18; 24-vi.-18; Italians recover ground, 29-vi.-18; 30-vi.-18; 2-vii.-18; 3-vii.-18

Asiago R. — Italian attack near, 28-i.-18

Asia Minor — Turkish troops bombarded in Adramyti Gulf 3-iii.-15; Russians bombard Heraclea, 8-iii.-15; Italian Note to Turkey demanding free departure of Italians, 3-viii.-15; Allied blockade, 25-viii.-15

" Asiatic Prince," s.s. — sunk, 30-v.-18

Askaris — 700 surrender S.E. of Chivata, 18-xi.-17

" Askold," Russian cruiser — arrives in Dardanelles, 25-iii.-15

Asolone, Mte. — Austrians capture, 18-xii.-17 : Italians recapture, 19-xii.-17; 21-xii.-17

" Aspenleaf," s.s. — mined, 30-xii.-16

Aspach-le-Bas — French occupy, 2-xii.-14

Aspach-le-Haut — French occupy, 2-xii.-14

Asquith, Mr. H. H. — moves adjournment of Government of Ireland Bill, 30-vii.-14; succeeded by Lord Kitchener as War Secretary, 5-viii.-14; Guildhall speech : " We shall never sheathe the sword . . ." 9-xi.-14; at Cardiff; on German 1912 overtures, 2-x.-14; in Parliament : moves £225,000,000 war credit, 16-xi.-14; presides over Cabinet Committee on food supply and prices, 24-i.-15; at New-castle : speech on munitions, 20-iv.-15; state-ment on aliens, 13-v.-15; statement on re-construction of Government, 19-v.-15; visits G.H.Q. in France, 30-v.-15; visits Grand Fleet at Cromarty, 7-viii.-15; at War Office during Lord Kitchener's absence in Near

Asquith, Mr. H. H. (continued) :—
East, 5-xi.-15; Guildhall speech on war, 9-xi.-15; member of new War Committee, 2-xi.-15; 11-xi.-15; proceeds to Dublin, 11-v.-16; moves £300,000,000 credit, 23-v.-16; urged by Mr. Lloyd George to reduce War Cabinet, 1-xii.-16; accepts reconstruction, 3-xii.-16; resigns, 5-xii.-16; confers with Mr. Lloyd George on war aims, 5-i.-18; motion to refer Gen. Maurice's charges defeated in Com-mons, 9-v.-18

Assevillers — French take, 3-vii.-16

" Assyria," s.s. — sunk, 26-viii.-17

Assyrians — British convoy reaches Sain Kala, 23-vii.-18

" Aster," H.M.S. — mined, 4-vii.-17

Astico — Italians fall back, 23-v.-16; counter-offensive, 12-vi.-16

Aston, Gen. — commands marine battalions at Ostend, 27-viii.-14; commands R.M. Brigade and Oxfordshire Hussars, 20-ix.-14; invalided, 2-x.-14

" Astoria," s.s. — sunk, 9-x.-16

" Astræa," H.M.S. — shells Dar-es-Salaam wireless station, 8-viii.-14

" Astrum," drifter — sunk, 9-vii.-16

" Asturias," H.S. — attacked by U20, 1-ii.-15; torpedoed, 21-iii.-17

" Athenia," s.s. — sunk, 16-viii.-17

" Athenic," s.s. — torpedoed, 19-ii.-18

Athens — Anti-Entente riots, 12-vi.-16; Allied troops landed, 17-x.-16; M. Venizelos in, 25-vi.-17; Anti-Venizelist outrages, 5-xii.-16, 6-xii.-16; Allied Note demands inquiry, 21-xii.-16; further Allied Note on demands, 31-xii.-16; Central Powers' Ministers in : departure demanded by Adm. du Fournet, 19-xii.-16

Athies — British take, 9-iv.-17

Atina — Russians landed at, 4-iii.-16

" Atlantian," s.s. — torpedoed, 3-xi.-17; sunk, 25-vi.-18

Atlantic — passage across reported safe, 14-viii.-14; s.s. " Galician " captured and released by A.M.C. " Kaiser Wilhelm der Grosse," 15-viii.-14; s.s. " Arlanza " cap-tured and released, 16-viii.-14

" Atlas," s.s. — sunk, 14-ii.-18

" Attentive," H.M.S. — attacked by U18, 27-ix.-14; supports Belgians in Yser battle, 17-x.-14; shells Belgian coast, 18-x.-14; hit in operations off Belgian coast, 7-ix.-15

" Attila," s.s. — captured, 25-viii.-14

Attilly — British take, 11-ix.-18

Auberive — French take, 17-iv.-17

Aubers — British take, 17-x.-14; 7th Division progress toward, 13-iii.-15; British attack ridge, 9-v.-15

Aubigny — Germans seize, 23-iii.-18

Aubvillers — taken by French, 23-vii.-18

" Auchencraig," s.s. — sunk, 12-i.-17

Auchin Farm — taken by French, 12-vii.-18

" Auckland Castle," s.s. — sunk, 24-viii.-18

Audenarde — Allies at, 1-xi.-18

" Aud," German auxiliary — arrives off Kerry, lands arms and munitions at Tralee, 20-iv.-16; scuttled, 21-iv.-16

" Audacious," H.M.S. — sunk, 27-x.-14; described in New York Press, 16-xi.-14; news in Germany, 26-xi.-14

Audeghem — Germans driven out, 26-ix.-14

" Augsburg," H.I.M.S. — bombards Libau, 2-viii.-14; mine-laying in Gulf of Finland, 17-viii.-14; in Gulf of Bothnia, 7-ix.-14

Augusta Victoria, German Empress — at Homburg, 18-viii.-18

Augustovo — fighting near, 1-2-x.-14; Germans defeated, 9-x.-14; Russians driven back, 19-viii.-15

Augustovo—Przemysl — Germans repulsed, 12-iii.-15; offensive checked, 13-iii.-15

Austria-Hungary and Serbia (continued) :— Minister; Minister leaves Belgrade, 25-vii.- 14; mediation refused; war declared on Serbia, 28-vii.-14; Sir E. Grey's final proposals passed over, 31-vii.-14

Austria-Hungary and United States — U-Boat policy; Note to U.S., 5-iii.-17; U.S. breaks with, 8-iv.-17; at war, 7-xii.-17

Dumba, Dr. — documents compromising: discovery causes public indignation, 6-ix.-15; recall demanded, 9-ix.-15; recalled, 17-ix.-15

" **Author**," s.s. — sunk, 13-i.-16

" **Author**," s.s. — damaged, 16-iii.-18

" **Autolycus**," s.s. — sunk, 12-iv.-18

Autrêches — German attacks beaten off, 17-i.-15; French advance near, 3-vii.-18

Autry — taken, 1-x.-18

" **Ava**," s.s. — sunk, 27-i.-17

" **Avanti**," s.s. — sunk, 2-ii.-18

Avarescu, Gen. (Rumania) — commands 2nd Army, 10-x.-16; forms Cabinet, 9-ii.-18

Aveh — Russians drive rebels from, 7-xii.-15

Aveluy Wood — British retake, 6-iv.-18

" **Avenger**," H.M.A.M.C. — sunk, 14-vi.-17

Avesnes — German G.H.Q. at, 18-iii.-18; council held, 20-iii.-18; British reach outskirts of Bapaume, 24-viii.-18; British occupy, 8 xi.-18

Avion — British enter, 28-vi.-17

Avlona — Italians occupy, 29-v.-15; Italians land, 15-xii.-15; LZ97 raids, 25-iv.-17; bridgehead captured by Austrians, 18-xi.-17; Austrian attacks, 6-i.-18; Italians force Vojusa, N. of, 8-vii.-18

" **Avocet**," s.s. — attacked by aircraft, 30-x.-15

Avocourt — German attack on front, 18-iii.-17; German failure, 2-vii.-17

Avocourt Redoubt — French regain, 29-iii.-16

Avocourt Wood — Germans carry, 20-iii.-16; French regain S.E. horn, 29-iii.-16; repulsed attack, 18-v.-16; further German attack, 19-v.-16; French take trenches near, 21-v.-16; German attack repulsed, 26-v.-16; French recovery at, 28-iii.-17; German attack, 18-vii.-17; French take, 20-viii.-17

Avre R. — French advance on 37½-mile front between Aisne and, 18-iii.-17; German progress, 29-iii.-18; take and lose Demnin, 30-iii.-18; British take prisoners, 1-iv.-18; French attack in valley, 18-iv.-18; Germans attack on 8-mile front, 24-iv.-18; attacks in valley fail, 24-iv.-18; French seize wood skirting, 2-v.-18; Germans withdraw on right bank, 4-viii.-18; French cross, 8-viii.-18

Avre Valley — German attack W. of; defeated by French, 11-v.-18; French gain in, 14-v.-18; advance, 23-vii.-18

" **Axminster**," s.s. — sunk, 13-xi.-17

Ayette — British line through, 26-iii.-18; taken by Germans, 27-iii.-18; Allied line W. of, 27-iii.-18; British take, 2-iv.-18

" **Aylevarroo**," s.s. — sunk, 7-x.-18

Aylmer, Gen. — to command Tigris line, 9-xii.-15; marches from Ali Gherbi to relieve Kut, 6-i.-16; in touch with Turks at Sheikh Saad, 7-i.-16; defeats Turks near, 8-i.-16; halts at, 10-i.-16; defeats Turks at " Wadi position " near Orah, 13-i.-16; attacks Turks at Umm-el-Hanna; held up, 21-i.-16; Gen. Lake joins at Umm-el-Hanna, 26-i.-16; attack Es Sinn: fails at Dujailah Redoubt: falls back, 8-iii.-16; Gen. Gorringe succeeds in command, 12-iii.-16

" **Aymeric**," s.s. — sunk, 30-v.-18

" **Ayr**," s.s. — sunk, 8-iii.-18

Azizieh — Gen. Townshend's advanced forces at, 3-x.-15; main force reaches, 23-x.-15; retreat to, 28-xi.-15; Turkish rout through, 27-ii.-17

Azores — Cable from Emden cut, 5-viii.-14

" **Aztec**," U.S. armed liner — torpedoed, 2-iv.-17

B.

Baalbek — entered, 9-x.-18

Babington, Gen. — commands 14th British Corps on Italian front, 21-x.-18

Babit, Lake — Russians forced back between Kemmern and, 31-x.-15; Russian counter-attack near, 6 xi.-15

Babuna Pass — fighting, 15-xi.-15

Babuna—Glava-Rajac — Serbians retire, 22-xi.-14

Bab Yunus — raided, 8-ii.-15

" **Bacchante**," H.M.S. — covers landing at Anzac Cove, 25-iv.-15

Bacher Valley (Dolomites) — Italian advance, 17-viii.-15

Bachmann, Adm. (Germany) — Chief of Naval Staff, 6-ii.-15; resignation refused, 27-viii.-15; transferred to Baltic command, 3-ix.-15

Bacon, Adm. — commands Dover Patrol, 13-iv.-15; leaves for Belgian coast, 22-viii.-15; squadron shells Belgian coast, 7-ix.-15; instructions to Thames estuary defence monitors, 20-xii.-15; fleet off Zeebrugge, 13-ix.-16; monitors bombarding Ostend, 5-vi.-17; superintends laying of net barrage off Belgian coast, 25-vii.-17; at bombardment of Ostend, 25-ix.-17; scheme for landing on Belgian coast, 15-x.-17; leaves command at Dover, 29-xii.-17; transferred to Ministry of Munitions, 11-i.-18

Bac St. Maur — Allies retire, 9-iv.-18; Germans cross Lys, 10-iv.-18

" **Badagri**," s.s. — sunk, 13-vii.-18

" **Baden**," H.I.M.S. — Kaiser visits Heligoland in, 18-viii.-17; sails for raid on convoy line, 23-iv.-18; Allies require instead of " Mackensen," 14-xii.-18

Baden, Grand Duke of — abdicates, 13-xi.-18

Baden, Prince Max of — Chancellor, 3-x.-18; peace overtures: replies to Pres. Wilson's inquiry as to authority, 12-x.-18; transfers Chancellorship to Herr Ebert, 9-xi.-18

Badenache, Mte. — Germans storm, 4-xii.-17

" **Badger**," H.M.S. — rams U19, 24-x.-14

" **Badminton**," s.s. — sunk, 23-vii.-16

Badonviller — Allied line at Armistice, 11-xi.-18

Bagamoyo — occupied by British, 15-viii.-16

Bagatelle — French take, 29-xi.-14; Germans attack, 7-8-ii.-15; progress, 2-iv.-15; 30-iv.-15; French progress near, 22-vii.-15

" **Bagdale**," s.s. — sunk, 1-v.-17

Baghdad — Turks retreat towards from Kut, 28-ix.-15; reach Ctesiphon: reinforced, 3-x.-15; Russians 23 marches from, 4-xii.-15; Persian rebels retreat towards, 20-xii.-15; air raid, 20-i.-17; Turks retreat along road, 24-ii.-17; British advance begun, 25-ii.-17; Turks routed on road, 27-ii.-17; broken before, 10-iii.-17; railway station occupied, 10-iii.-17; falls, 11-iii.-17; British 30 miles beyond, 13-iii.-17; British holding road to Enzeli, 15-viii.-18

Baghdad—Mosul road — British advance on, 11-v.-18

Baghdad railway — British air-raid on, 27-xii.-16; Amamus Tunnel complete, 31-i.-17

Baghdad—Samara railway — British success on, 8-iv.-17

Bahia — H.I.M.S. " Eber " at, 14-ix.-14; set on fire and sunk, 26-x.-17

Bahran — British reach, 1-vi.-15

Bahrein Islands — Gen. Barrett joins Gen. Delamain at, 14-xi.-14

Baillescourt Farm — taken, 7-ii.-17; progress N. of, 17-ii.-17

Bailleul — British at, 14-x.-14; Lahore (Indian) Division at, 22-x.-14; British take, 13-iv.-17; Germans pushing towards, 11-iv.-18; gain ground, 12-iv.-18; attacks repulsed, 14-iv.-18; falls to Germans, 15-iv.-18; Germans repulsed N.E. of, 23-iv.-18; attacks, 25-iv.-18; British advance, 18-viii.-18; entered, 30-viii.-18

Bailloud, Gen. (France) — commands Algerian Division at Dardanelles, 5-v.-15; relieves Gen. Gouraud in Gallipoli, 30-vi.-15

Bailly — Gen. Maunoury's Army to stand at, 18-ix.-14

Bainsizza Plateau — Italian gains S.E. of, 15-ix.-17; Austrians repulsed, 30-ix.-17; Italian progress, 20-viii.-17; 22-viii.-17; furious fighting, 28-viii.-17; Italian positions bombarded, 23-x.-17; prepare to evacuate, 25-x.-17; evacuate, 26-x.-17

Baisieux — taken by British, 6-xi.-18

Baker, Mr. (U.S.) — inspects 1st and 42nd Divisions on W. front, 19-iii.-18; inspects 2nd Division, 20-iii.-18; on despatch of troops to Europe: announces 500,000 estimate surpassed, 10-v.-18; says " 700,000 already sent," 10-vi.-18

Bakhmatch — taken, 14-iii.-18

Bakovice — taken, 1-xi.-15

Baku — Anti-Bolshevist " coup," 26-vii.-18; British detachments sent to, 15-viii.-18; 39th Brigade proceeds to; Gen. Dunsterville arrives, 17-viii.-18; Turks attack British force, 26-viii.-18; 31-viii.-18; 1-ix.-18; British evacuate, 14-ix.-18; Nuri Pasha enters, 16-ix.-18; warned to evacuate; troops concentrating at Enzeli for occupation, 9-xi.-18; Allied forces leave for, 16-xi.-18; British enter, 17-xi.-18; passes out of Gen. Marshall's command: maintained via Batum, 31-xii.-18

Bakuba — British at, 14-iii.-17

" **Baku Standard,**" **s.s.** — sunk, 11-ii.-18

" **Balance of Power**" **system** — M. Clemenceau in French Chamber asserts faith in, 29-xii.-18

" **Baldersby,**" **s.s.** — sunk, 28-ix.-18

Balfour, Mr. A. J. — member of War Committee, 11-xi.-15; meets Adm. Jellicoe at Rosyth, 27-xi.-16; Foreign Secretary, 11-xii.-16; reply to President Wilson's Peace Note, 17-i.-17; in Washington, 26-iv.-17; succeeded by Lord Northcliffe as head of British mission to U.S., 6-vi.-17; conference with Mr. Lloyd George and Pres. Wilson in London, 27-xii.-18; confers with Col. House in Paris, 31-xii.-18; at Allied discussion of Levant affairs, 20-iii.-19

" **Balgownie,**" **s.s.** — attacked by aircraft, 27-xi.-15

" **Balgray,**" **s.s.** — sunk, 20-ii.-18

Balkan Express — first: leaves Berlin, 15-i.-16

Balkans — Ballplatz memorandum, 4-vii.-14; presented to Kaiser, 5-vii.-14; Paris Conference ends, 26-vii.-17; Franco-Serb offensive against Bulgarians and German 11th Army, 15-ix.-18; fighting, 27-ix.-18; Germans fight Bulgarians, 4-x.-18

" **Ballarat,**" **H.M.S.** — sunk, 25-iv.-17

Ballin, Herr (Germany) — in London; converses with Lord Haldane and Sir E. Grey, 23-vii.-14

" **Ballogie,**" **s.s.** — sunk, 9-xi.-17

Baltic — H.I.M.S. " Blücher " " demonstration " cruise, 3-ix.-14; large scale naval operations discussed at British conference, 17-ix.-14; U-Boats in, 1-i.-15; 4-ii.-15; German 3rd High Sea Squadron exercising, 22-i.-15; German transports sunk, 29-vii.-15; 2-viii.-15; U26 lost in, 31-viii.-15; LZ88 scouting over, 27-vii.-16; 14-viii.-16; 3rd High Sea Squadron in, 16-v.-17; battle;

Baltic (continued) :—
Russian naval forces pressed back to Moon Sound; " Slava " lost; two German trawlers destroyed; two T.B.s blown up, 17-x.-17; Germans take Schilden Is.; four Russian vessels ashore; British submarine sinks German transport and torpedoes German Dreadnought, 20-x.-17; H.M. submarine C32 blown up, 24-x.-17; British mine-sweepers clear passage to Kiel, 25-xi.-18; light cruiser squadron at Copenhagen to superintend opening, 28-xi.-18; H.M.S. " Cassandra " mined, 4-xii.-18

" **Baltic,**" **s.s.** — attacked by U-Boat, 25-26-iv.-17

Baltic Committee — meets in Paris, 14-v.-19

Baltic Provinces — Germans invade, 26-iv.-15; German Settlement Law, 3-vii.-16; Kaiser instructs Herr von Kühlmann to demand at Brest-Litovsk, 7-ii.-17; Germans in, 22-ii.-18

Baltimore — UC " Deutschland " arrives, 8-vii.-16

Baluchistan — demonstration arranged, 4-vi.-18

Bamendu — Allies take, 22-x.-15

" **Bamse,**" **s.s.** — torpedoed, 17-iv.-18; sunk, 2-x.-18

Banat : see Temesvar, Banat of

Ban-de-Sapt — French repulse counter-attacks, 29-xi.-14; German attack, 10-ii.-15; take Hill 627, 22-vi.-15; French recapture, 8-vii.-15

" **Bandon,**" **s.s.** — sunk, 13-iv.-17

" **Bankfields,**" **s.s.** — sunk, 25-ix.-14

Banyo, Mt. — British take German positions, 6-xi.-16

Bapaume — German line hardens W. of, 6-x.-14; defences broken into, 1-vii.-16; air battle N.E. of: 30 British machines rout 40 Germans, 9-xi.-16; British advance towards, 27-ii.-17; 28-ii.-17; Germans fall back on, 13-iii.-17; British capture, 17-iii.-17; falls to Germans, 24-iii.-18; heavy fighting, 25-iii.-18; battle opens, 21-viii.-18; main attack, 23-viii.-18; outskirts reached at Avesnes, 24-viii.-18; road carried, 25-viii.-18; Beugnatre taken, 27-viii.-18; falls to British, 29-viii.-18

Bapaume—Cambrai road — fighting between Arras and, 23-iii.-17; British advance, 28-iii.-17; British success near, 2-iv.-17, 9-iv.-15; German counter-attack fails, 15-iv.-17

Bapaume—Péronne railway — British success on, 1-iv.-17

Bapaume—Péronne road — French advance across, 13-ix.-16; 8-x.-16; British attack heights in front, 12-x.-16

Bapaume ridge — Germans abandon forward crest, 13-iii.-17

Baralle — taken by British, 3-ix.-18

" **Baralong,**" **H.M.S.** — sinks U27, 19-viii.-15; sinks U41, 24-ix.-15; German memorandum, 28-xi.-15; British reply, 14-xii.-15; White Paper issued; German Note; British proposals rejected; reprisals threatened, 14-i.-16

Barani — British reoccupy, 28-ii.-16

Baranovitchi — Russians carry German positions E. of, 20-x.-15; Russian offensive, 2-vii.-16; Hindenburg's front pierced by Gen. Evert, 3-vii.-16; German counter-attack, 14-vii.-16; success against centre, 9-xi.-16; Russians yield at, 26-iii.-17

Baratoff, Gen. — at Kermanshah, 12-ii.-16; captures Bidesurkh—Sakhne Passes, 24-ii.-16; in touch with British at Ali Gharbi, 20-v.-16

" **Barbara,**" **s.s.** — sunk, 20-x.-16

" **Barbary,**" **s.s.** — sunk, 12-xi.-17

Barcelona — UC74 interned, 24-xi.-18

Bargela — British air-raid on, 21-xii.-16

" **Barham,**" **H.M.S.** — arrives at Scapa, 2-x.-15; collision, 1-xii.-15; in Jutland battle, 31-v.-16

Bari — air-raid, 1-vi.-15

Beskid Pass (Carpathians) — Russians beaten back near, 28-i.-15; battle in, 29-i.-15; Russians retire from, 3-ii.-15

Bessarabia — Germans gain footing, 1-viii.-17 Rumania — union with voted, 9-iv.-18

Bessarabia—Bukovina frontier — heavy fighting, 27-xii.-15

Bethencourt — British line through, 23-iii.-18

Béthincourt — German attack repulsed, 14-iii.-16; fails, 5-iv.-16; French evacuate salient, 8-iv.-16; French abandon road, 30-v.-16

Bethlehem — British advance, 8-xii.-17

Beth Horon — British advance N.W. of, 29-xii.-17

Bethmann-Hollweg, Herr von (Germany) — conference with Emperor William, 5-vii.-14; conference with Count Hoyos and Count Szögyeny, 6-vii.-14; "scrap of paper" interview, 4-viii.-14; in Reichstag: accuses England of originating the war, 2-xii.-14; Adm. von Pohl discusses air campaign against London, 5-ii.-15; issues new apologia for "scrap of paper" suggestion, 25-i.-15; on occupied territories as "pawns," 9-xii.-15; dismissal to be urged by Hindenburg and Ludendorff, 6-vii.-17; offer to resign refused by Kaiser, 10-vii.-17; Kaiser decides to dismiss, 13-vii.-17
Peace — instructs Count Bernstorff to accept Pres. Wilson's offices in promoting conference, 18-viii.-16; audience of Kaiser, 25-x.-16; Kaiser's letter on strength to perform "moral deed" of proposing peace, 31-x.-16; draft of joint terms with Austria approved by Kaiser, 8-xi.-16; announces offer in Reichstag, 12-xii.-16; draws up Vienna document, 27-iii.-17
U-Boat warfare — Herr Helfferich's memorandum, 5-viii.-15; misgivings cause dropping of proposals, 31-xii.-15; memorandum to Kaiser: expresses fear of U.S. intervention if policy is pursued, 29-ii.-16; decides to postpone policy, 6-iii.-16; decides policy is indispensable, 28-iii.-16; intimation to Adm. von Scheer, 30-vi.-16; Ludendorff urges to adopt unrestricted policy, 20-xii.-16; urged by Hindenburg to expedite inauguration, 23-xii.-16; maintains views that policy is one for which he is not responsible, 24-xii.-16; again urged by High Command not to delay, 25-xii.-16; agrees, 9-i.-17; expresses confidence in policy, 9-v.-17

Béthune — Indian troops in support, 19-x.-14; air-raid, 20-v.-15; German attempt at Lawe defeated, 11-iv.-18; British night operations N. of; gain German forward positions, 15-vi.-18

Béthune—La Bassée road — British raid S. of, 16-iv.-16

Beugnatre — taken by British, 27-viii.-18

Beugny — British line through, 23-iii.-18

Beugny—Ytres line — British reach, 18-iii.-17

Beyers, Gen. — routed by Gen. Botha, 27-x.-14; shot in attempt to swim Vaal R., 7-xii.-14

Beynon, Gen. — engaged on Swat R., 29-viii.-15

Bezonvaux — French take works, 15-xii.-16; gain village, 16-xii.-16; Germans attack between Fosses Wood and, 4-iii.-17; French trenches entered, 16-iii.-18; German retreat on 33-mile front from Norroy to, 15-ix.-18

Bezu — Franco-Americans reach, 22-vii.-18

Bezzecca heights — Italian success, 10-viii.-15

"Bhamo," s.s. — mined, 26-viii.-17

Biaches — French take, 9-vii.-16; German counter-attacks repulsed, 17-vii.-16; Allies on line, 24-iii.-18

Biache St. Vaast — British gain line, 7-x.-18

Biala — taken by Germans, 9-ii.-15

Biala R. — Germans cross, 2-v.-15

Bialystok — air-raids, 24-ix.-14; 20-vii.-15; 5-viii.-15; 11-viii.-15; German advance, 12-viii.-15; Russians partly evacuate, 16-viii.-15; railway cut at Bielsk, 18-viii.-15; taken by Prussians, 26-viii.-15

"Biarritz," H.M. minelayer — lays first anti-U-Boat minefield, 23-v.-16

Bidesurkh Pass — Russians take, 24-ii.-16

Biefvillers — British carry, 24-viii.-18

Bielgorod — Germans at, 10-iv.-18

Bieliaeff, Gen. (Russia) — War Minister, 16-i.-17

Bielsk — railway cut, 18-viii.-15; Germans advance S. of, 22-viii.-15

Bigsworth, Squadron Cmdr. — destroys U-Boat, 26-viii.-15

Bihucourt — British carry, 23-viii.-18

Bikanir, Maharajah of — delegate to Peace Conference; arrives in England, 13-xii.-18; leaves for Paris, 11-i.-19

Bilhem — British take, 24-iv.-17

Binche — 5th Cavalry Brigade under Gen. Chetwode at, 21-viii.-14

Bingham, Cmdr. E. B. S. — awarded V.C., 31-v.-16

Biramulo — Germans defeated, 3-vii.-16

Bir Asur — British reach, 21-ix.-18

"Birchgrove," s.s. — attacked, 20-v.-17

"Birchleaf," s.s. — torpedoed, 23-ii.-18

"Birchwood," H.M. collier — sunk, 3-i.-18

"Birdoswald," s.s. — sunk, 26-vi.-18

Birdwood, Gen. — welcomed in London, 19-xii.-18

Bir el Abd — Turks retire to, 8-viii.-16; counter-attack repulsed, 9-viii.-16; abandon, 11-viii.-16

Bir el Bayud — Turks routed near, 11-viii.-16

Bir el Hassana — Turks captured, 20-ii.-17

Bir el Magdhaba — British take, 23-xii.-16

Bir Hakim — crew of s.s. "Tara" rescued from Senussi, 17-iii.-16

"Birkenhead," H.M.S. — joins 3rd Light Cruiser Squadron, 6-xi.-15

"Birkhall," s.s. — sunk, 23-i.-18

Bir Mazar — British air-raid, 13-vi.-16

"Birmingham," H.M.S. — sinks U15, 9-viii.-14; attacked by U-Boat, 20-vi.-15

Birnaville — taken, 1-x.-18

Birrell, Mr. A. — resigns, 3-v.-16

Bir Salmana — Anzac raid, 31-v.-16

"Birtley," s.s. — sunk, 4-i.-18

"Biruta," s.s. — sunk, 6-viii.-18

Biscupice — Germans break through, 29-vii.-15

"Bismarck" (German outpost leader) — sunk, 29-iii.-17

Bismarcksburg — Anglo-Belgian success near, 2-vi.16; Col. Murray occupies, 6-vi.-16

Bissing, Gen. von (Germany) — appointed Governor of Belgium, 23-xi.-14; death, 22-iv.-17

Bissolati, Signor (Italy) — resignation on Jugo-Slav question, 28-xii.-18

Bistritza River — Russians cross, 5-iii.-15; 8-vii.-17

Bitcharakhoff, Gen. — troops concentrating at Enzeli for occupation of Baku, 9-xi.-18; leaves Kasvin for Enzeli, 8-vi.-18; fights Mandjil Bridge battle against Kuchik Khan's Jangali levies, 12-vi.-18; leaves Enzeli for Alyat, 1-vii.-18; 3-vii.-18

Bitlis — Turks retire on, 21-v.-15; Armenian massacre, 2-vii.-15; Russians N.E. of, 1-iii.-16; in, 2-iii.-16

"Bittern," H.M.S. — sunk, 4-iv.-18

Bixschoote — French take, 31-vii.-17; gain N.W. of, 8-viii.-17; 9-viii.-17; gains E. of, 17-viii.-17; slight British advance N. of, 20-viii.-17; fighting near, 17-iv.-18

Bixschoote—Langemarcke — German gas attack, 22-iv.-15

Biyuk Anafarta Valley — important tactical feature captured, 28-viii.-15

"Blackcock," H.M. tug — wrecked, 18-i.-18

Bouchavesnes — road cut S. of; captured by French, 12-ix.-16; French progress, 7-x.-16; British raid S. of, 8-ii.-17; British take trenches, 4-iii.-17; German counter-attack fails, 5-iii.-17; British advance on ridge, 12-iii.-17; British take, 1-ix.-18

Bougainville (Solomon Islands) — occupied by Australians, 13-ix.-14

Bouleaux Wood — part taken, 15-ix.-16; Germans abandon, 25-ix.-16

Boulogne — First British troops landed, 9-viii.-14; Sir John French lands, 14-viii.-14; cleared by Royal Naval Transport Service, 16-ix.-14; air-raids, 26-ix.-14; 22-ix.-16; 25-ix.-16; 16-ii.-17; 25-ix.-17; 26-i.-18; 23-iii.-18; 26-iii.-18

Bourbon, Prince Sixte of — communicates Emperor Charles' first "peace letter" to Pres. Poincaré, 31-iii.-17

Bouresches — German attack broken S.E. of, 2-vi.-18

Bourevilles — Germans attack, 3-i.-15

Bourg — British at, 13-ix.-14

Bourlon — part of village taken by British, 24-xi.-17; Germans recover, 25-xi.-17; British advance towards, 27-xi.-17; carried, 27-ix.-18

Bourlon Wood — British take part, 21-xi.-17; 24-xi.-17; advance W. of, 29-xi.-17; evacuate, 5-xii.-17; carried, 27-ix.-18

Boursies — British take, 9-iv.-17; German post E. of: carried, 10-xii.-17

Boûssoit — Allied line at Armistice, 11-xi.-18

"Bouvet," French battleship — with Dardanelles Squadron, 31-i.-15; damages bridge over Carack R., 2-iii.-15; enters Dardanelles to cover bombardment of Narrows, 7-iii.-15; mined, 18-iii.-15

Bouzencourt — Allies on line, 27-iii.-18

Bovent — carried, 10-x.-16

"Bowes Castle," s.s. — sunk, 18-viii.-14

"Boxer," H.M.S. — sunk, 8-ii.-18

"Boy Alfred" (smack) — engages U-Boat, 1-ii.-17

Boyana — French T.B.D. "Fresnel" aground at, 29-xii.-15

Boy-Ed, Capt. (Germany) — requested to leave U.S., 3-xii.-15; recalled, 10-xii.-15

Boyelles — British line through, 23-iii.-18; 24-iii.-18; fighting, 30-iii.-18; taken by British, 23-viii.-18

Boyle, Lieut-Cmdr. — in E14: sinks Turkish gunboat in Sea of Marmora, 27-iv.-15; sinks Turkish transport, 29-iv.-15; given V.C., 18-v.-15

"Boynton," s.s. — sunk, 24-ix.-17

Brabant-sur-Meuse — German attack, 21-ii.-16; French evacuate, 23-ii.-16

Braches — French attack from, 8-viii.-18

"Bracondale," H.M.S.V. — sunk, 7-viii.-17

"Bradford City," H.M.S.V. — sunk, 16-viii.-17

"Braemar Castle," H.S. — mined, 23-xi.-16

Braila — Germans approaching, 17-xii.-16; checked by Russians, 18-xii.-16; Mackensen 25 miles from: German 9th Army held up, 19-xii.-16; Germans attack bridgehead, 24-xii.-16; Germans held before, 25-xii.-16; advance, 30-xii.-16; repulsed near, 31-xii.-16; Russo-Rumanian positions pierced, 4-i.-17; falls, 5-i.-17; Germans advance N.W. of 6-i.-17

Braine — Franco-Americans cross Vesle R., 7-viii.-18

Braintree — air-raid, 21-ii.-15

"Bramham," s.s. — mined, 19-vii.-17

Brandenburg — formation of Soviet Council forbidden, 7-xi.-18

"Brandenburg," s.s. — interned at Trondhjem, 28-ix.-14

Brandon, Lieut. — bombs Zeppelin, 31-iii.-16; D.S.O., 1-x.-16

Branksome Hall," s.s. — torpedoed, 11-iv.-17; sunk, 14-vii.-18

"Brantingham," s.s. — sunk, 4-x.-16

Brasso — Rumanians take, 29-viii.-16; success between Hermannstadt and, 3-x.-16; retreat towards, 5-x.-16; Austro-Germans recapture, 7-x.-16; Rumanians resist S. of, 10-x.-16

Bratiano, M. (Rumania) — resigns, 6-ii.-18

"Braunschweig," German patrol vessel — sunk, 25-iii.-16

"Braunton," s.s. — sunk, 7-iv.-16

"Bravalla," Swedish s.s. — sunk, 5-ii.-17

Braye — German assaults defeated, 17-v.-17

Bray-sur-Somme — Gen. de Castelnau halted, 26-ix.-14; French advance along road, 9-vii.-16; Allies on line, 25-iii.-18; taken by Germans, 26-iii.-18; new British attack; German counter-attack N. of, 22-viii.-18; taken by Australians, 23-viii.-18

Braye-en-Laonnais — French take, 18-iv.-17; German gain N. of, 22-vi.-17; German local gain, 8-vii.-17; French recovery, 9-vii.-17

"Bray Head," s.s. — sunk, 14-iii.-17

Brazil:—
Germany — breaks with, 9-iv.-17; neutrality revoked, ships in port taken over, 2-vi.-17
Navy — Adm. Bronti to command vessels in European waters, 30-i.-18

"Brecknockshire," s.s. — sunk, 15-ii.-17

Bremen — Spartacist riots ended, 7-i.-19

"Bremen," H.I.M.S. — sunk, 17-xii.-15

"Bremen" ("merchant" U-Boat) — to travel to U.S., 17-ix.-16

"Bremse," H.I.M.S. — surrendered, 21-xi.-18

"Brenda," s.v. — sunk, 7-i.-17

Brenta — fighting, 10-vi.-17; Italians evacuate part of Val Sugana, 12-xi.-17; Austrians take Mte. Fontana Secca, 21-xi.-17; Austro-Germans repulsed, 25-xi.-17; 26-xi.-17

Brenta R. — Italians fall back, 23-v.-16; Germans attack towards, 4-xii.-17; Austrians attack E. of, 18-xii.-17; Italian advance E. of valley, 14-i.-18; attack, 28-i.-18

"Brentwood," s.s. — mined, 12-i.-17

Brescia — bombed, 25-viii.-15

"Breslau," H.I.M.S. — joins "Goeben," 1-viii.-14; ordered to Constantinople, 3-viii.-14; bombards Bône and Philippeville; outdistances British warships, 4-viii.-14; at Messina: ordered to Pola or Atlantic, 5-viii.-14; leaves for Constantinople; chased, 6-viii.-14; chased; engaged by "Gloucester"; escapes, 7-viii.-14; coals at Denusa, 8-viii.-14; in Dardanelles, 10-viii.-14; enters Black Sea, 21-ix.-14; Adm. Troubridge acquitted by court-martial, 14-xi.-14; Russian Black Sea Fleet engage, 18-xi.-14; bombards Yalta, 8-ii.-15; long-range action with Russian Fleet off Crimea, 3-iv.-15; bombards Black Sea ports; sinks H.S. "Ypered," 5-vii.-16; sinks H.M. monitor "Raglan": later driven into minefield and sunk, 20-i.-18

Brest — Pres. Wilson lands, 13-xii.-18

Brest-Litovsk — raided by LZ79, 10-viii.-15; Germans closing on, 15-viii.-15; Germans cross Bug R. N.W. of, 16-viii.-15; railway cut, 17-viii.-15; outer defences pierced by Austro-Germans, 18-viii.-15; Russian line penetrated, 24-viii.-15; falls, 25-viii.-15; Russians driven nearly to Kobryn, 27-viii.-15; Russo-German Peace: see under Peace — Russia

Brestovica Valley — Italian progress, 2-ix.-17

"Bretwalda," s.s. — sunk, 13-xii.-16

"Breynton," s.s. — torpedoed, 21-xi.-17

Briand, M. (France) — forms Ministry, 28-x.-15; in London, 9-vi.-16; reconstructs Cabinet, 11-xii.-16

Briansk — Germans reach heights between Narev and Bug, 15-viii.-15

Bridoux, Gen. — killed, 17-ix.-14

Brie — Somme bridge repaired, 18-iii.-17

Brieulles — Americans reach, 28-ix.-18

Brieulles-sur-Bar — taken by Americans, 3-xi.-18

Briggs, Squad.-Cmdr. — brought down at Friedrichshaven, 21-xi.-14

Brighton — King and Queen visit wounded Indians, 9-i.-15

" Brighton Queen," H.M. mine-sweeper — sunk, 6-x.-15

" Brigitta," s.s. — mined, 4-xii.-17

" Brilliant," H.M.S. — hit, 28-x.-14; blockship: run ashore in Ostend raid, 23-iv.-18

Brimont — French take trenches near, 4-v.-17

Brimont Fort — captured, 5-x.-18

Brindisi — air-raid, 1-vi.-15

Brioche — French carry, 12-ix.-16

Briquenay — taken by Americans, 2-xi.-18

" Brisbane River," s.s. — sunk, 17-iv.-17

" Bristol," H.M.S. — pursues and engages H.I.M.S. " Karlsruhe," 6-viii.-14; sinks two German transports off Falkland Islands, 8-xii.-14; engages Austrian naval forces, 15-v.-17

" Bristol City," s.s. — sunk, 16-xii.-17

" Britannia," H.M.S. — aground, 26-i.-15; refitting, 31-i.-15; torpedoed, 9-xi.-18

" Britannia," s.s. — sunk by U-Boat, 2-iv.-17

" Britannic," H.S. — mined, 21-xi.-16

British Empire :—

King's message, 19-xi.-18

Peace Conference (Paris) — to have five delegates, 15-i.-19

" British Monarch," s.s. — mined, 4-viii.-17

" British Princess," s.s. — torpedoed, 4-iii.-18

" British Star," s.s. — torpedoed, 26-iii.-18

" British Sun," s.s. — sunk, 1-v.-17

" British Viscount," s.s. — sunk, 23-ii.-18

" British Yeoman," s.v. — sunk, 26-ii.-17

Broadstairs — German air-raid, 9-ii.-16; 29-ii.-16; German T.B.D. raid, 25-ii.-17; 1-iii.-17

Brock, Adm. — in H.M.S. " Princess Royal " in Jutland battle, 31-v.-16; 1-vi.-16

Brockdorff-Rantzau, Count (Germany) — at Versailles, 29-iv.-19; declares Germany refused to admit whole war guilt, 7-v.-19; leaves for Spa, 17-v.-19; returns to Versailles with German reply, 19-v.-19; leaves for Spa with other delegates, 22-v.-19; returns to Versailles, 8-vi.-19; receives Allied reply; leaves for Weimar, 16-vi.-19; declines to sign treaty, 20-vi.-19

Brod — Serbs gain footing, 11-x.-16; taken, 17-x.-16

" Broderick," s.s. — sunk, 29-iv.-18

" Brodholme," s.s. — attacked by U-Boat, 10-vi.-18

" Brodmead," s.s. — torpedoed, 7-ix.-17

" Brodmore," s.s. — sunk, 27-ii.-17

" Brodness," s.s. — sunk, 31-iii.-17

" Brodstone," s.s. — sunk, 15-viii.-17

Brody — Austrians enter, 1-ix.-15; advance from, 2-ix.-15; Russian attack, 24-vii.-16; Austrians evacuate, 25-vii.-16; Russian progress towards, 26-vii.-16; Russians capture, 28-vii.-16; 20,000 prisoners, 29-vii.-16; Austrians fall back S. of, 31-vii.-16; Russian progress W. of; 3,000 prisoners, 5-viii.-16; Russian progress S. of, 6-viii.-16; fighting S.W. of, 30-ix.-16; Russians attack between Tarnapol and, 5-x.-16; German attack, 31-vii.-17

Brody—Dubno — Russians forced across border near, 6-ix.-15

" Broke," H.M.S. — collision, 17-xii.-14; in Jutland battle, 31-v.-16; sinks H.I.M. T.B.D. G85, 21-iv.-17; at bombardment of Ostend, 25-ix.-17; Bacon and Ronarc'h in: superintend laying of net barrage off Belgian coast, 25-vii.-17

Bronti, Adm. — to command Brazilian Fleet in European waters, 30-i.-18

" Bronwen," s.s. — sunk, 24-ix.-16

Broodseinde — part of height taken, 4-x.-17; British raid S.E. of, 6-x.-17

" Brookby," s.s. — sunk, 19-vi.-17

Brooking, Gen. — force attacked by Arabs at Shatt-el-Hai, 7-ii.-16; routs Arabs at Butaniyeh, 9-ii.-16; at Ana, 28-ii.-18

Brouchy — Germans seize, 23-iii.-18

Browning, Adm. — head of inter-Allied Mission to superintend execution of Armistice, 25-xi.-18; arrives at Wilhelmshaven, 4-xii.-18; inspects British merchantmen at Hamburg, 10-xii.-18; leaves for England, 18-xii.-18

Bruay — taken, 23-x.-18

Bruges — Gen. Rawlinson at, 7-x.-14; Germans pass, 14-x.-14; British air-raid, 12-ii.-15; French air-raid, 11-iv.-15; German raid N. of, 11-vi.-16; Capt. Fryatt shot, 27-vii.-16; bombed, 1-vi.-17; air camps bombarded, 3-vi.-17; Belgians close to, 18-x.-8; occupied, 19-x.-18

Bruges Canal — blockships sunk at entrance, 23-iv.-18

Bruges Docks — British airmen bomb T.B.D.s and U-Boats, 2-ii.-17; bomb ships, 3-ii.-17; further raids, 11-vii.-17; 23-iii.-18

" Brumaire," s.s. — sunk, 24-vii.-17

" Brummer," H.I.M.S. — sinks two British T.B.s, 17-x.-17; surrenders, 21-xi.-18

Brunsbüttel — High Sea Fleet moved to Cuxhaven, 9-viii.-15

Brunswick — munition factories : strikes, 28-vi.-16

Brunswick, Duke of — abdicates, 8-xi.-18

Brusiloff, Gen. (Russia) — takes Tarnopol, 27-viii.-14; advancing in Galicia, 28-viii.-14; occupies Halicz, 29-viii.-14; holds Carpathian passes, 28-xi.-14; leads Russian advance from Pripet—Rumanian frontier, 4-vi.-16; on Zlota Lipa, 15-viii.-16; appointed C.-in-C., 4-vi.-17; attacks Brzezany, 1-vii.-17; asked to resign, 15-v.-17; succeeded as C.-in-C. by Korniloff, 1-viii.-17

Brusnik — occupied, 22-xi.-15

Brussels — occupied by Germans, 20-viii.-14; Gen. von Lüttwitz appointed military commandant, 20-viii.-14; levy of £8,000,000 imposed, 22-viii.-14; Gen. von Kraewel appointed commandant, 23-viii.-14; air-sheds bombed by Allies, 19-xii.-14; 24-xii.-14; Gen. von Sauberzweig succeeds Gen. von Kraewel, 1-x.-15; raided by British aeroplanes, 2-viii.-16; 11-viii.-16; municipal council resists attempt to impart Flemish bias to city administration, 29-x.-17; Germans hoist red flag, 10-xi.-18; M. Max returns from captivity, 15-xi.-18; Belgian troops enter, 19-xi.-18; King and Queen of the Belgians enter, 22-xi.-18

" Brussels," s.s. — under Capt. Fryatt: escapes from U133, 28-iii.-15; chased by U-Boat; escapes; second encounter, 11-vi.-15; third encounter, 15-vi.-15; fourth encounter, 29-vi.-15; missed by torpedo, 20-vii.-15; captured by German T.B.: taken into Zeebrugge, 23-vi.-16; Capt. Charles Fryatt shot, 27-vii.-16

Bry — taken by British, 4-xi.-18

Bryan, Mr. W. J. (U.S.) — denies U.S. partiality to Allies, 24-i.-15; succeeded as Secretary of State, 8-vi.-15

Bryce, Lord — report on German outrages published, 12-v.-15

Brzezany — Russians drive wedge through German line near, 23-xi.-14; Russian line broken, 27-viii.-15; Gen. Brussiloff S. of, 15-viii.-16; Russians before, 3-ix.-16; German counter repulsed S. of, 1-x.-16; Russian success S. of, 2-x.-16; Russian raid S. of, 28-i.-17; " Red " Army attacks on 20-mile front, 1-vii.-17; progress, 2-vii.-17; 3-vii.-17; further fighting, 5-vii.-17; 1,000 more prisoners, 6-vii.-17; Russian retreat stayed near, 20-vii.-17

Buchanan, Sir G. — returns to England from Petrograd, 8-i.-18

Bucquoy — British progress S. of, 5-iii.-17; Germans beaten off, 28-iii.-18; strong attacks; heavy losses, 5-iv.-18; fighting, 9-v.-18; British raid: Tanks first used in night operations, 22-vi.-18; Germans abandon, 14-viii.-18; British reach, 21-viii.-18

Budapest — revolution: see under Hungary

Budrus-Sheikh Obeid — British advance between, 12-xii.-17

" Buffalo," s.s. — sunk, 18-vi.-17

" Buffalo," s.s. — sunk, 13-ix.-18

Buftea — Central Powers and Rumania, Treaty concluded at, 5-iii.-18

Bug R. — Russians retire towards, 1-ix.-14; Austro-German offensive, 29-vi.-15; Austro-Germans cross near Sokal, 18-vii.-15; driven back, 21-vii.-15; Germans reach junction, 6-viii.-15; progress towards, 12-viii.-15; Germans repulsed, 13-viii.-15; Germans reach Briansk heights, 15-viii.-15; Austro-Germans cross at Vlodava, 15-viii.-15; Germans cross at Drohiczyn, 16-viii.-15

Bukarest — air raids, 28-viii.-16; 4-ix.-16; 24-ix.-16; 25-ix.-16; 26-ix.-16; 27-ix.-16; 30-ix.-16; 23-x.-16; 1-xi.-16; 14-xi.-16; 20-xi.-16; 22-xi.-16; 5-xii.-16; Mackensen 50 miles from, 26-xi.-16; 17 miles from, 28-xi.-16; Germans nearing, 30-xi.-16; battle before, 1-xii.-16; 2-xii.-16; 3-xii.-16; Rumanians blow up arsenal, 4-xii.-16; Germans outside, 5-xii.-16; falls to Mackensen, 6-xii.-16; Peace Treaty with Central Powers signed at, 7-v.-18; King and Queen enter, 1-xii.-18

Bukarest-Tchernavoda — Rumanian territory S. of: held by Mackensen, 13-xii.-16

Bukoba — successful British raid, 21-vi.-15; captured, 25-vi.-15; British occupy, 2-vii.-16

Bukovina — Russians take Czernowitz, 15-ix.-14; Russians re-occupy, 31-x.-14; Austrians again evacuate Czernowitz, 26-xi.-14; Russian advance, 1-i.-15; further successes, 2-i.-15; Suczava taken, 3-i.-15; Russians take Kimpolung, 6-i.-15; Russians occupy Kirlibaba Pass, 16-i.-15; Austrian counter-offensive, 20-i.-15; Russians holding Kirlibaba Pass, 21-i.-15; Austrians recapture, 22-i.-15; Austrians recapture Kimpolung, 6-ii.-15; Austrians reach Suczava Valley, 7-ii.-15; Austrians retake Czernowitz, 17-ii.-15; Russians retire, 9-ii.-15; Austrians reach Sereth, 11-ii.-15; Austrians retreat, 6-iii.-15; Austrians fail to cross Pruth R., 17-iii.-15; heavy fighting at Ocna, 4-iv.-15; great Austro-German offensive opened, 13-vii.-15; fighting near Czernowitz, 14-viii.-15; fighting on frontier, 27-xii.-15; Russian success, 28-xii.-15; gain near Czernowitz, 4-i.-16; 5-i.-16; 19-i.-16; 2-ii.-16; 3-ii.-16; Russians clear, 23-vi.-16; Russian success, 3-i.-17; take 1,000 prisoners, 31-i.-17; Austrian attacks fail, 21-ii.-17; Russian recovery, 28-ii.-17; German advance, 1-viii.-17; 2-viii.-17; fall of Czernowitz, 3-viii.-17; progress, 4-viii.-17; 5-viii.-17; 26-viii.-17

Bulair — shelled from Xeros Gulf, 1-iii.-15; Fort Sultan bombarded, 2-iii.-15; bombarded, 11-iii.-15

" Buletown," H.M. collier — sunk, 8-ix.-16

Bulfin, Gen. — takes over 1st Division, 31-x.-14; wounded, 1-xi.-14

Bulgaria — Austro-German alliance: treaty signed, 4-viii.-14; announces neutrality, 3-xi.-14; German loan (£3,000,000), 2-ii.-15; irregulars attack Serbians at Valandovo, 1-iv.-15; declares war on Rumania, 1-x.-16; military convention with Central Powers signed, 4-ix.-15; Entente Note to, 14-ix.-15; mobilised; announces armed neutrality, 19-ix.-15; German officers

Bulgaria (continued) :—
arriving in, 1-x.-15; troops mass on Serbia frontiers, 2-x.-15; Russian ultimatum demands open break " with the enemies the Slav cause and of Russia," 3-x.-1 British ultimatum to, 4-x.-15; troops cross Serbian frontier E. and S.E. of Nish, 11-x.-15; declares war on Serbia 14-x.-15; Great Britain declares war 15-x.-15; France declares war 16-x.-1 Aegean coast blockaded, 16-x.-15; Italy declares war, 17-x.-15; forces join German at Krivivir, 5-xi.-15; surrenders, 30-ix.-18 King Ferdinand — abdicates, 4-x.-18 Ministry (Radoslavoff) — resignation; Malinoff Premier, 18-vi.-18 Operations: see various fronts and names places Peace: see Peace Turkey — modifies Treaty of Pera favour, 22-vii.-15

Bulgaria, Prince Boris of — at Spa, 11-viii.-1 King Ferdinand abdicates in favour, 4-x.-

Bulgarian front — British troops in, 25-ix.-1 Allies bombard, 14-ix.-18; Bulgarians in fr retreat, 18-ix.-18; retreat on nearly 100-m front, 22-ix.-18; Serb cavalry near frontie 25-i.-18 (see also names of places)

" Bulgarian," s.s. — sunk, 20-i.-17

Bullard, Gen. (U.S.) — commands 3rd Arm Corps, 3-viii.-18; 22-ix.-18; commands ne 7th Army, 12-x.-18

Bullecourt — British Tanks penetrate; evac ated, 11-iv.-15; penetrate Hindenburg li near, 3-v.-17; further progress, 4-v.-1 7-v.-17; 12-v.-17; German success W. 15-v.-17; captured by Territorials, 17-v.-1 British attacked, 20-v.-17; progress, 21-v.-1 section of line N.W. of, captured, 15-vi.-1 fighting round, 16-vi.-17; thrusts nea 20-xi.-17; Germans attack near, 12-xii.-1 British improve position, 13-xii.-17; Germ attack E. of, 5-i.-18; taken by German 21-iii.-18; British take and lose, 30-viii.-1 retaken, 1-ix.-18

Bullets, explosive — Russians protest again use by Germans, 20-i.-15

Bülow, Marshal von (Germany) — commar 2nd Army, 2-viii.-14; 14-viii.-14; tal over command of von Kluck's 1st Army a von Marwitz's Cavalry Corps, 18-viii.-1 von Kluck again under, 10-ix.-14; supersed in command of 2nd Army; retired, 4-iv.-1 created Field-Marshal, 27-i.-15

Bultfontein — S. African rebels defeate 14-xi.-14

" Bulwark," H.M.S. — blown up in Medwa 26-xi.-14;

" Bulysses," s.s. — sunk, 20-viii.-17

Burbach — furnaces bombarded, 22-i.-17

" Burdigala," French auxiliary — min 14-xi.-16

" Buresk " (late British collier) — destroy by H.M.S. " Sydney," 9-xi.-14

Burgas — Russian Fleet bombards, 21-x.-1 Turkish munition ship sunk, 16-ix.-16

Burian, Baron (Austria-Hungary) — appoint Minister for Foreign Affairs, 13-i.-15; German G.H.Q. at Pless, 17-x.-16; succeed by Count Czernin, 22-xii.-16; succeeds Cou Czernin, 15-iv.-18; in Berlin: adheres Austro-Polish solution, 11-vi.-18; confers w Kaiser at Spa, 15-viii.-18; notifies Berlin intention of Austria to take separate pea action, 30-viii.-18; Count Hertling (sta ment), 16-ix.-18; resigns, 24-x.-18

" Burnby," s.s. — sunk, 26-ii.-17

Burney, Adm. — commands H.M.S. " Lc Nelson," 7-viii.-14; arrives at Scapa; to co mand 1st Battle Squadron, 21-xii.-14; illne 25-xii.-14; resumes command, 28-xii.-14; H.M.S. " Marlborough " in Jutland batt

Chaume Wood (continued) :—
French success, 19-xi.-17; German attack fails, 12-i.-18

Chauny — French take, 19-iii.-17; Germans take, 24-iii.-18; French withdraw near, 6-iv.-18; French take, 6-ix.-18

Chavignon — French gain, 22-x.-17; -taken, 23-x.-17

Chavonne — British at, 13-ix.-14; French take part of, 16-iv.-17; capture, 18-iv.-17

"Cheerful," H.M.S. — mined, 30-vi.-17

"Cheford," s.s. — sunk, 14-iv.-18

Chemical Warfare Supplies — committee (inter-Allied) formed, 6-iii.-18

Chemin-des-Dames — Germans repelled, 17-ix.-14; French attack, 16-iv.-17; Germans driven back on, 19-iv.-17; French across W. end, 20-iv.-17; progress, 21-iv.-17; German counter-attacks repulsed, 26-iv.-17; French capture, 5-v.-17; German attacks, 20-v.-17; 7-vi.-17; 14-vii.-17; furious artillery battle: German attack repulsed, 22-vii.-17; German retreat, 1-xi.-17; French occupy, 2-xi.-17; German attacks N. of repulsed, 8-ii.-18; Germans take, 27-v.-18; Kaiser views battlefield from, 30-v.-18; evacuated, 11-x.-18; Franco-Italian advance across, 12-x.-18

Chêne-la-Reine — Germans reach; French regain, 17-vii.-18

Chennery Bayonville — taken by Americans, 1-xi.-18

Chenois — German attack, 11-vii.-16

Chenois Wood — French recovery, 22-vi.-16; 25-vi.-16

Cheppy — French raids near, 16-iii.-18

Chérisy — British enter; abandon, 3-v.-17; take, 27-viii.-18

"Chertsey," s.s. — sunk, 26-iv.-17

Cheshire — Zeppelin raid, 27-xi.-16

"Chester," H.M.S. — in Jutland battle, 31-v.-16; completes repairs, 29-vii.-16

"Chesterfield," H.M. fleet messenger — sunk, 13-v.-18

"Chesterfield," s.s. — sunk, 18-v.-18

Chetwode, Gen. — commanding 5th Cavalry Brigade at Binche, 21-viii.-14

Chevilly — French enter, 30-viii.-18

"Cheviot Range," s.s. — sunk, 21-ii.-18

Chevreux — French take, 6-v.-17; carry trench lines E. of, 22-v.-17; Germans attack, 12-x.-17; French occupy, 1-xi.-17

"Chic," s.s. — sunk, 13-iv.-16

"Chicago," s.s. — sunk, 8-vii.-18

"Chicago City," s.s. — torpedoed, 23-v.-17

Chikaldir Bridge — British air-raid, 27-xii.-16

"Chikara," H.M.A.T. — sinks UC41, 21-viii.-17

Chile :—
"Dresden," H.I.M.S. — destruction off Juan Fernandez: protest, 24-iii.-15; British apology, 16-iv.-15

Chilly — French take, 4-ix.-16; French raid S. of, 2-xi.-16

Chilwell — munition works blown up, 5-x.-17

Chimay — French forces enter Belgium near, 14-viii.-14; French approach, 10-xi.-18; Allied line at Armistice, 11-xi.-18

China — breaks with Germany, 13-iii.-17 declares war on Austria and Germany, 14-viii.-17
East, Far — agreement with Japan for preservation of peace, 25-iii.-18; agreement with Entente and Japan, 15-v.-18 United States and Japan — agreement, 2-xi.-17

Chinese — volunteers in fight with Bolshevists, 12-iii.-18

Chios — Turkish coast bombarded opposite, 27-vi.-15

Chipilly — Germans cross to S. bank of Somme, 27-iii.-18; Germans regain, 9-viii.-18

Choisy Hill — retaken for fifth time by French, 3-vi.-18

Choisy salient — French abandon, 12-vi.-18

"Chirripo," s.s. — mined, 28-xii.-17

Chirumba — Germans at, 17-xii.-17

Chivata (G.E. Africa) — Germans prepare leave, 14-xi.-17; British occupy, 15-xi.-1 Germans and Askaris surrender, 18-xi.-17

Chivy — French take, 18-iv.-17

Chocheprat, Adm. — member of French W Mission to U.S., 15-iv.-17

Chocolate Hill — British take, 7-viii.-15

Chorok R. — Turks driven back west 18-i.-15

Chortkoff — Russian success at, 9-ix.-15

Christian, Adm. — southern force forme 9-viii.-14; at Ostend, 22-viii.-14

Christiania — German bomb plot discovere 25-vi.-17

Christmas Island — Adm. von Spee at, 7-ix.-

Chuignes — taken by Australians, 23-viii.-18

Chuignolles — taken by Australians, 23-viii.-

"Chulmleigh," s.s. — sunk, 14-ix.-17

"Chupra," H.M.T. — damaged in actio 22-iii.-18

Churchill, Mr. W. S. — confers with Ad Jellicoe at Loch Ewe, 17-ix.-14; visits J. French on Aisne, 26-ix.-14; arrives Antwerp, 3-x.-14; attends war counc 6-x.-14; second visit to Sir J. French France, 7-xii.-14; stigmatises Germ raiders as " baby-killers," 20-xii.-14; repl to Sir J. French's appeal for naval aid Belgian coast, 20-xii.-14; telegram to Sir French re development of Zeebrugge U-Boat base, 2-i.-15; Minister of Munitio 17-vii.-17

"Chyebassa," s.s. — torpedoed, 8-xii.-17

Cierges — Anglo-French capture, 1-viii.-18

Ciez Kovice — Germans take, 2-v.-15

Cilicia — Armenians deported, 27-vii.-15

"Cilicia," s.s. — mined, 12-ii.-17

"Cimbrier," s.s. — torpedoed, 8-ii.-18

Cisna — Russians occupy, 4-iv.-15

"Citta di Messina," Italian auxiliary — sur 21-vi.-16

"Citta di Palermo," Italian s.s. — min 8-i.-16

"City of Adelaide," s.s. — sunk, 11-viii.-18

"City of Athens," s.s. — mined, 10-viii.-17

"City of Baroda," s.s. — sunk, 4-vi.-17

"City of Birmingham," s.s. — sunk, 27-xi.-1

"City of Brisbane," s.s. — sunk, 13-viii.-18

"City of Cairo," s.s. — U.-Boat atta 11-xi.-16

"City of Cambridge," s.s. — sunk, 3-vii.-17

"City of Canton," s.s. — U-Boat atta 18-vii.-17

"City of Corinth," s.s. — sunk, 21-v.-17

"City of Edinburgh," s.s. — U-Boat atta 25-x.-16

"City of Exeter," s.s. — mined, 11-vi.-17

"City of Florence," s.s. — sunk, 20-vii.-17

"City of Glasgow," s.s. — sunk, 1-ix.-18

"City of Lahore," s.s. — U-Boat atta 24-xi.-15

"City of Lucknow," s.s. — torpedo 29-iv.-16; sunk, 21-xii.-17

"City of Manchester," s.s. — detached fr Indian convoy, 9-xi.-14

"City of Marseilles," s.s. —U-Boat atta 23-xi.-15

"City of Oran," s.s. — U-Boat atta 31-xii.-16

"City of Oxford," s.s. — journeys, disguised man of war, to Scape to join Special Serv Squadron, 7-xii.-14

"City of Paris," s.s. — sunk, 4-iv.-17

"City of Perth," s.s. — sunk, 11-vi.-17

"City of Winchester," s.s. — sunk, 6-viii.-

"City of Winchester," s.s. — torpedo 15-iv.-18

Ciulnita — air-raid, 5-x.-16

Cividale — falls to Austro-Germans, 27-x.-17

"Civilian," s.s. — sunk, 6-x.-17

Daniels, Mr. J. (U.S.) — agrees to send 32 T.B.D.s to European waters, 20-vi.-17; on creation of " incomparably the greatest navy in the world," 30-xii.-18

Dankl, Gen. (Austria) — enters Poland at Krasnik, 10-viii.-14

" Danton," French Dreadnought — torpedoed, 19-iii.-17

Danube — British picket boat torpedoes Austrian monitor " Körös," 22-iv.-15; German attempt to cross at Semendria: repulsed, 2-x.-15; Austro-Germans begin to cross, 7-x.-15; Germans cross, 9-x.-15; Austro-Germans cross in force, 10-x.-15; navigation reopened, 4-xi.-15; Austrians retire at Orsova, 1-ix.-16; Rumanians take Orsova, 3-ix.-16; Rumanians bombard Widin, Lom Palanka, and Rahova, 8-ix.-16; Mackensen crosses at Sistovo, 23-xi.-16; Bulgarians cross E. of Bukarest, 8-xii.-16; Russo-Rumanians withdraw across, 23-xii.-16; Bulgarians cross opposite Tulcea, 22-i.-17; driven across by Russians, 23-i.-17; French near Widin, 19-x.-18; Serbians reach near Semendria, 29-x.-18; Germans on line, 3-xi.-18; Serbians cross near Semendria, 9-xi.-18

Danube Is. — Germans take, 8-x.-16

Danube Trench — British take, 16-ix.-16

" Danubian," s.s. — mined, 20-iii.-17

Danzig — H.M.S. " Coventry " leaves Copenhagen for, 20-xii.-18; British Naval Mission in, 3-i.-19

Polish troops — transport through: discussed at Paris Peace Conference, 21-iii.-19; Gen. Noudant presents Note to German Armistice Commission demanding, 26-iii.-19; Germans refuse landing, 28-iii.-19; Council of Four consult Marshal Foch and Gens. Wilson and Diaz, 31-iii.-19; negotiations at Spa, 2-iv.-19; 3-iv.-19; Allies' right established and transport of troops arranged, 4-iv.-19

" Danzig," H.I.M.S. — mined, 18-v.-15

Danzig Bay — German High Sea Squadrons in, 11-x.-17

Dardanelles — open to German warships, 4-viii.-14; H.I.M.SS " Goeben " and " Breslau " enter, 10-viii.-14; German naval aid asked for by Adm. Souchon, for defence, 16-viii.-14; H.M.S. " Indomitable " leaves, 19-viii.-14; closed, 1-x.-14; forts bombarded by Anglo-French squadrons, 3-xi.-14; Turkish battleship " Messudiyeh " torpedoed by B11, 13-xii.-14; B9 enters, but forced to retire, 14-xii.-14; French submarine " Saphir " sunk, 17-i.-15; French Squadron placed under orders of Adm. Carden, 31-i.-15; forts bombarded, 19-ii.-15; 20-ii.-15; 25-ii.-15; Straits swept for four miles, 25-ii.-15; progress in, 1-iii.-15; 2-iii.-15; 3-iii.-15; demolition parties landed, 4-iii.-15; new attack from Gulf of Xeros over Gallipoli Peninsula, 5-iii.-15; Fort L magazine blown up, 5-iii.-15; Narrows bombarded; two forts out of action, 7-iii.-15; French battleships enter, 7-iii.-15; British battleships enter. 8-iii.-15; H.M.S. " Amethyst " damaged by Turkish gunfire in Sari Siglar Bay, 13-iii.-15; reconnaissance by French submarine " Coulomb," 14-iii.-15; Vice-Adm. de Robeck succeeds Vice-Adm. Carden, 16-iii.-15; approaches swept by Allied minesweepers, 17-iii.-15; Allied naval attack on forts: H.M.SS. " Irresistible " and " Ocean " and French " Bouvet " mined; H.M.S. " Inflexible " and French " Gaulois " damaged: losses made good by H.M.SS. " Queen " and " Implacable," 18-iii.-15; Russian cruiser " Askold " arrives, 25-iii.-15; French battleship " Henri IV." arrives, 27-iii.-15; " Juaréguiberry " arrives, 28-iii.-15; French T.B.D. Flotilla at, 14-iv.-15; E15 sunk, 15-iv.-15; ammunition: War Office divert supplies from France,

Dardanelles (continued) :—
22-iv.-15; B.E.F. leaves Mudros for, 24-iv.-15; French cruiser " Jeanne D'Arc " arrives, 24-iv.-15; " Latouche-Tréville " arrives, 25-iv.-15; AE2 torpedoes Turkish gunboat, 25-iv.-15; French submarine " Joule " mined, 1-v.-15; Gen. Bailloud's Algerian Division reinforcing, 5-v.-15; Gen. Sarrail succeeds Gen. Gourand, 6-viii.-15; Turkish gunboat sunk, 10-viii.-15; Turkish transport sunk by British seaplane, 12-viii.-15; French transport torpedoed off Cape Helles, 4-vii.-15; French submarine " Mariotte " sunk, 26-vii.-15; French aeroplanes bomb Akbachi Slimai and Chanak, 30-viii.-15; E7 sunk, 4-ix.-15; Commission: interim report issued, 8-iii.-17; forts to be occupied under Turkish Armistice terms, 30-x.-18; H.M.S. " Shark " and French T.B.D. " Mangini " enter, for Constantinople, 10-xi.-18; H.M.S. " Superb " in, 12-xi.-18

Dardanus, Fort — bombarded from Asiatic side, 26-ii.-15; bombarded, 6-iii.-15

Dar-es-Salaam — bombarded, 8-viii.-14; 13-viii.-14; 28-xi.-14; 2-i.-15; guns of H.I.M.S. " Königsberg " mounted, 11-vii.-15; surrenders, 4-ix.-16

Darfur — Sultan: see Ali Dinar

" Darius," s.s. — sunk, 13-vi.-17

" Dartmoor," s.s. — sunk, 27-v.-17

" Dartmouth," H.M.S. — joins 2nd Light Cruiser Squadron, 28-xii.-14; in action with Austrian light forces, 15-v.-17

Daucourt, Capt. (France) — bombs Krupp's Essen works, 24-ix.-16

Davenscourt — taken by Germans, 27-iii.-18

" David Lloyd George," s.s. — torpedoed, 17-xi.-17

Davis, Mr. J. W. (U.S. Ambassador) — arrives in London, 14-xii.-18

" Daybreak," s.s. — sunk, 24-xii.-17

Dead Sea — British patrols reach, 26-ii.-18; Arabs occupy Kerak, 7-iv.-18

Deal — R.N.D. in camp, 10-x.-14; air raids, 19-iii.-16; 3-v.-16

Debeney, Gen. (France) — 1st Army covering Roye-Moreuil, 23-iii.-18; commanding 1st Army placed under Sir D. Haig, 28-vii.-18; attacking in battle of Amiens, 8-viii.-18; captures Roye, 27-viii.-18

Deccan Horse — charge near Bois des Foureaux, 14-vii.-16

De Chair, Adm. — establishes Northern Patrol, 6-viii.-14; hoists flag in H.M.A.M.C. " Alsatian " as commander of 10th (Merchant) Cruiser Squadron for blockade duties, 3-xii.-14

Decorations, Orders, &c. :

British:
Distinguished Service Medal (Naval) instituted, 19-x.-14
Garter — enemy sovereigns, &c., struck off roll, 23-v.-15
Military Cross — instituted, 28-xii.-14
Victoria Cross — first award: five officers and four men decorated, 16-xi.-14; — Boyle, Lieut-Cmdr., 18-v.-15; — Canadian (first), 23-iv.-15; — Holbrook, Lieut. N., 21-xii.-14; — Indian (first), 26-i.-15; — Jutland battle awards, 31-vi.-16; — Robinson, Lieut., 3-ix.-16

French:
Croix de Guerre — instituted, 8-iv.-15
Legion of Honour — awards, 13-i.-15; 14-vi.-18; Gens. Haig and Smith-Dorrien appointed Grand Officers, 13-i.-15; Gen. Dubail appointed Grand Chancellor, 14-vi.-18

German — Iron Cross reinstituted for war services, " 1914," 5-viii.-14

Dedeagatch — British Fleet bombards, 21-x.-15; Allied ships shell, 18-i.-16

THE TIMES DIARY AND INDEX OF THE WAR. 231

Dikeli -- field battery silenced, 4-iii.-15

" Dilar de Larrinaga," s.s. — sunk, 4-v.-17

Dillingen — British air-raid, 26-xii.-16

Dinant — German failure at, 12-viii.-14; Prussian cavalry division checked, 15-viii.-14

" Diomed," s.s. — sunk, 22-viii.-15

" Diomed," s.s. — sunk, 21-viii.-18

" Diplomat," s.s. — sunk, 18-ix.-14

" Director," German s.s. — sunk, 11-x.-16

Dispatches: see under Western front, and names of battles

Diterichs, Gen. (Russia) — with Czecho-Slovaks; in control at Vladivostok, 29-vi.-18

Dittmann, Herr (Germany) — arrested, 31-i.-18; withdraws from Berlin Government, 29-xii.-18

Dixmude — French Marine Brigade at, 15-x.-14; German attack held, 16-x.-14; King Albert at, 18-x.-14; strong German attacks, 19-x.-14; fail, 21-x.-14; repulsed, 23-x.-14; 25-x.-14; Germans take after 3 weeks' battle, 10-xi.-14; Germans fails to cross Yser at, 2-xii.-14; Belgians cross Yser, 23-xii.-14; German attack fails, 8-iii.-15; Belgian progress, 14-iii.-15; Germans take Cloister-Hoek, 1-iv.-15; German raft attack S. of repulsed, 9-iv.-15; German attack near: fails, 12-iv.-15; Germans attack Franco-Belgians S. of: fail to break through, 26-iv.-15; Dunkirk bombarded from, 28-iv.-15; Anglo-Belgian attack from Ploegsteert to near, 28-ix.-18; occupied, 29-ix.-18; Belgians pass, 1-x.-18; Allied advance on front, 14-x.-18

Dixmude—Nieuport — French and Belgians between, 19-x.-14

Djemal Pasha (Turkey) — size of force, 3-ii.-15

" Djemnah," s.s. — sunk, 14-vii.-18

Dneister R. — Russian offensive, 6-ix.-14; battle ends, 12-ix.-14; Russian counter-attack, 9-v.-15; Germans forced back on front, 15-v.-15; Russian success S. of, 29-v.-15; Austrian defeat, 2-vi.-15; Austro-German army cross, 6-vi.-15; Germans driven across, 9-vi.-15; Russians retake Zuravno, 11-vi.-15; Austro-Germans again checked round Zuravno, 23-vi.-15; Russians retreating, 27-vi.-15; heavy Austro-German losses, 16-vi.-15; Russian progress, 3-ii.-16; cross to W. bank, 9-ii.-16; force line, 12-vi.-16; Germans cross S. of Halicz; repulsed, 11-ii.-17; bitter Russian resistance S. of, 29-vii.-17

Dobell, Gen. — off Duala, 23-ix.-14; reports conquest of Cameroons, 16-ii.-16; commands Eastern forces, 26-iii.-17; 27-iii.-17

Doberdo — Italians repulsed, 8-ix.-15; attack, 21-x.-15; advance E. of, 11-viii.-16

Dobritch — captured by Bulgaro-Germans, 4-ix.-16; fighting, 8-ix.-16

Dobropolie — Serbs capture advance Bulgar positions, 3-v.-18; Franco-Serb advance on, 16-ix.-18

Dobropolie—Moglena sector — Serb progress, 30-viii.-17

Dobrudja — Russian troops in, 30-viii.-16; Bulgarians cross border, 1-ix.-16; Bulgarian offensive, 2-ix.-16; Russo-Rumanians and Bulgaro-Germans in contact, 4-ix.-16; Bulgarians take Tutrakan, 6-ix.-16; fighting at Dobritch, 8-ix.-16; Rumanians retire, 14-ix.-16; Russo-Rumanians retire, 16-ix.-16; Bulgaro-Germans held, 19-ix.-16; lull, 20-ix.-16; Mackensen in, 24-ix.-16; Rumanian progress, 25-ix.-16; Mackensen's centre and right repulsed, 1-x.-16; Rumanian success, 3-x.-16; 4-x.-16; Mackensen's new offensive, 19-x.-16; 20-x.-16; success; Russo-Rumanian retreat; railway cut, 21-x.-16; German pressure weakening, 26-x.-16; Gen. Sakharoff commanding in, 1-xi.-16; furious fighting, 3-xii.-16; German pursuit in, 16-xii.-16; Russo-Rumanian retirement, 17-xii.-16; Russian withdrawal, 21-xii.-16; Russo-Rumanians withdraw across Danube, 23-xii.-16; Germans

Dobrudja (continued) :—
clearing, 24-xii.-16; further German success, 1-i.-17; Allies evacuate, 5-i.-17; Germans organise Northern defences, 6-i.-17; ceded to Bulgaria, 4-iii.-18

Dobrynka — Russian line penetrated, 24-viii.-15

" Dockleaf," s.s. — mined, 3-vi.-17

Dodoma — British reach Central Railway, 29-vii.-16

Dogger Bank — battle, 24-i.-15; Admiralty reports safe return of all ships engaged in battle, 26-i.-15; preliminary telegraphic report issued, 27-i.-15; dispatch published, 3-iii.-15

Doignies — British carry, 2-iv.-17; taken by Germans, 21-iii.-18

Doiran — Bulgarians enter, 12-xii.-15; French bombard, 9-viii.-16; 10-viii.-16; French take " Tortoise Hill," 15-viii.-16; British advance in sector, 12-iii.-17; progress, 25-iv.-17; 14-v.-17; Allies bombard front from Monastir to, 14-ix.-18

Doiran, Lake — Anglo-Greek troops attack W. and E. of, 18-ix.-18; Bulgarians retreat on nearly 100-mile front between Monastir and, 22-ix.-18

Doldjeli — British in contact, 17-viii.-16

Dolina — battle, 22-ii.-15; Russian advance towards, 12-iii.-17

Dolomites — Italians take Cortina, 30-v.-15; gain footing on Col de Lana, 4-viii.-15; advance on Bacher Valley, 17-viii.-15; capture Col di Lana, 7-xi.-15; successes, 22-viii.-16; Austrian attacks fail, 21-v.-17

Domesnes — Russians land and repulse Germans, 22-x.-15

" Dominion," H.M.S. — 12in. guns reported cracked, 25-viii.-14; sent to Devonport, 2-ix.-14

Dominion Battery — King George visits, 13-viii.-16; fires on Ostend, 27-vi.-17

Dominions (see also Canada, etc.) — Premiers invited to " Special War Conference of the Empire," 25-xii.-16

Dommary Baroncourt station — U.S. air-raid on, 13-vi.-18

Dompierre — German attack fails, 28-i.-16; 29-i.-16; French capture, 1-vii.-16

Don — British air-raid, 20-ii.-16

Don, R. — Cossack rising, 9-xii.-17; Germans enter Donetz region W. of, 2-v.-18

" Don Arturo," s.s. — sunk, 24-vi.-17

" Don Diego," s.s. — sunk, 21-v.-17

Don—Douai — junctions bombed by British airmen, 13-iii.-15

" Donegal," H.M.S. — leaves Scapa to cruise White Sea route and protect Archangel trade, 17-xi.-15; protects White Sea route, 22-xi.-15; sunk, 17-iv.-17

" Don Emilio," s.s. — sunk, 1-vii.-17

Donetz region — Germans enter, 2-v.-18

Donon Crest — French 1st Army reaches, 14-viii.-14

Doornberg — De Wet defeats Union troops, 7-xi.-14

" Doris," H.M.S. — raids Ascalon, 15-xii.-14; blows up bridge near Deurt Yol, 21-xii.-14; destroys s.s. " Odessa," 24-xii.-14; landing party distributes food at Ruad Island, 22-i.-15; landing party raids Alexandretta, 25-i.-15; shells barracks at Deurt Yol: 450 Turkish casualties, 10-iii.-15

Dormans — Germans reach Marne near, 31-v.-18; Allies cross Marne at Chassines—Passy, 22-vii.-18

Dornach — poison-gas factory bombed, 26-viii.-15

Dorna Watra — Germans attack Russo-Rumanian army junction, 15-x.-16; slight progress, 16-x.-16; fighting, 20-x.-16; Russian reverse, 27-x.-16; success S. of, 6-xi.-16; Austrian success near, 27-ii.-17

" Dorothy," s.s. — sunk, 24-ii.-17

Dumarea — Russo-Rumanians at, 9-xi.-16

Dumba, Dr. (Austria) — discovery of documents compromising, 6-ix.-15; U.S. demand recall, 9-ix.-15; recalled, 17-ix.-15

" **Dunaff Head,**" s.s. — attacked by U-Boat, 2-vi.-18

Dunayetz — Russians advancing on Cracow, 13-xi.-14; Austro-German mass offensive, 1-v.-15; 2-v.-15; crossing of Dunayetz begun, 3-v.-15; Austrian advance near Tarnov, 18-ii.-15; progress, 10-v.-15.

" **Dundalk,**" s.s. — sunk, 14-x.-18

" **Dundee,**" H.M.A.M.C. — operating with 3rd Cruiser Squadron, 17-ii.-16; leaves Scapa disguised as merchantman, 15-viii.-16; sinks German raider, 16-iii.-17

" **Dunedin,**" s.s. — mined, 23-xii.-17

Dunkirk — British D.S.C. and French Croix de Guerre conferred, 15-x.-18
Air-raids, 30-xii.-14; 6-i.-15; 10-i.-15; 22-i.-15; 27-i.-15; 26-v.-15; 30-xi.-15; 2-iv.-16; 19-v.-16; 20-v.-16; 21-v.-16; 22-v.-16; 23-viii.-17; 3-ix.-17; 24-ix.-17; 25-ix.-17; effect, 28-ix.-17; further raids, 26-i.-18; 20-iii.-18; 26-iii.-18; casualties, 15-x.-18; aeroplanes brought down, 22-i.-15; 25-v.-17
Bombardments — by German T.B.D.s, 25-iii.-17; 25-iv.-17; 19-x.-17; 21-iii.-18; by long-range guns, 6-xii.-14; 28-iv.-15; 27-vi.-17; 15-x.-18

" **Dunmore Head,**" s.s. — sunk, 27-iv.-17

" **Dunrobin,**" s.s. — sunk, 24-xi.-17

" **Dunsley,**" s.s. — sunk, 19-viii.-15

Dunsterville, Gen. — force repulses frontier raid in Mohmand country, 5-ix.-15; leaves Karachi for Baghdad, 6-i.-18; leaves Baghdad on special mission to Baku, 27-i.-18; at Enzeli, 17-ii.-18; returns to Hamadan, 20-ii.-18; at Kasvin, 1-vi.-18; force under defeats Jangali attack, 20-vii.-18; arrives at Baku, 17-viii.-18

" **Dupetit-Thouars,**" French cruiser — torpedoed, 7-viii.-18

Durah — British advance near, 18-i.-18

" **Durango,**" s.s. — sunk, 26-viii.-17

Durazzo — Albanians bombard, 10-iv.-15; Serbians enter, 4-vii.-15; evacuate, 17-vii.-15; bombarded, 6-xii.-15; Austrians capture, 27-ii.-16; Austrian T.B.D.s escape from engagement in Adriatic, 22-v.-18; bombarded, 2-x.-18; occupied, 14-x.-18

Durham — Zeppelin raids, 15-vi.-15; 1-iv.-16; 5-iv.-16; 9-viii.-16; 27-xi.-16; 13-iii.-18

" **Durward,**" s.s. — sunk, 21-i.-15

Dury — taken by British, 2-ix.-18

Düsseldorf — British air-raid, 22-ix.-14

Dutoff, Gen. (Russia) — Cossack rising under, 9-xii.-17

Dutumi — action at, 10-ix.-16

Duval (" Bonnet Rouge ") — sentenced to death, 13-v.-18

Duweidar — Turco-German attack repulsed, 23-iv.-16

" **Dux,**" s.s. — sunk, 8-v.-18

Dvaelbank — French take, 26-x.-17

Dvina R. — Count Schmettow's 5th Cavalry Corps formed, 21-viii.-15; Germans attack Friedrichstadt bridgehead, 29-viii.-15; Germans storm Friedrichstadt bridgehead, 3-ix.-15; Russians attacked on, 11-ix.-15; two years' position warfare begins, 29-ix.-15; Austro-German crossing begun, 7-x.-15; Germans active, 17-x.-15; advance, 18-x.-15; Germans capture bank, 20-x.-15; attacks near Dahlen Island, 11-xi.-15; 16-xi.-15; recover Bersemunde, 24-xi.-15; German activity: Russian line withdrawn, 22-viii.-17; forced by Germans, 1-ix.-17; Russian line lost up to Friedrichstadt, 5-ix.-17; Germans cross, 18-ii.-18; withdraw on wide front, 22-x.-17

Dvinsk — Russians retire near, 2-viii.-15; evacuating, 10-viii.-15; evacuated, 11-viii.-15;

Dvinsk (continued) :—
renewed offensive on, 18-ix.-15; heavy fighting, 20-ix.-15; German reverse near, 25-ix.-15; fighting continued, 29-ix.-15; Germans attack, 1-x.-15; fresh threat to, 2-x.-15; desperate fighting, 3-x.-15; 6-x.-15; 8-x.-15; Russian attack; LZ85 raids, 12-x.-15; German success, 22-x.-15; slight progress, 26-x.-15; Russian counter-offensive, 31-x.-15; success near Platonovka, 3-xi.-15; German reverse, 5-xi.-15; German air-raid, 15-xi.-15; Russians in outskirts of Illukst, 29-xi.-15; repulsed near Lake Drisviaty, 15-xii.-15; German air-raids, 15-i.-16; 18-i.-16; LZ86 raids, 4-ii.-16; Russian attack, 18-iii.-16; Germans fail S. of, 19-iii.-16; Russians progress S. of, 20-iii.-16; air-raids, 26-iv.-16; 28-iv.-16; Germans attack, 28-iv.-16; Russian reverse, 29-iv.-16; air-raids, 27-vi.-16; 29-vii.-16; 17-i.-17; 18-vi.-17; Russian withdrawal, 23-vii.-17; Germans occupy, 18-ii.-18

" **Dwinsk,**" s.s. — sunk, 18-vi.-18

" **Dykland,**" s.s. — sunk, 22-iv.-17

Dyle R. — Belgians retire, 8-viii.-14

E.

" **Earl of Elgin,**" s.s. — sunk, 7-xii.-17

East, Far — China and Japan to co-operate in resisting influences likely to endanger peace, 25-iii.-18; agreement between Entente, Japan, and China, 15-v.-18

East Coast: see under Great Britain

" **Eastern City,**" s.s. — sunk, 9-iv.-16

Eastern Front — Russians penetrate German territory between Kalish and Thorn; Austro-German offensive between Baltic and Bukovina, 13-vii.-15; first suspension of hostilities, 2-xii.-17; armistice, 7-xii.-17 (see various fronts and names of places)

" **Eastern Prince,**" s.s. — sunk, 30-viii.-17

" **Eastfield,**" s.s. — sunk, 27-xi.-17

" **Eastgate,**" s.s. — rescued from U-Boat, 5-i.-17

East Indies — Dutch Government to send convoy, 16-iv.-18; 29-iv.-18

" **Eastlands,**" s.s. — sunk, 25-i.-18

" **Eastpoint,**" s.s. — sunk, 9-iii.-17

East Riding: see under Yorkshire

Eaucourt l'Abbaye — British advance E. of, 27-ix.-16; taken, 1-x.-16; Germans regain footing, 2-x.-16; British recapture, 3-x.-16; British progress, 5-x.-16; mill captured between Le Sars and, 6-x.-16

" **Eavestone,**" s.s. — sunk, 3-ii.-17

Eben, Gen. von (Germany) — commanding 1st (Prussian) Army Corps in taking of Bialystok, 26-viii.-15

" **Eber,**" H.I.M.S. — at Bahia, 14-ix.-14; set on fire and sunk, 26-x.-17

Ebert, Herr (Germany) — in Reichstag, on annexations, 28-v.-15; president of Socialist group, 20-xii.-15; becomes Chancellor, 9-xi.-18; forms joint Socialist Ministry, 10-xi.-18; orders army to obey officers, 12-xi.-18; ratifies Peace Treaty, 9-vii.-19

" **Eboe,**" s.s. — attacked by U-Boat, 7-iv.-18

Ebolowa—Akonolinga — Germans evacuate, 18-i.-16

" **Echunga,**" s.s. — sunk, 5-ix.-17

Eckau — German attack repulsed, 27-ix.-15; Germans cross near Grünwald, 14-x.-15

Eckermann, Adm. (Germany) — receives Kaiser's instructions as to High Sea Fleet, 3-x.-14; invalided, 19-vii.-15

Eckerö — German expedition arrives off, 5-iii.-18

Ecourt — British enter, 4-ix.-18

Ecoust St. Mein — British carry, 2-iv.-17; taken by Germans, 21-iii.-18

Ecuries — French advance, 4-ii.-15; 9-v.-15

" **Eddie,**" s.s. — sunk, 16-ii.-17

234   THE TIMES DIARY AND INDEX OF THE WAR.

Edea — Allies occupy, 26-x.-14
" Eden," H.M.S. — sunk, 18-vi.-16
" Edernian," s.s. — sunk, 20-viii.-17
" Edina," s.s. — sunk, 17-viii.-17
Edinburgh — bombed, 2-iv.-16
" Edlington," s.s. — sunk, 23-ix.-18
Edmonds, Flight-Lieut. — sinks Turkish transport, 12-viii.-15
" Edurna," s.s. — torpedoed, 5-vii.-17
Edwards, Gen. — occupies Nanungu, 19-v.-18; drives Germans westward from Nanungu-Mahua, 22-v.-18; von Lettow surrenders to, 25-xi.-18
" Egg, The " — position: British storm, 12-iv.-17
Egri Palanka — Bulgarians take, 17-x.-15
" Egusa," British auxiliary yacht — sunk, 28-iv.-16
Egypt — British Protectorate proclaimed; Sir A. H. McMahon High Commissioner, 17-xii.-14; Khedive appointed (see Hussein Kamel Pasha); Sultan deposed, 18-xii.-14; Gen. Allenby appointed Special High Commissioner, 21-iii.-19; in Cairo, 25-iii.-19; U.S. recognises Protectorate, 22-iv.-19
Ministry — Sir Hussein Rushdi Pasha to form, 9-iv.-19
Nationalists — Zaghlul Pasha and three others; arrested, 8-iii.-19; deported to Malta; riots in Cairo, 9-iii.-19; 14-iii.-19; 25-iii.-19; 1-iv.-19; 3-iv.-19; Zaghlul Pasha and associates released, 7-iv.-19; deputation to Paris leaves; Zaghlul Pasha joins at Malta, 11-iv.-19
Operations — Turkish advance begun, 26-i.-15; " second invasion " fails, 11-viii.-16: see also Palestine, Sinai and names of places
British Command — Gen. Murray succeeds Gen. Maxwell, 19-iii.-16; Gen. Allenby succeeds Gen. Murray, 29-vi.-17
Western — Arabs routed near Mersa Matruh, 11-xii.-15; 13-xii.-15; 3,000 defeated at, 25-xii.-15; Senussi dispersed at Halazih, 23-i.-16; defeated at Agagia, 26-ii.-16; British reoccupy Barani, 28-ii.-16; Sollum reoccupied, 14-iii.-16; Senussi defeated at Girba, 4-ii.-17; British occupy Siwa, 5-ii.-17
Sultan: see Abbas Hilmi Pasha, and Hussein Kamel Pasha
" Egyptiana," s.s. — sunk, 9-vi.-17
" Egyptian Prince," s.s. — sunk, 12-v.-17
" Egyptian Transport," s.s. — attacked by U-Boat, 1-i.-18
Eichhorn, Marshal von (Germany) — commanding new 10th Army, 26-i.-15; promoted Field-Marshal, 18-xii.-17; commands Kieff Army Group, 31-iii.-18; orders Ukrainian peasants to sow the land, 1-v.-18; assassinated, 30-vii.-18
Eider Light — German fleet puts out to, 19-vii.-15
Eifel — German 3rd Army concentrated, 14-viii.-14
Eiffel Tower — Eight bombs dropped near, 22-v.-15
18th Division: see under Army — Divisions
Einem, Gen. von (Germany) — to command 3rd Army, 12-ix.-14
Eisner, Kurt — assumes control in Munich, 8-xi.-18
" Ekaterina II.," Russian battleship: see " Svobodnaya Rossiya "
Ekaterinburg — Tsar Nicholas removed to, 1-v.-18; murdered at, 16-vii.-18; Sir C. Eliot at, 5-x.-18
Ekaterinoslav — Germans at, 2-iv.-18
" El Argentino," s.s — mined, 26-v.-16
El Arish — British raid, 18-v.-16; air-raids, 13-vi.-16; 19-vi.-16; Germans retire, 11-viii.-16; British occupy, 21-xii.-16

" Elax," H.M. oiler — sunk, 10-x.-16
Elbasan — Allies advance, 22-vii.-18; captur 7-x.-18; Italians at, 9-x.-18
" Elbing," H.I.M.S. — sunk in Jutla battle, 31-v.-16
" Eleanor," H.M. mine-carrier — su 12-ii.-18
" Elele," s.s. — sunk, 18-vi.-17
Eliot, Sir C. — appointed High Commissio in Siberia, 16-viii.-18; at Ekaterinbu 5-x.-18
El Fasher — British force advances 15-v.-16; occupies, 23-v.-16
" Elford," s.s. — mined, 18-v.-17
El-Kafr — fighting, 28-iii.-18
El Kantara — skirmish near, 26-i.-15; Tu attempt to bridge canal, 3-ii.-15; skirmi 7-iv.-15
El Kubri — Turkish raid on Suez Canal z stopped by Indian troops and Lancasl T.F. battery, 23-iii.-15
" Ella Sayer," s.s. — sunk, 29-iv.-18
" Ellaston," H.M. collier — sunk, 16-iii.-18
Elles, Gen. — to command Tanks in Fran 29-ix.-16; order to Tank Corps bef Cambrai battle, 19-xi.-17
" Elmgrove," s.s. — sunk, 29-v.-16
" Elmleaf," s.s. — attacked by U-Bc 24-xii.-17
" Elmmoor," s.s. — sunk, 23-v.-17
" Eloby," s.s. — sunk, 19-vii.-17
" Elsinore," s.s. — sunk, 1-ix.-14
" Elsiston," s.s. — sunk, 19-x.-17
" Elswick Grange," s.s. — attacked by Boat: reached port, 17-v.-18
" Elswick Lodge," s.s. — sunk, 20-viii.-17
" Elvaston," s.s. — torpedoed, 15-vi.-17
" Elysia," s.s. — attacked by U-Bc 24-v.-18
" El Zorro," H.M. oiler — sunk, 28-xii.-15
Embermènil — Germans take, 20-iv.-15
" Emden," H.I.M.S. — leaves Tsingt 31-vii.-14; captures s.s. " Ryasan," 10-v 14; joins Adm. von Spee at Pagan Isla 12-viii.-14; in Bay of Bengal, 10-ix.- sinks s.s. " Diplomat," 13-ix.-14; sinks " Trabboch " and " Clan Matheso 14-ix.-14; bombards Madras, 22-ix.- captures and sinks British steam 25-ix.-14; off Pondicherry, 28-ix.-14; Malabar coast, 30-ix.-14; collier sunk H.M.S. " Yarmouth," 16-x.-14; si " Mousquet " and " Zhemchug," 28-x.- destroys wireless station at Cocos Isla 9-xi.-14; destroyed by H.M.S. " Sydne 9-xi.-14
" Emden II.," H.I.M.S. — surrend 21-xi.-18
" Emdleton," s.s. — sunk, 11-ix.-17
" Emma," s.s. — sunk, 20-iv.-17
Emmich, Gen. von (Germany) — atta Liège, 4-viii.-14; enters, 7-viii.-14; recei Pour le Mérite, 7-viii.-14; superseded as c mander of 10th (Prussian) Army Col 22-xii.-15
" Emperor of India," H.M.S. — at Berehav 1-xii.-14; joins 4th Battle Squadr 10-xii.-14
" Ems," German s.s. — sunk, 19-vi.-16
Ems R. — 6 German submarines transferred 3-ix.-14; U37 sunk, 22-vi.-15
" Engadine," H.M. seaplane carriei arrangements for attack on Tond Zeppelin base: result, 4-v.-16; in Jutl battle: sends up first seaplane for rec naissance in action, 31-v.-16
Enghien — first British aeroplane shot do 22-viii.-14
" England," s.s. — sunk, 23-v.-17
Englefontaine — carried, 26-x.-18

English Channel — French mine N.E.,
2-xi.-14; 16 German aeroplanes seen,
10-i.-15; two German seaplanes brought
down, 11-vi.-17
"English Monarch," s.s. — sunk, 18-vi.-17
English-speaking Union — founded, 4-vii.-18
"Enidwen," s.s. — sunk, 8-vi.-17
"Ennismore," s.s. — sunk, 29-xii.-17
Enos — Allied naval attack on, 8-iv.-15;
Anglo-French force at, 22-iv.-15
Enver Pasha (Turkey) — on Dardanelles and
German warships, 4-viii.-14; visits Batum,
18-iv.-18; requested to withdraw from all
Caucasus territories other than Kars, Batum,
and Ardahan by German High Command,
9-vi.-18; Hindenburg telegraphs regarding
starving Armenians, 29-vii.-18; reply,
3-viii.-18
Enzeli — Gen. Dunsterville at, 17-ii.-18; Gen.
Bitcherakoff leaves for, 8-vi.-18; leaves for
Alyat, 1-vii.-18; 3-vii.-18; British Mission at,
4-viii.-18; British holding road from Baghdad, 15-viii.-18; British return to, 14-ix.-18;
British troops concentrating for occupation
of Baku, 9-xi.-18; Allied forces leave for
Baku, 16-xi.-18
Epéhy — British advance beyond, 16-iv.-17;
auxiliary thrusts near, 20-xi.-17; British
resistance, 21-iii.-18; taken by Germans,
22-iii.-18; British reach edge, 9-ix.-18; battle,
12-ix.-18
Epéhy-Peizères — British take, 1-iv.-17
Epénancourt — British occupy Somme bank
from Péronne to, 18-iii.-17
Epernay — German retirement towards, 9-ix.-
14; LZ77 raids, 25-i.-16; Germans progress
towards, 16-vii.-18; 17-vii.-18; Germans
yielding on Marne R., 26-vii.-18
Epieds — Franco-Americans reach, 22-vii.-18
Epinal — LZ87 raids, 23-ii.-16
Epinoy — British advance E. of, 4-x.-18
Epirus — Italians occupy Yanina, 8-vi.-17
"Eptalofos," s.s. — sunk, 23-iii.-17
Equancourt — British take, 27-iii.-17
"Era," H.M. trawler — sunk, 11-vi.-16
"Era," s.s. — sunk, 1-v.-18
Ercavallo Peak — Italians on, 7-viii.-15
Erches — Germans reach, 26-iii.-18
Ercloo — Allies at, 3-xi.-18
"Erebus," H.M. monitor — bombards Belgian
coast, 12-ix.-16; 13-ix.-16; bombards Ostend,
5-vi.-17; takes up Belgian coast patrol,
27-vii.-17; bombards Ostend, 21-vii.-17; hit
by motor-boat, 28-x.-17
"Eretria," s.s. — mined, 13-v.-16
"Eric Calvert," s.s. — sunk, 22-iv.-18
"Erik," s.s. — sunk, 25-viii.-18
"Erin," H.M.S. (ex-Turkish "Reshadiey")
— joins Grand Fleet, 17-ix.-14
Erivan — Armenian Parliament opened,
1-viii.-18
Ermenonville Wood — Germans abandon guns,
1-ix.-14
"Ermine," H.M.S. — sunk, 2-viii.-17
"Erne," H.M.S. — lost, 6-ii.-15
Ernécourt — H.Q. 2nd French Colonial Corps,
30-viii.-18
"Eros," s.s. — sunk, 17-viii.-18
Erquelines — Allied line at Armistice, 11-xi.-18
"Errington Court," s.s. — mined, 7-vi.-17
Ervillers — taken by British, 23-viii.-18
Erzberger, Herr (Germany) — Armistice
delegate; leaves for front, 6-xi.-18; asks for
immediate armistice: refused, 8-xi.-18;
renewal of armistice; leaves for Treves,
8-xii.-18; at Spa to confer with Marshal
Foch on Danzig question, 2-iv.-19; forms
Government, 22-vi.-19
Erzinjan — Russian progress towards, 12-vii.-
16; 20-vii.-16; falls, 25-vii.-16
Erzrum — Russian advance checked, 13-i.-15;
Armenians deported, 14-vi.-15; Russians
drive Turks back on, 17-i.-16; take another
fort, 13-ii.-16; 14-ii.-16; 15-ii.-16; falls,

Erzrum (continued) :—
16-ii.-16; Russians carry positions W. of,
8-vii.-16; Turks 20-30 miles W. of,
12-vii.-16; Baiburt captured by Russians,
15-vii.-16; Turks retake, 11-iii.-18
Erzrum—Mush — Russian advance on, 27-i.-16
"Escrick," s.s. — sunk, 16-viii.-18
Eseka — Allies occupy, 30-x.-15
Esjberg — U16 at; damaged, 6-xii.-14
"Eskimo," s.s. — captured; taken to Ger-
many, 26-vii.-16
"Esmeraldas," s.s. — sunk, 10-iii.-17
Esnes — British 4th Division at, 26-viii.-14
Espain — taken, 23-x.-18
"Esperanza de Larrinaga," s.s. — attacked by
U-Boat, 13-v.-18
Espérey, Gen. Franchet d' (France) — com-
manding 1st Corps 5th Army at Dinant,
15-viii.-14; instructed to attack northward,
4-ix.-14; commands in Franco-Serb offensive,
15-ix.-18; Bulgarian armistice: see under
Peace — Bulgaria — Armistice
Essad Pasha — to administer Albania, 5-x.-14
Es Salt — taken by British, 25-iii.-18; retire,
31-iii.-18; advance S. of, 30-iv.-18;
Australians capture, 1-v.-18; Turks repulsed,
2-v.-18; British withdraw, 3-v.-18; British
reach, 23-ix.-18
Es Samrah — occupied, 25-ix.-18
Essarts — British advance towards, 14-iii.-17
Essen — bombed, 24-ix.-16; 7-vii.-17; staff
reduced at Krupp's works, 1-xii.-18
Essen, Adm. (Russia) — commands British
submarines, 30-x.-14; death, 20-v.-15
Essex — air-raids, 16-iv.-15; 4-vi.-15; 12-viii.-
15; 17-viii.-15; 11-ix.-15; 12-ix.-15; 31-iii.-
16; 25-iv.-16; 25-viii.-16; 30-ix.-16; 5-vi.-17;
13-vi.-17; 4-vii.-17; 22-vii.-17; 12-viii.-17;
24-ix.-17; 30-ix.-17; 1-x.-17; 29-x.-17;
31-x.-17; 6-xii.-17; 18-xii.-17; 29-i.-18
Essigny — Germans occupy, 21-iii.-18
Essigny-le-Petit — taken by French, 8-x.-18
Es Sinn — Gen. Aylmer attacks, 8-iii.-16;
British advance through, 13-xii.-16
"Essonite," s.s. — sunk, 1-ii.-17
Estaires — Allies retire, 9-iv.-18; Germans
cross Lys, 10-iv.-18; British forced back,
11-iv.-18
Estaires—La Bassée road — Germans pushed
off, 15-x.-14
Esthonia — Diet meets at Reval, 14-vii.-17;
independence proclaimed, 28-xii.-17; Republic proclaimed, 24-ii.-18; Germans in,
27-ii.-18; Germans occupy, 5-iii.-18; Allied
recognition of independence sought, 17-iii.-19
Bolshevists — proclaim republic, 15-xii.-18;
appeal to Britain for arms against, 6-i.-19;
offensive begun, 15-ii.-19; proposed
Prinkipo conference: see under Russia
Estienne, Gen. (France) — to command
Tanks, 30-ix.-16
Estrées — taken by French, 4-vii.-16; con-
solidated, 5-vii.-16; French take trenches S.
of, 19-vii.-16; French progress, 24-vii.-16;
26-vii.-16; 1-viii.-16; 13-viii.-16; 21-viii.-16;
Germans take, 26-iii.-18; British take,
1-x.-18
"Estrella," s.s. — mined, 5-iii.-18
Etaing — British attack on 6-mile front,
2-ix.-18
"Etal Manor," s.s. — sunk, 19-ix.-17
Etaples — air-raids, 25-iv.-16; 1-x.-16; British
hospitals bombed, 19-v.-18
Eth — taken by British, 4-xi.-18
"Ethel," s.s. — sunk, 16-ix.-18
"Ethel and Millie," H.M. armed fishing craft
— sunk, 15-viii.-17
"Ethel Duncan," H.M. collier — sunk,
18-x.-16
"Ethelinda," s.s. — sunk, 29-i.-18
"Etonian," s.s. — sunk, 23-iii.-18
Etricourt — British carry, 4-ix.-18
"Etton," H.M. collier — mined, 20-ix.-16

Fère-Champenoise — attacked by French, 9-ix.-14; Gen. Foch at, 10-ix.-14

Fère-en-Tardenois — Sir J. French at, 12-ix.-14; Germans reach, 30-v.-18; French advance towards, 23-vii.-18; 24-vii.-18; taken, 28-vii.-18; fighting, 29-vii.-18; advance along road, 1-viii.-18

Fère Forest — Allied progress along Marne, 24-vii.-18; taken, 25-vii.-18

Fergusson, Gen. — invalided, 22-x.-14; troops under break through Quéant—Pronville defences, 3-ix.-18; arrives at Cologne as Military Governor, 11-xii.-18

" Ferndene," s.s. — sunk, 24-iv.-17

" Fernmoor," s.s. — sunk, 17-iv.-17

Ferries — train Channel service opened, 28-ii.-18

" Ferrona," s.s. — sunk, 28-x.-17

Ferryman's House (Yser) — skirmish near, 10-vii.-15

Fesmy — taken by British, 4-xi.-18

Festubert — hard fighting at, 13-x.-14; Germans capture trenches, 29-x.-14; battle begun, 9-v.-15; suspended, 10-v.-15; resumed, 15-v.-15; British advance, 16-v.-15; British consolidated, 17-v.-15; progress, 18-v.-15; 22-v.-15; 23-v.-15; 24-v.-15; ends, 25-v.-15; British success E. of, 16-vi.-15; British raids, 28-i.-17; trenches recovered, 19-iv.-18

Fetesti — LZ101 raids, 24-x.-16

Feuchy — British take, 9-iv.-17

Feuillères — French take, 3-vii.-16

Fey-en-Haye — French recapture trenches, 8-vii.-15; attack on 12-mile front between Xivray and, 12-ix.-18

Fife (Nyasaland) — skirmish near, 17-v.-15; von Lettow crosses into Rhodesia, 2-xi.-18

51st (Highland) Division — see under Army — Divisions

Fiji — volunteers leave for England, 1-i.-15

Filain — French advance, 25-x.-17

Finance — Triple Entente agreement, 6-ii.-15; see also under various country headings

Finland :—
Bolshevists — conflict between Finnish troops and " Red " Guards, 25-i.-18; " Reds " capture Helsingfors, 28-i.-18; domination spreads, 15-ii.-18; " Red " revolution, 27-i.-19
" Crown " — Prince Frederick Charles of Hesse accepts offer, 9-ix.-18

Finland, Gulf of — German warships minelaying in, 17-viii.-14; Russian T.B.D.s " Ispoluitelni " and " Letuchi " founder, 16-xii.-14

Finland and Germany — peace, 7-iii.-18; German expedition proposed, 2-iii.-18; arrives off Eckerö, 5-iii.-18; lands, 12-iii.-18; prepares to advance on Murman railway, 3-vii.-18

" Firedrake," H.M.S. — captures UC5, 27-iv.-16; sinks UC51, 13-xi.-17

" Firefly," H.M.S. — disabled; abandoned, 1-xii.-15; recaptured, 26-ii.-17

Fireships — German attempt to use on Ancre R., 3-ii.-15

" Firfield," s.s. — sunk, 16-vii.-17

Firman Pasha, Prince — Persian Premier, 25-xii.-15

1st Army Corps: see under Army — Corps

" Fiscus," s.s. — sunk, 20-xii.-17

" Fisgard II.," H.M.S. — lost, 17-ix.-14

Fisher, Lord — First Sea Lord, 29-x.-14; resignation refused, 14-v.-15; accepted, 22-v.-15; chairman of Inventions Board, 5-vii.-15

Fisher, Lce.-Cpl. — first Canadian to win V.C. in war, 23-iv.-15

Fisher, Mr. A. (Australia) — appointed High Commissioner in England, 26-x.-15

" Fisher Girl," H.M. drifter — sinks U20, 17-xii.-16

Fishing-boats (British) — 8 sunk by Germans, 22-viii.-14; 16 captured by German raiders off E. Coast, 26-viii.-14; attacked by U-Boat E. of Shetlands; 16 sunk, 23-vi.-15

Fismes — Allied advance, 3-viii.-18; French reach Vesle, E. of; taken by Americans, 4-viii.-18; Vesle R. crossed, 7-viii.-18

Fismettes — taken by Americans, 9-viii.-18

FitzClarence, Gen. — sends 2nd Worcesters to retake Gheluvelt, 31-x.-14; killed, 11-xi.-14

Fiume — Hungarian troops mutiny, 24-x.-18; U.S. battalion at, 17-xi.-18; occupied by D'Annunzio, 12-ix.-19; Council declares for independence, 15-xii.-19

Flamborough Head — U86 leaves for, 17-v.-17

" Flamenco," s.s. — sunk, 6-ii.-16

Flame-throwers — Germans attack with, 26-ii.-15; success at Hooge, 30-vii.-15

" Flamma," s.s. — mined, 10-vii.-17

Flanders — activity, 19-xi.-14; German attack slackening, 20-xi.-14; rain impedes operations, 2-i.-15; snowstorms, 19-i.-15; 127 small U-Boats for, 4-ii.-15; first stage of battle, 7-vi.-17; artillery activity towards coast, 23-vi.-17; intense artillery fighting, 10-vii.-17; 22-vii.-17; 25-vii.-17; 29-vii.-17; second phase, 31-vii.-17; 24-viii.-17; second phase ends, 25-viii.-17; third stage, 20-ix.-17; position-warfare until April 30: begun, 1-i.-18; German raids, 1-iii.-18; two French divisions transferred to heights, 9-iv.-18; Allied progress, 15-x.-18

Flanders Coast — occupation by German Naval Corps, 20-x.-14; abandonment: Gen. Ludendorff's statement, 18-ix.-18; evacuation of U-Boat base ordered, 29-ix.-18

" Flandre," French Dreadnought — launched, 20-x.-14

Flaucourt — French take, 3-vii.-16

" Flavia," s.s. — sunk, 24-viii.-18

" Flawyl," s.s. — sunk, 2-v.-18

Fleetwood — U21 off, 30-i.-15

Fléron — falls, 13-viii.-14

Flers — taken by British, 15-ix.-16; progress, 21-ix.-16; 27-ix.-16

Flesquières — taken by British, 20-xi.-17; salient abandoned, 22-iii.-18; taken by British, 27-ix.-18

Fleurbaix — taken, 2-x.-18

Fleury — Germans occupy, 23-vi.-16; French progress, 24-vi.-16; German attack, 26-vi.-16; Germans capture, 11-vii.-16; French gain, 19-vii.-16; 22-vii.-16; 2-viii.-16; French retake, 3-viii.-16; Germans take and lose, 4-viii.-16; French progress, 7-viii.-16; Germans repulsed, 19-viii.-16; French progress, 3-ix.-16; 4-ix.-16; German attack repulsed, 27-ix.-16

" Flimston," s.s. — sunk, 18-xii.-16

" Flirt," H.M.S. — sunk, 26-x.-16

" Florentia," s.s. — sunk, 29-vi.-18

" Floridian," s.s. — sunk, 4-ii.-17

Florina — occupied, 2-v.-16; Serbians in contact S.E. of, 17-viii.-16; Bulgarians occupy, 18-viii.-16; fighting, 19-viii.-16; heights carried, 18-ix.-16; taken, 18-ix.-16; Allies advance from, 2-x.-16

" Florrieston," s.s. — sunk, 20-iv.-18

" Fluent," s.s. — mined, 20-vii.-17

" Flushing," U.S. s.s. — bombed by German aeroplane, 28-iv.-15

Foch, Marshal (France) — 20th Corps under falls back, 20-viii.-14; commanding 9th Army interposed between 5th and 4th Armies, 27-viii.-14; instructed to attack towards Sézanne Fère, 4-ix.-14; carries Sézanne Plateau: attacks Fère, 9-ix.-14; at Fère-Champenoise, 10-ix.-14; enters Chalons, 11-ix.-14; 2nd and 10th Armies placed under, 30-ix.-14; at Doullens, 8-x.-14; created G.C.B., 1-xii.-14; commanding in Somme battle, 1-vii.-16; advances along Bray-Péronne road, 9-vii.-16; Chief of Staff, 15-v.-17; confers with War Cabinet in London, 23-xi.-17; to be member of Military Committee of Allied Political Council, 9-xi.-17; to remain

France (continued) :—

Military mission — under Col. Huguet arrives in London, 10-viii.-14

Ministry — M. Millerand, War Minister; M. Delcassé, Foreign Minister, 27-viii.-14; M. Delcassé resigns, 13-x.-15; Ministry resigns: Briand Cabinet formed, 28-x.-15; Gen. Roques succeeds Gen. Gallieni as War Minister, 16-iii.-16; Ministry reconstructed, 11-xii.-16; Gen. Lyautey resigns as War Minister, 14-iii.17; Ministry resigns, 17-iii.-17; Ribot Cabinet formed, 19-iii.-17; Adm. Lacaze resigns as Minister of Marine, 2-viii.-17; Painlevé Cabinet formed, 11-ix.-17; falls, 13-xi.-17; Clemenceau Cabinet formed, 16-xi.-17

Motor-car service — Bar-le-Duc—Verdun road —statistics, 31-iii.-16

Munitions — agreement with Great Britain, 8-x.-15; Minister appointed, 3-xi.-15

Security against unprovoked attacks by Germany — Marshal Foch dissatisfied with Peace Treaty guarantees, 6-v.-19; Treaties with Great Britain and United States: signed by Mr. Lloyd George and Pres. Wilson, 28-vi.-19

Shipping — requisitioned, 10-iii.-18

Socialists — to attend Stockholm Conference, 28-v.-17; passports refused, 1-vi.-17

War Council — reconstructed, 11-xii.-16; 12-xii.-16; 17-iii.-17

Yellow Book — issued, 1-xii.-14

France (Army) — preliminary concentration completed, 12-viii.-14; new line established, 1-iii.-15; operations: see various fronts and names of places

African army — transported, 30-vii.-14; 3-viii.-14

Algerian Corps — transferred to, 12-viii.-14; reinforcing at Dardanelles, 5-v.-15

Armies — **1st**: reaches Donon Crest, 14-viii.-14; at Schirmeck, 16-viii.-14; 16th Division, 8th Corps, takes Saarburg, 18-viii.-14; holding fast on Vosges front, 25-viii.-14; 4-ix.-14; covering Roye-Moreuil, 23-iii.-18; under Gen. Debeney, on Avre, 30-vi.-18; placed under Sir D. Haig, 28-vii.-18; attacking in battle of Amiens, 8-viii.-18; takes St. Quentin, 1-x.-18; Germans withdraw before, 5-xi.-18; — **2nd**: Gen. de Castelnau commanding; invades Lorraine, 16-viii.-14; attacking Mörchingen, 18-viii.-14; falls back, 19-viii.-14; covering Nancy, 4-ix.-14; Kaiser watches German attack on before Nancy, 5-ix.-14; reformed, 20-x.-14; attacks at Verdun, 20-viii.-17; under Gen. Hirschauer, on right of Gens. Fayolle, Maistre, and Castelnau Group, 30-vi.-18; relieved on Argonne front by Gen. Pershing's army, 22-ix.-18; march to Rhine begun, 17-xi.-18; — **3rd**: unsuccessfully engaged astride Belgian frontier, 22-viii.-14; falling back across Meuse, 26-viii.-14; Gen. Sarrail commanding; to attack westward from S.W. of Verdun, 4-ix.-14; relieved by British 5th, 20-i.-18; covering Noyon and Oise R., 23-iii.-18; under Gen. Humbert, at Nouvron, 30-vi.-18; strikes on German flank below Montdidier, 9-viii.-18; Germans withdraw before, 5-xi.-18; — **4th**: unsuccessfully engaged astride Belgian frontier, 22-viii.-14; 9th Army interposes, 27-viii.-14; to hold German 4th Army, 4-ix.-14; occupies Vitry, 10-ix.-14; advancing; takes Souain, 14-ix.-14; under Gen. Gouraud, E. of Reims, 30-vi.-18; holding Germans in battle positions, 15-vii.-18; on Argonne front, 22-ix.-18; Germans withdrawn before, 5-xi.-18; march to Rhine begun, 17-xi.-18; — **5th**: enters Belgium, 14-viii.-14; 1st Corps checks Prussian Guards at Dinant, 15-viii.-14; retires from

France (Army) :—

Armies (continued) :—

Charleroi, 22-viii.-14; 9th Army interposes, 27-viii.-14; defeats three German Corps, 29-viii.-14; to prepare attack northward, 4-ix.-14; passes through La Ferté Gaucher, 7-ix.-14; crosses Petit-Morin, 8-ix.-14; advance at Château-Thierry, 9-ix.-14; attacks Craonne Plateau, 14-ii.-14; 16-ix.-14; first Tanks in action with, 16-iv.-17; under Gen. Berthelot, W. of Reims, 30-vi.-18; commander changed, 14-x.-18; Germans withdraw before, 5-xi.-18; — **6th**: takes over in Somme Valley, 27-viii.-14; to attack towards Château-Thierry, 4-ix.-14; begins battle of Ourcq, 5-ix.-14; Germans driven back, 7-ix.-14; reinforced from Paris; Germans driven across Ourcq, 9-ix.-14; crosses Aisne, 13-ix.-14; carries line at Compiègne —Soissons, 14-ix.-14; driven back on Aisne, 15-ix.-14; clinging to German flank about Noyon, 16-ix.-14; regains ground between Soissons—Compiègne, 17-ix.-14; U.S. 2nd Division in position on front, 2-vi.-18; Gen. Degoutte to command, 15-vi.-18; at Marne R., 30-vi.-18; — **7th**: under Gen. Boissoudez, on right of Gens. Fayolle, Maistre, and Castelnau Group, 30-vi.-18; — **8th**: under Gen. Gérard, on right of Gens. Fayolle, Maistre, and Castelnau Group, 30-vi.-18; in new group for attack on Metz, 27-x.-18; march to Rhine begun, 17-xi.-18; — **9th**: Gen. Foch commanding; interposed between 5th and 4th Armies, 27-viii.-14; to attack towards Sézanne—Fère, 4-ix.-14; thrust back on right, 8-ix.-14; carries Sézanne Plateau, 9-ix.-14; advancing, 14-ix.-14; falls back on Reims, 17-ix.-14; 18-ix.-14; under Gen. Mitry, on Marne R., 30-vi.-18; holds Epernay, 17-vii.-18; — **10th**: under Gen. Maud'huy, brought up around Arras—Lens, 30-ix.-14; under Gen. Mangin, at Ourcq R., 30-vi.-18; reaches Mont de Paris, 18-vii.-18; Tanks engaged in area, 18-vii.-18; in new group for attacks on Metz, 27-x.-18; march to Rhine begun, 17-xi.-18

Re-grouped — under Gens. Fayolle, Maistre, and Castelnau, 30-vi.-18

Artillery — in action on Mte. Grappa, 13-xii.-17

Commander-in-Chief — Gen. Joffre appointed, 3-xii.-15; Gen. Nivelle appointed, 12-xii.-16; Gen. Pétain appointed, 15-v.-17

Corps — **1st**: checks Prussian Guard at Dinant, 15-viii.-14; reinforces at Verdun, 24-ii.-16; — **9th**: relieves British 1st Corps in Ypres salient, 27-x.-14; — **16th**: saves Kemmel and regains W. part of Wytschaete, 1-xi.-14; relieves U.S. 3rd Corps on Veslé, 8-ix.-18; — **17th**: in Verdun salient, 22-ix.-18; — **20th**: reinforces at Ypres, 4-xi.-14; at Verdun, 24-ii.-16; — **33rd**: mentioned in Army Orders, 9-v.-15; — Colonial Corps, 2nd: in Woevre, 22-ix.-18

Equipment — deficiency, 13-vii.-14

G.H.Q. — at Vitry-le-François, 25-viii.-14; at Beauvais, 10-i.-17; at Compiègne, 4-iv.-17; 15-v.-17

Gas: see under Gas

George V., King — visits; issues Order of the Day, 27-x.-15

Italy — troops arrive in, 3-xi.-17; Gen. Fayolle to command, 9-xi.-17

Staff, Chief of — Gen. de Castelnau appointed, 9-xii.-15; Gen. Pétain appointed, 29-v.-17; Gen. Foch appointed, 15-v.-17; to remain, 4-xii.-17

Tanks: see Tanks

France (Navy) — fleet to watch H.I.M.S. "Goeben" and protect transport of African Army, 3-viii.-14; at Malta, 12-viii.-14

Battleships and cruisers: see their names (index)

Dardanelles Squadron: placed under orders of Adm. Carden, 31-i.-15; command changed, 15-v.-15

2nd Cruiser Squadron — guarding Dover Straits, 3-viii.-14

Submarines: see Submarines

Syrian Squadron formed, 31-i.-15

T.B.s — 300: mined, 1-xi.-16; — 331: sunk, 17-vi.-15; — 333: sunk, 12-iii.-18

T.B.D.s — engage Austrian light naval forces in Adriatic, 15-v.-17; — "Aventurier": under Adm. Hood; engages German positions at Lombaertzyde, 30-x.-14; — "Bisson": sinks Austrian U3, 13-viii.-15; — "Bouclier": in action with German T.B.D.s 21-iii.-18; — "Boutefeu": mined, 15-v.-17; — "Branlebas": mined, 5-x.-15; 9-xi.-15; — "Capitaine Mehl": engagement with German T.B.D.s, 27-x.-17; — "Catapulte": sunk in collision, 18-v.-18; — "Dague": mined, 24-ii.-15; — "Etandard": sunk, 25-iv.-17; — "Fantassin": sunk, 5-vi.-16; — "Fourché": sunk, 21-vi.-16; — "Fresnel": aground at Boyana, 29-xii.-15; — "Intrépide": under Adm. Hood; engages German positions at Lombaertzyde, 30-x.-14; — "Magon": engagement with German T.B.D.s, 27-x.-17; 21-iii.-18; — "Mangini": enters Dardanelles, 10-xi.-18; — "Mehl": in action with German T.B.D.s, 21-iii.-18; — "Mousquet": sunk, 28-x.-14; — "Renaudin": sunk, 18-iii.-16; — "Yatagan": sunk, 7-xii.-16

France and Germany — territory not to be annexed if Britain remains neutral, 29-vii.-14; ultimatum as to neutrality, and French reply, 31-vii.-14; territory violated, 2-viii.-14; war declared; Ambassador leaves Paris, 3-viii.-14; French Ambassador leaves Berlin, 3-viii.-14

France and Italy — naval convention, 10-v.-15

France and United States — mission leaves Paris, 15-iv.-17; war affairs: organised by M. Tardieu, 19-vi.-18

Francilly—Selency — British take, 2-iv.-17; French take, 24-ix.-18

Francis Ferdinand, Archduke — assassinated, 28-vi.-14; body arrives at Trieste, 1-vii.-14; funeral, 4-vii.-14; result of inquiry, 13-vii.-14

Francis Joseph, Emperor of Austria — letter to Emperor William, 4-vii.-14; 5-vii.-14; Kaiser communicates peace views to, 1-xi.-16; death, 21-xi.-16

François, Gen. von — 1st Prussian Corps under retiring on Königsberg, 20-viii.-14; commands 8th Army, 8-x.-14; superseded 7-xi.-14; commands Prussian Reserve Corps, 24-xi.-14

"Franconia," H.M.T. — torpedoed, 4-x.-16

Frankenau — Germans defeated, 23-viii.-14

Frankfurt — air raid, 21-viii.-18

"Frankfurt," H.I.M.S. — surrenders, 21-xi.-18

"Franklyn," s.s. — sunk, 2-v.-18

Fransart — Anglo-French progress towards, 16-viii.-18

"Franz Fischer," s.s. — sunk, 1-ii.-16

Frasnoy — taken by British, 4-xi.-18

"Frauenlob," H.I.M.S. — sunk in Jutland battle, 31-v.-16

Frederick, Archduke — retired, 11-ii.-17

"Freedom of Seas" — conversation between Mr. Lloyd George and M. Clemenceau on British naval assistance to France, and Pres. Wilson's concurrence, mentioned by M. Clemenceau in French Chamber, 29-xii.-18

Frégicourt — French advance to outskirt 25-ix.-16; taken, 26-ix.-16; French progres 28-ix.-16

Freiburg — French air-raids, 5-xii.-14 15-iv.-15; 30-vii.-15; 6-ix.-15; Allied raid 14-iv.-17; 13-iii.-18

Freikofel — Italians take, 9-vi.-15

Fremantle, Adm. — in H.M.S. "Hibernia, 6-xi.-15

Frémicourt — fighting, 29-viii.-18

French, Lord — designated C.-in-C. of eventu B.E.F. to France, 30-vii.-14; at Boulogn 14-viii.-14; visits Pres. Poincaré, 15-viii.-14 confers with Gen. Joffre, 16-viii.-14; at I Cateau, 17-viii.-14; at Bavai, 24-viii.-14 confers with Gen. Joffre, 29-viii.-14; 1 Dammartin, 31-viii.-14; confers with Lor Kitchener in Paris, 1-ix.-14; at Mortcerf an Melun, 4-ix.-14; 5-ix.-14; at Coulommier 9-ix.-14; at Fère-en-Tardenois, 12-ix.-14 proposes transfer of British from Aisne 1 left flank of Allied line in West, 29-ix.-14 G.H.Q. transferred from Fère-en-Tardeno to Abbeville, 8-x.-14; transferred to S Omer, 12-x.-14; inspects H.A.C., 9-xi.-14 invested with O.M. by King, 3-xii.-14; M Churchill's second visit to, 7-xii.-14; Adm Hood visits, 13-xii.-14; receives messag from Mr. Churchill, 20-xii.-14; orders fo mation of 1st and 2nd Armies, 25-xii 14; decides on change in command (Lahore division, 26-xii.-14; confers wit Gen. Joffre at Chantilly, 27-xii.-14; propose amalgamation of British and Belgian armie 28-xii.-14; Mr. Churchill's telegram to, o development of Zeebrugge as U-Boat bas 2-i.-15; suggests offensive for recapture o Ostend and Zeebrugge, 3-i.-15; memorandur from War Council regarding possibility o stalemate in France and Flanders, 9-i.-15 Gen. Joffre's memorandum to regardin operations towards Ostend—Zeebrugge 19-i.-15; reports capture of 400 yards o trenches at Neuve Chapelle; also 75 prisoners, 10-iii.-15; in statement publishe in "The Times" says: "The protraction c the war depends entirely upon the supply c men and munitions," 27-iii.-15; War Offic direct diversion of 20 per cent. ammunitio to the Dardanelles, 22-iv.-15; German us of gas: reports uselessness of protes 4-v.-15; unlimited ammunition supply state ment, 14-v.-15; "Order of the Day, 30-ix.-15; retires from command of arm in France and Flanders, 15-xii.-15 appointed to Home Command, 15-xii.-15 farewell to army in France, 18-xii.-15 appointed Lord-Lieutenant of Ireland 5-v.-18

Dispatches — first, 9-ix.-14; of Sept. 1 and Oct. 8, 19-x.-14; Ypres, 20-xi.-14 Nov., 1914, to Feb., 1915, 16-ii.-15; (April 5, 16-iv.-15; Loos, 1-xi.-15

"French Prince," s.s. — sunk, 15-ii.-17

Frenzela Gorge — Austrian defeat abou 11-ii.-18

Frescati — French airmen bomb airshed 26-xii.-14

"Freshfield," s.s. — sunk, 5-viii.-18

Fresnes — German attacks, 11-vii.-15; Ge mans take, 7-iii.-16; Allied line E. of ε armistice, 11-xi.-18

Fresnoy — British carry, 3-v.-17; German recapture with heavy loss, 8-v.-17

Fresnoy-le-Petit — British take, 9-iv.-17

Fresnoy-les-Roye — Anglo-French progress t wards, 16-viii.-18

Freytag-Loringhoven, Gen. von (Germany) - appointed Quarter-Master General, 27-i.-15

Frezenberg — Germans take ridge, 8-v.-15 British take, 31-vii.-17; British progress N ef, 6-ix.-17; ground lost, 7-ix.-17

Fricourt — German attack repulsed, 3-vi.-16; British threaten, 1-vii.-16; taken, 2-vii.-16; trenches carried, 7-vii.-16

"Friedrich der Grosse," H.I.M.S. — passes into North Sea, 31-vii.-14; Adm. von Pohl's flag hoisted, 3-ii.-15; engine defects, 17-vii.-15; in Jutland battle, 31-v.-16; 1-vi.-16; mutiny in, 18 viii.-17; surrendered, 21-xi.-18

"Friedrich Karl," H.I.M.S. — sunk, 16-xi.-14

Friedrichshaven — British air-raid: Squad.-Cmdr. Briggs brought down, 21-xi.-14; French air-raid on, 28-iv.-15

Friedrichstadt — bridgehead attacked by Germans, 29-viii.-15; stormed, 3-ix.-15; Russian line lost up to, 5-ix.-17

Friedrich Wilhelm (New Guinea) — occupied, 24-ix.-14

"Frimaire," s.s. — sunk, 15-iii.-17

Frise — French lose, 28-i.-16; recover, 11-ii.-16; French capture, 1-vii.-16; Allies on line, 25-iii.-18

Frisian Coast — British naval light forces in action with German aircraft, 11-viii.-18

Friuli Plain — Austro-Germans enter, 27-x.-17

Froidement Farm — Germans gain and lose footing near, 1-vii.-17

Frommel, Gen. (Germany) — commands mixed group, 27-ix.-14

Fruges — United States 2nd Army Corps formed at, 25-vi.-18

Fryatt, Capt. — in s.s. "Brussels" escapes from U133, 28-iii.-15; captured by German T.B. and taken into Zeebrugge, 23-vi.-16; court-martialled and shot, 27-vii.-16

"Fulda," German minesweeper — sunk, 14-v.-17

"Fulmer," s.s. — attacked by aircraft, 6-ix.-15

Fumban — Allies take, 2-xii.-15

Fumin Wood — French recovery, 22-vi.-16; 25-vi.-16; Germans gain footing, 11-vii.-16; French recover, 28-x.-16

Funchal — U-Boats bombard, 3-xii.-16; 12-xii.-17

Furceni — Allies evacuate, 11-viii.-17

"Furious," H.M.S. — laid down, 8-vi.-15; launched, 15-viii.-16; escorts airmen in bombing of Tondern, 19-vii.-18

Furka — Bulgarians attack: lose 8,000 men, 11-xii.-15

Furnes — German aeroplane bombards, 2-xi.-14; German long-range bombardment, 8-xii.-14

"Fürst Bismarck," H.I.M.S. — attacked by E1, 18-x.-14

G.

Gaba Tepe — Turkish post bombarded, 15-iv.-15; British land, 25-iv.-15

"Gadsby," s.s. — sunk, 1-vii.-15

"Gafsa," s.s. — sunk, 16-vi.-16

"Gafsa," s.s. — sunk, 28-iii.-17

"Gaillardia," H.M.S. — mined, 22-iii.-18

Galata Bridge (Constantinople) — blown up, 1-viii.-15

"Galatea," H.M.S. — shoots down L7, 4-v.-16; attacked, 12-vii.-16

Galatz. — LZ101 raids, 25-xii.-16

"Galcka," H.S. — mined, 28-x.-16

Galicia — Russians enter Sokol, 14-viii.-14; take Tarnopol: Austrians fall back on Lemberg, 27-viii.-14; battle of Lemberg, 1-ix.-14; Austrians defeated, 2-ix.-14; Russians holding Drohobycz oilfields, 14-ix.-14; advance on Przemysl, 16-ix.-14; Jaroslav attacked, 20-ix.-14; Russians invest Przemysl, 22-ix.-14; Jaroslav falls, 23-ix.-14; Krosno and Dukla Pass taken, 28-ix.-14; oilfields in Russian hands, 28-ix.-14; Russians fall back, 10-x.-14; Austrians advance, 4-x.-14; Russians retire, 6-x.-14; Austrian defeat at Jaroslav, 4-xi.-14; Russians investing

Galicia (continued) :—
Przemysl, 11-xi.14; cavalry N. of Cracow, 12-xi.-14; 13-xi.-14; Austrians defeated between Cracow—Czestochowa, 22-xi.-14; Russian successes towards Cracow, 28-xi.-14; 1-xii.-14; 3-xii.-14; take Wielitza, 4-xii.-14; bombard N. Cracow forts, 7-xii.-14; Austrian counter-attack: Russians fall back to Miditza—Dunayetz rivers, 8-xii.-14; Austrians seize Dukla Pass: Russians retire almost to R. San, 12-xii.-14; battle for Cracow ending, 13-xii.-14; Austrian sortie from Przemysl, 15-xii.-14; regain Lupkov Pass, 18-xii.-14; sorties at Przemysl fail, 18-xii.-14; 22-xii.-14; defeated at Tarnov, 25-xii.-14; offensive broken, 26-xii.-14; retreat, 29-xii.-14; 31-xii.-14 advance through Yablonitza Pass, 12-ii.-15; take Nadvorna, 14-ii.-15; retake Kolomea, 16-ii.-15; heavy fighting, 17-ii.-15; advance near Tarnov, 18-ii.-15; sortie at Przemysl, 19-ii.-15; battle at Stanislau and Dolina, 22-ii.-15; Stanislau recaptured, 3-iii.-15; Russians cross Bistritza, 5-iii.-15; Russians penetrate outer defences of Przemysl, 13-iii.-15; break Austrian line near Smolnik, 15-iii.-15; last Austrian sortie from Przemysl, 18-iii.-15; defence ending: further Russian success near Smolnik, 20-iii.-15; Przemysl falls: Russians take 126,000 prisoners and 700 guns, 22-iii.-15; Austro-German mass offensive from Dunayetz—San Rs.: Gorlice—Tarnov, 1-v.-15; take Gorlice, Ciezkovice and cross Biala R.: Russians retire on Visloka R., 2-v.-15; Dunayetz crossing begun, 3-v.-15; Austrians enter Tarnov, 5-v.-15; cross Visloka R. at Jaslo: Russians retire on R. San, 7-v.-15; Austro-Germans checked at Sanok, 10-v.-15; Prussian Guard takes Jaroslav, 14-v.-15; Kolomea recovered, 14-v.-15; Nadvorna recovered, 15-v.-15; Austro-Germans cross San, 17-v.-15; Russians driven from Sieniava, 18-v.-15; Przemysl bombarded, 20-v.-15; Zajrody taken, 25-v.-15; Sieniava recaptured, 17-v.-15; Przemysl retaken by Austro-Germans, 3-vi.-15; advance between San and Moscica, 13-vi.-15; Russians retreat from Grodek line, 19-vi.-15; Austro-Germans take Rava Russka and Zolkiev, 20-vi.-15; occupy Halicz, 27-vi.-15; storm Gnila—Lipa line and cross near Rohatyn; advance from Tomaszov; Russians retreat, 30-vi.-15; retire from Gnila—Lipa to Zlota—Lipa line, 3-vii.-15; Austro-Germans reach Zlota—Lipa line, 4-vii.-15; held, 11-vii.-15; fighting, 14-viii.-15 27-viii.-15; Russian success on Strypa R., 30-viii.-15; Austrians enter Brody, 1-ix.-15; advance, 2-ix.-15; Russians on Sereth R., 2-ix.-15; Austrians reach Sereth, 3-ix.-15; Russians forced across border between Brody—Dubno, 6-ix.-15; victory near Tarnopol—Trembovla, further successes, 8-ix.-15; 9-ix.-15; Austrian offensive fails, 12-ix.-15; Russian advance at Tarnopol, 13-ix.-15; and along Sereth, 14-ix.-15; Germans driven across Strypa, 15-ix.-15; Russians pierce line at Hajvoronka; cross Strypa, 11-x.-15; fighting, 12-x.-15; 14-x.-15; Russians take Chartorysk, 18-x.-15; success at Tarnopol, 30-x.-15; Polish Legion fights as Austrian unit on Linsingen's front, 1-xi.-15; Russians driven out of Chartorysk, 15-xi.-15; Austro-Germans driven across Styr, 1-xii.-15; Russians repulsed, 17-xii.-15; Russian offensive, 24-xii.-15; 31-xii.-15; 1-i.-16; 5-i.-16; take Chartorysk, 7-i.-16; struggle for, 8-i.-16; cross W. bank of Dneister, 9-ii.-16; Russian advance, 3-vi.-16; progress, 4-vi.-16; 29-vi.-16; advance from Kolomea, 4-vii.-16; Germans retreat to Koropiec R., 6-vii.-16; Gen. Lechitsky at

Germany (Army):—
  Armies (continued):—
    front, 5-ix.-15; Gen. von Gallwitz in
    command, 30-ix.-15; invades Serbia,
    6-x.-15; crosses Danube, 9-x.-15; Gen.
    von Winckler commanding, 10-viii.-16; in
    action, 15-ix.-18; on Save–Danube line,
    3-xi.-18; — **12th:** formed in Poland; Gen.
    Gallwitz in command, 7-viii.-15; Gen.
    von Fabeck takes over, 17-ix.-15;
    22-ix.-15; dissolved, 3-x.-16; — **14th:** Gen.
    O. von Below in command, 9-ix.-17; com-
    mand lapses, 23-i.-18; — **17th:** formed
    under Gen. von Below, 1-ii.-18; attacking
    in Somme battle, 21-iii.-18; — **18th** (new):
    Gen. von Hutier in command, 27-xii.-17;
    in new army group, 6-viii.-18; — **19th:**
    formed under Gen. von Bothmer, 4-ii.-18
  Artillery — long-range bombardment of
    Paris, 23-iii.-18; 24-iii.-18; 25-iii.-18;
    29-iii.-18; 27-v.-18; 5-viii.-18; 9-viii.-18
  Bavarians — at Hollebeke, 30-x.-14; 15th
    Chasseurs battalion: participate in Turco-
    German Caucasus expedition until Armis-
    tice, 7-vi.-18; begin homeward march from
    Caucasus, 6-xi.-18
  Casualties: see Appendix I.
  Coast defence — Gen. von Heeringen to
    command, 28-viii.-16; H.Q. lapses, 16-xi.-18
  Corps — Alpine (Prusso-Bavarian): formed
    for service in Tirol, 21-v.-15; transferred
    to Serbian front, 13-x.-15; arrives,
    30-x.-15; reinforced in Champagne,
    10-iv.-16; on Verdun front, 28-v.-16; on
    Isonzo front, 15-ix.-17; — "Asia Corps":
    formed, 2-vii.-17; remnants interned at
    Haida Pasha, Hadikof, and Prinkipo,
    17-xi.-18; — Beskid Corps: formed, 28-iii.-
    15; — Cavalry: three on right wing of
    6th Army, 15-x.-14; — naval: in right
    wing of 4th Army, 17-x.-14; — Reserve:
    three in right wing of 4th Army, 17-x.-14;
    — **1st** Corps takes Bialystok, 26-viii.-15; —
    2nd (Cavalry): broken up, 28-xii.-14; —
    3rd: engaged on German right (W.
    front), 17-x.-14; Gen von Lüttwitz super-
    seded in command by Gen. von Kraewel,
    25-xi.-14; withdrawn from Verdun front,
    16-iii.-16; Gen. von Lüttwitz succeeds
    Gen. von Lockow, 25-xi.-16; — **4th:** trans-
    ferred from 1st Army front to 6th
    Army, 28-ix.-14; Gen. von Kraewel com-
    manding, 25-ii.-17; — **4th** (Cavalry):
    command broken up, 14-xii.-14; — **5th**
    (Cavalry): formed on Dvina front,
    21-viii.-15; — **6th** (Cavalry): formed,
    18-viii.-15; — **10th:** Gen. von Lüttwitz
    supersedes Gen. von Emmich, 22-xii.-15;
    arrives in Champagne from Russia,
    25-x.-15; — **13th:** reinforces on Cham-
    pagne front, 28-ix.-15; — **15th:** in
    right wing of 4th Army, 17-x.-14; Gen.
    Ilse to command, 25-v.-17; — **17th:**
    engaged at Grojetz, 9-x.-14; — **19th:** at
    Lille, 12-x.-14; — **21st:** Gen. von Hutier
    succeeds Gen. F. von Below, 4-iv.-15; —
    22nd to **27th** reserve corps formed,
    25-viii.-14; — **24th:** from Ypres reinforces
    Mackensen at Lask-Pabience, 30-xi.-14; —
    25th: with 3rd Prussian Guard
    Division: heavily engaged at Rzgov,
    21-xi.-14; cut off: break through Russian
    line at Brzezany, 24-xi.-14; Gen. Grömer
    commanding, 20-xii.-17; — **39th, 40th,**
    and **41st:** formed, 24-xii.-14; — 41st re-
    inforces 11th Army in Galicia, 16-iv.-15
  Divisions — Baltic: landed at Hangö,
    3-iv.-18; — **1st.** (Landwehr): captures
    outer forts of Grodno, 1-ix.-15; — **5th**
    (Brandenburg) from Aisne: reinforces on
    Champagne front, 24-ix.-15; costly attacks
    at Douaumont in Verdun battle, 25-ii.-16;
    on Isonzo front, 15-ix.-17; — **11th**

Germany (Army):—
  Divisions (continued):—
    (Landwehr), 22-viii.-15; — **105th:** trai
    ferred to Black Sea coast, 1-xii.-15
  East, in — Gen. von Hindenburg appoint
    C.-in-C., 1-xi.-14
  G.H.Q. at Luxemburg, 30-viii.-14;
    Charleville, 28-ix.-14; at Thielt: bomb
    by British aeroplane, 1-xi.-14; at Mézièr
    —Charleville: bombed by French airme
    14-iv.-15; moved to Pless, 4-v.-1
    9-ix.-16; transferred to Kreuznach, 19-i
    17; Kaiser at, 8-xi.-16; Adm. von Sche
    visits, 22-xi.-16; Count Hertling's men
    randum on military functions in politic
    decisions, 12-i.-18; moved to Avesn
    18-iii.-18; counting on "victory" with a
    of reinforcements of 200,000 men fr
    other fronts, 30-vi.-18; transferred
    Cassel, 13-xi.-18; premeditated devastati
    in France: M. Klotz before Paris Pea
    Conference on, 10-ii.-19
  Groups — new: formed on E. fro
    9-ii.-15; 5-viii.-15; — Beseler gro
    formed, 21-vii.-15; dissolved, 20-viii.-1
    — Crown Prince's group: formed
    W. front, 26-ix.-15; — Gallw
    group: formed, 19-vii.-16; dissolve
    28-viii.-16; formed at Verdun, 1-i.-18;
    Kieff group: Gen. Count Kirchbach co
    manding, 8-viii.-18; Marshal von Eichho
    assumes command, 31-iii.-18; — Mackens
    group in Rumania: dissolved, 1-vii.-18;
    Tirol group broken up, 15-vi.-18;
    W. group: formed, 28-viii.-16
  High Command — requests Enver Pash
    withdrawal from all Caucasus territori
    save Kars, Batum, and Ardahan, 9-vi.-18
  Landsturm called up, 15-viii.-14; demobilis
    tion and dissolution, 31-xii.-18
  Officers — Hindenburg issues manifesto
    behalf, 25-xii.-18
  Operations: see various fronts and names
    places
  Peace offer — order to be issued with: ca
    for unrelaxed effort, 8-xii.-16
  "Pill-boxes" — first encountered, 16-viii.-
  Propaganda service — for "enlightenment
    of troops at front: created, 9-vii.-17; i
    structions issued, 25-vii.-17; 29-vii.-17
  Prussian Guard Corps — reinforces 6
    Army, 23-ix.-14; reinforces new Germ
    11th Army in Galicia, 16-iv.-15; returns
    6th Army, 2-ix.-15; command: chang
    24-i.-17; 1st and 2nd Divisions on Russi
    front, 19-vii.-17; Prince Eitel Friedrich
    command of 1st Division, 20-viii.-18;
    Reserve Corps: transferred from W. to
    front, 26-viii.-14; merged in Gen. v
    Gallwitz's new army group, 9-ii.-15; rece
    stituted on E. front, 17-iv.-16; caval
    division transferred to Poland, 16-vii.-15
  Quarter-master General — Gen. von Freyt
    Loringhoven appointed, 27-i.-15; Ge
    Ludendorff appointed, 29-viii.-16
  Reinforcements — of 200,000 men fr
    Austria, Ukraine, Palestine, &c., 30-vi.-
  Tactics — front line lightly held: policy fi
    applied on Western front, 16-viii.-17
  Tanks — messages to have priority, 8-ix.-1
  Soviet formed at Malines, 11-xi.-18; order
    to obey officers, 12-xi.-18
  Staff — Chief: Gen. von Falkenhayn co
    firmed, 3-xi.-14; Gen. von Hindenbu
    appointed, 29-viii.-16
  Uniform — "field-grey": Kaiser decrees u
    in peace as well as war, 21-ix.-15
Germany (Navy) — Fleet returns from N
    way, 26-vii.-14; warships abroad "warned
    26-vii.-14; mobilises at Kiel, 29-vii.-1
    operations against French N. coast to
    disputed, 3-viii.-14; activity in North S

Germany (Navy):—
T.B.D.s (continued) :—
— G88: torpedoed, 7.-iv.-17; — G101, 103, 104, and V106: sink 6 merchant ships and convoying destroyer and trawlers, 12.-xii.-17; — G102: damaged, 15.-ii.-18; — G194: sunk, 25.-iii.-16; — G196: sunk, 26.-vii.-15; — S20: sunk, 5.-vi.-17; — S22: mined, 25.-iii.-16; — S27: mined, 16.-v.-17; — S33: sunk, 4.-x.-18; — S35: sunk, 31.-v.-16; — S90: sinks Japanese cruiser "Takchiho," 17.-x.-14; — S115: sunk, 17.-x.-14; — S116: sunk, 6.-x.-14; — S117, 118, and 119: sunk, 17.-x.-14; — V4: sunk in Jutland battle, 31.-v.-16; — V25: in Gulf of Bothnia, 7.-ix.-14; — V26: rescues part of crew of H.I.M.S. "Magdeburg," 26.-viii.-14; — V27 and 29: sunk in Jutland battle, 31.-v.-16; — V30: mined, 21.-xi.-18; — V48: sunk in Jutland battle, 31.-v.-16; — V63: tows U93 to Wilhelmshaven, 11.-v.-17; — V69: in action with British light forces, 23.-i.-17; leaves Ymuiden, 11.-ii.-17; —V187: sunk, 28.-viii.-14; — V191: sunk, 17.-xii.-15; — V191: sunk by British submarine, 17.-xii.-15
Torpedoes — number manufactured and fired, 30.-ix.-18
Transports — two sunk in Falkland Islands battle by H.M.S. "Bristol" and A.M.C. "Macedonia," 8.-xii.-14; one sunk in Baltic, 4.-vi.-15; 8.-x.-15; 5 sunk and one driven ashore in Baltic, 16.-x.-15
Trawler outposts — 5th Light Cruiser Squadron raids: 14 captured 1 sunk, 6.-x.-15
U-Boats: see under Submarines — German
Vessels: see their names (index)
Germany and Russia — telegrams exchanged without effect; Tsar seeks to stop general mobilisation, 29.-vii.-14; Russian proposal to Germany to stop mobilising if Austria waived demands touching Serbian Monarchy not communicated to Vienna, 30.-vii.-14; Russia summoned to stop mobilising, 31.-vii.-14; Germany declares war, 1.-viii.-14
Bolshevists — Envoy Joffe expelled from Berlin, 5.-xi.-18; transfers money to Socialist Cohn for revolutionary propaganda, 6.-xi.-18; arms purchased with Bolshevist money, 21.-x.-18
Brest-Litovsk peace: see under Peace — Russia and Central Powers
Gevgeli — Bulgarians enter, 12.-xii.-15; French carry first Bulgarian lines on heights W. of, 10.-x.-16; taken, 22.-ix.-18; Vardar Valley captured from Gradsko to, 24.-ix.-18
Gevgeli—Doiran — British in action, 30.-x.-15
"G. Garibaldi," Italian cruiser — sunk, 8.-vii.-15
"Ghazee," s.s. — sunk, 4.-ii.-17
Gheluvelt — German attacks beaten off, 29.-x.-14; ground gained E. of, 29.-x.-14; lost: retaken by 2nd Worcesters, 31.-x.-14; gallant British resistance to desperate Prussian Guard attack, 11.-xi.-14; British progress towards, 26.-x.-17; occupied, 29.-ix.-18
Gheluvelt—Landvoorde — German 15th Corps fighting at, 30.-x.-14
Ghent — entered by Germans, 12.-x.-14; Allies nearing, 3.-xi.-18; Belgians on line, 9.-xi.-18; enter, 10.-xi.-18; Allied line at Armistice, 11.-xi.-18
Ghislenghien — Allied line at Armistice, 11.-xi.-18
Ghistelles — British air-raid, 16.-ii.-15; German airship sheds bombed, 2.-vii.-15; French aeroplanes bomb, 31.-v.-17; air camps bombarded, 3.-vi.-17; German air-raider brought down, 24.-ix.-17; British air-raid, 4.-i.-18

Ghoraniyeh — Turkish attacks near bridge, 11.-iv.-18
"Ghurka," H.M.S. — sinks U8, 4.-iii.-15
Giardina, Gen. (Italy) — member of Versailles Committee, 8.-ii.-18
"Gibel-Hamam," s.s. — sunk, 14.-ix.-18
Gibeon — Germans defeated by Union forces, 28.-iv.-15
"Gibraltar," s.s. — sunk, 12.-ix.-17
Giffécourt — French take, 3.-iv.-17
Ginchy — British advance towards, 18.-viii.-16; 24.-viii.-16; progress N.W. of, 27.-viii.-16; German attack round, 31.-viii.-16; British recovery, 1.-ix.-16; gained and lost, 3.-ix.-16; British hold outskirts, 5.-ix.-16; captured 9.-ix.-16; German counter fails, 10.-ix.-16
"Gipsy," H.M.S. — assists in destruction of U48, 24.-xi.-17
"Giralda," s.s. — sunk, 28.-viii.-18
Girba — Senussi defeated, 4.-ii.-17
"Girdleness," s.s. — sunk, 2.-v.-18
"Gisella," s.s. — mined, 17.-iv.-17
Giudicaria — Austro-German attack repulsed 3.-xi.-17
Giurgiu — captured, 27.-xi.-16
Givenchy — British left at, 15.-x.-14; violent attack, 7.-xi.-14; five days' battle begun 18.-xii.-14; Indians attack, 19.-xii.-14; Germans take part of, 20.-xii.-14; retaken by British, 20.-xii.-14; British support Indians and re-establish line, 21.-xii.-14; battle dying down, 22.-xii.-14; secured by British 22.-xii.-14; recapture of positions completed 23.-xii.-14; British repulse attack, 25.-i.-15; Allied line E. of pushed forward; British co-operate in French advance on right 13.-ii.-15; British take trenches, 3.-vi.-15 4.-vi.-15; British attack N.E. of: fail to hold 15.-vi.-15; feint attack, 25.-ix.-15; wood Germans gain footing in British line 21.-ii.-16; British recovery, 22.-ii.-16; German attack: British trenches seized, 22.-vi.-16 Germans enter; expelled, 9.-iv.-18; German attacks round defeated, 18.-iv.-18; trenches recovered, 19.-iv.-18
Givenchy-en-Gohelle — French progress in wood, 10.-x.-15; British attack at, 9.-iv.-17 take, 13.-iv.-17
Givenchy — Neuve Chapelle — Fauquissart - British retire on line, 22.-x.-14
Givet — falls, 31.-viii.-14
Givet—Longwy — French armies unsuccessfully engaged, 22.-viii.-14
"Gladiator," s.s. — sunk, 19.-viii.-15
"Gladys Royle," s.s. — sunk, 9.-i.-17
"Glasgow," H.M.S. — escapes from Coronel battle, 1.-xi.-14; with H.M.S. "Cornwall" sinks H.I.M.S. "Leipzig" off Falkland Islands, 8.-xii.-14; with H.M.S. "Kent" and A.M.C. "Orama" sinks H.I.M.S. "Dresden" off Juan Fernandez, 14.-iii.-15
"Glatton," H.M.S. — blown up, 16.-ix.-18
Glatz — M. Max interned, 12.-x.-14; transferred to Celle, 27.-xi.-15
"Glaucus," s.s. — sunk by U-Boat, 3.-vi.-18
"Gleaner of the Sea," H.M. drifter - destroys, UB3, 24.-iv.-16
"Glenalmond," s.s. — sunk, 9.-iv.-16
"Glenamoy," s.s. — attacked by U-Boat 1.-ii.-18
"Glenarm Head," s.s. — sunk, 4.-i.-18
"Glenart Castle," H.S. — mined, 1.-iii.-18 sunk, 26.-ii.-18
"Glenartney," s.s. — sunk, 5.-ii.-18
"Glenbridge," s.s. — torpedoed, 27.-xi.-17
"Glencarron," s.s. — sunk, 19.-ii.-18
"Glencliffe," s.s. — sunk, 12.-iv.-17
"Glencluny," s.s. — sunk, 27.-iv.-17
Glencorse Wood — British enter, 10.-viii.-17 back in, 11.-viii.-17; British attack, 16.-viii.-17; fierce fighting, 24.-viii.-17; take 20.-ix.-17

" **Glenfoyle**," H.M. special service ship — sunk, 18-ix.-17

" **Glengyle**," s.s. — sunk, 1-i.-16

" **Glenlee**," s.s. — sunk, 9-viii.-18

" **Glenmoor**," s.s. — sunk, 6-xi.-15

" **Glenogle**," s.s. — sunk, 27-iii.-17

" **Glenstrae**," s.s. — sunk, 28-vii.-17

" **Glitra**," s.s. — sunk, 20-x.-14

" **Gloaming**," s.v. — captured and sunk, 26-viii.-18

" **Glorious**," H.M.S. — laid down, 1-v.-15; launched, 20-iv.-16; commissioned, 14-x.-16

" **Gloucester**," H.M.S. — sights H.I.M.S. " Goeben " and " Breslau," 6-viii.-14; abandons chase, 7-viii.-14; in 2nd Light Cruiser Squadron, 28-xii.-14

" **Gloucester Castle**," H.S. — torpedoed, 30-iii.-17

" **Gloxinia**," Tyne trawler — sunk, 1-iv.-15

" **Gneisenau**," H.I.M.S. — ordered to await instructions, 6-vii.-14; Admiral Cradock ordered to concentrate a force to meet, 14-ix.-14; bombards Papeete, 22-ix.-14; sinks French gunboat " Zélée," 22-ix.-14; in Coronel battle, 1-xi.-14; sunk, 8-xii.-14

Gnila—Lipa — Russians opposite Halicz, 4-ix.-16; Germans attack, 19-x.-16

" **Goathland**," s.s. — sunk, 4-vii.-17

" **Goeben**," H.I.M.S. — off Syrian coast, 28-vi.-14; ordered to Pola, 6-vii.-14; Brindisi, 1-viii.-14; ordered to Constantinople, 3-viii.-14; bombards Bône and Philippeville; out-distances British warships, 4-viii.-14; at Messina: ordered to Pola or Atlantic, 5-viii.-14; leaves for Constantinople; chased, 6-viii.-14; challenged by H.M.S. " Gloucester "; escapes, 7-viii.-14; coals at Denusa, 8-viii.-14; in Dardanelles, 10-viii.-14; in Black Sea, 22-ix.-14; escape: Adm. Troubridge recalled for inquiry, 19-ix.-14; acquitted by Court-Martial, 14-xi.-14; Russian Black Sea fleet engages, 18-xi.-14; bombards Batum, 11-xii.-14; long-range action off Crimea, 3-iv.-15; bombards Black Sea ports; sinks H.S. " Ypered," 5-vii.-15; bombed by British airmen, 9-vii.-17; sinks H.M. monitor " Raglan ": driven ashore and attacked by British aircraft, 20-i.-18; refloated: towed to Constantinople, 27-i.-18; interned, 5-xii.-18

Goethals, Gen. (U.S.) — Director of Purchase, Storage, and Traffic, 16-iv.-18

" **Golconda**," s.s. — safeguard for Austrian passengers: requested by Austria against danger from own U-Boats, 7-xii.-15; sunk, 3-vi.-16

Goldap — Russians take, 10-xi.-14

Gold Coast — force landed at Lome, Togoland, 12-viii.-14

" **Goldfinch**," H.M.S. — wrecked, 19-ii.-15

" **Goldmouth**," H.M. oiler — sunk, 31-iii.-16

" **Goliath**," H.M.S. — bombards Dar-es-Salaam, 2-i.-15; sunk, 13-v.-15

Golitzin, Prince (Russia) — becomes Premier, 8-i.-17

" **Golo II**," French auxiliary — torpedoed, 22-viii.-17

Goltz, Marshal von der (Germany) — appointed Governor-General of occupied Belgium, 23-viii.-14; superseded, 23-x.-14; assumes Turco-German command in Mesopotamia, 24-xi.-15; inspects Turkish lines before Kut, 15-i.-16; death, 19-iv.-16

Golubovitch, M. (Ukraine) — elected President, 20-xi.-17

Gombin—Lodz — Russians retire on, 15-xi.-14

Gomel — entered, 1-iii.-18

Gomiécourt — approaches to: taken by French, 7-xi.-16; taken by British, 23-viii.-18

Gommecourt — British raid trenches, 23-iii.-16; attack on 20-mile front, 1-vii.-16; reached but not held, 1-vii.-16; occupied, 27-ii.-17;

Gommecourt (continued) :—
British advance E. of, 28-ii.-17; German retreat, 4-iii.-17; British progress E. and N.E. of, 13-iii.-17

Gonnelieu — British at, 20-iv.-17; positions penetrated, 30-xi.-17; recovered, 1-xii.-17

Gontrode — Zeppelin sheds bombed, 25-v.-15

Goodenough, F. Comm. — in command of H.M.S. " Southampton " visiting Stavanger, 10-viii.-14; commands Light Cruiser Squadron in battle of Heligoland Bight, 28-viii.-14

" **Good Hope**," H.M.S. — Adm. Cradock's flag transferred to, 13-viii.-14; sunk in Coronel battle, 1-xi.-14

" **Good Hope**," s.s. — sunk, 19-x.-17

" **Goodwood**," s.s. — sunk, 21-viii.-17

" **Goorkha**," H.S. — mined, 17-x.-17

Goremykin, M. (Russia) — succeeded as Premier, 1-ii.-16; arrested, 13-iii.-17

Gorizia — Italians advance on, 24-v.-15; attack, 7-vii.-15; success, 20-vii.-15; retire near, 28-vii.-15; success near, 1-xi.-15; assaults on, 20-xi.-15; progress towards, 30-xi.-15; centre forced back N.W. of, 27-iii.-16; recovery, 28-iii.-16; falls to Italians, 9-viii.-16; King of Italy visits, 21-viii.-16; advance E. of, 20-ix.-16; heights E. of cleared, 1-xi.-16; Austrians attack E. of, 9-ii.-17; Italian line re-established, 11-ii.-17; Austrian progress S. of, 26-iii.-17; Italian attack, 14-v.-17; progress in E., 15-v.-17; further gains, 20-v.-17; fighting E. of, 27-v.-17; Italian successes, 28-viii.-17; heavy fighting N.E. of, 4-ix.-17; 5-ix.-17; Italian pressure, 7-ix.-17; falls, 28-x.-17

Gorlice — Germans take, 2-v.-15

Gorlice—Tarnov — Austro-Germans mass offensive, 1-v.-15

Görlitz — Greek 4th Army Corps sent to after surrendering, 27-viii.-16

Gorringe, Gen. — defeats Turks and Arabs at Nasiriyeh, 24-vii.-15; commands Kut Relief Force, 12-iii.-16; takes Turkish positions 20 miles from Kut, 5-iv.-16; carries Dujailar Redoubt, 19-v.-16; succeeded by Gen. Maude, 11-vii.-16

" **Gorsemore**," s.s. — sunk, 22-ix.-18

Goschen, Sir E. — " scrap of paper," interview, 4-viii.-14

Gothland — German mine-layer " Albatross " chased ashore, 2-vii.-15; German warships off, 2-iii.-18

Goudberg — Canadians capture, 6-xi.-17

Gough, Gen. — commands Cavalry Corps, 2nd Division, 9-x.-14; commands 7th Division, 27-v.-15; commands from La Boisselle to Serre in Somme battle, 2-vii.-16; relieves French 3rd Army, 20-i.-18; to organise new defence lines, 28-iii.-18

Gounaris, M. (Greece) —forms Ministry, 9-iii.-15; majority in Greek elections, 19-xii.-15

Gouraud, Gen. (France) — wounded, 30-vi.-15; Gen. Sarrail takes over command of Dardanelles force, 6-viii.-15; commanding 4th Army in second battle of Marne, 15-vii.-18; retakes Prunay, 18-vii.-18; re-occupies old positions E. of Reims, 22-vii.-18; commands 4th Army Corps, 22-ix.-18

Gouy — taken, 3-x.-18

Gouzeaucourt — British take, 12-iv.-17; progress N. of, 17-iv.-17; British positions penetrated; Germans driven back, 30-xi.-17; British reach edge of, 9-ix.-18; attack on 16-mile front, 18-ix.-18; taken, 28-ix.-18

Gouzeaucourt Wood — British take, 12-ix.-18

" **Governor**," s.s. — sunk, 14-iii.-17

Goworowo — battle begun, 4-viii.-15

" **Gowrie**," s.s. — sunk, 10-x.-17

Gradekovo — Bolshevist raid, 19-viii.-18

Great Britain:—

Ministry (Lloyd George) (continued) :—
Reconstruction; Mr. Churchill: munitions;
Mr. Montagu: India, 17-vii.-17; Mr.
Henderson resigns: succeeded by Mr.
Barnes, 11-viii.-17; Lord Milner: war
secretary, 18-iv.-18; Lord Rothermere
resigns as air minister: Sir W. Weir
appointed, 26-iv.-18

War Cabinet — Mr. Lloyd George urges
Mr. Asquith to establish, 1-xii.-16; Mr.
Asquith resigns, 5-xii.-16; Mr. Lloyd
George forms, 11-xii.-16; French
ministers confer in London, 28-v.-17;
U.S. mission confers, 20-xi.-17; Sir E.
Carson enters, 17-vii.-17; resigns,
21-i.-18; Mr. Chamberlain joins, 18-iv.-18

Munitions: see Munitions

Munitions, Ministry of — Adm. Bacon
transferred to, 11-i.-18

National service — Government decide to
institute, 18-xii.-16; scheme, 6-ii.-17

National Relief Fund — reached £4,001,000,
2-xii.-14

Navy: see Navy

Parliament — opened, 11-xi.-14; prorogued,
18-ix.-14; reassembles, 2-ii.-15; opposition
offer support, 2-viii.-15; secret sitting: on
London air-raid, 9-vii.-17; prorogued,
King's message: "The vigorous prosecution of the war must be our sole
endeavour," 22-xii.-16; dissolved, 25-xi.-18;
200 members send telegram to Mr. Lloyd
George, 8-iv.-19; reply by Mr. Lloyd
George: another telegram from 200
members, 9-iv.-19

Women members — Bill passes Lords,
15-xi.-18

Press — to be influenced in German sense,
12-vii.-14; Press Bureau formed, 11-viii.-
14; Censor's powers to be limited,
25-xi.-14; Press Bureau closed, 30-iv.-19

Propaganda — Lord Beaverbrook minister,
10-ii.-18; Hindenburg issues warning
against, 2-ix.-18

Registration, national — Bill introduced,
29-vi.-15; passed, 14-vii.-15; register taken,
15-viii.-15

Riots — anti-German: in Liverpool, 10-v.-15;
in London, 10-v.-15; 11-v.-15; 12-v.-15

Royal House — foreign titles abolished,
9-vi.-17; assumes name of Windsor,
17-vii.-17

Royal Marines: see Royal Marines

Shipping: see under Shipping

Trading with enemy (neutral countries) —
memorandum, 24-vi.-15; proclamation,
29-ii.-16

Great Britain and France — Lord Derby
appointed ambassador, 18-iv.-18

Great Britain and Germany — overtures
(1912): Mr. H. H. Asquith on, 2-x.-14

Great Bursted — Zeppelin brought down,
23-ix.-16

" Great City," s.s. — torpedoed, 19-vi.-17

" Greatham," s.s. — sunk, 22-i.-18

" Greavesash," s.s. — sunk, 26-ii.-18

Greece:—

Allied Powers — Britain offers Cyprus in
return for participation, 17-x.-15; refuses,
21-x.-15; Greece guarantees security of
troops, 25-xi.-15; troops withdrawn across
frontier, 13-xii.-15; French troops landed
at Corfu; Greek protest, 11-i.-16; Note
demanding demobilisation; fresh elections;
new Government; and dismissal of Anti-
Entente officials; demands accepted,
21-vi.-16; Adm. du Fournet demands
Central Powers' ministers' departure from
Athens; surrender of military material,
19-xi.-16; demands surrender of mountain

Greece:—

Allied Powers (continued) :—
batteries and other material, 24-xi.-16;
King Constantine interviewed, 26-xi.-16;
surrender of fleet demanded, 10-x.-16;
troops landed at Piræus: King Constantine offers six batteries instead of ten,
1-xii.-16; crisis, 2-xii.-16; Athens riots,
5-xii.-16; 6-xii.-16; blockade until compensated for, 7-xii.-16; Allied Note:
demands complete demobilisation: control
of public works, and release of Venizelists,
11-xii.-16; ultimatum demanding withdrawal of Greek troops from Thessaly,
14-xii.-16; accepted, 15-xii.-16; Note to:
in addition to previous demands: inquiry
into Athens riots and prohibition of
Reservists meetings, 21-xii.-16; further
Allied Note on previous demands,
31-xii.-16; new Allied Note: 48 hours
time limit, 8-i.-17; demands accepted,
10-i.-17; 16-i.-17; demand abdication of
King Constantine, 11-vi.-17; abdicates,
12-vi.-17

Army — mobilised, 23-ix.-15; chief of staff
changed, 26-viii.-16; 4th Army Corps
surrendered; sent to Görlitz, 27-viii.-16;
mutiny at Lamia suppressed, 1-ii.-18

Blockade — by Allies, 19-xi.-15; 16-vi.-16;
19-ix.-16; in force until Athens outrages
compensated, 7-xii.-16; suspended, 16-vi.-17

Bulgaria — irregulars over frontier, 9-xii.-15;
raid, 18-iv.-16; driven back on frontier by
Serbians, 24-vii.-16; Venizelist attacks on,
5-v.-17; 10-v.-17

Central Powers — King Constantine's wireless message to Berlin intercepted,
10-xii.-16; cut off, 18-ii.-17; break with,
30-vi.-17

Chamber — dissolved, 11-xi.-15

Constantinists — arrested, 1-ii.-18

Elections — Venizelist victory, 13-vi.-15;
Gounarist victory, 19-xii.-15

Ministry — M. Venizelos resigns, 6-iii.-15;
Gounaris ministry, 9-iii.-15; M. Venizelos
forms ministry, 21-viii.-15; M. Zaimis
forms, 7-x.-15; resigns, 3-xi.-15; M.
Skouloudis's ministry formed, 4-xi.-15;
resigns, 21-vi.-16; Zaimis Cabinet formed,
21-vi.-16; resigns, 11-ix.-16; Kalogeropoulos
ministry formed, 16-ix.-16; resigns,
3-x.-16; Lambros Cabinet formed, 8-x.-16;
conference to establish government under
M. Venizelos, 23-vi.-17; M. Zaimis
resigns, 24-vi.-17; Venizelos Cabinet
formed, 26-vi.-17

Venizelists — provisional government at
Salonika, 29-ix.-16; 18-x.-16; outrages on,
5-xii.-16; 6-xii.-16; Allies Note demands
release, 11-xii.-16; troops land at Hermopolis, 12-xii.-16; warrant issued for arrest
of M. Venizelos on treason charge,
17-xii.-16; Allies recognise government,
18-xii.-16; Allied Note demands release,
21-xii.-16

" Greeleen," s.s. — sunk, 22-ix.-17

" Greenbank," s.s. — sunk, 3-vi.-17

Green Crassier — Canadians in, 23-viii.-17

Greenland Hill — British progress, 5-vi.-17;
take, 27-viii.-18

" Greenwich," s.s. — sunk, 5-xii.-17

" Greif," German raider — sunk, 29-ii.-16

" Greldon," s.s. — sunk, 8-x.-17

" Greltoria," s.s. — sunk, 27-ix.-17

" Grenadier," s.s. — sunk, 23-ii.-17

Grenadier Guards — 3rd and 4th battalions
arrive in France, 31-viii.-15

Grenay—Vermelles — British attack, 25-ix.-15

Grenfell, Capt. F. H. — commands H.M.S.
" Penshurst," 14-i.-17

" Gresham," s.s. — sunk, 26-iv.-18

" Gretaston," s.s. — sunk, 30-iv.-17

Hariana Lancers (7th) — in rearguard action, 29-xi.-15
Haricot Redoubt — taken, 28-v.-15; French capture and lose for fourth time, 4-vi.-15; regain, 21-vi.-15
Harington, Gen. — Deputy Chief, Imperial General Staff, 29 iv.-18
"Harleywood," s.s. — torpedoed, 17-vii.-18
"Harmatris," s.s. — sunk, 9-iii.-16
"Harmattan," s.s. — mined, 5-v.-17
"Harmonides," s.s. — attacked by U-Boat, 20-i.-18
"Harold," s.v. — sunk, 21-vii.-17
"Harpalion," s.s. — torpedoed, 24-ii.-15
"Harpalyce," s.s. — Belgian relief ship: sunk, 10-iv.-15
"Harpathian," s.s. — sunk, 5-vi.-18
Harp Position, The — British take, 9-iv.-17
Harrington — shelled by U-Boat, 16-viii.-15
"Harrovian," s.s. — sunk, 16-iv.-16
"Hartland," s.s. — torpedoed, 22-xi.-17
Hartlepool — bombed, 13-iii.-18
"Hartley," s.s. — attacked by seaplanes, 9-vii.-17
Hartmannsweilerkopf — French attack, 19-i.-15; heavy fighting near, 20-i.-15; Germans carry, 21-i.-15; struggle round, 22-i.-15; French attack, 5-iii.-15; German second line reached, 24-iii.-15; French carry fortified summit, 26-iii.-15; fail at, 12-iv.-15; Germans retake: French regain crest, 26-iv.-15; successes, 20-ix.-15; 15-x.-15; 21-xii.-15; Germans regain footing, 22-xii.-15; further French successes, 23-xii.-15; 30-xii.-15; German attack repulsed, 10-xi.-17
Hartwig, M. (Russia) — death, 10-vii.-14
Harunabad — Russians take, 18-iii.-17
Harwich — German air-raids, 6-vi.-15; 12-vi.-15; 23-v.-17; 4-vii.-17; 22-vii.-17; first batch of surrendered U-Boats arrive, 20-xi.-18; further batches arrive, 21-xi.-18; 22-xi.-18; 24-xi.-18; 27-xi.-18
"Haslingden," s.s. — attacked by seaplanes, 9-vii.-17; sunk, 12-v.-18
Haspres — British line extends to, 12-x.-18
Hassan Kala — Russians take, 20-i.-16
Hasuur — Union forces occupy, 1-iv.-15
"Hatasu," s.s. — sunk, 27-ix.-18
Hatfield — first Tank trial at, 29-i.-16; King George inspects at, 8-ii.-18
"Hathor," s.s. — sunk, 26-viii.-17
Hattencourt — Allies on line, 25-iii.-18; Germans take, 26-iii.-18
Haucourt — Germans gain at, 22-iii.-16; won, 5-iv.-16; British S. of, 20-iii.-17; taken by Canadians, 30-viii.-18
Haucourt—Malancourt — Germans repulsed, 28-iii.-16
Haudromont Wood — German attack, 25-v.-16; French recovery, 26-v.-16
"Haulwen," s.s. — sunk, 9-vi.-17
Haumont Wood — Germans take, 21-ii.-16; French retake part: evacuate village, 22-ii.-16
Hausen, Gen. von (Germany) — commanding 3rd Army, 2-viii.-14; 14-viii.-14; succeeded, 12-ix.-14
Haussy — German reaction about, 16-x.-18
Haut, Mont — French take: fail to hold, 18-iv.-17; regain, 14-vii.-17; German assault defeated, 15-vii.-17
Hautebraye — French local operations near, 17-vi.-18
Haute Chevauchée — Germans advance, 7-vii.-15
Haute Deule Canal — British cross, 15-x.-18; 17-x.-18
Hautmont — British occupy, 8-xi.-18
"Haverford," s.s. — attacked by U-Boat, 12-vi.-17; torpedoed, 26-vi.-17
Havre — communications threatened, 29-viii.-14; cleared by Royal Naval Transport

Havre (continued) :—
Service, 16-ix.-14; Belgian Government at, 13-x.-14; U-Boats appear off, 29-xi.-14; Belgian powder factory blown up, 11-xii.-15
Havrincourt — British loss and recovery near, 1-ix.-17; taken by British, 20-xi.-17; battle; British take, 12-ix.-18
Havrincourt Wood — British penetrate, 8-iv.-17; progress, 22-iv.-17; 23-iv.-17; New Zealanders reach N. fringe, 4-ix.-18; British carry high ground N. of overlooking Hindenburg Line, 9-ix.-18
"Hawk," H.M. armed trawler — rams and sinks U14, 5-vi.-15
"Hawke," H.M.S. — sunk, 15-x.-14
"Haworth," s.s. — sunk, 17-vii.-17
"Haydn," s.s. — sunk, 29-ix.-15
Haynecourt — carried by British, 27-ix.-18
"Hazard," H.M.S. — sunk, 28-i.-18
Hazebrouck — attacked, 9-x.-14; British 3rd Corps at, 12-x.-14; Lahore Division concentrated W. of, 20-x.-14
"Headcliffe," s.s. — repels U-Boat attack, 6-iv.-18
"Headlands," s.s. — sunk, 12-iii.-15
"Healdton," U.S. s.s. — sunk, 21-iii.-17
"Heatherside," s.s. — sunk, 24-viii.-17
"Hebburn," s.s. — sunk, 25-ix.-18
Hebron — Turks retreat on, 9-xi.-17; 10-xi.-17; British occupy, 7-xii.-17
Hébuterne — French advance near, 7-vi.-15; progress, 8-vi.-15; 11-vi.-15; 13-vi.-15; British take prisoners, 1-iv.-18; 5-iv.-18; Germans evacuate positions in sector, 14-viii.-18
Hedjaz, King of — master of Akaba—Hedjaz railway country, 12-vii.-17; Medina occupied in name of, 13-i.-19
Hedjaz railway — Arabs attack, 6-i.-18; British threaten, 21-ii.-18; Turks hold bridgehead, 23-ii.-18; British advance, 22-iii.-18; 25-iii.-18; cavalry approaching Amman, 26-iii.-18; Arabs occupy 53 miles of S. of Maan, 24-iv.-18; advance towards, 30-iv.-18; damage N. of Maan, 3-v.-18; demolish part N. and S. of Maan, 12-v.-18; British occupy positions, 25-ix.-18
Hedjef — murderers surrender, 18-iii.-18
"Hedwig von Wissmann," German s.s. — sunk, 9-ii.-16
Heeringen, Gen. von (Germany) — commanding 7th Army, 2-viii.-14; 14-viii.-14; transferred to Aisne, 12-ix.-14; to command Coast Defence, 28-viii.-16
"Heinrich Rathjen," German outpost vessel — mined, 15-v.-17
"Hela," H.I.M.S. — sunk, 12-ix.-14
"Helenus," s.s. — torpedoed, 1-xii.-17
Helfferich, Herr (Germany) — memorandum to Chancellor regarding suspension of U-Boat blockade, 5-viii.-15; in Reichstag on unrestricted U-Boat warfare: claims 1,600,000 tonnage sunk, 28-iv.-17; succeeds Count Mirbach at Moscow; transfers seat of mission to Pskoff, 12-viii.-18
"Helga," H.M.S. — destroys Liberty Hall by gunfire, 26-iv.-16
"Helgoland," Austrian cruiser — bombards railway and coast round Viesti-Manfredonia, 24-v.-15; sinks French submarine "Monge," 29-xii.-15
"Helgoland," H.I.M.S. — damaged in Jutland battle, 2-vi.-16
Heligoland — British submarine patrol instituted, 5-viii.-14; U-Boats return from scouting cruise, 11-viii.-14; bombardment and capture discussed at Loch Ewe conference, 17-ix.-14; British cruiser off, 24-xi.-14; German High Seas Fleet trip to, 21-iv.-15; High Sea Fleet cruise, 6-vi.-15; 25th anniversary of German installation, 10-viii.-15; U-Boat "Deutschland" leaves

Heligoland (continued) :—
for U.S., 23-vi.-16; U53 returns from U.S., 28-x.-16; Kaiser visits, 18-viii.-17; air station inspected by Allied Commission, 9-xii.-18

Heligoland Bight — completely blockaded by Grand Fleet during transport of troops to France, 16-viii.-14; covering movement to be carried out, 25-viii.-14; battle, 28-viii.-14; swept by Harwich force, 10-ix.-14; British carry out reconnaissance, 17-i.-15; British operations abandoned, 28-i.-15; British lay mines, 11-v.-15; 8-xi.-15; first mines laid from British submarine: by E41 in, 22-vi.-16; E23 attacks German warships, 19-viii.-16; British T.B.D.s sweep; three armed trawlers destroyed, 28-iii.-18; light forces engaged, 20-iv.-18; E45 lays mines, 24-iv.-18; British and German air forces engaged: one German shot down, 19-vi.-18

Helldorf, Capt. (Germany) — courier during Armistice negotiations; leaves for Spa, 8-xi.-18; held up on Capelle road by German bombardment; 9-xi.-18; reaches Spa; leaves, 10-xi.-18; reaches German delegates, 11-xi.-18

Helles, Cape — fort bombarded, 19-ii.-15; fort shattered, 25-ii.-15; British landing, 25-iv. 15; advance from, 27-iv.-15; Allied attack from, 7-viii.-15; H.M.S. "Goliath" sunk off 13-v.-15; French transport "Carthage" torpedoed, 4-vii.-15; Allies repulse Turkish attack, 7-i.-16; evacuated, 8-i.-16

"Helmsmuir," s.s. — sunk, 3-xii.-15

Helsingfors — Adm. Nepenin shot, 10-iii.-17; Red Guards capture, 28-i.-18; 29-i.-18; 7 British submarines destroyed, 3-iv.-18; Germans occupy, 13-iv.-18

Helvetsluis — UB6 aground off: interned, 12-iii.-16

Hem — French win, 5-vii.-16; capture fortified work near, 2-viii.-16; carry trenches, 7-viii.-16; seize wood near, 8-viii.-16; German counter-attack repulsed, 9-viii.-16; British progress, 29-viii.-18

"Hemisphere," s.s. — sunk, 28-xii.-14

Henderson, Mr. — member of new War Cabinet, 11-xii.-16; on special mission to Russia, 29-v.-17; Soviet Council's reply to letter explaining scope of International Socialist Conference, 12-vi.-17; attitude at Labour Party Conference: Government view causes resignation from Cabinet, 11-viii.-17

Henin — British line through, 26-iii.-18

Heninel — British storm, 12-iv.-17; British capture high ground, 26-viii.-18

Henin-sur-Cojeul — British cavalry in touch with Germans, 19-iii.-17; British carry, 2-iv.-17; British capture, 24-viii.-18

"Henley," s.s. — sunk, 10-iv.-18

"Henri IV.," French battleship — arrives in Dardanelles, 27-iii.-15

"Henry James," s.s. — mined, 16-vii.-17

Heraclea — bombarded, 8-iii.-15; Russian Black Sea Fleet again bombards, 15-iv.-15

Herbeboise — German attack, 21-ii.-16; French evacuate, 23-ii.-16

Herbecourt — taken by French, 2-vii.-16; British take, 31-iii.-17

Herbertshöhe — Australians leaving for, 31-viii.-14; German headquarters captured, 11-ix.-14

Herbignies — taken by British, 4-xi.-18

Herchies — Allied line at Armistice, 11-xi.-18

"Hercules," H.M.S. — completes turbine repairs, 19-iii.-16; sunk, 30-xii.-17

"Herdis," s.s. — sunk, 29-vi.-18

Herleville — taken by Australians, 23-viii.-18

Herlies — British take, 17-x.-14

Hermada, Mte. — furious fighting, 20-viii.-17; Italian progress, 30-viii.-17

"Hermann," H.I.M. auxiliary — sunk 14-vi.-16

Hermann line — Germans on, 21-x.-18

Hermannstadt — Austrians evacuate, 10-ix.-16; Rumanian success between Brasso and, 3-x.-16

"Hermes," H.M.S. — sunk, 31-x.-14

Hermies — British take, 9-iv.-17

"Hermione," s.s. — mined, 14-iv.-17

Hermopolis — Venizelist troops land, 12-xii.-16

"Heron," s.s. — sunk, 30-ix.-17

"Heron Bridge," H.M. collier — sunk, 16-v.-18

Herr — Allies on line, 24-iii.-18

Hertfordshire — air-raids, 3-ix.-16; 1-x.-16

Hertling, Count (Germany) — declines to succeed Herr von Bethmann-Hollweg as Chancellor, 13-vii.-17; appointed Chancellor, 1-xi.-17; announces preparedness to treat with Bolshevists, 29-xi.-17; on military functions in political decisions: detailed memorandum to G.H.Q., 12-i.-18; reply to Mr. Wilson and Mr. Lloyd George on war aims, 24-i.-18; vetoes G.H.Q.'s proposal to occupy Zeeland province, 21-iv.-18; Crown Prince Rupprecht of Bavaria in letter to: says he is sceptical of German victory: advises contentment with Eastern gains, 1-vi.-18; replies that hope of collapse of one of Western Powers should not yet be abandoned, 5-vi.-18; vetoes proposal to extend field of unrestricted U-Boat warfare, 2-vii.-18; proposal again urged, 16-vii.-18; attends conference at Spa, 13-viii.-18; 15-viii.-18; explains risk of direct offer of peace, 3-ix.-18; on Count Burian's peace step and appeal to Dutch mediation, 16-ix.-18; resigns, 30-ix.-18

Hervilly — British take, 31-iii.-17

"Hesperian," s.s. — sunk, 4-ix.-15

"Hesperides," s.s. — sunk, 25-iv.-17

Hesse, Prince Frederick Charles of — accepts offer of Finnish "Crown," 9-ix.-18

Het Sas — French progress near, 14-v.-15; French recover, 15-v.-15

Heudicourt — British take, 30-iii.-17; taken and lost by British, 30-viii.-18; retaken, 1-ix.-18

Hewlett, Flight.-Cmdr. — missing after Cuxhaven raid, 25-xii.-14; picked up by Dutch trawler, 31-xii.-14

Heyst — British ships bombard, 24-ix.-15

"Hibernia," H.M.S. — in heavy sea, 6-xi.-15; reports 12-in. gun cracked, 11-ix.-14

"Hickla," Norwegian s.s. — sunk, 31-i.-17

"Hidalgo," s.s. — sunk, 28-viii.-17

"Highcliffe," s.s. — sunk, 3-ix.-18

"Highflyer," H.M.S. — brings "Tubantia" into Plymouth, 4-viii.-14; at Lisbon, 9-viii.-14; sinks "Kaiser Wilhelm der Grosse," 26-viii.-14

"Highland Brae," s.s. — captured and scuttled, 14-i.-15

"Highland Brigade," s.s. — sunk, 7-iv.-18

"Highland Corrie," s.s. — mined, 14-viii.-15; sunk, 16-v.-17

"Highland Harris," s.s. — sunk, 6-viii.-18

"Highland Hope," s.s. — sunk, 14-ix.-14

"Highland Prince," s.s. — sunk, 11-iv.-18

High Wood — British take, 15-ix.-16

"Hilary," H.M.A.M.C. — sunk, 26-v.-17

"Hildawell," s.s. — mined, 20-xii.-16

Hill 10 (Gallipoli) — stormed and carried, 6-viii.-15

Hill 60 (Gallipoli) — Anzac advance against, 27-viii.-15; secured, 29-viii.-15

Hill 60 (Ypres) — British take, 17-iv.-15; consolidated: repulse German counterattacks, 18-iv.-15; German attempt on, 19-iv.-15; Germans still attacking, 20-iv.-15; 21-iv.-15; German gas attack repulsed, 1-v.-15; Germans recapture after heavy gas attack, 5-v.-15; British regain some trenches, 6-v.-15; carried, 4-ix.-18

Hoxa — first line of U-Boat obstructions completed, 29-xii.-14

Hoyos, Count (Austria-Hungary) — leaves Vienna for Berlin with autograph letter from Emperor Francis Joseph to Kaiser and Ballplatz Memorandum on Balkan policy, 4-vii.-14; conference with Herr Zimmermann and Herr von Bethmann-Hollweg, 6-vii.-14

Hoy Sound — anti-U-Boat obstructions completed, 19-ii.-15

"Huelva," s.s. — sunk, 23-vii.-17

Hughes, Lieut. — lands from E11 and blows up portion of Anatolian railway, 21-viii.-15

Hughes, Mr. W. M. (Australia) — Prime Minister, 26-x.-15; leaves for Paris, 11-i.-19

Huguet, Col. (France) — military mission under, arrives in London, 10-viii.-14

Hull — air raids, 6-vi.-15; 5-iii.-16; 9-viii.-16; 12-ii.-18

Hulluch — German gas attack S. of, 27-iv.-16; British capture outskirts, 25-ix.-15; take trenches, 13-x.-15; German attack fails, 19-x.-15; slight German success, 31-xii.-15; German attacks, 14-v.-16; British raid opposite, 9-i.-17; air raids, 25-i.-17

Hulua, Mt. — K.A.R. engage Gen. von Lettow near, 6-ix.-18

Humber — U-Boats detached to watch, 14-viii.-14; H.M.SS. "Invincible" and "New Zealand" stationed in, 18-viii.-14; approaches mined by German minelayers, 26-viii.-14; H.M.S. "Speedy" mined, 3-ix.-14

"Humber," H.M. monitor — ordered to Ostend, 12-x.-14; supports Belgians in Yser battle, 17-x.-14; shells Belgian coast, 18-x.-14

Humbert, Gen. (France) — commanding 3rd Army covering Noyon and Oise R., 23-iii.-18; commanding 3rd Army below Montdidier, 9-viii.-18; advances, 21-viii.-18; 5-ix.-18

Hunding line — fighting, 14-x.-18; French penetrate on 3-mile front, 19-x.-18

Hungary:—
Army — mutiny, 20-x.-18; 24-x.-18
Austria: see Austria
Blockade — raised, 4-viii.-19
Ministry — Tisza resigns, 22-v.-17; Weckerle resigns, 24-x.-18; Karolyi forms, 17-xi.-18; resigns, 21-iii.-19
National Council — formed, 25-x.-18
Republic — proclaimed, 30-x.-18; Karolyi provisional President, 12-i.-19
Revolution — Soviet Government formed at Budapest: Bela Kun Foreign Minister; offer of military alliance accepted by Moscow Soviet, 22-iii.-19; Gen. Smuts at Budapest, 4-iv.-19; leaves, 5-iv.-19; elections, 7-iv.-19; counter-revolution suppressed, 24-vi.-19; Allied warning to Soviets, 26-vii.-19; fall of Bela Kun, 1-viii.-19; fall of provisional Cabinet; Archduke Joseph "State Governor," 6-viii.-19; Supreme Council refuses to countenance appointment, 22-viii.-19; Archduke Joseph resigns, 23-viii.-19
Rumania — attack, 20-vii.-19; nearing Budapest, 1-viii.-19; Budapest occupied, 2-viii.-19; present ultimatum to Goverment embodying armistice terms, 5-viii.-19; Budapest evacuated, 13-xi.-19
Frontier — readjusted, 4-iii.-18
Russia — cavalry raids, 28-ix.-14; 2-xii.-14; 31-xii.-14

Hungaro-Rumanian neutral zone — discussed by Paris Peace Conference, 25-ii.-19

"Hungerford," s.s. — sunk, 16-iv.-18

"Hunsbridge," s.s. — sunk, 7-ix.-17

"Hunsbrook," s.s. — attacked by U-Boat, 22-xii.-17

"Hunsdon," s.s. — sunk, 18-x.-18

"Hunsgrove," s.s. — sunk, 8-vi.-18

"Hunstanton," s.s. — sunk, 4-iv.-17

Huntingdonshire — Zeppelin raid, 3-ix.-16

"Huntscraft," s.s. — torpedoed, 6-vii.-18

"Huntsfall," s.s. — sunk, 2-x.-16

"Huntsgulf," s.s. — torpedoed, 18-xi.-17

"Huntsland," s.s. — sunk, 6-vi.-18

"Huntsman," s.s. — sunk, 25-ii.-17

"Huntsmoor," s.s. — sunk, 20-ii.-18

"Huntstrick," s.s. — sunk, 8-vi.-17

"Huronian," s.s. — torpedoed, 28-xii.-15

"Hurunui," s.s. — sunk, 18-v.-18

"Hurst," s.s. — sunk, 3-x.-17

"Hurstside," s.s. — sunk, 4-vii.-17

Hurtebise — Germans take part of salient, 17-vi.-17; French on Craonne Ridge, N of, 25-vi.-17; Germans beaten off E. attack defeated, 19-vii.-17; French prog N.W. of, 31-viii.-17; Germans att 12-x.-17

Hurtebise Farm — French take, 16-iv.-17

Husiatyn — Germans reach Russian from round, 28-vii.-17; withdraw, 13-ix.-17

"Hussa," H.M.S. — bombards Turkish c opposite Chios, 27-vi.-15

Hussarek, Baron von (Austria) — appoi Premier, 24-vii.-18; proclaims reconstruc of Dual Monarchy, 1-x.-18

Hussars (14th) — in rearguard action, 29 15; squadron under Gen. Bitcherakoff Mandjil Bridge battle, 12-vi.-18

Hussein Kamel Pasha, Prince — appoi Khedive of Egypt, 18-xii.-14; attem assassination, 8-iv.-15; bomb thrown 9-vii.-15

Hutier, Gen. von (Germany) — commands (Prussian) Army Corps, 4-iv.-15; comm 8th (Riga) Army, 22-iv.-17; 1-ix.-17; s seded, 12-xii.-17; commands 18th A 27-xii.-17; in Somme battle, 21-iii.-18 Noyon battle, 9-vi.-18

Huwaish Gorge — British cavalry in posi 27-x.-18

Huy — Germans take, 12-viii.-14

"Hyacinth," H.M.S. — bombarded Ta 15-viii.-15

"Hyacinthus," s.s. — attacked by U-E 25-xii.-17

Hyderabad Redoubt — British take, 9-iv.-1

Hydrophones — use by British subma 14-v.-17

"Hylas," s.s. — sunk, 15-viii.-17

"Hyndford," s.s. — wards off U-Boat, 6-

"Hyperia," s.s. — sunk, 28-vii.-18

"Hythe," H.M. minesweeper — sunk, 28-

I.

"Iberian," s.s. — sunk, 30-vii.-15

"Ibuki," H.I.J.M.S. — joins British (squadron, 26-viii.-14; escorts Australian voy, 1-xi.-14; escorts New Zealand transp 9-xi.-14

"Iceland," H.M. armed trawler — des German seaplanes, 9-vii.-17

Ickau — Turks advance, 11-x.-15

"Idaho," s.s. — sunk, 19-viii.-18

Ideals — Prusso-German: against A Saxon: Kaiser's speech at G.H.Q. brating 30th anniversary of acces 15-vi.-18

"Idomeneus," s.s. — torpedoed, 15-ix.-17

"Ikalis," s.s. — sunk, 7-vi.-17

"Ikaria," s.s. — sunk, 30-i.-15

"Ikbal," s.s. — sunk, 29-iv.-17

"Ikeda," s.s. — sunk, 21-iii.-18

Ikua–Styr line — Russians cross, 6-vi.-16

"Ilderton," s.s. — sunk, 24-x.-17

Ili — Germans reach, 11-viii.-18

Ilkeston — Zeppelin raid on, 31-i.-16

"I'll Try," British smack — engages U-I 1-ii.-17

Illukst — Germans take, 23-x.-15; Russians approach, 4-xi.-15; Russian success, 29-xi.-15

Ilse, Gen. (Germany) — to command 15th (Prussian) Corps, 25-v.-17

Ilse, Lake — Russian counter-offensive between Lake Sventen and, 31-x.-15

"**Iiston**," s.s. — sunk, 30-vi. 17

"**Ilvington Court**," s.s. — sunk, 6-xii.-17

"**Imber**," s.s. — torpedoed, 13-vii.-18

Imecourt — taken by Americans, 1-xi.-18

"**Immingham**," H.M. store-carrier — sunk, 6-vi.-15

"**Imperatritsa Maria**," Russian battleship — blown up, 20-x.-16

"**Imperial**," s.s. — sunk, 8-viii.-16

Imperial Camel Corps — with Anzacs: take Turkish position at Rafa, 9-i.-17

"**Imperial Transport**," s.s. — sunk, 11-iv.-17

Imperial War Conference: see under Great Britain

"**Implacable**," H.M.S. — at Dardanelles, 18-iii.-15; covers landing at X. Beach, 25-iv.-15

Inchy — British advance, 3-ix.-18

"**Indefatigable**," H.M.S. — 2-viii.-14; 4-viii.-14; enters Ægean, 10-viii.-14; maintains blockade, 19-viii.-14; bombards Dardanelles forts, 3-xi.-14; at Rosyth, 24-iii.-15; sunk in Jutland battle, 31-v.-16

India:—

 Army:—
  Bikanir Camel Force — skirmish with Bedouins at Katiyeh, 21-xi.-14
  Expeditionary force — convoy sails for France, 28-viii.-14; second convoy sails, 20-ix.-14; force landed at Marseilles, 26-ix.-14; convoy diverted to Liverpool, 22-x.-14; Imperial Service Cavalry Brigade and infantry brigades leave for France and Egypt, 2-xi.-14; transports detached, 9-xi.-14; field corps: commander, 27-x.-14; force leaves France, 28-xii.-15
  Fighting: see under various fronts and names of places
  Lahore Division — concentrated W. of Hazebrouck, 20-x.-14; at Bailleul, 22-x.-14; at Ypres: relieve Canadians, 26-iv.-15; in Palestine, 13-iv.-18
  Meerut (7th) Division — transferred to Palestine, 6-iv.-18
  Mutiny — Light Infantry, 15-ii.-17
  Poona (6th) Division — Gen. Townshend to command, 23-iv.-15
  Transport — armoured cars and mechanical transport: first use, 9-x.-15
  Victoria Cross — first decorated, 16-i.-15
  North-West frontier — North Waziristan Militia engaged in Tochi Valley, 29-xi.-14; Bannu Column, with Waziristan Militia, defeats Khostwal Lashkar threatening Miranshah, 26-iii.-15; Khaibar Column repulses a raid at Peshawar, 18-iv.-15; Malakand Column engaged on Swat R., 29-viii.-15; Mohmand raid repulsed at Shabkadar, 9-x.-15; raid at Chakdara repulsed, 27-x.-15
 Registration ordinance, 6-ii.-17
 Rowlatt Acts — "passive resistance" riots in Delhi, 3-iii.-19; continue, 11-iv.-19; Mr. Gandhi advises suspension of "passive resistance," 18-iv.-19

"**India**," H.M.A.M.C. — sunk, 8-viii.-15

"**India City**," s.s. — sunk, 12-iii.-15

"**Indian Prince**," s.s. — sunk, 4-ix.-14

India Office — Military Secretary, 26-ix.-14

"**Indien**," s.s. — sunk, 8-ix.-15

Indigo — crop acquired by British Government, 12-iii.-15

"**Indomitable**," H.M.S. — 2-viii.-14; 4-viii.-14; enters Ægean, 10-viii.-14; ordered to leave Dardanelles for Gibraltar, 19-viii.-14; bombards Dardanelles forts, 3-xi.-14; joins

"**Indomitable**," H.M.S. (continued) :—
 Battle Cruiser Fleet at Rosyth, 26-xii.-14; in Dogger Bank battle; tows H.M.S. "Lion" home, 24-i.-15; refitting, 31-i.-15; in Jutland battle, 31-v.-16

"**Indore**," s.s. — torpedoed, 25-vii.-18

"**Industrial**," s.s. — sunk, 4-x.-18

Infantry Hill — stormed by British, 14-vi.-17; fighting, 18-vi.-17; 19-vi.-17; German attack, 2-viii.-17; British recovery, 3-viii.-17

"**Inflexible**," H.M.S. — enters Ægean, 10-viii.-14; leaves Malta for home, 18-viii.-14; assists in sweeping Heligoland Bight, 10-ix.-14; leaves Devonport to sail under Adm. Sturdee, 5-xi.-14; in Falkland Islands battle, 8-xii.-14; supports attack on Dardanelles forts, 5-iii.-15; damaged, 18-iii.-15; joins Battle Cruiser Fleet, 19-vi.-15; in Jutland battle, 31-v.-16

Ingelmünster — taken, 16-x.-18

Ingenohl, Adm. von (Germany) — C.-in-C. High Sea Fleet, 31-vii.-14; asks for transfer to Baltic, 12-ix.-14; receives Kaiser's instructions as to High Sea Fleet, 3-x.-14; supercession under discussion, 23-xii.-14; superceded by Adm. von Pohl, 3-ii.-15

"**Inglemoor**," s.s. — sunk, 1-vii.-15

"**Ingleside**," s.s. — sunk, 8-v.-18

"**Inkosi**," s.s. — sunk, 28-iii.-18

"**Inniscarra**," s.s. — sunk, 12-v.-18

"**Innisfallen**," s.s. — sunk, 23-v.-18

Inovlodz (Poland) — Germans fighting rearguard action, 30-xii.-14

Insterburg — Germans evacuate, 23-viii.-14; Gen. Rennenkampf retiring on, 31-viii.-14; raided by ZIV., 9-ix.-14; retaken by Germans, 11-ix.-14; German Eastern H.Q. removed to, 5-ii.-15

Inter-Allied Labour Conference (Westminster) — memorandum on war aims: published, 24-ii.-18

"**Intrepid**," H.M.S. — blockship: sunk at entrance to Bruges Canal, 23-iv.-18

Inventions Board — Lord Fisher chairman, 5-vii.-15

Invergordon — Portsmouth floating dock arrives, 6-ix.-14; H.M.S. "Iron Duke" refits at, 1-x.-15; new floating dock arrives, 23-ix.-16

"**Inverness**," s.s. — attacked by U-Boat, 29-xii.-17

Inverness Copse — fierce fighting, 24-viii.-17; British take strong point N. of, 15-ix.-17; capture, 20-ix.-17

"**Inververbie**," H.M. collier — sunk, 14-ix.-16

"**Invincible**," H.M.S. — stationed in the Humber, 18-viii.-14; assists in sweeping Heligoland Bight, 10-ix.-14; leaves Cromarty to sail under Adm. Sturdee, 5-xi.-14; in Falkland Islands battle, 8-xii.-14; at Rosyth, 24-iii.-15; guns replaced, 30-iv.-15; Adm. Hood hoists flag, 26-v.-15; sunk in Jutland battle, 31-v.-16

"**Iolanthe**," s.s. — sunk, 4-i.-18

"**Iolo**," s.s. — sunk, 11-x.-16

"**Iolo**," s.s. — sunk, 17-ii.-17

"**Ionian**," s.s. — sunk, 20-x.-17

"**Ionic**," s.s. — attacked by U-Boat, 31-xii.-15

"**Ionna**," s.s. — torpedoed, 10-ix.-17

Ipek — captured, 6-xii.-15

"**Iphigenia**," H.M.S. — sunk at entrance to Bruges Canal, 23-iv.-18

Ipswich — LZ38 raids, 30-iv.-15

"**Iran**," s.s. — sunk, 7-viii.-17

Ireland:—
 Boyne celebrations, 14-vii.-14
 German plot — 150 Sein Feiners arrested, 17-v.-18; British Government paper published, 24-v.-18
 Home Rule — Bill: passed in Lords, 14-vii.-14; second reading in Commons, 30-vii.-14; conference summoned by King, 19-vii.-14; fails, 24-vii.-14

Kemmern — Russians forced back between Lake Babit and, 31-x.-15; Russians advance on, 7-xi.-15; Germans forced from, 10-xi.-15; occupied, 11-xi.-15; Russian advance W. of, 12-xi.-15; German retreat, 14-xi.-15; Russian success near, 16-vii.-16

Kemp (S. African rebel) — beaten off at Upington, 24-i.-15; surrenders, 3-ii.-15

Kenali — Serbs reach, 3-x.-16; Allies capture defences, 14-xi.-16

"Kendal Castle," s.s. — sunk, 15-ix.-18

Kengaver — British and Russian Consuls aided by Persian Cossacks, 26-x.-15

"Kenilworth," s.s. — sunk, 24-iv.-17

"Kenmare," s.s. — sunk, 2-iii.-18

"Kenmore," s.s. — sunk, 26-viii.-17

"Kennet," H.M.S. — damaged in action off Tsingtau, 23-viii.-14

"Kennett," s.s. — sunk, 22-ix.-16

"Kennington," s.s. — sunk, 12-vi.-18

Kent — German air-raids, 4-vi.-15; 17-viii.-15; 23-i.-16; 5-iii.-16; 25-iv.-16; 19-v.-16; 3-vii.-16; 2-viii.-16; 25-viii.-16; 3-ix.-16; 23-ix.-16; 16-iii.-17; 17-iii.-17; 5-vi.-17; 2-viii.-17; 2-ix.-17; 3-ix.-17; 24-ix.-17; 25-ix.-17; 30-ix.-17; 1-x.-17; 31-x.-17; 6-xii.-17; 18-xii.-17; 27-xii.-17; 29-i.-18; last air-raid on England, 17-vi.-18; T.B.D.s raid coast, 18-iii.-17

"Kent," H.M.S. — sinks H.I.M.S. "Nürnberg" off Falkland Islands, 8-xii.-14; sinks H.I.M.S. "Dresden" off Juan Fernandez, 14-iii.-15

Kephez, Cape — forts bombarded, 1-iii.-15

Kerak — occupied by Arabs, 7-iv.-18

Kerensky, M. (Russia) — Minister of Justice, 14-iii.-17; War Minister, 16-v.-17; visits front, 1-vii.-17; forms National Ministry, 6-viii.-17; dismisses Gen. Korniloff, 8-ix.-17; virtual dictator, 10-ix.-17; generalissimo, 11-ix.-17; Government entrusted to Council under, 15-ix.-17; forms Coalition Government, 7-x.-17; forces defeated at Tsarskoe Selo, 13-xi.-17; escapes from Gatchina, 14-xi.-17; at London Labour conference, 26-vi.-18

Kereves Dere — French attack, 6-vi.-15; 7-v.-15; French take heights near, 21-vi.-15; French reach mouth, 12-vii.-15

Kerman — British column enters, 13-vi.-16

"Kerman," s.s. — torpedoed, 27-ii.-18

Kermanshah — Russians pursue Persian rebels to, 17-xii.-15; 20-xii.-15; Turks reinforce rebels at, 14-i.-16; Gen. Baratoff at, 12-ii.-16; Turks retreat on, 24-ii.-16; Russians take, 26-ii.-16; Turks claim recapture, 1-vii.-16; Russian attack between Hamadan and, 5-iii.-17; occupied, 13-iii.-17

Kernan, Gen. (U.S.) — succeeded by Gen. Harbord in charge of supply services at Tours, 31-vii.-18

Kerry — Sir Roger Casement arrives off, 20-iv.-16

Keyes, Adm. — attends naval conference at Loch Ewe, 17-ix.-14; appointed to command at Dover, 29-xii.-17; appointed acting viceadm., 1-i.-18; commanding in raid off Zeebrugge—Ostend, 23-iv.-18; lands at Ostend, 17-x.-18; Freedom of Dover presented, 12-xii.-18

Kezdi — Rumanians advance toward, 27-vii.-17

Kezdi Vasarhely — Rumanians take, 29-viii.-16

Khabarovsk — Japanese at, 5-ix.-18

Khadairi Bend — operations: begun, 5-i.-17

Khalil Pasha — invites Gen. Townshend to surrender Kut, 10-iii.-16; discusses surrender of Kut with, 26-iv.-16

Khan Aby Rayat — occupied, 20-ii.-18

Khan Baghdadie — occupied, 10-iii.-18; Turkish army defeated, 26-iii.-18

Khanikin — British and Russians in touch near, 2-iv.-17; Russians occupy, 4-iv.-17; Russians report evacuation, 9-vii.-17

Kharkoff — Germans enter, 8-iv.-18; Gen. Denikin takes, 27-vi.-19

Khartum — L.50's non-stop flight from Yamboli, 30-xi.-17

"Kheir-ed-Din-Barbarossa," Turkish battleship —sunk, 9-viii.-15

"Khephren," s.s. — sunk, 16-vii.-17

"Khiva," s.s. — attacked by U-Boat, 29-iii.-17

Khizan — Russians occupy, 24-iii.-16

Kholm — Germans checked, 24-vii.-15; AustroGermans at, 31-vii.-15; success, 3-viii.-15; railway cut, 17-viii.-15; territorial concession: terms, 9-ii.-18

Khorasan — Turks reach, 25-xii.-14; defeated, 23-i.-15

Khriask — Russians take, 1-i.-16

Kiaochow — Japanese capture station, 13-ix.-14

Kiaochow Bay — blockade declared, 27-viii.-14; Japanese cruiser "Takachiho" sunk by German T.D.B. S90, 17-x.-14; Japanese T.B. 33 mined, 11-xi.-14

Kibata — Gen. Smuts gains ground N.W. of, 15-xii.-16

Kidete — British success, 16-viii.-16

Kidodi — British bar German retreat, 10-ix.-16

Kidugalla — Gen. von Lettow marches from Ubena to, 17-x.-16

Kieff — Bolshevists declare war on Rada, 26-i.-18; Germans advance towards, 20-ii.-18; 23-ii.-18; entered, 1-iii.-18; Gen. Skoropadsky at, 29-iv.-18; Marshal Eichhorn assassinated, 30-vii.-18; Hetman (Gen. Skoropadsky) overthrown, 14-xii.-18; Bolshevists capture, 3-ii.-19

Kiel — German raider "Möwe" at, 4-iii.-16; ships damaged in Jutland battle: sent for repair, 2-vi.-16; strike, 28-i.-18; Kaiser visits U-Boat School, 24-ix.-18; German 3rd High Sea Squadron passes to, 30-x.-18; seamen's demonstration, 3-xi.-18; red flag hoisted in ship; Herr Noske arrives, 4-xi.-18; minesweepers clear Baltic passage to, 25-xi.-18; Adm. Browning's squadron leaves for England, 18-xii.-18

Kiel Canal — completion: expedition ordered, 25-vii.-14; 3rd High Sea Squadron passes through, 22-i.-15

Kielce — Austrians occupy, 7-viii.-14; AustroGermans defeated, 3-xi.-14; retake, 12-v.-15; fighting, 16-v.-15

"Kieldrecht," s.s. — sunk, 15-vi.-18

Kifri — Russians advance on, 13-v.-17; Turks retire towards Jebel Hamrin, 3-xii.-17; British take Salkaltutan Pass, 4-xii.-17; British occupy, 28-iv.-18

Kigali — Belgians occupy, 6-v.-16; 12-v.-16

Kiggell, Gen. L. — succeeded as Chief of Staff to Sir D. Haig, 19-i.-18

Kigoma — taken by Belgians, 27-vii.-16

Kikombo — British occupy section of Central Railway, 30-vii.-16

"Kilbride," H.M. collier — sunk, 1-iii.-16

"Kilcoan," s.s. — sunk, 30-i.-15

"Kildare," s.s. — sunk, 12-iv.-17

"Kildonan," s.s. — sunk, 29-ix.-17

"Kildonan Castle," H.M.A.M.C. — attacked by U-Boat, 26-x.-16

Kilid Bahr — fort bombarded, 5-iii.-15

Kilimanjaro — von Lettow preparing for campaign, 3-ix.-14; fighting round, 24-iv.-15; British offensive, 5-iii.-16; Gen. Smuts advances towards, 7-iii.-16; area conquered, 21-iii.-16

Kilimatinde — British occupy, 31-vii.-16

Killingholme — arrival of 23 U.S. flying boats and personnel; based there, 30-v.-18

Killossa — captured, 22-viii.-16

"Kilmaho," s.s. — sunk, 16-v.-17

" **Lady Carrington**," s.s. — sunk, 12-xi.-16

" **Lady Cory-Wright**," H.M. mine-carrier — sunk, 26-iii.-18

" **Lady Ninian**," s.s. — sunk, 28-v.-16

" **Lady Olive**," H.M. special service ship — sunk, 19-ii.-17

" **Lady Patricia**," H.M. special service ship — sunk, 20-v.-17

" **Lady Plymouth**," s.s. — chased by U-Boat, 5-xi.-15

" **Laertes**," s.s. — escapes from U-Boat, 10-ii.-15; sunk, 1-viii.-17

La Fère — British retiring on, 28-viii.-14; 29-viii.-14; Germans reach, 30-viii.-14; Germans retreat on, 19-iii.-17; heavy fighting between St. Quentin and, 22-iii.-17; French defeat Germans, 23-iii.-17; French progress between Laon and, 27-iii.-17; French occupy, 13-x.-18

La Ferté Gaucher — French pass through, 7-ix.-14

La Ferté Milon — Germans at, 3-ix.-14; 8-ix.-14; British at, 10-ix.-14

Laffaux — French seize outskirts, 3-iv.-17; take, 19-iv.-17; progress: Mill taken, 5-v.-17; German assaults, 17-v.-17; slight gain, 1-vi.-17; French assault on Salient; German division succumbs to gas attack, 22-x.-17

La Fille Morte Mill — Germans capture, 7-vii.-15; temporary German gain, 13-vii.-15

La Folie — French reach, 26-ix.-15; progress, 1-x.-15; progress on ridges, 10-x.-15; 11-x.-15; Germans enter French trenches W. of, 8-ii.-16; British take farm and wood, 9-iv.-17; captured by British, 4-xi.-18

La Fontaine-aux-Charmes — Germans repulsed, 11-viii.-15

La Fontenelle — French storm defences, 24-vii.-15

" **Laforey**," H.M.S. — mined, 23-iii.-17

Lagarina Valley — Italian counter-offensive, 12-vi.-16

Lagnicourt — British carry, 26-iii.-17; 2-iv.-17; German counter-attack, 15-iv.-17; taken; British resistance round, 21-iii.-18

Lagny-Meaux — British at, 2-ix.-14

La Harazée — French relieved by U.S. Army, 22-ix.-18

Lahej — British force attacked, 4-vii.-15; British retire, 5-vii.-15; Turkish forces driven back from Shaikh Othman, 21-vii.-15

Laibach — Slav conference, 17-viii.-18

L'Aigle, Forêt de — French dent German line, 6-v.-15

Lajj — British reach, 20-xi.-15; 25-xi.-15; cavalry at, 5-iii.-17

Lake, Gen. — C.-in-C., Mesopotamia, 10-i.-16; reports S. bank of Tigris to Shatt-el-Hai clear of Turks, 20-v.-16

" **Lake Michigan**," s.s. — mined, 15-xi.-16; sunk, 16-iv.-18

Lala Baba Hill — stormed and carried, 6-viii.-15

La Maisonette Château — Germans penetrate, 29-x.-16

La Maisonette Château — Biaches front — French take, 18-x.-16

La Maisonette Farm — French progress, 9-vii.-16; captured, 10-vii.-16; German counter-attack repulsed, 17-vii.-16

La Malmaison — battle, 23-x.-17

Lambe, Cmdr. — commanding Dover—Dunkirk air forces, 5-viii.-15

Lambros, M. (Greece) — Premier, 8-x.-16; arrested, 1-ii.-18

Lamia — Greek Army mutinies: suppressed, 1-ii.-18

Lammasch, Prof. (Austria) — Premier, 27-x.-18

La Montagne — Germans force Crozat Canal, 22-iii.-18

" **Lampada**," s.s. — sunk, 8-xii.-17

Lancashire — air raids, 25-ix.-16; 12-iv.-18

Lancers, 15th — at Orleans, 3-x.-14

Lancourt — French raid W. of, 2-xi.-16

Landersbach — French take trenches, 27-viii.-15

" **Landonia**," s.s. — sunk, 21-iv.-18

Landrecies — German attack beaten off by 4th Guards Brigade, 25-viii.-14; British approach, 24-x.-18; take, 4-xi.-18

Landreville — taken by Americans, 1-xi.-18

Landships: see Tanks

" **La Negra**," s.s. — sunk, 3-ix.-17

Laneuveville — SLVII. raids, 21-ii.-16; Americans take, 4-xi.-18

" **Lanfranc**," H.S. — sunk, 17-iv.-17

Lang, Most Rev. Cosmo G., Archbishop of York — visits Grand Fleet at Scapa, 26-vi.-15

Langeland Belt — mined, 24-ix.-14

Langemarck — heavy fighting, 23-x.-14; French take, 4-xii.-14; Germans attack with gas; French E. of, retire to canal, 22-iv.-15; Germans take, 23-iv.-15; French air raid on, 13-ix.-15; British take, 16-viii.-17; progress E. and S.E. of, 27-viii.-17; Germans attack, 13-ix.-17; British advance between Hollebeke and, 21-ix.-17

Langle, Gen. de (France) — commanding 4th Army, 27-viii.-14

Langres — U.S. Tank School at, 8-i.-18

" **Languedoc**," French Dreadnought — laid down, 1-v.-15

Lanrezac, Gen. (France) — commanding 5th Army, 14-viii.-14; 4-ix.-14; 9th Army interposed between 5th and 4th, 27-viii.-14

Lansdowne, Lord — letter to " Daily Telegraph," 29-xi.-17

Lansing, Mr. (U.S.) — Secretary of State, 8-vi.-15; in Paris: with Mr. Wilson at sitting of Supreme War Council, 12-i.-19

" **Lanthorn**," s.s. — sunk, 22-v.-17

Laon — Germans reach, 30-viii.-14; French progress, 27-iii.-17; 1-iv.-17; French assault on Laffaux Salient, 22-x.-17; victory on Soissons road, 23-x.-17; German long-range gun shells Paris, 23-iii.-18; fired on by U.S. naval gun, 25-vii.-18; French occupy, 13-x.-18

Lao Shan Bay — British land, 23-ix.-14

La Panne — German air raid on, 20-xii.-15; Belgian hospital bombed, 7-vii.-14

Lapeyrère, Adm. Boué de (France) — takes fleet to sea, 3-viii.-14; commands Anglo-French naval forces in Mediterranean, 6-viii.-14; joins Adm. Troubridge's squadron, 15-viii.-14; commands " Courbet " in action near Cattaro, 16-viii.-14; relinquishes command, 11-x.-15

" **Lapland**," s.s. — mined: reached port, 7-iv.-17

La Pompelle — German gas attack, 19-x.-15

La Poterie Farm — British capture trench system on mile front, 11-vi.-17

La Quinque Rue — Canadians capture orchard position near, 20-v.-15; British gain S. of, 22-v.-15

La Quinque Rue—Béthune road — British reach, 18-v.-15

" **Larchmore**," s.s. — sunk, 3-vii.-15

Larissa — Franco-British at, 12-vi.-17

Larnaude, M. (France) — on League of Nations Committee of Revision, 26-iii.-19

" **La Rosarina**," s.s. — chased by U-Boat: first recorded escape by use of gun, 17-iv.-15

La Royère — French success, 30-vii.-17

Lassigny — French driven out, 25-ix.-14; re-take, 17-iii.-17; taken by Germans, 27-iii.-18; Allies on line W. of, 27-iii.-18; French advance, 31-vii.-18; French take Carnoy Farm, 11-viii.-18; Belval taken, 13-viii.-18; progress, 14-viii.-18; capture completed, 15-viii.-18

" **Lassoo**," H.M.S. — mined, 13-viii.-16

La Targette — captured, 9-v.-15

Lateaux Wood — taken by British, 20-xi.-17; regained by Germans, 30-xi.-17

" **Latouche-Tréville,**" **French cruiser** — arrives in Dardanelles, 25-iv.-15

Lauch — French progress N. of, 15-iv.-15

Lauch Valley — German offensive, 13-ii.-15

Lauenstein, Gen. von (Germany) — commanding Prussian 39th Corps, 24-xii.-14; commands force for thrust into Lithuania and Courland, 22-iv.-15; invades, 27-iv.-15

Launois — French storm German defences, 24-vii.-15

Laurence, Cmdr. — commands E1 in sinking of German transport, 29-vii.-15

" **Laurentic,**" **H.M.A.M.C.** — mined, 23-i.-17

La Vacquerie — taken by British, 20-xi.-17; Germans penetrate positions; regain, 30-xi.-17; slight British withdrawal, 3-xii.-17; German attacks round, 6-xii.-17; German trenches captured; British line improved, 7-xii.-17

Laval — French capture, 21-viii.-18

" **Lavender,**" **H.M. sloop** — sunk, 5-v.-17

Laventie — German raids near defeated, 11-iii.-18; Germans penetrate line, 9-iv.-18

" **Lavernock,**" **s.s.** — sunk, 17-ix.-18

" **Laverock,**" **H.M.S.** — casualty, 25-iii.-16; torpedoed, 1-iii.-17

Lavertine Valley — French penetrate, 28-vi.-18

Law, Mr. Bonar — member of War Committee, 11-xi.-15; King sends for on resignation of Mr. Asquith, 5-xii.-16; declines to form Ministry, 6-xii.-16; to lead Commons, 11-xii.-16; on German peace proposals: reiterates Mr. Asquith's statement, " The Allies require that there shall be adequate reparation for the past and adequate security for the future," 14-xii.-16; leaves for Paris, 11-i.-19

Lawambala—Lujenda Rs. — fighting at junction, 7-i.-18

Lawe — German attempt, 11-iv.-18; forced, 12-iv.18

Lawrence, Gen. — appointed Chief of Staff to Sir D. Haig, 19-i.-18; welcomed in London, 19-xii.-18

Lazarevatz — Austro-Serbian battle, 28-xi.-14

League of Nations — Pres. Wilson's speech at Guildhall, 28-xii.-18; Gen. Smuts's pamphlet, 10-i.-19; Peace Conference: adopts resolution on Pres. Wilson's motion, 25-i.-19; Pres. Wilson reads draft at, 14-ii.-19; Pres. Wilson's speech at Boston, 24-ii.-19; discussed by Pres. Wilson and Congress Foreign Relations Committee, 27-ii.-19; Pres. Wilson's speech in New York; Senator Lodge's resolution against, 4-iii.-19; Spain: first neutral to notify desire to join, 3-iv.-19; Geneva: to be seat, 10-iv.-19; covenant condemned by British Labour Party, 5-iii.-19; revised covenant approved by Peace Conference, 28-iv.-19; Sir J. E. Drummond appointed first secretary-general, 28-iv.-19 Committee, Select — holds first meeting, 3-ii.-19; completes first half of draft, 7-ii.-19; hears neutral delegates, 20-iii.-19; 21-iii.-19; first full meeting since reading of draft: amendment discussed, 22-iii.-19; accepts U.S. Monroe Doctrine clause; vetoes Japanese race equality resolution, 10-iv.-19; completes revision of new draft, 11-iv.-19

" **Leasowe Castle,**" **s.s.** — torpedoed, 20-iv.-17; sunk, 26-v.-18

Le Balcon — French take, 16-iv.-17

Lebanon — Deputation heard by Peace Conference, 15-ii.-19

Le Barque — occupied, 26-ii.-17; carried by British, 25-viii.-18

Le Cateau — Sir J. French at, 17-viii.-14; British falling back to, 25-viii.-14; battle: Allied forces engaged; British retiring, 26-viii.-14; second battle, 8-x.-18; Allies within 12 miles, 9-x.-18; captured, 10-x.-18;

Le Cateau (continued) :—
Anglo-French attack southward from, 17-x.-18; part carried, 17-x.-18; British-American advance, 18-x.-18; British attack on Lille front at, 20-x.-18

Le Catelet — British advance towards, 16-iv.-17; take, 3-x.-18

Lechitsky, Gen. (Russia) — advance towards Czernowitz, 10-vi.-16; in Czernowitz, 17-vi.-16; defeat Austrians on 25-mile front near Kolomea, 28-vi.-16; at Delatyn, 8-vii.-16; progress towards Stanislau, 7-viii.-16; 8-viii.-16; in Stanislau, 10-viii.-16; at Solotvina, 15-viii.-16

Le Clipon — British 1st Division withdrawn, 15-x.-17

Lecluse — taken by British, 3-ix.-18

" **Le Coq,**" **s.s.** — mined, 6-x.-17

Leczca — Germans occupy, 18-xi.-15

" **Ledbury,**" **s.s.** — sunk, 25-iii.-17

Ledebour, Herr (Germany) — attempt to set up Communist régime in Berlin, 6-i.-19

Ledeghem — British take, 2-x.-18

" **Leeds City,**" **s.s.** — sunk, 6-v.-18

" **Leelanaw,**" **s.s.** — torpedoed, 25-vii.-15

Le Forest — French take, 3-ix.-16; French press on E. of, 4-ix.-16; 5-ix.-16

Le Gheir—Hollebeke — British cavalry at, 19-x.-14

Le Hamel — taken by French, 19-viii.-18

Leicester — Zeppelin raid on, 5-iii.-16

" **Leicester,**" **H.M. store-carrier** — mined, 12-ii.-16

" **Leicestershire,**" **s.s.** — escapes from U-Boat, 7-ix.-15

Leigh-on-Sea — air-raid, 10-v.-15

Leinert, Deputy (Germany) — presides at Congress of Workmen's and Soldiers' Councils, 16-xii.-18

" **Leinster,**" **s.s.** — sunk, 10-x.-18

" **Leipzig,**" **H.I.M.S.** — sinks s.s. " Elsinore," 11-ix.-14; sinks s.s. " Bankfields," 25-ix.-14; in Coronel battle, 1-xi.-14; at Valparaiso, 13-xi.-14; sunk off Falkland Islands, 8-xii.-14

Leipzig Redoubt — British gain footing, 1-vii.-16; part carried, 7-vii.-16; advance, 19-vii.-16; German attack repulsed, 21-vii.-16; British carry, 18-viii.-16; advance across, 24-viii.-16

Leith — air-raid, 2-iv.-16

Leman, Gen. (Belgium) — taken prisoner, 15-viii.-14

Le Mans — advanced British base, 29-viii.-14; U.S. army corps awaiting re-embarkation, 19-xi.-18

Lembeni — British occupy, 24-v.-16

Lemberg — Austrians fall back on, 27-viii.-14; battle, 1-ix.-14; Austrians defeated, 2-ix.-14; evacuated, 3-ix.-14; Russians on Grodek line before, 14-vi.-15; battle begun, 17-vi.-15; Austro-Germans recapture, 22-vi.-15; Russians in retreat, 25-vi.-15; 27-vi.-15; Germans storm Gnila—Lipa line and cross near Rohatyn; Austro-Germans advance from Tomaszov and Russians retreat, 30-vi.-15; Austrian success N.E. of, 1-ix.-15; Russians advance on, 30-ix.-16; seized by Ukrainians, 1-xi.-18; Poles recover, 22-xi.-18; Poles retake from Ukrainians, 10-i.-19; Polish-Ukrainian truce, 22-ii.-19; ends; Ukrainians bombard town, 3-iii.-19; Poles relieve, 20-iii.-19

Lemerle — Italians lose, 9-vi.-16

Le Mesnil — French gain near, 25-ii.-15; French take trenches near, 26-ii.-15; progress, 9-iii.-15; success N.E., 11-ii.-16; gains held, 12-ii.-16

Le Mesurier, F. Comm. — commanding 4th Light Cruiser Squadron, 30-vi.-15

Lempire — British take, 5-iv.-17; 18-ix.-18

Lenin, M. (Russia) — organises Bolshevist Petrograd revolt, 16-vii.-17; revolt continued, 17-vii.-17; crushed, 18-vii.-17; presides at Bolshevist and Social Revolutionary Conference, 8-viii.-17; coup d'état in Petrograd, 7-xi.-17

Lennewaden — Russian success at, 21-ix.-15

Lens — occupied by Germans, 4-x.-14; 8-x.-14; British bombard, 25-vi.-16; British raid in region, 16-i.-17; advance towards, 12-iv.-17; 13-iv.-17; 14-iv.-17; 15-iv.-17; 16-iv.-17; 21-iv.-17; German trenches captured near, 5-v.-17; Germans repulsed, 7-v.-17; Canadian progress, 2-vi.-17; British progress on 2,500 yard front S.W. of; numerous British raids, 24-vi.-17; progress S.W. of, 26-vi.-17; 28-vi.-17; German defence captured on ½-mile front, 30-vi.-17; British setback, 2-vii.-17; British progress near, 6-viii.-17; attack: suburbs taken, 15-viii.-17; German counter-attack fails, 16-viii.-17; 18-viii.-17; Canadians carry positions near, 21-viii.-17; invested S.W. and N., 22-viii.-17; Canadians in Green Crassier, 23-viii.-17; British progress N.W. of, 6-ix.-17; advance S. of, 3-i.-18; Canadian raids, 12-ii.-18; 14-ii.-18; German attempts near, 3-iii.-18; Germans evacuate, 3-ix.-18; fighting on front, 7-ix.-18; Germans withdraw, 2-x.-18; British advance E. of and between Cambrai and, 4-x.-18; British progress between Scarpe and, 10-x.-18

"Leonardo da Vinci," Italian battleship — destroyed by explosion, 2-viii.-16

"Leonatus," s.s. — mined, 12-xii.-17

"Léon Gambetta," French cruiser — sunk, 27-iv.-15

"Leopard," German raider — sunk, 16-iii.-17

Leopoldshöhe — French air-raid on, 28-iv.-15

"Lepanto," s.s. — torpedoed, 23-x.-17

L'Epinette — British take, 12-iii.-15

Le Plémont — French widen salient N. of, 2-iv.-18

Le Port R. — Allies take, 6-vi.-18

Le Priez Farm — French take trench system S. of, 13-ix.-16; carried, 14-ix.-16; trench system N. of taken, 15-ix.-16

Le Quesnoy — taken by Germans, 25-iii.-18; taken by British, 4-xi.-18

Lersner, Baron von (Germany) — signs formal ratification of peace, 10-i.-20

Le Rutoire — French recover, 7-xii.-14

Le Sars — British capture mill between Eaucourt l'Abbaye and, 6-x.-16; take, 7-x.-16; attack on 5,000-yard front between Schwaben Redoubt and, 21-x.-16; Allies on line, 24-iii.-18; carried, 25-viii.-18

Lesbœufs — captured, 25-ix.-16; British advance, 7-x.-16; attack E. of, 23-x.-16; progress N.E. of, 28-x.-16; Anglo-French advance, 1-xi.-16; French capture trenches, 10-xi.-16

Les Corneilles — French take, 24-v.-15

Les Eparges — French attack, 17-ii.-15; success, 19-ii.-15; fighting, 24-ii.-15; progress, 27-iii.-15; German counter-attack repulsed, 28-iii.-15; French attack crest, 5-iv.-15; 7-iv.-15; take part of heights, 8-iv.-15; carry crest, 9-iv.-15; German counter-attacks repulsed, 11-iv.-15; German attacks repulsed, 24-iv.-15; German attacks, 19-vii.-15; 19-iv.-16; repulsed, 20-iv.-16; French raid near, 4-iii.-18

Leskovatz — Bulgarians take, 9-xi.-15

Les Loges — taken by French, 11-viii.-18

Lesmésnils — French take, 2-xii.-14

Les Quatre Bouquetaux — French take, 27-v.-15

Lesser Zab — Turks retire towards, 23-x.-18; British force, 25-x.-18

Lessines — Allied line at Armistice, 11-xi.-18

"Lestris," s.s. — captured; taken to Zeebrugge, 5-vii.-16

Le Transloy — British progress W. of 12-x.-16; attack, 5-xi.-16; success near, 27-i.-17; advanced post near rushed, 19-ii.-17; captured by British, 2-ix.-18

Le Tronquoy — captured, 30-ix.-18

Lettland — troops in action, 19-ix.-17; Republic proclaimed, 22-xi.-18; Allied recognition of independence sought, 17-iii.-19; operations against Bolshevists: capture Mitau, 19-iii.-19

Lettow-Vorbeck, Gen. von (Germany) — campaign: see Africa, East; summoned to surrender, 13-xi.-18; surrenders, 25-xi.-18

Leugenboom — long-range gun bombards Dunkirk, 27-vi.-17

Leury — French carry, 31-viii.-18

Leuze Wood — British gain footing, 4-ix.-16; held, 5-ix.-16; cleared, 6-ix.-16; ground captured, 9-ix.-16

Levant — discussed by Pres. Wilson, M. Clemenceau, Mr. Lloyd George, M. Pichon, Mr. Balfour, and Gen. Allenby, 20-iii.-19

"Leven," H.M.S. — sinks, UB35, 26-i.-18

Levergies — British take, 1-x.-18

Le Verguier — British take, 9-iv.-17; British resistance, 21-iii.-18; taken by Germans, 22-iii.-18; British storm outer defences, 18-ix.-18

Leveson, Adm. — Rear-Adm. in 2nd Battle Squadron, 15-i.-15; in H.M.S. "Orion" in Jutland battle, 31-v.-16; 1-vi.-16

"Leviathan," H.M.S. — in new 1st Cruiser Squadron, 7-xii.-14

Lewin, Gen. — at Altun Keupri, 31-x.-18

"Lewisham," s.s. — sunk, 14-v.-17

"Lexie," s.s. — sunk, 10-ix.-16

Leyton — Zeppelin raid, 17-viii.-15

Leytonstone — Zeppelin raid, 17-viii.-15

Lezachov — San crossed at, 17-v.-15

Liancourt — Allies on line, 25-iii.-18; Germans take, 26-iii.-18

Liaptcheff, M. (Bulgaria) — peace plenipotentiary, 28-ix.-18

Libau — bombarded, 2-viii.-14; 18-xi.-14; ZXIX. shot down, 25-i.-15; bombarded, 31-iii.-15; Germans advance on, 1-v.-15; occupy; governor appointed, 7-v.-15; German T.B.D. mined in harbour, 8-v.-15; Adm. von Tirpitz visits, 14-viii.-15; British naval force at, 3-xii.-18; returns to Copenhagen, 7-xii.-18; suggested by Germans as port for Gen. Hallers' Polish troops, 28-iii.-19

Libau—Dvinsk railway — Germans reach, 29-iv.-15; 30-iv.-15

Libau—Vilna railway — Germans forced back, 8-v.-15

Liberia — breaks with Germany, 8-v.-17; Monrovia shelled by U-Boat, 10-iv.-18; to have delegate at Paris Peace Conference, 15-i.-19

"Liberty," H.M.S. — sinks UC46, 8-ii.-17

"Libourne," s.s. — sunk, 29-ix.-18

Lichtervelde — taken, 16-x.-18

Lida — ZXII. raids, 13-ix.-15

Liebknecht, Herr (Germany) — visits Belgium, 24-viii.-14; votes against war credits, 2-xii.-14; 20-iii.-15; 20-viii.-15; supposed author of "Spartakus" letters, 27-i.-16; arrested, 1-v.-16; sent to penal servitude, 23-viii.-16; released, 21-x.-18; attempts to set up Communist régime in Berlin, 6-i.-19; killed in Berlin, 15-i.-19

Liége — attack begun, 4-viii.-14; air-raid, 5-viii.-14; penetrated by 14th German Infantry Brigade, 6-viii.-14; entered, 7-viii.-14; four forts fall, 13-viii.-14; Meuse reached N. of by von Kluck's leading corps, 14-viii.-14; last fort, Loncin, destroyed; Gen. Leman taken prisoner, 15-viii.-14; German Naval Corps replaces garrison, 31-viii.-14; British air-raid on, 22-v.-18

Liéramont — British take, 27-iii.-17

Lierre, Fort — falls, 1-x.-14

Liévin — British take, 14-iv.-17

Liggett, Gen. (U.S.) — commanding 1st Army Corps, 15-i.-18; 30-viii.-18; 22-ix.-18; 12-x.-18

"Light," H.M. drifter — assists in destruction of UB82, 17-iv.-18

"Lightning," H.M.S. — mined, 30-vi.-18

Lightship — sunk by U-Boat, 28-iii.-17

Ligny — British occupy, 27-ii.-17; Allies on line, 24-iii.-18; G.H.Q. U.S. 1st Army, 30-viii.-18

Ligny-en-Barrois — U.S. 3rd Army H.Q. constituted, 7-xi.-18

Ligny-Thilloy — Anzacs at, 3-iii.-17

Ligonya R. — Germans driven across, 12-vi.-18

Lihons — German attack broken, 19-xii.-14; taken by British, 9-viii.-18; fighting, 11-viii.-18; British attack on 30-mile front, 23-viii.-18

Likungo R. — Germans cross, 1-vii.-18; 5-vii.-18; 24-viii.-18

"Lilac," H.M. mine-sweeper — mined, 18-viii.-15

Lille — German cavalry in, 26-viii.-14; abandoned by French, 27-viii.-14; German line hardens, 6-x.-14; bombarded, 8-x.-14; 10-x.-14; German 19th Corps at, 12-x.-14; Allies shell, 7-ii.-16; unemployed invited to "volunteer" for work, 25-iii.-16; forcible levy of workers ordered, 11-iv.-16; impressment begun, 22-iv.-16; press-gangs thanked by Crown Prince of Bavaria, 29-iv.-16; British cross Haute Deule Canal S.W. of, 15-x.-18; falls; British 5th Army enter, 17-x.-18

Limanowa — Austrians begin battle, 5-xii.-14

Liman von Sanders, Gen. (Germany) — takes over Yildirim command, 25-ii.-18

Limburg (Dutch) —retreating Germans pass through, 13-xi.-18

"Lime Branch," s.s. — torpedoed, 13-iv.-17

"Limeleaf," s.s. — torpedoed, 19-iv.-17

"Limerick," s.s. — sunk, 28-v.-17

Lincoln — air-raids, 5-iii.-16; 31-iii.-16; 24-iv.-16; 28-vii.-16; 31-vii.-16; 3-ix.-16

Lincolns, 2nd — joins convoy, 3-x.-14

Lincolnshire — air-raids, 5-iii.-16; 31-iii.-16; 24-iv.-16; 28-vii.-16; 31-vii.-16; 3-ix.-16; 23-ix.-16; 25-ix.-16; 1-x.-16; 24-ix.-17; 12-iv.-18

"Lincolnshire," s.s. — sunk, 29-iii.-17

"Linda Blanche," s.s. — sunk, 30-i.-15

Lindi — British ships shell, 20-iii.-15; heavy fighting near, 3-viii.-17; Germans pressed, 21-ix.-17; Allies attack column, 25-ix.-17; fighting, 1-x.-17

Linge — trenches captured, 22-viii.-15

Lingenkopf — French advance, 26-vii.-15; French success, 27-vii.-15; Germans attack French, 2-viii.-15; Germans repulsed, 7-viii.-15

Lingekopf—Barrenkopf — German attacks repulsed, 9-ix.-15

"Linkmoor," H.M. collier — sunk, 20-ix.-15

Linsingen, Gen. von (Germany) — commands new Southern Army on E. front, 11-i.-15; commands Bug Army, 6-vii.-15; loses 8,000 prisoners, 6-vii.-16; defeated on Slonuvka R., 25-vii.-16; army group on Hindenburg's front, 30-vii.-16; suspension of hostilities on front, 2-xii.-17; forbids formation of Soviet councils, 7-xi.-18

Lioma — Germans engaged, 30-viii.-18

"Lion," H.M.S. — in Dogger Bank battle; damaged; towed home, 24-i.-15; reaches Rosyth, 31-i.-15; repairing, 31-i.-15; in Tyne, 9-ii.-15; returns to Rosyth, 7-iv.-15; with 1st and 2nd Battle Cruiser Squadrons covers mine-laying operations in the Bight, 10-ix.-15; supports Harwich force in Horn

"Lion," H.M.S. (continued):—
Reef operations, 18-x.-15; supports Skagerrak sweeping, 6-xi.-15; in Jutland battle, 31-v.-16; sweeps towards Naze; proceeds to Scapa, 30-ix.-16

Lipno — German offensive near, 30-i.-16

Lipsk — Germans storm, 29-viii.-15

Liquid fire — Germans use in W. Poland, 7-iii.-15; use by Germans in Alsace, 6-iii.-15

Liquorice factory — Turks fall back to, 4-ii.-17; British carry trenches, 10-ii.-17

Lisbon — rising, 6-xii.-17; President assassinated, 14-xii.-18

"Lismore," s.s. — sunk, 12-iv.-17

Lissa — bombarded by French, 17-ix.-14; Italians land, 3-xi.-18

Lithuania — German offensive in preparation, 22-iv.-15; advance on Shavli, 26-iv.-15; 27-iv.-15; Germans reach Libau—Dvinsk railway; Russians retire on Mitau, 29-iv.-15; Germans reach Shavli, Muravievo, and Radzivilishki, 30-iv.-15; enter Shavli and advance on Libau, 1-v.-15; German advance on Mitau, 3-v.-15; checked, 5-v.-15; retire from; occupy Libau: governor appointed, 7-v.-15; destroyer mined in Libau harbour; forced back at Zejny on Libau-Vilna railway, 8-v.-15; Germans retire from Shavli, 11-v.-15; Russians take Kindovary, 27-v.-15; Germans checked near Shavli, 9-vi.-15; Russian offensive, 16-iii.-16; 26-iii.-16; German 10th Army in, 16-xi.-18; German bid for sympathies by institution of "national" council, 30-v.-17; plan developed, 21-vii.-17; Bolshevists demand self-determination and withdrawal of German troops, 2-i.-18; Allied recognition of independence sought, 17-iii.-19

Liktera — British cavalry advance to, 19-ix.-18

Little Fisher Bank — Grand Fleet sweeps down to, 18-iv.-15; 3rd Light Cruiser Squadron sweeps down to, 1-x.-15; 10-x.-15; Harwich force operates off, 31-x.-15

Litzmann, Gen. (Germany) — commanding Prussian Reserve Corps, 24-xii.-14

Liubichevatz — Austro-Germans and Bulgarians in touch, 26-x.-15

Liumnitza — French and Venizelists gain ground, 10-v.-17

Livenza R. — Italians reach, 6-xi.-17; Austrian rout, 30-x.-18

Liverpool — anti-German riots, 10-v.-15

"Liverpool," H.M.S. — bombed by aeroplane, 24-xi.-14 develops serious boiler trouble: first of many ships to do so, 12-xii.-14

Livonia — Wenden raided, 28-iv.-16; Russians holding at Segewold, 13-ix.-17; Germans occupy, 5-iii.-18

"Livonia," s.s. — sunk, 3-xii.-17

Lizerne — Germans attack with gas; take bridge S. of, 23-iv.-15; French and Belgians recover, 24-iv.-15; Germans recover, 25-iv.-15; French regain, 27-iv.-15

Lizerne—Het Sas — French advance, 4-v.-15

Lizzana Castle — Austrians destroy, 4-viii.-15

"Lizzie Westoll," s.s. — sunk, 17-vi.-17

"Llancarvan," s.s. — sunk, 16-v.-18

"Llandovery Castle," H.S. — chased by U-Boat, 8-vi.-15; sunk, 27-vi.-18

"Llandrindod," s.s. — sunk, 18-v.-17

"Llandudno," s.s. — sunk, 1-viii.-17

"Llangorse," s.s. — sunk, 8-ix.-16

"Llanishen," s.s. — sunk, 8-viii.-17

"Llewellyn," H.M.S. — sinks UC19, 4-xii.-16

"Llongwen," s.s. — sunk, 18-vii.-16

Lloyd, Sir W. F. (Newfoundland) — leaves for Paris, 11-i.-19

Lloyd George, Mr. D. — "silver bullet" speech 8-ix.-14; announces £350,000,000 War Loan, 17-xi.-14; outlines liquor control proposals,

Lloyd George, Mr. D. (continued) :—
29-iv.-15; Minister of Munitions, 16-vi.-15; member of War Committee, 11-xi.-15; War Secretary, 6-vii.-16; urges Mr. Asquith to establish small War Cabinet, 1-xii.-16; Mr. Asquith accepts reconstruction scheme, 3-xii.-16; threat to resign causes break-up of Asquith Ministry, 5-xii.-16; agrees to form Ministry, 6-xii.-16; forms, 11-xii.-16; on German peace offer and new cabinet's war policy: "restitution, reparation, and a guarantee against repetition" demanded; Government to call Imperial conference; control shipping and mining and institute National Service, 18-xii.-16; attends Rome conference, 5-i.-17; conference with M. Ribot and Baron Sonnino: at St. Jean de Maurienne, 19-iv.-17; at conference in Paris, 6-v.-17; proceeds to Italy, 4-xi.-17; in Paris on need for Allied War Council, 12-xi.-17; defends scheme; announces destruction of 5 U-Boats in one day, 19-xi.-17; on Russian collapse and Italian defeat: says fresh obligations imposed upon Great Britain, 20-xii.-17; speech on war aims, 5-i.-18; statement on military situation; Versailles decisions, 12-ii.-18; 19-ii.-18; on Gen. Robertson, 19-ii.-18; announces Gen Foch's appointment as Allied C.-in-C., 30-iii.-18; at Edinburgh on U-Boat campaign; British ship construction, 23-v.-18; announces agreement on Armistice terms, 6-xi.-18; conference with Pres. Wilson and Mr. Balfour in London, 27-xii.-18; leaves for Paris, 11-i.-19; returns, 8-ii.-19; in Parliament: denies recognition of Bolshevists, 12-ii.-19; discusses Levant affairs, 20-iii.-19; member of Council of Four, 24-iii.-19; King Albert confers with in Paris, 2-iv.-19; telegram sent by 200 M.P.s urging firmness on indemnity question, 8-iv.-19; replies stating he will stand by pledges; another telegram signed by 200 M.P.s urges refusal to recognise Moscow Government, 9-iv.-19; in Parliament: on Peace Conference, 16-iv.-19; signs Franco-British Treaty, 28-vi.-19; leaves France for England, 29-vi.-19; in Parliament: on Treaty, 3-vii.-19; signs formal ratification of peace, 10-i.-20

" **Llwyngwair,**" **s.s.** — sunk, 26-iv.-18

Lochow, Gen. von (Germany) — Kaiser confers Pour le Mérite order, 13-i.-15; superseded in command of 3rd Prussian Army Corps, 25-xi.-16; in acting-command of 5th Army, 1-xii.-16

" **Locksley Hall,**" **s.s.** — sunk, 12-v.-17

Locon — British advance, 9-viii.-18

Locquinol — taken by British, 4-xi.-18

Locre — Allies pressed back towards; four German attacks defeated, 26-iv.-18; British minor success S.W. of, 3-v.-18; French advance E. and N.E. of: reach obectives on 2½-mile front, 20-v.-18; German attack repulsed, 27-v.-18

Lodge, Senator (U.S.) — anti-League of Nations resolution in Senate, 4-iii.-19

Lody, Lieut. (Germany) — shot in Tower, 6-xi.-14

Lodz — raided by ZV., 11-viii.-14; Russians regain, 28-x.-14; battle begun, 16-xi.-14; Germans reach Strykow, 17-xi.-14; Germans approaching, 18-xi.-14; fighting E. and S.E. of, 20-xi.-14; German 25th Reserve Corps and 3rd Prussian Guard Division heavily engaged S.E. of, 21-xi.-14; battle continues, 22-xi.-14; Russians drive wedge through German line E. of: near Brzezany, 23-xi.-14; German 25th Reserve Corps and 3rd Prussian Guard Division cut off: break through Russian line at Brzezany, 24-xi.-14; Russians evacuating, 27-xi.-14; Germans

Lodz (continued) :—
bombard, 29-xi.-14; 25th Reserve Corps reinforces Mackensen S.W. of, 30-xi.-14; Germans in suburbs, 1-xii.-14; Germans enter, 6-xii.-14; German 9th Army engaged, 17-xii.-14

" **Lofoten,**" **s.s.** — sunk, 3-ii.-18

Loftus Jones, Cmdr. — awarded V.C., 31-v.-16

Loges Wood — French progress, 16-viii.-18

Loivre — French take, 16-iv.-17; 3-x.-18

Lol Kissale — British take, 6-iv.-16

Lomax, Gen. — fatally wounded at Ypres, 31-x.-14

Lombaertzyde — evacuated, 20-x.-14; British bombard, 21-x.-14; Belgians reoccupy, 22-x.-14; Germans retake, 28-x.-14; engaged by French vessels under Adm. Hood, 30-x.-14; Germans lose and retake, 4-xi.-14; Allies advance towards, 15-xii.-14; Belgians take trenches near, 27-xii.-14; British ships bombard, 1-x.-15; Germans penetrate British positions: driven out, 10-vii.-17; German attack S. of, 19-vii.-17

Lombray — French reach, 20-viii.-18

Lome — Gold Coast Force landed, 12-viii.-14

Lomie — French occupy, 25-vii.-15

Lomja — Russian counter-attack near, 21-ii.-15

Lomnica R. — Austro-Germans behind, 9-vii.-17

Lom Palanka — Rumanians bombard, 8-ix.-16

" **Lompoc,**" **s.s.** — torpedoed, 21-iv.-18; 28-viii.-18

Lomzha — Germans storm Fort 4, 9-viii.-15; Germans take, 10-viii.-15

Loncin — last Liége fort to be destroyed, 15-viii.-14

London :—

Air-raids — inhabitants warned, 28-xii.-14; campaign discussed by Adm. von Pohl and Herr von Bethmann-Hollweg, 5-i.-15; Kaiser authorises use of airships for raids, 9-i.-15; first raid, 31-v.-15; further raids, 17-viii.-15; 7-ix.-15; 8-ix.-15; 13-x.-15; 2-iv.-16; 25-iv.-16; 25-viii.-16; (attempted), 31-viii.-16; raid, 3-ix.-16; 23-ix.-16; 1-x.-16; first aeroplane raid: one raider down in France, 28-xi.-16; daylight raid, 13-vi.-17; raid prevented by bad weather, 17-vi.-17; daylight raid: four raiders down on return journey, 7-vii.-17; (secret sitting of House of Commons, 19-vii.-17); further raids, 4-ix.-17; 24-ix.-17; 25-ix.-17; 29-ix.-17; 30-ix.-17; 1-x.-17; 19-x.-17; 31-x.-17; 6-xi.-17; 18-xii.-17; 28-i.-18; 29-i.-18; 16-ii.-18; 17-ii.-18; 18-ii.-18; 7-iii.-18; thirty-second and last: five raiders destroyed, 19-v.-18

Defences — in charge of Adm. Sir P. Scott, 13-ix.-15; area formed, 31-viii.-17

Anti-German riots, 10-v.-15; 11-v.-15; 12-v.-15

Army commanders — welcomed on return from W. front, 19-xii.-18

Peace — proclaimed in City and St. James's Palace, 2-vii.-19; National Thanksgiving at St. Paul's Cathedral, 6-vii.-19; Armistice anniversary celebrated, 11-xi.-19

Ration order — first, 25-ii.-18

Munition factory explodes, 19-i.-17

" **London,**" **s.s.** — sunk by U-Boat, 23-vi.-18

London, Declaration of — German reply to U.S. Note, 16-ii.-15; rescinded, 8-vii.-16

London, Pact of — Triple Entente Powers agree not to make separate peace, 5-ix.-14; Japan adheres to, 19-x.-15; Italy adheres to, 1-xii.-15; Allies protest against any breach of by Russia, 23-xi.-17

London Scottish — arrive in France, 30-ix.-14; first Territorials in action: engage with "unshaken" losses at Messines, 31-x.-14

Lone Pine — taken, 6-viii.-15

Longatte — British carry, 2-iv.-17; taken by Germans, 21-iii.-18

Longavesnes — British take, 27-iii.-17

" Longhirst," s.s. — sunk, 23-ii.-17

Longpont — German failure at, 5-vi.-18; French regain, 12-vii.-18

Longueval — taken by British, 14-vii.-16; partially recaptured, 18-vii.-16; heavy fighting, 19-vii.-16; orchard recovered, 27-vii.-16; last German positions taken, 28-vii.-16; taken by British, 27-viii.-18

Longuyon — U.S. naval gun in action, 25-vii.-18

Longwy — falls to German 5th Army, 26-viii.-14

Lonsdale, Private — death sentence commuted, 11-i.-15

Loos — battle: British attack S. of La Bassée Canal to E. of Grenay—Vermelles: capture Hohenzollern Redoubt, Hulluch outskirts, Loos village, and Hill 70; French gain Souchez cemetery and remainder of the Labyrinth, 25-ix.-15; gains consolidated: French capture Souchez and reach La Folie, 26-ix.-15; British attack progresses E. of Loos: pushed back between Fosse 8 and Hohenzollern Redoubt, 27-ix.-15; further British progress facing German third line: Guards carry Chalk Pit near Hill 70; French relieve British between Double Crassier—Loos, 28-ix.-15; German pressure near Hohenzollern Redoubt: French carry Hill 140 on Vimy, 29-ix.-15; battle continued, 20-ix.-15; French progress on La Folie heights, 1-x.-15; Germans recapture part of Hohenzollern Redoubt, 3-x.-15; indecisive actions, 5-x.-15; strong German counter-attacks on Loos repulsed: British gain trench at Cité St. Eloi: French lose ground near Double Crassier, 8-x.-15; severe fighting, 9-x.-15; French progress in Souchez valley, Givenchy-en-Gohelle wood, and La Folie ridges, 10-x.-15; progress N.E. of Souchez and on La Folie heights, 11-x.-15; British take trenches at Vermelles—Hulluch and main trench of Hohenzollern Redoubt; 46th Division engaged, 13-x.-15; German counter-attack at Hohenzollern Redoubt repulsed, 14-x.-15; German attack at quarries, Hulluch, and Hohenzollern Redoubt fail, 19-x.-15; Germans explode mines near, 30-xii.-15; German attack N.W. of repulsed, 27-i.-16; fight at Hohenzollern Redoubt, 2-iii.-16; 26-iii.-16; gas attack N. of defeated, 29-iv.-16; German attacks at Hohenzollern Redoubt, 14-v.-16; raid on British trenches S. of: repulsed, 5-i.-17; British raids, 14-i.-17; 17-i.-17; 21-i.-17; 26-i.-17; German raids beaten off, 14-ii.-17; British attacks, 13-iv.-17; 14-iv.-17; attack N.E. of, 15-viii.-17

Dispatch — issued, 1-xi.-15

Loos—Fampoux — British gains, 18-iv.-17

" Lord Charlemont," s.s. — sunk, 19-iv.-18

" Lord Derby," s.s. — sunk, 28-xii.-17

" Lord Leitrim," H.M. drifter — sinks UB31, 2-v.-18

" Lord Nelson," H.M.S. — commander, 7-iii.-14; bombards Narrows, 7-iii.-15

" Lord Ormonde," s.s. — torpedoed, 20-iii.-18

" Lord Roberts," s.s. — sunk, 21-vi.-17

" Lord Stewart," s.s. — sunk, 16-ix.-18

" Lord Strathcona," s.s. — bombed in Dunkirk dock, 20-v.-16

" Lord Tredegar," s.s. — sunk, 17-ix.-16

" Lorle," s.s. — sunk, 11-vi.-18

" Lorna," H.M. armed yacht — sinks UB74, 26-v.-18

Lorraine — entered by French, 6-viii.-14; advance, 10-viii.-14; invaded by 2nd Army, 16-viii.-14; 15th (Prussian) Corps

Lorraine (continued) :—
transferred to Aisne, 12-ix.-14; Germans retake Embermenil, 20-iv.-15; two years' position warfare begun, 31-v.-15; German attack in Parroy Forest, 16-vii.-15; position-warfare until Armistice: begun, 10-i.-18; French raids, 20-ii.-18; Honved Division in, 13-ix.-18

Losice — Russians reach, 14-viii.-15; entered, 15-viii.-15

" Lotusmere," H.M. collier — sunk, 2-x.-16

Loughborough — Zeppelin raid on, 31-i.-16

Lough Swilly — Grand Fleet base transferred to, 17-x.-14; H.M.S. " Iron Duke " at, 22-x.-14; temporarily obstructed against U-Boat attack, 23-x.-14

" Louis," H.M.S. — wrecked, 31-x.-15

Loupart Wood — British in, 13-iii.-17; British carry, 24-viii.-18

Louppy — Allied line at Armistice, 11-xi.-18

Louvain — occupied by Germans, 19-viii.-14; street fighting, 25-viii.-14; destruction begun, 26-viii.-14

" Louvain," H.M. armed steamer — sunk, 20-i.-18

Louvemont — French take, 15-xii.-16

Louveral — British carry, 2-iv.-17; 10-iv.-17; Germans take, 21-iii.-18

Louvignies — taken by British, 4-xi.-18

Lovatchy — Austrians resist at, 19-vi.-16

Lovicz — German centre beyond, 14-x.-14

Lovtchen, Mt. — Austrian assault supported by warships, 9-i.-16; take, 10-i.-16

" Lowdale," s.s. — sunk, 20-iv.-17

Lowestoft — s.s. " Tunisiana " sunk off, 23-vi.-15; air-raid on, 20-ii.-16; naval raids, 25-iv.-16; 26-xi.-16

Lowicz — Germans on defensive W. of, 25-xi.-14; Austrians support Mackensen at Limanowa, 5-xii.-14; Russian stand at, 11-xii.-14; taken by Germans, 17-xii.-14

Lowicz—Lodz — Germans prepare fresh thrust into Poland at, 10-xi.-14

Lowicz—Lodz—Petrikov — German advance on line, 26-xi.-14

Lowry, Adm. — C.-in-C. coast of Scotland: inaugurates new anti-U-Boat operation, 23-v.-15

" Lowther Castle," s.s. — mined, 14-vi.-17

" Lowther Grange," s.s. — sunk, 20-ix.-18

Lowther Rock, Pentland Firth — H.M. armed steamer " Duke of Albany " aground, 7-vi.-15; H.M.S. " Blonde " ashore, 10-viii.-16

" Lowtyne," H.M. auxiliary — sunk, 10-vi.-18

" Loyal," H.M.S. — sinks German T.B.D.s, 17-x.-14

Lubartov — Austrians bombard Hill 183, 6-viii.-15; take hill, 7-viii.-15

Lublin — Austrian check, 2-ix.-14; Austro-German offensive towards, 4-vii.-15; Russian counter-attacks, 11-vii.-15; Germans checked, 24-vii.-15; heavy fighting, 19-vii.-15; Austro-Germans enter, 30-vii.-15; bombard Hill 183, 6-viii.-15; advance, 23-viii.-15

Lublin—Lutsk — army group moved forward, 28-viii.-14

Lubonia — Russians take Hill 1002 near, 21-iv.-15

Luce R. — British take prisoners, 1-iv.-18

" Lucellum," s.s. — torpedoed, 3-xii.-16

" Luciston," s.s. — mined, 29-xi.-16; attacked by U-Boat, 24-xii.-17

Ludd — Gen. Allenby advances N.E. of, 15-xii.-17

Ludendorff, Gen. (Germany) — Quartermaster 2nd Army; penetrates Liége, 6-viii.-14; occupies Liége citadel, 7-viii.-14; receives Pour le Mérite, 7-viii.-14; appointed Chief of Staff to Gen. von Hindenburg in E. Prussia, 22-viii.-14; arrives at Marienburg, 23-viii.-14; designated Chief of Staff

Ludendorff, Gen. (Germany) (continued):—
to 9th Army, 15-ix.-14; 18-ix.-14; on
E. front, 5-ii.-15; ordered to resume
offensive in Poland, 1-vii.-15; Chief of Staff,
5-viii.-15; appointed Quarter-master, 29-viii.-
16; provisional agreement to peace proposals,
5-xi.-16; urges upon Chancellor that unrestricted U-Boat warfare could no longer be
delayed, 20-xii.-16; arrives in Berlin to urge
dismissal of Chancellor, 6-vii.-17; telegraphs
resignation to Kaiser, 12-vii.-17; summoned
to Berlin, 13-vii.-17; issues confidential instruction warning against spread of " political
propaganda " in Army, 25-vii.-17; issues
detailed programme for patriotic propaganda
in Army, 29-vii.-17; Kaiser discusses new
Russian frontier with, 2-i.-18; congratulates
Gen. Hoffmann on Brest-Litovsk speech,
12-i.-18; urges rapid decisions at Brest-
Litovsk, 5-ii.-18; at Homburg, on coming
offensive: promises Kaiser victory, 13-ii.-18;
declares impossibility of further working with
von Kühlmann, 1-vii.-18; refers to battle of
Amiens as " the Black Day of the German
Army," 8-viii.-18; attends conference at Spa,
13-viii.-18; 15-viii.-18; statement on abandonment of Flanders coast, 18-ix.-18; agrees to
request for armistice, 28-ix.-18; informed of
peace negotiations, 29-ix.-18; tenders resignation, 26-x.-18; successor appointed, 27-x.-18
Lüderitz Bay — abandoned by Germans,
10-viii.-14; occupied by British, 18-ix.-14
" **Ludgate,**" **s.s.** — mined, 26-vii.-17
" **Ludlow,**" **H.M. mine-sweeper** — mined,
29-xii.-16
Ludwig, King of Bavaria — at Sofia, 8-ix.-18;
escapes into Austria, 7-xi.-18; abdicates,
13-xi.-18
Ludwigshafen — air-raids, 26-v.-15; 7-vii.-17
" **Lugano,**" **s.s.** — sunk, 2-x.-17
" **Luis,**" **s.s.** — sunk, 12-iv.-18
Luisenhof farm — occupied, 25-ii.-17
Lujenda valley — British occupy, 3-ii.-18
Lukigura, R. — Germans defeated, 24-vi.-16
Lukoff, Gen. (Bulgaria) — peace plenipoten-
tiary, 28-ix.-18
Lukov — Germans seize railway junction,
12-viii.-15
Lukuledi — Germans driven into interior,
10-vi.-17; skirmish, 21-x.-17
Lukuledi R. — s.s. " Präsident " blown up,
29-vii.-15; heavy fighting, 3-viii.-17
Lukwa, R. — Russians pursue Austrians to,
8-vii.-17
" **Lulea,**" **German s.s.** — sunk, 10-x.-15
" **Lumina,**" **s.s.** — sunk, 6-xi.-15
" **Lundy Island,**" **s.s.** — sunk, 10-i.-17
Lunéville — bombed, 3-viii.-14; Germans enter,
22-viii.-14; French reoccupy, 12-ix.-14;
German attack E. of defeated, 24-iii.-18
Luninetz — air-raid, 3-v.-18
Lupembe — Germans defeated, 30-x.-16;
19-xi.-16
Lupkov Pass — Austrians regain, 18-xii.-14;
Russians recover, 25-xii.-14; Austrians driven
from, 21-ii.-15; Russians capture: 1,700
prisoners, 26-iii.-15
Lurio, R. — Germans retire to, 24-iv.-18;
driven S. across, 28-v.-18
" **Lusitania,**" **s.s.** — arrives at Liverpool
flying American flag, 6-ii.-15; German
warning against sailing published in U.S.
Press, 30-iv.-15; sunk by U20: 1,198
drowned, 7-v.-15; anti-German riots in
London and Liverpool, 10-v.-15; U.S.
first Note to Germany, 14-v.-15; reply:
asserts she carried guns, 30-v.-15; Kaiser confers with advisers, 31-v.-15; second Note to
Germany, 9-vi.-15; German reply, 8-vii.-15;
third Note, 23-vii.-15; Germany offers com-
pensations for U.S. victims, 10-ii.-16; settlement deferred, 17-ii.-16

Lusse — Germans driven from summit betwee[n]
Wissenbach and, 19-ii.-15
Lutende — fighting, 30-vi.-17
Lutsk — Germans occupy, 31-vii.-15; Russian
re-occupy, 23-ix.-15; Russians again evacuate
28-ix.-15; Russians take, 6-vi.-16; attac[k]
near, 14-v.-16; fighting round, 18-vi.-16
19-vi.-16; Austro-German progress, 2-vii.-16
Russian success, 4-vii.-16; battle N. of
6-vii.-16; Russians reach line Gorodok–
Manievitche—Zogarovka and approache[s]
Stokhod R., 7-vii.-16; Russians break S.W
face of salient opposite Vladimir—Volynsk–
Brody on 12-mile front; 13,000 prisoners
15-vii.-16; Austrians defeated; 4,00[0]
prisoners, 20-vii.-16; Germans driven ove[r]
Styr R.; 14,000 prisoners, 21-vii.-16
Russians break German first line; 9,00[0]
prisoners, 27-vii.-16; Germans attack W. of
27-ix.-16; Russian attacks W. of, 2-x.-16
progress, 30-x.-16; Germans occupy, 18-ii.-1[8]
Lütterbach — French air-raid on, 9-ix.-15
Lüttwitz, Gen. von (Germany) — appointe[d]
Military Commander of Brussels, 20-viii.-14
orders arrest of M. Max, 26-ix.-14; super
seded as Commandant of Brussels, 23-xi.-14
as commander of 3rd Prussian Army Corps
25-xi.-14; to command 10th Prussian Army
Corps, 22-xii.-15; commands 3rd Prussian
Army Corps, 25-xi.-16
" **Lützow,**" **H.I.M.S.** — sunk in Jutlan[d]
battle, 31-v.-16
" **Lux,**" **s.s.** — sunk, 2-ii.-17
Luxburg, Count (Germany) — handed pass
ports, 12-ix.-17
Luxemburg — invaded by 8th German Army
Corps, 3-viii.-14; German 4th Army concen
trated in, 14-viii.-14; German G.H.Q. at
30-viii.-14; Americans reach, 21-xi.-18; enter
22-xi.-18; advance guard reaches German
frontier, 23-xi.-18; British reach Germa[n]
frontier N. of, 24-xi.-18
Luxemburg, Princess Adelaide of — abdicates
15-i.-19
Luxemburg, Princess Charlotte of — accession
French Government notified, 15-i.-19
Luxemburg, Rosa — killed in Berlin, 15-i.-19
" **Luxor,**" **s.s.** — sunk, 19-iii.-18
" **Luz Blanca,**" **s.s.** — sunk, 5-viii.-18
Luznica ridge — Italian advance, 23-vii.-15
Lvoff, Prince (Russia) — Premier, 14-iii.-17
head of Coalition, 16-v.-17; resigns, 22-vii.-17
" Russian Political Conference " in Paris
denies Bolshevist claim to represent Russia
8-ii.-19
Lyautey, Gen. (France) — resigns as War
Minister, 14-iii.-17; again becomes War
Minister, 11-xii.-17
" **Lychnis,**" **H.M.S.** — sinks U64, 17-vi.-18
" **Lycia,**" **s.s.** — sunk, 11-ii.-17
Lyck — Germans pressing, 9-ix.-14; taken by
Russians, 8-x.-14; retaken by Germans
13-x.-14; raided by ZVI., 1-ii.-15; Germans
near, 13-ii.-15; captured, 14-ii.-15
" **Lydie,**" **s.s.** — sunk, 9-ii.-15
" **Lynburn,**" **s.s.** — mined, 29-viii.-17
Lyncker, Gen. von (Germany) — conference
with Emperor William, 5-vii.-14
" **Lynorta,**" **s.s.** — sunk, 11-viii.-17
" **Lynx,**" **H.M.S.** — mined, 9-viii.-15;
damaged in engagement with H.I.M.S.
" Hamburg," 16-xii.-14
Lys Canal — Germans on, 21-x.-18; Franco-
Belgian attack; crossed, 22-x.-18
Lys R. — British reach, 15-x.-14; German
Army in line, 17-x.-14; Allies advantage on
line, 6-i.-15; British advance from, 31-vii.-17;
battle, 9-iv.-18; Allies retire between Estaires
—Bac St. Maur, 9-iv.-18; Gen. Foch's orders
as battle developed, 9-iv.-18; Germans cross
between Estaires—Bac St. Maur, 10-iv.-18;
push on towards Bailleul, 11-iv.-18; success-

" **Marmion**," **H.M.S.** — sunk by collision, 21-x.-17

" **Marmion**," **s.s.** — sunk, 26-viii.-17

Marmora, Sea of — AE2 in, 26-iv.-15; E11 in: sinks Turkish gunboat, 27-iv.-15; sinks Turkish transport, 29-iv.15; Turkish gunboat, 3-v.-15; Turkish steamer driven ashore, 13-v.-15; Turkish storeship sunk, 2-vi.-15; E14 sinks dhows, 20-vi.-15; E7 in, 30-vi.-15; in action with Turkish gunboat, 7-vii.-15; Turkish steamer sunk at Mudania, 10-vii.-15; two dhows sunk, 11-vii.-15; Turkish trains shelled near Kava Burnu, 17-vii.-15; Mudania shelled, 18-vii.-15; four dhows sunk, 19-vii.-15; dhow sunk, 21-vii.-15; E7 returns from cruise, 21-vii.-15; Turkish destroyer "Yar Hissar" reported sunk, 6-ix.-15; vessels sunk by British submarine, 4-xii.-15

" **Marmora**," **H.M.A.M.C.** — sunk, 23-vii.-18

Marne R. — Germans cross, 2-ix.-14; Allies hardening, 2-ix.-14; British retire across, 3-ix.-14; Allies behind, 4-ix.-14; Germans drawing S.E. across towards Paris, 4-ix.-14; German withdrawal S. of ordered, 5-ix.-14; first battle begun: general Allied offensive, 6-ix.-14; left progressing, 7-ix.-14; 8-ix.-14; German retirement to Aisne ordered, 9-ix.-14; battle progressing, 9-ix.-14; British cross, 9-ix.-14; German retirement admitted, 10-ix.-14; battle ended, 10-ix.-14; British 6th Division concentrated S. of, 14-ix.-14; German progress towards, 29-v.-18; reach at Château-Thierry—Dormans, 31-v.-18; French counter-attack, 2-vi.-18; second battle, 15-vii.-18; Germans cross at Fossoy, 15-vii.-18; progress to Reuil, towards Epernay, 16-vii.-18; reach Nanteuil—Pourcy; driven out by Italians, 17-vii.-18; Allies advance S. of, 18-vii.-18; Allies retake Montvoisin, 19-vii.-18; German re-cross, 20-vii.-18; progress, 21-vii.-18; Allies cross at Chassins—Passy; Germans retreat, 22-vii.-18; progress, 23-vii.-18; 24-vii.-18; Germans yielding, 26-vii.-18

Marne—Reims — Allies regain ground, 7-vi.-18

Maroilles — taken by British, 5-xi.-18

" **Marquette**," **H.M.T.** — chased by U-Boat; escapes, 25-v.-15; sunk, 23-x.-15

Marrières Wood — French occupy part, 5-ix.-16; captured by French, 12-ix.-16; stand by S. Africans; lost, 24-iii.-18

" **Mars**," **s.s.** — sunk, 8-vii.-18

" **Marseillaise**," **French cruiser** — F. to Adm. Rouyer in Dover Straits, 3-viii.-14

Marshall, Capt. — murdered, 21-iii.-18

Marshall, Gen. — to succeed Gen. Maude in Mesopotamia, 24-xi.-17; takes Salkaltutan Pass, 4-xii.-17; crosses Nahrin R. and drives Turks from Kara Tepe, 5-xii.-17; occupies Hit, 9-iii.-18; defeats Turks at Khan Baghdadie, 26-iii.-18; reaches Tauk R., 30-iv.-18; enters Kirkuk, 7-v.-18; ordered to attack Turkish 6th Army, 7-x.-18; Baku and Krasnovodak pass out of command of, 31-xii.-18

Marshall Islands — Adm. Spee in, 19-viii.-14; proceeding E. of, 29-viii.-14; occupied by Japanese, 6-x.-14

" **Marstonmoor**," **s.s.** — sunk, 14-iv.-18

Marteville — taken, 30-iii.-17

Martinpuich — British advance, 17-vii.-16; gain crest of ridge, 4-viii.-16; further progress, 6-viii.-16; British capture small salient S. of, 30-viii.-16; taken, 15-ix.-16; progress N. of, 18-ix.-16; 20-ix.-16; 28-ix.-16; carried, 25-viii.-18

Marwitz, Gen. von der (Germany) — commands cavalry screen in Belgium, 6-viii.-14; 2nd Cavalry Corps placed under command of Gen. von Bülow, 18-viii.-14; cavalry under, on Scheldt, W. of Renaix, 23-viii.-14; cavalry placed under direct orders of 1st

Marwitz, Gen. von der (Germany) (continued): Army: diverted to Tournai and Denain, 24-viii.-14; attacks British, 1-ix.-14; guarding southern flank on Marne, 8-ix.-14; commands 38th Reserve Corps, 28-xii.-14; commands 6th (Prussian) Army Corps, 7-xi.-15; commands 2nd Army, 17-xii.-16; attacks at Cambrai, 30-xi.-17; commanding 2nd Army in Somme battle, 21-iii.-18

Mary, Queen — visits wounded Indians at Brighton, 9-i.-15; returns to London after 10 days in France, 14-vii.-17; present at Thanksgiving at St. Paul's, 6-vii.-19

" **Mary**," **H.M. drifter** — sinks UC78, 2-v.-18

" **Mary Baird**," **s.s.** — mined, 18-v.-17

Masaryk, Prof. (Czecho-Slovakia) — appointed President, 15-xi.-18; arrives in London from New York, 29-xi.-18; leaves for Prague, 6-xii.-18; in Paris; received by M. Poincaré, 7-xii.-18; takes oath, 22-xii.-18; in Prague: calls for better communications between Allies and Czecho-Slovakia, 6-i.-19

" **Mascota**," **s.s.** — sunk, 29-iii.-17

" **Mashalla**," **s.v.** — sunk, 22-iv.-18

" **Mashobra**," **s.s.** — sunk, 15-iv.-17

Masnières — Germans take Lateau Wood, 30-xi.-17; British withdraw from salient, 1-xii.-17; taken, 30-ix.-18

Massey, Mr. (New Zealand) — Peace Conference delegate; in England, 19-i.-19

Massiges — fighting round, 5-xi.-15; German assault between Tahure and, 15-ii.-17; German attacks, 15-vii.-18

Massiges Plateau — French top, 25-ix.-15; French advance N. of, 1-x.-15

" **Massouda**," **s.v.** — sunk by U-Boat, 11-v.-18

" **Mastiff**," **H.M.S.** — ashore, 30-v.-17

" **Maston**," **s.s.** — sunk, 13-viii.-17

" **Masunda**," **s.s.** — sunk, 28-ii.-16

Masurian campaign — battle, 5-ix.-14; Hindenburg piercing line, 7-ix.-14; battle continued, 8-ix.-14; 9-ix.-14; ends on E. Prussian frontier, 15-ix.-14; new German 10th Army formed, 26-i.-15; Hindenburg issues orders for winter battle, 5-ii.-15; battle opens, Russians attacked on Pilkallen—Gumbinnen—Johannisburg front, 7-ii.-15; battle ends, 22-ii.-15

" **Matador**," **s.s.** — sunk, 3-vii.-17

Matajur, Mte. — captured by Austro-Germans, 25-x.-17

Matamondo — British reach, 9-viii.-16; Germans defeated, 11-viii.-16

" **Matchless**," **H.M.S.** — damaged by mine, 9-xi.-15; brought into Dover in sinking condition, 29-v.-17

Matchukovo — German-Bulgar posts driven in, 21-iii.-16; Bulgarian raid at, 1-iii.-16

Matchva Plain — Serbians evacuate, 8-xi.-14

" **Matheran**," **s.s.** — mined, 26-i.-17

Matsui, Mr. (Japan) — signs formal ratification of peace, 10-i.-20

" **Matunga**," **s.s.** — sunk, 6-viii.-17

Matz, R. — Germans cross, 12-vi.-18

Matz Valley — German progress, 9-vi.-18

Maubeuge — British aeroplanes arrive, 13-viii.-14; invested by Germans, 25-viii.-14; falls, 7-ix.-14; British reach outskirts, 8-xi.-18; Guards enter, 9-xi.-18

Maubeuge—Givry — 1st Corps under Gen. Haig at, 21-viii.-14

Maubeuge—Jenlain — British fall back to, 24-viii.-14

Maubeuge—Sars la Bruyère — 2nd Corps under Gen. Smith-Dorrien at, 21-viii.-14

Maude, Gen. F. S. — commands 14th Infantry Brigade, 29-x.-14; commands Tigris column, 11-vii.-16; commands W. of Kut, 10-ii.-17; clears Turks from Dahra Bend, 15-ii.-17; captures Kut-el-Amara, 24-ii.-17; captures Baghdad, 11-iii.-17; death, 18-xi.-17

Maud'huy, Gen. (France) — 16th Division under takes Saarburg, 18-viii.-14; commands 10th Army, 30-ix.-14; advances on Douai, 1-x.-14; retires on Arras, 4-x.-14; attacks N. of Arras, 17-xii.-14

Maunoury, Gen. (France) — commanding 6th Army; on Allied left in Somme valley, 27-viii.-14; to attack towards Château-Thierry, 4-ix.-14; begins battle of Ourcq, 5-ix.-14; Gen. von Kluck facing, 6-ix.-14; stands at Soissons—Bailly, 18-ix.-14; troops take Hills 132 and 151, 8-i.-15; wounded; invalided, 12-iii.-15; Governor of Paris, 2-xi.-15

Maure — taken, 28-ix.-18

Maurepas — French reach outskirts, 30-vii.-16; part taken, 12-viii.-16; 18-viii.-16; German line shortened, 18-viii.-16; French success N. of, 22-viii.-16; French complete capture, 24-viii.-16; attack from, 3-ix.-16

Maurice, Gen. — letter to Press attributes mis-statement to British Ministers with regard to military position, 7-v.-18; Mr. Asquith's motion to refer charges defeated in Commons, 9-v.-18

"Mavisbrook," s.s. — sunk, 17-v.-18

Max, M. (Belgium) — arrest ordered, 26-ix.-14; conveyed to Namur, 27-ix.-14; interned at Glatz, 12-x.-14; transferred to Celle, 27-xi.-15; returns from captivity, 15-xi.-18

Maxwell, Gen. — succeeded in Egypt command by Gen. A. Murray, 19-iii.-16

Mayo, Adm. (U.S.) — C.-in-C. U.S. Atlantic Fleet; witnesses bombardment of Ostend; flag hoisted in H.M.S. "Broke"; first occasion U.S. admiral under fire in British warship, 25-ix.-17; leaves England, 25-xi.-18

Mazinde — British at, 8-vi.-16

Mbemkuru R. — Germans driven to, 21-ix.-17

Mbemkuru valley — Germans retire to, 19-vii.-17

Meaureau — taken by British, 5-xi.-18

Meaux — Germans attacked by French, 5-ix.-14

Mebaricourt — British take, 9-viii.-18

Mecca — Arabs penetrate, 13-vi.-16; masters of, 21-vi.-16

"Mechanician," H.M. escort ship — sunk, 20-i.-18

Mecklenburg, Grand Duke of — abdicates, 14-xi.-18

Medals: see Decorations

"Medea," Dutch s.s. — sunk, 25-iii.-15

Medeazza — Italian gain near, 28-v.-17

"Media," s.s. — attacked by U-Boat, 18-v.-18

Medina — Arabs repulsed, 13-vi.-16; occupied in name of King of Hedjaz, 13-i.-19

"Medina," s.s. — sunk, 28-iv.-17

Mediterranean — two Italian cruisers sunk by Austrian U-Boat, 8-vii.-15; UB1 lost in, 31-viii.-15; German submarines sent to Pola, 31-viii.-15; vessels sunk: see their names

Allied command — appointments, 18-viii.-14; change, 20-ix.-14

Allied policy — conference in London, 22-i.-17

"Medjidieh," Turkish cruiser — mined, 3-iv.-15

"Medora," s.s. — sunk, 2-v.-18

"Medusa," H.M.S. — lost, 25-iii.-16

"Megantic," s.s. — chased by U-Boat, 30-v.-15; 2-iv.-16; 28-xi.-16; torpedo misses, 24-ii.-17

"Meggie," s.s. — captured and taken to Germany, 24-vi.-17

Mekran Mission — returns to Chahbar, 2-ii.-17

"Melampus," H.M.S. — destroys JC16, 23-x.-17

"Melanie," s.s. — sunk, 16-vi.-18

"Melbourne," H.M.S. — leaves Samoa, 31-viii.-14; escorts Australian convoy, 1-xi.-14; escorts New Zealand transports, 9-xi.-14

"Melford Hall," s.s. — sunk, 22-vi.-17

Melicocq — Germans enter and lose, 12-vi.-18

"Meline," s.s. — torpedoed, 23-iii.-18

"Melita," s.s. — attacked by U-Boat, 25-vii.-

Melun — Sir J. French at, 4-ix.-14; 5-ix.-14

Memel — Russians occupy, 18-iii.-15; Germans retake, 21-iii.-15; suggested Germans as port for Gen. Haller's Polish troops, 28-iii.-19

"Memling," s.s. — sunk, 3-x.-17

"Memphian," s.s. — sunk, 8-x.-17

Mengiennes — fired on by U.S. naval gun, 25-vii.-18

Menin — trenches taken on road, 30-vii.-1; Allied air-raid on, 4-i.-18; British within miles, 30-ix.-18; taken, 15-x.-18

Menin—Roulers — British advance on: fail, 19-x.-14; Anglo-Belgians reach, 29-ix.-18

"Menzaleh," s.s. — sunk, 5-vi.-18

Mercatel — British attack, 23-viii.-18

Mercer, Gen. — commands 3rd Canadian Division, 20-xi.-15; killed, 2-vi.-16

"Mercian," H.M.T. — attacked by U-Boat, 11-xi.-15

Mercier, Cardinal (Belgium) — forbidden circulate Pastoral Letter, 3-i.-15

Merckem — Belgians drive Germans back t 6-iv.-15; taken by French, 27-x.-17

"Merida," s.s. — attacked by U-Boat, 4-vii.-

"Merioneth," s.s. — sunk, 3-vi.-17

"Merionethshire," s.s. — sunk, 27-v.-18

Merisov — heavy fighting, 18-ix.-16

Merris — Australians raid, 11-vii.-18; captur 30-vii.-18

Mersa Matruh — Arabs routed near, 11-xii.-1 13-xii.-15; defeated, 25-xii.-15

Mersa Moresa — Italians land, 4-v.-16

"Mersario," s.s. — sunk, 1-x.-17

Mersea Island — Zeppelin brought dow 23-ix.-16

"Merton Hall," s.s. — sunk, 11-ii.-18

Merv — Bolshevists repulsed at, 16-i.-1 Bolshevists capture, 23-v.-19

Merville — British surrender, 11-iv.-18; Germ attacks repulsed, 14-iv.-18; fighting, 13-v.-1 British success N.W. of, 20-v.-18; Briti advance, 9-viii.-18; enter, 19-viii.-18

"Mesaba," s.s. — sunk, 1-ix.-18

Mesnil — German attack repulsed, 21-iv.-18

Mesnil, Butte de — French take "I Courtine," 24-x.-15; German counter-atta fails, 25-x.-15; 30-x.-15

Mesnil-les-Hurlus — French take wood nea 1-i.-15

Mesopotamia (see also Kut-el-Amara, Tigri &c.) — British expedition originated, 26-i 14; British repulse Turkish attacks Saniyeh, 11-xi.-14; Turks defeated at Sah 17-xi.-14; Turks evacuate Basra, 21-xi.-1 British occupy, 22-xi.-14; British force wi naval flotilla fails to take Kurna; Meze destroyed by H.M. ships, 4-xii.-14; Briti rout Turks opposite Kurna, 7-xii.-14; Tur surrender Kurna, 9-xii.-14; heavy fightii N.W. of Basra, 3-iii.-15; Lord Crev announces reinforcements for Ahwaz—Kurn 16-iii.-15; Turks attack at Kurna and Ahwa 11-iv.-15; at Shaiba, 12-iv.-15; routed Shaiba, 14-iv.-15; British advance: occu; Nakaila, 17-iv.-15; British occupy Kutunie 11-xi.-15; British forces concentrated 18-xi.-15; British occupy Zeur, 19-xi.-1 Turco-German command assumed Marshal von der Goltz, 24-xi.-15; Briti cavalry in rearguard action, 29-xi.-1 British reach Umm-al-Tubal, 30-xi.-1 rearguard action at Umm-al-Tuba 1-xi.-15; Russians capture Mush 18-ii.-16; British at D Akhlat, Abbas, 31-iii.-17; British occupy Dekwa Sindia, 31-iii.-17; British in touch wi Russians on Diala R., 2-iv.-17; Russia

"Möwe," **German raider** (continued) :—
s.s. "Governor," 14-iii.-17; returns to Kiel, 22-iii.-17; total of vessels captured, 22-iii.-17
Moyenneville — British reach, 21-viii.-18
Moy-sur-Oise — French take, 4-iv.-17
"**Moyune**," s.s. — sunk, 12-iv.-18
Mozambique — Gen. von Lettow-Vorbeck in, 1-xii.-17; German retreat into, 27-xii.-17; 7-i.-18; 11-i.-18; 12-i.-18; 21-i.-18; 3-ii.-18; British heavily engaged N.E. of; German losses, 11-iv.-18; Germans retire to Lurio R., 24-iv.-18; fighting, 5-v.-18; 19-v.-18; 22-v.-18; 28-v.-18; 12-vi.-18; 16-vi.-18; 18-vi.-18; 1-vii.-18; 2-vii.-18; Manungu: German H.Q.: occupied by Gen. Edwards, 19-v.-18
Mozely — taken, 24-ii.-15
Mpapua — British occupy, 12-viii.-16
Mrogoro — British advance, 23-viii.-16; Germans evacuate, 24-viii.-16; British enter, 26-viii.-16; German retreat barred, 10-ix.-16
Muanza — Gen. Crewe captures, 14-vii.-16
Mudania — E7 sinks Turkish steamer, 10-vii.-15; shelled, 18-vii.-15
Mudra, Gen. von (Germany) — commands 1st (Reims) Army, 18-vi.-18; relieved, 12-x.-18
Mudros — Gen. Ian Hamilton returns to, 7-iv.-15; B.E.F. leaves for Dardanelles, 24-iv.-15; H.M.T. "Southland" beached, 2-ix.-15; Gen. Monro leaves, 30-xii.-15; air-raids, 20-iii.-17; 24-iv.-17; Turkish envoys arrive, 26-x.-18; armistice signed, 30-x.-18
"**Muirfield**," s.s. — sunk, 11-vii.-17
Mukhmas — British advance 2 miles on 6-mile front, 14-ii.-18
Mülhausen: see Mulhouse
Mülheim — air-raids on, 2-iv.-15; 21-iv.-15; 26-viii.-15
Mulhouse — entered by French, 8-viii.-14; first battle, 9-viii.-14; second battle, 19-viii.-14; French again evacuate, 25-viii.-14; French air-raid, 18-iii.-16; Kaiser explains peace offer in speech to troops, 13-xii.-16; President Poincaré and M. Clemenceau enter, 10-xii.-18
Müller, Herr Hermann (Germany) — signs Peace Treaty, 28-vi.-19
"**München**," H.I.M.S. — torpedoed, 19-x.-16
Munich — French air-raid, 17-xi.-16; strike, 30-i.-18; Kurt Eisner assumes control, 8-xi.-18
"**Munificent**," s.s. — sunk, 1-iii.-17
Munitions:—
Ammunition — ships of Grand Fleet disembark 50 per cent. of rifle ammunition to cover Army deficiency, 31-viii.-14; agreement between Government and trade unions: no cessation of work, 19-iii.-15; Sir J. French in statement published in "The Times" says: "The protraction of the war depends entirely on the supply of men and munitions," 27-iii.-15; Mr. Asquith's Newcastle speech, 20-iv.-15; shell shortage at Festubert, 9-v.-15; statement sent from G.H.Q. in France by desire of Sir J. French, 14-v.-15; Lord Kitchener's speech, 18-v.-15; consignments sent from France to Russia, 17-xi.-15; King's message to workers, 21-v.-15; British artillery fire 65,000 tons in three days, 29-ix.-18
Anglo-French agreement, 8-x.-15
Münster — French bombard, 19-vi.-15; French advance towards, 20-vii.-15; second battle, 26-vii.-15; French success at Lingenkopf, 27-vii.-15; Allied line at Armistice, 11-xi.-18
"**Munster**," H.M.S. — rescues crew of H.M.A.M.C. "Alcantara," 29-ii.-16
Muravievo — Germans reach, 30-iv.-15
"**Murcia**," s.s. — sunk, 2-xi.-18
"**Murex**," H.M. oiler — sunk, 21-xii.-16
"**Muriel**," s.s. — sunk, 17-ix.-18
Murman Coast — Allied force on, 12-vii.-18

Murman railway — Germans in Finland prepare to advance on, 3-vii.-18
Murmansk — Gen. Rawlinson to co-ordinate British withdrawal, 31-vii.-19
Murray, Col. — occupies Bismarckburg, 8-vi.-16
Murray, Gen. — appointed C. in-C. Mediterranean E.F., 21-xii.-15; 19-i.-16; commands in Egypt, 19-iii.-16; succeeded by Gen. Allenby, 29-vi.-17
Mush — Armenian massacre, 10-vii.-15; Russians capture, 18-ii.-16; recapture, 23-viii.-16; Turks announce Russian evacuation, 30-iv.-17
Mushaidieh — Turkish position captured, 15-iii.-17
Mushroom Valley — Gen Botha routs De Wet, 11-xi.-14
Musile — Austrians cross Piave near, 15-vi.-18; sole part of Piave right bank unrecovered, 23-vi.-18; remaining Austrians disposed of, 24-vi.-18
Muslimieh Junction — occupied, 28-x.-18
Mwembe — German defeat, 7-i.-18; Gen von Lettow reaches, 17-ix.-18
Mwenzo — von Lettow enters Rhodesia, 2-xi.-18
"**Myrmidon**," H.M.S. — mined, 25-ii.-17
"**Myrmidon**," s.s. — torpedoed, 7-ix.-17
"**Myrtle Branch**," s.s. — sunk, 11-iv.-18
Mystery ships: see under Navy — Q ships

N.

Nablus: see Shechem
Nadvorna — Austrians take, 14-ii.-15; fighting near, 17-ii.-15; Russians recover, 15-v.-15
Nagwamira — Gen. von Lettow at, 28-ix.-18
Nahrin R. — British across; Turks driven out of Kara Tepe, 5-xii.-17
"**Nailsea Court**," s.s. — sunk, 19-i.-17
"**Nairn**," s.s. — sunk, 27-viii.-17
Nairobi — Gen. Stewart arrives, 3-ix.-14
Nakaila — British occupy, 17-iv.-15
Nakhl — Turks captured, 20-ii.-17
Nakob — British force overcome by German raiders, 17-ix.-14
Namacurra — Germans attack Anglo-Portuguese force at, 2-vii. 18
Namirue R. — Germans cross, 22-vii.-18
Namur — besieged by Germans, 22-viii.-14; entered, 23-viii.-14; fall of last two forts, 26-viii.-14; Belgian troops transferred to Antwerp, 30-viii.-14; British air-raid, 11-viii.-16
"**Namur**," s.s. — sunk, 29-x.-17
Nancy — battle of Grand Couronné, 31-viii.-14; Gen. de Castelnau instructed to cover, 4-ix.-14; Kaiser watches German attack before, 5-ix.-14; heavy fighting, 7-ix.-14; 8-ix.-14; Germans bombard, 9-ix.-14; sector cleared, 13-ix.-14; Germans repulsed E. of, 27-x.-14; 8th Brigade R.F.C. to operate from, 31-x.-17; French raid E. of, 20-ii.-18
Air-raids, 13-x.-14; 24-xii.-14; 25-xii.-14; 28-iii.-15; 4-vi.-15; 5-vi.-15; 15-vi.-15; 31-vii.-15; 1-viii.-15; 8-ix.-15; 12-ii.-18
Nanesti — Germans take, 19-i.-17
Nangwale — Germans at, 2-xii.-17
"**Nantes**," s.s. — sunk, 1-v.-18
Nanteuil — Germans reach, 17-vii.-18
Nanteuil-la-Fosse — French take, 18-iv.-17
Nantucket Light — Eight vessels torpedoed off, 8-x.-16
Nanungu — Germans defeated W. of, 5-v.-18; Gen. Edwards occupies, 19-v.-18; drives Germans westwards from, 22-v.-18
Napier, Adm. — commanding 2nd Light Cruiser Squadron, 28-xii.-14
Napoleon, Fort — bombarded, 2-iii.-15
"**Narbrough**," H.M.S. — wrecked, 12-i.-18

Navy (British):—
Battle cruiser squadrons (continued):—
Moore commanding, 15-i.-15; Adm. Pakenham succeeds Adm. Moore, 31-iii.-15; operations in Skagerrak, 28-vii.-15; cover mine-laying operations in the Bight, 10-ix.-15; operations in Skagerrak, 26 i.-16; in Jutland battle, 31-v.-16; 1-vi.-16; sweeps towards the Naze, 4-ix.-16; — **3rd:** cruise in centre of North Sea, 5-iii.-16; in Jutland battle, 31-v.-16; 1-vi.-16; — **4th:** in Jutland battle, 31-v.-16; 1-vi.-16; — **5th:** in Jutland battle, 31-v.-16; 1-vi.-16

Light cruiser squadron — sweeps across to Skagerrak; warships attacked by U-Boats, 20-vi.-15; leave to meet airships for joint exercises, 7-x.-16; — **1st:** sweeps out Skagerrak, 6-xi.-15; convoys seaplane-carriers for attack on Tondern Zeppelin base, 4-v.-16; operates off Norway, 3-xi.-16; operates in Skagerrak, 26-i.-16; operates off Naze, 14-vi.-16; — **2nd:** formed; Adm. Napier in command, 28-xii.-14; sweeps out Skagerrak, 6-xi.-15; leaves for two days' sweep to eastward of Little Fisher Bank, 8-xii.-15; at sea to intercept returning Zeppelin raiders, 2-iv.-16; in Jutland battle, 31-v.-16; 1-vi.-16; proceeds westward of Little Fisher Bank; sweeps to the Naze, 26-vii.-16; sweeps towards the Naze, 4-ix.-16; — **3rd:** sweeps down to Little Fisher Bank, 1-x.-15; 10-x.-15; operations off Dogger Bank, 24-xii.-15; off Norway, 17-ii.-16; search for German raiders, 12-xii.-17; — **4th:** formed; composition, 30-vi.-15; leaves Scapa to cruise off Norwegian coast, 6-viii.-15; operating off Norway, 10-v.-16; in Jutland battle, 31-v.-16; 1-vi.-16; proceeds towards Udsire Light; meets convoy of merchant ships and escorts to Rattray Head, 12-viii.-16; — **5th:** captures 14 German trawlers and sinks one, 6-x.-15; — **10th:** (Merchant) Cruiser Squadron: in Shetlands, 6-viii.-14; blockade duties in northern waters: Adm. de Chair hoists flag in "Alsatian" as commander, 3-xii.-14; intercept neutral ships intending to evade blockade, 15-xii.-15; report of work, 18-i.-15

Dardanelles — Vice-Adm. Carden relinquishes command: succeeded by Vice-Adm. de Robeck, 16-iii.-15

Decoy trawlers — inaugurated, 23-v.-15

Destroyers — first use for mine-sweeping, 1-ix.-15; sweep to Norway with H.M.S. "Comus," 19-iii.-16; Chase German T.B.D.s back to Zeebrugge, 20-iii.-16; action with Germans off Belgian coast, 16-v.-16; operate off Naze, 14-vi.-16; operate off Norway, 3-xi.-16; engage U84: drive back damaged to port, 22-ii.-17; engage German T.B.D.s in channel, 25-ii.-17; action in German Bight: German T.B.D.s and two minesweepers damaged, 16-viii.-17; search for German raiders, 12-xii.-17; action with Germans off Belgian coast, 27-vi.-18; O46: wrecked, 27-iii.-15; — O64: wrecked in Ægean, 21-xii.-15; — No. 11: mined, 10-iii.-16; — "Abdiel": sweeps in Heligoland Bight, 28-iii.-18; — "Ardent": collision with "Fortune," 13-x.-15; sunk, 31-v.-16; — "Ariel": sinks U12, 10-iii.-15; sinks UB29, 6-xii.-16; sweeps in Heligoland Bight, 28-iii.-18; mined, 2-viii.-18; — "Arno": sunk, 23-iii.-18; — "Attack": sunk, 30-xii.-17; — "Botha": operates with T.B.D.s and 1st Light Cruiser

Navy (British):—
Destroyers (continued):—
Squadron off Norway, 3-xi.-16; engagement with German T.B.D.s, 27-x.-17; sinks German T.B.D.s, 21-iii.-18; — "Christopher": in action with U Boat, 7-viii.-15; — "Fairy": sinks UC49, 30-v.-18; sinks UC75; afterwards sunk, 31-v.-18; — "Ferret": sweeps in Heligoland Bight, 28-iii.-18; — "Fortune": collision with "Ardent," 13-x.-15; sunk in Jutland battle, 31-v.-16; — "Garry": engages U-Boat in Holm Sound, 3-xii.-14; — "Lance": at sinking of "Königin Luise," 5-viii.-14; sinks German T.B.D.s, 17-x.-14; — "Landrail": at sinking of "Königin Luise," 5-viii.-14; — "Legion": sinks German T.B.D.s, 17-x.-14; sweeps in Heligoland Bight, 28-iii.-18; — "Lennox": sinks German T.B.D.s, 17-x.-14; — "Lizard": action with H.I.M.SS. "Goeben" and "Breslau": former driven ashore and latter sunk, 20-i.-18; — "Llewellyn": damaged in action, 18-iii.-17; — "Marne": sinks UB124, 20-vii.-18; — "Mary Rose": sunk, 17-x.-17; — "Medea": sinks UC18, 12-iii.-17; destroys U-Boat, 25-viii.-18; — "Melpomene": hit by shell, 24-iv.-16; — "Mentor": engagement with German T.B.D.s, 27-x.-17; — "Michael": collision, 27-iii.-16; — "Moresby": in Jutland battle, 31-v.-16; destroys U110, 15-iii.-18; — "Morris": in action with German T.B.D.s, 21-iii.-18; — "Nestor": sunk in Jutland battle, 31-v.-16; — "Nomad": sunk in Jutland battle, 31-v.-16; — "North Star": sinks German motor-boat, 28-x.-17; sunk, 23-iv.-18; — "Petard": damaged in Jutland battle, 31-v.-16; — "Phœnix": sunk by U-Boat, 14-v.-18; — "Recruit I.": sunk, 1-v.-15; — "Rifleman": aground in fog; docked, 22-v.-15; rescues crew of s.s. "Ivernia," 1-i.-17; — "Shark": sunk in Jutland battle, 31-v.-16; — "Sparrowhawk": sunk in Jutland battle, 31-v.-16; — "Strongbow": sunk, 17-x.-17; — "Talisman": attacked by U-Boat, 24-i.-16; — "Telemachus": sweeps in Heligoland Bight, 28-iii.-18; — "Tigress": action with H.I.M.SS. "Goeben" and "Breslau": former driven ashore and latter sunk, 20-i.-18; — "Tipperary": sunk in Jutland battle, 31-v.-16; — "Turbulent": sunk in Jutland battle, 31-v.-16; — "Usk": assists in blockade of Kiaochow Bay, 27-viii.-14; — "Vanquisher": sweeps in Heligoland Bight, 28-iii.-18; — "Vehement": mined, 2-viii.-18

Docks, floating — arrive at Invergordon, 6-ix.-14; 28-ix.-16

Dover Patrol — command: Adm. Bacon succeeds Adm. Hood, 13-iv.-15; King inspects, 23-ix.-15; Adm. Keyes succeeds Adm. Bacon, 29-xii.-17

Dreadnought Battle Fleet — strength reduced for period, 31-x.-14; three days' cruise for gunnery and battle exercises, 10-i.-15; on three days' cruise in northern part of North Sea, 7-iii.-15; starts on cruise near Shetlands, 11-vii.-15; leaves Scapa for cruise W. of Orkneys, 2-xi.-15

Drifter patrol boats — first unit arrives at Dover, 4-i.-15; increase during 1917, 31-xii.-17; — No. 83: claims hitting of U-Boat, 27-vii.-15; — G and E: sink UB4, 11-viii.-15; — P12: sunk, 4-xi.-18; — P26: mined, 10-iv.-17; — P51: destroys U61, 26-iii.-18; — P56: sinks U87,

Navy (British) :—

Drifter patrol boats (continued) :—
25-xii.-17 ; — P57 : rams UC47, 18-xi.-17 ; — P62 : sinks U84, 26-i.-18

Dutch coast, off — forces intercept 6 German steamers: four captured, two driven ashore, 16-vii.-17

East coast defence — 3rd Battle and 3rd Cruiser Squadrons based at Rosyth, 20-xi.-14

"Firefly" gunboat class — assemble at Abbadan, 24-viii.-15

George V., King — message, 3-vi.-16

Guns — 12in.: of H.M.SS. "King Edward VII." and "Dominion" reported cracked, 25-viii.-14 ; and H.M.S. "Hibernia," 11-ix.-14 ; — 15in.: mounted in H.M.S. "Queen Elizabeth," 25-ii.-15

Grand Fleet — puts to sea, 4-viii.-14 ; commander, 4-viii.-14 ; hold North Sea, 5-viii.-14 ; completes three-day cruise off N.E. Scotland and Norway, 5-ix.-14 ; puts to sea from Loch Ewe, 7-ix.-14 ; off Little Fisher Bank, 20-ix.-14 ; sweeps back to northward in front of 40 miles, 21-ix.-14 ; in position in North Sea to protect first Canadian convoy, 3-x.-14 ; west of Orkneys, 11-x.-14 ; returns to Scapa ; cruisers sweep down to Dogger Bank, 12-x.-14 ; moved out to W. of Orkneys, 16-x.-14 ; bases transferred, 17-x.-14 ; securely based for first time, 23-x.-14 ; leaves Lough Swilly for Scapa, 3-xi.-14 ; at Scapa, 4-xi.-14 ; — mine-sweeping gunboats detached for service off Belgian coast, 4-xii.-14 ; small margin over German High Sea Fleet, 12-xii.-14 ; puts to sea to intercept return of German vessels raiding East coast, 16-xii.-14 ; returns to Scapa, 19-xii.-14 ; abandons sweep, 26-xii.-14 ; reinforced ; destroyer strength, 19-ii.-15 ; H.M.S. "Faulknor" and six T.B.D.s detached to hunt U-Boats in Irish Sea, 12-iii.-15 ; carries out strategical exercises, 18-iii.-15 ; returns to bases, 19-iii.-15 ; three days' cruise in centre of North Sea, 11-iv.-15 ; H.M.S. "Warspite" joins at Scapa, 13-iv.-15 ; in North Sea: swoop down to Little Fisher Bank, 18-iv.-15 ; returns to bases: refuelled for sweep to Danish coast, 21-iv.-15 ; whole fleet on two days' sweep in central North Sea, 17-v.-15 ; sweep for two days' down to Dogger Bank, 29-v.-15 ; put to sea for battle exercises in northern waters, 11-vi.-15 ; visited by Archbishop of York, 26-vi.-15 ; visited by King, 7-vii.-15 ; movements handicapped by miner's strike, 15-vii.-15 ; exercised, 13-x.-15 ; H.M.S. "Canada" joins, 15-x.-15 ; battle exercises, 1-xii.-15 ; leaves Scapa, 10-ii.-16 ; 26-ii.-16 ; Russian Press representatives visit, 1-iii.-16 ; sweep in North Sea, 6-iii.-16 ; puts to sea in heavy gale and snow, 25-iii.-16 ; battle exercises, 29-iii.-16 ; puts to sea and moves to Horn Reef to cover relaying of Russian Baltic minefield, 21-iv.-16 ; sweep interrupted by fog, 22-iv.-16 ; returns to base ; puts to sea for southward sweep, 24-iv.-16 ; leaves bases to cover air operation off Horn Reef and detain High Sea Fleet, 2-v.-16 ; supports attack on Tondern Zeppelin base, 4-v.-16 ; puts out into North Sea, 30-v.-16 ; in Jutland battle, 31-v.-16 ; 1-vi.-16 ; returns to bases, 2-vi.-16 ; King George visits, 14-vi.-16 ; addresses officers and men on board H.M.S. "Iron Duke," 15-vi.-16 ; Admiralty approves proceedings in Jutland battle, 4-vii.-16 ; proceeds on cruise for battle exercises N. and E. of Shetlands, 17-vii.-16 ; sweep in southern waters ; H.M.S. "Iron Duke" attacked, 18-viii.-16 ; concentrates near "Long Forties,"

Navy (British) :—

Grand Fleet (continued) :—
steering southward ; H.M.S. "Notting ham " attacked by U-Boat and sunk Zeppelin reported ; High Sea Flee chased ; H.M.S. "Falmouth" sunk pursuit abandoned, 19-viii.-16 ; leaves fo battle exercises between Orkneys an Shetlands and Norway, 20-ix.-16 ; cruis in northern waters, 24-xi.-16 ; Adm Jellicoe issues Farewell Order, 28-xi.-16 Adm. Beatty C.-in-C., 29-xi.-16 ; disbanded 7-iv.-19

Harwich force — Adm. Tyrrwhitt in com mand, 11-viii.-14 ; operates off Horn Ree 18-x.-15 ; off Little Fisher Bank, 31-x.-15 three days' operations off Danish coas 20-xii.-15 ; at sea to intercept Zeppelin 2-ii.-16 ; puts to sea, 10-ii.-16 ; sails for a attack on Tondern, 24-iii.-16 ; in Jutlan battle, 1-vi.-16 ; abandons pursuit of Hig Sea Fleet, 19-viii.-16 ; chases 11 German T.B.D.s back into Zeebrugge, 10-v.-17

Hydrophones — use by submarines, 14-v.-17 perfected: supply increased during 1917 31-xii.-17

Light forces — two-day sweep in Skagerral 16-viii.-15 ; sweep up Norwegian coast an back, 12-vii.-16 ; 17-vii.-16 ; 24-vii.-16 1-viii.-16 ; 20-ix.-16 ; sweep towards Hor Reef, 21-vii.-16 ; sweep to southward o German North Sea minefield, 26-ix.-16 sweep from Rosyth to Little Fisher Ban and back, 17-x.-16 ; reconnaissance i North Sea, 28-x.-16 ; encounter wit German T.B.D. division, 23-i.-17 ; i action with German aircraft, 11-viii.-18

Mediterranean Fleet — at Malta, 1-viii.-14 under French C.-in-C., 18-viii.-14

Mine-laying — result of 1917 operation: 31-xii.-17 ; see also Mines

Mine-net division — off N. Goodwins attacked by German aircraft ; aeri: torpedo first used, 19-iv.-17

Mine-sweeping — result of 1917 operation: 31-xii.-17

Monitors — ordered to Ostend, 12-x.-14 Thames estuary: Adm. Bacon's instruc tions, 20-xii.-15 ; — M15 : sunk, 11-xi.-17 — M21 ; mined, 20-x.-18 ; — M24 : joir Dover Patrol, 7-x.-15 ; sinks German moto boat, 28-x.-17 ; — M25 : joins Dove Patrol, 6-ix.-15 ; — M26 : joins Dove Patrol, 19-x.-15 ; — M27 : joins Dove Patrol, 6-xi.-15 ; — M28 : sunk, 20-i.-16 ; - M30 : sunk, 13-v.-16 ; — "Lord Clive " bombards Zeebrugge, 23-viii.-15 ; Adm Bacon's flag in, 7-ix.-15 ; Rear-Adm. d Marliave's flag in, 26-i.-16 ; bombard Belgian coast, 8-ix.-16 ; 11-ix.-16 15-ix.-16 ; — "Marshal Ney ": in attac on Belgian coast, 25-ix.-15 ; detailed fc defence of Downs, 2-iv.-17 ; engage German T.B.D.s, 27-iv.-17 ; — "Marsh: Soult ": bombards Belgian coast, 27-xii 15 ; 8-ix.-16 ; 11-ix.-16 ; 13-ix.-16 ; takes u Belgian coast patrol, 27-vii.-17 ; - "Mersey ": supports Belgians in Yse battle, 17-x.-14 ; shells Belgian coas 18-x.-14 ; hit and damaged, 28-x.-14 attacks H.I.M.S. "Königsberg," 4-vii 15 ; ordered to Ostend, 12-x.-14 ; - "Prince Eugène ": bombards Belgia coast, 9-ix.-16 ; — "Prince Rupert " bombards Belgian coast, 25-viii.-15 9-ix.-16 ; 11-ix.-16 ; 13-ix.-16 ; shelled an straddled, 10-x.-16 ; — "Raglan " sunk, 20-i.-18 ; — "Severn ": ordere to Ostend, 12-x.-14 ; supports Belgians i Yser battle, 17-x.-14 ; shells Belgian coas 18-x.-14 ; attacks H.I.M.S. "Königsberg. 4-vii.-15 ; — "Sir John Moore ": bon bards Belgian coast, 23-viii.-15 ; 12-ix.-16 13-ix.-16 ; — "Terror ": bombards Belgia

Nyassa, Lake — s.s. "Von Wissmann" captured by British launch, 13-viii.-14
"Nyassa," s.s. — sunk, 24-xi.-17
Nyassaland — Germans take Kisi, 10-ix.-14; driven out, 12-ix.-14; fighting near Fife, 17-v.-15; Germans driven to Rovuma border, 30-vi.-17
"Nymphe," H.M.S. — collision with H.M.S. "Nemesis," 17-iii.-15

O.

"Oakleaf," H.M. oiler — sunk, 25-v.-17
"Oakleaf," s.s. — sunk, 25-vii.-17
Oberndorf — Mauser works bombed, 12-x.-16
Oberndorff, Count (Germany) — Armistice delegate; leaves for front, 6-xi.-18; delegate for renewal of Armistice; leaves for Treves, 9-xii.-18
"Oberon," s.s. — torpedoed, 3-iv.-17
Obozerskaya — in Allied hands, 6-ix.-18
Obrenovatz — Austrians attack Germans, 6-viii.-14
Observation Ridge — British take, 9-iv.-17
"Obwasi," s.s. — sunk, 8-vii.-17
"Ocean," H.M.S. — lands Marines at Fao, 8-xi.-14; bombards forts on Cape Kephez, 1-iii.-15; mined in Dardanelles, 18-iii.-15
"Oceanic," H.M.A.M.C. — commissioned, 31-viii.-14; wrecked, 8-ix.-14
"Ocean Roamer," H.M. drifter — sinks UB31, 2-v.-18
Ochrida — Serbians retreat along road, 2-xii.-15; Italian advance S. of, 16-i.-17; Allied pressure in region, 10-ix.-17; 12-ix.-17
Ociva — Germans at, 14-vii.-18
Ocna — heavy fighting at, 4-iv.-15; Russian success S.W. of, 17-ii.-17; Germans repulsed, 16-viii.-17; in outskirts, 19-viii.-17
Odensholm — naval action off: H.I.M.S. "Magdeburg" blown up; H.I.M.S. "Augsburg" and U3 engaged Russian cruisers 26-viii.-14
Odessa — Turco-German warships bombard, 29-x.-14; Turkish cruiser "Medjidieh" mined off, 3-iv.-15; Germans reach, 12-iii.-18; Allies evacuate, 6-iv.-19
"Odessa," s.s. — destroyed, 24-xii.-14
"Odin," H.M.S. — bombards Fao, 8-xi.-14
Oesel Islands — Germans occupy most of, 12-x.-17; Germans take Arensburg, 13-x.-17; naval action between Dagö Is. and, 14-x.-17; German progress; Russian garrison partly escape; 3,500 prisoners claimed, 15-x.-17; whole in German hands; 10,000 prisoners claimed, 16-x.-17
Offenburg — air-raid, 12-ii.-18
Oghratina — Turks retire, 8-viii.-16
Oginski Canal — Austro-Germans driven behind, 23-ix.-15
Oie Hill — French take, 21-viii.-17
"Oilfield," H.M. oiler — sunk, 16-iii.-18
Oil pipe-line — Clyde to Forth: laying arranged, 9-iii.-18; commenced, 11-vii.-18
Oise R. — Germans approaching, 30-viii.-14; fierce fighting, 26-iv.-14; French advance between Andéchy and, 17-iii.-17; French advance to W. bank, 24-iii.-17; Germans attack on 50-mile front, 21-iii.-18; 2nd Army covering, 23-iii.-18; French withdraw, 7-iv.-18; retire S. of, 8-iv.-18; Germans fail to cross at Vingré, 5-vi.-18; new German army group formed on front, 6-viii.-18; German attacks, 7-viii.-18; French take Ribécourt, 14-viii.-18; progress, 16-viii.-18; 18-viii.-18; French attack N. of, 19-viii.-18; 20-viii.-18; advance, 21-viii.-18; 22-viii.-18; line held, 23-viii.-18; French reach line, 10-x.-18; Germans retreat on front from Argonne to, 13-x.-18; Anglo-French 2 mile advance N. of, 17-x.-18; French attack in German salient between Serre and, 18-x.-18;

Oise R. (continued) :—
French attack on 25-mile front between Aisne and, 25-x.-18; Germans retreat toward Hirson, 27-x.-18; battle, 4-xi.-18
Oise—Aisne Canal — Germans retire, 22-x.-17; 25-x.-17; 5-xi.-18
Oise—Marne — Germans hold, 1-vi.-18
Oise valley — Germans flood, 23-iii.-17
Oisy — British advance on front, 4-xi.-18
Oitoz Pass — Rumanian successes, 19-x.-16; 24-x.-16; heavy fighting, 28-xii.-16
Oitoz Valley — Austrians repulsed, 13-x.-16
O'Kelly, Mr. J. T. — Sinn Fein "envoy" in Paris, 24-ii.-19
"Okement," s.s. — sunk, 17-ii.-17
"Okhla," s.s. — mined, 29-vii.-17
"Oku," H.M. trawler — sinks U74, 27-v.-16
Olai — Russians take, 6-xi.-15; fighting 19-x.-15
"Oldambt," Dutch s.s. — rescued from Germans, 1-xi.-16
"Oldenburg," H.I.M.S. — tows disabled "Moltke," 24-iv.-18
"Older," Norwegian s.s. — in charge of German prize-crew; intercepted by H.M.A.M.C. "Otway," 18-xi.-16
"Oldfield Grange," s.s. — torpedoed, 7-vi.-17; sunk, 11-xii.-17
Olita — evacuated by Russians, 26-viii.-15
"Olive," s.s. — sunk, 22-vii.-16
"Olive Branch," s.s. — sunk, 2-ix.-17
Oliver, Adm. — appointed Deputy-Chief of Naval War Staff, 4-v.-17
Olizy — Germans seize, 23-iii.-18; French take 15-x.-18; Franco-American advance, 1-xi.-18
Olti — Russians defeat Turks, 4-iv.-15
"Olympic," s.s. — stands by H.M.S. "Audacious," 27-x.-14; U-Boat attacks 1-x.-15; 23-ii.-16; 28-ii.-16; sinks U103 12-v.-18
Oman — Arab attack on British repelled 11-i.-15
"Omrah," s.s. — sunk, 12-v.-18
Onega — mutiny, 23-vii.-19
"Onslow," H.M.S. — in Jutland battle damaged, 2-vi.-16; destroys UB17, 25-ii.-18
"Onward," H.M. trawler — sunk, 11-vi.-16
"Oola," H.M. collier — sunk, 26-x.-16
"Oopack," s.s. — sunk, 4-x.-18
Oosttaverne — British capture, 7-vi.-17; British line advanced E. of, 9-vii.-17
"Opal," H.M.S. — wrecked, 12-i.-18
"Ophelia," H.I.M.S. — captured, 17-x.-14 condemned by Prize Court, 21-v.-15
"Ophelia," H.M.S. — destroys UB83, 10-ix.-1
Oppy — line: British thrust against, 28-iv.-17 progress: trench system taken, 29-iv.-17 German positions taken, 28-vi.-17; British gain, 7-x.-18
"Oracle," H.M.S. — sinks, U44, 12-viii.-17
Orah — Wadi position near: Turks defeated 13-i.-16
"Orama," H.M.A.M.C. — with H.M.SS "Glasgow" and "Kent": sinks H.I.M.S. "Dresden," 14-iii.-15; sunk, 19-x.-17
Oran — three British motor-boats lost; s.s "Achaia" torpedoed, 8-ix.-16
Orange Hill — taken by British, 26-viii.-18
"Orangemoor," s.s. — bombed, 3-ix.-17
Orany — Germans reach, 31-viii.-15; fierce fighting, 2-ix.-15
"Orator," s.s. — sunk, 8-vi.-17
"Orfordness," s.s. — sunk, 20-vii.-18
Orient Army — Gen. Franchet d'Espere commands, 15-ix.-18
"Oriflamme," s.s. — mined, 25-xi.-17
"Origen," s.s. — sunk, 30-vi.-18
"Oriole," s.s. — sunk, 30-i.-15
"Orion," H.M.S. — with Grand Fleet 9-ix.-14; in Jutland battle, 31-v.-16
"Orissa," s.s. — sunk, 25-vi.-18

Peace Conference (continued):—

Scavenius heard, 21-i.-19; decision to send civil and military mission to Poland: invites Russian factions to confer at Prinkipo **Is.**, 22-i.-19; German colonies discussed, 28-i.-19; 29-i.-19; Polish and Czecho-Slovakian claims heard, 29 i. 10; provisional arrangement for German colonies and occupied territory in Asiatic Turkey, 30-i.-19; Allied delegates to visit Teschen: Serb and Rumanian delegates heard on Banat question, 31-i.-19; Czecho-Polish Teschen agreement, 1-ii.-19; Greek claims heard, 3-ii.-19; 4-ii.-19; referred to special committee, 4-ii.-19; Emir Feisul heard, 6-ii.-19; German premeditated destruction of French territory: M. Klotz heard on, 10-ii.-19; Belgian claims heard, 11-ii.-19; Syria: Dr. Howard Bliss and Chekri Ganem heard, 13-ii.-19; Lebanon deputation heard, 15-ii.-19; Yugo-Slavs heard, 18-ii.-19; Danish Schleswig claims heard, 21-ii.-19; Albanian case heard, 24-ii.-19; Hungaro-Rumanian neutral zone discussed, 25-ii.-19; Armenian claims heard, 26-ii.-19; Marshal Foch on final armistice terms, 1-iii.-19; Montenegrin case heard, 5-iii.-19; Belgian Commission report on revision of 1839 Treaty, 8-iii.-19; transport of Gen. Haller's troops through Danzig discussed, 21-iii.-19; Polish Commission's report, 22-iii.-19; U.S. League of Nations clause consecrating Monroe Doctrine accepted; Japanese race equality resolution vetoed, 10-iv.-19; War Responsibility Commission's Report presented; findings against Central Powers, 22-iv.-19; Economic Council decides on blockade of Germany in event of refusal to sign, 12-v.-19; military terms for Austria discussed, 15-v.-19; M. Padarewski heard on Polish frontiers, 5-vi.-19; Allied reply presented to Germans, 16-vi.-19; Council of Four: formed, 24-iii.-19; first meeting, 25-iii.-19; concludes first survey of terms, 28-iii.-19; consults Marshal Foch and Gens. Wilson and Diaz on landing of Polish troops at Danzig, 31-iii.-19; decide to raise blockade for Poland, Esthonia, Turkey, German-Austria, Bulgaria, Czecho-Slovakia, and new Serbian and Rumanian territories, 1-iv.-19; Syria and Arabia considered, 12-iv.-19; Pres. Wilson's statement on Adriatic: Italian delegation withdraws, 23-iv.-19; Signor Orlando leaves Paris, 24-iv.-19; Shantung agreement, 30-iv.-19; Council of Three: disposes of German colonies, 6-v.-19; Signor Orlando returns, 6-v.-19; Council of Four decides on conditional recognition of Adm. Koltchak, 26-v.-19; considers German counter proposals to Treaty, 30-v.-19; last meeting of Council of Three, 28-vi.-19

Plenary sittings — first meeting fixed by Supreme War Council, 13-i.-19; delegates: number allotted to nations, 15-i.-19; 17-i.-19; Press regulations settled, 17-i.-19; sitting opened by Pres. Poincaré; M. Clemenceau permanent president, 18-i.-19; second sitting: Pres. Wilson's motion on League of Nations resolution adopted, 25-i.-19; third sitting: Pres. Wilson reads draft of League of Nations covenant, 14-ii.-19; fourth sitting: draft convention for International Labour Legislation approved, 11-iv.-19; fifth sitting: revised League of Nations covenant approved, 28-iv.-19; sixth sitting: Treaty communicated to Allied delegates not concerned in drafting; Marshal Foch dissatisfied with guarantees for French securities, 12-v.-19

" **Peace Mission** " (U.S.A.) — see under Ford, Mr. Henry

" **Pearl**," **s.s.** — sunk, 23-ix.-16

Pearse — Irish rebel leader: surrenders, 29-iv.-16

Pecinka, Mt. — Austrian line taken, 14-viii.-16

" **Pegasus**," **H.M.S.** — shells Dar-es-Salaam wireless station, 8-viii.-14; sunk, 20-ix.-14

Pégoud (French airman) — killed, 31-viii.-15

" **Pegu**," **s.s.** — mined, 8-vii.-17

Peirse, Vice-Adm. — at bombardment of Yeni Kale, 5-iii.-15

Peissant — British 1st Corps extended to, 22-viii.-14

Pelagosa — French bombard, 17-ix.-14; Italians occupy, 25-vii.-15; Austrians attack, 17-viii.-15

Pellé, Gen. (France) — evacuates Noyon, 25-iii.-18

" **Pellew**," **H.M.S.** — disabled, 12-xii.-17

Pelves — taken by Canadians, 28-viii.-18

" **Pendennis**," **s.s.** — captured, 8-vii.-16

" **Penelope**," **s.s.** — sunk, 24-viii.-17

" **Penhale**," **s.s.** — sunk, 18-v.-17

" **Penhallow**," **s.s.** — sunk, 12-vi.-18

" **Peninsula**," **s.s.** — sunk, 25-vii.-17

" **Penistone**," **s.s.** — sunk, 11-viii.-18

" **Pennyworth**," **s.s.** — attacked by U-Boat, 15-v.-18

" **Penshurst**," **H.M.S.** — sinks UB19, 30-xi.-16; sinks UB37, 14-i.-17; sunk, 25-xii.-17

" **Penpol**," **s.s.** — captured and taken to Germany, 19-vi.-17

" **Pentwyn**," **s.s.** — sunk, 16-x.-18

" **Pentyrch**," **s.s.** — sunk, 18-iv.-18

" **Penvearn**," **s.s.** — sunk, 1-iii.-18

Pera, Treaty of — Turkey modifies in favour of Bulgaria, 22-vii.-15

" **Pera**," **s.s.** — sunk, 19-x.-17

" **Peresviet**," **Russian battleship** — mined, 3-i.-17

Perim — Turks attempt to land; driven off, 16-xi.-15

" **Perla**," **s.s.** — sunk, 10-vi.-17

Perm — Bolshevists take, 24-xii.-18; 1-vii.-19

Pernambuco — s.s. " Indian Prince " sunk off, 4-ix.-14

" **Pernambuco**," **German s.s.** — sunk, 18-x.-16

Pernant — Germans capture, 3-vi.-18

Pernau — attempted German landing, 20-viii.-15; villages S. of shelled, 3-ix.-17

Péron — French cross, 26-x.-18

Péronne — Germans at, 29-viii.-14; occupy, 24-ix.-14; French attack towards, 1-vii.-16; French capture villages on road, 3-vii.-16; French take Biaches, 9-vii.-16; French take Hill 76, 12-ix.-16; Anglo-French advance toward, 1-xi.-16; falls to British, 18-iii.-17; British occupy Somme bank from Epénancourt to, 18-iii.-17; British on line from Canizy to, 19-iii.-17; British line through, 23-iii.-17; falls to Germans, 24-iii.-18; heavy fighting, 25-iii.-18; British progress, 29-viii.-18; Somme crossed, 30-viii.-18; Australians take Mont St. Quentin, 31-viii.-18; falls, 1-ix.-18; French cross S. of Péronne, 3-ix.-18; British progress, 4-ix.-18

" **Perseus**," **s.s.** — mined, 21-ii.-17

Pershing, Gen. (U.S.) —to take division to France, 19-v.-17; sails from New York, 28-v.-17; arrives in London, 8-vi.-17; in France, 13-vi.-17; at Clermont; offers Gen. Foch all available forces, 28-iii.-18; telegraphs Gen. Foch's answer to U.S. War Department, 29-iii.-18; commanding 1st Army sector, 30-viii.-18; transfers command of 1st Army to Gen. Liggett, 12-x.-18; enters Luxemburg, 21-xi.-18; in London, 15-vii.-19

Persia:—

Government — Prince Firman Firma premier, 25-xii.-15

Great Britain — agreement signed, 9-viii.-19

Shah — receives Allied Ministers, 12-xi.-15

Turco-German intrigues — Turks seize Tabriz, 13-i.-15; driven out, 30-i.-15; reach Urmia, 16-iv.-15; Russians occupy Mian-

Pichon, M. (France) — on Allied Russian policy, 24-xii.-18; at discussion on Levant affairs with Pres. Wilson, M. Clemenceau, Mr. Lloyd George, and others, 20-iii.-19

Pieris — Isonzo crossed near, 5-vi.-15

Pierremand — Germans claim, 7-iv.-18

Pierrepont — taken by French, 9-viii.-18

Piesteritz — German State nitrogen plant laid down, 1-iv.-15

Pietra Rossa — Italians carry Hill 92, 23-v.-17

" Pikepool," s.s. — torpedoed, 16-ii.-18

Pilkem — Germans take British trenches, 22-x.-14; recovered, 23-x.-14; German attacks at, 12-ii.-16; British take, 31-vii.-17

Pillkallen — Russians advancing in neighbourhood, 25-i.-15; Russian right outflanked near, 9-ii.-15

" Pilot Me," H.M. drifter — at destruction of UB82, 17-iv.-18

Pilsudski, Gen. (Poland) — to form Ministry, 12-xi.-18

Pimple, The — British take, 12-iv.-17

" Pincher," H.M.S. — wrecked, 24-vii.-18

" Pinewood," s.s. — sunk, 17-ii.-18

" Pinmore," s.v. — sunk, 19-ii.-17

" Pinna," s.s. — torpedoed, 12-ii.-17

Pinon — French advance, 25-x.-17

Pinsk — Austro-Germans occupy, 15-ix.-15; driven behind Oginski Canal, 23-ix.-15; Germans repulsed, 26-ix.-15; Russian success near, 28-xi.-15

Pinzano — Austro-Germans force Tagliamento N. of; 6,000 prisoners, 4-xi.-17

Piræus — Allied naval demonstration, 1-ix.-16; four German steamers seized, 2-ix.-16; Adm. du Fournet lands troops; Allies withdraw after fighting, 1-xii.-16

Pirmasens — British air-raid on junction, 11-xii.-17

Pirrie, Lord — Controller-General of Mercantile Shipbuilding, 20-iii.-18

Pitesti — Falkenhayn at, 29-xi.-16; Rumanians retire along railway, 2-xii.-16

Pitirim, Archbishop (Russia) — arrested, 13-iii.-17

" Planudes," s.s. — mined, 20-i.-17

Platana — Russians land, 16-iv.-16; Turks at, 18-ii.-18

Platonovka — Russian success near, 3-xi.-15; German reverse, 5-xi.-15

Plava — fighting near, 9-vi.-15; positions held by Italians, 18-vi.-15; advance, 21-vii.-15; Italian progress, 15-v.-17; Austrian first line carried: Italians cross Isonzo N. of, 19-viii.-17

" Plawsworth," s.s. — sunk, 13-vii.-18

Plehwe, Gen. (Germany) — commands army group, 28-viii.-14

Pleschen — Russians cut railway at, 9-xi.-14

Pless — German G.H.Q. moved to, 4-v.-15; war council held, 31-viii.-16; military and naval council held, 3-ix.-16; German G.H.Q. transferred to, 9-ix.-16

Plettenberg, Gen. von (Germany) — succeeded in command of Prussian Guard Corps, 24-i.-17

Plezzo — Italians storm Monte Rombon, 27-viii.-15

Plezzo Basin — Italian success in, 4-ix.-15

Plock — German advance, 14-x.-14; Russians take Serpets, 13-i.-15; Germans take, 15-ii.-15; Russian defeat, 17-ii.-15; Russian counter-attack near, 21-ii.-15

Plœcken — progress in region, 29-x.-17

Ploegsteert — German attempts between Armentières and, 23-i.-17; British pressed back, 10-iv.-18; yield ground, 11-iv.-18; carried, 4-ix.-18; Anglo-Belgian attack from Dixmude to, 28-ix.-18

Ploegsteert Wood — British drive back German attack, 13-v.-16; German raid N.E. of, 22-i.-17

Ploesti — Germans advance towards, 4-xii.-16; take, 6-xii.-16; Rumanians pressed back E. of, 9-xii.-16; recovery, 10-xii.-16; Germans 20 miles E. of, 11-xii.-16

Ploesti—Bukarest line — Germans on: bar Rumanian retreat from Predeal, 7-xii.-16

Plotsk — sharp fighting round, 17-xi.-14

Plumer, Gen. Lord — commands British troops in Italy, 10-xi.-17; returns to France, 10-iii.-18; commands in attack at Dixmude-Wervicq, 14-x.-18; crosses German frontier, 1-xii.-18; welcomed in London, 19-xii.-18; telegram to Mr. Lloyd George describing bad food condition in W. Germany; urges relief, 8-iii.-19

Plunkett, Count — arrested, 17-v.-18

Pltiskow, Gen. von (Germany) — 11th Army Corps transferred to E. front, 26-viii.-14

Podgora — Italians attack spur, 15-vi.-15; attack ridge, 3-vii.-15; capture part, 20-vii.-15; take ridge, 21-x.-15; take Podgora, 6-viii.-16

Podolia — Germans on frontier, 2-viii.-17

Poelcappelle — Germans take, 20-x.-14; fight for height, 4-x.-17; taken, 9-x.-17; British retire between Wallemolen and, 10-x.-17; Anglo-French advance, 22-x.-17; British advance, 26-x.-17; 30-x.-17; German raid, 2-ii.-18

Pohl, Adm. von (Germany) — returns to Berlin, 25-vii.-14; memorandum from Adm. von Tirpitz, 16-ix.-14; High Seas Fleet: receives Kaiser's instructions, 2-x.-14; conveys to officials at Wilhelmshaven, 3-x.-14; reports Scarborough raid to Kaiser, 23-xii.-14; discusses air campaign against London with Herr von Bethmann-Hollweg, 5-i.-15; assumes command of High Seas Fleet, 3-ii.-15; Adm. Bachmann succeeds as Chief of Naval Staff, 6-ii.-15; instructs U-Boats not to attack large passenger ships, 6-vi.-15; urges naval authorities not to make concessions in conduct of U-Boat blockade, 26-vi.-15; new Chief of Staff appointed, 19-vii.-15; Kaiser refuses resignation, 3-ix.-15; last expedition with High Seas Fleet in 1915, 24-x.-15; invalided, 9-i.-16; death, 23-ii.-16

Poincaré, M. (France) — leaves Dunkirk to visit Tsar, 13-vii.-14; at Kronstadt, 20-vii.-14; in Paris, 29-vii.-14; visited by Sir J. French, 15-viii.-14; visits Sir J. French, 5-x.-14; presents colours to Marine Brigade, 11-i.-15; visits Verdun front, 1-iii.-16; Emperor Charles's first " peace letter " communicated to, 31-iii.-17; receives President Masaryk, 7-xii.-18; enters Strasbourg, 9-xii.-18; enters Mulhouse, 10-xii.-18; opens first formal meeting of Peace Conference at Paris, 18-i.-19

Poivre — Germans entrenched on ridge, 29-ii.-16; failure E. of, 4-iii.-16; Germans repulsed on heights, 20-iii.-16; French take ridge, 15-xii.-16

Pola — French submarine " Curie " captured near, 28-xii.-14; air-raids, 30-v.-15; 12-vii.-15; German submarine base, 31-viii.-15; Italian T.B.D. raid, 1-xi.-16; German U-Boats leave for Germany, 28-x.-18; others destroyed to avoid surrender, 31-x.-18

" Polamhall," s.s. — sunk, 7-v.-17

Poland — proclamation by Grand Duke Nicholas, 14-viii.-14; Tsar calls conference to discuss future, 6-ii.-17; Bolshevists demand self-determination, 21-i.-18; German withdrawal demanded for referendum, 21-i.-18; civil and military missions to Peace Conference Paris report, 22-iii.-19
Council of Regency — appointed by Austro-German patent, 12-ix.-17
Frontiers — M. Paderewski before Paris Peace Conference, 5-vi.-19

Poland (continued) :—

Independence — proclaimed independent State with an hereditary Monarchy and constitution by Germany and Austria-Hungary, 5-xi.-16; Russian Provisional Government guarantees, 30-iii.-17; Cracow Congress: resolution, 28-vi.-17; Austria adheres to, 11-vi.-18; Great Britain recognises Republic, 27-ii.-19

Ministry — Gen. Pilsudski to form, 12-xi.-18; M. Paderewski forms, 16-i.-19; recognised by Great Britain, 27-ii.-19

Operations: see Russian front

Relief — Inter-Allied Commission: approved by Inter-Allied Supreme Council of Supply and Relief, 20-i.-19

Republic — Directorate formed, 6-xi.-18

Poland and Czecho-Slovakia — Teschen dispute: see Teschen

Poland—Ukrainian war — Poles take Lemberg, 10-i.-19; truce at Lemberg, 22-ii.-19; end of truce: Ukrainians bombard Lemberg, 3-iii.-19; Poles relieve Lemberg, 20-iii.-19

" **Polar Prince**," **s.s.** — sunk, 18-ix.-17

Polazzo Plateau — Italians repulsed, 2-viii.-15

" **Polbrae**," **s.s.** — sunk, 4-v.-18

Polderhoek Château — Germans enter British trench: part regained, 14-xii.-17; Germans attack near, 8-iii.-18

" **Poldown**," **s.s.** — sunk, 9-x.-17

" **Polescar**," **s.s.** — bombed, 25-ix.-17; torpedoed, 5-viii.-18

" **Polesley**," **s.s.** — sunk, 21-ix.-18

" **Policastra**," **s.s.** — torpedoed, 9-ix.-18

" **Politania**," **s.s.** — sunk, 18-viii.-17

Polivanoff, Gen. (Russia) — War Minister, 26-vi.-15; superseded, 29-iii.-16

" **Poljames**," **s.s.** — sunk, 2-x.-18

" **Polleon**," **s.s.** — sunk, 22-iii.-18

" **Polo**," **s.s.** — sunk, 12-ii.-18

Poloshko — Serb cavalry reach, 18-ix.-18

Polotsk — Germans reach Vilna—Dvinsk railway near, 16-ix.-15

" **Polpero**," **s.s.** — torpedoed, 19-vii.-18

Poltava — Germans occupy, 29-iii.-18

" **Polvarth**," **s.s.** — sunk, 20-xii.-17

" **Polvena**," **s.s.** — sunk, 17-x.-17

" **Polwell**," **s.s.** — sunk, 5-vi.-18

" **Polyanthus**," **s.s.** — destroys UB17, 25-ii.-18

Polygon Wood — Germans occupy, 24-x.-14; retain only small part, 11-xi.-14; British take part, 20-ix.-17; Germans penetrate lines between Tower Hamlets and; ejected, 25-ix.-17; rest taken, 26-ix.-17; German attack from Ypres—Menin road to, 1-x.-17; Germans repulsed between Tower Hamlets and, 3-x.-17; German attack E. of fails, 7-x.-17; British gains S.W. of, 3-xii.-17; German strong point S.E. of carried, 13-iii.-18

" **Pomeranian**," **s.s.** — sunk, 15-iv.-18

" **Pommern**," **H.I.M.S.** — sunk in Jutland battle, 31-v.-16

Pommières — taken by French, 22-viii.-18

" **Pomona**," **s.s.** (Belgian relief ship) — sunk by U-Boat, 12-iv.-15

Pompelle, Fort de la — French lose and retake, 1-vi.-18

Pongwe — Germans defeated, 18-vi.-16

Poniewiecz — Germans take, 25-vii.-15; Russians retire E. of, 2-viii.-15

Pont-à-Mousson — French penetrate Bois-le-Prêtre near, 8-xii.-14; Bois-le-Prêtre in French hands, 17-i.-15

Pont Arcy — British at, 13-ix.-14; Germans reach, 27-v.-18

Pont Givart — French cross Suippe, 7-x.-18

" **Pontiac**," **s.s.** — sunk, 21-iv.-17

" **Pontiac**," **s.s.** — sunk, 28-iv.-17

Pont l'Evêque — French take, 28-viii.-18

Pontoise — French advance, 21-viii.-18

Pontru — British take, 9-iv.-17

" **Ponus**," **H.M. oiler** — wrecked, 3-xi.-16

Pope: see Benedict XV.

Poperinghe — Germans reach, 4-x.-14

Porquericourt — French take, 28-viii.-18

" **Port Adelaide**," **s.s.** — sunk, 3-ii.-17

Port Amelia — British column at, 12-i.-18

" **Port Campbell**," **s.s.** — sunk, 7-iv.-18

" **Port Curtis**," **s.s.** — sunk, 7-vii.-17

" **Port Hardy**," **s.s.** — sunk, 6-vii.-18

" **Porthkerry**," **s.s.** — sunk, 20-v.-17

" **Portia**," **H.M. fleet messenger** — su 2-viii.-15

" **Port Jackson**," **s.s.** — sunk, 28-iv.-17

" **Port Kembla**," **s.s.** — sunk, 18-ix.-17

Portland — H.M.S. " Fisgard II." lost 17-ix.-14

" **Portloe**," **s.s.** — sunk, 20-iv.-17

" **Port Nicholson**," **s.s.** — mined, 15-i.-17

Porto Buso — Italians raid, 24-v.-15

Porto Corsini — shelled, 24-v.-15

Port Said — Home Counties Territor Division detained at, 11-xi.-14; air-rai 8-v.-15; 21-v.-16; " through " convoy fr England started, 31-x.-17

Port-sur-Seille — Americans on front, 30-vi 18; U.S. 4th Corps at, 22-ix.-18

Portugal — German shipping seized, 23-ii.- Germany breaks with, 9-iii.-16; Germa declares war, 10-iii.-16

Army — ready to leave for W. fro 9-xi.-16; reported in action on W. fro 17-vi.-17; German raid on front n Neuve Chapelle, 1-iii.-18; counter pe trates second line, 9-iii.-18; German r near Laventie defeated, 11-iii.-18; 2 Division attacked, 9-iv.-18

Ministry — provisional: formed under I Sidonio Paes, 6-xii.-17

President: see Machado, Dr. B., and Pa Dr. S.

" **Portugal**," **H.S.** — torpedoed, 31-iii.-16

" **Port Victor**," **s.s.** — torpedoed, 26-ix.-17

" **Portwood**," **s.s.** — torpedoed, 8-viii.-18

Posen — Russian cavalry enter, 9-xi.-14; G man Eastern H.Q. removed to Intersbu 5-ii.-15

" **Posen**," **H.I.M.S.** — damaged in Jutla battle, 31-v.-16; escorts expedition to F land, 5-iii.-18

" **Potaro**," **s.s.** — captured and scuttled, 10-i.-

Poti — Germans land, 18-vi.-18

Potiorek, Marshal (Austria) — commands troc invading Serbia, 7-ix.-14

Potters Bar — airship brought down, 1-x.-16

Pourcy — Germans reach, 17-vii.-18

" **Powhatan**," **s.s.** — sunk, 6-iv.-17

Pozarevatz — Austro-Germans take, 14-x.-15

Pozières — outskirts captured by British, 15-v 16; British advance, 17-vii.-16; street figl ing, 22-vii.-16; British capture greater pa 23-vii.-16; fighting continues, 24-vii.-1 British complete capture; approach Hill 16 25-vii.-16; trench captured N. of, 26-vii.-1 progress near, 28-vii.-16; British advar against German second line, 4-viii.-18 6-viii.-16; gains, 9-viii.-16; Germans repulse 10-viii.-16; British advance N.W. of, 12-vii 16; Germans enter part of captured trench 13-viii.-16; German counter-attacks repulse 17-viii.-16

Praga — Russians driven out, 9-viii.-15

Prahovo — Bulgarians advance on, 23-x.-1 take, 24-x.-15

Pralea — Rumanian advance S.W. of, 15-i.-

Prasalon, Mte. — taken by Austro-Germa 16-xi.-17

" **Präsident**," **s.s.** — blown up, 29-vii.-15

Predeal — Rumanians retire on, 7-x.-16; G mans at, 12-x.-16; Austrians on front ridge, 14-x.-16; Austrians at, 23-x.-16; G man success W. of, 5-xi.-16; Rumani retreat barred, 7-xii.-16

Predeal Pass — Austrians repulsed, 13-x.-16; invaders in, 21-x.-16; progress, 22-x.-16; 24-x.-16; Austrian success, 31-x.-16; violent Austrian attacks, 2-xi.-16; severe fighting, 16-xi.-16

Premeli — Italians at, 9-x.-16

"Prense," H.I.M.S. — sinks two British T.B.D.s, 17-x.-17

Préseau — taken by British, 2-xi.-18

"President Kruger," s.s. — arrives at Baku with Gen. Dunsterville on board, 17-viii.-18

"President Lincoln," U.S. transport — sunk, 31-v.-18

Press Bureau: see under Great Britain

Pressoire — French take, 7-xi.-16

Preux-au-Sart — taken by British, 4-xi.-18

Priaforá Mountain — Italians take, 25-vi.-16

Prilep — Serbians hold between Veles and, 1-xi.-15; Bulgarians advance on, 14-xi.-15; falls, 16-xi.-15; Serb cavalry near, 18-ix.-18; carried, 23-ix.-18

"Primo," s.s. — sunk, 26-xi.-14

"Primo," s.s. — sunk, 18-ix.-18

"Primula," H.M. sloop — sunk, 1-iii.-16

"Prince Abbas," s.s. — sunk, 9-vii.-17

"Prince George," H.M.S. — attacks in Dardanelles, 3-iii.-15; shells Besika, 4-iii.-15; supports Dardanelles attack, 4-iii.-15

Prince Heinrich Hill (Tsingtau) — carried, 28-ix.-14

"Princess Alberta," H.M. fleet messenger — sunk, 21-ii.-17

"Princess Irene," H.M. auxiliary — destroyed, 27-v.-15

"Princess Irma," s.s. — attacked by aircraft, 27-ii.-18

"Princess Margaret," H.M. minelayer — operations, 8-xi.-15; 3-v.-16

Princess Patricia's Canadian Light Infantry — gallantry at Ypres, 8-v.-15

"Princess Royal," H.M.S. — leaves 1st Battle Cruiser Squadron to protect first convoy of Canadians, 28-ix.-14; meets convoy, 10-x.-14; leaves to reinforce N. American station, 11-xi.-14; returns to Grand Fleet, 1-i.-15; in Dogger Bank battle; F. to Adm. Beatty, 24-i.-15; leaves Rosyth to support operations in Heligoland Bight, 28-i.-15; in Jutland battle, 31-v.-16; sunk by U-Boat, 26-v.-18

"Principe Umberto," Italian transport — sunk, 9-vi.-16

Prinkipo — remnants of German Asia Corps interned, 17-xi.-18; proposed conference of Russian factions at; see under Russia

"Prinz Adalbert," H.I.M.S. — torpedoed and damaged, 2-vii.-15; sunk by E8, 23-x.-15

"Prinz Eitel Friedrich," H.I.M.A.M.C. — leaves Tsingtau, 10-viii.-14; joins Adm. Spee at Pagan Island, 12-viii.-14; chases s.s. "Colusa," 1-xi.-14; sinks s.s. "Charcas," 5-xii.-14; sinks s.v. "William P. Frye," 28-i.-15; at Newport News, 11-iii.-15; interned, 8-iv.-15

"Prinz Eugen," Austrian Dreadnought — torpedoed, 9-vi.-18

"Prinz Regent Luitpold," H.I.M.S. — in 3rd High Sea Squadron, 26-xii.-14; mutiny, 18-viii.-17; surrenders, 21-xi.-18

Prisches — taken by British, 5-xi.-18

Prishtina — falls, 23-xi.-15

Prisoners (see also names of battles) :—

Allies — statistics, 1-x.-18; 5-x.-18

Disabled — exchange arranged through U.S., 6-i.-15; British and German exchanged, 15-ii.-15

Germany — statistics, 3-iii.-16

British — statistics, 22-viii.-17; first batch leaves for England, 21-xi.-18

Condition — German Government apprised, 20-xi.-18

Russians — statistics, 22-ii.-15

Prisoners (continued) :—

Great Britain — statistics, 19-x.-16; 1-vi.-17; 22-viii.-17; 15-xi.-17; and Appendix II.

German — segregation of U-Boat crews: Germans threaten reprisals, 2-iv.-15; 39 British officers arrested as reprisals, 12-iv.-15; crews again treated as ordinary prisoners, 12-vi.-15

Lonsdale, Private: see Lonsdale, Private Statistics: see Appendix II.

Prittwitz und Gaffron, Gen. von (Germany) — commands 8th Army, 2-viii.-15; informs Germans G.H.Q. of impossibility of maintaining position E. of the Vistula, 20-viii.-14; relinquishes command, 22-viii.-14

Prizrend — taken, 30-xi.-15

"Professor Woermann," s.s. — captured, 22-viii.-14

Pronville — British break through defences, 3-ix.-18

Propaganda: see under various countries

"Prophet," s.s. — sunk, 14-xi.-17

Prosnes — German gas attack, 19-x.-15

"Protector," British pilot cutter — mined, 31-xii.-16

Protopopoff, M. (Russia) — arrested, 13-iii.-17

"Provence II.," French auxiliary — sunk, 26-ii.-16

Provins — Germans scouting to southward, 5-ix.-14

Proyart — Germans take, 27-iii.-18

"Prudentia," H.M. oiler — sunk, 12-i.-16

Prunay — French advance, 15-i.-15; 17-iv.-17; German attacks, 15-vii.-18; French pushed slightly back, 16-vii.-18; Germans defeated S. of, 17-vii.-18; retaken by French, 18-vii.-18

Prussia — Amnesty proclaimed, 4-viii.-14; 23-xi.-18; Kaiser promises franchise reform, 7-iii.-17; equal franchise after next election, 11-vii.-17; republic: programme, 13-xi.-18; Upper House of Diet abolished, 15-xi.-18; Independent Socialists withdraw from Government, 3-i.-19

Prussia, East — Russians cross frontier, 2-viii.-14; invaded by Russian 1st Army, 7-viii.-14; Russian Niemen Army cross frontier, 16-viii.-14; battle at Gumbinnen, 19-viii.-14; battle ends: 1st Prussian Corps retiring on Königsberg, 20-viii.-14; retirement continues; Gen. Samsonoff's 2nd Army invading Allenstein district, 21-viii.-14; Gen. von Hindenburg to command 8th German Army in, 22-viii.-14; Russians advance, 24-viii.-14; battle of Tannenburg begun: Samsonoff engages Hindenburg at Allenstein—Mlava, 26-viii.-14; Samsonoff's right being turned by Hindenburg's army, 27-viii.-14; Hindenburg ordered to clear, 31-viii.-14; Russians re-enter, 2-xi.-14; drive Germans back, 4-xi.-14; Russians reach Eydtkuhnen—Stallupönen, 8-xi.-14; take Goldap and penetrate German territory between Kalisch—Thorn, 10-xi.-14; threaten Thorn, 13-xi.-14; checked, 14-xi.-14; Russians levy war-tax, 15-xi.-14; defeated at Soldau, 18-xi.-14; advance on, 11-i.-15; 12-i.-15; advancing in neighbourhood of Pillkallen, 25-i.-15; Lyck raided, 1-ii.-15; Germans in Johannisburg, 8-ii.-15; take Biala, 9-ii.-15; Germans near Lyck, 13-ii.-15; Germans take Lyck; Russians driven out of E. Prussia, 14-ii.-15; Germans take Tauroggen, 18-ii.-15; Russians occupy Memel, 18-iii.-15; Germans retake, 21-iii.-15; in Tauroggen, 29-iii.-15

Prussia, Prince Eitel Friedrich of — in command of 1st Prussian Guard Division, 20-viii.-18

Prussia, Prince Henry of — hoists flag in H.I.M.S. "Blücher," 3-ix.-14; removed from British Royal Naval List, 5-xi.-14

"Prut," Russian minelayer — sunk, 29-x.-14

Pruth, R. — Austrians fail to cross, 17-iii.-15; Austro-Germans cross, 12-vi.-15

"**Royalist**," **H.M.S.** — in 4th Light Cruiser Squadron, 30-vi.-15

Royal Marine Brigade — landed at Dunkirk, 20-ix.-14; proceeds to Antwerp, 2-x.-14; landed at Fao by H.M.S. "Ocean," 8-xi.-14; see also Marines

Royal Naval Air Service — assist at Dardanelles bombardment, 19-ii.-15; anti-U-Boat patrols; operations, 8-xii.-17; amalgamated into R.A.F., 1-iv.-18

Royal Naval Division — to be formed, 17-viii.-14; takes over Crystal Palace, 8-ix.-14; arrive at Dunkirk for Antwerp, 4-x.-14; at Antwerp, 6-x.-14; part cross into Holland; interned, 9-x.-14; re-embarked at Ostend; sent to Deal, 10-x.-14; total strength, 15-viii.-15; men interned in Holland leave for England, 14-xi.-18

Royal Naval Transport Services — clears Boulogne, Havre, and Rouen, 16-ix.-14

Royal Naval Volunteer Reserve — drafts for R.N.D. moved into Crystal Palace, 8-ix.-14

"**Royal Sceptre**," **s.s.** — captured and released by H.I.M.S. "Karlsruhe," 27-x.-14; attacked by U-Boat, 2-vii.-18

Roye — French raid German communications to E. from, 17-ix.-14; Gen. de Castelnau halted, 26-ix.-14; fighting near, 2-x.-14; German line hardens W. of, 6-x.-14; Germans repulsed near, 5-xi.-14; British line opposite, 26-ii.-17; advance from Arras to Roye road, 17-iii.-17; retaken, 17-iii.-17; French 1st Army covering, 23-iii.-18; lost, 26-iii.-18; French progress on road, 10-viii.-18; advance, 11-viii.-18; 12-viii.-18; 16-viii.-18; 17-viii.-18; falls, 27-viii.-18

Royhan — heavy fighting, 20-vii.-15; Germans cross Narev R., 23-vii.-15; Germans storm, 24-vii.-15

Ruad Island — British landing party distribute food, 22-i.-15; French occupy, 31-viii.-15

Ruaha R. — British bar German retreat, 10-ix.-16

Ruanda — Germans raid Belgian post, 24-ix.-14; Belgian advance, 8-v.-16; Belgians occupy Kigali, 6-v.-16

Rubescourt—St.   Maur — French counter-attack, 11-vi.-18

"**Rubio**," **s.s.** — mined, 25-ii.-18

Rudnik ridge — Austrians gain foothold; Serbians counter-attack, 3-xii.-14; 4-xii.-14; Austrians routed, 5-xii.-14; retreat, 6-xii.-14

"**Ruel**," **s.s.** — sunk, 21-viii.-15

Ruffey, Gen. (France) — commanding 3rd Army falling back across Meuse, 26-viii.-14

Rufiji R. — British occupy Mafia Islands, 10-i.-15; H.I.M.S. "Königsberg" attacked by monitors, 4-vii.-15; 6-vii.-15; destroyed, 11-vii.-15; British on N. bank, 5-i.-17; progress on, 20-i.-17; Maj. Wintgens captured, 22-v.-17

Rügen — H.I.M.S. "Gazelle" damaged by Russian submarine, 25-i.-15

Ruhungu — British reach, 12-viii.-16

Rumancourt — taken by British, 3-ix.-18

Rumania — Austria-Hungary declares war, 27-viii.-16; Germany declares war, 28-viii.-16; Turkey declares war, 30-viii.-16; Bulgaria declares war, 1-ix.-16

Austro-German army of occupation — Marshal Mackensen in command, 11-v.-18; dissolved, 1-vii.-18; evacuation demanded, 9-xi.-18

Bessarabia: see under Bessarabia

Distress — relief: Inter-Allied Commission approved, 20-i.-19

Finance — credit (£4,000,000) voted, 4-viii.-15; — loan (£5,000,000) from Great Britain, 27-i.-15

Government — at Jassy, 6-xii.-16

Rumania (continued) :—

Hungary — Hungarians attack, 20-vii.-19; Rumanians nearing Budapest, 1-viii.-19; Budapest occupied, 2-viii.-19; ultimatum to Government embodying armistice terms, 5-viii.-19; Budapest evacuated, 13-xi.-19

King: see Ferdinand

Ministry — Bratiano Cabinet resigns, 6-ii.-17; Averescu Cabinet formed, 9-ii.-18

Royal family — leaves Jassy, 11-viii.-17

Rumania (operations) — Bulgarians cross Dobrudja, 1-xi.-16; Rumanians take Orsova, 3-ix.-16; fighting in Dobrudja; town captured, 4-ix.-18; Bulgarians take Tutrakan, 6-ix.-16; German 9th Army under Falkenhayn, 6-ix.-16; fighting at Dobritch; Rumanian bombardment, 7-ix.-16; Rumanians take Toplitza, 9-ix.-16; cross Aluta R. retire in Dobrudja, 14-ix.-16; Austrian counter in Transylvania, 15-ix.-16; Rumanians evacuate Petroseny; lull in Dobrudja, 20-ix.-16; Austrians reach Vulcan Pass, 21-ix.-16; Austrians in Roter Turm Pass, 23-ix.-16; Rumanian progress in Dobrudja, 25-ix.-16; Austrians carry W. side of Roter Turm Pass, 26-ix.-16; Germans fail to cross Danube at Korabia; Bukarest bombed, 30-ix.-16; Mackensen repulsed, 7-x.-16; Rumanians cross Danube at Rahova, 1-x.-16; Rumanian rally S. of Roter Turm Pass, 2-x.-16; capture 13 guns; withdraw from Rahova, 3-x.-16; retreat towards Brasso, 5-x.-16; retire on Predeal—Orsova; Austro-Germans capture Brasso and Szekeley Udvarhely, 7-x.-16; Germans take Törzburg and Danube Is., 8-x.-16; Rumanian retreat, 9-x.-16; Austro-Germans in Törzburg Pass, 10-x.-16; Germans at Predeal, 12-x.-16; Austrians repulsed, in Predeal—Vulcan Passes, 13-x.-16; German attack at Dorna Watra, 14-x.-16; capture Gyimes Pass, 16-x.-16; checked in Gyimes Pass, 17-x.-16; Rumanian success, 18-x.-16; new German offensive in Dobrudja, 19-x.-16; fighting in Gyimes Pass, 19-x.-16; Rumanians lose Tuzla; fighting at Dorna Watra, 20-x.-16; Russo-Rumanian retreat in Dobrudja; Germans cut railway, 21-x.-16; Rumanians evacuate Constanza, 22-x.-16; further withdrawal, 23-x.-16; successes at Roter Turm—Oitoz Passes: invaders capture Vulcan Pass, 24-x.-16; Austrians take Predeal town and Germans take Tchernavoda, 25-x.-16; further Rumanian retirement, 26-x.-16; successful counter-attacks in Uza Valley, Törzburg Pass, and Jiul Valley, 27-x.-16; Austro-German advance S. of Roter Turm Pass, 28-x.-16; Rumanian counter-attacks, 29-x.-16; 30-x.-16; 31-x.-16; Austro-German pressure in passes, 1-xi.-16; 2-xi.-16; Russian fleet bombards Constanza, 4-xi.-16; German successes in passes, 5-xi.-16; fighting in passes, 6-xi.-16; 8-xi.-16; 9-xi.-16; 10-xi.-16; 11-xi.-16; 12-xi.-16; 13-xi.-16; 14-xi.-16; Germans through Törzburg Pass, in Rumanian territory in Roter Turm and Vulcan Passes, 15-xi.-16; Rumanian retreat in passes continued, 16-xi.-16; 18-xi.-16; 19-xi.-16; fall of Craiova, 21-xi.-16; fighting at Orsova, 22-xi.-16; Germans take Simnitza, 23-xi.-16; cut off Orsova garrison, 25-xi.-16; take Rymnik, 26-xi.-16; Giurgiu and Curtea de Arges, 27-xi.-16; approach Bukarest, 28-xi.-16; 29-xi.-16; 30-xi.-16; Arges battle, 1-xii.-16; 2-xii.-16; 3-xii.-16; Bukarest arsenal blown up, 4-xii.-16; Germans outside Bukarest, 5-xii.-16; take, 6-xii.-16; advance from, 7-xii.-16; 8-xii.-16; 9-xii.-16; 10-xii.-16; 11-xii.-16; 13-xii.-16; 15-xii.-16; 16-xii.-16; 17-xii.-16; 18-xii.-16; 19-xii.-16; 21-xii.-16; 22-xii.-16; 23-xii.-16; take Tulcea, 24-xii.-16; before Braila, 25-xii.-16; fighting continued

Rumania (operations) (continued) :—
26-xii.-16; Austro-Germans take Rimnic
Sarat, 27-xii.-16; further progress, 28-xii.-16;
30-xii.-16; 31-xii.-16; 1-i.-17; take Jujila,
3-i.-17; enter Macin, 4-i.-17; take Braila,
5-i.-17; advance from, 6-i.-17; take Focsani,
8-i.-17; Austro-Germans driven across Putna,
10-i.-17; Turks storm Mihalea, 12-i.-17;
Mackensen checked, 16-i.-17; Rumanian success, 17-i.-17; Austro-Germans take Nanesti,
19-i.-17; gains: line, 23-i.-17; Allied counter,
27-i.-17; 30-i.-17; 31-i.-17; 23-vii.-17;
27-vii.-17; 28-vii.-17; 29-vii.-17; checked,
6-viii.-17; Austro-German progress, 7-viii.-17;
8-viii.-17; 9-viii.-17; 10-viii.-17; 11-viii.-17;
12-viii.-17; Rumanian counter, 12-viii.-17;
13-viii.-17; Austro-German advance continued, 15-viii.-17; checked, 16-viii.-17;
17-viii.-17; continued, 19-viii.-17; 28-viii.-17;
checked, 31-viii.-17
Rumania and Russia — agreement signed,
18-ix.-14
Rumania and United States — Minister leaves
Rumania, 13-i.-17
Rumeli Medjidieh Tabia, Fort — bombarded,
8-iii.-15
Rumilly — British break line, 2-x.-18
" Runo," s.s. — mined, 5-ix.-14
Runö Is. — raided by LZ88, 6-ix.-16; German
detachments landed, 15-x.-17
" Runswick," s.s. — sunk, 18-iv.-18
" Ruomi," German s.s. — sunk by E19, 3-xi.-16
Rupel, Fort — Bulgaro-Germans occupy,
26-v.-16
" Ruperra," s.s. — sunk, 20-vi.-17
Rushdi Pasha, Sir Hussein (Egypt) — to form
new Cabinet, 9-iv.-19
" Russell," H.M.S. — joins Grand Fleet,
7-viii.-14; mined, 27-iv.-16
Russia — prepares to mobilise on Austrian
frontier, 25-vii.-14; general mobilisation,
31-vii.-14 (see Germany and Russia); sale of
alcohol prohibited, 16-ix.-14; Turkey declares
war on, 14-xi.-14; protest against German
atrocities, 20-i.-15; ultimatum to Bulgaria,
3-x.-15; Note to Allies: confirms intention to
continue war, 3-v.-17; out of war, 10-ii.-18;
no fighting or negotiation, 11-ii.-18
Allied Powers — policy: M. Pichon on,
24-xii.-18
Bolshevists — and Social Revolutionary Conference under Lenin, 8-viii.-17; Lenin's
coup d'état in Petrograd, 7-xi.-17; Kerensky's forces defeated at Tsarskoe Selo,
13-xi.-17; escapes from Gatchina, 14-xi.-17;
right of peoples to self-determination proclaimed, 15-xi.-17; boycott Constituent
Assembly, 11-xii.-17; disperse, 13-xii.-17;
ultimatum to Ukraine, 17-xii.-17; order
arrest of Rumanian King, 15-i.-18; Constituent Assembly refuses dictation by,
18-i.-18; dissolve Constituent Assembly,
19-i.-18; declare war on Kieff Rada,
26-i.-18; Red Guards fight with Finnish
troops, 25-i.-18; capture Helsingfors,
28-i.-18; 29-i.-18; counter-revolution in W.
Siberia, 19-vi.-18; take Perm, 24-xii.-18;
occupy Riga, 2-i.-19; and Vilna, 4-i.-19;
advance from Vilna, 11-i.-19; repulsed at
Merv, 16-i.-19; Allies near Shenkursk retire before, 25-i.-19; Soviet rule at Kharkoff, 28-i.-19; retire at Tarasevo, 30-i.-19;
Bolshevists take Kieff, 3-ii.-19; reply to
Prinkipo proposal, 6-ii.-19; defeated at
Kadish, 7-ii.-19; Russian Political Conference drives claim to represent, 8-ii.-19;
mission from International Socialist Conference (Berne) agreed to, 20-ii.-19; Caspian
flotillas surrender to Allies, 24-ii.-19; Adm.
Koltchak takes Ufa, 14-iii.-19; Esthonians,
Letts, Ukrainians, and Lithunians seek
help of Allies against, 17-iii.-19; Letts capture Mitau, 19-iii.-19; Budapest Soviets

Russia:—
Bolshevists (continued) :—
offer of alliance accepted, 22-iii.-19; Bol-
shevists repulsed on Archangel front,
1-iv.-19; capture Merv, 23-v.-19; drive
Adm. Koltchak's left wing on Ufa,
4-vi.-19; capture Ufa, 9-vi.-19; Gen.
Denikin takes Kharkoff from, 27-vi.-19;
Tsaritsyn, 30-vi.-19; Adm. Koltchak loses
Perm to, 1-vii.-19; Ekaterinburg, 14-vii.-19;
Adm. Koltchak in retreat, 16-vi.-19; Gen.
Denikin takes Kharkoff, 27-vi.-19; Bol-
shevists capture Perm, 1-vii.-19; Adm.
Koltchak withdraws from Omsk, 15-xi.-19
Great Britain, recognition by — denied by
Mr. Lloyd George in Parliament,
12-ii.-19; 200 M.P.s send telegram to
British Peace Conference delegation
urging non-recognition, 9-iv.-19
Church — separation from State, 15-xii.-17
Constituent Assembly — meets in Petrograd:
boycotted by Bolshevists, 11-xii.-17; dispersed by Bolshevists, 13-xii.-17; refuses
dictation by Bolshevists, 18-i.-18; Bolshevists dissolve, 19-i.-18
Cossacks — rising, 9-xii.-17; Gen. Kaledin
resigns headship of Don Cossacks in favour
of Gen. Alexieff, 4-ii.-18
Council of Peasants — appeal to army,
7-vi.-17
Duma — convened, 1-viii.-15; prorogued,
29-xii.-16; 12-iii.-17; Tsar opens, 22-ii.-16;
occupied by Red Guard, 4-xii.-17
Federation — Congress (Kieff): border
peoples' vote in favour, 21-ix.-17
Frontier, new — Kaiser discusses with Hindenburg and Ludendorff, 2-i.-18
Government (National: Lvoff) — elected,
12-iii.-17; names, 14-iii.-17; Moscow
adheres to, 14-iii.-17; recognised by Great
Britain, France, and U.S., 24-iii.-17;
guarantees Polish independence, 30-iii.-17;
pledges itself to continuance of war, 1-v.-17;
vote of confidence in: passed by Petrograd
Soviet Council, 5-v.-17; Minister of War
and Marine: resigns, 13-v.-17
Government (Coalition: Lvoff) — formed,
16-v.-17; declares against separate peace,
19-v.-17; Ukrainian policy: four Cadet
Ministers resign, 15-vii.-17; Prince Lvoff
resigns: succeeded by M. Kerensky,
22-vii.-17
Government (National: Kerensky) — formed,
6-viii.-17
Government (Council of Five) — formed,
15-ix.-17
Government (Coalition: Kerensky) —
formed, 7-x.-17
Government (Archangel) — rejects Prinkipo
proposal, 27-i.-19; represented on " Russian
Political Conference " in Paris, 8-ii.-19
Government (Ekaterinodar) — represented on
" Russian Political Conference " in Paris,
8-ii.-19
Government (Koltchak) — represented on
" Russian Political Conference " in Paris,
8-ii.-19; recognition: decision of Council of
Four, 26-v.-19; reply to Allies' Note,
12-vi.-19; Gen. Denikin recognises as
supreme head, 12-vi.-19
Grand Dukes — bodies found, 29-ix.-18
Great Britain — Mr. Henderson on special
mission, 29-v.-17; reply to Note of May 3,
11-vi.-17; policy: Lord Milner defends,
19-xii.-19; Bolshevists (see under Bolshe-
vists above)
Japan — agreement with published, 8-vii.-16
Military position — Gen. Korniloff at All-
Russia Conference on, 28-viii.-17
Ministry — Gen. Polivanoff War Minister,
26-vi.-15; M. Stuermer succeeds M.
Goremykin as Premier, 1-ii.-16; M.

x

Russian front (continued) :—
wedge through German line E. of Lodz near Brzezany, 23-xi.-14; German 25th Reserve Corps and 3rd Prussian Guard Division cut off : break through Russian line at Brzezany, 24-xi.-14; Germans on defensive near Strykow —Glowno and W. of Lowicz, 25-xi.-14; German retreat completed near Rzgov: advance on Lowicz—Lodz—Petrikov, 26-xi.-14; Russians evacuating Lodz, 27-xi.-14; Germans bombard Lodz, 29-xi.-14; Mackensen reinforced by 25th Reserve Corps at Lask-Pabiance begins battle of Lowicz, 30-xi.-14; Germans in suburbs of Lodz, 1-xii.-14; Mackensen's Lowicz attack supported by Austrians giving battle at Limanowa, 5-xii.-14; Germans enter Lodz, 6-xii.-14; second German attack on Warsaw, 7-xii.-14; battle continues, 9-xii.-14; Russian stand at Lowicz, 11-xii.-14; Warsaw battle continued, 13-xii.-14; Russian stand 30 miles S.W. of, 16-xii.-14; Germans take Lowicz, 17-xii.-14; Russians attacked along Lower Bzura—Ravka line, 19-xii.-14; Russian stand on Lower Bzura, 20-xii.-14; Germans fail to cross, 21-xii.-14; Germans cross Bzura but fail to advance, 23-xii.-14; Germans defeated at Skiernevice, 27-xii.-14; Germans fighting rearguard action at Bolimov and Movlodz, 30-xii.-14; Austro-German retreat, 31-xii.-14; further Russian successes on Bzura front, 2-i.-15; German attack repulsed on Ravka R., 7-i.-15; Russians take Skempe, 20-i.-15; German offensive near Lipno, 30-i.-15; German offensive along Ravka line near Bolimov, 31-i.-15; 1-ii.-15; German pressure, 2-ii.-15; Russians regain Gumin: German offensive weakening, 3-ii.-15; Germans take Serpets, 11-ii.-15; Russians counter-attack near Plock and Lomja, 21-ii.-15; success near Bolimov, 24-ii.-15; Germans bombard Ossovietz, 25-ii.-15; Germans retire from Przasnysz, 2-iii.-15; Germans mass forces between Thorn and Mlava, 5-iii.-15; Germans use liquid fire, 7-iii.-15; new offensive begun, 9-iii.-15; Germans attack towards Niemen R., 10-iii.-15; repulsed at Augustovo—Przasnysz, 12-iii.-15; offensive checked, 13-iii.-15; fail to take Przasnysz and make no progress towards Niemen, 14-iii.-15; Russian counter-attack along Orzec R., 15-iii.-15; Germans abandon Ossovietz, 21-iii.-15; Russians advancing to Suvalki, 9-iv.-15; Germans repulsed at Ossovietz, 14-iv.-15; Austro-German offensive between Viedrz and Bug, 29-vi.-15; Kaiser orders resumption of offensive, 1-vii.-15; Austro-Germans capture Zamosc and Krasnik, 1-vii.-15; Austro-German offensive stayed near Krasnik, 4-vii.-15; Austro-Germans defeated N.E. of Krasnik, 5-vii.-15; 9-vii.-15; German attack on Ravka R., 6-vii.-15; Austro-German attack, 10-vii.-15; Russian counter-attacks at Lublin, 11-vii.-15; Germans capture Przasnysz; Russians retire from Narev R.; German thrust towards Riga, 14-vii.-15; Prussian Guard Cavalry Division transferred from Belgium, 16-vii.-15; Russians forced back to Narev Fortress line, 17-vii.-15; heavy fighting on Lublin front, 19-vii.-15; German break through on Lublin-Kholm railway at Biscupice, 29-vii.-15; Russians retiring; Austro-Germans in Lublin, 30-vii.-15; Austro-Germans at Kholm, 31-vii.-15; German success on Bobr R., near Ossovietz, 6-viii.-15; New German 12th Army formed, 7-viii.-15; Germans enter Siedlce; seize Lukov railway junction, 12-viii.-15; Russians retiring from Siedlce reach Losice, 14-viii.-15; Germans between Bug and Jasiolda, 19-viii.-15; Ossovietz occupied by Prussians; Russians retire from Niemen—Bobr, 22-viii.-15; Austro-Germans advance E. from Lublin; enter Kovel, 23-viii.-15; Austro-German,

Russian front (continued) :—
advance on Vilna: reaches Orany: occupy Lutsk and cross Styr, 31-viii.-15; Grodno: outer forts captured, 1-ix.-15; falls: fierce fighting at Orany, 2-ix.-15; Russian local recovery at Grodno: Germans storm Friedrichstadt bridgehead, 3-ix.-15; strike N.W. of Vilna at Novo Troki: take Volkovisk, 7-ix.-15; Vilna—Dvinsk battle begun, 9-ix.-15; Germans reach Utsiany: force Russians back E. of Grodno, 12-ix.-15; cut Vilna—Petrograd railway at Svientsiany: Russians at Vilna threatened with envelopment, 14-ix.-15; Austro-Germans occupy Pinsk: offensive towards Rovno developing, 15-ix.-15; Vilna almost encircled: German cavalry reaches Vilna—Minsk railway between Molodechna—Polotsk, 16-ix.-15; Russians retire between Vilia—Pripet: Austro-German Rovno offensive checked, 17-ix.-15; Vilna falls: renewed attacks on Dvinsk: Bavarians repulsed at Slonim: Austro-Germans retire at Rovno, 18-ix.-15; reach Smorgon: Russian counter-stroke at Smorgon—Molodechna, 19-ix.-15; heavy fighting at Vilna—Dvinsk—Riga, 20-ix.-15; successful Russian retreat from Vilna: success at Lennewaden: Germans driven from Smorgon, 21-ix.-15; Russians holding, 22-ix.-15; re-occupy Vileika and Lutsk: drive Austro-Germans behind Oginski Canal, 23-ix.-15; German assault between Lake Drisviaty—Dvina repulsed, 24-ix.-15; reverse near Dvinsk: Russians take Drisviaty, 25-ix.-15; straighten line N.W. of Dubno: repulse Germans near Pinsk: success round Vileika, 26-ix.-15; repulse German attacks at Eckau and W. of Vileika, 27-ix.-15; forced back in Pripet area: evacuate Lutsk, 28-ix.-15; Dvinsk fighting continues: two years' position warfare on Lower Dvina begun, 29-ix.-15; German advance stayed, 30-ix.-15; attack Dvinsk and Smorgon, 1-x.-15; fresh threat to Dvinsk, 2-x.-15; desperate fighting S. of Dvinsk, 3-x.-15; Russian advance between Smorgon—Lake Drisviaty, 4-x.-15; fighting near Smorgon, 5-x.-15; German assaults on Dvinsk: fierce fighting at Grunwald, 6-x.-15; fighting at Garbunovka, 7-x.-15; close fighting before Dvinsk, 8-x.-15; desperate struggle for Garbunovka, 9-x.-15; Germans driven from, 10-x.-15; Russians attack at Dvinsk—Smorgon: take Visniovtchyk, 12-x.-15; Germans cross Eckau: Russian success at Vessolovo, 14-x.-15; Russians repulsed at Gross Eckau, 16-x.-15; Germans active on Dvina line, 17-x.-15; heavy fighting on Styr: Germans advance on Dvina, 18-x.-15; fighting at Olai, 19-x.-15; Russians carry German positions at Baranovitchi: Germans capture Dvina bank E. of Riga, 20-x.-15; German success near Dvinsk, 22-x.-15; take Illutsk, 23-x.-15; slight success near Dvinsk, 26-x.-15; success at Garbunovka, 28-x.-15; Russian offensive in south, 31-xii.-15; great German concentration on Riga—Dvinsk front, 23-iii.-17; hostilities resumed, 18-ii.-18; German advance into heart of Russia, 19-ii.-18; German military movements end, 3-iii.-18

Russian Political Conference (Paris) — under Prince Lvoff and representing Archangel, Omsk, and Ekaterinodar Governments: denies Bolshevist claims to represent Russia, 8-ii.-19

" Russian Prince," s.s. — torpedoed; reaches port, 8-vi.-17

Russky, Gen. (Russia) — enters Sokol, 14-viii.-14; advancing in Galicia, 28-viii.-14; falls back, 10-x.-14; retires, 20-xii.-15

Rustam — operations begun against hostile tribesmen, 21-viii.-15

Rustchuk — Rumanian division across Danube at Rahovo, 1-x.-16; bombarded, 10-ix.-16

" **Rustington,"** **s.s.** — sunk, 25-vii.-17
Ruter Gat — E45 lays mines, 24-iv.-18
" **Ruth Hickman,"** **s.s.** — sunk, 24-v.-18
Rutland — Zeppelin raid on, 5-iii.-16
Ruyaulcourt — taken by New Zealanders, 4-ix.-18
Ruyaulcourt Fins — taken, 30-iii.-17
" **Ruysdael,"** **s.s.** — sunk, 7-ix.-18
" **Ryasan,"** **s.s.** — captured; armed as German raider and renamed " Cormoran," 10-viii.-14
" **Rydal Hall,"** **s.s.** — sunk, 1-xii.-17
Rymnik — German progress near, 8-xi.-16; captured, 26-xi.-16
Rypin — raided by ZV., 25-viii.-14
" **Rytonhall,"** **s.s.** — sunk, 2-ix.-17
Rzgov — Germans heavily engaged, 21-xi.-14; retreat completed after desperate fighting, 26-xi.-14

S.

Saarbrücken — French air-raids, 9-viii.-15; 6-ix.-15; Allied raids, 25-i.-18; 5-ii.-17
Saarburg — taken by French, 18-viii.-14; French driven out, 19-viii.-14; evacuated, 20-viii.-14
Saar Valley — Germans at Versailles suggest provision of coal instead of cession of area, 13-v.-19; further German Note on, 16-v.-19; German proposal rejected, 24-v.-19
" **Saba,"** **s.s.** — mined, 8-iii.-18
Sabatino — Italians take, 6-viii.-16
" **Sabbia,"** **s.s.** — sunk, 20-iv.-16
" **Sabia,"** **s.s.** — sunk, 24-xi.-17
Sabot Wood — French gain footing, 7-iii.-15; in French hands, 14-iii.-15; French take, 27-ix.-15
" **Sachem,"** **s.s.** — attacked by U-Boat, 15-xii.-17
Sadani — British occupy, 1-viii.-16
" **Saga,"** **s.s.** — sunk, 14-ii.-18
" **Sagamore,"** **s.s.** — sunk, 3-iii.-17
Saghir Dere — British attacked near coast, 28-vi.-15
Sagrado — attacked, 10-vi.-15; Italians fail to cross river at, 15-vi.-15; Italians gain crossing of Isonzo R.; town captured, 25-vi.-15
Sahain — action at, 15-xi.-14
Sahil — Turks defeated at, 17-xi.-14
Saillisel — French take, 19-x.-16; British progress between St. Pierre Vaast Wood and, 15-iii.-17
Sailly — French progress to, 8-x.-16; taken, 28-ix.-18
Sailly-le-Sec — British line through, 26-iii.-18
Sailly-Saillisel — French progress W. of, 12-x.-16; in outskirts, 15-x.-16; French progress, 16-x.-16; taken, 18-x.-16; attacks repulsed, 21-x.-16; French gain Ridge 128, W. of, 22-x.-16; carry trench system N.W. of, 29-x.-16; recapture most of, 5-xi.-16; hand-to-hand fight at, 8-xi.-16; French progress, 11-xi.-16; complete recapture, 12-xi.-16; British reach top of ridge, 8-ii.-17; trench captured, 28-ii.-17; British take, 1-ix.-18
" **Sailor Prince,"** **s.s.** — sunk, 2-x.-15
" **Saima,"** s.s. — sunk, 8-vi.-18
Sain Kala — British convoy reaches, 23-vii.-18
St. Agnan — American recovery N. of, 16-vii.-18; Germans reach heights, 18-vii.-18
St. André — British air-raid on junction, 9-v.-15
" **St. Andrew,"** **H.S.** — chased by U-Boat, 25-ii.-15
" **St. Andrews,"** **s.s.** — sunk, 13-vi.-17
St. Aubert — British win high ground, 11-x.-18
St. Aubin — taken by French, 22-viii.-18
" **Saint Barchan,"** **s.s.** — sunk, 21-x.-18
Saint-Clément — German airship brought down, 19-x.-17
St. Croix R. — bridge across partially blown up; arrest, 2-ii.-15
St Denis (Paris) — bombed, 11-v.-15
St. Denis Westrem — British aeroplanes r 2-viii.-16; aerodrome bombed, 3-vi.-15-vi.-17; 27-ix.-17
St. Dié — German 7th Army transferred Aisne from, 12-ix.-14; bombarded by G mans, 27-xii.-14
" **St. Dimitrios,"** **s.s.** — sunk, 20-iii.-18
St. Edouard, Cité — British enter, 16-iv.-17
Ste. Elizabeth, Cité — British take, 15-viii.-
Ste. Euphraise — British advance, 24-vii.- bitter fighting, 29-vii.-18
St. Eloi — Germans take, 10-xi.-14; Germ capture trenches, 14-ii.-15; regained, 15-ii.- Germans take part of, 14-iii.-15; British covery, 15-iii.-15; further German attack pulsed, 17-iii.-15; British raid, 19-i.- British successes, 27-iii.-16; 3-iv.-16; fighti 28-iii.-16; Germans win crater, 6-iv.- British retake crater, 10-iv.-16; Germ gain at, 19-iv.-16; German defences storn 7-vi.-17
St. Eloi, Cité (Artois) — British gain Gern trench, 8-x.-15
St. Emile, Cité — British take, 15-viii.-17
St. Emilie — taken by Germans, 22-iii.-18
St. Gabriele, Mte. — Italian progress, 30-v 17; pressure, 1-ix.-17; gain ground, 4-ix.- Austrian counters repulsed, 9-ix.-17
St. Gemme — taken by Allies, 30-vii.-18
" **St. George,"** **H.M.S.** — shells Rim 24-v.-15
St. Georges (Argonne) — taken by Americ 1-xi.-18
St. Georges (Flanders) — Allies reco 28-xii.-14; German counter-attack f 29-xii.-14; French consolidate, 4-i.-15
St. Germain — Austrian Peace Delegation 14-v.-19; incomplete Draft of Treaty sented, 2-vi.-19; Treaty presented, 20-vii. signed, 10-ix.-19
St. Gobain Forest — evacuated, 13-x.-18
St. Hilaire — Americans capture, 10-xi.-18
St. Hilaire—St. Souplet road — French wood on, 27-ix.-15
St. Hubert (Argonne) — Germans capt 15-x.-14; heavy fighting, 22-i.-15
St. Hubert (Flanders) — taken by Bri 2-xi.-18
St. Jacques Capelle — German attack by repulsed by French marines, 9-iv.-15
St. Jansbeek — French attack, 26-x.-17
St. Janshoek — British advance E. 30-viii.-17
St. Jean — taken, 9-x.-17
St. Jean de Maurienne — conference bet Mr. Lloyd George, M. Ribot, and B Sonnino, 19-iv.-17
St. Julien — German gas attack against Fr Colonials and Canadians: capture wood of, 22-iv.-15; capture, 24-iv.-15; Northun land Brigade enter for a time, 26-iv.-15; attack near: repulsed, 2-v.-15; British 31-vii.-17; lose, 1-viii.-17; retake, 3-viii advance on front from Tower Hamlets to E. of, 26-ix.-17
St. Laurent, Cité — British take, 15-viii.-1
St. Laurent Fampoux — British take, 9-iv
St. Léger — taken by Germans, 22-iii British capture, 24-viii.-18
" **St. Leonards,"** **s.s.** — mined, 15-xi.-16
" **St. Louis,"** **French cruiser** — bom Gaza, 12-iv.-15; arrives at Dardan 10-v.-15
St. Martin's Cathedral (Ypres) — destr 3-vi.-15
St. Ménéhould — taken by Germans, 3-i headquarters removed to Montfaucon, 1 14; Crown Prince's attack towards rep 3-x.-14

St. Mihiel — Germans attack, 23-ix.-14; occupied, 25-ix.-14; salient maintained for four years, 25-ix.-14; French artillery destroy German bridge, 27-i.-15; French attack S. of, 5-iv.-15; 6-iv.-15; slight advance, 21-iv.-15; German success at Vaux Féry, 6-vii.-15; German attacks on Fresnes, 11-vii.-15; last German bridge destroyed, 13-xii.-15; German floating mines fished up at, 10-iii.-16; French gain, 13-iii.-17; battle; 16,000 prisoners taken, 12-ix.-18; salient flattened out, 13-ix.-18; part taken by Americans, 7-xi.-18

St. Nazaire — British base transferred to, 29-viii.-14; 6th Division landed at, 11-ix.-14; U.S. 1st Division at, 26-vi.-17

St. Omer — British 1st Corps leaves for, 11-x.-14; G.H.Q. at, 12-x.-14; British 27th Division concentrating, 23-xii.-14

St. Paul's Rocks — s.s. " Maple Branch " sunk S.W. from, 13-ix.-14; s.s. " Highland Hope " sunk, 14-ix.-14

St. Petersburg: see Petrograd

St. Pierre, Cité — British take, 14-iv.-17

St. Pierre Aigle — French take, 1-vii.-18

St. Pierre Divion — British storm, 13-xi.-16

St. Pierre Vaast Wood — French advance to edge, 26-ix.-16; entered, 27-ix.-16; French attack, 5-xi.-16; further advance, 6-xi.-16; Germans abandon trenches near, 14-iii.-17; British progress between and Saillisel, 15-iii.-17; occupied in part, 16-iii.-17; British reach W. edge, 1-ix.-18; captured, 2-ix.-18

St. Pol — British Aircraft Depôt demolished: decentralised, 28-ix.-17

St Quentin — British reach line, 27-viii.-14; Germans retreat on, 19-iii.-17; French cavalry within 5 miles, 20-iii.-17; heavy fighting between La Fère and, 22-iii.-17; French defeat Germans, 23-iii.-17; French advance towards, 25-iii.-17; Allied advance on, 31-iii.-17; 1-iv.-17; 2-iv.-17; 3-iv.-17; 4-iv.-17; 5-iv.-17; 7-iv.-17; operations near, 9-iv.-17; 13-iv.-17; 14-iv.-17; 15-iv.-17; 16-iv.-17; German attack, 18-vii.-17; defeated, 19-vii.-17; German attempts N. and S. of, 3-iii.-18; Germans occupy Essigny, Benay, and Quessy, S. of, 21-iii.-18; Germans break positions W. and S.W. of, 22-iii.-18; British in new positions S. and W. of, 23-iii.-18; French advance, 5-ix.-18; German resistance, 8-ix.-18; Anglo-French attack towards, 24-ix.-18; British 4th Army engaged N. of, 29-ix.-18; falls, 1-x.-18; attack on 21-mile front between Cambrai and, 8-x.-18; 23 German divisions defeated by British, 9-x.-18; French advance 5 miles E. of, 9-x.-18

St. Quentin Canal — British reach, 23-iv.-17; fighting, 18-ix.-18

St Rémy — taken, 9-ii.-15

" Saint Ronald," s.s. — sunk, 19-ix.-17

St. Roque, Cape — s.s. " Strathroy " sunk off, 31-viii.-14

" St. Seiriol," H.M. minesweeper — mined, 25-iv.-18

St. Souplet — French lose and recapture advanced work near, 7-xii.-15

" St. Theodore," s.s. — captured by " Möwe ": converted into raider, 12-xii.-16; sinks s.v. " Jean," 30-xii.-16

St. Thierry heights — Allies hold, 28-v.-18

St. Trond — fighting in streets, 9-viii.-14

" St. Ursula," s.s. — sunk, 12-xii.-16

Saisa — Germans and Belgians in action, 6-ix.-15

Saizerais — G.H.Q. U.S. 1st Corps, 30-viii.-18

Sakharoff, Gen. (Russia) — commanding on Galician front, 5-vii.-16; commanding in Dobrudja, 1-xi.-16

Sakhne Pass — Russians take, 24-ii.-16

Salaita — Gen. van Deventer occupies, 9-iii.-16

" Saldanha," s.s. — sunk, 18-iii.-18

Saliff — British take, 12-vi.-17

Salkaltutan Pass — taken by British, 4-xii.-17

" Salmonpool," s.s. — sunk, 1-vi.-16

Salonika — British 10th Division lands at invitation of Greek Government, 5-x.-15; 20,000 Allied troops at, 7-x.-15; Gen. Sarrail at, 13-x.-15; reinforcements arrive, 4-xii.-15; Greece to keep one division, 11-xii.-15; fortified, 13-xii.-15; German air-raid; enemy Consuls arrested, 30-xii.-15; King Peter at, 1-i.-16; LZ85 raids, 31-i.-16; 17-iii.-16; Germano-Bulgar outposts driven in N. of, 21-iii.-16; state of siege, 3-vi.-16; Russian troops at, 30-vii.-16; Allied offensive, 10-viii.-16; first Italian contingent arrives, 11-viii.-16; French take " Tortoise Hill," 15-viii.-16; Russian troops on front, 25-viii.-16; Venizelist revolt, 30-viii.-16; air-raids, 27-ii.-17; 4-iii.-17; fire: great damage, 18-viii.-17; Allied offensive suspended, 24-v.-17; activity on front, 8-viii.-17; Allied advance on Struma, 16-iv.-18; withdraw from villages, 18-iv.-18; Gen. Franchet D'Espèrey succeeds Gen. Guillaumat in command, 8-vi.-18: see also Macedonia

Salonika Harbour — airship destroyed by Allied fleet, 4-v.-16

Salonika—Uskub—Nish railway — Bulgarian attack on progressing: 100 miles of line captured, 21-x.-15

" Salsette," s.s. — sunk, 20-vii.-17

" Salta," H.S. — mined, 10-iv.-17

" Salvia," H.M. sloop — sunk, 20-vi.-17

" Samara," s.s. — sunk, 19-viii.-15

Samaria — British reach, 21-ix.-18

Samarra — Gen. Maude attacked near, 21-iv.-17; occupies station, 23-iv.-17

Sambre R. — French advance towards, 15-viii.-14; Allies abandon line, 24-viii.-14; British progress between Scheldt R. and, 24-x.-18; battle, 1-xi.-18; 4-xi.-18; German retreat, 5-xi.-18

Same — Gen. Smuts occupies, 25-v.-16

Samoa — New Zealand troops landed at Apia, 30-viii.-14; Adm. Patey leaves, 31-viii.-14; Adm. Spee's squadron off, 14-ix.-14

Samogneux — French evacuate, 23-ii.-16; French take, 21-viii.-17; French attack, 25-xi.-17; French trenches penetrated, 16-iii.-18

Samos — coast opposite bombarded, 4-viii.-15

" Samoset," H.M. oiler — sunk, 20-iii.-18

Samson, Cmdr. — commands armed motor-car attack on Uhlans near Doullens, 16-ix.-14

Samsonoff, Gen. (Russia) — commanding 2nd Army, 21-viii.-14; killed, 30-viii.-14

Samsun — Armenians deported, 27-vi.-15

San R. — Austrians attempt to cross, 18-x.-14; Austrians retiring towards, 10-ix.-14; Russians force, 14-ix.-14; Russians fall back, 12-xii.-14; Russians retire on, 7-v.-15; Russians behind, 14-v.-15; Austro-German crossing begins, 16-v.-15; cross at Jaroslav and Lezachov, 17-v.-15; ends, 23-v.-15; Austro-German advance between Moscisca and, 13-vi.-15; advance on right bank, 15-vi.-15

" San Andres," s.s. — sunk, 2-ix.-18

Sancy — French advance near, 20-iv.-17; 21-iv.-17

" Sanda," H.M. yacht — sunk, 25-ix.-15

Sanders, Lieut. — in H.M. Q. schooner " Prize ": engages U93, capturing commander and two men, 30-iv.-17

Sandfontein — British reverse, 26-ix.-14; rebels defeated, 8-xi.-14

" Sandhurst," s.s. — sunk, 6-v.-18

" San Diego," U.S. cruiser — mined, 19-vii.-18

Sandomir — taken by Russians, 18-ix.-14

San Dona di Piave — Italians cross Lower Piave, 29-x.-18

" Sandon Hall," s.s. — sunk, 1-i.-18

Scheer, Adm. (Germany) — transferred to 3rd German High Sea Squadron, 26-xii.-14; acting C.-in-C. German High Seas Fleet, 9-i.-16; C.-in-C., 15-i.-16; in H.I.M.S. "Friedrich der Grosse" in Jutland battle, 31-v.-16; 1-vi.-16; report on repairs to fleet, 2-vi.-16; at German G.H.Q. at Pless, 22-xi.-16; at Oldenburg: decorates Capt. Strasser, 30-viii.-17; sails with High Sea Fleet for raid on convoy line, 23-iv.-18; Chief of Naval Staff, 2-viii.-18; at G.H.Q., Spa, 10-ix.-18; interview with Gen. Ludendorff, 18-ix.-18

Scheidemann, Herr (Germany) — censured for visiting Belgium, 14-xi.-15; on annexations, 9-xii.-15; proclaims republic, 9-xi.-18; resigns ministry, 20-vi.-19

Scheldt R. — Gen. von der Marwitz's cavalry on, 23-viii.-14; Belgian Army withdrawn across, 6-x.-14; Germans cross at Termonde, 7-x.-14; three German T.B.D.s put to flight, 23-vii.-16; Germans on line, 21-x.-18; British progress between Sambre R. and, 24-x.-18; German retreat on line, 5-xi.-18; British cross, 7-xi.-18; 8-xi.-18

Neutrality question: see under Belgium

Scheldt Canal — British gain ground on E. bank, 21-xi.-17; Germans retire; British cross, 5-x.-18

Scherpenberg — Allies stand, 26-iv.-18; French recovery, 29-iv.-18

Schilden Is. — Germans take, 20-x.-17

Schirmeck — French 1st Army at, 16-viii.-14

"Schlesien," German s.s. — captured: sent to Plymouth, 6-viii.-14

Schleswig-Holstein — German airship sheds raided, 25-iii.-16; British bomb Tondern, 19-vii.-18; Danish claims heard by Paris Peace Conference, 21-ii.-19

Schmettow, Count (Germany) — commanding 5th Cavalry Corps on Dvina front, 21-viii.-15

Schmidt, F. Adm. (Germany) — succeeds Adm. Eckermann as Chief of Staff, 19-vii.-15; on H.I.M.S. "Moltke," 11-x.-17

Schnee, Governor (G.E. Africa) — loses baggage retreating before Gen. Edwards, 22-v.-18

"Scholar," s.s. — sunk by U-Boat, 18-v.-18

Scholtz, Gen. von (Germany) — commands 8th Army, 26-v.-15

Schönbrunn — Emperor Charles at, 2-xi.-18

Schouwen Bank — T.B.D. action, 23-i.-17

Schratzmännele — French capture trenches on crest, 18-viii.-15; carried, 22-viii.-15

Schröder, Adm. von (Germany) — commands Naval Corps at Liége, 31-viii.-14

Schubert, Gen. von (Germany) — commands 8th Army, 18-ix.-14; superseded, 8-x.-14; commands 7th Army, 28-viii.-16; succeeded, 11-iii.-17

Schwaben Redoubt — part carried, 27-ix.-16; most of taken, 28-ix.-16; German attack fails, 7-x.-16; British progress, 14-x.-16; German attacks defeated, 20-x.-16; British attack on 5,000 yards front between Le Sars and, 21-x.-16

Schwidden — Russians cross frontier, 2-viii.-14

Scilly Is. — s.s. "Wayfarer" torpedoed by U-Boat off, 11-iv.-15

Sclechka, Mts. — fighting, 22-ix.-18

"Scorpion," H.M.S. — sinks Turkish mine-layer, 2-xi.-14

Scotland — air-raids, 2-iv.-16; 2-v.-16

Scott, Adm. Sir P. — in command of London air defences, 13-ix.-15

"Scott," H.M.S. — sunk, 15-viii.-18

"Scottish Hero," s.s. — sunk, 10-vi.-17

"Scottish Monarch," s.s. — sunk, 29-vi.-15

Scott-Kerr, Brig.-Gen. — wounded, 18-ix.-14

"Sculptor," s.s. — attacked by U-Boat; wrecked, 17-v.-18

Scutari — Serbian Government moved to, 24-xi.-15

"Seagull," H.M.S. — sunk, 30-ix.-18

"Seagull," s.s. — sunk, 17-iii.-18

Seaham — s.s. "Holtby" mined off, 30-viii.-14

Seaham Harbour — bombarded, 11-vii.-16

"Sea King," H.M. trawler — destroys UC66, 12-vi.-17

"Seang Choon," s.s. — sunk, 10-vii.-17

"Sea Ranger," H.M. trawler — sinks U74, 27-v.-16

"Seatonia," s.s. — sunk, 1-xi.-16

"Seattle," s.s. — bombed in Dunkirk dock, 19-v.-16

Sebastopol — Turco-German warships bombard, 29-x.-14; raided by SLX., 27-vii.-16; Germans at, 1-v.-18; Allied squadron off, 27-xi.-18; Allies evacuate, 28-iv.-19

"Sebek," s.s. — sunk, 21-iv.-17

Sebourg — taken by British, 4-xi.-18

Sec, Mt. — taken, 12-ix.-18

2nd Army Corps: see under Army — Corps

2nd Division: see under Army — Divisions

"Secondo," s.s. — sunk, 27-ix.-16

Sedan — Germans enter, 25-viii.-14; Americans advance towards, 5-xi.-18; in outskirts, 6-xi.-18; Allied line at Armistice, 11-xi.-18

"Sedbergh," s.s. — torpedoed, 9-xii.-17

Sedd-ul-Bahr — fort shattered, 25-ii.-15; marines landed to complete destruction, 26-ii.-15; s.s. "River Clyde" run ashore, 25-iv.-15; British carry village, castle, and Hill 141, 26-iv.-15

"Seeadler" (German raider) — sinks vessels, 9-i.-17; 10-i.-17; 19-ii.-17; 26-ii.-17; 11-iii.-17; wrecked, 2-viii.-17

Seeckt, Gen. von (Germany) — plans Soissons operation, 13-i.-15; Chief of Staff to Gen. von Mackensen, 16-iv.-15

Seeheim — Union forces occupy, 18-iv.-15

Seely, Gen. — assumes command of Canadian Cavalry Brigade, 31-xii.-14

Segewold — Russians hold at, 13-ix.-17

Seicheprey — French raid near, 7-i.-18; lost and regained by Americans, 19-iv.-18

Seidler, Dr. von (Austria) — announce Parliamentary Government impossible, 3-v.-18; succeeded as Premier, 24-vii.-18

"Seistan," s.s. — sunk, 23-x.-17

Seitz, Governor (G.S.W. Africa) — surrenders to Gen. Botha, 9-vii.-15

Selborne, Lord — announces that Navy has submarine menace "well in hand," 26-viii.-15

Selency — British take, 2-iv.-17; British progress near, 24-ix.-18; captured, 25-ix.-18

Selle R. — British line extends to Haspres, 12-x.-18; battle, 17-x.-18; line forded by Tanks, 17-x.-18; British attack on front; passage forced, 20-x.-18

Selo — Austrian line penetrated near, 20-viii.-17

Selous, Capt. F. C. — killed in action, 4-i.-17

Selow, Capt. von (Germany) — armistice delegate; leaves for front, 6-xi.-18

Selzaete — Allied line at Armistice, 11-xi.-18

Semakh — occupied, 25-ix.-18

"Semantha," s.s. — sunk, 14-x.-17

Semendria — German attempt to cross Danube at: repulsed, 2-x.-15; cross, 9-x.-15; 10-x.-15; Serbians reach Danube, 29-x.-18; cross, 9-xi.-18

Semenoff, Gen. (Russia) — Cossacks in touch with Czechs, 2-ix.-18

Semlin — Serbians occupy, 10-ix.-14; evacuated, 17-ix.-14

Semuy — taken by French, 1-xi.-18

Sende — French take, 25-x.-15

Sengern — Germans take, 14-ii.-15

Senones — French advance near, 27-i.-15; Allied line at Armistice, 11-xi.-18

Sensée Canal — British on, 12-x.-18

Sensée R. — British advance, 24-iv.-17; take Sart woods, 27-viii.-18; British-American battle from St. Quentin to N. of, 29-ix.-18; crossed, 18-x.-18

Senussi — tribesmen massacre Italians at Tripoli, 23-vii.-15; dispersed at Halazin, 23-i.-16; S. Africans defeat at Agagia, 26-ii.-16; crew of s.s. " Tara " rescued from : at Bir Hakim, 17-iii.-16; defeated by British armoured car column, 4-ii.-17; dispersed, 5-ii.-17

Sept — Germans take trenches, 13-ii.-16

Sequehart — British take, 3-x.-18

" Sequoya," s.s. — torpedoed, 23-iii.-18

Seraincourt — German reserves bombed, 27-x.-18

Serajevo — Archduke Ferdinand and wife assassinated, 28-vi.-14; report of inquiry, 13-vii.-14; Serbs move on, 22-ix.-14; Count Tisza's arrogant speech at, 22-ix.-14

Serapeum — Turks attempt to bridge canal, 3-ii.-15

Serbia (see Austria-Hungary and Serbia) — Government at Nish, 25-vii.-14; breaks with Turkey, 3-xi.-14; necessity for sacrifices recognised, 24-viii.-15; Government at Mitrovitza, 13-xi.-15; at Scutari, 24-xi.-15; Yugo-Slavs press for union, 25-x.-18
Army — H.Q. at Valievo, 11-xi.-14; removed to Kraguyevatz, 11-xi.-14; at Krushevatz, 21-x.-15; fighting : see Serbia (operations), and other fronts.

Serbia (operations) — Austrian military movements on frontier, 12-vii.-14; Austrians cross Drina, 13-viii.-14; Austrians take Shabatz, 16-viii.-14; Austrian setback, 17-viii.-14; defeated on Yadar R. and driven across Drina, 18-viii.-14; defeat completed, 19-viii.-14; Serbians evacuate Matchva Plain and fall back to Kolubara line, 8-xi.-14; Austrians take Valievo, 19-xi.-14; take Milovatz and Strazhara, 20-xi.-14; Serbians retire on Babuna—Glava-Rajac, 22-xi.-14; battle at Lazarevatz, 28-xi.-14; evacuation of Belgrade begun, 29-xi.-14; battle for Belgrade ridges, 1-xii.-14; Austrians take Belgrade, 2-xii.-14; gain footing on Rudnik ridge : Serbian counter-attack, 3-xii.-14; 4-xii.-14; Austrians routed, 5-xii.-14; retreat, 6-xii.-14; defeated S. of Belgrade, 8-xii.-14; Serbians pursue and retake Valievo, 9-xii.-14; pursuit continues, 11-xii.-14; retreating Austrians cross Drina R., 12-xii.-14; Austrian rout, 13-xii.-14; Serbians claim 60,000 prisoners and nearly 200 guns, 15-xii.-14; first German troops in line on front, 24-v.-15; German 11th Army concentrating, 5-ix.-15; Mackensen takes over new army group against, 18-ix.-15; masses men and guns on frontier : Gen. von Gallwitz commands new German 11th Army against, 30-ix.-15; Bulgarians mass on frontiers; German attempt to cross Danube at Semendria repulsed by Serbians, 2-x.-15; artillery action on Belgrade—Save front, 4-x.-15; invasion by Austro-Germans under Mackensen, 6-x.-15; begin to cross Dvina, Save, and Danube, 7-x.-15; enter Belgrade, 8-x.-15; Austrians occupy Belgrade; Germans cross Danube below Semendria, 9-x.-15; Austro-Germans cross in force and capture Belgrade heights, 10-x.-15; Bulgarians cross frontier E. and S.E. of Nish, 11-x.-15; Greece refuses aid : Austro-German progress S. of Belgrade, 12-x.-15; Germans reinforced by Prusso-Bavarian Alpine Corps, 13-x.-15; Bulgaria declares war, 14-x.-15; Pozarevatz taken by Austro-Germans, 14-x.-15; French and Bulgarians engaged at Valandovo; Bulgarians occupy Vrania, 15-x.-15; Bulgarians repulse Franco-Serbians at Valandovo; Austro-Germans 10 miles S. of Belgrade, 16-x.-15; Austro-Germans 15 miles S. of Belgrade; Bulgarians force Timok Valley : take Egri Palanka and cut railway at Vrania, 17-x.-15; Austro-Germans 20 miles S. of Belgrade take Obrenovatz; fierce fight-

Serbia (operations) (continued) :—
ing between Bulgars and Serbs at Vrania, 18-x.-15; Austro-Germans 25 miles S. of Belgrade; Bulgarians occupy Veles; Allies at Strumnitza—Krivolak, 20-x.-15; Bulgarian attack on Salonika—Nish railway progressing, 100 miles captured; occupy Kumanovo; French repulse Bulgars near Rabrovo, 21-x.-15; again repulsed; occupy Uskub and in touch with Allies at Krivolak; Austrians occupy Shabatz, 22-x.-15; Germans cross Danube and Orsova; Bulgarians advance on Prahovo—Negotin, 23-x.-15; take Prahovo and Negotin, 24-x.-15; Franco-Serbs recapture Veles and threaten Uskub; Bulgarians retire on Ishtip; Austrians occupy Kladovo, 25-x.-15; Austro-Germans and Bulgarians in touch at Liubichevatz; reach within 20 miles of Kraguyevatz; Serbians retire through Zaitchar—Kraguyevatz, 26-x.-15; Austrians cross Drina E. of Vishegrad; Bulgars take Zaitchar; Montenegrins fighting, 27-x.-15; Bulgarians recapture Veles; French occupy Strumnitza, 29-x.-15; Prusso-Bavarian Alpine Corps arrives; British in action at Gevgeli—Doiran; Bulgarians attack Krivolak, 30-x.-15; chief arsenal falls to Austro-Germans, 1-xi.-15; Bulgarians take Kalavat, 3-xi.-15; Germans cross W. Morava R., 7-xi.-15; Austro-Germans threaten Mitrovitza, 17-xi.-15; Serbs retreat towards Albania, 23-xi.-15; German army refused free passage through Serbia, 26-xi.-15; H.Q. report flight of Serbs and " main operations closed," 28-xi.-15

Serbia, Prince Alexander of — army under defeats Austrians on Yadar R., 18-viii.-14; remains Regent, 25-xi.-18

Serbia and Rumania — Banat question : see Temesvar, Banat of

" Serbino," s.s. — sunk, 16-viii.-15

Seres — British progress towards, 6-x.-16; cavalry 2 miles from, 10-x.-16; capture three villages S. of, 25-x.-17

Sereth R. — Austrians reach, 11-ii.-15; Russians on, 2-ix.-15; Austrians reach, 3-ix.-15; Russian victory at Tarnopol—Trembovla, 7-ix.-15; 8-ix.-15; further successes at Trembovla and Chortkoff, 9-ix.-15; Austro-Germans retire from, 11-ix.-15; further Russian offensive, 14-ix.-15; Russians cross, 19-vi.-16; cross towards Lemberg—Odessa railway, 10-viii.-16; Germans advance to, 6-i.-17; checked, 16-i.-17; last German effort against Rumanian line, 19-i.-17; Germans held on Galatz—Focsani line, 23-i.-17; Russian retreat on, 21-vii.-17; Germans cross S. of Tarnopol, 23-vii.-17; progress, 15-viii.-17

Serfontein — S. African rebel : Gen. Botha demands unconditional surrender, 5-xii.-14; surrender, 8-xii.-14

Sergy — Allies win, 29-vii.-18

Seringes — taken by Americans, 31-vii.-18

Serpets — Russians take, 13-i.-15; Germans take, 11-ii.-15

Serqueux — German airship brought down, 19-x.-17

" Serrana," s.s. — sunk, 22-i.-18

Serre — reached by British, 1-vii.-15; Gen. Gough commanding British in Somme battle, 2-vii.-16; Germans in British post N.W. of, 13-i.-17; German attacks fail, 31-i.-17; British gain on S. slopes, 4-ii.-17; German attempts frustrated, 11-ii.-17; 13-ii.-17; British occupied, 25-ii.-17; British take 230 prisoners, 30-iii.-18; Germans abandon, 14-viii.-18; French attack in German salient between Oise and, 19-x.-18; French advance on front, 22-x.-18

Serre R. — Germans retreat towards Hirson, 27-x.-18

Silesia — Hindenburg ordered to relieve threat to, 31-viii.-14

Silistria — taken by Bulgaro-Germans, 10-ix.-16

" Silksworth Hall," s.s. — sunk, 10-iv.-16

" Silverash," s.s. — sunk, 6-x.-15

" Silverdale," s.s. — sunk, 8-iii.-18

Silvertown — munition factory explodes, 19-i.-17

" Silvia," s.s. — sunk, 23-viii.-15

Simbirsk — Czecho-Slovaks at, 25-vii.-18

" Simla," s.s. — sunk, 2-iv.-16

Simmitza — Germans take, 23-xi.-16

Simon, Sir J. — resigns, 31-xii.-15

" Simoon," H.M.S. — torpedoed, 23-i.-17

Sims, Adm. (U.S.) — hoists flag at Queenstown, 17-vi.-17; present at surrender of German Fleet, 21-xi.-18

Sinai Peninsula — Bedouin raid, 29-x.-14; Turks invade, 16-i.-15; skirmish near El Kantara; Turks appear opposite Ismalia, 2-ii.-15; 26-i.-16; attempt to bridge canal; raid in canal zone repulsed, 3-ii.-15; 23-iii.-15; Turkish force at Tor annihilated, 12-ii.-15; skirmish near El Kantara, 7-iv.-15; British air-raid on Turkish camps, 16-iv.-15; Australian reconnaissance, 13-iv.-16; Turco-German attack at Duweidar, 23-iv.-16; Anzacs occupy Katiyeh, 26-iv.-16; Turkish camp at Bayoud stormed, 9-v.-16; British raid on El Arish, 18-v.-16; Anzac raid at Bir Salmana, 31-v.-16; Turks entrenched at Oghratina—Mageibra, 31-vii.-16; advance between Katia and Hamisah, 3-viii.-16; retire from Oghratina to Bir el Abd, 8-viii.-16; counter-attack at Bir el Abd repulsed, 9-viii.-16; routed near Bir el Bayud; Bir el Abd abandoned; retire to El Arish, 11-viii.-16; British occupy El Arish, 21-xii.-16; capture Bir el Magdhaba, 23-xii.-16; Turkish detachments captured at Bir el Hassana and Nakhl, 20-ii.-17; Turks abandon strong position W. of Shalal, 5-iii.-17: see also Suez Canal, Palestine, &c.

" Sindoro," s.s. — sunk: British delegates to Hague Prisoners' Conference aboard, 6-vi.-18

Singapore — Indian Light Infantry mutiny, 15-ii.-15

Singes, Mt. des — French take, 15-ix.-18

Sinha, Lord (India) — delegate to Peace Conference, 13-xii.-18

Sinigaglia — shelled, 24-v.-15

" Sirdar," armed launch — bombards Fao, 8-xi.-14

" Sir Francis," s.s. — sunk, 7-vi.-17

" Sirius," H.M.S. — blockship: run ashore in Ostend raid, 23-iv.-18

Siroka Njivo — Italians at, 26-viii.-17

Sisemol, Mte. — German attacks from towards Brenta R., 4-xii.-17; Austrians capture, 6-xii.-17; French take, 24-x.-18

Sissonne — taken, 14-x.-18; French advance between Château-Porcien and, 26-x.-18

Sisteron — German airship brought down, 19-x.-17

Sistovo — Germans cross Danube at, 23-xi.-16

Sivas — Armenians deported, 25-vi.-15

" Sivoutch," Russian gunboat — sunk, 18-viii.-15

Sivry — Allied line at Armistice, 11-xi.-18

Siwa — occupied by British, 5-ii.-17

" Sjaelland," s.s. — sunk, 25-v.-17

Skagerrak — British cruiser squadrons sweep down to entrance, 4-ix.-14; British naval operations, 28-vii.-15; light forces two-day sweep, 16-viii.-15; swept out, 6-xi.-15

" Skaraas," s.s. — sunk, 23-v.-18

Skempe — Russians take, 20-i.-15

Skiernevice — Germans defeated, 27-xii.-14; unsuccessful gas attack by German 9th Army, 2-v.-15

Skoropadsky, Gen. (Ukraine) — at Kieff, 29-iv.-18; in Berlin, 5-ix.-18

Skouloudis, M. (Greece) — Premier, 4-xi.-15; resigns, 21-vi.-16; arrested, 1-ii.-18

Skutari — Austrians occupy, 23-i.-16; Italians enter, 31-x.-18

Slatina — Germans take, 27-xi.-16

" Slava," Russian battleship — lost, 17-x.-17

Slave labour — German G.H.Q. advise army commands of impending orders for organising, 2-iv.-16

Slonim — Germans repulsed, 18-ix.-15

Slonuvka R. — Germans defeated, 25-vii.-16

Smalls, The — U28 sinks s.s. " Aguila " off, 27-iii.-15

" Smeul," Rumanian T.B. — sunk, 17-v.-17

Smith-Dorrien, Gen. — commands 2nd Army Corps, 17-viii.-14; at Maubeuge—Sars-la-Bruyères, 21-viii.-14; on La Bassée Canal, 11-x.-14; to command 2nd Army, 25-xii.-14; appointed Grand Officer of Legion of Honour, 13-i.-15; to command in E. Africa, 14-xii.-15; relinquishes E. African command, 9-ii.-16

Smolnik — Russians break Austrian line near, 15-iii.-15; further Russian success near, 20-iii.-15

Smorgon — Germans reach, 19-ix.-15; driven out, 21-ix.-15; Germans attack, 1-x.-15; Russian advance near, 4-x.-15; fighting near, 5-x.-15; Russian attack, 12-x.-15; German attacks fail, 5-vi.-16; penetrate Russian trenches: driven out, 20-vi.-16; Russian offensive, 2-vii.-16; withdrawal, 23-vii.-17

Smorgon—Molodechna — Russian counter-stroke at, 19-ix.-15

Smuts, Gen. (S. Africa) — commands in E. Africa, 9-ii.-16; proceeds to Italy, 4-xi.-17; League of Nations pamphlet, 10-i.-19; at Budapest, 4-iv.-19; leaves for Paris, 5-iv.-19

Smyrna — forts silenced, 6-iii.-15; bombarded by warships and aeroplanes, 6-iv.-15; 22-iv.15; coast bombarded at Sighadjik, 3-viii.-15; Italians prevented from leaving, 19-viii.-15

Smyrna Gulf — Turkish minelayer destroyed by H.M.SS. " Wolverine " and " Scorpion," 2-xi.-14; bombardment, 5-iii.-15; 6-iii.-15

Smyth-Pigott, Squad.-Cmdr. — Commands air-raid on Constantinople—Adrianople, 14-iv.-16

" Snaefell," H.M. armed steamer — sunk, 5-vi.-18

" Snapdragon," H.M.S. — destroys UB68, 4-x.-18

" Sneaton," H.M. collier — sunk, 3-iv.-16

Snettisham — German air-raid, 19-i.-15

Sniatyn — Russians take, 13-vi.-16; falls, 30-vii.-17

Snow, Gen. — invalided, 21-ix.-14

" Snowdon," s.s. — sunk, 19-v.-18

" Snowdonian," s.s. — sunk, 31-vii.-17

" Snowdon Range," s.s. — sunk, 28-iii.-17

Socialists:—

Berne conference, 3-ii.-19; Soviet Government agrees to proposed visit of mission from, 20-ii.-19

Stockholm conference — French to attend, 28-v.-17; passports refused, 1-vi.-17; Russian Soviet Council replies to letter explaining scope, 17-vi.-17; British Labour Party to send delegates, 10-viii.-17; passports refused, 13-viii.-17; attitude of Blackpool Trade Union Congress, 4-ix.-17

" Soderham," German s.s. — sunk, 18-x.-16

Sofia — Austro-German terms for Treaty of alliance with Bulgaria signed, 4-viii.-14; bombed, 21-iv.-16; Germans fight Bulgarians near, 4-x.-18

" Sofie," s.s. — sunk, 3-ii.-18

Soignies — Germans at, 23-viii.-14

Soissons — Germans moving through, 2-ix.-14; British reach Aisne near, 11-ix.-14; recaptured by Allies, 13-ix.-14; French carry Aisne line at, 14-ix.-14; shelled and on fire, 15-ix.-14; French regain ground, 17-ix.-14;

Soissons (continued) :—

Gen. Maunoury to stand at, 18-ix.-14; French take Hills 132 and 151, 8-i.-15; Germans bombard cathedral, 9-i.-15; counter-attacks in area, 9-i.-15; French progress at Hill 132, 10-i.-15; German counter-attack N. of, 11-i.-15; French pushed back from Hills 132 and 151 to Aisne R., 12-i.-15; Germans recapture Hills 132 and 151 and gain Vrégny heights, 13-i.-15; French withdraw to S. of Aisne R., 14-i.-15; German progress checked, 15-i.-15; German attacks at Autrêches beaten off, 17-i.-15; Germans fail to cross Aisne R., 29-i.-15; bombarded, 28-ii.-15; 1-iii.-15; cathedral bombarded, 22-iii.-15; 23-iii.-15; German attack at Fontenoy, 16-vii.-15; German attack fails, 13-ii.-16; 14-ii.-16; 30-i.-17; French progress N. of, 22-iii.-17; French success N. of, 3-iv.-17; advance N. and N.E. of, 11-iv.-15; attack, 16-iv.-17; victory on Laon road, 23-x.-17; Germans take, 29-v.-18; held at outlets from, 30-v.-18; French local operations N.W. of, 17-vi.-18; Allied offensive Fontenoy—Belleau; Mont de Paris reached, 18-vii.-18; progress, 19-vii.-18; 20-vii.-18; 23-vii.-18; falls, 2-viii.-18; Allies cross Aisne R. E. of, 4-viii.-18; French capture Laval, 21-viii.-18; progress above, 21-viii.-18

Soissons—Craonne — German first positions between: carried by French, 16-iv.-17

Soissons—Laon road — German attack across, 8-vii.-17; German retreat between Grand-Pré and, 11-x.-18

Soissons—Noyon salient — flattened by Germans, 31-v.-18; German attacks, 3-vi.-18

Soissons—Reims — German attack between, 27-v.-18

Sokol — Gen Russky enters, 14-viii.-14; Austro-Germans cross Bug R. near, 18-vii.-15; driven back, 21-vii.-15; German attacks repulsed, 25-vi.-16

Solarolo, Mte. — taken, 24-x.-18

Soldau — skirmish with Russian cavalry, 5-viii.-14; Russian defeat, 18-xi.-14

Solesmes — Germans at, 26-viii.-14

Solesmes—Le Cateau road — British reach, 10-x.-18

Solf, Dr. (Germany) — at Foreign Office, 3-x.-18; resigns, 30-xii.-18; entreats Pres. Wilson to mitigate terms of Armistice, 11-xi.-18; 12-xi.-18; presses hastening of food relief, 15-xi.-18; requested to address Allies and not Pres. Wilson, 16-xi.-18; appeals to Allies, 18-xi.-18

Sollum — Gen. Peyton reoccupies, 14-iii.-16

Solomon Islands — Australians occupy Bougainville, 13-ix.-14

Solotvina — Russians at, 15-viii.-16

" Solway Queen," s.s. — sunk, 2-iv.-18

" Somerset," s.s. — sunk, 26-vii.-17

Somme R. — French 6th Army in valley, 27-viii.-14; fierce fighting, 26-ix.-14; German attack broken near Lihons, 19-xii.-14; slight French gain at La Boisselle, 17-i.-15

First battle — 70 raids and 40 gas attacks made in week preceding, 24-vi.-16; artillery preparation on whole W. front, 24-vi.-16; 26-vi.-16; 29-vi.-16; Franco-British advance N. and S.; attack on 20-mile front; Montauban and Mametz captured; Fricourt threatened; footing gained in Leipzig Redoubt; Gommecourt, Serre, and Grandcourt reached, 1-vii.-16; British take Fricourt and progress near La Boisselle; French take Curlu and Herbecourt, 2-vii.-16; British capture La Boisselle; French take Chapître Wood, Feuillères, Buscourt, and Flaucourt; Assevillers taken; prisoners total 12,300, 3-vii.-16; further French advance; Belloy-en-Santerre, Estrées, and Sormont Farm taken; British take Bernafay Woods and Caterpillar Wood, 4-vii.-16; outskirts of

Somme R. :—

First battle (continued) :—

Contalmaison reached, 5-vii.-16; British carry trench on 1,000 yards front E. of La Boisselle; German counter-attack defeated S.W. of Thiepval, 6-vii.-16; trenches carried at Fricourt; Prussian Guard beaten E. of Contalmaison; part of Leipzig Redoubt carried, 7-vii.-16; British enter Ovillers and Trônes Wood; French take Hardecourt, 8-vii.-16; British capture Maltz Horn Farm, 9-vii.-16; French in outskirts of Barleux and in Belloy-en-Santerre, 9-vii.-16; British hold Contalmaison, 10-vii.-16; capture of first German defence system complete; 7,500 prisoners, 11-vii.-16; British hold Mametz Wood, 12-vii.-16; S. Trônes Wood consolidated, 13-vii.-16; British attack second line; carried on 4-mile front; British cavalry charge, 14-vii.-16; Delville Wood taken by South Africans; over 2,000 prisoners, 15-vii.-16; German positions captured N.W. of Bazentin-le-Petit Wood; part of Ovillers garrison surrenders; British withdraw from Foureaux Wood, 16-vii.-16; British complete capture of Ovillers; German counter-attacks repulsed at Biaches and La Maisonette Farm, 17-vii.-16; German counter-attacks against Longueval and Delville Wood, 18-vii.-16; heavy fighting on Longueval—Delville Wood front; lost ground recaptured; British advance S. of Thiepval and E. of Leipzig Redoubt, 19-vii.-16; British advance 1,000 yards N. of Bazentin—Longueval line; French advance: Estrées—Vermand Ovillers carried; 3,000 prisoners, 20-vii.-16; British withdraw from Bois de Foureaux; German attack on Leipzig Redoubt repulsed; attack at Soyécourt, 21-vii.-16; British attack along Pozières—Guillemont front, 26-vii.-16; French progress S. of Estrées and N. of Vermand Ovillers, 24-vii.-16; Pozières in British hands, 25-vii.-16; British carry trench N. of Pozières—Bazentin-le-Petit; French progress at Estrées; fighting at Soyécourt, 26-vii.-16; fighting at Longueval, 27-vii.-16; whole of Delville Wood recaptured; German positions at Longueval taken, 28-vii.-16; Anglo-French advance E. from Delville Wood; British enter Guillemont but withdraw; French capture Monacu Farm, 30-vii.-16; French gain between Estrées—Belloy-en-Santerre, 1-viii.-16; French captures between Hem—Monacu Farm, 2-viii.-16; British gains N. of Bazentin-le-Petit, 3-viii.-16; British advance against German second line N. and W. of Pozières; gain trench near Mouquet Farm, 4-viii.-16; further British progress, 6-viii.-16; British attack Guillemont, 7-viii.-16; King George visits front, 8-viii.-16; British continue against Guillemont; line advanced 400 yards; French advance E. of Hill 139; seize wood N. of Hem, 8-viii.-16; British gain 200 yards on 600-yard front N.W. of Pozières, 9-viii.-16; British advance N. of Bazentin-le-Petit, 11-viii.-16; British advance N.W. of Pozières, 12-viii.-16; French progress S.W. of Estrées; Germans enter part of captured trenches W. of Pozières, 13-viii.-16; artillery duel, 14-viii.-16; French advance; mile of trenches taken; Guillemont—Maurepas road reached 16-viii.-16; British capture trench N.W. of Bazentin; German counter attacks repulsed at Pozières, 17-viii.-16; British advance on 11-mile front; Thiepval—Guillemont and towards Ginchy; Leipzig Redoubt carried; French take more of Maurepas and Calvary Hill; German line shortened at Guillemont—Maurepas, 18-viii.-16; British established outside Mouquet Farm and penetrate Guillemont, 21-viii.-16; French

Somme R.:—
First battle (continued) :—
progress near Cléry and E. of Soyécourt and
S.W. of Estrées, 21-viii.-16; German counter
on Guillemont station repulsed, 23-viii.-16;
French capture all Maurepas; British across
Leipzig salient, and on edges of Delville
Wood, 24-viii.-16; British progress N.W.
of Ginchy, 27-viii.-16; German attempts
near Guillemont and Foureaux Wood
defeated; British capture small salient S. of
Martinpuich, 30-viii.-16; German attack
round Foureaux Wood and Ginchy; advanced
British trench reached, 31-viii.-16; British
recovery, 1-ix.-16; Anglo-French attack;
British take part of Mouquet Farm and all
Guillemont; Ginchy gained and lost; French
attack from Maurepas, take Le Forest and
trenches; over 2,000 prisoners, 3-ix.-16;
German second line in British hands;
Wedge Wood captured, footing gained in
Leuze Wood; French press E. of Le Forest;
500 more prisoners; French attack from
Barleux to Chaulnes; 2,700 prisoners,
4-ix.-16; British extend 1,500 yards E.
of Guillemont; hold Leuze Wood—
Falfemont Farm and Ginchy outskirts;
French advance E. of Le Forest; storm
Hôpital Farm, occupy part of Marrières
Wood, and progress E. of Cléry, 5-ix.-16;
Leuze Wood cleared; French successes,
6-ix.-16; further French success round
Deniécourt, 7-ix.-16; British capture
Ginchy and ground between it and Leuze
Wood, 9-ix.-16; German counter round
Ginchy—Mouquet Farm fails, 10-ix.-16;
French advance N. from S. of Combles;
Hill 145, Marrières Wood, and German
trench system up to Bapaume—Péronne road
taken; Brioche, Bouchavesnes, and Hill 76
carried, 1,500 prisoners, 12-ix.-16; first
British Tanks in action: British take Flers,
Martinpuich, Courcelette, all High Wood,
part Bouleaux Wood; French capture
trenches at Rancourt and Le Priez Farm,
15-ix.-16; British extend gains; take Danube
Trench and Mouquet Farm strong work,
16-ix.-16; French take Vermand Ovillers—
Berny, 17-ix.-16; Combles Quadrilateral
captured by British; French take Deniécourt,
18-ix.-16; British take trenches near Flers,
21-ix.-16; British take Lesbœufs—Morval;
French take Rancourt—Le Priez Farm and
Hills 120 and 130, 25-ix.-16; British penetrate
Thiepval; carry Zollern Redoubt—Mouquet
Farm; French take Frégicourt and reach St.
Pierre Vaast Wood; Combles taken by
Franco-British, 26-ix.-16; British capture
Thiepval and parts of Schwaben and Stuff
Redoubts; French enter St. Pierre Vaast
Wood, 27-ix.-16; British take Thiepval
cemetery and most of Schwaben Redoubt;
French progress, 28-ix.-16; British gain
Destremont Farm, 29-ix.-16; hold most of
Thiepval ridge, 30-ix.-16; take Eaucourt
l'Abbaye, 1-x.-16; French advance at Morval,
4-x.-16; British take Le Sars, 7-x.-16;
French take Bovent, Ablaincourt, and most of
Chaulnes Wood, 10-x.-16; French in Sailly-
Saillisel, 15-x.-16; progress at, 16-x.-16;
take Sailly and whole La Maisonette
Château—Biaches front, 18-x.-16; Saillisel,
19-x.-16; British take all Stuff Redoubt
and Regina Trench; French in
Chaulnes Wood; repulse German counter
on Sailly-Saillisel, 21-x.-16; gain Ridge
128, 22-x.-16; British attack at Lesbœufs—
Gueudecourt, 23-x.-16; German counter on
Stuff Redoubt repulsed, 26-x.-16; British
progress near Lesbœufs, 28-x.-16; French
carry trench system near Sailly-Saillisel,
29-x.-16; Anglo-French advance on Péronne
road, 1-xi.-16; British capture trench near

Somme R.:—
First battle (continued) :—
Gueudecourt; French raid W. of Lancourt,
2-xi.-16; recapture most of Saillisel; attack
St. Pierre Vaast Wood; British progress near
Butte de Warlencourt, 5-xi.-16; French
progress in St. Pierre Vaast Wood, 6-xi.-16;
take Ablaincourt—Pressoine and Gomiécourt
approaches; further British progress; German
attack on Beaumont Hamel repulsed,
7-xi.-16; hand-to-hand fight at Saillisel,
8-xi.-16; British air victory over Bapaume,
9-xi.-16; French capture trenches near
Lesbœufs; German counters on Saillisel and
Deniécourt repulsed, 10-xi.-16; French progress at Saillisel; British take Farmers
Road; German attack S.E. of Berny repulsed, 11-xi.-16; French complete capture of
Saillisel, 12-xi.-16; British captures: total
since July 1, 18-xi.-16; Sir D. Haig's
dispatch, 29-xii.-16; Germans retire N. and
S. of, 14-iii.-17; British advance, 16-iii.-17;
13 villages captured N. and S., 17-iii.-17;
W. bank occupied from Péronne to Epénan-
court, 18-iii.-17; position of British line,
19-iii.-17; Germans in retreat to Hindenburg
line, 21 iii.-17
Second battle (battle for Amiens) —
Germans attack British on 50-mile
front between Scarpe—Oise; British
defences penetrated; Germans took
Bullecourt, Noreuil, Longatte, Ecoust St.
Mein, Doignies, Lagnicourt, Louverval,
Roussoy, Hargicourt, Villeret, Templeux,
Maissliny; Essigny, Benay and Quessy
occupied; British resistance at Epéhy and
Le Verguier and round Lagnicourt, 21-iii.-18;
Germans break through positions W. and
S.W. of St. Quentin; forced Crozat Canal at
Jussy-Quessy—La Montagne; took Tergnier;
British stand at Fontaine-les-Clercs; N. from
St. Quentin Germans took Holmon Wood,
Caulaincourt, Le Verguier, Roisel, St.
Emilie, Villers Faucon, Epéhy, and St.
Léger; British retire to Somme line; abandon
Flesquières salient, 22-iii.-18; Ham falls to
Germans; British in new positions S. and W.
of St. Quentin; Germans seize Aubigny,
Brouchy, Ollezy, &c.; French in action
on right, 23-iii.-18; fall of Péronne
and Bapaume to Germans; stand by S.
Africans in Marrières Wood; Germans take
Nesle, Guiscard, and Chauny, 24-iii.-18;
heavy fighting between Péronne—Bapaume;
Germans reach 1916 line; French evacuate
Noyon, 25-iii.-18; Gen. Grant organises
force for defence of British line S. of,
25-iii.-18; fighting N. of dies down; heavy
German attacks S. of; Roye, Chaulnes,
Hattencourt, Liancourt, Estrées, and Bray
lost; in S.W. corner Germans take Le
Quesnoy and reach Erches; British cling to
Andéchy on flank and hold up advance;
British, French, and Americans in action,
26-iii.-18; British line held N. of; Albert
lost; N. of Ancre, Ablainzeville, and Ayette
taken by Germans; Germans aiming at
Amiens cross to S. bank between Cerisy-
Chipilly; British forced out of Proyart,
Framéviller, and Morcourt; further S.
Lassigny, Andéchy, Davenescourt, and
Montdidier, 27-iii.-18; Gen. Rawlinson com-
manding forces S. of; Gen. Gough to
organise new British defence lines, 28-iii.-18;
German attack in Scarpe Valley towards
Vimy Ridge repulsed with heavy loss;
Germans beaten off S. of Scarpe in Bucquoy
sector; progress towards Amiens as far as
Hamel; French progress in Montdidier
sector, 28-iii.-18; German progress between
Albert—Avre R., 11 miles from Amiens,
29-iii.-18; fighting N. of at Boiry—Boyelles;
Germans repulsed with loss; near Serre

"**Stanhope,**" s.s. — sunk, 17-vi.-17
Stanislau — fighting near, 21-ii.-15; battle, 22-ii.-15; Russians recapture, 3-iii.-15; Russian progress towards, 1-vii.-16; 7-viii.-16; 8-viii.-16; 9-viii.-16; falls, 10-viii.-16; attack extending towards, 6-vii.-17; Russians break Austrian front W. of, 8-vii.-17; 17 miles from, 11-vii.-17; evacuated, 23-vii.-17; falls to Austro-Germans, 24-vii.-17
"**Star,**" H.M.S. — destroys UB115, 29-ix.-18
"**Stathe,**" s.s. — sunk, 26-ix.-16
"**Staunch,**" H.M.S. — sunk, 11-xi.-17
Steele, Gen. — commands 2nd Canadian Division, 25-v.-15; succeeded by Gen. Turner, 17-viii.-15
"**Steelville,**" H.M. collier — sunk, 3-i.-18
Steenbeek R. — French cross, 10-viii.-17; British progress, 14-viii.-17; French across, 16-viii.-17
Steenstraate — Germans attack with gas: French retire to canal, 22-iv.-15; Germans take bridge, 23-iv.-15; French progress near, 14-v.-15; Germans shell, 10-ix.-15; attacks, 12-ii.-16; French take, 31-vii.-17
Steenwerck — British forced back, 11-iv.-18; Germans abandon, 31-viii.-18
Steenvoorde — French cavalry ordered to 9-iv.-18
Stein, Gen. von (Germany) — commands Prussian 14th Reserve Corps, 14-ix.-14
Steinbach — French recover part, 31-xii.-14; 3-i.-15; recapture completed, 4-i.-15
Stenay — Americans take Laneuville, 4-xi.-18; entered, 9-xi.-18; Allied line at Armistice, 11-xi.-18
"**Stephanotis,**" s.s. — sunk, 25-iv.-17
"**Stephen Furness,**" H.M. armed steamer — sunk, 13-xii.-17
Stern, Col. — resigns as Controller of Mechanical Warfare (Tanks) Department, 16-x.-17
"**Stettin,**" H.I.M.S. — damaged, 28-viii.-14
Steuben, Gen. von (Germany) — commands 11th Army, 15-ix.-18
Stewart, Gen. — arrives at Nairobi, 3-ix.-14
"**Stirling Castle,**" H.M. auxiliary — sunk, 26-ix.-16
Stock Exchange, London — closed since July 30; opened, 4-i.-15
"**Stockforce,**" H.M. special service ship — sunk, 30-vii.-18
Stockhod R. — Russians retire from, 18-vi.-16; Russian offensive on line, 4-vii.-16; battle, 6-vii.-16; Russians approach, 7-vii.-16; Russians win crossings, 9-vii.-16; German resistance, 10-vii.-16; renewed Russian offensive, 28-vii.-16; Russian captures total 9,000 prisoners, 30-vii.-16; Russians on Sitovitche—Yanovka line, 2-viii.-16; Russian advance, 19-viii.-16; Germans carry bridgehead, 3-iv.-17; artillery activity, 3-vii.-17
Stolniki — German 9th Army engaged in ten days' battle about, 5-iii.-16
Stolpce — ZXII. raids, 7-iii.-16
"**Stolt-Nielsen,**" s.s. — sunk, 11-iii.-18
"**Stonecrop,**" H.M.S. — engages U-Boat, 17-ix.-17
Stopford, Gen. — commanding at Suvla Bay landing, 6-viii.-15; succeeded by Gen. de Lisle, 15-viii.-15
Stossweiler — Germans take, 21-ii.-15
"**Stralsund,**" H.I.M.S. — within 40 miles of Yarmouth: chased by British forces, 17-viii.-14
Strassbourg — German 7th Army concentrated, 14-viii.-14; French air-raid on, 16-iv.-15; 19-iv.-15; French enter, 25-xi.-18; M. Poincaré enters, 9-xi.-18
"**Strassburg,**" H.I.M.S. — within 40 miles of Yarmouth: chased by British forces, 17-viii.-14; assists in sinking of British fishing-boats in North Sea, 22-viii.-14; in Gulf of Bothnia, 7-ix.-14

Strasser, Capt. (Germany) — commands raids on Harwich and E. Anglia, 23-v.-17; invested with order Pour le Mérite, 30-viii.-17; on board L70 in raid on England, 5-viii.-18
"**Strathalbyn,**" s.s. — mined, 9-xii.-16
"**Strathallen,**" s.s. — sunk, 2-ix.-16
"**Strathcarron,**" H.M. collier — sunk, 8-vi.-15
"**Strathcona,**" s.s. — sunk, 13-iv.-17
"**Strathfillan,**" s.s. — Belgian relief ship: bombed by German aircraft: missed, 21-iii.-15
Strathie Point — German raider "Möwe" lays mines near, 2-i.-16
"**Strathray,**" s.s. — sunk, 31-viii.-14
"**Strathtay,**" s.s. — sunk, 6-ix.-16
Strazhara — Austrians take, 20-xi.-14
Strickland, Gen. — commanding 1st Division withdrawn from Le Clipon, 15-x.-17
"**Strombus,**" s.s. — attacked by U-Boat, 4-vi.-18
Struga — Bulgarians enter, 12-xii.-15
Struma R. — British on, 8-vi.-16; Bulgarian thrust E. of; Greek 4th Army Corps surrenders, 27-viii.-16; British cross; Bulgarians driven from villages E. of R., 10-ix.-16; British seize part of Bulgarian line, 30-ix.-16; Bulgarian counter defeated, 2-x.-16; British advance, 7-x.-16; success: capture 3 villages, 31-v.-16; operations, 5-xi.-16; British withdraw on left bank owing to malaria, 16-vi.-17; British capture villages S. of Seres, 25-x.-17; Allied advance, 16-iv.-18; withdraw from villages, 18-iv.-18
Strumnitza — French occupy, 29-x.-15; British lose front trenches, 6-xii.-15; retire, 7-xii.-15; British in Bulgaria 6 miles S. of, 25-ix.-18
Strumnitza—Krivolak — Allies at, 20-x.-15
Stryj — Austro-Germans take, 31-v.-15
Strykow — Germans reach, 17-xi.-14
Strykow-Glowno — Germans on defensive near, 25-xi.-14
Strypa R. — Russian success, 30-viii.-15; Austrians driven back towards, 8-ix.-15; Austro-Germans retire to, 11-ix.-15; Austrian offensive collapses behind, 12-ix.-15; Russians cross 11-x.-15; take Visniovtchyk, 12-x.-15; driven back across, 13-x.-15; Austro-Germans checked, 14-x.-15; fighting, 31-x.-15; Russians cross, 1-xi.-15; Russians repulse Austrians, 17-xii.-15; Russian offensive, 24-xii.-15; take trenches on, 31-xii.-15; offensive continues, 5-i.-16; Russians cross, 8-vi.-16; Russians take 2,000 prisoners, 12-vii.-16
Stuermer, M. (Russia) — Premier, 1-ii.-16; arrested, 13-iii.-17
Stuff Redoubt — British carry part, 27-ix.-16; progress, 15-x.-16; German attacks defeated, 20-x.-16; British carry, 21-x.-16; German attack repulsed, 26-x.-16; British occupy ground between Grandcourt and, 6-ii.-17
Sturdee, Adm. — attends naval conference at Loch Ewe, 17-ix.-14; leaves as C.-in-C. S. Atlantic to search for Adm. von Spee, 5-xi.-14; leaves for Falkland Isles, 11-xi.-14; at St. Vincent, 17-xi.-14; defeats Adm. von Spee off Falkland Islands, 8-xii.-14; joins Grand Fleet; commands 4th Battle Squadron, 28-iii.-15; dispatch published, 3-iii.-15; in H.M.S. "Benbow" in Jutland battle, 31-v.-16; 1-vi.-16
"**Sturgeon,**" H.M.S. — destroys UB54, 11-iii.-18
Stürgkh, Count (Austria) — shot, 21-x.-16
"**Sturton,**" s.s. — sunk, 7-ii.-18
Stuttgart — air-raids, 22-ix.-15; 16-ix.-17
Styr R. — Germans lose positions near Kolki, 8-xi.-15; Russian victory, 9-xi.-15; Russians reoccupy Chartorysk, 19-xi.-15; Germans cross, 31-viii.-15; Austrian offensive collapses

Styr R. (continued) :—
behind, 12-ix.-15; Austro-Germans driven across, 2-xii.-15; Russians driven across, 15-xi.-15; cross near Chartorysk, 31-xii.-15; Russians drive Austrians across, 1-i.-16; offensive continues, 5-i.-16; Germans driven over, 21-vii.-16

Styr—Stockhod line — German counter-attack fails, 16-vi.-16; Russian offensive, 4-vii.-16; battle, 6-vii.16

" Subadar," s.s. — sunk, 27-vii.-18

Submarines :—
Austrian — sink Italian cruisers " Amalfi " and " G. Garibaldi," 8-vii.-15; sink Italian submarine " Nereide," 15-viii.-15; sink French destroyer " Renaudin," 18-iii.-16; s.s. " Mashobra," 15-iv.-17; torpedo French submarine " Circé," 20-viii.-18; — **U3:** sunk, 13-viii.-15; — **U5:** sinks French cruiser " Léon Gambetta," 27-iv.-15; — **U11:** bombed by French airman, 1-vii.-15; — **U12:** sunk, 11-viii.-15; — **U17:** torpedoes Italian T.B.D. " Impetuoso," 10-vii.-16

British — sink German T.B.D., 26-vii.-15; blow up Galata Bridge, Constantinople, 1-viii.-15; sink German transport in Baltic, 2-viii.-15; sink Turkish battleship " Kheir-ed-Din-Barbarossa," 9-viii.-15; sink Turkish gunboat " Berk-i-Salvet," 10-viii.-15; torpedo Turkish supply ship " Isfahan," 23-viii.-15; in Baltic: sink German transport, 8-x.-15; German s.s. " Lulea," 10-x.-15; sink 5 German transports: drive 1 ashore, 16-x.-15; sink 2 German steamers, 18-x.-15; 19-x.-15; 4 steamers, 27-x.-15; sink H.I.M.S. " Bremen " and T.B.D. VI91, 17-xii.-15; 9 in position off Horn Reef, Vyl Light, and Terschelling, 3-v.-16; anti-U-Boat patrol of Shetlands—Heligoland line, 5-iv.-16; operate in Skagerrak against German decoy vessels, 26-x.-16; sink German transport and torpedo German Dreadnought in Baltic, 20-x.-17; — **AE1:** lost, 19-ix.-14; — **AE2:** enters Dardanelles: torpedoes Turkish gunboat, 25-iv.-15; in Sea of Marmora, 26-iv.-15; sunk, 30-iv.-15; — **B3:** attacked by U-Boat, 2-x.-14; — **B9:** enters Dardanelles: forced to retire: 14-xii.-14; — **B10:** sunk, 9-viii.-16; — **B11:** torpedoes Turkish battleship " Messu-diyeh " in Dardanelles; commander given V.C., 13-xii.-14; — **C** class act with decoy trawler, 23-v.-15; 4 leave the Nore for Archangel, 3-viii.-16; 4 at Kronstadt, 19-ix.-16; — **C3:** blown up against Zee-brugge Mole, 23-iv.-18; — **C6:** pursues U-Boat by use of hydrophones, 14-v.-17; — **C7:** sinks UC68, 5-iv.-17; — **C15:** sinks UC65, 3-xi.-17; — **C17:** lays off Zeebrugge to register tidal curves, 21-ix.-17; — **C19:** attempts to ram U-Boat, 1-iii.-17; 4-iii.-17; — **C24:** sinks U40, 23-vi.-15; — **C25:** attacked by seaplanes, 6-vii.-18; — **C26:** destroyed, 3-iv.-18; — **C27:** sinks U23, 20-vii.-15; destroyed, 3-iv.-18; — **C29:** mined, 29-viii.-15; — **C31:** lost, 4-i.-15; — **C32:** ashore and blown up, 24-x.-17; — **C33:** lost, 4-viii.-15 — **C34:** sunk by U52, 21-vii.-17; — **C35:** destroyed, 3-iv.-18; — **D2:** lost, 25-xi.-14; — **D3:** sunk, 15-iii.-18; — **D4:** sinks UB72, 12-v.-18; — **D5:** mined, 3-xi.-14; — **D6:** sunk, 28-vi.-18; — **D7:** leaves for 10 days' cruise in Skagerrak, 9-i.-16; operates in, 21-ii.-16; in Kattegat, 5-iii.-16; 25-v.-16; sinks U45, 12-ix.-17; — **D8:** cruise off Norway, 5-ii.-16; — **E:** two operate in Baltic, 15-x.-14; — **E1:** in Baltic: attacks H.I.M.S. " Fürst Bismarck," 18-x.-14; in Danzig Bay, 20-x.-14; at Libau, 21-x.-14;

Submarines:—
British (continued) :—
at Lapvig under Russian Adm. Essen's orders, 30-x.-14; sinks German transport, 29-vii.-15; torpedoes H.I.M.S. " Moltke," 18-viii.-15; destroyed, 3-iv.-18; — **E3:** sunk, 18-x.-14; — **E4:** in battle of Heligo-land Bight, 28-viii.-14; — **E5:** in battle of Heligoland Bight, 28-viii.-14; lost in North Sea, 7-iii.-16; — **E6:** in battle of Heligo-land Bight, 28-viii.-14; mined, 26-xii.-15; — **E7:** in battle of Heligoland Bight, 28-viii.-14; in Sea of Marmora, 30-vi.-15; sinks Turkish steamer and two dhows, 2-vii.-15; in action with Turkish gunboat, 7-vii.-15; sinks Turkish steamer, 10-vii.-15; sinks two dhows, 11-vii.-15; fires torpedo at Constantinople arsenal, 15-vii.-15; shells Turkish trains near Kava Burnu, 17-vii.-15; 22-vii.-15; shells Mudania, 18-vii.-15; sinks four dhows, 19-vii.-15; sinks dhow, 21-vii.-15; returns from cruise, 24-vii.-15; sunk in Dardanelles, 4-ix.-15; — **E8:** in battle of Heligoland Bight, 28-viii.-14; sinks H.I.M.S. " Prinz Adalbert," 23-x.-15; destroyed, 3-iv.-18; — **E9:** in battle of Heligoland Bight, 28-viii.-14; sinks H.I.M.S. " Hela," 12-ix.-14; sinks S116, 6-x.-14; passes into Baltic, 20-x.-14; at Libau, 22-x.-14; at Lapvig under Russian Adm. Essen's orders, 30-x.-14; sinks German T.B.D., 29-i.-15; sinks German transport, 4-vi.-15; torpedoes and damages H.I.M.S. " Prinz Adalbert," 2-vii.-15; sinks s.ss. " Soderham " and " Per-nambuco," 18-x.-16; sinks s.ss. " Johannes Russ " and " Dal Alfven," 19-x.-16; destroyed, 3-iv.-18; — **E10:** lost, 18-i.-15; **E11:** fails to enter Baltic: returns to base, 22-x.-14; five British airmen taken on board during Cuxhaven raid, 25-xii.-14; sinks Turkish gunboat, 23-v.-15; sinks Turkish transport and storeship, 24-v.-15; torpedoes Turkish steamer, 25-v.-15; 31-v.-15; sinks Turkish supply ship, 28-v.-15; 2-vi.-15; torpedoes Turkish troop-ship, 7-vi.-15; shells Turkish reinforce-ments, 7-viii.-15; 18-viii.-15; Lieut. Hughes lands and blows up portion of Anatolian railway, 21-viii.-15; — **E12:** sinks Turkish munition ship, 16-ix.-16; — **E13:** wrecked after being shelled, 18-viii.-15; German apology to Denmark, 24-viii.-15; — **E14:** in Sea of Marmora: sinks Turkish gunboat, 27-iv.-15; sinks Turkish transport, 29-iv.-15; Turkish gun-boat, 3-v.-15; sinks Turkish transport with 6,000 troops, 10-v.-15; drives Turkish steamer ashore, 13-v.-15; returns from Sea of Marmora; commander given V.C.; crew decorated, 18-v.-15; sinks dhows in Sea of Marmora, 20-vi.-15; shells Turkish reinforcements, 7-viii.-15; sunk, 28-i.-18; — **E15:** sunk in Dardanelles, 15-iv.-15; — **E16:** leaves Aberdeen for coast of Norway, 12-ix.-15; sinks U6, 15-ix.-15; lost, 22-viii.-16; — **E17:** cruises in Kattegat, 12-xi.-15; wrecked, 6-i.-16; — **E18:** lost in Baltic, 24-v.-16; — **E19:** sinks German T.B.D., 14-x.-15; sinks German merchantman, 3-x.-16; sinks German s.s. " Lulea," 10-x.-16; sinks 5 ore-laden vessels in Baltic, 11-x.-16; sinks H.I.M.S. " Ancona," 2-xi.-16; sinks German s.s. " Rouomi," 3-xi.-16; destroyed, 3-iv.-18; — **E20:** sunk, 6-xi.-15; — **E21:** sinks Austrian ammunition transport, 30-vi.-18; — **E22:** sunk, 25-iv.-16; — **E23:** attacks H.I.M.S. " Der-fflinger," 19-viii.-16; torpedoes H.I.M.S. " Westfalen," 19-viii.-16; reports German ships steering west, 19-viii.-16; — **E24:**

Submarines:—
German (continued) :—

"Majestic," 27-v.-15; torpedoes 7 Dutch vessels, 22-ii.-17; — **U22:** transferred to the Ems, 3-ix.-14; visits the Minch, 24-xi.-14; encountered in Cuxhaven raid, 25-xii.-14 — **U23:** sunk, 20-vii.-15; — **U24:** transferred to the Ems, 3-ix.-14; torpedoes H.M.S. "Formidable," 1-i.-15; surrendered, 1-xii.-18; — **U26:** sinks Russian cruiser "Pallada," 11-x.-14; lost in Baltic, 31-viii.-15; — **U27:** torpedoes E3, 18-x.-14; sinks H.M.S. "Hermes," 31-x.-14; sinks s.s. "Arabic," 19-viii.-15; sunk, 19-viii.-15; — **U28:** transferred to the Ems, 3-ix.-14; sinks s.s. "Aguila" off the Smalls, 27-iii.-15; under Cmdr. von Forstner torpedoes s.s. "Falaba": drowning people jeered at, 28-iii.-15; tows Swedish sailing ship with crew of "Meteor," 9-viii.-15; lost, 2-ix.-17; — **U29:** captures s.s. "Adenwen," 11-iii.-15; attempts to attack 1st Battle Squadron and rammed and sunk by H.M.S. "Dreadnought," 18-iii.-15; — **U30:** encountered in Cuxhaven raid, 25-xii.-14; in Irish Sea, 18-ii.-15; attempts to salve: J1 attacks forces protecting operations, 4-xi.-16; surrendered, 1-xii.-18; — **U31:** found adrift with crew dead, 31-i.-15; — **U33—39:** sent to Pola, 31-viii.-15; — **U33:** Capt. Fryatt shot for alleged attempt to ram, 27-vii.-16; — **U34:** destroyed, 8-xi.-18; — **U35:** sinks H.M. sloop "Primula," 1-iii.-16; at Cartagena with autograph letter from Kaiser to King of Spain, 21-vi.-16; torpedoes minesweeper, 2-x.-16; sinks auxiliary, 4-x.-16; with another: sinks s.ss. "Brisbane River," "Corfu," and "Fernmoor," 17-iv.-17; sinks s.s. "Trekieve," 18-iv.-17; s.s. "Sowwell," 19-iv.-17; with another: sinks s.ss. "Lowdale" and "Nentmoor," 20-iv.-17; surrendered, 1-xii.-18; — **U36:** sunk, 25-vii.-15; — **U37:** sunk, 22-vi.-15; — **U38:** torpedoes French gunboat "Surprise," 3-xii.-16; mined, 8-ii.-18; — **U39:** bombed by French airmen: towed into and interned in Cartagena harbour, 18-v.-18; — **U40:** sunk, 23-vi.-15; — **U41:** sunk, 24-ix.-15; — **U43:** sinks collier, 2-x.-16; surrendered, 1-xii.-18; — **U44:** under Lt.-Cmdr. P. Wagenfuhr: sinks s.s. "Belgian Prince": crew deliberately drowned, 31-vii.-17; sunk by H.M.S. "Oracle," 12-viii.-17; — **U45:** sunk, 12-ix.-17; — **U46:** in Jutland battle, 1-vi.-16; surrendered, 1-xii.-18; — **U47:** destroyed, 31-x.-18; — **U48:** destroyed; papers secured by Dover Salvage Corps, 24-xi.-17; — **U51:** torpedoed and destroyed, 14-vii.-16; — **U52:** sinks H.M.S. "Nottingham," 19-viii.-16; sinks C34, 21-vii.-17; surrendered, 1-xii.-18; — **U53:** leaves Heligoland for U.S., 17-ix.-16; passes N. of Shetlands, 20-ix.-16; at Newport (Rhode Is.), 7-x.-16; torpedoes eight vessels; starts return to Germany, 8-x.-16; returns to Heligoland, 28-x.-16; sinks vessels, 22-i.-17; 28-i.-17; 29-i.-17; 31-i.-17; 2-ii.-17; 3-ii.-17; 4-ii.-17; 5-ii.-17; — **U54:** sinks s.s. "Justicia," 20-vii.-18; surrendered, 1-xii.-18; — **U55:** surrendered, 1-xii.-18; — **U56:** destroyed by Russian patrol vessels, 2-xi.-16; — **U57:** surrendered, 1-xii.-18; — **U58:** sunk, 17-xi.-17; — **U59:** sunk, 14-v.-17; — **U60:** at sinking of U.S. s.s. "Housatonic," 3-ii.-17; surrendered, 1-xii.-18; — **U61:** destroyed, 26-iii.-18; — **U62:** reports capture of commander of H.M. Q12, 30-iv.-17; — **U63:** at sinking of H.M.S. "Falmouth," 19-viii.-16; sunk,

Submarines:—
German (continued) :—

1-xi.-17; — **U64:** sunk, 17-vi.-18; — **U65:** destroyed, 31-x.-18; — **U66:** at sinking of H.M.S. "Falmouth," 19-viii.-16; destroyed, 1-x.-17; — **U67:** surrendered, 1-xii.-18; —**U69:** sunk, 12-vii.-17; — **U70:** surrendered, 1-xii.-18; — **U72:** destroyed, 31-x.-18; — **U73:** destroyed, 31-x.-18; — **U74:** sunk, 27-v.-16; — **U75:** mined, 10-xii.-17; — **U76:** sunk, 26-i.-17; — **U77:** lost, 7-vii.-16; — **U78:** sunk, 28-x.-18; — **U79:** surrendered, 1-xii.-18; — **U81:** sunk, 1-v.-17; — **U83:** at sinking of Allied vessels, 4-ii.-17; sunk, 17-ii.-17; — **U84:** engaged by British T.B.D.; driven home damaged, 22-ii.-17; sunk, 26-i.-18; — **U85:** sunk, 12-iii.-17; — **U86:** leaves for Flamborough Head, 17-v.-17; surrendered, 1-xii.-18; — **U87:** sunk, 25-xii.-17; — **U89:** sunk, 12-ii.-18; — **U90:** surrendered, 1-xii.-18; — **U91:** surrendered, 1-xii.-18; — **U92:** mined, 9-ix.-18; — **U93:** engaged by H.M. Q schooner "Prize": commander and two men captured, 30-iv.-17; returns to Heligoland; total tonnage sunk by to April 30, 9-v.-17; towed to Wilhelmshaven, 11-v.-17; — **U94:** surrendered, 1-xii.-18; — **U95:** lost, 31-i.-18; — **U96:** rams and sinks UC69, 6-xii.-17; surrendered, 1-xii.-18; — **U97:** mined, 21-xi.-18; — **U98:** surrendered, 1-xii.-18; — **U100:** sunk, 26-i.-18; surrendered, 1-xii.-18; — **U101:** surrendered, 1-xii.-18; — **U102:** mined, 30-ix.-18; — **U103:** sunk, 12-v.-18; — **U104:** sunk, 25-iv.-18; — **U105:** surrendered, 1-xii.-18; — **U106:** destroyed, 1-x.-17; — **U107:** surrendered, 1-xii.-18; — **U108:** surrendered, 1-xii.-18; — **U110:** destroyed, 15-iii.-18; — **U111, 112, 113, 114, 117, 118, 119, 120, 121, 123, 125, 126,** surrendered, 1-xii.-18; — **U133:** chases s.s. "Brussels," 28-iii.-15; — **U135, 139, 141:** surrendered, 1-xii.-18; — **U154:** sunk, 11-v.-18; — **U156:** mined, 25-ix.-16; — **U157:** interned in Norway, 11-xi.-18; — **U160, 161, 162, 163, 164:** surrendered, 1-xii.-18; — **UA1:** surrendered, 1-xii.-18; — **UB1:** lost, 31-viii.-15; — **UB3:** destroyed, 24-iv.-16; — **UB4:** sunk, 11-viii.-15; — **UB6:** aground off Helvetsluis: interned, 12-iii.-16; — **UB7:** lost, 31-x.-16; — **UB10:** destroyed, 30-ix.-18; — **UB12:** mined, 31-viii.-18; — **UB13:** sunk, 31-iii.-16; — **UB15:** lost, 31-v.-16; — **UB16:** sunk, 10-v.-18; — **UB17:** destroyed, 25-ii.-18; — **UB18:** sinks E22, 25-iv.-16; mined, 17-xi.-17; — **UB19:** sunk, 30-xi.-16; — **UB20:** sunk, 29-vii.-17; — **UB21:** surrendered, 1-xii.-18; — **UB22:** mined, 19-i.-18; — **UB24:** surrendered, 1-xii.-18; — **UB25:** surrendered, 1-xii.-18; — **UB26:** sunk, 5-iv.-16; — **UB27, 28:** surrendered, 1-xii.-18; — **UB29:** sunk, 6-xii.-16; — **UB31:** sunk, 2-v.-18; — **UB32:** destroyed, 16-viii.-17; — **UB33:** mined, 11-iv.-18; — **UB34:** surrendered, 1-xii.-18; — **UB35:** sunk, 26-i.-18; — **UB36:** lost, 30-vi.-17; — **UB37:** sunk, 14-i.-17; — **UB39:** destroyed, 17-v.-17; — **UB40:** destroyed, 30-ix.-18; — **UB41:** blown up, 5-x.-17; — **UB44:** destroyed, 30-vii.-16; — **UB45:** lost, 30-x.-16; — **UB46:** mined, 16-xii.-16; — **UB48:** destroyed, 31-x.-18; — **UB52:** sunk, 23-v.-18; — **UB53:** mined, 3-viii.-18; — **UB54:** destroyed, 11-iii.-18; — **UB55:** mined, 22-iv.-18; — **UB56:** mined, 19-xii.-17; — **UB57:** mined, 14-viii.-18; — **UB58:** mined, 10-iii.-18; — **UB59:** destroyed, 30-ix.-18; — **UB60:** surrendered, 1-xii.-18; — **UB61:** mined, 29-xi.-17; — **UB62:** surrendered, 1-xii.-18; — **UB63:** sunk, 28-i.-18; — **UB64:** attacks s.s.

Submarine warfare — first phase, 1-viii.-14; measures against; arrangements, 12-x.-14; no British merchantmen sunk during December, 31-xii.-14; first attack without warning, 30-i.-15; Irish Sea sailings restricted, 1-ii.-15; sailings resumed, 2-ii.-15; second phase, 4-ii.-15; commanders addressed by Kaiser, 4-ii.-15; action postponed, 15-ii.-15; " blockade " of Great Britain, 18-ii.-15; exempted route between Lindesnäs and Tyne marked for Danish and Swedish ships, 18-ii.-15; U.S. and Italian flags to be immune, 20-ii.-15; instructed to use caution with U.S. and Italian ships 22-ii.-15; attack Folkestone-Boulogne night packets, 23-ii.-15; British Admiralty issue instructions applicable to vessels carrying defensive armament, 25-ii.-15; free route for Scandinavian ships abolished; area to be free from mines, 7-iii.-15; favoured treatment of Scandinavian vessels suspended, 30-iii.-15; order to commanders eliminating necessity for warning, 2-iv.-15; discrimination for neutrals, 18-iv.-15; 24-iv.-15; British anti-U-Boat operation inaugurated, 23-v.-15; operations against British passenger ships to continue, 31-x.-15; Germany informed U.S. would regard abandonment of blockade as appeal to public conscience, 2-vi.-15; Kaiser agrees no large passenger ships be sunk, 5-vi.-15; instructions to U-Boats issued 6-vi.-15; Adm. von Pohl urges authorities not to make concessions, 26-vi.-15; Herr Helfferich's memorandum to Chancellor, 5-viii.-15; restrictions regarding passenger ships, 24-viii.-15; Lord Selborne announces that Navy has menace " well in hand, 26-viii.-15; Count Bernstorff's statement regarding attacks on passenger ships 26-viii.-15; blockade duty stopped, 27-viii.-15; commanders ordered not to sink small passenger ships without warning, 30-viii.-15; Adm. von Pohl's resignation refused, 3-ix.-15; policy: Kaiser addresses Cabinet Order on, 7-ix.-15; second phase ended 30-ix.-15

Unrestricted campaign: Gen. von Falkenhayn declares in favour of, 30-xii.-15; advocates in Memorandum, 31-xii.-15; Note to U.S.: offers reparation for " damages caused by death or injuries to American citizens," 7-i.-16; Naval Staff declares for, 13-i.-16; Memorandum urges, 12-ii.-16; Bethmann-Hollweg's Memorandum to Kaiser: expresses fear of U.S. intervention if policy is pursued, 29-ii.-16; Kaiser and Chancellor decide to postpone 6-iii.-16; Kaiser and Naval Staff

Suvla (continued) :—
advance towards Anafarta, 9-viii.-15; further attack fails, 10-viii.-15; British progress, 12-viii.-15; Gen. Stopford succeeded by Gen. de Lisle; 500 yards advance, 15-viii.-15; further attack on Anafarta fails, 21-viii.-15; further advance, 26-viii.-15; withdrawal : begun, 10-xii.-15; successfully effected, 19-xii.-15

Suzanne — British capture, 26-viii.-18

Suzoy — French take, 28-viii.-18

Sventen, Lake — Russian counter-offensive between Lake Ilse and, 31-x.-15

Sventsiansk — Germans cross Niemen R. near, 24-ii.-15

Svidniki — German counter-attacks round, 18-vi.-16

Svientsiany — Germans cut railway at, 13-ix.-15

" Svobodnaya Rossiya " (ex " Ekaterina II."), Russian battleship — torpedoed by Russian T.B.D. " Kertch," 18-vi.-18

Swakopmund — abandoned by Germans, 10-viii.-14; Union forces occupy, 14-i.-15; Gen. Botha takes over 200 prisoners and some field guns at Riet, near, 20-iii.-15

" Swanmore," s.s. — sunk, 25-iv.-17

" Swan River," s.s. — sunk, 27-ix.-17

Swat R. — Malakand Column engaged, 29-viii.-15

Sweden — Germany to inform war imminent; gravity to own destiny, 23-vii.-14; British intercept steamer, 3-iv.-16; German decoration for Charge d'Affaires in Mexico: letter published, 13-ix.-17

" Swedish Prince," s.s. — sunk, 17-viii.-16

" Swift," H.M.S. — attacked by U9, 15-x.-14; joins Dover Patrol, 31-xii.-15; sinks H.I.M. T.B.D. G42, 21-iv.-17

" Swiftsure," H.M.S. — escorts Indian convoy, 20-ix.-14; attacked, 25-v.-15; engages Dardanelles forts 8 and 9, 2-iii.-15; bombards post on Gaba Tepe, 15-iv.-15; covers landing at X Beach, 25-iv.-15

" Swift Wings," H.M. collier — sunk, 1-ix.-16

Switha Sound — first line of U-Boat obstructions completed, 12-i.-15

Switzerland — mobilisation, 8-viii.-14; peace Note to belligerents, 22-xii.-16; declines to sever relations with Germany, 5-ii.-17; Herr Hoffman resigns as Foreign Minister, 18-vi.-17; general strike collapses, 14-xi.-18

" Sycamore," s.s. — sunk, 25-viii.-17

" Sydney," H.M.A.S. — escorts Australian convoy, 1-xi.-14; escorts New Zealand transports: destroys H.I.M.S. " Emden," 9-xi.-14

Sykes, Maj.-Gen. Sir P. — with British column : enters Kerman, 13-vi.-16

Sylt — air raid E. of, 25-iii.-16

" Sylvanian," s.s. — sunk, 24-vi.-17

Syria — Deurt Yol barracks bombarded by H.M.S. " Doris ": 450 Turkish casualties, 10-iii.-15; Allied blockade, 25-viii.-15; King of Hedjaz master of country between Akaba—Hedjaz railway, 12-vii.-17; fighting: see Palestine and names of places (index); Council of Four consider question, 12-iv.-19

Syrmia — invaded by Serbians, 6-ix.-14; Jarak taken, 12-ix.-14

" Szechuen," s.s. — sunk, 10-v.-18

Szekeley Udvarhely — Austro-Germans recapture, 7-x.-16

" Szent Istvan," Austrian Dreadnought — torpedoed, 9-vi.-18

Szögyény, Count (Austria-Hungary) — presents Emperor Francis Joseph's letter and Balkan Memorandum to Kaiser, 5-vii.-14; confers with Herr von Bethmann-Hollweg and Herr Zimmermann, 6-vii.-14

Sztropoko — Russians occupy, 4-iv.-15

T.

" T. R. Thompson," s.s. — sunk, 29-iii.-18

Tabir — British capture Turkish post, 22-xi.-

Tabor — British progress near, 8-vi.-18

Tabora — Belgians at, 19-ix.-16; Germ retreat on: reaches Kitunda, 6-v.-17

Tabriz — Turks seize, 13-i.-15; driven o 30-i.-15; Turks claim, 14-vi.-18; drive Miane post, 5-ix.-18

Tafile — Hedjaz Arabs defeat Turks, 26-i.-18

Taganrog — Germans reach, 28-iv.-18

Tagliamento R. — Italians retiring, 28-x.-1 rearguard action, 30-x.-17; Italians behin 60,000 prisoners claimed, 31-x.-17; pressu on line, 2-xi.-17; forced N. of Pinzai 4-xi.-17; retreat on Piave, 5-xi.-17; rea Livenza R., 6-xi.-17; Austro-Germans read 30-xi.-17; British on, 3-xi.-18; America force, 4-xi.-18

" Tagona," s.s. — sunk, 16-v.-18

Tagus — German ships dismantled, 9-viii.-14

Tahiti — Germans bombard Papeete, 22-ix.-1

Tahure — Germans assault between Massig and, 15-ii.-17; German salient won betwe Butte du Mesnil and, 13-ii.-18; Germ attempt near, defeated, 18-ii.-18

Tahure, Butte de — French engage Germ second line, 29-ix.-15; French take, 6-x.-1 gain S.E. of, 7-x.-15; Germans fail 8-x.-15; recapture, 30-x.-15

Tahure—Somme-Py — German success, 13-i 16; French recovery, 16-ii.-16

" Tainui," s.s. — torpedoed, 8-iv.-18

" Takachiho," H.I.J.M.S. — sunk, 17-x.-14

" Take Care," H.M. armed motor trawler chases U-Boat from Start Bay, 19-xii.-17

Talaat Pasha (Turkey) — informs Prin Hohenlohe that Armenian question " longer exists," 31-viii.-15; in Chamber: equality of Ottoman Empire peoples, 15-ii.-1 at Brest-Litovsk Conference, 8-i.-18

" Talawa," s.s. — torpedoed, 5-v.-17

Talgert, F. Cmdr. (Germany) — surrende battle cruisers, 21-xi.-18

Talou Hill — French take, 20-viii.-17

" Tamele," s.s. — sunk, 16-vii.-17

Tammerfors — taken by Finnish White Guar 3-iv.-18

" Tampa," U.S. auxiliary — torpedoe 26-viii.-18

" Tanfield," s.s. — torpedoed, 15-iv.-18

Tanga — British landed at, 2-xi.-14; action Ras Kasone, 3-xi.-14; British reverse, 4-x 14; guns of H.I.M.S. " Königsberg mounted, 11-vii.-15; bombarded, 15-viii.-1 occupied by British, 7-vii.-16

Tanganyika, Lake — German ships sun 26-xii.-15; 9-ii.-16; Belgians take Kigon 27-vii.-16; Ujiji occupied, 2-viii.-16; 3-viii.-1 " Graf von Götzen " destroyed, 2-viii.-16

" Tangistan," s.s. — sunk, 9-iii.-15

Tauk R. — British reach, 30-iv.-18

Tanks:—
British — committee formed, 24-ii.-15; fir " Mother " completed, 26-i.-16; first ta at Hatfield, 29-i.-16; King George inspec 8-ii.-16; Mr. D'Eyncourt's Committ thanked for evolving, 10-ii.-16; Gen. E commands in France, 29-ix.-16; battalio formation arrangements, 4-iii.-17; Ad Moore to be controller of Mechanical W fare Department, 16-x.-17; 700 Mark delivered in France, 31-x.-17
French — first in action (Aisne battl 16-iv.-17
Operations — first British in action, 15-16; Arras battle: allotments, 8-iv.-17; action, 10-iv.-17; 11-iv.-17; 12-iv.-17; action at Gaza, 17-iv.-17; Gen. Ell special order before Cambrai battle, 19-17; in action facing Cambrai, 20-xi.-

" Titian," **s.s.** — sunk, 26-viii.-17

Titu — Rumanian 1st Army driven beyond, 3-xii.-16

Tobolsk — ex-Tsar Nicholas sent to, 15-viii.-17; removed from, 1-v.-18

Tochi Valley — North Waziristan Militia engaged, 29-xi.-14

Togoland — Franco-British force in, 8-viii.-14; Gold Coast force landed at Lome, 12-viii.-14; conquered, 26-viii.-14

" **Tokomaru,**" **s.s.** — sunk, 30-i.-15

" **Toledo,**" **s.s.** — destroyed, 5-x.-17

Tolmino — Italians advance to Monfalcone, 22-vii.-15; Italians advance towards, 18-viii.-15; positions bombarded, 23-x.-17

Tomaszov — Austro-Germans advance, 30-vi.-15

Tomba — Austrian retirement, 4-i.-18

Tomlin, Capt. — appointed S.N.O., Ramsgate, 21-i.-15

Tomorica — Franco-Italian offensive, 6-vii.-18; prisoners taken, 6-vii.-18; 10-vii.-18

" **Tonawanda,**" **s.s.** — torpedoed, 2-vi.-17

Tondarecar — Germans storm, 4-xii.-17

Tondern — air attack: preparations, 24-iii.-16; Zeppelin base attacked, 4-v.-16; bombed, 19-vii.-18

Toplitza — fighting, 14-xi.-15; taken by Rumanians, 9-ix.-16

Tor — Turkish force annihilated, 12-ii.-15

Toraro, Monte — Italians lose, 19-v.-16

" **Torcello,**" **s.s.** — sunk, 15-vii.-17

Torchin — Russians take, 12-vi.-16

" **Torilla,**" **s.s.** — attacked and chased, 3-xii.-15

" **Tornado,**" **H.M.S.** — mined, 23-xii.-17

" **Toro,**" **s.s.** — sunk, 12-iv.-17

Torpedoes — German: statistics, 30-ix.-18

" **Torrent,**" **H.M.S.** — mined, 23-xii.-17

" **Torr Head,**" **s.s.** — sunk, 20-iv.-17

" **Torridge,**" **s.s.** — sunk, 6-ix.-16

" **Torrington,**" **s.s.** — sunk, 8-iv.-17

Tortoise Hill (Doiran) — taken by French, 15-viii.-16

" **Tortuguero,**" **s.s.** — sunk, 26-vi.-18

Tory Island — s.s. " Manchester Commerce " mined near, 26-x.-14; s.s. " Tritonia " sunk off, 19-xii.-14

Törzburg — Germans take, 8-x.-16

Törzburg Pass — Austro-Germans on frontier ridge, 10-x.-16; Rumanians retreat; invaders 6 miles within territory, 13-x.-16; Germans held, 16-x.-16; Rumanian success S. of, 18-x.-16; Germans within, 20-x.-16; violent fighting, 24-x.-16; Rumanians repulse violent attack, 26-x.-16; counter-attack successfully, 27-x.-16; invaders checked, 31-x.-16; German heavy guns through, 15-xi.-16; severe fighting, 16-xi.-16

" **Tottenham,**" **s.s.** — sunk, 4-viii.-16

Toul — to be pledged to Germany: ultimatum to France, 31-vii.-14; U.S. troops lose and regain Seicheprey, 19-iv.-18; H.Q. U.S. 4th Corps, 30-viii.-18; U.S. 2nd Army H.Q. at, 12-x.-18

Tourcoing — British air-raid on railway, 26-iv.-15; press-gangs thanked by Crown Prince of Bavaria, 29-iv.-16; British E. of, 18-x.-18

Tournai — German Cavalry Corps diverted to, 24-viii.-14; taken by 4th Cavalry Division, 24-viii.-14; British reach outskirts, 21-x.-18; Germans fall back N. of, 3-xi.-18; British occupy part, 8-xi.-18; occupation completed, 9-xi.-18

Tours — U.S. Army Supply Services at, 16-ii.-18; Gen. Rogers, U.S. Army, Q.M.G. at, 22-vii.-18; Gen. Harbord in charge of U.S. Supply Services, 31-vii.-18

Tower Hamlets (Ypres) — positions won S. of, 21-ix.-17; German penetrate lines between Polygon Wood and; ejected, 25-ix.-17; British advance on front from ridge to E. of St.

Tower Hamlets (Ypres) (continued) :—
Julien, 26-ix.-17; spur captured, 26-ix.-17; Germans repulsed between Polygon Wood and, 3-x.-17

" **Towneley,**" **s.s.** — sunk, 31-i.-18

Townshend, Gen. — arrives at Basra to command 6th (Poona) Division, 23-iv.-15; returns to Basra after sick leave, 21-viii.-15; instructed to occupy Kut-el-Amara, 23-viii.-15; leaves for Amarah, 25-viii.-15; at Amarah, 28-viii.-15; occupies Kutunieh, 11-xi.-15; forces concentrate at Kutunieh, 18-xi.-15; leaves Kutunieh, 19-xi.-15; reaches Lajj, 20-xi.-15; advances on Ctesiphon, 21-xi.-15; retreats from Ctesiphon, 25-xi.-15; 28-xi.-15; 30-xi.-15; fights rearguard action, 1-xii.-15; force, after 40-mile march, reaches Shumran bend, 2-xii.-15; reaches Kut-el-Amara after retreat of 90 miles, 3-xii.-15; cavalry sent down Tigris, 6-xii.-15; reports Kut can hold out 27 days, 22-i.-16; discovers hidden native stores: able to hold out 84 days, 25-i.-16; Khalil Pasha invites surrender of, 10-iii.-16; discusses with, 26-iv.-16; surrenders, 29-iv.-16 (see Kut-el-Amara); leaves Baghdad for Constantinople, 12-v.-16; at Constantinople, 3-vi.-16; at Mitylene, 20-x.-18

" **Trabboch,**" **s.s.** — sunk, 14-ix.-14

Tracy-le-Val — French take, 13-xi.-14; German counter-attacks fail, 19-xi.-14; 7-xii.-14; 7-viii.-18; French advance, 18-viii.-18

Trade — running as usual, 14-viii.-14; U.S Note to Great Britain, 29-xii.-14; British preliminary reply, 7-i.-15; neutral: British memorandum, 24-vi.-15; black lists withdrawn, 14-v.-19

" **Trader,**" **s.s.** — sunk, 13-i.-16

Trades Union Congress — Stockholm Congress: see under Stockholm

Tralee — arms and munitions landed, 20-iv.-16; Sir Roger Casement lands: captured, 21-iv.-16

Transchorok — Russian success, 9-iii.-15

Transylvania — heavy fighting at Merisov, 18-ix.-16; Austrians reach Vulcan Pass, 22-ix.-16; Austrians moving on Roter Turm Pass, 24-ix.-16; 25-ix.-16; Austrians carry W. side, 26-ix.-16; Rumanian success, 3-x.-16; Germans capture Gyimes Pass, 16-x.-16; Rumanians cross frontier, 28-viii.-16; Austrians retreat; Rumanians take Petroseny, Brasso, and Kezdi Vasarhely, 29-viii.-16; take Toplitza, 9-ix.-16; Austrians evacuate Hermannstadt, 10-ix.-16; Rumanians advance, 14-ix.-16; Austrian counter-attack, 15-ix.-16; fighting in passes, 12-x.-16; Rumanians vote unconditional union with Rumania, 1-xii.-18

" **Transylvania,**" **s.s.** — sunk, 4-v.-17

Trebizond — Russians land W. of, 16-iv.-16; bombarded, 21-iv.-15; 8-ii.-15; Armenians deported, 26-vi.-15; Russians destroy bridges, 18-ii.-16; Russians 30 miles from, 27-iii.-16; falls, 17-iv.-16; Baibart captured by Russians, 15-vii.-16; Turks 8 miles from, 18-ii.-18; recaptured, 24-ii.-18

" **Tredegar Hall,**" **s.s.** — sunk, 23-x.-17

" **Tregenna,**" **s.s.** — sunk, 26-xii.-17

" **Trekieve,**" **s.s.** — sunk, 18-iv.-17

" **Trelissick,**" **s.s.** — sunk, 15-vii.-17

" **Treloske,**" **s.s.** — sunk, 29-viii.-17

" **Trelyon,**" **s.s.** — mined, 21-vii.-17

Trembovla — Russian success at, 9-ix.-15; Russian retreat pivoting on, 25-vii.-17

" **Tremeadow,**" **s.s.** — sunk, 19-i.-17

Tremiti — bombarded, 23-vii.-15

Trench feet — first cases developed in British Army: 20,000 men invalided during winter, 21-xi.-14

Trench mortars — first employed by Germans at Fléron, 13-viii.-14

Trent — Italians occupy, 3-xi.-18

Trentino — Austria offers Italy rectification of frontier, 2-iv.-15; Austrians blow up bridges, 24-v.-15; Italians occupy Monte Altissimo, 25-v.-15; capture Ala and Grado, 27-v.-15; advance in Adige Valley, 1-vi.-15; Italians take Monticello, 8-vii.-15; capture Malga Sarta and Costa Della, 9-vii.-15; on Ercavallo Peak, 7-viii.-15; Italian success in, 4-ix.-15; Italian success on Adamello Range, 11-iv.-16; 29-iv.-16; Austrian bombardment, 14-v.-16; assault: Italian centre retires, 15-v.-16; Austrian gains at Rovereto, 16-v.-16; Italians rally at Zuguna Torta, 17-v.-16; evacuate, 18-v.-16; Italians lose Monte Toraro—Spitz Tonezza, 19-v.-16; evacuate Armentera ridge, 20-v.-16; fall back between Astico—Brenta R., 23-v.-16; on S. Posina ridge, 24-v.-16; strong Austrian pressure, 25-v.-16; Italians driven from heights E. of Val d'Assa, 26-v.-16; Austrians on Sette Communi plateau, 27-v.-16; Italians evacuate Asiago and Arsiero, 29-v.-16; violent Austrian assaults, 30-v.-16; Italians withdraw at Posina—Asiago, 31-v.-16; heavy Austrian attack on left of centre, 1-vi.-16; offensive held, 3-vi.-16; attacks S. of Posina fail, 4-vi.-16; also S. and S.W. of Asiago, 7-vi.-16; Italians lose Monte Lemerle, 9-vi.-16; counter-attacks in Largarina Valley and Posina—Astico front, 12-vi.-16; capture trenches E. of Monfalcone, 14-vi.-16; Austrian attack on Monte Pau fails, 15-vi.-16; Italian progress, 16-vi.-16; Asiago, Priafora, and Cengio mountains taken, 25-vi.-16; re-occupy Arsiero—Posina, 26-vi.-16; progress, 27-vi.-16; success at Mt. Pasubio, 9-x.-16; Austrian attacks repulsed, 19-x.-16; Austrian reverse, 13-vi.-17; Italian success, 19-vi.-17; Austro-Germans take Asiago ruins, 9-xi.-17; attempts repulsed, 14-xi.-17; Marshal von Hötzendorf relieved of command, 16-vii.-18

Trepoff, M. (Russia) — Premier: in Duma: announces Allies acknowledgment of Russia's claim to Constantinople, 2-xii.-16; resigns, 8-i.-17

Trescault — British take part, 22-iv.-17; remainder, 23-iv.-17; again take, 12-ix.-18

Tresnoy — British take, 6-x.-18

" **Trevarrack**," s.s. — sunk, 16-xi.-16

" **Treveal**," s.s. — sunk, 4-ii.-18

" **Trevean**," s.s. — sunk, 22-i.-17

" **Trevelyan**," s.s. — torpedoed, 19-xii.-17

" **Treverbyn**," s.s. — sunk, 3-ix.-17

Treves — air-raids, 3-vi.-17; 7-vii.-17; 25-i.-18; 27-i.-18; 18-ii.-18; 21-viii.-18; Americans enter, 1-xii.-18; German delegates for renewal of Armistice leave for, 9-xii.-18; renewal discussed, 12-xii.-18; renewed, 14-xii.-18; Convention signed, 16-i.-19; Marshal Foch presents terms of final Armistice renewal to Germans at, 14-ii.-19; agreement signed, 16-ii.-19

Treviso — U.S. infantry battalion at, 29-x.-18

" **Trident**," s.s. — sunk, 7-viii.-16

Trieste — Italians land, 3-xi.-18; relief: Inter-Allied Commission: approved by Inter-Allied Supreme Council of Supply and Relief, 20-i.-19

Trieste Gulf — Austrian line shelled by monitors, 24-v.-17; two Austrian battleships torpedoed, 9-xii.-17

" **Trinidad**," s.s. — sunk, 22-iii.-18

Tripoli — Italians massacred by Senussi tribesmen, 23-vii.-15; rebels advance on Zuara, 13-i.-17

Tripolis — occupied, 13-x.-18

" **Tritonia**," s.s. — sunk, 19-xii.-14

" **Tritonia**," s.s. — sunk, 27-ii.-17

" **Triumph**," H.M.S. — assists in blockade of Kiaochow Bay, 27-viii.-14; silences Bismarck Forts at Tsingtau, 1-xi.-14; bombards forts on

" **Triumph**," H.M.S. (continued) :—Cape Kephez, 1-iii.-15; attacks in Dardanelles, 3-iii.-15; covers landing at Anzac Cove, 25-iv.-15; torpedoed, 25-v.-15

" **Triumph**," fishing vessel — captured and converted into raider, 20-viii.-18; captures fishing vessel, 25-viii.-18

" **Trocas**," s.s. — sunk, 19-i.-18

" **Trojan Prince**," s.s. — sunk, 23-ii.-17

Trondhjem — H.I.M.S. " Brandenburg " interned, 28-ix.-14; German auxiliary " Berlin " interned at, 16-xi.-14

Trônes Wood — British enter, 8-vii.-15; British capture Maltz Horn Farm, 9-vii.-16; German counter-attacks, 10-vii.-16; British fail to hold N. end of wood, 11-vii.-16; British progress, 12-vii.-16; consolidated, 13-vii.-16; capture completed, 14-vii.-16

Trotha, Rear-Adm. von (Germany) — Chief of Naval Staff, 15-i.-16

Trotsky, M. (Russia) — evades formal Treaty with Central Powers, 10-ii.-18; informs Allies of armistice, 6-xii.-17; at Brest-Litovsk as chief Soviet delegate to peace conference, 7-i.-18; agrees to continue negotiations, 10-i.-18; leaves Brest-Litovsk, 20-i.-18; on German peace condition: " a demand for a most monstrous annexation," 23-i.-18; returns to Brest-Litovsk, 29-i.-18; intimates Russia would neither fight nor negotiate, 11-ii.-18

Trotus Valley — Russian advance, 10-xii.-16; Austro-Germans take positions between Uzal Valley and, 8-iii.-17; Rumanian setback S. of, 26-iii.-17; Rumanian retirement, 8-viii.-17; 10-viii.-17; 11-viii.-17; Rumanian offensive, 12-viii.-17; progress, 13-viii.-17; heavy fighting, 17-viii.-17; German progress, 19-viii.-17

Troubridge, Adm. — to shadow H.I.M.S. " Goeben " and watch Adriatic, 2-viii.-14; squadron under joined at entrance to Adriatic by French main fleet, 15-viii.-14; to command ships in Mediterranean, 18-viii.-14; blockade maintained by ships under, 19-viii.-14; recalled, 19-ix.-14; acquitted by court-martial, 14-xi.-14

" **Trowbridge**," s.s. — sunk, 14-xi.-17

Troyes — Germans converging on, 4-ix.-14

Troyon, Fort — bombarded by Germans, 8-ix.-14; refuses surrender, 9-ix.-14; German attack fails, 10-ix.-14; siege raised, 12-ix.-14; British advance, 14-ix.-14; British pressed, 18-ix.-14; attacked, 20-ix.-14; German surprise attack, 10-iii.-16

Trumbitch, Dr. (Serbia) — visits Italian G.H.Q., 17-iv.-18

" **Trunkby**," H.M. collier — sunk, 27-v.-16

Tsaritsyn — Gen Denikin takes, 30-vi.-19

Tsarskoe Selo — ex-Tsar prisoner at, 22-iii.-17

Tsavo — Germans repulsed, 7-ix.-14

Tschirschky, Herr von (Germany) — reports to Berlin Austrian desire for " thorough reckoning " with Serbs, 30-vi.-14; reprimanded for " lukewarmness," 8-vii.-14

Tseniovka — trench line carried by " Red " Army, 1-vii.-17

Tshogowall R. — Gen. Smuts occupies German camp on, 4-i.-17

Tsingtau — s.s. " Ryasan " renamed " Cormoran " after capture leaves, 10-viii.-14; Japanese squadron proceeds to blockade 23-viii.-14; T.B.D. " Kennet " damaged in action, 23-viii.-14; Japanese occupy islands off, 27-viii.-14; Japanese landed, 2-ix.-14; British force leaves Tientsin, 19-ix.-14; outposts driven in, 26-ix.-14; bombarded 29-ix.-14; German attack fails, 30-ix.-14; Japanese permit civilian evacuation, 15-x.-14; general Allied attack, 16-x.-14; land bombardment, 31-x.-14; Bismarck Forts silenced by H.M.S. " Triumph," 1-xi.-14; Austrian

Villers-Ghislain — British 3rd Division holding salient, 22-viii.-14; British take, 18-iv.-17; capture post near, 13-xii.-17; take, 30-ix.-18

Ville-sur-Ancre — Australians raid, 18-v.-18; Australian 2nd Division takes, 19-v.-18

Ville-sur-Tourbe — Germans fail, 15-v.-15

Villette — German Financial Delegation meets Economic Council at, 1-iv.-19

Vilna — Germans progress towards, 29-viii.-15; 31-viii.-15; Russians retire N.W. of, 11-ix.-15; Russians threatened with envelopment, 13-ix.-15; Germans cross Vilia N.E. of, 15-ix.-15; almost encircled, 16-ix.-15; fall, 18-ix.-15; heavy fighting, 20-ix.-15; successful Russian retreat, 21-ix.-15; Russian offensive E. of, 22-vii.-17; Bolshevists occupy, 4-i.-19

Vilna—Dvinsk — battle begun, 9-ix.-15; Germans concentrate, 11-ix.-15; railway cut by Germans, 13-ix.-15; railway reached by German cavalry at Molodechna—Polotsk, 16-ix.-15; heavy fighting, 20-ix.-15

"Vimeira," s.s. — sunk, 12-v.-18

Vimy — fighting in sector, 12-ii.-16; British take, 13-iv.-17

Vimy ridge — French reach La Folie, 26-ix.-15; carry Hill 140 on, 29-ix.-15; progress on La Folie, 1-x.-15; 10-x.-15; 11-x.-15; British explode mines and take trenches, 15-v.-16; Germans capture crater, 17-v.-16; carry British trenches, 21-v.-16; all except Hill 145 taken by British, 9-iv.-17; German attack towards; repulsed, 28-iii.-18

Vineyard (Gallipoli) — British gain trenches between Gully Ravine and, 15-xi.-15

Vincennes — Bolo Pasha shot, 17-iv.-18

"Vindex," seaplane carrier — arrangements for attack on Tondern Zeppelin base; result, 4-v.-16

"Vindictive," H.M.S. — captures s.s. "Schlesien," 6-viii.-14; runs alongside Zeebrugge Mole; storming party landed, 23-iv.-18; sunk as blockship at Ostend, 10-v.-18

Vingrè — Germans fail to cross Oise at, 5-vi.-18

"Vinovia," s.s. — sunk, 19-xii.-17

"Virent," s.s. — sunk, 24-viii.-18

"Virgen del Socorro," Spanish schooner — leaves Vigo for German waters, 8-x.-16

"Virginia," s.s. — sunk, 16-vii.-16

"Viribus Unitis," Austrian Dreadnought — arrives at Trieste with bodies of Archduke Ferdinand and wife, 1-vii.-14; torpedoed, 31-x.-18

Visé — set on fire, 4-viii.-14

Vis-en-Artois — taken by British, 27-viii.-18

Vishegrad — attacked by Serbo-Montenegrins, 12-viii.-14; 14-ix.-14; Montenegrins take, 12-xii.-14; Austrians cross Drina E. of, 27-x.-15

Visloka, R. — Russians retire on, 2-v.-15; 4-v.-15; Austrians cross at Jaslo, 7-v.-15

Visniovtchyk — Russians take, 12-x.-15

Vistula R. — German G.H.Q. informed of impossibility of maintaining position E. of, 20-viii.-14; Russian offensive, 6-ix.-14; battle ends, 12-ix.-14; Russians pursue Germans across, 22-x.-14; Russians advancing along take Serpets, 13-i.-15; progress, 14-i.-15; 16-i.-15; German advance N. of, 15-ii.-15; Russians driven across N. of Ivangorod, 22-vii.-15; Germans force between Warsaw and Ivangorod, 28-vii.-15; fall of Novo-Georgievsk, 19-viii.-15

Vitry — occupied by French, 10-ix.-14

Vitry-le-François — first conference between Gen. Joffre and Sir J. French held, 16-viii.-14; French G.H.Q. at, 25-viii.-14

Vittorio — Italians capture, 29-x.-18

Viviani, M. (France) — member of French War Mission to U.S., 15-iv.-17

Vladimir Volynsk — German attacks, 31-viii.-16

Vladivostok — Japanese and British marines at, 5-iv.-18; Japan decides to land troops, 2-viii.-18; British land, 3-viii.-18; Japanese land, 11-viii.-18; Gen. Otani commanding expedition, 16-viii.-18; Gen. Diterichs and Czecho-Slovaks in control, 29-vi.-18

Vlodava — Germans repulsed, 13-viii.-15; Austro-Germans reach; Bug crossed, 15-viii.-15

Vodice, Mte. — Italians on summit, 18-v.-17; fierce fighting; 7000 Austrian prisoners, 19-v.-17; further Italian gains, 20-v.-17; Austrian attacks repulsed, 28-v.-17

Vojusa — Italians force, 8-vii.-18

Volga — Czecho-Slovaks at Simbirsk, 25-vii.-18

"Volga," s.s. — torpedoed, 14-v.-17

Volhynia — Austro-Germans enter Kovel, 23-viii.-15; German attacks at Vladimir Volynsk, 31-viii.-16 German attacks W. of Lutsk, 27-ix.-16

Volkovisk — Germans take, 7-ix.-15

"Volnay," s.s. — mined, 14-xii.-17

"Volodia," s.s. — sunk, 21-viii.-17

Vologda — U.S. Embassy removed to, 13-iii.-18

"Voltaire," s.s. — sunk, 2-xii.-16

Voncq — taken by French, 1-xi.-18

"Von Der Tann," H.I.M.S. — bombards Scarborough and Whitby, 16-xii.-14; in Jutland battle, 31-v.-16; to assist in raid on Sunderland, 18-viii.-16; surrendered, 21-xi.-18

"Von Wissmann," German armed steamer — captured, 13-viii.-14; destroyed, 30-vi.-15

Voormezeele — German attacks defeated, 26-iv.-18; Germans take and lose, 27-iv.-18; defeated on 10-mile front, 29-iv.-18; attack, 8-v.-18; defeated, 9-v.-18; 27-v.-18

Vosges — French holding passes, 15-viii.-14; Gen. Dubail's 1st Army holding fast, 25-viii.-14; 4-ix.-14; sector cleared, 13-ix.-14; French repulse counter-attacks at Ban-de-Sapt, 29-xi.-14; Germans bombard St. Dié, 27-xii.-14; French advance near Senones, 27-i.-15; German success, 19-ii.-15; Germans take Hill 627, 22-vi.-15; French recapture trenches between Fey-en-Haye and Bois-le-Prêtre, and Hill 627, 8-vii.-15; storm German La Fontenelle—Launois defences, 24-vii.-15; gain footing on Sondernach crest, 17-viii.-15; capture trenches on Schratzmännele crest, 18-viii.-15; carried, 22-viii.-15; German attacks at Lingenkopf—Barrenkopf repulsed, 9-ix.-15; position warfare until Armistice, 10-i.-18

"Vosges," s.s. — shelled and sunk in Channel, 27-iii.-15

Vouziers — French reach, 12-x.-18; Franco-American advance, 1-xi.-18

Vozarci — Franco-Serb armies pass, 21-ix.-18

Voyennes — British line through, 23-iii.-18

Vrania — Bulgarians occupy, 15-x.-15; cut railway at, 17-x.-15; fierce fighting between Serbs and Bulgars, 18-x.-15

Vrata ridge — carried, 14-vi.-15

Vrégny — French occupy, 8-xi.-14; Germans gain heights, 13-i.-15; French progress, 26-iii.-17; advance on, 30-iii.-17; French reduce salient, 18-iv.-17; 19-iv.-17; 20-iv.-17; Allies hold on plateau, 28-v.-18; Germans extended, 29-v.-18

Vrigné — French cross Meuse near, 10-xi.-18

"Vronwen," s.s. — sunk, 29-viii.-17

Vrsik Crest — Italians progress, 17-viii.-15

Vulcan Pass — Austrians reach, 22-ix.-16; repulsed, 13-x.-16; captured, 24-x.-16; Rumanian retreat, 26-x.-16; counter-attack, 27-x.-16; pursuit of invaders, 30-x.-16; Rumanians holding in, 1-xi.-16; success, 2-xi.-16; German progress, 13-xi.-16; Rumanians retreat, 14-xi.-16; Germans progress, 15-xi.-16; severe fighting, 16-xi.-16; Germans extend S. of, 19-xi.-16

Vyfweegn — air camps bombarded, 3-vi.-17
Vyl Light — submarines in position off, 3-v.-16

W.

" **W. Harkess**," s.s. — sunk, 22-x.-16
" **W. C. McKay**," s.s. — sunk, 10-i.-18
" **W. S. Bailey**," H.M. trawler — sinks UB63, 28-i.-18
" **Wabasha**," s.s. — torpedoed, 6-vii.-17
Wadai — British operations on border, 6-xi.-16
Wadi Auja — British secure ground 3 miles N. of, 14-iii.-18
Wadi Ghuzzeh — successful British attack from, 17-iv.-17
Wadi Hesi — British pressing on to, 7-xi.-17; Turks evacuate, 9-xi.-17
Wadi Khuweilfeh — Turkish lines captured, 6-xi.-17
Wadi Sheria — Turkish lines captured, 6-xi.-17
Wadi Sukereir — Turks driven from, 13-xi.-17
Wadi Surar — Turks retire on, 13-xi.-17
Waelhem, Fort — falls, 1-x.-14
Wagenfuhr, Lt.-Cmdr. P. (Germany) — in U44: sinks s.s. "Belgian Prince" and deliberately drowns crew, 31-vii.-17
Wahle, Gen. von (Germany) — in engagement at Mahiwa, 15-x.-17; captured, 18-x.-18
Waht — Turco-Arab force driven out by British Aden Column, 25-ix.-15
" **Waihemo**," s.s. — sunk, 17-iii.-18
" **Waikawa**," s.s. — sunk, 19-x.-17
" **Waipara**," s.s. — torpedoed, 4-viii.-18
" **Wairuna**," s.s. — sunk, 2-vi.-17
" **Waitemata**," s.s. — sunk, 14-vii.-18
Waldersee, Gen. Count (Germany) — relinquishes position as Chief of Staff, 22-viii.-14
Wales — miners' strike, 15-vii.-15
Wales, Prince of — National Relief Fund: appeal, 7-viii.-14; joins B.E.F., 16-xi.-14; with King on 70-mile tour of British front, 2-xii.-14; in Paris, 28-xi.-18; at Ypres, 8-xii.-18
Walk — Germans at, 22-ii.-18
Wallace, Gen. — disperses Senussi at Halazin, 23-i.-16
Wallachia — German pursuit in, 16-xii.-16; further Allied retreat, 24-xii.-16; fierce struggle, 26-xii.-16
Wallemolen — British retire between Poelcappelle and, 10-x.-17
" **Wallsend**," s.s. — sunk, 14-viii.-18
Walmer — German air-raid on, 20-ii.-16
Walney Is. — Messrs. Vickers works shelled by U21, 30-i.-15
Walsall — Zeppelin raid on, 31-i.-16
" **Walter Leonhardt**," German s.s. — sunk, 11-x.-16
Wami R. — Gen. Smuts' forces cross at Dakawa, 18-viii.-16
Wancourt — British storm, 12-iv.-17; British line through, 26-iii.-18; taken, 26-viii.-18
" **Waneta**," s.s. — sunk, 30-v.-18
Wangenheim, Baron von (Germany) — Ambassador to Turkey; invalided, 30-vii.-15; death, 25-x.-15
" **Wapello**," s.s. — sunk, 15-vi.-17
" **War Arabis**," s.s. — sunk, 9-ix.-18
" **War Baron**," s.s. — sunk, 5-i.-18
War Cabinet: see Great Britain — Ministry
" **War Clover**," s.s. — sunk, 19-x.-17
" **War Council**," H.M. collier — sunk, 16-x.-18
" **War Crocus**," s.s. — sunk, 8-vii.-18
Ward, Sir J. (New Zealand) — Peace Conference delegate: in England, 19-i.-19
" **War Deer**," s.s. — torpedoed, 30-vii.-18
" **War Firth**," s.s. — sunk, 4-ix.-18
Wargnies-le-Grand — taken by British, 4-xi.-18
Wargnies-le-Petit — taken by British, 4-xi.-18
" **War Grange**," s.s. — attacked by U-Boat, 15-v.-18
" **War Helmet**," s.s. — sunk, 19-iv.-18

" **Warilda**," H.S. — sunk, 3-viii.-18
" **War Knight**," s.s. — mined after collision; on fire; beached, 24-iii.-18
Warlencourt — British advance beyond, 2-iii.-17; British carry, 25-viii.-18
Warlencourt, Butte de — British progress near, 5-xi.-16; 7-xi.-16; local advance E. of, 14-xi.-16; further advance; some ground lost, 16-xi.-16
Warlencourt-Eaucourt — occupied, 25-ii.-17
Warmbad — Union forces occupy, 3-iv.-15
" **War Monarch**," s.s. — sunk, 14-ii.-18
Warneford, Lieut. — bombs Gontrode Zeppelin sheds, 25-v.-15; destroys Zeppelin, 7-vi.-15
" **Warner**," H.M. special service ship — sunk, 13-iii.-17
Warneton — British progress towards, 11-vi.-17; 12-vi.-17; Australian raid near, 10-ii.-18; British raid, 3-iii.-18; Australian raid, 4-iii.-18
" **War Panther**," s.s. — attacked by U-Boat, 30-v.-18
" **War Patrol**," s.s. — sunk, 10-viii.-17
" **Warren**," s.s. — sunk, 1-iv.-17
Warrender, Adm. — relieved of command of 2nd Battle Squadron, 16-xii.-15
" **Warrior**," H.M.S. — in new 1st Cruiser Squadron, 7-xii.-14; sunk in Jutland battle, 31-v.-16; 1-vi.-16
" **War Roach**," s.s. — torpedoed, 2-xi.-18
Warsaw — Hindenburg to strike towards, 31-viii.-14; Germans concentrated for advance on, 27-ix.-14; Mackensen S.E. of Blonie position, 12-x.-14; advance on, 14-x.-14; first battle: begun, 15-x.-14; Germans 7 miles from, 16-x.-14; saved by arrival of Russian reinforcements, 17-x.-14; Germans retire from 18-x.-14; 19-x.-14; Russian offensive, 20-x.-14; Germans retreat, 21-x.-14; Russian pursuit, 22-x.-14; Germans approach, 18-xi.-14; second German attack, 7-xii.-14; battle continued, 9-xii.-14; 13-xii.-14; Russian stand 30 miles S.W. of, 16-xii.-14; Germans cross Bzura R.; fail to advance, 23-xii.-14; German offensive arrested, 25-xii.-14; direct attack on abandoned, 26-xii.-14; Germans retire from Bzura—Ravka line, 28-xii.-14; Germans 30 miles from, 6-i.-15; Russian retreat to Blonie line, 18-vii.-15; threatened, 21-vii.-15; Russians preparing for evacuation, 25-vii.-15; Germans force Vistula, 28-vii.-15; Germans held W. of, 1-viii.-15; Prince Leopold of Bavaria attacking, 3-viii.-15; civilians evacuating, 4-viii.-15; Germans enter, 5-viii.-15; Russians driven out of Praga; cross Vieprz S. of, 9-viii.-15; Germans take junction of Ostrolenka—Petrograd—Warsaw railways, 11-viii.-15; German progress towards Bug R., 12-viii.-15; Gen. von Beseler appointed Governor-General, 24-viii.-15; appointment terminated, 18-xi.-18; Allied mission at, 12-ii.-19
Air raids, 25-ix.-14; 26-ii.-15; 1-iii.-15; 10-iii.-15; 15-iv.-15; 23-iv.-15; 22-vii.-15; 31-vii.-15
" **War Song**," s.s. — sunk, 15-i.-18
" **Warspite**," H.M.S. — joins Grand Fleet at Scapa, 13-iv.-15; rejoins, 23-xi.-15; damaged in collision, 1-xii.-15; damaged in Jutland battle, 31-v.-16; returns to Rosyth, 2-vi.-16; collision; damaged, 24-viii.-16
" **War Swallow**," s.s. — sunk, 16-vii.-18
" **War Thistle**," s.s. — attacked by U-Boat, 17-i.-18
" **War Tune**," s.s. — sunk, 9-xii.-17
" **Warturm**," s.s. — torpedoed, 25-iii.-18
Warwick — Zeppelin raid, 12-iv.-18
" **Warwickshire**," s.s. — torpedoed, 10-iv.-18
Washington, George — tomb: Pres. Wilson's address to Diplomatic Corps at, 4-vii.-18
Wassigny — taken, 18-x.-18

William II., German Emperor (continued):—
Submarine warfare — addresses U-Boat commanders at Wilhelmshaven, 4-ii.-15; orders postponement, 15-ii.-15; at German G.H.Q., Pless; confers with advisers on first U.S. "Lusitania" Note; decides U-Boats continue against British passenger ships, 31-v.-15; addresses Cabinet Order on policy, 7-ix.-15; visits Wilhelmshaven, 23-ii.-16; Bethmann-Hollweg's Memorandum to, 29-ii.-16; decides to postpone policy, 6-iii.-16; decides policy indispensable, 7-iii.-16; defers decision, 31-viii.-16; agrees to "unrestricted" policy: Order to Admiralty Staff: "I command that unrestricted U-Boat warfare shall be instituted with the utmost energy on February 1," &c., 9-i.-17; at Spa: vetoes proposal to extend field, 2-vii.-18; speech at Kiel on campaign, 24-iv.-18
" **William Middleton**," **s.s.** — attacked by U-Boat, 23-xii.-16
" **William P. Frye**," **U.S. s.v.** — sunk by Germans, 28-i.-15; U.S. note to Germany demanding £45,610 indemnity, 5-iv.-15
Williams, Gen. — wounded, 2-vi.-15
" **Willingtonia**," **s.s.** — sunk, 25-viii.-18
" **Willow Branch**," **H.M. special service ship** — sunk, 25-iv.-18
Wilson, Gen. Sir A. — commands in Suez Canal zone, 16-xi.-14
Wilson, Field-Marshal Sir Henry — member of Military Committee of Supreme Allied Political Council, 9-xi.-17; Chief of Imperial General Staff, 16-ii.-18; at Doullens, 25-iii.-18
Wilson, Capt. Stanley — captured, 6-xi.-15
Wilson, President Woodrow (U.S.) — speech at Philadelphia: " . . . too proud to fight," 10-v.-15; denounces pro-Germans, 7-ii.-15; invites neutrals to break with Germany, 4-ii.-17; armed neutrality resolution obstructed in Senate, 4-iii.-17; summons Congress: grave questions of national policy, 20-iii.-17; asks Congress to declare a state of war with Germany, 2-iv.-17; signs Conscription Act, 18-v.-17; decides to send army division to France, 19-v.-17; message to Russian Government defining war aims, 10-vi.-17; on army: says over 1,000,000 men sailed for France, 2-viii.-18; address to Diplomatic Corps at Washington's tomb, 4-vii.-18; message to Congress: "our object is to win the war," 4-xii.-17; authorises seizure of Dutch ships in U.S. ports, 20-iii.-18; signs Man Power Bill, 31-viii.-18; demands German capitulation, 13-x.-18; entreated to mitigate Armistice terms, 11-xi.-18; 12-xi.-18; promises Germans conditional food relief, 13-xi.-18; Dr. Solf presses hastening of food relief, 15-xi.-18; Dr. Solf requested to address messages to Allies, 4-xi.-18; leaves for Europe, 4-xii.-18; lands at Brest, 13-xii.-18; receives Freedom of Paris, 16-xii.-18; arrives in England, 26-xii.-18; in London: conference with Mr. Lloyd George and Mr. Balfour, 27-xii.-18; further conference; at Guildhall on League of Nations, 28-xii.-18; visits Manchester, 29-xii.-18; leaves for Paris, 31-xii.-18; in Rome, 3-i.-19; returns to Paris, 7-i.-19; with Mr. Lansing sits with Allied Supreme War Council, 12-i.-19; resolution on League of Nations adopted at Paris Peace Conference, 25-i.-19; suggests Australasian mandate for German Pacific Is., 29-i.-19; Jugo-Slav offer to submit Adriatic question to: Italy refuses, 10-ii.-19; reads draft of League of Nations at Paris Peace Conference, 14-ii.-19; leaves France for U.S., 16-ii.-19; at Boston: defends League of Nations, 24-ii.-19; at Washington: discusses League of Nations with Congress Foreign Relations Committee, 27-ii.-19; in New York on

Wilson, President Woodrow (continued):—
League of Nations, 4-iii.-19; sails for Europe, 5-iii.-19; in Paris, 14-iii.-19; discusses Levant affairs with Allied representatives, 20-iii.-19; member of Council of Four, 24-iii.-19; King Albert visits in Paris, 4-iv.-19; withdraws from Adriatic discussion, 21-iv.-19; leaves Paris for Brussels, 17-vi.-19; signs Franco-American Treaty, 28-vi.-19; leaves France for U.S., 29-vi.-19; arrives in U.S.; prepares for Treaty campaign, 8-vii.-19
" Freedom of Seas " — conversation between M. Clemenceau and Mr. Lloyd George: concurrence mentioned by M. Clemenceau in French Chamber, 29-xii.-18
Peace — Count Bernstorff instructed that Germany would accept good offices in promoting conference, 18-viii.-16; terms: suggests intimation of views by belligerents, 20-xii.-16; German reply, 26-xii.-16; Allied reply, 10-i.-17; message to Congress, 22-i.-17; reply to Pope's Note, 29-viii.-17; " 14 points " message to Congress: declares policy and says: " Treatment accorded to Russia by her sister-nations will be the acid-test of their goodwill," 8-i.-18; in Congress: on separate negotiations, 11-ii.-18; reply to Austrian proposal, 16-ix.-18 Kaiser favours appeal to, 29-ix.-18; German Notes to, 4-x.-18; 5-x.-18; reply, 9-x.-18; final reply, 23-x.-18
President — re-elected, 7-xi.-16
Submarine warfare: see Submarine warfare
" **Wilton**," **s.s.** — attacked by U-Boat, 30-vi.-18
" **Wilton Hall**," **s.s.** — sunk, 16-vii.-16
" **Wimmera**," **s.s.** — mined, 26-vi.-18
" **Wimpole**," **H.M. trawler** — destroys UB17, 25-ii.-18
Winckler, Gen. von (Germany) — commands 11th Army, 10-viii.-16
Windau — Germans bombard and lose torpedo-boat, 28-vi.-15; German gunboat attacked by Russian seaplanes, 2-viii.-15
Windhuk — occupied, 12-v.-15
Windsor — British Royal House assumes name, 17-vii.-17
" **Windsor**," **s.s.** — sunk, 21-viii.-15
" **Windsor Hall**," **s.s.** — sunk, 17-i.-18
" **Winifredian**," **s.s.** — mined, 17-iv.-17
Winterfeld, Gen. von (Germany) — Armistice delegate: leaves for front, 6-xi.-18
Wintgens, Maj. (Germany) — captured by Belgians, 22-v.-17
Wirballen — taken, 10-ii.-15
" **Wirral**," **s.s.** — sunk, 12-v.-17
Wissenbach — Germans driven from summit between Lusse and, 19-ii.-15
Wloclawek — Germans begin battle, 11-xi.-14; 9th Army engaged, 17-xii.-14
Woevre — French take St. Remy, 9-ii.-15; French attack on Les Eparges spur, 17-ii.-15; success, 19-ii.-15; fighting, 24-ii.-15; progress at Les Eparges, 27-iii.-15; German counter-attack repulsed, 28-iii.-15; French take Regniéville, 3-iv.-15; attack crest of Les Eparges, 5-iv.-15; 7-iv.-15; carry crest, 9-iv.-15; German counter-attacks repulsed, 11-iv.-15; French attacks fail near Maizeray, 13-iv.-15; French repulse Germans at Les Eparges, 24-iv.-15; Germans attack at Les Eparges, 19-iv.-16; French raids, 24-i.-17; activity, 11-iv.-17; German attacks N. of repulsed, 8-ii.-18; French raid, 4-iii.-18; Germans gain and lose foothold at Bois Brulé, 19-iii.-18; Austrian 35th Division on front, 9-viii.-18
" **Wolf**," **German raider** — captures H.M. oiler " Turritella," 27-ii.-17; sinks s.s. " Jumna," 1-iii.-17; s.s. " Wordsworth," 11-iii.-17; s.v. " Dee," 30-iii.-17; sinks s.s. " Wairuna," 2-vi.-17; s.s. " Mongolia " sunk by mine laid

Yudenitch, Gen. (Russia) — fails before Petrograd, 26-x.-19

Yugo-Slavs — independence proclaimed, 29-x.-18; delegates press for union with Serbia—Montenegro, 25-xi.-18; claim heard at Paris Peace Conference, 18-ii.-19; abstain from signing Austrian Treaty, 10-ix.-19; abstain from signing Bulgarian Treaty, 26-xi.-19; sign Treaties, 5-xii.-19; Adriatic question: see under Adriatic

Yuksanki — H.M.A.M.C. " Arlanza " reaches, 29-x.-15

Yusupoff, Prince (Russia) — Rasputin murdered in palace, 29-xii.-16

" Yzer," s.s. — sunk, 20-vii.-16

Z.

" Zaanstroom," Dutch s.s. — seized and taken into Zeebrugge by Germans, 21-iii.-15

Zab, Lesser — Turks driven over, 11-v.-18

" Zafra," H.M. collier — sunk, 8-iv.-16

Zaghlul Pasha — arrested, 8-iii.-19; deported to Malta, 9-iii.-19; released, 7-iv.-19; joins Egyptian Nationalist delegation to Paris, 11-iv.-19; in Paris, 20-iv.-19

Zagora — Italian success near, 1-xi.-15

Zagrody — Austro-Germans take, 25-v.-15

Zahlek — occupied, 6-x.-18

" Zaïda," auxiliary yacht — sunk, 17-viii.-16

Zaimis, M. (Greece) — Premier, 7-x.-15; forms Cabinet, 21-vi.-16; resigns, 11-ix.-16; 24-vi.-17

Zaitchar — Serbians retire through, 26-x.-15; Bulgarians take, 27-x.-15

Zaleszczyki — Russians force Dniester line at, 12-vi.-16; falls, 30-vii.-17

" Zambesi," s.s. — sunk, 1-iv.-17

Zamosc — captured by Austro-Germans, 1-vii.-15

Zandvoorde — British advance towards, 22-xi.-17

" Zanoni," s.s. — sunk, 12-v.-17

" Zara," s.s. — sunk, 13-iv.-17

Zboroff — Russians capture heights, 3-vii.-17

Zbrucz R. — German advance near Russian frontier, 1-viii.-17; Russian resistance, 12-viii.-17

" Zealandia," H.M.S. — reports sinking of U-Boat, 10-ix.-14; in heavy sea, 6-xi.-15

Zeebrugge — British 7th Division land, 7-x.-14; Allies evacuate, 12-x.-14; British naval squadron bombards, 23-xi.-14; British air-raids, 12-ii.-15; 16-ii.-15; 1-vi.-15; development as U-Boat base; Mr. Churchill's telegram, 2-i.-15; Sir J. French suggests offensive for recapture, 3-i.-15; Gen. Joffre's memorandum regarding operations towards, 19-i.-15; bombed by British airmen, 22-i.-15; bombed by Allied airmen, 8-iv.-15; bombarded by British ships, 23-viii.-15; 24-ix.-15; 3-x.-15; 17-x.-15; Allied air-raid on, 18-iii.-16; 20-iii.-16; bombarded, 24-iv.-16; s.s. " Lestris " captured and taken to, 5-vii.-16; British seaplane shot down and captured, 23-vii.-16; British air-raids, 28-xi.-16; 11-xii.-16; 4-iv.-17; 5-iv.-17; 7-iv.-17; naval and aerial raid, 12-v.-17; French aeroplane bombs U-Boat base, 31-v.-17; bombed by British, 1-vi.-17; air camps bombarded, 3-vi.-17; Dover C.M.B.s attack Mole, 22-viii.-17; bombed, 12-ix.-17; 30-ix.-17; German T.B.D.s chased, 21-iii.-18; naval raid; blockships sunk; submarine sunk

Zeebrugge (continued) :—
against Mole, 23-iv.-18; British air-raid, 2-v.-18; German T.B.D. sunk during British air-raid, 22-v.-18; Belgians occupy, 19-x.-18; King George visits, 9-xii.-18

Zeeland — proposed German occupation of province, 21-iv.-18

Zeltunlik — powder mills shelled, 15-vii.-15

Zejny — Germans forced back, 8-v.-15

Zele — Germans held up, 7-x.-14

" Zélée," French gunboat — sunk, 22-ix.-14

Zenker, Capt. (Germany) — conference with Kaiser, 5-vii.-14

Zenson — Germans establish bridgehead, 12-xi.-17; fighting, 16-xi.-17; Italians recover sector, 20-vi.-18; Italians cross Lower Piave, 29-x.-18

Zenson loop — Austrian landing prevented, 11-ii.-18

" Zent," s.s. — sunk, 5-iv.-16

" Zenta," Austrian cruiser — sunk, 16-viii.-14

Zeppelin, Count (Germany) — death, 8-iii.-17

Zeppelins: see under Aerial warfare — German fleets — Airships

" Zermatt," s.s. — sunk, 24-vii.-17

Zeur — occupied, 19-xi.-15

Zevenkote — Germans occupy, 4-v.-15

" Zhemchug," Russian cruiser — sunk by H.I.M.S. " Emden," 28-x.-14

Zhitomir — Germans reach, 24-ii.-18

Zhmerinka — Germans take, 2-iii.-18

" Zillah," s.s. — sunk, 22-x.-17

Zillebeke — Germans enter British trenches, 2-vi.-16; Canadians recover, 13-vi.-16

Zillebeke—Zandvoorde road — British line advanced, 1-viii.-17

Zimmermann, Herr (Germany) — conference with Kaiser, 5-vii.-14; with Count Hoyos and Count Szögeny, 6-vii.-14; Foreign Secretary, 22-xi.-16; succeeded as Foreign Secretary, 6-viii.-17

" Zinal," s.s. — sunk, 17-viii.-18

Zloczow — Russian line penetrated, 14-ii.-17; line re-established, 15-ii.-17; Russian positions pierced, 19-vii.-17

Zlota—Lipa — fighting, 14-viii.-15; Gen Brusiloff S. of Brzezany, 15-viii.-16; Russian success, 29-viii.-16

Zolkiev — Austro-Germans take, 20-vi.-15

Zollern Redoubt — carried by British, 26-ix.-16

Zombrovo — Germans take, 12-viii.-15

Zomo, Mte. — Austrians storm, 5-xii.-17

" Zone," s.s. — sunk, 30-vii.-17

Zonnebeke — artillery duel, 1-i.-15; Germans occupy, 4-v.-15; British take, 26-ix.-17

Zonnebeke—St. Julien—Langemarck—Bixschoote — British 1st Corps reaches line 21-x.-14

" Zoroaster," s.s. — mined, 29-xii.-16

" Zrinyi," Austrian battleship — shells Sinigaglia, 24-v.-15

Zuara — Italians defeat rebels, 13-i.-17

" Zubian," H.M.S. — joins Dover Patrol 2-vii.-17; sinks UC50, 4-ii.-18; see Appendix IV.

Zugna Torta — Austrian gain, 16-v.-16; Italian rally, 17-v.-16; evacuate, 18-v.-16

Zuravno — Austro-Germans take, 5-vi.-15 Germans defeated near, 9-vi.-15; Russian victory near develops, 10-vi.-15; retaken 11-vi.-15; Austro-Germans again checked 23-vi.-15

Zweibrücken — air-raid, 16-iii.-18

" Zylpha," H.M. special service ship — sunk 15-vi.-17

www.ingramcontent.com/pod-product-compliance
Lightning Source LLC
Chambersburg PA
CBHW060838100426
42814CB00016B/414/J